SCHUBERT: THE COMPLETE SONG TEXTS

SCHUBERT:
THE COMPLETE SONG TEXTS

Texts of the Lieder and Italian Songs,
with English Translations

by

RICHARD WIGMORE

Foreword by Dietrich Fischer-Dieskau

SCHIRMER BOOKS

A Division of Macmillan, Inc.

New York

Compilation and translation © 1988 by Richard Wigmore

First American edition published in 1988 by
Schirmer Books
A Division of Macmillan, Inc.

Schirmer Books
A Division of Macmillan, Inc.
866 Third Avenue, New York, N.Y. 10022

First published in Great Britain by
Victor Gollancz Limited
London

Library of Congress Catalog Card Number: 88-11653

Printed in Great Britain

printing number
1 2 3 4 5 6 7 8 9 10

Library of Congress Cataloging-in-Publication Data
Schubert, Franz, 1797-1828.
Schubert — the complete song texts.

Includes index.
1. Songs — Texts.   I. Wigmore, Richard.   II. Title.
ML54.6.S39W52   1988   784.3'05   88-11653
ISBN 0-02-872911-0

CONTENTS

To Ania

FOREWORD

Collected here are the texts of all Schubert's well-loved songs, with exact English translations. I am delighted that modern English versions are now available for the benefit of English-speaking singers and listeners. The book will also afford a greater understanding of Schubert's original texts when, as sometimes happens, the songs are sung in a free English version. I wish Richard Wigmore's translations the widest possible circulation.

DIETRICH FISCHER-DIESKAU

PREFACE

Assembled here, for the first time, are texts and prose
translations of all Schubert's surviving completed solo songs, both
German and Italian, for voice and piano. It also seemed natural to
include the songs calling for obbligato wind — *Auf dem Strom*
(with horn) and *Der Hirt auf dem Felsen* (with clarinet) — and a
few pieces originally composed for operas, such as the two arias
from *Claudine von Villa Bella*, which have found their way into
the Peters edition of Schubert's songs. In certain early strophic
songs some verses have been omitted, partly because no singer
today would risk testing his audience's patience by performing,
complete, a song such as *Idens Schwanenlied*, with its seventeen
verses. Moreover, we cannot always be sure exactly how many
verses of a particular song Schubert intended to be sung;
sometimes he would simply write out the first verse of the poem
and put repeat marks at the end. But with these few exceptions all
the songs, including the extended ballads, are translated in full.

All translation is a more or less uncomfortable compromise; and
the greater the poem, the greater the compromise. No English
rendering can do more than hint at the rolling majesty of Goethe's
Grenzen der Menschheit or the epigrammatic subtlety of the
Heine poems — though, at the other end of the spectrum, no
translation could possibly conceal the banality and bathos of
Adelwold und Emma, the longest and arguably the worst poem set
by Schubert. With the needs of the singer, the student and the
listener in mind, I have attempted to provide clear, straightfor-
ward translations that remain close to the originals without
descending into stilted translation-ese. Wherever possible the
original line order has been followed, though not to the point
where the resultant English would have been excessively con-
torted. Where the text set by Schubert is a fairly free translation
from the English, as in the case of the Shakespeare and Scott
songs, a literal rendering of the German is followed by the original
English poem; but where the German is a more or less faithful
translation of an English text, as with the Ossian songs, the

English original is printed alongside the German.

The texts are arranged alphabetically, by German (or Italian) title (in German the articles *Ein*, *Eine* and *Das*, *Der*, *Die* are included in the title). In the case of identical titles the alphabetical order is by poet. Although the fourteen songs published posthumously under the title *Schwanengesang* were not conceived by Schubert as a cycle, they appear together in editions of the songs and are frequently performed as a group. For convenience, therefore, they are treated here as a single collection, though individual titles are cross-referenced.

I should like to thank my publishers, Livia Gollancz and David Burnett, for their encouragement during this project; many musician friends, and in particular Jacek Strauch, for their valuable suggestions; and Dietrich Fischer-Dieskau, who first kindled my enthusiasm for Schubert's *Lieder*, for kindly agreeing to provide a foreword.

RICHARD WIGMORE

WIMBLEDON
LONDON

THE SONG TEXTS

Abendbilder / Nocturne

JOHANN PETER SILBERT

D 650 (1819)

Still beginnt's im Hain zu tauen,
Ruhig webt der Dämm'rung Grauen
Durch die Glut
Sanfter Flut,
Durch das Grün umbuschter
  Auen,
So die trunk'nen Blicke schauen.

Sieh', der Raben Nachtgefieder
Rauscht auf ferne Eichen nieder;
Balsamduft
Haucht die Luft.
Philomelens Zauberlieder,
Hallet zart die Echo wider.

Horch! des Abendglöckleins Töne
Mahnen ernst der Erde Söhne,
Dass ihr Herz
Himmelwärts,
Sinnend ob der Heimat Schöne,
Sich des Erdentands entwöhne.

Durch der hohen Wolken Riegel
Funkeln tausend
  Himmelssiegel,
Lunas Bild
Streuet mild
In der Fluten klaren Spiegel
Schimmernd Gold auf Flur und Hügel.

Von des Vollmonds Widerscheine
Blitzet das bemooste, kleine
Kirchendach.
Aber ach!
Ringsum decken Leichensteine
Der Entschlummerten Gebeine.

Ruht, o Traute! von den Wehen,
Bis beim grossen Auferstehen
Aus der Nacht
Gottes Macht
Einst uns ruft, in seiner Höhen
Ew'ge Wonnen einzugehen.

Softly, dew begins to fall in the grove,
Gently the grey dusk
Weaves through the red glow
Of the calm waters,
And through the green meadows, fringed
  with bushes,
That distort before the eye.

See, the ravens' nocturnal flight
Descends with a swish on distant oaks;
The air breathes
A balmy fragrance.
Echo tenderly repeats
Philomel's magic songs.

Hark! The vesper-bell
Solemnly urges the sons of earth,
To forgo all earthly dross
And turn their hearts
Towards heaven,
Reflecting upon that fair dwelling-place

A thousand celestial stars
Sparkle through chinks in the barrier of
  high clouds;
The moon
Shines gently
In the clear mirror of the waters,
Tinging hill and meadow with gold.

The mossy roof of the little church
Gleams in the reflection
Of the full moon.
But all around
Tombstones cover
The bones of the departed.

Rest, beloved ones, from your cares,
Until, at the Great Resurrection,
God in His might
Calls us from the night
To eternal bliss
On high

Abendlied / Evening Song

MATTHIAS CLAUDIUS

D 499 (1816)

Der Mond ist aufgegangen,
Die goldnen Sternlein prangen
Am Himmel hell und klar;
Der Wald steht schwarz und schweiget,
Und aus den Wiesen steiget

The moon is up,
The golden stars shine
Bright and clear in the heavens.
The woods lie dark and silent,
And from the meadows, uncannily,

Der weiße Nebel wunderbar.	The white mist rises.
Wie ist die Welt so stille,	How still the world is,
Und in der Dämmrung Hülle	And in dusk's mantle
So traulich und so hold!	How intimate and tender,
Als eine stille Kammer,	Like a peaceful room
Wo ihr des Tages Jammer	Where you may sleep and forget
Verschlafen und vergessen sollt.	The day's cares.
Seht ihr den Mond dort stehen?	Do you see the moon there?
Er ist nur halb zu sehen,	It is only half visible,
Und ist doch rund und schön!	And yet it is so round and fair.
So sind wohl manche Sachen,	Thus it is with many things:
Die wir getrost belachen,	We thoughtlessly mock them
Weil unsre Augen sie nicht sehn.	Because we cannot see them.
Wir stolze Menschenkinder	We proud sons of men
Sind eitel arme Sünder,	Are but poor sinners,
Und wissen gar nicht viel;	And know very little;
Wir spinnen Luftgespinste,	We spin airy fantasies
Und suchen viele Künste,	And seek to master many arts,
Und kommen weiter von dem Ziel.	Yet move further from our goal.
Gott, laß dein Heil uns schauen,	God, may we behold Your grace,
Auf nichts Vergänglichs trauen,	Mistrust all that is transitory,
Nicht Eitelkeit uns freun!	And delight not in vanity.
Laß uns einfältig werden,	May we attain simplicity,
Und vor dir hier auf Erden	And before You here on earth
Wie Kinder fromm und fröhlich sein!	Live as children, pious and cheerful.

Abendlied / Evening Song

FRIEDRICH LEOPOLD, GRAF ZU STOLBERG-STOLBERG

D 276 (1815)

Gross und rotentflammet schwebet	The sun hovers, massive and flaming red,
Noch die Sonn am Himmelsrand,	On the sky's edge,
Und auf blauen Wogen bebet	And upon the blue waves
Noch ihr Abglanz bis zum Strand;	Its reflection glistens, touching the shore.
Aus dem Buchenwalde hebet	From the beechwood the moon rises,
Sich der Mond, und winket Ruh'	Heralding peace
Seiner Schwester Erde zu.	To her sister earth.
In geschwollnen Wolken ballet	On the swollen clouds
Dunkler sich die rote Glut,	The red glow darkens,
Zarter Farbenwechsel wallet	Delicately changing colours
Auf der Roggenblüte Flut;	Play on the sea of burgeoning rye;
Zwischen schwanken Halmen schallet	Among the slender blades of grass
Reger Wachteln heller Schlag,	The lively quails' bright call echoes,
Und der Hirte pfeift ihm nach.	Answered by the shepherd's pipe.

Abendlied / Evening Song

POET UNKNOWN

D 382 (1816)

Sanft glänzt die Abendsonne	The evening sun shines gently
Auf diese stille Flur	On these silent meadows,

Und strahlet Ruh und Wonne	Shedding peace and joy
Auf jede Kreatur.	Over every creature.
Sie zeichnet Licht und Schatten	It traces light and shadow
Auf die beblümte Au,	Upon the flower-decked pastures,
Und auf den grünen Matten	And on the verdant fields
Blitzt der kristallne Tau.	The crystal dew sparkles.

Hier in der Zephyrn Spiele	Here, amid the play of zephyrs
Beim frohen Vogelchor,	And the happy choir of birds
Hier steigen Hochgefühle	My breast surges
In meiner Brust empor.	With elation.
Ich atme süsse Freuden	I breathe in sweet delights
Auf diesem Tempel ein,	In this temple;
Mich fliehen Gram und Leiden	Grief and sorrow flee
Im milden Abendschein.	In the gentle light of evening.

Dir, der die Abendröte	To you, who spread the red glow of evening
Am Himmel ausgespannt	Over the heavens,
Und süsses Nachtgeflöte	And brought the sweet song of the night
Auf diese Flur gesandt,	To these meadows,
Dir sei dies Herz geweihet,	To you I dedicate this heart
Das reiner Dank durchglüht,	Glowing with pure gratitude;
Es schlage noch erfreuet,	May it still beat joyfully
Wenn einst das Leben flieht.	When life ceases.

Abendlied der Fürstin / The Princess's Evening Song

JOHANN MAYRHOFER

D 495 (1816?)

Der Abend rötet nun das Tal,	The evening tinges the valley with red;
Mild schimmert Hesperus.	Hesperus gleams softly.
Die Buchen stehen still zumal,	The beech trees stand silent,
Und leiser rauscht der Fluß.	And the river murmurs more softly.

Die Wolken segeln goldbesäumt	The clouds, fringed with gold,
Am klaren Firmament;	Sail across the clear sky;
Das Herz, es schwelgt, das Herz, es träumt,	The heart swells, the heart dreams,
Von Erdenqual getrennt.	Free from earthly sorrow.

Auf grünem Hügel hingestreckt,	The huntsman, stretched out on the green hillside,
Schläft sanft der Jäger ein —	Falls sound asleep;
Doch plötzlich ihn der Donner weckt,	But suddenly he is woken by thunder,
Und Blitze zischen drein.	And the hiss of lightning.

Wo bist du, heilig Abendrot,	Where are you, sacred evening glow?
Wo, sanfter Hesperus?	Where are you, gentle Hesperus?
Es wandelt sich in Schmerz und Not	Thus every pleasure
Ein jeglicher Genuß.	Turns to grief and distress.

Abendlied für die Entfernte / Evening Song for the Distant Beloved

AUGUST WILHELM VON SCHLEGEL

D856 (1825)

Hinaus mein Blick! hinaus ins Tal!	Gaze out, eyes, gaze out to the valley!
Da wohnt noch Lebensfülle;	There abundant life still dwells.
Da labe dich im Mondenstrahl	Refresh yourself there in the moonlight,
Und an der heil'gen Stille.	And in the sacred peace.
Da horch nun ungestört, mein Herz,	Listen, heart, now undisturbed,
Da horch den leisen Klängen,	Listen to the soft sounds
Die, wie von fern, zu Wonn' und Schmerz	That press upon you, as from afar,
Sich dir entgegen drängen.	For joy and for sorrow.
Sie drängen sich so wunderbar,	They teem in so wondrously,
Sie regen all mein Sehnen.	They arouse all my longing.
O sag' mir Ahnung, bist du wahr?	This intimation, is it real?
Bist du ein eitles Wähnen?	Or is it a vain illusion?
Wird einst mein Aug' in heller Lust,	Will my eyes one day smile in pure pleasure,
Wie jetzt in Tränen, lächeln?	As they do now in tears?
Wird einst die oft empörte Brust	Will blessed peace one day
Mir sel'ge Ruh umfächeln?	Caress my heart, so often incensed?
Wenn Ahnung und Erinnerung	When presentiment and memory
Vor unserm Blick sich gatten,	Are joined before our eyes,
Dann mildert sich zur Dämmerung	Then at twilight
Der Seele tiefster Schatten.	The soul's deepest shadows grow softer.
Ach, dürften wir mit Träumen nicht	Ah, if we could not
Die Wirklichkeit verweben,	Interweave reality with dreams,
Wie arm an Farbe, Glanz und Licht	How poor you would be, human life,
Wärst du, o Menschenleben!	In colour, lustre and light!
So hoffet treulich und beharrt	Thus the heart remains constant, hoping faithfully
Das Herz bis hin zum Grabe;	Unto the grave;
Mit Lieb' umfaßt's die Gegenwart,	With love it embraces the present,
Und dünkt sich reich an Habe.	And deems itself rich in possessions.
Die Habe, die es selbst sich schafft,	The possessions which it creates itself
Mag ihm kein Schicksal rauben;	No fate can snatch from it.
Es lebt und webt in Wärm' und Kraft,	It lives and works in warmth and strength,
Durch Zuversicht und Glauben.	Through trust and faith.
Und wär in Nacht und Nebeldampf	And if all around lies dead
Auch Alles rings erstorben,	In night and mist,
Dies Herz hat längst für jeden Kampf	This heart has long ago won
Sich einen Schild erworben.	A shield for every battle.
Mit hohem Trotz im Ungemach	In adversity it endures its fate
Trägt es, was ihm beschieden.	With lofty defiance.
So schlummr' ich ein, so werd' ich wach,	And so I fall asleep, so I awake,
In Lust nicht, doch in Frieden.	If not in joy, yet in peace.

Abendröte / Sunset

FRIEDRICH VON SCHLEGEL

D690 (1820?)

Tiefer sinket schon die Sonne,
Und es atmet alles Ruhe,
Tages Arbeit ist vollendet,
Und die Kinder scherzen munter.
Grüner glänzt die grüne Erde,
Eh' die Sonne ganz versunken.
Milden Balsam hauchen leise
In die Lüfte nun die Blumen,
Der die Seele zart berühret,
Wenn die Sinne selig trunken.
Kleine Vögel, ferne Menschen,
Berge, himmelan geschwungen,
Und der grosse Silberstrom,
Der im Tale schlank
   gewunden,
Alles scheint dem Dichter redend,
Denn er hat den Sinn gefunden:
Und das All ein einzig
   Chor,
Manches Lied aus einem Munde.

The sun sinks deeper,
All things breathe peace;
The day's work is finished
And the children play merrily.
The green earth shines greener
Before the sun goes down.
The flowers softly breathe
Into the air sweet balm
That tenderly caresses the soul
While the senses are drunk with rapture.
Small birds, people in the distance,
Mountains soaring heavenwards,
And the great silver river
That winds its slender course through the
   valley:
All seem to speak to the poet,
For he has divined their meaning;
And the whole world becomes a single
   choir,
Singing many a song with one voice.

Abends unter der Linde / Evening beneath the Linden Tree

LUDWIG KOSEGARTEN

First version: D235 (1815)
Second version: D237 (1815)

Woher, o namenloses Sehnen,
Das den beklemmten Busen presst?
Woher, ihr bittersüssen Tränen,
Die ihr das Auge dämmernd nässt?
O Abendrot, o Mondenblitz,
Flimmt blasser um den Lindensitz.

Es säuselt in dem Laub der Linde;
Es flüstert im Akazienstrauch.
Mir schmeichelt süss, mir schmeichelt
   linde
Des grauen Abends lauer Hauch.
Es spricht um mich wie Geistergruss;
Es geht mich an wie Engelkuss.

Whence this nameless longing
That oppresses my troubled heart?
Whence these bittersweet tears
That veil my eyes in moisture?
O evening glow, o glittering moon,
Cast a paler light beneath the linden tree.

The leaves of the linden tree rustle,
The acacia whispers.
Sweetly, gently, I am
   caressed
By the warm evening breeze.
All around it is as if spirits greet me,
And I am touched by an angel's kiss.

Abendständchen: an Lina / Evening Serenade: To Lina

GABRIELE VON BAUMBERG

D265 (1815)

Sei sanft, wie ihre Seele,
Und heiter, wie ihr Blick,

Be as gentle as her soul,
And as serene as her gaze,

O Abend! und vermähle
Mit seltner Treu das
   Glück.

O evening, and reward
Such uncommon constancy with
   happiness!

Wenn alles schläft, und trübe
Die stille Lampe scheint,
Nur Hoffnungslose Liebe
Noch helle Tränen weint:

When all sleep,
The silent lamp burns dimly,
Only hopeless love
Often sheds its shining tears.

Will ich, laß mir's gelingen!
Zu ihrem Fenster gehn,
Ein Lied von Liebe singen;
Und schmachtend nach ihr sehn.

If only I may succeed in my desire
To go to her window,
Sing a song of love,
And gaze soulfully at her!

Vielleicht, daß Klagetöne
Von meinem Saitenspiel
Mehr wirken auf die Schöne,
Mehr reizen ihr Gefühl;

Perhaps the sorrowful tones
Of my strings
Will touch the fair maiden more deeply,
And stir her feelings.

Vielleicht daß meine Saiten
Und meine Phantasie'n
Ein Herz zur Liebe leiten,
Das unempfindlich schien.

Perhaps my strings
And my improvisations
Will awaken love in a heart
That seemed unfeeling.

Wenn sie, im sanften
   Schlummer
Durch Lieder gern gestört,
Halb träumend meinen Kummer
Und meine Leiden hört;

When, happily aroused from gentle
   slumber
By my songs,
She hears, half-dreaming,
My grief and suffering,

Dann bang, und immer bänger,
Von ihrem Lager steigt,
Und was er litt, ihr Sänger,
Sich selber überzeugt:

Then she will rise from her bed,
Ever more anxious,
Realizing
How her minstrel has suffered.

Dann leucht' aus deiner Höhe
Herab, geliebter Mond!
Daß ich die Tränen sehe,
Die meinen Schmerz belohnt.

Then, beloved moon, shine down
From on high,
That I may see her tears
Reward my pain.

Abendstern / The Evening Star

JOHANN MAYRHOFER

D806 (1824)

Was weilst du einsam an dem Himmel,
O schöner Stern? und bist so mild;
Warum entfernt das funkelnde
   Gewimmel
Der Brüder sich vor deinem Bild?
»Ich bin der Liebe treuer Stern,
Sie halten sich von Liebe fern.«

Why do you linger all alone in the sky,
Fair star? For you are so gentle;
Why does the host of sparkling
   brothers
Shun your sight?
'I am the faithful star of love;
They keep far away from love.'

So solltest du zu ihnen gehen,
Bist du der Liebe, zaud're nicht!
Wer möchte denn dir widerstehen?
Du süsses eigensinnig Licht.
»Ich säe, schaue keinen Keim,
Und bleibe trauernd still daheim.«

If you are love,
You should go to them without delay!
For who could resist you,
Sweet, wayward light?
'I sow no seed, I see no shoot,
And remain here, silent and mournful.'

Abschied / Farewell

JOHANN MAYRHOFER

D 475 (1816)

Über die Berge zieht ihr fort,
Kommt an manchen grünen Ort;
Muss zurücke ganz allein,
Lebet wohl! es muss so sein.

Scheiden, meiden, was man liebt,
Ach wie wird das Herz betrübt!
O Seenspiegel, Wald und Hügel
   schwinden all;
Hör' verschwimmen eurer Stimmen
   Widerhall.

Lebt wohl! klingt klagevoll,
Ach wie wird das Herz betrübt.
Scheiden, meiden was man liebt;
Lebt wohl! klingt klagevoll.

You go over the mountains
And come upon many a green spot;
I must return all alone,
Farewell, it must be so.

Parting, leaving that which we love,
Ah, how it grieves the heart.
Glassy lakes, woods and hills all
   vanish;
I hear the echo of your voices fade
   away.

The lament sounds: 'Farewell!'
Ah, how it grieves the heart.
Parting, leaving that which we love;
The lament sounds: 'Farewell!'

Abschied / Farewell

LUDWIG RELLSTAB

see Schwanengesang no. 7

Abschied von der Erde / Farewell to the Earth

ADOLF VON PRATOBEVERA

D 829 (1826)

Leb' wohl, du schöne Erde!
Kann dich erst jetzt versteh'n,
Wo Freude und wo Kummer
An uns vorüberweh'n.

Leb' wohl, du Meister Kummer!
Dank dir mit nassem Blick!
Mit mir nehm' ich die Freude,
Dich lass' ich hier zurück.

Sei nur ein milder Lehrer,
Führ' alle hin zu Gott,
Zeig' in den trübsten Nächten
Ein Streiflein Morgenrot!

Lasse sie die Liebe ahnen,
So danken sie dir noch,
Der früher und der später,
Sie danken weinend doch.

Dann glänzt das Leben heiter,
Mild lächelt jeder Schmerz,
Die Freude hält umfangen
Das ruhige, klare Herz.

Farewell, beautiful earth!
I can understand you only now,
When joy and sorrow
Pass away from us.

Farewell, Master Sorrow!
I thank you with moist eyes!
Joy I take with me,
You I leave behind.

Be a kindly teacher
And lead all men to God;
In the darkest nights
Reveal a gleam of dawn!

Let them know what love is
And they will be thankful;
Some sooner, others later
Will thank you with tears.

Then life will be radiantly happy;
Every sorrow will smile gently,
And joy will hold in its embrace
The pure, tranquil heart.

Abschied von der Harfe / Farewell to the Harp

JOHANN GAUDENZ VON SALIS-SEEWIS

D 406 (1816)

Noch einmal tön', o Harfe,
Die nur Gefühle tönt!
Verhalle zart und leise
Noch jene Schwanenweise,
Die auf der Flut des Lebens
Uns mit der Not versöhnt.

Im Morgenschein des Lebens
Erklangst du rein und hell!
Wer kann den Klang verwahren?
Durch Forschen und Erfahren
Verhallet und versieget
Des Liedes reiner Quell.

In spätern Jugendjahren
Hallt es schon zart und bang,
Wie Finkenschlag im Märze;
Mit des Entknospens Schmerze
Erbeben Herz und Saiten
Voll Liebe und Gesang!

Am Sommertag des Lebens
Verstummt das Saitenspiel!
Aus sehnsuchtsvoller Seele
Lockt's noch, wie Philomele,
Schon seltner, aber rührend,
Nur Schwermut und Gefühl.

O schlag' im dunkeln Busen
Der ernsten Abendzeit!
Will um das öde
   Leben
Des Schicksals Nacht sich weben,
Dann schlag' und wecke Sehnsucht
Nach der Unsterblichkeit!

Sound once more, o harp;
You express only emotion!
Softly, tenderly,
Let that swan song fade away
Which in the flood of life
Reconciles us to our misery.

In the dawn of life
You resounded, pure and bright!
Who can preserve that sound?
With our searchings, our experience,
The pure source of your song
Fades and runs dry.

In later youth
It sounds, tender and anxious,
Like the finch's song in March;
With the pain of budding growth
The heart and strings quiver,
Filled with love and song!

In the summertime of life
The strings fall silent.
From a yearning soul
They still call, like the nightingale,
More rarely now, yet touching us,
All melancholy and tenderness.

O sound in the dark heart
Of solemn eventide!
When the darkness of fate would spin
   its web
Around life's barrenness,
Then sound forth, and awaken longing
For immortality!

Abschied von einem Freunde / Farewell to a Friend

FRANZ SCHUBERT

D 578 (1817)

Lebe wohl! Du lieber Freund!
Ziehe hin in fernes Land,
Nimm der Freundschaft trautes Band —
Und bewahr's in treuer Hand!
Lebe wohl! Du lieber Freund!

Lebe wohl! Du lieber Freund!
Hör' in diesem Trauersang
Meines Herzens innern Drang,
Tönt er doch so dumpf und bang.
Lebe wohl! Du lieber Freund!

Farewell, dear friend!
Go forth to a distant land,
Take this cherished bond of friendship
And keep it faithfully,
Farewell, dear friend!

Farewell, dear friend!
Hear in this mournful song
The yearning of my inmost heart,
Muffled and anxious.
Farewell, dear friend!

Lebe wohl! Du lieber Freund!	Farewell, dear friend!
Scheiden heißt das bitt're Wort,	Parting is a bitter word,
Weh, es ruft Dich von uns fort	Alas, it calls us you from us
Hin an den Bestimmungsort.	To the place decreed for you.
Lebe wohl! Du lieber Freund!	Farewell, dear friend!

Lebe wohl! Du lieber Freund!
Wenn dies Lied Dein Herz ergreift,
Freundes Schatten näher schweift,
Meiner Seele Saiten streift.
Lebe wohl! Du lieber Freund!

Farewell, dear friend!
If this song should stir your heart,
My friendly spirit shall hover close by,
Touching the strings of my soul.
Farewell, dear friend!

Adelaide / Adelaide

FRIEDRICH VON MATTHISSON

D95 (1814)

Einsam wandelt dein Freund im
　Frühlingsgarten,
Mild vom lieblichen Zauberlicht
　umflossen,
Das durch wankende Blütenzweige
　zittert,
Adelaide

In solitude your lover walks in the
　spring garden
Gently bathed in the lovely magic
　light
That shimmers through the swaying
　branches in blossom,
Adelaide!

In der spiegelnden Flut, im Schnee der
　Alpen,
In des sinkenden Tages Goldgewölke,
Im Gefilde der Sterne strahlt dein Bildnis,
Adelaide

In the mirroring waters, in the Alpine
　snows,
In the golden clouds of the dying day,
In the meadows of stars your image shines,
Adelaide!

Abendlüftchen im zarten Laube
　flüstern,
Silberglöckchen des Mai's im Grase
　säuseln,
Wellen rauschen und Nachtigallen flöten:
Adelaide!

Evening breezes whisper in the tender
　leaves,
Silver bells of May rustle in the
　grass,
Waves plash and nightingales sing:
Adelaide!

Einst, o Wunder! entblüht auf meinem
　Grabe
Eine Blume der Asche meines Herzens;
Deutlich schimmert auf jedem Purpur-
　blättchen:
Adelaide!

One day, miraculously, a flower from the
　ashes of my heart
Shall bloom upon my grave;
On every tiny purple leaf shall glimmer
　clearly:
Adelaide!

Adelwold und Emma / Adelwold and Emma

FRIEDRICH ANTON BERTRAND

D211 (1815)

Hoch und ehern schier von Dauer,
Ragt' ein Ritterschloß empor;
Bären lagen an dem Tor
Beute schnaubend auf der Lauer,
Türme zingelten die Mauer
Gleich den Riesen — bange Schauer

A knight's castle, ancient and lofty,
Towered up boldly;
Bears lay at the gate,
Snorting, awaiting their prey.
Turrets arose from the walls
Like giants; eerily the wind

Wehten brausend, wie ein Meer,
Von den Tannenwipfeln her.

Aber finstrer Kummer nagte
Mutverzehrend um und an
Hier am wackern deutschen Mann,
Dem kein Feind zu trotzen wagte;
Oft noch eh der Morgen tagte,
Fuhr er auf vom Traum, und fragte —
Jetzt mit Seufzer — jetzt mit Schrei,
Wo sein teurer Letzter sei?

» Vater! Rufe nicht dem Lieben «
Flüstert einstens Emma drein —
» Sieh, er schläft im Kämmerlein
Sanft and stolz — was kann ihn
    trüben? «
» Ich nicht rufen? — sind nicht die Sieben
Meiner Söhn' im Kampf geblieben?
Weint' ich nicht schon fünfzehn Jahr
Um das Weib, das euch gebar? «

Emma hört's und schmiegt mit Beben
Weinend sich an seine Brust.
» Vater! sieh dein Kind —
    ach früh
War dein Beifall mein Bestreben! «
Wie, wenn, Trosteswort zu geben,
Boten Gottes niederschweben,
Führt der Holden Red' und Blick
Neue Kraft in ihn zurück.

Heiter preßt er sie ans Herze:
» O vergib, daß ich vergaß,
Welchen Schatz ich noch besaß,
Übermannt von meinem Schmerze!
Aber sprachst du nicht im Scherze —
Wohl dann! bei dem Schein der Kerze
Wandle mit mir einen Gang
Stracks den düstern Weg entlang. « . . .

Zitternd folgte sie, bald
    gelangen
Sie zur Halle, graus und tief,
Wo die Schar der Väter schlief;
Rings im Kreis' an Silberspangen
Um ein achtes
    hergehangen,
Leuchteten mit bleichem bangen
Grabesschimmer fort und fort
Sieben Lämplein diesem Ort.

Unter'n Lämplein war's von Steinen . . .
Traun! erzählen kann ich's nicht,
War's so traurig zugericht,
War's so ladend ach zum Weinen.
» Bei den heiligen Gebeinen,
Welchen diese Lämplein scheinen «
Ruft er laut — » beschwör' « ich dich,
Traute Tochter, höre mich.

Gusted from the fir-tops,
Like the roaring sea.

But black care constantly gnawed away
At the spirit
Of the valiant German knight
Whom no foe dared defy
Often, before the morning dawned,
He would awaken from his dream and ask,
Now sighing, now crying out,
'Where is my beloved youngest boy?'

'Father, do not call to the dear boy,'
Emma now whispers.
'See, he is asleep in his little room,
Gentle and proud — what can trouble
    him?'
'You ask me not to call? Have not seven
Of my sons died in battle?
Have I not for fifteen years
Mourned the woman who bore you?'

Emma listens, and nestles,
Trembling and weeping, against his breast.
'Father, behold your child! Ah, since I was
    young
I have sought to win your approval!'
And, as when God's messengers
Gently descend to bring words of comfort,
So the fair maiden's words and look
Give him new strength.

Cheered, he presses her to his heart:
'O forgive me, that I,
Overwhelmed by grief, forgot
What treasure I still possessed!
But you did not speak in jest.
And now, by candlelight
Walk with me straightway
Along the dark path.'

Trembling, she followed him; soon they
    reached
The deep and terrible vault
Where their forefathers slept;
Arranged in a circle, seven lamps —
The eighth was lacking — hanging on silver
    clasps
Illuminated this place constantly
With pale, troubled,
Sepulchral gleam.

Beneath the lamps were stones . . .
Forsooth! I cannot relate it!
It was so mournful in appearance,
Such an invitation to weeping.
'By the holy remains
For which these lamps shine,'
He cries loudly, 'I entreat you
To hear me, beloved daughter.

Mein Geschlecht seit grauen Zeiten
War — wie Rittermännern ziemt —
Keck, gestreng' und fast berühmt;
In des Grabes Dunkelheit
Sank die Reih' von Biederleuten —
Sanken die, so mich
  erfreuten,
Bis einst der Posaune
  Hall
Sie wird wecken allzumal.

Nie vergaßen deine Brüder
Dieser großen Ahnen Wert;
Reich und Kaiser schäzt' ihr Schwert
Wie ein deckendes Gefieder;
Ach die Tapfern sanken nieder!
Gib sie, Tochter, gib sie wieder
Mir im wackern Bräutigam,
Dir erkiest aus Heldenstamm.

Aber Fluch!«. . . . Und mit dem Worte
Gleich als jagt ihn Nacht und Graus —
Zog er plötzlich sie hinaus
Aus dem schauervollen Orte. . . .
Emma wankte durch die Pforte:
»Ende nicht die Schreckensworte!
Denk' an Himmel und Gericht!
O verwirf, verwirf mich nicht!«

Bleich, wie sie, mit bangem
  Zagen
Lehnt des Ritters Knappe hier;
Wie dem Sünder wird's ihm schier,
Den die Schrecken Gottes schlagen;
Kaum zu atmen tät er wagen —
Kaum die Kerze vorzutragen
Hatte, matt und fieberhaft,
Seine Rechte noch die Kraft.

Adelwolden bracht als
  Waise
Mitleidsvoll auf seinem Roß
Einst der Ritter nach dem Schloß
Heim von einer fernen Reise —
Pflegte sein mit Trank und Speise,
Tät' ihn hegen in dem Kreise
Seiner Kinder — oft und viel
War er tummelnd ihr Gespiel.

Aber Emma . . . seine ganze
Zarte Seele webt' um sie,
War es frühe Sympathie?
Froh umwand sie seine Lanze
Im Turnier mit einem Kranze —
Schwebte leichter dann im Tanze
Mit dem Ritter, keck und treu,
Als das Lüftchen schwebt im Mai.

Rosig auf zum Jüngling blühte
Bald der Niedre von Geschlecht;
Edler lohnte nie ein Knecht

'Since the misty past men of my lineage
Have been bold, stern and renowned,
As befits knights;
Honourable men,
Whom I cherished,
Have one by one descended into the grave's
  darkness,
Until the day when the sound of the
  trumpet
Shall awaken them all.

'Your brothers never forgot
The merit of these great forebears.
Their swords, like protective plumage,
Revered the emperor and his realm;
Alas, these brave men have perished!
My daughter, restore them to me
In the form of a valiant bridegroom
Chosen from a race of heroes.

'But a curse . . . !' And with these words,
As if stricken by darkness and horror,
He suddenly dragged her
Out of the fearful place. . . .
Emma staggered through the gate:
'Do not finish your terrible words!
Think of heaven, of the Last Judgment!
Do not, ah do not reject me!'

As pale as the maiden, fearful and
  apprehensive,
The knight's squire lurks here;
He feels almost as a sinner
Struck by the terrors of God.
He hardly dares breathe;
His right hand, weak and feverish,
Scarcely has the strength
To carry the candle.

Adelwold . . . the knight once took pity
  on him
As an orphan, and brought him on his horse
From distant parts.
Home to his castle
He tended him with food and drink,
And raised him among
His own children; long and often
Did they romp about together.

But Emma . . . his whole tender soul
Wove around her;
Was it the first sign of love?
In the tournament she gaily
Crowned his lance with a wreath,
And then she would dance
With the bold and true horseman
More blithely than the wafting May breeze.

Soon the boy of lowly birth
Blossomed into a fine young man;
Never did a vassal reward more nobly

Seines Pflegers Vatergüte;
Aber heiß und heißer glühte —
Was zu dämpfen er sich mühte;
Fester knüpft' ihn, fester ach!
An das Fräulein jeden Tag.

Fest und fester sie an ihren
Süßen trauten Adelwold.
»Was sind Wappen, Land, und Gold —
Sollt'ich Arme dich verlieren?
Was die Flitter, so mich zieren?
Was Bankete bei Turnieren?
Wappen, Land, Geschmuck, und Gold
Lohnt ein Traum von Adelwold!«

So das Fräulein, wenn der Schleier
Grauer Nächte sie umfing;

Doch mit eins, als Emma heute
Spät noch betet, weint, und wacht,
Steht, gehüllt in Pilgertracht,
Adelwold an ihrer Seite:
»Zürne nicht, Gebenedeite!
Denn mich treibt's, mich treibt's ins Weite!
Fräulein, dich befehl ich Gott!
Dein im Leben und im Tod!

»Leiten soll mich dieser Stecken
Hin in Zions heilges Land —
Wo vielleicht ein Häuflein Sand
Bald den Armen wird bedecken . . .
Meine Seele muß erschrecken,
Durch Verrat sich zu beflecken
An dem Mann, der, mild und groß
Her mich trug in seinen Schoß.

»Selig träumt' ich einst als Knabe
Engel — ach vergib es mir!
Denn ein Bettler bin ich schier;
Nur dies Herz ist meine Habe.«
»Jüngling — ach an diesem Stabe
Führst du treulos mich zum Grabe,
Du würgest — Gott verzeih es dir!
Die dich liebte für und für!«

Und schon wankte der Entzückte
Als des Fräuleins keuscher Arm —
Ach so weiß, so weich und warm!
Sanft ihn hin zum Busen drückte . . .
Aber fürcherterlicher blickte —
Was ihm schier ihr Kuß entrückte;
Und vom Herzen, das ihm schlug,
Riß ihn schnell des Vaters Fluch.

»Lindre, Vater, meine Wunde —
Keinen Laut aus deinem Munde!

The paternal kindness of his guardian.
But the feelings he sought to quell
Glowed more and more warmly;
Each day, alas, they bound him more firmly
To the maiden.

And she, too, became more and more
closely bound
To her dear, sweet Adelwold.
'What do I care for a coat of arms, for land
and gold,
If I, poor maiden, should lose you?
What do I care for the finery that
adorns me,
For banquets at tournaments?
One dream of Adelwold is worth
A coat of arms, land, jewels and gold!'

So mused the maiden, when the veil
Of dark nights enveloped her.

But this night, as Emma stays awake,
Praying and weeping,
Adelwold all of a sudden appears
At her side, dressed as a pilgrim.
'Do not be angry, blessed one,
For I am driven far from here!
Sweet maiden, God be with you!
I am yours in life and in death!

'This staff shall lead me
Into the Holy Land of Zion,
Where, perhaps, a mound of sand
Will soon cover this poor man . . .
My soul recoils at the thought
Of being stained with the betrayal
Of the man who, in his kindness and
greatness,
Took me to his bosom.

'As a boy I once dreamed blissfully . . .
My angel — O forgive me,
For I am almost a beggar;
This heart is my only possession.'
'Sweet youth, with this staff
You would faithlessly lead me to the grave;
You would kill her — God forgive you! —
Who would love you for ever!'

And already the enraptured youth wavered
As the maiden's chaste arm,
So white, so soft, so warm,
Pressed him gently to her breast . . .
But the feelings aroused in him by her
mere kiss
Seemed more terrible still;
And swiftly her father's curse
Tore him from the heart that beat for him.

'Father, ease my pain —
There is no sound from your lips,

Keine Zähr' in dieser Stunde!	No tears at this hour,
Keine Sonne, die mir blickt!	No sun to gaze upon me,
Keine Nacht, die mich erquickt!«	No night to refresh me!'
Gold, Gestein, und Seide nimmer,	She swears that henceforth
Schwört sie, fort zu legen an;	She will never don gold, jewels or silk;
Keine Zofe darf ihr nahn,	Neither maid nor squire
Und kein Knappe jetzt und nimmer;	May approach her, now and for ever more;
Oft bei trautem Mondesschimmer	Often, by the moonlight she loved,
Wallt sie barfuß über	She goes, barefoot, on a pilgrimage,
Trümmer,	through ruins
Wild verwachsen, steil und	That are wild and overgrown, steep and
rauh,	bleak,
Noch zur hochgelobten Frau.	To the revered Lady.
Ritter! ach schon weht vom Grabe	Knight! Ah, already the wind of death
Deiner Emma Todtenluft!	Blows from your Emma's grave.
Schon umschwärmt der Väter Gruft	Already screech owls and ravens
Ahnend Käuzlein, Eul' und	Flock around your forefathers' tombs,
Rabe; —	sensing death;
Weh dir weh! an seinem Stabe	Unhappy man! With his staff
Folgt sie willig ihm zum Grabe	She follows him gladly to the grave,
Hin, wo mehr denn Helm und Schild	Where, more than helmet and shield,
Liebe, Treu' und Tugend gilt. . . .	Love, constancy and virtue are prized.
Selbst dem Ritter tät sich senken	Even the knight now bowed his head
Tief und tiefer jetzt das Haupt;	Lower and lower;
Kaum daß er der Mähr noch glaubt;	He scarcely had faith in his mare now;
Seufzen tät er jetzt — jetzt denken,	He sighed, and wondered
Was den Jüngling konnte kränken? —	What could be troubling the youth —
Ob ein Spiel von Neid und Ränken? —	Was it envy and intrigue,
Ob? . . . Wie ein Phantom der Nacht	Was it . . .? As from a nocturnal phantom,
Schreckt'ihn — was er jetzt	He recoils in horror from the thought that
gedacht.	now struck him.
Hergeführt auf schwülen Winden,	Borne on the sultry winds,
Muß ein Strahl die Burg	A thunderbolt must have set fire to the
entzünden,	castle.
Tosend gleich den Wogen wallen	Roaring like the waves
Rings die Gluten — krachend	The flames rage all around — pillars and
dräun	arches,
Säul und Wölbung, Balk' und	Crossbeams and stones threaten
Stein,	straight away
Stracks in Trümmer zu zerfallen;	To crash down in ruins.
Angstruf und Verzweiflung schallen	Cries of terror and despair echo
Grausend durch die weiten Hallen:	Horribly through the vast halls:
Stürmend drängt und atemlos	Breathless, servant and squire
Knecht und Junker aus dem Schloß.	Rush out of the castle.
»Richter! ach verschone!«	'Lord, my Judge! Ah, spare me!'
Ruft der Greis mit starrem Blick —	Calls the old man, staring fixedly —
»Gott! mein Kind! — es bleibt zurück! —	'Lord! My child — she remains within! —
Rettet — daß euch Gott einst lohne! —	Save her, may God reward you!
Gold und Silber, Land und Frohne,	Gold and silver, land and farm,
Jede Burg, die ich bewohne,	Every castle I possess —
Ihrem Retter zum Gewinn —	All these shall be her rescuer's reward.
Selbst dies Leben geb' ich hin für sie.«	I would even sacrifice my life for her.'
Gleiten ab von tauben Ohren	His distressed cries
Tät des Hochbedrängten Schrei; —	Fall on deaf ears;

Aber plötzlich stürzt herbei,
Der ihr Treue
    zugeschworen —
Stürzt nach den entflammten Toren —
Gibt mit Freuden sich verloren;
Jeder staunend fern und nah
Wähnt' ein Blendwerk, was er sah.

Glut an Glut! und jedes Streben
Schien vergebens! — endlich faßt
Er die teure, süße Last,
Kalt und sonder Spur von Leben;
Doch beginnt ein leises Beben
Herz und Busen jetzt zu heben;
Und durch Flamme, Dampf und Graus
Trägt er glücklich sie hinaus.

Purpur kehrt auf ihre Wangen,
Wo der Traute sie geküßt. . . .
»Jüngling! sage, wer du bist —
Ich beschwöre dich — der Bangen;
Hält ein Engel mich umfangen,
Der auf seinem Erdenflug
Meines Lieben Bildnis trug?«

Starr zusammenschrickt der Blöde —
Denn der Ritter noch am Tor
Lauscht mit hingewandtem Ohr
Jedem Laut der süßen Rede;

Doch den Zweifler tät
    ermannen
Bald des Ritters Gruß und Kuß
Dem im süßesten
    Genuß
Hell der Wonne Zähren rannen:
»Du es, du, sag' an, von wannen?
Was dich konnt' von mir verbannen?
Was dich — nimmer lohn' ich's dir —
Emma wiedergab und mir?«

»Deines Fluchs mich zu entlasten
War es Pflicht, daß ich entwich,
Eilig, wild und fürchterlich
Trieb's mich sonder Ruh und Rasten;
Dort im Kloster, wo sie praßten,
Labten Tränen mich und Fasten,
Bis der frommen Pilger Schar
Voll zum Zug versammelt war.

Doch mit unsichtbaren Ketten
Zog mich plötzlich Gottes Hand
Jetzt zurück von Land zu Land
Her zur Burg, mein Teuerstes zu retten,
Stürme mich beflügelt hätten, —
Nimm sie, Ritter, nimm und
    sprich
Das Urteil über mich.«

Emma harrt, in düstres Schweigen,
Wie in Mitternacht gehüllt;

But suddenly he appears —
The man who has vowed to be faithful
    to her.
He rushes to the flaming gates,
And would gladly lose his life;
All are astonished, near and far,
Believing what they see to be an illusion.

Flame upon flame! All efforts
Seem in vain! Then, at last,
He holds his dear, sweet burden,
Cold and without trace of life;
But then, with a slight trembling,
Her heart and breast begin to rise,
And through flames, smoke and terror
He carries her safely out.

Crimson returned to her cheeks
Where her beloved has kissed her. . . .
'Sweet youth! Tell me in my distress
Who you are, I entreat you;
Am I embraced by an angel
Who, on his flight to earth,
Has assumed the form of my love?'

The bashful youth is paralysed with fear,
For at the gate the knight
Listens with attentive ears
To every word of her sweet speech.

But the doubting youth's courage was
    quickly restored
By the knight's welcoming kiss;
Down the old man's cheeks streamed
    shining tears
Of joy and sweetest pleasure.
'Is it you? Tell me whence you have come.
What could have driven you away from me?
What has restored you to Emma and to me?
For this I can never reward you.'

'It was my duty to escape,
In order to release myself from your curse.
In fear I was driven onwards,
Swiftly, harshly and without respite.
In the monastery, where they feasted,
Tears and fasting consoled me
Until the band of devout pilgrims
Was assembled for the journey.

But, with invisible chains
God's hand suddenly drew me
Back through one land after another
To this castle, to rescue my beloved!
It was as if the wind had given me wings.
Take her now, noble knight, and
    pronounce
Judgment on me.'

Emma waits, shrouded in a silence
As dark as midnight;

Starrer denn ein Marmorbild,
Harren furchterfüllte Zeugen;
Denn es zweifelten die Feigen,
Ob den Ritterstolz zu beugen
Je vermöcht' ein hoher Mut
Sonder Ahnenglanz und Gut.

»Dein ist Emma! ewig dein! — längst
    entscheiden
Tät der Himmel; rein wie
    Gold
Bist du funden, Adelwold —
Groß in Edelmut und Leiden;
Nimm! — ich gebe sie mit Freuden;
Nimm! — der Himmel tät entscheiden —
Nannte selbst im Donnerlaut
Sie vor Engeln deine Braut.

»Nimm sie hin mit Vatersegen;
Ihn wird neben meine Schuld —
Ach mit Langmut und Geduld!
Der einst kommt, Gericht zu hegen,
Auf die Prüfungswage legen —
Mir verzeihn um
    euretwegen,
Der von eitlem Stolz befleckt,
Beid' euch schier ins Grab gestreckt.«

Fest umschlungen jetzt von ihnen,
Blickt der Greis zum
    Himmel auf:
»Fröhlich endet sich mein Lauf!«
Spuren der Verklärung schienen
Aus des Hochentzückten Mienen —
Und auf dampfenden Ruinen
Fügt' er schweigend' ihre Hand
In das langersehnte Band.

More rigid than marble statues
The fearful onlookers wait.
For the fainthearted among them doubted
That a noble heart alone,
Without wealth or ancestral glory,
Could ever bend the knight's pride.

'Emma is yours, yours for ever! Thus
    heaven
Has long since decreed; you are deemed
    to be
As pure as gold, Adelwold,
And great in magnanimity and suffering;
Take her! With joy I give her to you;
Take her! Heaven has decreed it!
In a peal of thunder, before angels,
Heaven itself named her as your bride.

'Take her with a father's blessing!
He who shall come one day to judge me
Will lay that blessing on the scales
Alongside my guilt —
May he show patience and forbearance! —
And forgive me for what I have done
    to you;
For, sullied by vain pride,
I all but drove you both to the grave.'

Warmly embraced by the pair,
The old man now looks up to
    heaven:
'Thus my days end joyfully!'
Transfigured happiness shone
From the youth's enraptured features,
And amid the smoking ruins
He silently took her hand
To seal the long-desired bond.

Alinde / Alinde

JOHANN FRIEDRICH ROCHLITZ

D904 (1827)

Die Sonne sinkt ins tiefe Meer,
Da wollte sie kommen.
Geruhig trabt der Schnitter einher,
Mir ist's beklommen.

»Hast, Schnitter, mein Liebchen nicht
    gesehn?
Alinde, Alinde!«
«Zu Weib und Kindern muss ich gehn,
Kann nicht nach andern Dirnen sehn;
Sie warten mein unter der
    Linde.«

The sun sinks into the deep ocean,
She was due to come.
Calmly the reaper walks by.
My heart is heavy.

'Reaper, have you not seen my
    love?
Alinde!'
'I must go to my wife and children,
I cannot look for other girls.
They are waiting for me beneath the linden
    tree.'

Der Mond betritt die Himmelsbahn,
Noch will sie nicht kommen.
Dort legt ein Fischer das Fahrzeug an,
Mir ist's beklommen.

»Hast, Fischer, mein Liebchen nicht
    gesehn?
Alinde, Alinde!«
»Muss suchen, wie mir die Reusen stehn,
Hab nimmer Zeit nach Jungfern zu gehn,
Schau, welch einen Fang ich finde.«

Die lichten Sterne ziehn herauf,
Noch will sie nicht kommen.
Dort eilt der Jäger in rüstigem Lauf,
Mir ist's beklommen.

»Hast, Jäger, mein Liebchen nicht
    gesehn?
Alinde Alinde!«
»Muss nach dem bräunlichen Rehbock
    gehn,
Hab nimmer Lust nach Mädeln zu sehn;
Dort schleicht er im Abendwinde.«

In schwarzer Nacht steht hier der Hain,
Noch will sie nicht kommen.
Von allen Lebend'gen irr ich allein,
Bang und beklommen.

»Dir, Echo, darf ich mein Leid gestehn:
Alinde, Alinde!«
»Alinde,« liess Echo leise herüberwehn;
Da sah ich sie mir zur Seite stehn:
»Du suchtest so treu, nun
    finde!«

The moon entered its heavenly course,
She still does not come.
There a fisherman lands his boat.
My heart is heavy.

'Fisherman, have you not seen my
    love?
Alinde!'
'I must see how my oyster baskets are,
I never have time to chase after girls;
Look what a catch I have!'

The bright stars appear,
She still does not come.
The huntsman rides swiftly along.
My heart is heavy.

'Huntsman, have you not seen my
    love?
Alinde!'
'I must go after the brown
    roebuck,
I never care to look for girls;
There he goes in the evening breeze!'

The grove lies here in blackest night,
She still does not come.
I wander alone, away from all mankind,
Anxious and troubled.

'To you, Echo, I can confess my sorrow:
Alinde!'
'Alinde,' came the soft echo;
Then I saw her at my side.
'You searched so faithfully. Now you
    find me.'

Alles um Liebe / All for Love

LUDWIG KOSEGARTEN

D 241 (1815)

Was ist es das die Seele füllt?
Ach Liebe füllt sie, Liebe!
Sie füllt nicht Gold noch Goldes Wert,
Nicht was die schnöde Welt begehrt;
Sie füllt nur Liebe! Liebe!

Und hüllte Todesfinsternis,
Dich, meines Lebens Sonne,
Und stürb' ich, nur von ihr gemeint,
Von ihr beklagt, von ihr beweint,
So stürb ich wohl mit Wonne.

Viel besser ist's, jung, kräftig, kühn
Im Arm der Liebe sterben,
Als ungeliebt und liebelos
In dumpfer Freuden mattem Schoß
Veralten und verderben.

What is it that fills the soul?
Ah, it is love!
Not gold, nor the worth of gold,
Nor the desires of this base world,
Love alone fills the soul!

And if the darkness of death
Shrouded you, sun of my life,
And if I died cherished,
Mourned and lamented by you alone,
Then I would die in bliss.

It is far better to die in the arms of love,
Young, vigorous and bold,
Than to grow old and decline,
Unloved and loveless,
In the lap of weary, faded joys.

Als ich sie erröten sah / When I Saw her Blush

BERNHARD AMBROS EHRLICH

D 153 (1815)

All mein Wirken, all mein Leben
Strebt nach dir, Verehrte, hin!
Alle meine Sinne weben
Mir dein Bild, o Zauberin!

Du entflammest meinen Busen
Zu der Leier Harmonie,
Du begeisterst mehr als Musen
Und entzückest mehr als sie!

Ach, dein blaues Auge strahlet
Durch den Sturm der Seele mild,
Und dein süßes Lächeln malet
Rosig mir der Zukunft Bild.

Herrlich schmückt des Himmels
  Grenzen
Zwar Auroras Purpurlicht,
Aber lieblicheres Glänzen
Überdeckt dein Angesicht,

Wenn mit wonnetrunknen Blicken,
Ach, und unaussprechlich schön
Meine Augen voll Entzücken
Purpurn dich erröten sehn.

All that I do, all that I am
Is for you, my adored one!
All my senses weave
An image of you, enchantress!

You kindle within my heart
The sweet sounds of the lyre,
You inspire me more than the Muses,
And, more than they, delight me!

Your blue eyes shine tenderly
Through the tempest of the soul,
And your sweet smile paints
A rosy image of my future.

Though the horizon is
  adorned
By Aurora's crimson glow,
A still fairer radiance
Suffuses your countenance,

When, with ecstatic glances,
My delighted eyes
See the ineffable beauty
Of your crimson blush.

Alte Liebe rostet nie / Old Love Never Dies

JOHANN MAYRHOFER

D 477 (1816)

Alte Liebe rostet nie,
Hört ich oft die Mutter sagen;
Alte Liebe rostet nie,
Muß ich nun erfahrend klagen.

Wie die Luft umgibt sie mich,
Die ich einst die Meine nannte,
Die ich liebte ritterlich,
Die mich in die Ferne sandte.

Seit die Holde ich verlor,
Hab' ich Meer und Land gesehen, —
Vor der schönsten Frauen Flor
Durft ich unerschüttert stehen.

Denn aus mir ihr Bildnis trat,
Zürnend, wie zum Kampf mit ihnen;
Mit dem Zauber, den sie hat,
Mußte sie das Spiel gewinnen.

Old love never dies,
I often heard my mother say —
Old love never dies,
With experience I must now sadly agree.

She envelops me like the air,
She whom I once called my own,
Whom I loved chivalrously,
Who sent me into the wide world.

Since I lost my beloved
I have travelled on sea and land —
Before the fairest flower of womanhood
I could only stand unmoved.

For her image arose from within me,
Angrily, as if in opposition to them;
With the magic she possesses
She had to win the contest.

Da der Garten, dort das Haus,
Wo wir oft so traulich kos'ten!
Seh' ich recht? sie schwebt
    heraus—
Wird die alte Liebe rosten?

There is the garden, there the house
Where we once caressed so lovingly!
Am I seeing things? She glides out
    towards me—
Will old love never die?

Am Bach im Frühling / By the Stream in Spring

FRANZ VON SCHOBER

D 361 (1816?)

Du brachst sie nun, die kalte Rinde,
Und rieselst froh und frei dahin,
Die Lüfte wehen wieder linde,
Und Moos und Gras wird neu und grün.

Now you have broken the frozen crust,
And ripple along, free and happy;
The breezes blow mild again,
Moss and grass are fresh and green.

Allein, mit traurigem Gemüte
Tret ich wie sonst zu deiner Flut,
Der Erde allgemeine Blüte
Kommt meinem Herzen nicht zu gut.

Alone, with sorrowful spirit,
I approach your waters as before;
The flowering of the whole earth
Does not gladden my heart.

Hier treiben immer gleiche Winde,
Kein Hoffen kommt in meinen Sinn,
Als daß ich hier ein Blümchen finde,
Blau, wie sie der Erinnrung blühn.

Here the same winds forever blow,
No hope cheers my spirit,
Save that I find a flower here,
Blue, as the flowers of remembrance.

Am ersten Maimorgen / On the First May Morning

MATTHIAS CLAUDIUS

D 344 (1816?)

Heute will ich fröhlich, fröhlich sein,
Keine Weis' und keine Sitte hören;
Will mich wälzen, und für Freude schrein,
Und der König soll mir das nicht wehren.

Today I shall be merry, merry;
I shall hear no wisdom and no moralizing.
I shall run about and shout for joy;
And even the king will not stop me.

Am Fenster / At the Window

JOHANN GABRIEL SEIDL

D 878 (1826)

Ihr lieben Mauern, hold und traut,
Die ihr mich kühl umschliesst,
Und silberglänzend niederschaut,
Wenn droben Vollmond ist!

Dear, familiar walls,
You enclose me within your coolness,
And gaze down with silvery sheen
When the full moon shines above.

Ihr saht mich einst so traurig da,
Mein Haupt auf schlaffer Hand,
Als ich in mir allein mich sah,
Und Keiner mich verstand.

Once you saw me here so sad,
Head buried in weary hands,
Looking only within myself,
Understood by no one.

Jetzt brach ein ander Licht heran,
Die Trauerzeit ist um,
Und Manche zieh'n mit mir die Bahn
Durch's Lebensheiligtum.

Now a new light has dawned,
The time of sadness is past,
And many join me on my path
Through this sacred life.

Sie raubt der Zufall ewig nie
Aus meinem treuen Sinn,
In tiefster Seele trag' ich sie,
Da reicht kein Zufall hin.

Du Mauer wähnst mich trüb wie
    einst,
Das ist die stille Freud;
Wenn du vom Mondlicht widerscheinst,
Wird mir die Brust so weit.

An jedem Fenster wähnt ich dann
Ein Freundeshaupt, gesenkt,
Das auch so schaut zum Himmel an,
Das auch so meiner denkt.

Chance will never steal them
From my faithful heart;
I carry them deep in my soul,
Where fate cannot penetrate.

Wall, you imagine I am as gloomy as I
    once was:
That is my silent joy.
When you reflect the moonlight
My heart swells.

Then I imagine I see at every window
A friendly face, lowered,
That then gazes heavenwards,
Thinking of me too.

Am Flusse / By the River

JOHANN WOLFGANG VON GOETHE

First version: D 160 (1815)
Second version: D 766 (1822)

Verfliesset, vielgeliebte Lieder,
Zum Meere der Vergessenheit!
Kein Knabe sing' entzückt euch
    wieder,
Kein Mädchen in der Blütenzeit.

Ihr sanget nur von meiner Lieben;
Nun spricht sie meiner Treue Hohn.
Ihr wart ins Wasser eingeschrieben;
So fliesst denn auch mit ihm davon.

Flow away, beloved songs,
Into the sea of oblivion.
No enraptured youth, no maiden in the
    springtime of life
Will ever sing you again.

You told only of my beloved,
Now she pours scorn on my constancy.
You were inscribed upon the water;
Then with the water flow away.

Am Grabe Anselmos / At Anselmo's Grave

MATTHIAS CLAUDIUS

D 504 (1816)

Dass ich dich verloren habe,
Dass du nicht mehr bist,
Ach! dass hier in diesem Grabe
Mein Anselmo ist,
Das ist mein Schmerz!
Seht, wie liebten wir uns beide,
Und, solang ich bin, kommt Freude
Niemals wieder in mein Herz.

That I have lost you,
That you are no more,
That my Anselmo lies
Here in this grave:
That is my sorrow!
See, we loved each other,
And as long as I live joy
Will never return to my heart.

Am Meer / By the Sea

HEINRICH HEINE

see Schwanengesang no. 12

Am See / By the Lake

FRANZ VON BRUCHMANN

D746 (1817?)

In des Sees Wogenspiele
Fallen durch den Sonnenschein
Sterne, ach, gar viele, viele,
Flammend leuchtend stets hinein.

Into the lake's play of waves,
Through the sunlight,
Stars, o so many stars,
Fall ceaselessly, flaming, gleaming.

Wenn der Mensch zum See geworden,
In der Seele Wogenspiele
Fallen aus des Himmels Pforten
Sterne, ach, gar viele, viele.

If man becomes a lake,
Stars, o so many stars,
Will fall from the gates of heaven
Into the play of waves within his soul.

Am See / By the Lake

JOHANN MAYRHOFER

D124 (1814)

Sitz' ich im Gras am glatten See,
Beschleicht die Seele süsses Weh,
Wie Äolsharfen klingt mich an
Ein unnennbarer Zauberwahn.

When I sit in the grass by the smooth lake,
Sweet sorrow steals through my soul,
As if by Aeolian harps, I am moved
By nameless magical sounds.

Das Schilfrohr neiget seufzend sich,
Die Uferblumen grüssen mich,
Der Vogel klagt die Lüfte wehn,
Vor Schmerzenslust möcht' ich vergehn!

The bulrushes bow, sighing,
The flowers on the bank greet me,
A bird laments, breezes blow,
I would die of sweet grief!

Wie mir das Leben kräftig quillt
Und sich in raschen Strömen spielt.
Wie's bald in trüben Massen gärt
Und bald zum Spiegel sich verklärt.

How vigorously life flows around me,
Playing in rapid currents,
Now fermenting in a dark mass,
And now as bright as a mirror.

Bewusstsein meiner tiefsten Kraft,
Ein Wonnemeer in mir erschafft.
Ich stürze kühn in seine Flut
Und ringe um das höchste Gut.

An awareness of my deepest powers
Creates waves of joy within me.
I plunge boldly into the waters
And strive for the highest good.

O Leben, bist so himmlisch schön,
In deinen Tiefen, in deinen Höh'n!
Dein freundlich Licht soll ich nicht sehn,
Den finstren Pfad des Orkus gehn?

O life, you are so celestially beautiful,
In your depths and your peaks!
Shall I not see your fair light,
Shall I follow the black course to Hades?

Doch bist du mir das Höchste nicht,
Drum opfr' ich freudig dich der Pflicht;
Ein Strahlenbild schwebt mir voran,
Und mutig wag' ich 's Leben dran!

Yet you are not my highest ideal,
And I joyfully sacrifice you to duty.
A radiant image draws me onwards,
For it I will bravely risk my life.

Das Strahlenbild ist oft betränkt,
Wenn es durch meinen Busen brennt
Die Tränen weg vom Wangenrot,
Und dann in tausendfachem Tod.

This radiant image is often moist,
When through my heart it burns away
The tears from my red cheeks,
As I die a thousand deaths.

Du warst so menschlich, warst so hold,	You were so humane, so gracious,
O grosser deutscher Leopold,	So great a German, Leopold;*
Die Menschheit fühlte dich so ganz	Mankind felt your goodness to the full,
Und reichte dir den Opferkranz.	And handed you the sacrificial wreath.
Und hehr geschmückt sprangst du hinab,	Nobly adorned, you leapt down,
Für Menschen in das Wellengrab.	For men's sake, to death in the waves.
Vor dir erbleicht, o Fürstensohn,	Son of princes,
Thermopylae und	Thermopylae and Marathon pale
Marathon.	before you.
Das Schilfrohr neiget seufzend sich,	The bulrushes bow, sighing,
Die Uferblumen grüssen mich,	The flowers on the bank greet me,
Der Vogel klagt, die Lüfte wehn,	A bird sings, breezes blow,
Vor Schmerzeslust möcht' ich vergehn.	I would die of sweet grief.

Am Strome / By the River

JOHANN MAYRHOFER

D 539 (1817)

Ist mir's doch, als sei mein Leben	It seems to me that my life
An den schönen Strom gebunden;	Is bound to the fair river;
Hab' ich Frohes nicht an seinem Ufer,	Have I not known joy
Und Betrübtes hier empfunden?	And sorrow on its banks?
Ja, du gleichest meiner Seele;	Yes, you are like my soul;
Manchmal grün und glatt gestaltet,	Sometimes green and unruffled,
Und zu Zeiten herrschen Stürme	And sometimes lashed by storms,
Schäumend, unruhvoll, gefaltet.	Foaming, agitated, furrowed.
Fliessest zu dem fernen Meere,	You flow to the distant sea,
Darfst allda nicht heimisch werden;	And cannot find your home there.
Mich drängt's auch in mildre Lande,	I, too, yearn for a more welcoming land;
Finde nicht das Glück auf Erden.	I can find no happiness on earth.

Amalia / Amalia

FRIEDRICH VON SCHILLER

D 195 (1815)

Schön wie Engel voll Walhallas	Fair as angels filled with the bliss of
Wonne,	Valhalla,
Schön vor allen Jünglingen war er,	He was fair above all other youths;
Himmlisch mild sein Blick, wie	His gaze had the gentleness of heaven, like
Maiensonne,	the May sun
Rückgestrahlt vom blauen Spiegelmeer.	Reflected in the blue mirror of the sea.
Seine Küsse — paradiesisch Fühlen!	His kisses were the touch of paradise!
Wie zwei Flammen sich ergreifen, wie	As two flames engulf each other,
Harfentöne in einander spielen	As the sounds of the harp mingle
Zu der himmelvollen Harmonie —	In celestial harmony,

*The Duke of Brunswick, who drowned on 27 April 1785 while attempting to save his threatened
  subjects from a flooded dam.

Stürzten, flogen, schmolzen Geist in Geist
  zusammen,
Lippen, Wangen brannten, zitterten,
Seele rann in Seele — Erd' und Himmel
  schwammen
Wie zerronnen um die
  Liebenden!

Er ist hin — vergebens, ach vergebens
Stöhnet ihm der bange Seufzer nach!
Er ist hin, und alle Lust des Lebens
Rinnet hin in ein verlor' nes Ach!

So our spirits rushed, flew and fused
  together;
Lips and cheeks burned, trembled,
Soul melted into soul, earth and
  heaven
Swam, as though dissolved, around
  the lovers!

He is gone — in vain, ah in vain
My anxious sighs echo after him!
He is gone, and all life's joy
Ebbs away in one forlorn cry!

Ammenlied / *The Nurse's Song*

MICHAEL LUBI

D 122 (1814)

Am hohen, hohen Turm,
Da weht ein kalter Sturm:
Geduld! die Glöcklein läuten,
Die Sonne blinkt von weiten.
Am hohen, hohen Turm,
Da weht ein kalter Sturm.

Around the high tower
A cold gale blows.
Patience! The bells ring,
The sun gleams from afar.
Around the high tower,
A cold gale blows.

Im tiefen, tiefen Tal,
Da rauscht ein Wasserfall:
Geduld! ein bißchen weiter,
Dann rinnt das Bächlein heiter.
Im tiefen, tiefen Tal,
Da rauscht ein Wasserfall.

In the deep valley
A waterfall rushes.
Patience! A little further on
The brooklet flows merrily.
In the deep valley
A waterfall rushes.

Am kahlen, kahlen Baum,
Deckt sich ein Täubchen kaum,
Geduld! bald blühn die Auen,
Dann wird's sein Nestchen bauen.
Am kahlen, kahlen Baum,
Deckt sich ein Täubchen kaum.

In the bare tree
A dove scarcely finds shelter.
Patience! Soon the meadows will bloom,
And then it will build its nest,
In the bare tree
A dove scarcely finds shelter.

Dich friert, mein Töchterlein!
Kein Freund sagt: komm herein!
Laß unser Stündchen schlagen,
Dann werden's Englein sagen.
Das beste Stübchen gibt
Gott jenem, den er liebt.

You are frozen, my little daughter!
No friend asks you to come in!
Let our hour come.
Then angels will invite you in.
God gives his best room
To those he loves.

Amphiaraos / *Amphiaraos*

THEODOR KÖRNER

D 166 (1815)

Vor Thebens siebenfach gähnenden
  Toren
Lag im furchtbaren Brüderstreit
Das Heer der Fürsten zum Schlagen
  bereit,

Outside Thebes' seven gaping
  gates
Lay, in grim fraternal strife,
The princes' armies, ready for
  battle,

Im heiligen Eide zum Morde
  verschworen.
Und mit des Panzers blendendem Licht
Gerüstet, als gält' es, die Welt zu
  bekriegen,
Träumen sie jauchzend von Kämpfen
  und Siegen,
Nur Amphiaraos, der Herrliche, nicht.

Denn er liest in dem ewigen Kreise der
  Sterne,
Wen die kommenden Stunden feindlich
  bedrohn.
Des Sonnenlenkers gewaltiger Sohn
Sieht klar in der Zukunft nebelnde
  Ferne.
Er kennt des Schicksals verderblichen
  Bund,
Er weiss, wie die Würfel, die eisernen,
  fallen,
Er sieht die Moira mit blutigen Krallen;
Doch die Helden verschmähen den
  heiligen Mund.

Er sah des Mordes gewaltsame Taten,
Er wusste, was ihm die Parze spann.
So ging er zum Kampf, ein verlor'ner
  Mann,
Von dem eig'nen Weibe schmählich
  verraten.
Er war sich der himmlischen Flamme
  bewusst,
Die heiss die kräftige Seele
  durchglühte;
Der Stolze nannte sich
  Apolloide,
Es schlug ihm ein göttliches Herz in
  der Brust.

»Wie? — ich, zu dem die Götter geredet,
Den der Wahrheit heilige Düfte umwehn,
Ich soll in gemeiner Schlacht vergehn,
Von Periklymenos' Hand getötet?
Verderben will ich durch eig'ne Macht,
Und staunend vernehm' es die kommende
  Stunde
Aus künftiger Sänger geheiligtem Munde,
Wie ich kühn mich gestürzt in die ewige
  Nacht.«

Und als der blutige Kampf begonnen,
Und die Eb'ne vom Mordgeschrei
  widerhallt,
So ruft er verzweifelnd: »Es naht mit
  Gewalt,
Was mir die untrügliche Parze gesponnen.
Doch wogt in der Brust mir ein göttliches
  Blut,
Drum will ich auch wert des Erzeugers
  verderben.«

And pledged to murder in sacred
  oath.
Clad in dazzling armour,
As if intent on conquering the
  world,
They dream joyfully of battle and
  victory,
All but the noble Amphiaraos.

For in the eternal course of stars he
  reads
Whom the coming hours threaten with a
  hostile fate.
The mighty offspring of the sun's master
Sees clearly into the mists of the distant
  future.
He understands destiny's pernicious
  bond,
He knows how the iron dice
  fall,
He beholds Fate with her bloody claws;
Yet the heroes scorn his sacred
  words.

He saw monstrous deeds of murder,
He knew what Fate was spinning for him.
Thus he went to battle, a man
  doomed,
Shamefully betrayed by his own
  wife.
He was aware of the heavenly
  flame
Which burned fiercely through his
  great soul;
The proud man called himself the son
  of Apollo,
A godlike heart beat in his
  breast.

'What? I, whom the gods have addressed,
Bathed in the holy scent of truth,
Am to perish in mean battle,
Slain by Periclymenos' hand?
I wish to die by the power of my own hand.
Future ages will hear,
  amazed,
From the sacred lips of minstrels
How I plunged boldly into eternal
  night.'

And when the bloody fight commenced,
And the plain echoed with murderous
  cries,
He called in despair: 'What unerring Fate
  has spun for me
Now approaches with mighty force.
But divine blood flows in my
  breast,
Thus will my death be worthy of my
  progenitor.'

Und wandte die Rosse auf Leben und Sterben,	And he turned his horses, for life or for death,
Und jagt zu des Stromes hochbrausender Flut.	And sped to the river's surging flood.

The stallions snort fiercely, the chariot
rattles loudly,

Wild schnauben die Hengste, laut rasselt der Wagen,
Das Stampfen der Hufe zermalmet die Bahn.
Und schneller und schneller noch rast es heran,
Als gält' es, die flüchtige Zeit zu erjagen.
Wie wenn er die Leuchte des Himmels geraubt,
Kommt er in Wirbeln der Windsbraut geflogen;
Erschrocken heben die Götter der Wogen
Aus schäumenden Fluten das schilfichte Haupt.

The stallions snort fiercely, the chariot rattles loudly,
Stamping hooves pound the track.
Faster and faster they approach,
As if striving to catch fleeting Time itself.
As if he had stolen the torch of heaven
He rushes onwards in a seething whirlwind.
Horrified, the gods of the waves
Raise their reed-covered heads from the foaming floods.

Doch plötzlich, als wenn der Himmel erglühte,
Stürzt ein Blitz aus der heitern Luft,
Und die Erde zerreisst sich zur furchtbaren Kluft;
Da rief laut jauchzend der Apolloide:
»Dank dir, Gewaltiger! fest steht mir der Bund.
Dein Blitz ist mir der Unsterblichkeit Siegel;
Ich folge dir, Zeus!« — und er fasste die Zügel
Und jagte die Rosse hinab in den Schlund.

But suddenly, as if the heavens were ablaze,
A thunderbolt falls from the clear air,
The earth is ripped open, a terrifying chasm appears.
Then, in jubilation, the son of Apollo cried aloud:
'I thank you, mighty one! My covenant stands firm.
Your thunderbolt is my seal of immortality.
I follow you, Zeus!' And he seized the reins
And spurred his horses down into the abyss.

An Chloen / To Chloe

JOHANN GEORG JACOBI

D 462 (1816)

Bei der Liebe reinsten Flammen
Glänzt das arme Hüttendach:
Liebchen! ewig nun beisammen!
Liebchen! träumend oder wach!

With the purest flames of love
The humble cottage roof shines.
Sweetheart, now we are together eternally,
Sweetheart, dreaming or awake!

Und wir teilen alle Freuden,
Sonn' und Mond und Sternenglanz;
Allen Segen, alles Leiden,
Arbeit und Gebet und Tanz.

And we shall share all our joys,
Sun, moon and starlight;
Each blessing, each sorrow,
Work, and prayer, and dancing.

So, bei reiner Liebe Flammen,
Endet sich der schöne Lauf;
Ruhig schweben wir zusammen,
Liebchen, Liebchen! himmelauf.

Thus, with the flames of pure love,
Shall the fair course end.
Peacefully we shall float together,
Sweetheart, towards heaven.

An den Frühling / To Spring

FRIEDRICH VON SCHILLER

First version: D 283 (1815)
Second version: D 587 (1817)

Willkommen, schöner Jüngling!
Du Wonne der Natur!
Mit deinem Blumenkörbchen
Willkommen auf der Flur!

Ei, ei! Da bist ja wieder!
Und bist so lieb und schön!
Und freun wir uns so herzlich,
Entgegen dir zu gehn.

Denkst auch noch an mein Mädchen?
Ei, Lieber, denke doch!
Dort liebte mich das Mädchen,
Und's Mädchen liebt mich noch!

Für's Mädchen manches Blümchen
Erbat ich mir von dir —
Ich komm' und bitte wieder,
Und du? Du gibst es mir.

Welcome, fair youth,
Nature's delight!
Welcome to the meadows
With your basket of flowers!

Ah, you are here again,
So dear and lovely!
We feel such heartfelt joy
As we come to meet you.

Do you still think of my sweetheart?
Ah, dear friend, think of her!
There my girl loved me,
And she loves me still!

I asked you for many flowers
For my sweetheart —
I come and ask you once more,
And you? You give them to me.

An den Mond / To the Moon

JOHANN WOLFGANG VON GOETHE

First version: D 259 (1815)
Second version: D 296 (1819?)

Füllest wieder Busch und Tal
Still mit Nebelglanz,
Lösest endlich auch einmal
Meine Seele ganz.

Breitest über mein Gefild
Lindernd deinen Blick,
Wie des Freundes Auge mild
Über mein Geschick.

Jeden Nachklang fühlt mein Herz
Froh- und trüber Zeit,
Wandle zwischen Freud und Schmerz
In der Einsamkeit.

Fliesse, fliesse, lieber Fluss!
Nimmer werd ich froh;
So verrauschte Scherz und
    Kuss,
Und die Treue so.

Rausche, Fluss, das Tal entlang,
Ohne Rast und Ruh,
Rausche, flüstre meinem Sang
Melodien zu,

Once more you silently fill wood and vale
With your hazy gleam,
And at last
Set my soul quite free.

You cast your soothing gaze
Over my fields;
With a friend's gentle eye
You watch over my fate.

My heart feels every echo
Of times both glad and gloomy.
I hover between joy and sorrow
In my solitude.

Flow on, beloved river!
I shall never be happy:
Thus have laughter and kisses rippled
    away,
And with them constancy.

Murmur on, river, through the valley,
Without cease,
Murmur on, whispering melodies,
To my song,

Wenn du in der Winternacht	When on winter nights
Wütend überschwillst,	You angrily overflow,
Oder um die	Or when you bathe the springtime
Frühlingspracht	splendour
Junger Knospen quillst.	Of the young buds.
Selig, wer sich vor der Welt	Happy he who, without hatred,
Ohne Hass verschliesst,	Shuts himself off from the world,
Einen Freund am Busen hält	Holds one friend to his heart,
Und mit dem geniesst,	And with him enjoys
Was, von Menschen nicht gewusst	That which, unknown to
Oder nicht bedacht,	And undreamt of by men,
Durch das Labyrinth der Brust	Wanders by night
Wandelt in der Nacht.	Through the labyrinth of the heart.

An den Mond / To the Moon

LUDWIG HEINRICH CHRISTOPH HÖLTY

D 193 (1815)

Geuss, lieber Mond, geuss deine	Beloved moon, shed your silver
Silberflimmer	radiance
Durch dieses Buchengrün,	Through these green beeches,
Wo Phantasien und Traumgestalten	Where fancies and dreamlike images
Immer vor mir vorüberfliehn!	Forever flit before me.
Enthülle dich, dass ich die Stätte finde,	Unveil yourself, that I may find the spot
Wo oft mein Mädchen sass,	Where my beloved sat,
Und oft, im Wehn des Buchbaums und	Where often, in the swaying branches of the
der Linde,	beech and lime,
Der goldnen Stadt vergass.	She forgot the gilded town.
Enthülle dich, dass ich des Strauchs mich	Unveil yourself, that I may delight in the
freue,	whispering bushes
Der Kühlung ihr gerauscht,	That cooled her,
Und einen Kranz auf jeden Anger streue,	And lay a wreath on that meadow
Wo sie den Bach belauscht.	Where she listened to the brook.
Dann, lieber Mond, dann nimm den	Then, beloved moon, take your veil once
Schleier wieder,	more,
Und traur um deinen Freund,	And mourn for your friend.
Und weine durch den Wolkenflor	Weep down through the hazy
hernieder,	clouds,
Wie ein Verlassner weint!	As one forsaken weeps.

An den Mond / To the Moon

LUDWIG HEINRICH CHRISTOPH HÖLTY

D 468 (1816)

Was schauest du so hell und klar	Why do you gaze down, so bright and clear,
Durch diese Apfelbäume,	Through these apple trees,
Wo einst dein Freund so selig war	Where once your friend was so happy,
Und träumte süsse Träume?	Dreaming sweet dreams?
Verhülle deinen Silberglanz,	Veil your silvery radiance,

Und schimmre, wie du schimmerst,
Wenn du den frühen Totenkranz
Der jungen Braut beflimmerst!

Du blickst umsonst so hell und klar
In diese Laube nieder;
Nie findest du das frohe Paar
In ihrem Schatten wieder!
Ein schwarzes, feindliches Geschick
Entriss mir meine Schöne!
Kein Seufzer zaubert sie zurück
Und keine Sehnsuchtsträne!

O wandelt sie hinfort einmal
An meine Ruhestelle,
Dann mache flugs mit trübem Strahl
Des Grabes Blumen helle!
Sie setze weinend sich aufs Grab,
Wo Rosen niederhangen,
Und pflücke sich ein Blümchen ab,
Und drück' es an die Wangen.

And glimmer as you do
When you shine upon the funeral wreath
Of the young bride.

In vain you gaze down, so bright and clear,
Into this arbour.
Never again will you find the happy pair
Beneath its shade.
Dark, hostile fate
Tore my beloved from me.
No sighs, no tears of longing
Can conjure her back.

If one day she should come
To my resting place,
Then, swiftly, with your sombre light
Make bright the flowers on my grave.
May she sit weeping on my grave
Where roses droop,
And pluck a flower,
And press it to her cheek.

An den Mond in einer Herbstnacht / To the Moon on an Autumn Night

ALOIS SCHREIBER

D 614 (1818)

Freundlich ist dein Antlitz,
Sohn des Himmels!
Leis sind deine Tritte
Durch des Äthers Wüste,
Holder Nachtgefährte!
Dein Schimmer ist sanft und
   erquickend,
Wie das Wort des Trostes
Von des Freundes Lippe,
Wenn ein schrecklicher Geier
An der Seele nagt.

Manche Träne siehst du,
Siehst so manches Lächeln,
Hörst der Liebe trauliches Geflüster,
Leuchtest ihr auf stillem Pfade;
Hoffnung schwebt auf deinem Strahle,
Herab zum stillen Dulder,
Der verlassen geht
Auf bedorntem Weg.

Du siehst auch meine Freunde,
Zerstreut in fernen Landen;
Du giessest deinen Schimmer
Auch auf die frohen Hügel,
Wo ich oft als Knabe hüpfte,
Wo oft bei deinem Lächeln
Ein unbekanntes Sehnen
Mein junges Herz ergriff.
Du blickst auch auf die Stätte,
Wo meine Lieben ruhn,

Your face is kind,
Son of heaven.
Softly you move
Through the airy waste,
Fair companion of the night.
Your shimmering light is gentle and
   refreshing,
Like a word of comfort
From the lips of a friend
When a terrifying vulture
Gnaws at the soul.

You see many a tear
And many a smile;
You hear lovers' intimate whispers
As you shine for them on their quiet way;
On your beams hope streams down
To the silent sufferer,
Wandering all alone
On the thorny patch.

You see my friends, too,
Scattered in distant lands;
You shed your light
Upon the happy hills
Where I often played as a boy,
And where, as you smiled down,
An unknown longing
Often seized my youthful heart.
You gaze also upon the place
Where my loved ones rest,

Wo der Tau fällt auf ihr Grab,
Und die Gräser drüber wehn
In dem Abendhauche.

Doch dein Schimmer dringt nicht
In die dunkle Kammer,
Wo sie ruhen von des Lebens Müh'n,
Wo auch ich bald ruhen werde!
Du wirst geh'n
Und wiederkehren,
Du wirst seh'n
Noch manches Lächeln;
Dann werd' ich nicht mehr lächeln,
Dann werd' ich nicht mehr weinen,
Mein wird man nicht mehr gedenken
Auf dieser schönen Erde.

Where the dew falls on their graves
And the grass above them
Blows in the evening breeze.

But your light does not penetrate
The dark chamber
Where they rest from life's toil,
And where I, too, shall soon rest.
You will go
And return again,
You will see
Many more smiles.
Then I shall smile
And weep no more;
I will no longer be remembered
On this fair earth.

An den Schlaf / *To Sleep*

JOHANN PETER UZ (?)

D 447 (1816)

Komm, und senke die umflorten
    Schwingen,
Süsser Schlummer, auf den müden
    Blick!
Segner! Freund! in deinen Armen
    dringen
Trost und Balsam auf's verlorne
    Glück.

Come, and lay your gossamer
    wings,
Sweet slumber, upon my weary
    eyes.
Benefactor, friend! In your
    arms
Comfort and balm come to my lost
    happiness.

An den Tod / *To Death*

CHRISTIAN FRIEDRICH DANIEL SCHUBART

D 518 (1817)

Tod, du Schrecken der Natur,
Immer rieselt deine Uhr:
Die geschwung'ne Sense blinkt,
Gras und Halm und Blume sinkt.

Mähe nicht ohn' Unterschied,
Dieses Blümchen, das erst blüht,
Dieses Röschen, erst halbrot;
Sei barmherzig, lieber Tod!

Tod, wann kommst du, meine Lust?
Ziehst den Dolch aus meiner Brust?
Streifst die Fesseln von der Hand?
Ach, wann deckst du mich mit Sand?

Komm, o Tod, wenn's dir gefällt,
Hol' Gefang'ne aus der Welt:
Komm, vollende meine Not;
Sei barmherzig, lieber Tod!

Death, terror of nature,
Your hour-glass trickles ceaselessly;
The swinging scythe flashes,
Grass, stalk and flower fall.

Do not mow down indiscriminately
This little flower just bloomed,
This rose half-opened;
Be merciful, dear death!

Death, when will you come, my joy,
To draw the dagger from my breast,
And slip the fetters from my hands?
Ah, when will you cover me with sand?

Come, death, if it pleases you,
Take the prisoners from this world.
Come, end my distress;
Be merciful, dear death!

An die Apfelbäume, wo ich Julien erblickte

LUDWIG HEINRICH CHRISTOPH HÖLTY

D 197 (1815)

Ein heilig Säuseln,
Und ein Gesangeston
Durchzittre deine Wipfel,
O Schattengang, wo bang und
    wild
Der ersten Liebe selige Taumel
Mein Herz berauschten.

Die Abendsonne
Bebte wie lichtes Gold
Durch Purpurblüten,
Bebte wie lichtes Gold
Um ihres Busens Silberschleier;
Und ich zerfloss in Entzückungsschauer.

Nach langer Trennung
Küsse mit Engelkuss
Ein treuer Jüngling hier
Das geliebte Weib,
Und schwör in diesem Blütendunkel
Ew'ge Treue der Auserkornen.

Ein Blümchen sprosse,
Wann wir gestorben sind,
Aus jedem Rasen,
Welchen ihr Fuss berührt,
Und trag' auf jedem seiner Blätter
Meines verherrlichten Mädchens
    Namen.

To the Apple Trees where I Caught Sight of Julia

Let solemn murmuring
And the sound of singing
Vibrate through the tree-tops above you,
O shaded walk, where, fearful and
    impassioned,
The blissful frenzy of first love
Seized my heart.

The evening sun
Shimmered like brilliant gold
Through purple blossoms,
Shimmered like brilliant gold
Around the silver veil on her breast.
And I dissolved in a shudder of ecstasy.

After long separation
Let a faithful youth
Kiss with an angel's kiss
His beloved wife,
And in the darkness of this blossom
Pledge eternal constancy to his chosen one.

May a flower bloom,
When we are dead,
From every lawn
Touched by her foot.
And may each of its leaves
Bear the name of my exalted
    love.

An die Entfernte / To the Distant Beloved

JOHANN WOLFGANG VON GOETHE

D 765 (1822)

So hab' ich wirklich dich verloren?
Bist du, o Schöne, mir entflohn?
Noch klingt in den gewohnten Ohren
Ein jedes Wort, ein jeder Ton.

So wie des Wandrers Blick am Morgen
Vergebens in die Lüfte dringt,
Wenn, in dem blauen Raum verborgen,
Hoch über ihm die Lerche singt:

So dringet ängstlich hin und
    wieder
Durch Feld und Busch und Wald mein
    Blick;
Dich rufen alle meine Lieder:
»O Komm, Geliebte, mir zurück!«

Have I really lost you?
Have you fled from me, fairest love?
Every word, every tone
Still sounds in my well-accustomed ears.

As in the morning the traveller's gaze
Searches the heavens in vain
When, concealed in the blue firmament,
The lark sings high above him:

So my gaze searches anxiously back and
    forth
Through field, thicket and
    woodland;
All my songs call out to you:
'Come back to me, beloved!'

An die Freude / Ode to Joy

FRIEDRICH VON SCHILLER

D 189 (1815)

Freude, schöner Götterfunken,
Tochter aus Elysium,
Wir betreten feuertrunken,
Himmlische, dein Heiligtum.
Deine Zauber binden wieder,
Was die Mode streng geteilt;
Alle Menschen werden Brüder,
Wo dein sanfter Flügel weilt.

Joy, fair divine spark,
Daughter of Elysium,
We enter your sanctuary,
Heavenly one, drunk with ardour.
Your magic will reunite,
What custom has harshly severed.
All men become brothers
Where your gentle wings hover.

Seid umschlungen, Millionen!
Diesen Kuss der ganzen Welt!
Brüder, überm Sternenzelt
Muss ein lieber Vater wohnen.

Be embraced, ye millions!
This kiss is for the whole world!
Brothers, above the starry vaults
A loving father must dwell.

Wem der grosse Wurf gelungen,
Eines Freundes Freund zu sein,
Wer ein holdes Weib errungen,
Mische seinen Jubel ein!
Ja — wer auch nur eine Seele
Sein nennt auf dem Erdenrund!
Und wer's nie gekonnt, der stehle
Weinend sich aus diesem
   Bund!

He who has had the good fortune,
To give and receive friendship,
He who has found a loving wife,
Let him add his jubilant voice!
Yes — whoever on this earth
Calls but one living soul his own!
And let him who cannot do so
Creep away, weeping, from this
   brotherhood!

Was den grossen Ring bewohnet,
Huldige der Sympathie!
Zu den Sternen leitet sie,
Wo der Unbekannte thronet.

Let all who inhabit this great globe
Pay homage to sympathy!
It leads to the stars,
Where the unknown being is enthroned.

Freude trinken alle Wesen
An den Brüsten der Natur,
Alle Guten, alle Bösen
Folgen ihrer Rosenspur.
Küsse gab sie uns und Reben,
Einen Freund, geprüft im Tod;
Wollust ward dem Wurm gegeben,
Und der Cherub steht vor Gott.

All creatures drink joy
From nature's breasts,
All men, good and evil,
Follow her rosy trail.
She gave us kisses, and the vine,
And a friend, tried in death.
Lust was granted to the worm,
And the Cherub stands before God.

Ihr stürzt nieder, Millionen?
Ahnest du den Schöpfer, Welt?
Such ihn überm Sternenzelt!
Über Sternen muss er wohnen.

Ye millions, do you bow down?
World, do you sense your Creator?
Seek Him beyond the starry vaults!
He must dwell above the stars.

An die Freunde / To my Friends

JOHANN MAYRHOFER

D 654 (1819)

Im Wald, im Wald da grabt mich ein,
Ganz stille, ohne Kreuz und Stein:
Denn was ihr türmet, überschneit
Und überwindet Winterszeit.
.

Bury me in the forest,
Silently, without cross or stone;
For whatever you raise up
Winter storms will cover with snow.

Und wann die Erde sich verjüngt
Und Blumen meinem Hügel bringt,
Das freut Euch, Guten, freuet Euch,
Dies alles ist dem Toten gleich.

Doch nein, denn Eure Liebe spannt
Die Äste in das Geisterland,
Und die Euch führt zu meinem Grab,
Zieht mich gewaltiger herab.

And when the earth grows young again,
Bringing flowers to my grave,
Rejoice, good friends, rejoice;
All this is nothing to the dead.

But no, for your love extends
Its branches into the land of spirits,
And as it leads you to my grave,
It draws me more forcefully downwards.

An die Geliebte / To the Beloved

JOSEPH LUDWIG STOLL

D 303 (1815)

O dass ich dir vom stillen Auge
In seinem liebevollen Schein
Die Tränen von der Wange sauge,
Eh sie die Erde trinket ein!

Wohl hält sie zögernd auf der Wange
Und will sie heiss der Treue weihn.
Nun ich sie so im Kuss empfange,
Nun sind auch deine Schmerzen mein,
   ja mein!

Oh that from your silent eyes,
In their loving radiance,
I might drink the tears from your cheek
Before the earth absorbs them!

They remain hesitantly on your cheek,
Which they dedicate warmly to constancy.
Now, as I receive them in my kiss,
Your sorrows, too, are
   mine.

An die Harmonie / To Harmony

JOHANN GAUDENZ VON SALIS-SEEWIS

D 394 (1816)

Schöpferin beseelter Töne!
Nachklang dem Olymp enthallt!
Holde, körperlose Schöne,
Sanfte geistige Gewalt,
Die das Herz der Erdensöhne
Kühn erhebt und mild umwallt!
Die in inn'rer Stürme Drange
Labt mit stillender Magie,
Komm mit deinem Sühngesange,
Himmelstochter Harmonie!

Seufzer, die das Herz erstickte,
Das, misskannt, sich endlich
   schloss —
Tränen, die das Aug' zerdrückte,
Das einst viel umsonst vergoss,
Dankt dir wieder der Entzückte,
Den dein Labequell umfloss.
Der Empfindung zarte Blume,
Die manch frost'ger Blick versengt,
Blüht, erquickt im Heiligtume
Einer Brust, die du getränkt.

Creator of inspired music!
Echo, sounding from Olympus!
Gracious, disembodied beauty,
Gentle spiritual power
Who boldly uplifts and tenderly envelops
The hearts of mortals,
Who with soothing magic
Quells the tempests within us,
Come with your comforting music,
Harmony, daughter of heaven.

For sighs, suppressed by the heart
That, misunderstood, at length became
   closed;
For tears, forced back by eyes
That had once wept so much in vain,
I thank you again, enraptured,
Lapped by your healing stream.
The tender flower of feeling,
Blighted by many a frozen look.
Blossoms, refreshed in the shrine
Of a heart nurtured by you.

An die Laute / To the Lute

JOHANN FRIEDRICH ROCHLITZ

D905 (1827)

Leiser, leiser, kleine Laute,
Flüstre, was ich dir vertraute,
Dort zu jenem Fenster hin!
Wie die Wellen sanfter Lüfte,
Mondenglanz und Blumendüfte,
Send es der Gebieterin!

Neidisch sind des Nachbars Söhne,
Und im Fenster jener Schöne
Flimmert noch ein einsam Licht.
Drum noch leiser, kleine Laute:
Dich vernehme die Vertraute,
Nachbarn aber, Nachbarn
nicht!

Play more softly, little lute,
Whisper what I secretly told you
To that window there!
Like the ripple of gentle breezes,
Like moonlight and the scent of flowers,
Convey your secret to my mistress.

My neighbour's sons are envious,
And at the fair lady's window
A solitary lamp flickers.
So play still more softly, little lute:
That my beloved may hear you,
But the neighbours — no, not the
neighbours!

An die Leier / To my Lyre

FRANZ VON BRUCHMANN

D737 (1822–3?)

Ich will von Atreus' Söhnen,
Von Kadmus will ich singen!
Doch meine Saiten tönen
Nur Liebe im Erklingen.

Ich tauschte um die Saiten,
Die Leier möcht ich tauschen!
Alcidens Siegesschreiten
Sollt ihrer Macht entrauschen!

Doch auch die Saiten tönen
Nur Liebe im Erklingen!
So lebt denn wohl, Heroen!
Denn meine Saiten tönen,
Statt Heldensang zu drohen,
Nur Liebe im Erklingen.

I would sing of Atreus' sons,
Of Cadmus,
But my strings bring forth
Only sounds of love.

I have changed the strings,
I should like to change the lyre!
Alcides' victorious march
Should ring out from its might!

But these strings, too
Bring forth only sounds of love!
Farewell, then, heroes!
For my strings,
Instead of threatening with heroic songs,
Bring forth only sounds of love.

An die Musik / To Music

FRANZ VON SCHOBER

D547 (1817)

Du holde Kunst, in wieviel grauen
Stunden,
Wo mich des Lebens wilder Kreis
umstrickt,
Hast du mein Herz zu warmer Lieb
entzunden,
Hast mich in eine bessre Welt entrückt!

Beloved art, in how many a bleak
hour,
When I am enmeshed in life's tumultuous
round,
Have you kindled my heart to the warmth
of love,
And borne me away to a better world!

Oft hat ein Seufzer, deiner Harf
  entflossen,
Ein süsser, heiliger Akkord von dir
Den Himmel bessrer Zeiten mir
  erschlossen,
Du holde Kunst, ich danke dir dafür!

Often a sigh, escaping from your
  harp,
A sweet, celestial chord
Has revealed to me a heaven of happier
  times,
Beloved art, for this I thank you!

An die Nachtigall / *To the Nightingale*

MATTHIAS CLAUDIUS

D497 (1816)

Er liegt und schläft an meinem Herzen,
Mein guter Schutzgeist sang ihn ein;
Und ich kann fröhlich sein und scherzen,
Kann jeder Blum' und jedes Blatts mich
  freun.
Nachtigall, Nachtigall, ach!
Sing mir den Amor nicht wach!

He lies sleeping upon my heart;
My kind tutelary spirit sang him to sleep.
And I can be merry and jest,
Delight in every flower and
  leaf.
Nightingale, ah, nightingale,
Do not awaken my love with your singing!

An die Nachtigall / *To the Nightingale*

LUDWIG HEINRICH CHRISTOPH HÖLTY

D 196 (1815)

Geuss nicht so laut der liebentflammten
  Lieder
Tonreichen Schall
Vom Blütenast des Apfelbaums
  hernieder,
O Nachtigall!

Do not pour out so loudly the sonorous
  strains
Of passionate love songs
From the blossom-covered boughs of the
  apple-tree,
O nightingale!

Du tönest mir mit deiner süssen Kehle
Die Liebe wach;
Denn schon durchbebt die Tiefen meiner
  Seele
Dein schmelzend »Ach«.

The singing from your sweet throat
Awakens love in me;
For already your melting
  sighs
Pierce the depths of my soul.

Dann flieht der Schlaf von neuem dieses
  Lager,
Ich starre dann
Mit nassem Blick und totenbleich
  und hager
Den Himmel an.

Then sleep once more shuns this
  bed,
And I stare,
Moist-eyed, drawn and deathly
  pale,
At the heavens.

Fleuch, Nachtigall, in grüne
  Finsternisse,
Ins Haingesträuch,
Und spend im Nest der treuen Gattin
  Küsse,
Entfleuch, Entfleuch!

Fly away, nightingale, to the green
  darkness
Of the grove's thickets,
And in your nest bestow kisses on your
  faithful spouse.
Fly away!

An die Natur / To Nature

FRIEDRICH LEOPOLD, GRAF ZU STOLBERG-STOLBERG

D 372 (1816?)

Süsse, heilige Natur,
Lass mich gehn auf deiner Spur,
Leite mich an deiner Hand,
Wie ein Kind am Gängelband!

Wenn ich dann ermüdet bin,
Sink' ich dir am Busen hin,
Atme süsse Himmelslust
Hangend an der Mutterbrust.

Ach! wie wohl ist mir bei dir!
Will dich lieben für und für;
Lass mich gehn auf deiner Spur,
Süsse, heilige Natur!

Sweet, holy nature,
Let me walk upon your pathway,
Lead me by the hand,
Like a child on the reins!

Then, when I am weary,
I shall sink down on your breast,
And breathe the sweet joys of heaven
Suckling at your maternal breast.

Ah, how happy I am to be with you!
I shall love you for ever;
Let me walk upon your pathway,
Sweet holy nature!

An die Sonne / To the Sun

GABRIELE VON BAUMBERG

D 270 (1815?)

Sinke, liebe Sonne, sinke!
Ende deinen trüben Lauf,
Und an deine Stelle winke
Bald den Mond herauf.

Herrlicher und schöner dringe
Aber Morgen dann herfür,
Liebe Sonn'! und mit dir bringe
Meinen Lieben mir.

Sink, dearest sun, sink!
End your dusky course,
And in your place quickly bid
The moon rise.

But tomorrow come forth
More glorious and more beautiful,
Dearest sun! And with you
Bring my love.

An die Sonne / To the Sun

CHRISTOPH AUGUST TIEDGE

D 272 (1815)

Königliche Morgensonne,
Sei gegrüßt in deiner Wonne,
Hoch gegrüßt in deiner Pracht!
Golden fließt schon um die Hügel
Dein Gewand; und das Geflügel
Eines jeden Waldes wacht.

Alles fühlet deinen Segen;
Fluren singen dir entgegen,
Alles wird Zusammenklang:
Und du hörest gern die Chöre
Froher Wälder, o so höre,
Hör' auch meinen Lobgesang.

Regal morning sun,
I greet you in your rapture,
I welcome you in your splendour!
Already your golden raiment
Drapes the hills,
And in every forest birds awaken.

Your blessing is felt by all;
The meadows sing to greet you,
All becomes harmonious.
And as you hear with delight the chorus
Of the happy forests, so, too,
Hear my song of praise.

An die Türen will ich schleichen / I shall Steal from Door to Door

JOHANN WOLFGANG VON GOETHE

see Harfenspieler III

An die untergehende Sonne / To the Setting Sun

LUDWIG KOSEGARTEN

D 457 (1816–17)

Sonne, du sinkst, sink in Frieden,
  o Sonne!
Still und ruhig ist deines Scheidens
  Gang,
Rührend und feierlich deines Scheidens
  Schweigen.
Wehmut lächelt dein freundliches Auge,
Tränen entträufeln den goldenen
  Wimpern;
Segnungen strömst du der duftenden
  Erde.
Immer tiefer, immer leiser,
Immer ernster, feierlicher
Sinkest du den Äther hinab.

Sonne, du sinkst, sink in Frieden,
  o Sonne!
Es segnen die Völker, es säuseln die
  Lüfte,
Es räuchern die dampfenden Wiesen
  dir nach;
Winde durchrieseln dein lockiges Haar;
Wogen kühlen die brennende Wange;
Weit auf tut sich dein Wasserbett.
Ruh' in Frieden, ruh' in Wonne!
Die Nachtigall flötet dir
  Schlummergesang.
Sonne, du sinkst, sink in Frieden,
  o Sonne!

Sun, you are sinking. Sink in peace,
  o sun!
Calm and tranquil is your
  parting,
Touching and solemn that parting's
  silence.
Sadness smiles from your kindly eyes,
Tears fall from your golden
  lashes;
You pour blessings upon the fragrant
  earth.
Ever deeper, ever softer,
Ever more grave and solemn,
You sink in the heavens.

Sun, you are sinking. Sink in peace,
  o sun!
The people bless you, the breezes
  whisper,
Mist drifts towards you from the hazy
  meadows;
The winds blow through your curly hair,
The waves cool your burning cheeks;
Your watery bed opens wide.
Rest in peace, rest in joy!
The nightingale is singing you
  lullabies.
Sun, you are sinking. Sink in peace,
  o sun!

An eine Quelle / To a Spring

MATTHIAS CLAUDIUS

D 530 (1817)

Du kleine grünumwachsne Quelle,
An der ich Daphne jüngst gesehn!
Dein Wasser war so still! und helle!
Und Daphnes Bild darin so schön!
O wenn sie sich noch mal am Ufer
  sehen lässt,
So halte du ihr schönes Bild doch fest;
Ich schleiche heimlich dann mit nassen
  Augen hin,
Dem Bild meine Not zu klagen;
Denn, wenn ich bei ihr selber bin,
Dann, ach dann kann ich ihr nichts sagen.

Little spring, mantled in green,
Where lately I saw Daphne!
Your water was so still and clear,
And Daphne's reflection so fair!
O, if she should appear once more on your
  banks,
Hold her fair image fast.
Then I will steal up furtively, with moist
  eyes,
To bewail my distress to her image;
For, when I am with her,
Ah, then I cannot say a word to her.

An Emma / To Emma

FRIEDRICH VON SCHILLER

D113 (1814)

Weit in nebelgrauer Ferne	Far in the grey, misty distance
Liegt mir das vergangne Glück,	Lies my past happiness,
Nur an Einem schönen Sterne	My eyes still linger lovingly
Weilt mit Liebe noch der Blick.	On one fair star alone.
Aber, wie des Sternes Pracht,	But, like that star's splendour,
Ist es nur ein Schein der Nacht.	It is merely an illusion of the night.
Deckte dir der lange Schlummer,	If the prolonged slumber
Dir der Tod die Augen zu,	Of death closed your eyes,
Dich besässe doch mein Kummer,	My sorrow would still possess you,
Meinem Herzen lebtest du.	You would live in my heart.
Aber ach! du lebst im Licht,	But, alas, you live in the light,
Meiner Liebe lebst du nicht.	Yet you do not live for my love.
Kann der Liebe süss Verlangen,	Emma, can love's sweet longing
Emma, kann's vergänglich sein?	Pass away?
Was dahin ist und vergangen,	That which is over and past, Emma,
Emma, kann's die Liebe sein?	Can that be love?
Ihrer Flamme Himmelsglut,	Does the celestial ardour of its flame
Stirbt sie wie ein irdisch Gut?	Perish like worldly goods?

An Laura, als sie Klopstocks Auf- erstehungslied sang / To Laura, when singing Klopstock's 'Ode on the Resurrection'.

FRIEDRICH VON MATTHISSON

D115 (1814)

Herzen, die gen Himmel sich erheben,	Hearts raised towards heaven,
Tränen, die dem Auge still entbeben,	Tears silently quivering from the eyes,
Seufzer, die den Lippen leis' entfliehn,	Sighs softly escaping from the lips,
Wangen, die mit Andachtsglut sich	Cheeks coloured with the fire of
malen,	devotion,
Trunkne Blicke, die Entzückung strahlen,	Enraptured looks, radiant in bliss:
Danken dir, o Heilverkünderin!	All thank you, harbinger of salvation!
Laura! Laura! Horchend diesen Tönen,	Laura! Listening to these strains
Müßten Engelseelen sich	The souls of angels must grow more
verschönen,	beautiful,
Heilige den Himmel offen sehn,	Saints behold the open gates of heaven,
Schwermutsvolle Zweifler sanfter	Melancholy doubters lament more
klagen,	softly,
Kalte Frevler an die Brust sich schlagen,	Heartless sinners beat their breasts
Und wie Seraph Abbadona flehn!	And pray like the seraph Abbadona.
Mit den Tönen des Triumphgesanges	With the strains of the triumphant song
Trank ich Vorgefühl des Überganges	I drank a foretaste of that passage
Von der Grabnacht zum	From the night of the grave to a
Verklärungsglanz!	transfigured radiance!
Als vernähm' ich Engelmelodieen,	It was as if I heard angels singing;
Wähnt' ich dir, o Erde, zu entfliehen,	I imagined I had escaped from you, earth,
Sah schon unter mir der Sterne Tanz!	And already saw the stars dance below me.

Schon umatmete mich des Himmels
   Milde,
Schon begrüßt' ich jauchzend die Gefilde,
Wo des Lebens Strom durch Palmen
   fleußt!
Glänzend von der nähern Gottheit
   Strahle
Wandelte durch Paradiesestale
Wonneschauernd mein entschwebter
   Geist!

I was embraced by Heaven's
   gentleness,
With joy I greeted the Elysian fields
Where the river of life flows through palm
   trees;
Glowing in the light of the Godhead
   close by,
My blissful, quivering spirit
Floated through the vales of
   Paradise.

An mein Herz / To my Heart

ERNST SCHULZE

D860 (1825)

O Herz, sei endlich stille!
Was schlägst du so unruhvoll?
Es ist ja des Himmels Wille,
Das ich sie lassen soll.

O heart! Be silent at last!
Why do you beat so restlessly?
For it is Heaven's will
That I should leave her.

Und gab auch dein junges Leben
Dir nichts als Wahn und Pein,
Hat's ihr nur Freude gegeben,
So mag's verloren sein.

Even though your youthful life
Gave you nothing but delusion and pain,
As long as it gave her joy
Then no matter if it was lost to you.

Und wenn sie auch nie dein Lieben
Und nie dein' Lieb' verstand,
So bist du doch treu geblieben,
Und Gott hat's droben erkannt.

And though she never understood
Your loving or your love,
You nevertheless remained faithful
And God above saw it.

Wir wollen es mutig ertragen,
So lang nur die Träne noch rinnt,
Und träumen von schöneren Tagen,
Die lange vorüber sind.

Let us bravely endure
As long as tears still flow,
And dream of fairer days
Long since past.

Und siehst du die Blüten erscheinen,
Und singen die Vögel umher,
So magst du wohl heimlich weinen,
Doch klagen sollst du nicht mehr.

When you see the blossoms appearing,
When the birds sing all around,
Then you may weep in secret
But you should complain no more.

Geh'n doch die ewigen Sterne
Dort oben mit goldenem Licht
Und lächeln so freundlich von ferne,
Und denken doch unser nicht.

For the eternal stars above
Move with a golden light,
Smiling kindly from afar
And yet with no thought for us.

An mein Klavier / To my Piano

CHRISTIAN FRIEDRICH SCHUBART

D342 (1816?)

Sanftes Klavier,
Welche Entzückungen schaffest du mir,
Sanftes Klavier!
Wenn sich die Schönen
Tändelnd verwöhnen,
Weih' ich mich dir,
Liebes Klavier!

Gentle piano,
What delights you bring me,
Gentle piano!
While the spoilt beauties
Dally,
I devote myself to you,
Dear piano!

Bin ich allein,
Hauch' ich dir meine Empfindungen ein,
Himmlisch und rein.
Unschuld im Spiele,
Tugendgefühle,
Sprechen aus dir,
Trautes Klavier!

Sing' ich dazu,
Goldener Flügel, welch' himmlische
  Ruh'
Lispelst mir du!
Tränen der Freude
Netzen die Saite!
Silberner Klang
Trägt den Gesang.

Sanftes Klavier!
Welche Entzückungen schaffst du
  in mir,
Goldnes Klavier!
Wenn mich im Leben
Sorgen umschweben;
Töne du mir,
Trautes Klavier!

When I am alone
I whisper my feelings to you,
Pure and celestial.
As I play, innocence
And virtuous sentiments
Speak from you,
Beloved piano!

When I sing with you,
Golden keyboard, what heavenly
  peace
You whisper to me!
Tears of joy
Fall upon the strings.
Silvery tone
Supports the song.

Gentle piano,
What delights you awaken within
  me,
Golden piano!
When in this life
Cares beset me,
Sing to me,
Beloved piano!

An Mignon / To Mignon

JOHANN WOLFGANG VON GOETHE

D 161 (1815)

Über Tal und Fluß getragen
Ziehet rein der Sonne Wagen.
Ach! sie regt in ihrem Lauf,
So wie deine, meine Schmerzen,
Tief im Herzen,
Immer morgens wieder auf.

Kaum will mir die Nacht noch frommen,
Denn die Träume selber kommen
Nun in trauriger Gestalt,
Und ich fühle dieser Schmerzen,
Still im Herzen,
Heimlich bildende Gewalt.

Schon seit manchen schönen Jahren
Seh' ich unten Schiffe fahren;
Jedes Kommt an seinen Ort;
Aber ach! die steten Schmerzen,
Fest im Herzen,
Schwimmen nicht im Strome fort.

Schön in Kleidern muß ich kommen,
Aus dem Schrank sind sie
  genommen,
Weil es heute Festtag ist;
Niemand ahndet, daß von Schmerzen
Herz im Herzen
Grimmig mir zerrissen ist.

Borne over valley and river
The sun's pure chariot moves on.
Ah, in its course it stirs
Your sorrows and mine,
Deep in our hearts,
Anew each morning.

The night brings me scant comfort,
For then my dreams themselves appear
In mournful guise,
And in my heart
I feel the secret, silent power
Of these sorrows grow.

For many a long year
I have watched the ships sail below.
Each one reaches its destination;
But, alas, the sorrows
That forever cling to my heart
Do not flow away in the current.

I must come in fine clothes;
They are taken from the
  closet,
Because today is a holiday.
No one guesses
That in my heart of hearts
I am racked by savage pain.

Heimlich muß ich immer weinen, Aber freundlich kann ich scheinen Und sogar gesund und rot; Wären tödlich diese Schmerzen Meinem Herzen, Ach! schon lange wär' ich tot.	Always I must weep in secret, Yet I can appear happy, Even glowing and healthy. If these sorrows could be fatal To my heart, Ah, I would have died long ago.

An Rosa I / To Rosa I

LUDWIG KOSEGARTEN

D315 (1815)

Warum bist du nicht hier, meine
  Geliebteste,
Dass mich gürte dein Arm, dass mich dein
  Händedruck labe,
Dass du mich pressest
An dein schlagendes Schwesterherz.
	Why are you not here, my
	  darling,
	That your arms may enfold me, that you
	  may press my hand to comfort me,
	That you may clasp me
	To your tenderly beating heart?

Matte labet der Quell, Müde der
  Abendstern,
Irre Wandrer der Mond, Kranke das
  Morgenrot
Mich erlabet, Geliebte,
Dein Umfangen am kräftigsten.
	The stream revives the faint, the evening
	  star the weary,
	The moon revives the lost traveller, the
	  sunrise the sick;
	But I, beloved, am best revived
	By your embrace.

Warum bist du nicht hier, meine
  Vertrauteste,
Dass dich gürte mein Arm, dass ich dir
  süssen Gruss
Lispl' und feurig dich presse
An mein schlagendes Bruderherz.
	Why are you not here, my
	  beloved,
	That my arm may embrace you, that I may
	  whisper
	A sweet greeting and press you ardently
	To my tenderly beating heart?

An Rosa II / To Rosa II

LUDWIG KOSEGARTEN

D316 (1815)

Rosa, denkst du an mich? Innig gedenk'
  ich dein!
Durch den grünlichen Wald schimmert das
  Abendrot.
Und die Wipfel der Tannen
Regt das Säuseln des
  Ewigen.
	Rosa, do you think of me? I think tenderly
	  of you.
	The evening light glimmers through the
	  green forest,
	And the pine-tops are stirred
	By the whisper of
	  eternity.

Rosa, wärest du hier, säh' ich im
  Abendrot
Deine Wangen getaucht, säh' ich vom
  Abendhauch
Deine Locken
  geringelt.
Edle Seele, mir wäre wohl!
	Rosa, if you were here I should see your
	  cheeks
	Bathed in the evening
	  glow,
	And your locks ruffled in the evening
	  breeze.
	Dearest soul, how happy I should be!

An Schwager Kronos / To Coachman Chronos

JOHANN WOLFGANG VON GOETHE

D 369 (1816?)

Spute dich, Kronos!	Make haste, Chronos!
Fort den rasselnden Trott!	Break into a rattling trot!
Bergab gleitet der Weg:	The way runs downhill;
Ekles Schwindeln zögert	I feel a sickening giddiness
Mir vor die Stirne dein Zaudern.	At your dallying.
Frisch, holpert es gleich,	Quick, away, never mind the bumping,
Über Stock und Steine den Trott	Over sticks and stones, trot
Rasch ins Leben hinein!	Briskly into life!
Nun schon wieder	Now once again
Den eratmenden Schritt	Breathless, at walking pace,
Mühsam berghinauf,	Struggling uphill;
Auf denn, nicht träge denn,	Up then, don't be sluggish,
Strebend und hoffend hinan!	Onwards, striving and hoping.
Weit, hoch, herrlich	Wide, lofty and glorious
Rings den Blick ins Leben hinein,	Is the view around into life,
Vom Gebirg zum Gebirg	From mountain range to mountain range
Schwebet der ewige Geist,	The eternal spirit glides,
Ewigen Lebens ahndevoll.	Bringing promise of eternal life.
Seitwärts des Überdachs Schatten	A shady roof
Zieht dich an	Draws you aside,
Und ein Frischung verheissender Blick	And the gaze of a girl
Auf der Schwelle des Mädchens da.	On the step, promising refreshment.
Labe dich! — Mir auch, Mädchen,	Refresh yourself! For me too, girl,
Diesen schäumenden Trank,	That foaming draught,
Diesen frischen Gesundheitsblick!	That fresh, healthy look.
Ab denn, rascher hinab!	Down then, down faster!
Sieh, die Sonne sinkt!	Look, the sun is sinking!
Eh sie sinkt, eh mich Greisen	Before it sinks, before the mist
Ergreift im Moore Nebelduft,	Seizes me, an old man, on the moor,
Entzahnte Kiefer schnattern	Toothless jaws chattering,
Und das schlotternde Gebein,	Limbs shaking,
Trunknen vom letzten Strahl	Snatch me, drunk with its last ray,
Reiss mich, ein Feuermeer	A sea of fire
Mir im schäumenden Aug,	Foaming in my eyes,
Mich geblendeten Taumelnden	Blinded, reeling,
In der Hölle nächtliches Tor.	Through hell's nocturnal gate.
Töne, Schwager, ins Horn,	Coachman, sound your horn,
Rassle den schallenden Trab,	Rattle noisily on at a trot.
Dass der Orkus vernehme: wir kommen,	Let Orcus know we're coming,
Dass gleich an der Tür	So that the innkeeper is at the door
Der Wirt uns freundlich empfange.	To give us a kind welcome.

An sie / To Her

FRIEDRICH GOTTLIEB KLOPSTOCK

D 288 (1815)

Zeit, Verkündigerin der besten Freuden,
Nahe selige Zeit, dich in der Ferne
Auszuforschen, vergoß ich
Trübender Tränen zu viel!

Time, herald of the greatest joys,
Blissful Time, now so near,
I have shed too many sorrowful tears
Seeking you in the far distance.

Und doch kommst du! O dich, ja Engel
senden,
Engel senden dich mir, die Menschen
waren,
Gleich mir liebten, nun lieben
Wie ein Unsterblicher liebt.

Yet you draw near, sent by
angels,
Sent to me by angels who were once
human,
Who loved like me, and now love
As immortals do.

Auf den Flügeln der Ruh in
Morgenlüften,
Hell vom Taue des Tags, der höher
lächelt,
Mit dem ewigen Frühling,
Kommst du den Himmel herab.

On wings of peace in the morning
breezes,
Bright with the dew of the day that smiles
more sublimely,
You descend from heaven
With the eternal spring.

Denn sie fühlet sich ganz und gießt
Entzückung
In dem Herzen empor die volle
Seele,
Wenn sie, daß sie geliebt wird,
Trunken von Liebe sichs denkt!

For she feels that she is
whole,
And her overflowing soul exudes rapture
within her heart
When, drunk with love,
She deems herself loved.

An Silvia / To Sylvia (from The Two Gentlemen of Verona)

WILLIAM SHAKESPEARE, translated by EDUARD VON BAUERNFELD

D 891 (1826)
A literal version of Bauernfeld's translation is given here. Shakespeare's original is printed below in italics.

Was ist Silvia, saget an,
Daß sie die weite Flur preist?
Schön und zart seh' ich sie nah'n,
Auf Himmelsgunst und Spur weist,
Daß ihr alles untertan.

What is Sylvia, tell me,
That the wide meadows laud her?
I see her draw near, fair and tender,
It is a mark of heaven's favour
That all are subject to her.

Ist sie schön und gut dazu?
Reiz labt wie milde
Kindheit;
Ihrem Aug' eilt Amor zu,
Dort heilt er seine Blindheit,
Und verweilt in süßer Ruh'.

Is she fair and kind as well?
Her charms refresh with child-like
gentleness;
Cupid hastens to her eyes,
There he cures his blindness
And lingers in sweet peace.

Darum Silvia, tön', o Sang,
Der holden Silvia Ehren;
Jeden Reiz besiegt sie lang,
Den Erde kann gewähren:
Kränze ihr und
Saitenklang!

Then to Sylvia let our song resound,
To fair Sylvia's glory!
She has long acquired every charm
That this earth can grant:
Bring her garlands, and the music of
strings!

53

Who is Sylvia, what is she
That all our swains commend her?
Holy, fair and wise is she.
The heavens such grace did lend her
That she might admired be.

Is she kind as she is fair?
For beauty lives with kindness.
Love doth to her eyes repair
To help him of his blindness,
And being helped, inhabits there.

Then to Sylvia let us sing,
That Sylvia is excelling.
She excels each mortal thing
Upon the dull earth dwelling.
To her let us garlands bring.

Andenken / Remembrance

FRIEDRICH VON MATTHISSON

D 99 (1814)

Ich denke dein,	I think of you
Wenn durch den Hain	When through the grove
Der Nachtigallen	The nightingales'
Akkorde schallen!	Harmonious song echoes!
Wann denkst du mein?	When do you think of me?
Ich denke dein	I think of you
Im Dämmerschein	In the twilight
Der Abendhelle	Of evening
Am Schattenquelle!	At the shady spring!
Wo denkst du mein?	Where do you think of me?
Ich denke dein	I think of you
Mit süsser Pein	With sweet pain,
Mit bangem Sehnen	With anxious longing,
Und heissen Tränen!	And burning tears!
Wie denkst du mein?	How do you think of me?
O denke mein,	Oh, think of me
Bis zum Verein	Until we meet
Auf besserm Sterne!	In a better world!
In jeder Ferne	However distant you are,
Denk ich nur dein!	I shall think only of you!

Antigone und Oedip / Antigone and Oedipus

JOHANN MAYRHOFER

D 542 (1817)

Antigone
Ihr hohen Himmlischen erhöret
Der Tochter herzentströmtes Flehen:
Laßt einen kühlen Hauch des Trostes
In des Vaters große Seele wehn.

Antigone
Ye gods on high,
Hear a daughter's heartfelt entreaty;
Let the cool breath of comfort
Waft into my father's great soul.

Genüget, euren Zorn zu sühnen,
Dies' junge Leben — nehmt es hin;
Und euer Rachestrahl vernichte
Die tiefbetrübte Dulderin.

This young life is sufficient to assuage
Your anger — take it;
And let your avenging blow
Destroy this deeply distressed sufferer.

Demütig falte ich die Hände —
Das Firmament bleibt glatt und rein,
Und stille ist's, nur laue Lüfte
Durchschauern noch den alten Hain.

Humbly I clasp my hands;
The firmament remains serene and clear,
And all is calm; now only mild breezes
Quiver through the ancient grove.

Was seufzt und stöhnt der bleiche Vater?
Ich ahn's — ein furchtbares Gesicht
Verscheucht von ihm den leichten
    Schlummer;
Er springt vom Rasen auf — er spricht:

Why does my pallid father sigh and moan?
I can guess — a terrible vision
Drives away his light
    sleep;
He starts up from the grass and speaks:

Oedip
Ich träume einen schweren Traum.
Schwang nicht den Zepter diese Rechte?
Doch Hoheit lös'ten starke Mächte
Dir auf, o Greis, in nicht'gen Schaum.

Oedipus
I dream a troubled dream.
Did not this right hand wield the sceptre?
But powerful forces reduced your majesty,
Old man, to mere foam.

Trank ich in schönen Tagen
    nicht
In meiner großen Väter
    Halle,
Beim Heldensang und Hörnerschalle,
O Helios, dein golden Licht,

In happy days, in the halls of my great
    fathers,
Amid the songs of heroes and the peal
    of horns,
Did I not drink
Your golden light, O Helios,

Das ich nun nimmer schauen kann?
Zerstörung ruft von allen Seiten:
»Zum Tode sollst du dich bereiten;
Dein irdisch Werk ist abgetan.«

Which now I can never see again?
Destruction calls from all sides:
'You are to prepare for death;
Your earthly task is done.'

Aria di Abramo / *Abraham's Aria*

PIETRO METASTASIO

D 33 no. 1 (1812)

Entra l'uomo allor che nasce
In un mar di tante pene,
Che si avezza dalle fasce
Ogni affanno a sostener.
Ma per lui si raro è il bene,
Ma la gioja è così rara,
Che a soffrir mai non impara
Le sorprese del piacer.

From the moment he is born
Man enters upon a sea of so much suffering
That he is accustomed from the cradle
To endure all misfortune.
But so rare is happiness for him,
So rare is joy,
That he never learns to experience
The surprise of pleasure.

Ariette der Claudine / *Claudine's Ariette**

JOHANN WOLFGANG VON GOETHE

D 239 no. 6 (1815)

Liebe schwärmt auf allen Wegen;
Treue wohnt für sich allein.
Liebe kommt euch rasch entgegen;
Aufgesucht will Treue sein.

Love roves everywhere;
Constancy lives alone.
Love comes rushing towards you;
Constancy must be sought.

*From Schubert's Singspiel *Claudine von Villa Bella*

Ariette der Lucinde / Lucinda's Ariette*

JOHANN WOLFGANG VON GOETHE

D 239 no. 3 (1815)

Hin und wieder fliegen die Pfeile;
Amors leichte Pfeile fliegen
Von dem schlanken goldnen Bogen;
Mädchen, seid ihr nicht getroffen?
Es ist Glück! Es ist nur Glück.

Warum fliegt er so in Eile?
Jene dort will er besiegen;
Schon ist er vorbei geflogen;
Sorglos bleibt der Busen offen;
Gebet acht! Er kommt zurück!

To and fro the arrows fly;
Cupid's light arrows fly
From the slender golden bow.
Maidens, are you not smitten?
It is chance! It is just chance!

Why does he fly with such haste?
He desires to conquer that maiden there;
Already he has flown by;
The heart remains open and carefree;
Take heed! He will be back!

Atys / Atys

JOHANN MAYRHOFER

D 585 (1817)

Der Knabe seufzt über's grüne
   Meer,
Vom fernenden Ufer kam er her,
Er wünscht sich mächtige Schwingen,
Die sollten ihn ins heimische Land,
Woran ihn ewige Sehnsucht mahnt,
Im rauschenden Fluge bringen.

»O Heimweh! unergründlicher
   Schmerz,
Was folterst du das junge Herz?
Kann Liebe dich nicht verdrängen?
So willst du die Frucht, die herrlich reift,
Die Gold und flüssiger Purpur streift,
Mit tödlichem Feuer versengen?

»Ich liebe, ich rase, ich hab'sie gesehn,
Die Lüfte durchschnitt sie im
   Sturmeswehn,
Auf löwengezogenem Wagen,
Ich musste flehn: o nimm mich mit!
Mein Leben ist düster und abgeblüht;
Wirst du meine Bitte versagen?

»Sie schaute mit gütigem Lächeln
   mich an;
Nach Thrazien zog uns das
   Löwengespann,
Da dien' ich als Priester ihr eigen.
Den Rasenden kränzt ein seliges
   Glück,
Der Aufgewachte schaudert zurück:
Kein Gott will sich hülfreich erzeigen.

With a sigh the youth gazes over the green
   sea;
He came from a distant shore,
And longs for mighty wings
That would take him in whirring flight
To the homeland
For which he yearns eternally.

'O longing for home, unfathomable
   pain,
Why do you torment the young heart?
Can love not drive you out?
Will you then scorch with your deadly fire
The fruit that ripens gloriously,
Kissed by gold and liquid purple?

'I live, I rage, I have seen her;
Like a whirlwind she swept through
   the air
In a chariot drawn by lions.
I had to entreat: Take me with you!
My life is bleak and grey.
Will you deny my plea?

'She looked upon me with a kindly
   smile;
The lions bore us off to
   Thrace
Where I serve as her priest.
The madman is filled with blissful
   happiness;
But when he awakes he recoils in fear:
There is no god to lend his aid.

*From Schubert's Singspiel *Claudine von Villa Bella*.

»Dort, hinter den Bergen im scheidenden
   Strahl
Des Abends entschlummert mein väterlich
   Tal;
O wär' ich jenseits der Wellen!«
Seufzet der Knabe. Doch
   Cymbelgetön
Verkündet die Göttin; er stürzt von
   Höh'n
In Gründe und waldige Stellen.

'There beyond the mountain, in the dying
   rays
Of evening, my native valley beings to
   slumber;
O that I might cross the waters!'
Thus sighs the youth. But the clash of
   cymbals
Proclaims the goddess; he plunges from the
   heights
Into the woods deep below.

Auf dem See / On the Lake

JOHANN WOLFGANG VON GOETHE

D 543 (1817?)

Und frische Nahrung, neues
   Blut
Saug ich aus freier Welt:
Wie ist Natur so hold und gut,
Die mich am Busen hält!

And I suck fresh nourishment and new
   blood
From the wide world;
How gracious and kindly is Nature
Who holds me to her breast!

Die Welle wieget unsern Kahn
Im Rudertakt hinauf,
Und Berge, wolkig himmelan,
Begegnen unserm Lauf.

The waves rock our boat up and down
To the rhythm of the oars,
And soaring, cloud-capped mountains
Meet us in our course.

Aug, mein Aug, was sinkst du nieder?
Goldne Träume, kommt ihr wieder?
Weg, du Traum! so gold du bist:
Hier auch Lieb und Leben ist.

My eyes, why are you cast down?
Golden dreams, will you return?
Begone, dream, golden as you are;
There is love here, and life too.

Auf der Welle blinken
Tausend schwebende Sterne,
Weiche Nebel trinken
Rings die türmende Ferne;

On the waves float twinkling
A thousand twinkling stars;
Soft mists drink up
The looming distances;

Morgenwind umflügelt
Die beschattete Bucht,
Und im See bespiegelt
Sich die reifende Frucht.

The morning breeze wings around
The shaded bay,
And in the lake
The ripening fruit is mirrored.

Auf dem Strom / On the River

LUDWIG RELLSTAB

D 943 (1828)

Nimm die letzten Abschiedsküsse,
Und die wehenden, die Grüsse,
Die ich noch ans Ufer sende,
Eh' Dein Fuß sich scheidend wende!
Schon wird von des Stromes Wogen
Rasch der Nachen fortgezogen,
Doch den tränendunklen Blick
Zieht die Sehnsucht stets zurück!

Take these last farewell kisses,
And the wafted greetings
That I send to the shore,
Before your foot turns to leave.
Already the boat is pulled away
By the waves' rapid current;
But longing forever draws back
My gaze, clouded with tears.

Und so trägt mich denn die Welle
Fort mit unerflehter Schnelle.
Ach, schon ist die Flur verschwunden,
Wo ich selig Sie
    gefunden!
Ewig hin, ihr Wonnetage!
Hoffnungsleer verhallt die Klage
Um das schöne Heimatland,
Wo ich ihre Liebe fand.

Sieh, wie flieht der Strand vorüber,
Und wie drängt es mich hinüber,
Zieht mit unnennbaren Banden,
An der Hütte dort zu landen,
In der Laube dort zu weilen;
Doch des Stromes Wellen eilen
Weiter ohne Rast und Ruh,
Führen mich dem Weltmeer zu!

Ach, vor jener dunklen Wüste,
Fern von jeder heitern Küste,
Wo kein Eiland zu erschauen,
O, wie faßt mich zitternd Grauen!
Wehmutstränen sanft zu bringen,
Kann kein Lied vom Ufer dringen;
Nur der Sturm weht kalt daher
Durch das grau gehobne Meer!

Kann des Auges sehnend Schweifen
Keine Ufer mehr ergreifen,
Nun so schau' ich zu den Sternen
Auf in jenen heil'gen Fernen!
Ach, bei ihrem milden Scheine
Nannt' ich sie zuerst die Meine;
Dort vielleicht, o tröstend Glück!
Dort begegn' ich ihrem Blick.

And so the waves bear me away
With relentless speed.
Ah, already the meadows
Where, overjoyed, I found her have
    disappeared.
Days of bliss, you are gone for ever!
Hopelessly my lament echoes
Round the fair homeland
Where I found her love.

See how the shore flies past,
And how mysterious ties
Draw me across
To land by yonder cottage,
To linger in yonder arbour.
But the river's waves rush onwards,
Without respite,
Bearing me on towards the ocean.

Ah, how I tremble with dread
At that dark wilderness,
Far from every cheerful shore,
Where no island can be seen!
No song can reach me from the shore,
To bring forth tears of gentle sadness;
Only the tempest blows cold
Across the grey, angry sea.

If my wistful, roaming eyes
Can no longer descry the shore,
I shall look up to the stars
There in the sacred distance.
Ah, by their gentle radiance
I first called her mine;
There, perhaps, o consoling fate,
There I shall meet her gaze.

Auf dem Wasser zu singen / To be Sung on the Water

FRIEDRICH LEOPOLD, GRAF ZU STOLBERG-STOLBERG

D774 (1823)

Mitten im Schimmer der spiegelnden
    Wellen
Gleitet, wie Schwäne, der wankende
    Kahn;
Ach, auf der Freude sanft schimmernden
    Wellen
Gleitet die Seele dahin wie der Kahn;
Denn von dem Himmel herab auf die
    Wellen
Tanzet das Abendrot rund um den
    Kahn.

Über den Wipfeln des westlichen
    Haines
Winket uns freundlich der rötliche
    Schein;

Amid the shimmer of the mirroring
    waves
The rocking boat glides, swan-
    like;
On gently shimmering waves of
    joy
The soul, too, glides like a boat.
For from the sky the setting
    sun
Dances upon the waves around the
    boat.

Above the tree-tops of the western
    grove
The red glow beckons kindly to
    us;

Unter den Zweigen des östlichen
   Haines
Säuselt der Kalmus im rötlichen Schein;
Freude des Himmels und Ruhe des
   Haines
Atmet die Seel' im errötenden
   Schein.

Ach, es entschwindet mit tauigem Flügel
Mir auf den wiegenden Wellen die
   Zeit.
Morgen entschwinde mit schimmerndem
   Flügel
Wieder wie gestern und heute die Zeit,
Bis ich auf höherem strahlendem Flügel
Selber entschwinde der wechselnden
   Zeit.

Beneath the branches of the eastern
   grove
The reeds whisper in the red glow.
The soul breathes the joy of
   heaven,
The peace of the grove, in the reddening
   glow.

Alas, with dewy wings
Time vanishes from me on the rocking
   waves.
Tomorrow let time again vanish with shim-
   mering wings,
As it did yesterday and today,
Until, on higher, more radiant wings,
I myself vanish from the flux of
   time.

Auf den Sieg der Deutschen / *On the Victory of the Germans*

POET UNKNOWN

D81 (1813)

Verschwunden sind die Schmerzen,
Weil aus beklemmten Herzen
Kein Seufzer wiederhallt.
Drum jubelt hoch, ihr Deutsche,
Denn die verruchte Peitsche
Hat endlich ausgeknallt.

Seht Frankreichs Creaturen,
Sie machten Deutschlands Fluren
Zum blutigen Altar!
Die gierige Hyäne
Fraß Hermanns edle Söhne
Durch mehr als zwanzig Jahr.

Es wurden Millionen
Vom Donner der Kanonen
Zum Jammer aufgeweckt,
Es lag auf Städt' und Flecken
Verwüstung, Todesschrecken,
Vom Satan ausgeheckt.

Der Kampf ist nun entschieden.
Bald, bald erscheint der Frieden
In himmlischer Gestalt.
Drum jubelt hoch, ihr Deutsche,
Denn die verruchte Peitsche
Hat endlich ausgeknallt.

Sorrow has vanished,
For no sighs echo
From oppressed hearts.
Then rejoice, Germans,
For the loathsome whip
Has finally cracked its last.

Behold the creatures of France!
They made Germany's meadows
A bloody altar!
The greedy hyena
Has devoured Germany's noble sons
For more than twenty years.

Millions were awakened
To a wretched plight
By the thunder of canons;
Over towns and villages
Lay devastation and the terror of death,
Conjured up by Satan.

But now the war is decided.
Soon peace will appear
In celestial form.
Rejoice, then, Germans,
For the loathsome whip
Has finally cracked its last.

Auf den Tod einer Nachtigall / On the Death of a Nightingale

LUDWIG HEINRICH CHRISTOPH HÖLTY

D 399 (1816)

Sie ist dahin, die Maienlieder tönte,
Die Sängerin,
Die durch ihr Lied den ganzen Hain
verschönte,
Sie ist dahin!
Sie, deren Ton mir in die Seele hallte,
Wenn ich am Bach,
Der durch Gebüsch im Abendgolde
wallte
Auf Blumen lag!

Sie gurgelte, tief aus der vollen Kehle,
Den Silberschlag:
Der Widerhall in seiner Felsenhöhle
Schlug leis' ihn nach.
Die ländlichen Gesäng' und
Feldschalmeien
Erklangen drein;
Es tanzeten die Jungfrau'n ihre Reihen
Im Abendschein.

She is no more, the songstress
Who warbled May songs,
Who adorned the whole grove with her
singing.
She is no more!
She whose notes echoed in my soul,
When I lay among flowers
By the brook that flowed through the
undergrowth
In the golden light of evening.

From the depths of her full throat
She poured forth her silver notes;
The echo answered softly
In the rocky caves.
Rustic melodies and pipers'
tunes
Mingled with her song,
As maidens danced
In the glow of evening.

Auf der Brücke / On the Bridge

ERNST SCHULZE

D 853 (1825?)

Frisch trabe sonder Ruh und Rast,
Mein gutes Ross, durch Nacht und
Regen!
Was scheust du dich vor Busch und Ast
Und strauchelst auf den wilden Wegen?
Dehnt auch der Wald sich tief und
dicht,
Doch muss er endlich sich erschliessen;
Und freundlich wird ein fernes
Licht
Uns aus dem dunkeln Tale grüssen.

Wohl könnt ich über Berg und
Feld
Auf deinem schlanken Rücken fliegen
Und mich am bunten Spiel der Welt,
An holden Bildern mich vergnügen;
Manch Auge lacht mir traulich zu
Und beut mir Frieden, Lieb und Freude,
Und dennoch eil ich ohne Ruh,
Zurück zu meinem Leide.

Denn schon drei Tage war ich fern
Von ihr, die ewig mich gebunden;
Drei Tage waren Sonn und Stern
Und Erd und Himmel mir
verschwunden.

Trot briskly on, my good horse,
Without pause for rest, through night and
rain!
Why do you shy at bush and branch,
And stumble on the wild paths?
Though the forest stretches deep and
dense,
It must at last open up;
And a distant light will greet us
warmly
From the dark valley.

I could cheerfully speed over mountain and
meadow
On your lithe back,
And enjoy the world's varied delights,
Its fair sights.
Many an eye smiles at me affectionately,
Offering peace, love and joy,
And yet, restlessly, I hasten
Back to my sorrow.

For three days now I have been far
From her, to whom I am eternally bound;
For three days sun and stars,
Earth and heaven have vanished
for me.

Von Lust und Leiden, die mein
  Herz
Bei ihr bald heilten, bald zerrissen
Fühlt ich drei Tage nur den Schmerz,
Und ach! die Freude musst ich missen!

Of the joy and sorrow which, when I was
  with her,
Now healed, now broke my heart,
I have for three days felt only the pain.
Alas, the joy I have had to forgo!

Weit sehn wir über Land und
  See
Zur wärmern Flur den Vogel fliegen;
Wie sollte denn die Liebe je
In ihrem Pfade sich betrügen?
Drum trabe mutig durch die Nacht!
Und schwinden auch die dunkeln
  Bahnen,
Der Sehnsucht helles Auge wacht,
Und sicher führt mich süsses
  Ahnen.

We watch the bird fly far away over land
  and sea
To warmer pastures.
How, then, should love ever
Be deceived in its course?
So trot bravely on through the night!
Though the dark tracks may
  vanish,
The bright eye of longing is awake,
And sweet presentiment guides me safely
  onwards.

Auf der Donau / *On the Danube*

JOHANN MAYRHOFER

D 553 (1817)

Auf der Wellen Spiegel schwimmt der
  Kahn,
Alte Burgen ragen himmelan,
Tannenwälder rauschen geistergleich,
Und das Herz im Busen wird uns
  weich.

The boat glides on the mirror of the
  waves;
Old castles soar heavenwards.
Pine-forests stir like ghosts,
And our hearts grow faint within our
  breasts.

Denn der Menschen Werke sinken all',
Wo ist Turm, wo Pforte, wo der
  Wall,
Wo sie selbst, die Starken,
  erzgeschirmt,
Die in Krieg und Jagden hingestürmt?

For the works of man all perish;
Where now is the tower, the gate, the
  rampart?
Where are the mighty themselves, in their
  bronze armour,
Who stormed forth to battle and the chase?

Trauriges Gesträuppe wuchert fort,
Während frommer Sage Kraft verdorrt:
Und im kleinen Kahne wird uns bang,
Wellen drohn wie Zeiten Untergang.

Mournful brushwood grows rampant
While the power of pious myth fades.
And in our little boat we grow afraid;
Waves, like time, threaten doom.

Auf der Riesenkoppe / *On the Giant Peak*

THEODOR KÖRNER

D 611 (1818)

Hoch auf dem Gipfel
Deiner Gebirge
Steh' ich und staun' ich,
Glühend begeistert,
Heilige Koppe,
Himmelanstürmerin!

High on the summit
Of your mountains
I stand and marvel
With glowing fervour,
Sacred peak,
You that storm the heavens.

Weit in die Ferne
Schweifen die trunknen
Freudigen Blicke;
Überall Leben,
Üppiges Streben,
Überall Sonnenschein.

My joyful,
Rapturous gaze
Scans the far distance.
Everywhere there is life,
Luxuriant growth,
Everywhere sunshine.

Blühende Fluren,
Schimmernde Städte,
Dreier Könige
Glückliche Länder
Schau' ich
  begeistert,
Schau' ich mit hoher
Inniger Lust.

Meadows in bloom,
Sparkling towns,
The happy realms
Of three kings:
These I behold
  with ardour,
And sublime,
Inward joy.

Auch meines Vaterlands
Grenze erblick' ich,
Wo mich das Leben
Freundlich begrüßte,
Wo mich der Liebe
Heilige Sehnsucht
Glühend ergriff.

I behold, too, the borders
Of my homeland,
Where life bade me
A friendly welcome.
Where the sacred longing
Of first love
Seized me with its fire.

Sei mir gesegnet
Hier in der Ferne
Liebliche Heimat!
Sei mir gesegnet
Land meiner Träume!
Kreis meiner Lieben,
Sei mir gegrüßt!

Beloved homeland,
I bless you
From afar.
I bless you,
Land of my dreams!
I greet you,
My loved ones!

Auf einen Kirchhof / *To a Churchyard*

FRANZ VON SCHLECHTA

D 151 (1815)

Sei gegrüsst, geweihte Stille,
Die mir sanfte Trauer weckt,
Wo Natur die bunte Hülle
Freundlich über Gräber deckt.

I greet you, holy stillness,
Which awakens within me gentle sorrow,
Where kindly nature drapes
Her bright mantle over graves.

Leicht von Wolkenduft getragen,
Senkt die Sonne ihren Lauf,
Aus der finstern Erde schlagen
Glühend rote Flammen auf!

Lightly borne by hazy clouds
The sun sinks in its course,
From the dark earth
Glowing red flames leap up!

Ach, auch ihr, erstarrte Brüder,
Habet sinkend ihn vollbracht;
Sankt ihr auch so herrlich nieder
In des Grabes Schauernacht?

Ah, you too, lifeless brothers,
Have sunk down to fulfil your course;
Did you, too, sink so gloriously
Into the dread night of the grave?

Schlummert sanft, ihr kalten Herzen,
In der düstern langen Ruh',
Eure Wunden, eure Schmerzen
Decket mild die Erde zu!

Slumber softly, cold hearts,
In your long, sombre peace;
Your wounds, your pain
Are gently covered by the earth!

Neu zerstören, neu erschaffen
Treibt das Rad der Weltenuhr.
Kräfte, die im Fels erschlaffen
Blühen wieder auf der Flur

Und auch du, geliebte Hülle,
Sinkest zuckend einst hinab,
Und erblühst in schönster Fülle
Neu, ein Blümchen auf dem Grab.

Wankst, ein Flämmchen durch die
    Grüfte,
Irrest flimmernd durch den Moor,
Schwingst, ein Strahl, dich in die Lüfte,
Klingest hell, ein Ton, empor!

Aber du, das in mir lebet,
Wirst auch du des Wurmes Raub?
Was entzückend mich erhebet,
Bist auch du nur eitel Staub?

Nein, was ich im Innern fühle,
Was entzückend mich erhebt,
Ist der Gottheit reine Hülle,
Ist ihr Hauch, der in mir lebt.

To destroy and to create anew
The wheel of the world's clock drives on;
Forces that languish in the rock
Blossom again in the meadows.

And you too, beloved mortal frame,
Will one day sink down, quivering,
And blossom anew in glorious fullness,
As a flower on the grave.

You will waver, as a flame, through the
    graves,
You will flicker, lost, across the moor;
As a shaft of light, you will pierce the air,
As a resonant tone, you will soar upwards.

But you, who live within me,
Will you, too, fall prey to the worm?
You who exalt and delight me,
Are you, too, but vain dust?

No, what I feel deep inside me,
What exalts and delights me
Is the pure spirit of the Godhead,
Is His breath, which lives within me.

Aufenthalt / Resting Place

LUDWIG RELLSTAB

see Schwanengesang no. 5

Auflösung / Dissolution

JOHANN MAYRHOFER

D 807 (1824)

Verbirg dich, Sonne,
Denn die Gluten der Wonne
Versengen mein Gebein;
Verstummet, Töne,
Frühlings Schöne
Flüchte dich und lass mich allein!

Quillen doch aus allen Falten
Meiner Seele liebliche Gewalten,
Die mich umschlingen,
Himmlisch singen.
Geh unter, Welt, und störe
Nimmer die süssen, ätherischen Chöre.

Hide yourself, sun,
For the fires of rapture
Burn through my whole being.
Be silent, sounds;
Spring beauty,
Flee, and let me be alone!

From every recess of my soul
Gentle powers well up
And envelop me
With celestial song.
Dissolve, world, and never more
Disturb the sweet ethereal choirs.

Augenlied / Song of the Eyes

JOHANN MAYRHOFER

D 297 (1817?)

Süße Augen, klare Bronnen!
Meine Qual und Seligkeit
Ist fürwahr aus euch gewonnen,
Und mein Dichten euch geweiht.

Sweet eyes, limpid fountains,
My torment and my bliss
Truly arise from you,
And my songs I dedicate to you.

Wo ich weile,
Wie ich eile,
Liebend strahlet ihr mich an;
Ihr erleuchtet,
Mir mit Tränen meine Bahn.

Where I linger,
When I hasten,
You smile upon me, radiant with love;
You illuminate my path,
And moisten it with your tears.

Treue Sterne, schwindet nimmer,
Leitet mich zum Acheron!
Und mit eurem letzten Schimmer
Sei mein Leben auch entfloh'n.

Faithful stars, never vanish;
Lead me to Acheron!
And with your last glimmer
May my life, too, fade away.

Aus »Diego Manazares«: Ilmerine / From 'Diego Manazares': Ilmerine*

FRANZ XAVER VON SCHLECHTA

D 458 (1816)

Wo irrst du durch einsame Schluchten
der Nacht,
Wo bist du, mein Leben, mein Glück?
Schon sind die Gestirne der Nacht
Aus tauendem Dunkel erwacht,
Und ach, der Geliebte kehrt noch nicht
zurück.

Why are you wandering through the lonely
ravines of the night?
Where are you, my life, my happiness?
Already the night stars
Have awoken from their dewy darkness,
And, alas, my beloved has not yet
returned.

Aus »Heliopolis« I / From 'Heliopolis' I

JOHANN MAYRHOFER

D 753 (1822)

Im kalten, rauhen Norden
Ist Kunde mir geworden
Von einer Stadt, der Sonnenstadt.
Wo weilt das Schiff, wo ist der Pfad,
Die mich zu jenen Hallen tragen?
Von Menschen konnt' ich nichts erfragen,
Im Zwiespalt waren sie verworren.
Zur Blume, die sich Helios
erkoren,
Die ewig in sein Antlitz blickt,
Wandt' ich mich nun, und ward
entzückt.

In the cold, harsh north
I learnt
Of a city, the city of the sun.
Where is the ship, where the path
That will take me to its courts?
Men could tell me nothing,
For they were entangled in conflict.
I then turned to the flower chosen by
Helios,
That forever gazes into his face,
And was
enchanted.

*Ilmerine is the heroine of von Schlechta's play *Diego Manazares*.

»Wende, so wie ich, zur Sonne
Deine Augen! Dort ist Wonne,
Dort ist Leben;
Treu ergeben
Pilgre zu und zweifle nicht:
Ruhe findest du im Licht.
Licht erzeuget alle Gluten,
Hoffnungspflanzen,
  Tatenfluten!«

'Like me, turn your eyes
To the sun! There is bliss,
There is life;
In true devotion
Make your pilgrimage, and do not doubt.
In the light you will find peace.
Light creates all ardour,
Begets flowers of hope and torrents
  of deeds!'

Aus »Heliopolis« II / From 'Heliopolis' II

JOHANN MAYRHOFER

D754 (1822)

Fels auf Felsen hingewälzet,
Fester Grund und treuer Halt;
Wasserfälle, Windesschauer,
Unbergriffene Gewalt.

Rock piled upon rock,
Firm ground and steady foothold;
Waterfalls, blasts of wind,
Uncomprehended power.

Einsam auf Gebirges Zinne,
Kloster wie auch Burgruine,
Grab' sie der Erinn'rung ein,
Denn der Dichter lebt vom
  Sein.

Solitary, on the mountain peak,
Stands a monastery and a ruined castle;
Etch them in the memory,
For the poet lives through
  existence.

Atme du den heil'gen Äther,
Schling die Arme um die Welt,
Nur dem Würdigen, dem Grossen
Bleibe mutig zugesellt.

Breathe the holy ether,
Clasp the world in your arms;
Boldly consort
Only with the worthy and the great.

Lass die Leidenschaften sausen
Im metallenen Akkord,
Wenn die starken Stürme brausen,
Findest du das rechte Wort.

Let the passions seethe
In brazen harmony.
When fierce tempests rage
You will find the right word.

Ave Maria / Ave Maria

SIR WALTER SCOTT, translated by ADAM STORCK

see Ellens Gesang III

Ballade / Ballad

JOSEPH KENNER

D134 (c.1815)

Ein Fräulein schaut vom hohen Turm
Das weite Meer so bang;
Zum trauerschweren
  Zitherschlag
Hallt düster ihr Gesang:
»Mich halten Schloss und Riegel fest,
Mein Retter weilt so lang.«

From the high tower a maiden
Looks anxiously down over the vast sea.
To the heavy, mournful chords of her
  zither
Her gloomy song resounds:
'Lock and bolt keep me captive here,
My saviour tarries so long.'

Sei wohl getrost, du edle Maid! Schau, hinterm Kreidenstein treibt In der Buchtung Dunkelheit Ein Kriegsboot herein: Der Aarenbusch, der Rosenschild, Das ist der Retter dein! Schon ruft des Hunen Horn Zum Streit hinab zum Muschelrain.	Take comfort, noble maid! Look, beyond the chalk cliff A warship approaches In the darkness of the bay; With eagle plumes, and rose-decked shield; Behold your saviour! Already the hero's horn Calls to battle on the shell-covered shore.
»Willkommen, schmucker Knabe, mir, Bist du zur Stelle kummen? Gar bald vom schwarzen Schilde dir Hau' ich die goldnen Blumen. Die achtzehn Blumen blutbetaut, Les' deine königliche Braut Auf aus dem Sand der Wogen, Nur flink die Wehr gezogen!«	'Welcome, fair youth, Have you reached your destination? Soon I shall cut the golden flowers From your black shield. Let the eighteen flowers, stained with blood, Be gathered by your royal bride From the sand washed by the waves. Quickly, draw your sword!'
Zum Turm auf schallt das Schwertgeklirr! Wie harrt die Braut so bang! Der Kampf dröhnt laut durchs Waldrevier, So heftig und so lang, Und endlich, endlich deucht es ihr, Erstirbt der Hiebe Klang.	The rattling of swords echoes up to the tower! How anxiously the bride waits! The clamour of battle resounded Long and fiercely. Then at length, it seems to her, The clash of weapons ceases.
Es kracht das Schloss, die Tür klafft auf, Die ihren sieht sie wieder; Sie eilt im atemlosen Lauf Zum Muschelplane nieder. Da liegt der Peiniger zerschellt, Doch weh, dicht neben nieder, Ach! decken's blutbespritzte Feld Des Retters blasse Glieder.	The lock is burst, the door opens, She sees her people once more; In breathless haste she runs down To the shell-covered shore. There lies her tormentor's mangled body. But alas! Close beside him Her saviour's pale limbs Cover the blood-bespattered field.
Still sammelt sie die Rosen auf In ihren keuschen Schoss Und bettet ihren Lieben drauf; Ein Tränchen stiehlt sich los Und taut die breiten Wunden an Und sagt: ich habe das getan!	Silently she gathers the roses In her chaste lap, And on them she lays her beloved. A tear falls, Bathing his gaping wounds And signifying: 'I have done the deed.'
Da frass es einen Schandgesell Des Raubes im Gemüt, Dass die, die seinen Herrn verdarb, Frei nach der Heimat zieht. Vom Busch, wo er verkrochen lag In wilder Todeslust, Pfeift schnell sein Bolzen durch die Luft, In ihre keusche Brust.	But an evil accomplice in her abduction Was tortured by the thought That she who destroyed his master Would return home freed. From the bush where he lay hidden In frenzied blood lust, His arrow whistled rapidly through the air Into her chaste heart.
Da ward ihr wohl im Brautgemach, Im Kiesgrund, still und klein; Sie senkten sie dem Lieben nach, Dort unter einem Stein, Den ihr von Disteln überweht. Noch nächst des Turmes Trümmern seht.	She was happy in her bridal chamber, Deep among the pebbles, small and silent; They lowered her to join her beloved Beneath a stone That, overgrown with thistles, You can still see beside the ruined tower.

Bei dem Grabe meines Vaters / At my Father's Grave

MATTHIAS CLAUDIUS

D 496 (1816)

Friede sei um diesen Grabstein her!
Sanfter Friede Gottes!
Ach, sie haben einen guten Mann
  begraben,
Und mir war er mehr;
Träufte mir von Segen, dieser Mann,
Wie ein Stern aus bessern Welten!
Und ich kann's ihm nicht vergelten,
Was er mir getan.

Er entschlief, sie gruben ihn hier ein.
Leiser, süsser Trost von Gott,
Und ein Ahnden von dem ew'gen Leben
Düft um sein Gebein!
Bis ihn Jesus Christus, gross und hehr,
Freundlich wird erwecken,
Ach, sie haben ihn begraben!
Einen guten Mann begraben,
Und mir war er mehr.

Peace be to this tombstone,
The tender peace of God.
Ah, they have buried a good
  man,
And to me he was still more.
He showered blessings upon me
Like a star from a better world;
And I can never repay
What he did for me.

He fell asleep, they buried him here.
May God's sweet, gentle comfort
And a presentiment of eternal life
Embalm his mortal remains,
Until Jesus Christ, great and glorious,
Lovingly wakens him.
Ah, they have buried him,
Buried a good man,
And to me he was still more.

Bei dir allein / With You Alone

JOHANN GABRIEL SEIDL

D 866 no. 2 (1828?)

Bei dir allein empfind' ich, dass ich lebe,
Dass Jugendmut mich schwellt,
Dass eine heit're Welt
Der Liebe mich durchbebe;
Mich freut mein Sein
Bei dir allein!

Bei dir allein weht mir die Luft so
  labend,
Dünkt mich die Flur so grün,
So mild des Lenzes Blüh'n,
So balsamreich der Abend,
So kühl der Hain,
Bei dir allein!

Bei dir allein verliert der Schmerz sein
  Herbes,
Gewinnt die Freud an Lust!
Du sicherst meine Brust
Des angestammten Erbes;
Ich fühl' mich mein
Bei dir allein!

With you alone I feel that I am alive,
That I am fired by youthful vigour,
That a bright world
Of love thrills through me;
I rejoice in my being
With you alone!

With you alone the breeze blows so
  refreshingly,
The fields seem so green,
The flowering spring so gentle,
The evening so balmy,
The grove so cool,
With you alone!

With you alone pain loses its
  bitterness,
Joy gains in sweetness!
You assure my heart
Of its natural heritage;
I feel I am myself
With you alone!

Beim Winde / When the Wind Blows

JOHANN MAYRHOFER

D 669 (1819)

Es träumen die Wolken, die Sterne, der
   Mond,
Die Bäume, die Vögel, die Blumen, der
   Strom,
Sie wiegen und schmiegen sich tiefer
   zurück,
Zur ruhigen Stätte, zum tauigen Bette,
   zum heimlichen Glück.

Doch Blättergesäusel und Wellengekräusel
   verkünden Erwachen;
Denn ewig geschwinde, unruhige Winde,
   sie stöhnen, sie fachen
Erst schmeichelnde Regung, dann wilde
   Bewegung;
Und dehnende Räume verschlingen die
   Träume.
Im Busen, im reinen, bewahre die
   Deinen;
Es ströme dein Blut,
Vor rasenden Stürmen besonnen zu
   schirmen
Die heilige Glut.

They dream — the clouds, stars,
   moon,
Trees, birds, flowers and
   stream;
Lulled, they nestle more deeply
   down
To peaceful places, dewy beds and secret
   happiness.

But rustling leaves and rippling waves
   herald the awakening;
For winds, eternally swift and restless,
   moan and stir,
First coaxing, then wildly
   agitated;
Dreams are engulfed by the expanding
   spaces.
Guard your dear ones in your pure
   heart;
Let your blood course,
That you may wisely protect the sacred
   glow
From raging storms.

Berthas Lied in der Nacht / Bertha's Nocturnal Song

FRANZ GRILLPARZER

D 653 (1819)

Nacht umhüllt
Mit wehendem Flügel
Täler und Hügel
Ladend zur Ruh'.

Und dem Schlummer
Dem lieblichen Kinde,
Leise und linde
Flüstert sie zu:

»Weißt du ein Auge,
Wachend im Kummer,
Lieblicher Schlummer,
Drücke mir's zu!«

Fühlst du sein Nahen?
Ahnest du Ruh?
Alles deckt Schlummer,
Schlummre auch du.

With fluttering wings
Night envelops
Valley and hill,
Bidding them rest.

And to Sleep
That sweet child,
She whispers
Softly and gently:

'If you know of an eye
That stays awake, grieving,
Sweet Sleep,
Close it for me!'

Do you feel him draw near?
Do you have a presentiment of peace?
Sleep makes all things well;
Then sleep also.

Blanka / Blanka

FRIEDRICH VON SCHLEGEL

D 631 (1818)

Wenn mich einsam Lüfte fächeln,
Muß ich lächeln,
Wie ich kindisch tändelnd kose
Mit der Rose.
Wären nicht die neuen Schmerzen,
Möcht ich scherzen;

Könnt'ich, was ich ahnde, sagen,
Würd' ich klagen,
Und auch bange hoffend fragen:
Was verkünden meine Loose?
Tändl' ich gleich mit Scherz und Rose,
Muß ich lächelnd dennoch klagen.

When, in my solitude, breezes fan me,
I must smile,
As, like a child, I playfully
Fondle the rose.
If it were not for this new suffering,
I should jest.

If I could say what I feel,
I should complain,
And ask with anxious hope
What my fate offers me.
Even if I jest, and dally with roses,
Still I must complain as I smile.

Blondel zu Marien / Blondel to Mary

POET UNKNOWN

D 626 (1818)

In düst'rer Nacht,
Wenn Gram mein fühlend Herz
umziehet,
Des Glückes Sonne mir entfliehet
Und ihre Pracht:
Da leuchtet fern
In feurig wonniglichem Glanze,
Wie in der Liebe Strahlenkranze,
Ein holder Stern.

Und ewig rein
Lebt unter Wonne, unter Schmerzen,
Im treuen liebevollen Herzen
Sein Widerschein.
So hold und mild
Wird unter tröstenden Gestalten
Auch in der Ferne mich umwalten
Dein Zauberbild.

In the dark night,
When grief envelops my tender
heart,
When the sun of happiness
And its splendour escape me,
A fair star
Shines in the distance,
With a fiery, joyous lustre,
Like a jewel in the radiant crown of love.

Amid joy and sorrow
Its reflection
Remains forever pure
Within my faithful, loving heart.
Thus your magic image,
Fair and gentle,
Will stay by me and comfort me
Though I am far away.

Blumenlied / Flower Song

LUDWIG HEINRICH CHRISTOPH HÖLTY

D 431 (1816)

Es ist ein halbes Himmelreich,
Wenn, Paradiesesblumen gleich,
Aus Klee die Blumen dringen;
Und wenn die Vögel silberhell
Im Garten hier, und dort am Quell,
Auf Blütenbäumen
  singen.

It is almost heaven
When, like blooms of paradise,
The flowers spring up from the clover;
And when with silvery voice
The birds sing on blossoming boughs
Here in the garden, and yonder by the
  stream.

Doch holder blüht ein edles Weib,
Von Seele gut und schön von Leib,
In frischer Jugendblüte.
Wir lassen alle Blumen stehn,
Das liebe Weibchen anzusehn
Und freun uns ihrer Güte.

But lovelier still blooms a noble lady,
Sweet of soul and fair of form,
In the freshness of youth.
We leave all the flowers be,
To gaze at that beloved lady
And to delight in her goodness.

Bundeslied / Song of Fellowship

JOHANN WOLFGANG VON GOETHE

D 258 (1815)

In allen guten Stunden,
Erhöht von Lieb' und Wein,
Soll dieses Lied verbunden
Von uns gesungen sein!
Uns hält der Gott zusammen,
Der uns hierher gebracht.
Erneuert unsre Flammen,
Er hat sie angefacht.

Whenever times are good,
Enhanced by love and wine,
Let us together
Sing this song.
God, who brought us here,
Binds us together,
And rekindles the flames
He first lit for us.

So glühet fröhlich heute,
Seid recht von Herzen eins!
Auf, trinkt erneuter Freude
Dies Glas des echten Weins!
Auf, in der holden Stunde
Stosst an, und küsset treu,
Bei jedem neuen Bunde,
Die alten wieder neu!

Then glow with happiness today,
Be truly united in your hearts.
Come, drink this glass of purest wine
To our renewed joy.
Come, at this sweet hour
Clink your glasses and, with a kiss,
At each new meeting
Renew our old bonds.

Mit jedem Schritt wird weiter
Die rasche Lebensbahn,
Und heiter, immer heiter
Steigt unser Blick hinan.
Uns wird es nimmer bange,
Wenn alles steigt und fällt,
Und bleiben lange, lange!
Auf ewig so gesellt.

With each step we move further
Along life's rapid course
And, ever cheerful,
Our eyes are raised heavenwards.
We shall never grow fearful,
Though all things rise and fall;
And long may we remain thus,
Eternally united.

Cavatine / Cavatina*

FRANZ VON SCHOBER

D 732 no. 13 (1821–2)

Wenn ich dich, Holde, sehe,
So glaub' ich keinem Schmerz,
Schon deine bloße Nähe
Beseligt dieses Herz.
Die Leiden sind
    zerronnen,
Die sonst die Brust gequält,
Es leuchten tausend Sonnen
Der lustenbrannten Welt.
Und neue Kräfte blitzen
In's trunkne Herz hinein,
Ja, ich will dich beschützen,
Ich will dein Diener sein.

When I behold you, fairest,
Then I no longer believe in sorrow;
Your mere presence
Makes my heart blissfully happy.
The suffering that once tormented my
    breast
Has vanished;
A thousand suns light up
This world inflamed with pleasure,
And new powers burn
Into my ecstatic heart;
Yes, I will protect you,
I will be your servant.

*From Schubert's opera *Alfonso und Estrella*

Clärchens Lied / Clärchen's Song

JOHANN WOLFGANG VON GOETHE

see Die Liebe

Cora an die Sonne / Cora to the Sun

GABRIELE VON BAUMBERG

D 263 (1815)

Nach so vielen trüben Tagen
Send' uns wiederum einmal,
Mitleidsvoll für unsre Klagen,
Einen sanften milden Strahl.

Liebe Sonne! trink den Regen,
Der herab zu stürzen dräut,
Deine Strahlen sind uns Segen,
Deine Blicke — Seligkeit.

Schein', ach scheine, liebe Sonne!
Jede Freude dank' ich dir;
Alle Geist- und Herzenswonne,
Licht und Wärme kommt von dir.

After so many gloomy days
Take pity on our plaint,
And send us once more
A soft, gentle ray of light.

Dear sun, drink up the rain
That threatens to pour down;
Your rays are a blessing to us,
Your glances bliss.

Shine, ah shine, dear sun!
All delight I owe to you;
Every joy of the spirit and the heart,
All light and warmth come from you.

Cronnan / Cronnan

JAMES MACPHERSON (OSSIAN), translated by EDMUND VON HAROLD

D 282 (1815)

Ich sitz bei der moosigten Quelle; am Gipfel des stürmischen Hügels. Über mir braust ein Baum. Dunkle Wellen rollen über die Heide. Die See ist stürmisch darunter. Die Hirsche steigen vom Hügel herab. Kein Jäger wird in der Ferne gesehen. Es ist Mittag: aber alles ist still. Traurig sind meine einsamen Gedanken. Erschienst du aber, o meine Geliebte, wie ein Wandrer auf der Heide! dein Haar fliegend im Wind hinter dir; dein Busen, hoch aufwallend!, deine Augen voll Tränen, für deine Freunde, die der Nebel des Hügels verbarg! Dich wollt ich trösten, o meine Geliebte, dich wollt ich führen zum Hause meines Vaters!

Aber ist sie es, die dort wie ein Strahl des Lichts, auf der Heide erscheint? Kommst du, o Mädchen, über Felsen, über Berge zu mir, schimmernd, wie im Herbste der Mond, wie die Sonne in der Glut des Sommers? Sie spricht: aber wie schwach ist ihre Stimme! wie das Lüftchen im Schilfe der See.

»Kehrst du vom Kriege schadlos zurück? Wo sind deine Freunde, mein Geliebter? Ich vernahm deinen Tod auf dem Hügel;

I sit by the mossy fountain; on the top of the hill of the winds. One tree is rustling above me. Dark waves roll over the heath. The sea is troubled below. The deer descend from the hill. No hunter at a distance is seen. It is mid-day; but all is silent. Sad are my thoughts alone. Didst thou but appear, O my love! a wanderer on the heath! Thy hair floating on the wind behind thee; Thy bosom heaving high; thine eyes full of tears for thy friends, whom the mist of the hill had concealed! Thee I would comfort my love, and bring thee to thy father's house!

But is it she that there appears, like a beam of light on the heath? Bright as the moon in autumn, as the sun in the glow of summer, comest thou, O maid, over rocks, over mountains to me? She speaks: but how weak her voice! like the breeze in the reeds of the lake!

'Returnest Thou safe from the war? Where are thy friends, my love? I heard of thy death on the hill; I heard and mourned thee, Shilric!' Yes, my fair, I return; but I alone of my race. Thou shalt see them no more: their graves I raised on the plain. But why art thou on the desert hill? Why on the

ich vernahm ihn, und beweinte dich!« Ja, meine Schönste, ich kehre zurück; aber allein von meinem Geschlecht. Jene sollst du nicht mehr erblicken: ich hab ihre Gräber auf der Fläche errichtet. Aber warum bist du am Hügel der Wüste? Warum allein auf der Heide? »O Shilric, ich bin allein! allein in der Winterbehausung. Ich starb vor Schmerz wegen dir. Shilric ich lieg erblaßt in dem Grab.«

Sie gleitet, sie durchsegelt die Luft; wie Nebel vorm Wind! Und, willst du nicht bleiben? Bleib, und Schau' meine Tränen! zierlich erscheinst du! im Leben warst du schön!

Ich will sitzen bei der moosigten Quelle; am Gipfel des stürmischen Hügels. Wenn alles um Mittag herum schweigt, dann sprich mit mir, o Vinvela! komm auf dem leichtgeflügelten Hauche! auf dem Lüftchen der Einöde, komm! laß mich, wenn du vorbeigehst, deine Stimme vernehmen; wenn alles um Mittag herum schweigt!

heath alone?

'Alone I am, O Shilric, alone in the winterhouse. With grief for thee I fell, Shilric; I am pale in the tomb.'

She flees, she sails away; as mist before the wind! and wilt thou not stay, Vinvela? Stay and behold my tears! fair thou appearest, Vinvela! fair thou wast; when alive! By the mossy fountain I will sit; on the top of the hill of winds. When mid-day is silent around. O talk with me, Vinvela! Come on the light winged gale! on the breeze of the desert, come! Let me hear thy voice, as thou passest, when mid-day is silent around!

Daphne am Bach / Daphne by the Brook

FRIEDRICH LEOPOLD, GRAF ZU STOLBERG-STOLBERG

D 411 (1816)

Ich hab' ein Bächlein funden
Vom Städtchen ziemlich weit,
Da bin ich manche Stunden
In stiller Einsamkeit.
Ich tät mir gleich erkiesen,
Ein Plätzchen kühles Moos;
Da sitz ich, und da fließen
Mir Tränen in den Schooß.

I have found a little brook
Quite far from the town;
There I pass many an hour
In quiet solitude.
I immediately chose
A patch of cool moss;
There I sit, as my tears
Flow down into my lap.

Für dich, für dich nur wallet
Mein jugendliches Blut;
Doch leise nur erschallet
Dein Nam' an dieser Flut.
Ich fürchte, daß mich täusche
Ein Lauscher aus der Stadt;
Es schreckt mich das Geräusche
Von jedem Pappelblatt.

My young blood pulses
For you, for you alone;
Yet your name echoes but softly
By these waters.
For I fear lest some eavesdropper
From the town should betray me;
I shudder at the rustling
Of every poplar leaf.

Ich wünsche mir zurücke
Den flüchtigsten Genuß;
In jedem Augenblicke
Fühl' ich den Abschiedskuß.
Es ward mir wohl und bange,
Als mich dein Arm umschloß,
Als noch auf meine Wange
Dein letztes Tränchen floß!

I long for the return
Of the most fleeting pleasure;
Every moment
I feel your parting kiss.
I was happy, and yet sad,
As your arms embraced me,
As your last tear
Fell on my cheeks.

Von meinem Blumenhügel
Sah' ich dir lange nach;

Long did I gaze after you
From my flower-decked hillside;

Ich wünschte mir die Flügel
Der Täubchen auf dem Dach;
Nun glaub' ich zu vergehen
Mit jedem Augenblick.
Willst du dein Liebchen sehen,
So komme bald zurück!

I yearned for the wings
Of the doves on the roof;
Now I feel I am fading away
With each moment.
If you wish to see your beloved,
Then come back soon!

Das Abendbrot / Sunset

ALOIS SCHREIBER

D 627 (1818)

Du heilig, glühend Abendrot!
Der Himmel will in Glanz zerrinnen;
So scheiden Märtyrer von hinnen,
Hold lächelnd in dem Liebestod.

Sacred glowing sunset!
The sky melts into radiance.
Thus do martyrs depart this life,
Serenely smiling as they die for their love.

Des Aufgangs Berge still und grau,
Am Grab des Tags die hellen Gluten;
Der Schwan auf purpurroten Fluten,
Und jeder Halm im Silbertau!

At dawn the mountains are grey and silent,
The flames glow brightly at the day's grave;
The swan glides on crimson waters
And every blade is bathed in silver dew.

O Sonne, Gottesstrahl, du bist
Nie herrlicher, als im
    Entfliehn!
Du willst uns gern hinüberziehn,
Wo deines Glanzes Urquell ist.

O sun, light of God, you are
Never more glorious than when you go
    down!
You would gladly draw us with you
To the source of your radiance!

Das Bild / The Image

POET UNKNOWN

D 155 (1815)

Ein Mädchen ist's, das früh und spät
Mir vor der Seele schwebet,
Ein Mädchen, wie es steht und geht,
Aus Himmelsreiz gewebet.

Day and night I see a maiden
In my mind's eye,
A maiden who stands and moves,
Woven from heaven's charms.

Ich seh's, wenn in mein Fenster mild
Der junge Morgen blinket,
Ich seh's, wenn lieblich, wie das
    Bild,
Der Abendstern mir winket.

I see her when, through my window,
The new morning shines gently
I see her when the evening star, as sweet as
    her image,
Beckons to me.

Mir folgt's, ein treuer Weggenoss',
Zur Ruh' und ins Getümmel,
Ich fänd' es in der Erde Schoss,
Ich fänd' es selbst im Himmel.

She follows me, a faithful companion,
Through calm and turmoil,
I would find her in the depths of the earth,
Or even in the sky.

Es schwebt vor mir in Feld und
    Wald,
Prangt überm
    Blumenbeete,
Und glänzt in Seraphims Gestalt
Am Altar, wo ich bete.

She hovers before me in the fields and
    the woods
She appears radiantly above the
    flower beds,
And shines, in the form of a seraph,
At the altar where I pray.

73

Allein das Bild, das spät und früh
Mir vor der Seele schwebet,
Ist's nur Geschöpf der Phantasie,
Aus Luft und Traum gewebet?

O nein, so warm auch Liebe mir
Das Engelbildnis malet,
Ist's doch nur Schatten von der Zier,
Die an dem Mädchen strahlet.

But this image, which day and night
Hovers before my mind's eye,
Is it only a figment of my imagination,
Woven from air and dreams?

Oh no, fondly though my love
Paints this angelic vision,
The vision is but a shadow of the beauty
Which irradiates the maiden.

Das Echo / The Echo

IGNAZ FRANZ CASTELLI

D 868 (1826?)

Herzliebe gute Mutter!
O grolle nicht mit mir,
Du sahst den Hans mich küssen,
Doch ich kann nichts dafür.
Ich will dir Alles sagen,
Doch habe nur Geduld,
Das Echo drauß' am Hügel
Beim Bügel,
Das ist an Allem Schuld.

Dearest mother,
Do not be angry with me.
You saw Hans kiss me,
But it was not my fault.
I will tell you everything,
But have patience;
The echo on yonder
Hillside
Is to blame for everything.

Ich saß dort auf der Wiese,
Da hat er mich gesehn,
Doch blieb er ehrerbietig
Hübsch in der Ferne stehn
Und sprach: »Gern trät' ich näher,
Nähmst du's nicht übel auf,
Sag, bin ich dir willkommen?«
»Kommen!«
Rief schnell das Echo drauf.

I was sitting out in the meadow;
There he saw me.
But he remained respectfully
At a distance,
Saying: 'I should gladly come nearer
If you would not take it amiss.
Say, would you welcome me?'
'Come!'
Resounded the echo quickly.

Dann kam er auf die Wiese,
Zu mir hin setzt er sich,
Hieß mich die schöne Liese,
Und schlang den Arm um mich,
Und bat, ich möcht' ihm sagen,
Ob ich ihm gut kann sein?
Das wär' ihm sehr erfreulich.
»Freilich!«
Rief schnell das Echo drein.

Then he came to the meadow
And sat down beside me;
He called me his fair Liese,
Put his arm around me,
And asked me to tell him
If I could be kind to him,
For that would please him very much.
'Of course!'
Resounded the echo quickly.

Dies hört er, und hat näher
Zu rücken mir gewagt,
Er glaubte wohl, ich hätte
Das Alles ihm gesagt:
»Erlaubst du, sprach er zärtlich,
Daß ich als meine Braut
Dich recht von Herzen küsse?«
»Küsse!«
Schrie jetzt das Echo laut.

Hearing this he ventured
Closer to me,
For he thought that I
Had spoken these words.
He said tenderly: 'Be my bride,
And let me kiss you
With all my heart.'
'Kiss!'
Called the echo loudly.

Nun sieh, so ist's gekommen,
Daß Hans mir gab den Kuß,
Das böse, böse Echo,
Es macht mir viel Verdruß;

So you see how it came about
That Hans gave me that kiss;
That wicked, wicked echo
Has caused me such trouble.

Und jetzo wird er kommen,
Wirst sehen, sicherlich,
Und wird von dir begehren
In Ehren
Zu seinem Weibe mich.

Ist dir der Hans, lieb Mutter,
Nicht recht zu meinem Mann,
So sag, daß ihm das Echo
Den bösen Streich getan.
Doch glaubst du, daß wir passen,
Zu einem Ehepaar,
Dann mußt du ihn nicht kränken,
Magst denken,
Daß ich das Echo war.

And now he will come for certain,
As you will see,
And he will ask you
With due deference
For my hand in marriage.

Dear mother, if you think
That Hans is not the right husband for me,
Then tell him that the echo
Has played this trick on him.
But if you think
That we make a fitting wedding pair,
Then you must not upset him.
You can think
That *I* was the echo.

Das Finden / The Find

LUDWIG KOSEGARTEN

D 219 (1815)

Ich hab' ein Mädchen funden,
Sanft, edel, deutsch und gut,
Ihr Blick ist mild und glänzend,
Wie Abendsonnenglut,
Ihr Haar wie Sommerweben,
Ihr Auge veilchenblau;
Dem Rosenkelch der Lippen
Entquillt Gesang wie Tau.

Ich hab' das edle Mädchen
An meiner Hand geführt,
Ich bin mit ihr am Staden
Des Bach's hinabspaziert.
Ich hab' sie liebgewonnen,
Ich weiss, sie ist mir gut,
Drum sei mein Lied ihr eigen,
Ihr eigen Gut und Blut.

I have found a maiden,
Gentle, noble, kind and German.
Her gaze is as tender and radiant
As the glow of the evening sun.
Her hair is like gossamer,
Her eyes are violet-blue.
From the rosy chalice of her lips
Pours song like the dew.

I took the noble maiden
By the hand,
I walked with her
Beside the brook.
I fell in love with her,
I know she is fond of me.
Therefore let my song be hers,
Her very own.

Das Fischermädchen / The Fisher Maiden

HEINRICH HEINE

see Schwanengesang no. 10

Das Geheimnis / The Secret

FRIEDRICH VON SCHILLER

First version: D 250 (1815)
Second version: D 793 (1823)

Sie konnte mir kein Wörtchen sagen,
Zu viele Lauscher waren wach;
Den Blick nur durft' ich schüchtern
    fragen,
Und wohl verstand ich; was er sprach.

She could not speak one word to me,
There were too many listening;
I could only shyly question the look in her
    eyes,
And well understood what it meant.

Leis' komm' ich her in deine Stille,	Softly I approach your silence,
Du schön belaubtes Buchenzelt,	Leafy beach grove,
Verbirg in deiner grünen Hülle	Beneath your green cloak
Die Liebenden dem Aug' der Welt!	Conceal the lovers from the eyes of the world.
Von Ferne mit verworr'nem Sausen	Far away, in whirring confusion,
Arbeitet der geschäft'ge Tag,	The bustling day is at work,
Und durch der Stimmen hohles Brausen	And through the empty buzz of voices
Erkenn' ich schwerer Hammer Schlag.	I discern the beat of heavy hammers.
So sauer ringt die kargen Lose	Thus man toils to wrest his meagre lot
Der Mensch dem harten Himmel ab;	From a cruel heaven.
Doch leicht erworben, aus dem Schosse	Yet happiness is easily won,
Der Götter fällt das Glück herab.	Falling from the lap of the gods.
Das ja die Menschen nie es hören	May people never hear
Wie treue Lieb' uns still beglückt.	How happy our true love makes us!
Sie können nur die Freude stören,	They can only mar our joy,
Weil Freude nie sie selbst entzückt.	Since they have never tasted joy themselves.
Die Welt wird nie das Glück erlauben,	The world will never permit happiness,
Als Beute wird es nur gehascht;	It can only be snatched;
Entwenden musst du's oder rauben,	You must seize it
Eh' dich die Missgunst überrascht.	Before envy catches you unawares.
Leis' auf den Zehen kommt's geschlichen,	It steals in on tiptoe,
Die Stille liebt es und die Nacht;	Cherishing silence and the night.
Mit schnellen Füssen ist's entwichen,	With rapid steps it flees
Wo des Verräters Auge wacht.	When the traitor lurks.
O schlinge dich, du sanfte Quelle,	Gentle fountain, envelop us
Ein breiter Strom um uns herum,	Like a broad stream,
Und drohend mit empörter Welle	And with angrily threatening waves
Verteidige dies Heiligtum!	Defend this sanctuary.

Das gestörte Glück / Troubled Happiness

THEODOR KÖRNER

D 309 (1815)

Ich hab' ein heisses junges Blut,	I'm young and hot-blooded,
Wie ihr wohl alle wisst,	As you all know,
Ich bin dem Küssen gar zu gut,	And very fond of kissing,
Und hab' noch nie geküsst;	Yet have never kissed;
Denn ist mir auch mein Liebchen hold,	For although my maiden cares for me
'S war doch, als wenn's nicht werden sollt:	It seems as though it will not happen:
Trotz aller Müh' und aller List,	In spite of all my efforts, all my cunning
Hab ich doch niemals noch geküsst.	I have never kissed her.
Des Nachbars Röschen ist mir gut;	Rosie, our neighbour's daughter, is fond of me;
Sie ging zur Wiese früh,	One morning she went to the fields,
Ich lief ihr nach und fasste Mut,	I ran after her, took courage
Und schlang den Arm um sie:	And put my arm around her;
Da stach ich an dem Miederband	But then I pricked my hand
Mir eine Nadel in die Hand;	On a pin in her bodice,
Das Blut lief stark, ich sprang nach Haus,	The blood gushed out, I rushed home,

Und mit dem Küssen war es aus.

And that was the end of kissing.

Und allemal geht mir's nun so;
O! dass ich's leiden muss!
Mein Lebtag werd' ich nimmer froh,
Krieg' ich nicht bald 'nen Kuss.
Das Glück sieht mich so finster an,
Was hab' ich armer Wicht getan?
Drum, wer es hört, erbarme sich,
Und sei so gut und küsse mich.

Every time it's the same;
How I suffer!
I shall never in my life be happy
If I don't get a kiss soon.
Fate is so unkind to me,
What have I, poor wretch, done?
So whoever hears this, take pity on me,
Be kind and kiss me.

Das Grosse Halleluja / The Great Hallelujah

FRIEDRICH GOTTLIEB KLOPSTOCK

D 442 (1816)

Ehre sei dem Hocherhabnen, dem Ersten,
   dem Vater der Schöpfung,
Dem unsre Psalmen stammeln,
Obgleich der wunderbare Er
Unaussprechlich, und undenkbar ist!

Glory be to the Exalted One, the First, the
   Father of Creation,
To whom we stammer our psalms,
Although He, the wondrous One,
Is ineffable and unthinkable.

Eine Flamme von dem Altar an dem
   Thron
Ist in unsere Seele geströmt!
Wir freuen uns Himmelsfreuden,
Dass wir sind und über Ihn erstaunen
   können!

A flame from the altar at the
   throne
Has entered our souls.
We taste the joys of heaven,
For we exist and can wonder at
   Him.

Ehre sei Ihm auch von uns an den Gräbern
   hier,
Obwohl an seines Thrones letzten Stufen
Des Erzengels niedergeworfene Krone
Und seines Preisgesanges Wonne tönt!

Glory be to Him also from us among the
   graves,
Although the archangel has set his crown
On the lowest steps of His throne,
And joyous songs hymn His praise.

Ehre sei, und Dank, und Preis dem
   Hocherhabnen, dem Ersten,
Der nicht begann, und nicht aufhören
   wird!
Der sogar des Staubs Bewohnern
   gab,
Nicht aufzuhören!

Glory, thanks and praise be to the Exalted
   One, the First,
Who had no beginning, and will have no
   end,
Who granted that even the creatures of
   the dust
Shall have no end.

Ehre Dir! Ehre Dir! Ehre Dir!
Hocherhabner! Erster,
Vater der Schöpfung!
Unaussprechlicher, o Undenkbarer!

Glory be to You,
Exalted One, the First,
Father of Creation!
Ineffable, Unthinkable One!

Das Heimweh / Longing for Home

1st verse: THEODOR HELL (pseudonym for KARL GOTTFRIED WINKLER)
2nd and 3rd verses: MAX KALBECK

D 456 (1816)

Oft in einsam stillen Stunden
Hab' ich ein Gefühl empfunden,

Often, in quiet, solitary hours,
I have experienced a feeling,

Unerklärbar, wunderbar,
Das wie Sehnsucht nach der Ferne,
Hoch hinauf in bess're Sterne,
Wie ein leises Ahnen war.

Wohl die alten Bäume wieder
Neigen ihre Wipfel nieder
Auf das Haus am Waldesrand.
Stille, stille! Lass mich lauschen!
Fernher tönt ein leises Rauschen:
Komm zurück ins Heimatland!

Wer soll meiner Liebe lohnen?
Dort, wo fremde Menschen wohnen
Geh ich nicht mehr ein und aus.
Droben in der Sternenräumen
Unter goldnen Himmelsbäumen
Wartet mein das Vaterhaus.

Inexplicable, marvellous,
Like a yearning for the far distance,
High above, on a better star,
Like a soft presentiment.

Again the old trees
Bow their heads
Over the house on the edge of the forest.
Hush! let me listen!
Far away a soft murmuring echoes:
Come back to your homeland!

Who will repay my love?
Yonder, where strangers dwell,
I shall no longer come and go.
Up above in the starry firmament,
Beneath the golden trees of heaven,
My home awaits me.

Das Heimweh / Homesickness

JOHANN LADISLAUS PYRKER

D 851 (1825)

Ach, der Gebirgssohn hängt
Mit kindlicher Lieb' an der Heimat.
Wie den Alpen geraubt hinwelket die
    Blume,
So welkt er ihr entrissen dahin.

Stets sieht er die trauliche Hütte,
Die ihn gebar, im hellen Grün umduften-
    der Matten;
Sieht das dunkele Föhrengehölz,
Die ragende Felswand über ihm,
Und noch Berg auf Berg in erschütternder
    Hoheit
Aufgetürmt und glühend im Rosen-
    schimmer des Abends.
Immer schwebt es ihm vor,
Verdunkelt ist alles um ihn her.

Ängstlich horcht er; ihm deucht,
Er höre das Muhen der Kühe vom nahen
    Gehölz
Und hoch von den Alpen herunter
    Glöcklein klingen;
Ihm deucht, er höre das Rufen der Hirten,
Oder ein Lied der Sennerin, die mit um-
    schlagender Stimme
Freudig zum Widerhall aufjauchzt
    Melodien des Alplands:
Immer tönt es ihm nach.

Ihn fesselt der lachenden Eb'nen Anmut
    nicht,
Er fliehet der Städte einengenden Mauern,
    einsam,

Ah, the son of the mountains clings
With a childlike love to his homeland.
As the flower wilts when plucked from the
    Alpine meadow,
So he wilts when he is torn away.

Always he sees the cosy cottage
Where he was born, amid fragrant,
    bright-green meadows;
He sees the dark pine-copse,
The rock face looming above him,
And mountain upon mountain, towering
    up in fearful majesty,
And glowing in the rosy light of
    evening.
Constantly they hover before his eyes,
All else around him is obscured.

He listens anxiously; he thinks
He hears the lowing of cattle in the nearby
    copse,
And bells tinkling from high on the
    alps;
He thinks he hears the call of shepherds
Or the song of a milkmaid who, with
    yodelling voice,
Joyfully sings her melodies to the echoing
    mountains.
Always it sounds in his ears.

The charm of the smiling plains cannot
    keep him;
All alone, he flees from the constricting
    walls of the town,

Und schaut aufweinend vom Hügel die
heimischen Berge;
Ach, es zieht ihn dahin mit unwider-
stehlicher Sehnsucht.

And, weeping, looks up from the hills
towards his native peaks;
Ah, he is drawn there with irresistible
longing!

Das Lied im Grünen / Song of the Green Countryside

FRIEDRICH REIL

D 917 (1827)

Ins Grüne, ins Grüne, da lockt uns der
Frühling,
Der liebliche Knabe,
Und führt uns am blumenumwundenen
Stabe
Hinaus, wo die Lerchen und Amseln so
wach,
In Wälder, auf Felder, auf Hügel zum
Bach,
Ins Grüne, ins Grüne.

To the green countryside!
Spring,
That sweet youth, invites us there,
And leads us with his flower-entwined
staff
To where larks and blackbirds
stir,
To woods and fields, over hills to the
brook,
To the green countryside!

Im Grünen, im Grünen, da lebt es sich
wonnig,
Da wandeln wir gerne
Und heften die Augen dahin schon von
ferne,
Und wie wir so wandeln mit heiterer
Brust,
Umwallet uns immer die kindliche Lust,
Im Grünen, im Grünen.

In the green countryside life is
blissful,
There we love to roam;
Even from afar we fix our eyes
on it,
And as we wander there with cheerful
hearts,
A childlike joy envelops us,
In the green countryside!

Im Grünen, im Grünen, da ruht man so
wohl,
Empfindet so Schönes,
Und denket behaglich an dieses und
jenes,
Und zaubert von hinnen, ach, was uns
bedrückt,
Und alles herbei, was den Busen entzückt
Im Grünen, im Grünen.

In the green countryside we find such
peace
And sense such beauty;
We contentedly dwell on this and
that,
Conjure away our
troubles,
And conjure up our hearts' delight,
In the green countryside!

Im Grünen, im Grünen, da werden die
Sterne
So klar, die die
Weisen
Der Vorwelt zur Leitung des Lebens uns
preisen,
Da streichen die Wölkchen so zart uns
dahin,
Da heitern die Herzen, da klärt sich der
Sinn
Im Grünen, im Grünen.

In the green countryside the
stars
Are so bright, those stars which the
wise men
Of old extolled as our life's
guidance.
The little clouds glide by so
tenderly,
Our hearts are cheered, and our senses
clear,
In the green countryside!

Im Grünen, im Grünen, da wurde manch
Plänchen
Auf Flügeln getragen,
Die Zukunft der grämlichen Ansicht
entschlagen,

In the green countryside many a little
plan
Takes wing,
And the future sheds its gloomy
aspect;

Da stärkt sich das Auge, da labt sich
  der Blick,
Sanft wiegen die Wünsche sich hin und
  zurück
Im Grünen, im Grünen.

Im Grünen, im Grünen am Morgen, am
  Abend
In traulicher Stille
Entkeimet manch Liedchen und manche
  Idylle
Und Hymen oft kränzt den poetischen
  Scherz,
Denn leicht ist die Lockung, empfänglich
  das Herz
Im Grünen, im Grünen.

O gerne im Grünen bin ich schon als
  Knabe
Und Jüngling gewesen
Und habe gelernt und geschrieben,
  gelesen
Im Horaz und Plato, dann Wieland und
  Kant,
Und glühenden Herzens mich selig
  genannt,
Im Grünen, im Grünen.

Ins Grüne, ins Grüne lasst heiter uns
  folgen
Dem freundlichen Knaben.
Grünt einst uns das Leben nicht
  fürder,
So haben wir klüglich die grünende Zeit
  nicht versäumt,
Und wenn es gegolten, doch glücklich
  geträumt,
Im Grünen, im Grünen.

The eye is strengthened and the gaze
  refreshed,
Our desires sway gently to and
  fro,
In the green countryside!

In the green countryside, morning and
  evening,
In the intimate stillness,
Many a song and many an idyll
  burgeons,
And Hymen often crowns the poetic
  dallying,
For it is easy to entice, and the heart is
  susceptible
In the green countryside!

I was glad to be in the green
  countryside
As a boy and as a youth,
Learnt and wrote, and
  read
Horace and Plato, then Wieland and
  Kant,
And with glowing heart counted myself
  happy,
In the green countryside.

Into the green countryside let us merrily
  follow
The friendly youth.
And when, one day, life no longer blossoms
  for us,
Then we shall have been wise enough not to
  miss the verdant years,
And shall have dreamed happily when the
  time was right,
In the green countryside!

Das Lied vom Reifen / Song of the Frost

MATTHIAS CLAUDIUS

D 532 (1817)

Seht meine lieben Bäume an,
Wie sie so herrlich stehn,
Auf allen Zweigen angetan
Mit Reifen wunderschön!

Von unten an bis oben 'naus
Auf allen Zweigelein
Hängt's weiss und zierlich, zart und
  kraus,
Und kann nicht schöner sein.

Ein Engel Gottes geht bei Nacht,
Streut heimlich hier und dort,
Und wenn der Bauersmann erwacht,
Ist er schon wieder fort.

Look how splendid
My beloved trees are,
Adorned on every branch
With beautiful frost!

From top to bottom
It hangs on every twig,
White and delicate, fragile and
  crisp.
Nothing could be lovelier.

An angel of God comes by at night,
Secretly scattering here and there,
And is already gone
When the farmer wakens.

Du Engel, der so gütig ist,
Wir sagen Dank und Preis,
O mach uns doch zum heil'gen Christ
Die Bäume wieder weiss!

O angel, who are so good,
We give you thanks and praise;
Make the trees white again for us
At Christmas time.

Das Mädchen / The Maiden

FRIEDRICH VON SCHLEGEL

D 652 (1819)

Wie so innig, möcht' ich sagen,
Sich der meine mir ergibt,
Um zu lindern meine Klagen,
Daß er nicht so innig liebt.

I should like to say that my beloved
Shows me such ardent devotion
In order to still my complaints
That he does not love me ardently.

Will ich's sagen, so entschwebt
es;
Wären Töne mir verliehen,
Flöss' es hin in Harmonien,
Denn in jenen Tönen lebt es.
Nur die Nachtigall kann sagen,
Wie er innig sich mir gibt,
Um zu lindern meine Klagen,
Daß er nicht so innig liebt.

When I am about to tell him, the words float
away;
If the power of music were granted me
My feelings would pour out in harmonies,
For they live in music.
Only the nightingale can say
What ardent devotion he shows me
In order to still my complaints
That he does not love me ardently.

Das Mädchen (Wenn mich einsam Lüfte fächeln) / The Maiden

FRIEDRICH VON SCHLEGEL

see Blanka

Das Mädchen aus der Fremde / The Maiden from Strange Parts

FRIEDRICH VON SCHILLER

First version: D 117 (1814)
Second version: D 252 (1815)

In einem Tal bei armen Hirten
Erschien mit jedem jungen Jahr,
Sobald die ersten Lerchen schwirrten,
Ein Mädchen schön und wunderbar.

To poor shepherds in a valley
Appeared each spring
With the first soaring larks,
A strange and lovely maiden.

Sie war nicht in dem Tal geboren,
Man wusste nicht, woher sie kam,
Doch schnell war ihre Spur verloren,
Sobald das Mädchen Abschied nahm.

She had not been born in the valley.
No one knew from where she came.
But when the maiden departed
They soon lost trace of her.

Beseligend war ihre Nähe
Und alle Herzen wurden weit,
Doch eine Würde, eine Höhe
Entfernte die Vertraulichkeit.

Her very presence was blissful
And all hearts opened to her,
Yet her dignity, her loftiness
Precluded familiarity.

Sie brachte Blumen mit und Früchte,
Gereift auf einer andern Flur,
In einem andern Sonnenlichte,
In einer glücklichern Natur;

She brought flowers, and fruit
Ripened in other fields,
Under another sun
In a happier countryside.

Und teilte jedem eine Gabe,
Dem Früchte, jenem Blumen aus,
Der Jüngling und der Greis am Stabe,
Ein jeder ging beschenkt nach Haus.

She bestowed her gifts on all,
Fruit on one, flowers on another,
The youth, the old man with his stick,
Each one went home enriched.

Willkommen waren alle Gäste,
Doch nahte sich ein liebend Paar,
Dem reichte sie der Gaben beste,
Der Blumen allerschönste dar.

All guests were welcome,
But if a loving couple approached
She would give them her finest gifts,
The fairest flowers of all.

Das Mädchen von Inistore / The Maid of Inistore

JAMES MACPHERSON (OSSIAN), translated by EDMUND VON HAROLD

D 281 (1815)

Mädchen Inistores, wein auf dem Felsen der stürmischen Winde! neig über Wellen dein zierliches Haupt, du, dem an Liebreiz der Geist der Hügel weicht; wenn er in einem Sonnenstrahl, des Mittags über Morvens Schweigen hingleitet. Er ist gefallen! der Jüngling erliegt bleich unter der Klinge Cuthullins! nicht mehr wird der Mut deinen Geliebten erheben, dem Blut der Gebieter zu gleichen. O Mädchen Inistores! Trenar, der zierliche Trenar ist todt! In seiner Heimat heulen seine Doggen; sie seh'n seinen gleitenden Geist. In seiner Halle sein Bogen ungespannt. Man hört auf dem Hügel seiner Hirsche keinen Schall!

Weep on the rocks of roaring winds, O maid of Inistore! Bend thy fair head over the waves, thou lovelier than the ghosts of the hills; when it moves, in a sun-beam, at noon, over the silence of Morven! He is fallen! thy youth is low! Pale beneath the sword of Cuthullin! No more shall valour raise thy love to match the blood of kings. Trenar, graceful Trenar died, O maid of Inistore! His dogs are howling at home! they see his passing ghost. His bow is in the hall unstrung. No sound is in the hills of his hinds.

Das Marienbild / Picture of the Virgin Mary

ALOYS SCHREIBER

D 623 (1818)

Sei gegrüßt, du Frau der Huld,
Und der reinen, schönen Minne,
Ohne Makel, ohne Schuld,
Und von demutsvollem Sinne!

Hail, gracious Lady
Of pure, fair love,
Without blemish, without guilt,
Humble in spirit.

Fromme Einfalt wölbte dir
Diese ärmliche Kapelle
In den Stamm der Eiche hier
Ohne Säulen, ohne Schwelle.

In pious simplicity
This lowly chapel was raised to you
In the trunk of this oak,
With neither pillars nor threshold.

Vögelein auf jedem Ast
Singen deinem Kindlein Lieder.
Durchs Gezweig im goldnen Glast
Steigen Engel auf und nieder.

On every bough
Birds sing their songs to your child;
Angels, bathed in golden radiance,
Move up and down amid the branches.

Und dem Herzen wird so
  leicht,
Wär es auch von Gram umsponnen,
Und dem Pilger wird gereicht
Labung aus dem Gnadenbronnen.

And the heart, though oppressed with
  grief,
Is made light;
And the pilgrim finds refreshment
At the fount of grace.

82

Wohl ein Hüttlein baut ich gern	I would fain build a little hut
Hier im stillen Waldesgrunde,	Here in the silent forest,
Daß mir dieser Meeresstern	That the star of the sea
Leuchte nun und jede Stunde;	Might shine for me now and always;
Daß in diesem kleinen Raum	That in this small space
Mir der Himmel angehöre,	Heaven might be mine,
Daß kein banger, böser Traum	And that no troubled, evil dream
Meinen letzten Schlummer störe.	Might disturb my last sleep.

Das Rosenband / The Rosy Ribbon

FRIEDRICH GOTTLIEB KLOPSTOCK

D 280 (1815)

Im Frühlingsgarten fand ich sie,	I found her in the spring garden,
Da band ich sie mit Rosenbändern:	And bound her with rosy ribbons;
Sie fühlt' es nicht und schlummerte.	Oblivious, she slept on.
Ich sah sie an; mein Leben hing	I looked at her; with that gaze
Mit diesem Blick an ihrem Leben:	My life was bound to hers:
Ich fühlt' es wohl und wusst' es nicht.	This I felt, yet did not know.
Doch lispelt' ich ihr sprachlos zu	But I whispered silently to her
Und rauschte mit den Rosenbändern.	And rustled the rosy ribbons.
Da wachte sie vom Schlummer auf.	Then she woke from her slumber.
Sie sah mich an; ihr Leben hing	She looked at me; with that gaze
Mit diesem Blick an meinem Leben,	Her life was bound to mine,
Und um uns ward Elysium.	And all around us was paradise.

Das Sehnen / Longing

LUDWIG KOSEGARTEN

D 231 (1815)

Wehmut, die mich hüllt,	Melancholy envelops me;
Welche Gottheit stillt	What god can still
Mein unendlich Sehnen!	My boundless longing?
Die ihr meine Wimper näßt,	It moistens my eyelashes,
Namenlosen Gram entpreßt,	And draws from me nameless grief.
Fließet, fließet Tränen!	Flow, tears, flow!
Mond, der lieb und traut	Moon, gazing fondly and tenderly
In mein Fenster schaut,	Through my window,
Sage, was mir fehle!	Say, what is the matter with me?
Sterne, die ihr droben blinkt,	Stars, shining up above,
Holden Gruß mir freundlich winkt,	Sending me your sweet, kindly greeting,
Nennt mir, was mich quäle!	Tell me what torments me!
Leise Schauer wehn,	The air quivers gently,
Süßes Liebeflehn	The sweet entreaty of love
Girrt um mich im Düstern.	Coos around me in the dusk.
Rosen- und Violenduft	The fragrance of roses and violets
Würzen rings die Zauberluft,	Spices the enchanted air,
Holde Stimmen flüstern.	Sweet voices whisper.

In der Ferne strebt,
Wie auf Flügeln schwebt
Mein erhöhtes Wesen.
Fremder Zug, geheime Kraft,
Namenlose Leidenschaft,
Laß, ach laß genesen!

Ängstender beklemmt
Mich die Wehmut, hemmt
Atem mir und Rede.
Einsam schmachten, o der Pein!
O des Grams, allein zu sein
In des Lebens Öde!

Ist denn, ach, kein Arm
Der in Freud' und Harm
Liebend mich umschlösse?
Ist denn, ach, kein fühlend Herz,
Keines, drinn in Lust und Schmerz
Meines sich ergösse?

Die ihr einsam klagt,
Einsam wenn es tagt,
Einsam wenn es nachtet,
Ungetröstet, ach, verächzt
Ihr das holde Dasein, lechzt,
Schmachtet und verschmachtet.

With a heightened sense of my existence
I strive for the far distance,
Soaring as if on wings.
A strange impulse, secret power,
Nameless passion,
Ah, let me be made well!

Melancholy oppresses me
Still more fearfully, stifling
My breath and my speech.
O the pain of languishing in solitude!
O the grief of being alone
In life's wilderness!

Is there then no arm
To embrace me fondly
In joy and sorrow?
Is there, alas, no tender heart
To which I may pour out my own
In pleasure and pain?

You who lament all alone,
Alone when day breaks,
Alone when night falls,
Disconsolate — ah you despise
This fair existence, you thirst,
Languish and pine away.

Das war ich / That was I

THEODOR KÖRNER

D 174 (1815)

Jüngst träumte mir, ich sah auf lichten
    Höhen
Ein Mädchen sich im jungen Tag
    ergehen,
So hold, so süss, dass es dir völlig glich.
Und vor ihr lag ein Jüngling auf den
    Knien,
Er schien sie sanft an seine Brust zu
    ziehen,
Und das war ich.

Doch bald verändert hatte sich die Szene,
In tiefen Fluten sah ich jetzt die
    Schöne,
Wie ihr die letzte, schwache Kraft
    entwich,
Da kam ein Jüngling hülfreich ihr
    geflogen,
Er sprang ihr nach und trug sie aus den
    Wogen,
Und das war ich!

So malte sich der Traum in bunten
    Zügen,
Und überall sah ich die Liebe siegen,

Recently I dreamt I saw on sunlit
    hills
A maiden wandering in the early
    morning,
So fair, so sweet, that she resembled you.
Before her knelt a
    youth,
He seemed to draw her gently to his
    breast;
And that was I.

But soon the scene had changed.
I now saw that fair maiden in the deep
    flood,
Her frail strength was deserting
    her.
Then a youth rushed to her
    aid,
He plunged after her and bore her from the
    waves.
And that was I.

The dream was painted in bright
    colours,
Everywhere I saw love victorious,

Und alles, alles drehte sich um dich!
Du flogst voran in ungebund'ner Freie,
Der Jüngling zog dir nach mit stiller
  Treue,
Und das war ich!

Und als ich endlich aus dem Traum
  erwachte,
Der neue Tag die neue Sehnsucht
  brachte,
Da blieb dein liebes, süsses Bild um mich.
Ich sah dich von der Küsse Glut
  erwarmen,
Ich sah dich selig in des Jünglings
  Armen,
Und das war ich!

And everything was centred on you!
You sailed on, free and unfettered,
The faithful youth followed you,
  silently,
And that was I.

And when at length I awoke from my
  dream,
The new day brought new
  longing.
Your dear, sweet image was still with me.
I saw you warmed by the fire of his
  kisses,
I saw you blissful in that youth's
  arms,
And that was I.

Das Weinen / Weeping

KARL GOTTFRIED VON LEITNER

D 926 (1827)

Gar tröstlich kommt geronnen
Der Tränen heil'ger Quell,
Recht wie ein Heilungs-Bronnen,
So bitter, heiß und hell,
Darum du Brust voll Wunden,
Voll Gram und stiller Pein,
Und willst du bald gesunden,
So tauche da hinein.

The sacred source of tears
Flows comfortingly,
Like a healing spring,
So bitter, hot and clear.
Therefore, my heart, full of wounds,
Grief and silent pain,
If you would recover quickly,
Immerse yourself there.

Es wohnt in diesen Wellen
Geheime Wunderkraft,
Die ist für wehe Stellen
Ein linder Balsamsaft.
Die wächst mit deinen Schmerzen,
Und fasset, hebt und rollt
Den bösen Stein vom Herzen,
Der dich zerdrücken wollt'.

A secret, magic power
Dwells in these waters
That is gentle balm
To wounds;
It increases with your suffering,
And seizes, lifts and rolls away
From your heart the evil stone
That would crush you.

Das hab' ich selbst empfunden
Hier in dem Trauerland,
Wenn ich, vom Flor umwunden,
An lieben Gräbern stand.
Da schalt in irrem Wähnen
Ich selbst auf meinen Gott,
Es hielten nur die Tränen
Der Hoffnung Schiffchen flott.

I have felt this myself,
Here in this land of sorrow,
When, swathed in crêpe,
I stood at the graves of dear ones.
There, in demented frenzy,
I cursed my God;
Only my tears kept
The ship of hope afloat.

Drum, hält dich auch umfangen
Der Schwermut trübste Nacht,
Vertrau' in allem Bangen
Der Tränen Zaubermacht.
Bald, wenn vom heißen Weinen
Dir rot das Auge glüht,
Wird neu der Tag erscheinen,
Weil schon der Morgen blüht.

Therefore, when you too are ensnared
In the darkest night of sorrow,
In your anguish trust
The magic power of tears.
Soon, when from bitter weeping
Your eyes glow red,
A new day will appear,
For already morning is radiant.

Das Zügenglöcklein / The Passing Bell

JOHANN GABRIEL SEIDL

D871 (1826?)

Kling' die Nacht durch, klinge,	Ring, ring the night through,
Süssen Frieden bringe	Bring sweet peace
Dem, für den du tönst!	To him you toll for!
Kling in weite Ferne,	Ring out in the far distance;
So du Pilger gerne	Thus you reconcile pilgrims
Mit der Welt versöhnst.	With the world.
Aber wer will wandern	But who would wish to journey
Zu den lieben andern,	To the loved ones
Die vorausgewallt?	Who have gone before?
Zog er gern die Schelle,	Though he gladly rang the bell,
Bebt er an der Schwelle,	He trembles on the threshold
Wann »Herein« erschallt.	When a voice cries 'Enter'.
Gilt's dem bösen Sohne,	Is it meant for the wicked son
Der noch flucht dem Tone,	Who still curses its sound
Weil er heilig ist?	Because it is sacred?
Nein, es klingt so lauter	No, it rings more loudly
Wie ein Gottvertrauer	When a man who trusts in God
Seine Laufbahn schliesst.	Concludes his life's journey.
Aber ist's ein Müder,	But if it is a weary man
Den verwaist die Brüder,	Deserted by his kin,
Dem ein treues Tier	Whose faith in the world
Einzig liess den Glauben	Has been saved
An die Welt nicht rauben,	Only by a faithful beast,
Ruf ihn, Gott, zu Dir!	Call him unto You, O God!
Ist's der Frohen einer,	If it is one of the blessed,
Der die Freuden reiner	Who partakes of the joys
Lieb' und Freundschaft teilt,	Of love and friendship,
Gönn' ihm noch die Wonnen	Then grant him yet bliss
Unter dieser Sonnen,	Beneath this sun,
Wo er gerne weilt!	Where he gladly tarries!

Daß sie hier gewesen / That She has been Here

FRIEDRICH RÜCKERT

D775 (1823?)

Daß der Ostwind Düfte	The east wind
Hauchet in die Lüfte,	Breathes fragrance into the air;
Dadurch tut er kund,	And so doing it makes known
Daß du hier gewesen!	That you have been here!
Daß hier Tränen rinnen,	Since tears flow here
Dadurch wirst du innen,	You will know,
Wär's dir sonst nicht kund,	Though you are otherwise unaware,
Daß ich hier gewesen!	That I have been here!

86

Schönheit oder Liebe,	Beauty or love:
Ob versteckt sie bliebe?	Can they remain concealed?
Düfte tun es und Tränen kund,	Fragrant scents and tears proclaim
Daß sie hier gewesen!	That she has been here!

Delphine / Delphine*

CHRISTIAN WILHELM VON SCHÜTZ

D857 no. 2 (1825)

Ach, was soll ich beginnen	Ah, how shall I begin,
Vor Liebe?	For love?
Ach, wie sie innig durchdringet	Ah, how profoundly it penetrates
Mein Innres!	My inmost being!
Siehe, Jüngling, das Kleinste	See, young man, the smallest part of me,
Vom Scheitel	From my head
Bis zur Sohl' ist dir einzig	To the soles of my feet,
Geweihet.	Is dedicated to you alone.
O Blumen! Blumen! verwelket,	O flowers, fade!
Euch pfleget	The soul
Nur, bis sie Lieb' erkennet,	Tends you
Die Seele.	Only until it knows love.
Nichts will ich tun, wissen and haben,	I wish to do nothing, know nothing, have nothing;
Gedanken	All I wish is to cherish
Der Liebe, die mächtig mich fassen,	Thoughts of love,
Nur tragen.	Which has held me in its power.
Immer sinn' ich, was ich aus Inbrunst	I forever reflect on what else I might do
Wohl könne tun,	In my ardour,
Doch zu sehr hält mich Liebe im Druck,	But love holds me too tightly in its grasp,
Nichts läßt sie zu.	It permits me nothing.
Jetzt, da ich liebe, möcht' ich erst brennen,	Now that I am in love I desire first to burn,
Und sterbe.	Then to die.
Jetzt, da ich liebe, möcht ich hell brennen,	Now that I am in love I desire first to burn brightly,
Und welke.	Then to wither.
Wozu auch Blumen reihen und wässern?	What is the good of planting rows of flowers and watering them?
Entblättert!	They are stripped of their leaves!
So sieht, wie Liebe mich entkräftet,	Thus he sees
Sein Spähen.	How love weakens me.
Der Rose Wange will bleichen,	The rose's cheek will fade,
Auch meine.	And so, too, will mine.
Ihr Schmuck zerfällt, wie verscheinen	Her lustre is ruined, as clothes
Die Kleider.	Grow threadbare.
Ach Jüngling, da du mich erfreuest	Ah, young man, if you bring me joy
Mit Treue,	With your devotion,
Wie kann mich mit Schmerz so bestreuen	How can that joy fill me
Die Freude?	With such pain?

Dem Unendlichen / To the Infinite One

FRIEDRICH GOTTLIEB KLOPSTOCK

D291 (1815)

| Wie erhebt sich das Herz, wenn es dich, | How the heart surges when it thinks of you, |
| Unendlicher, denkt! wie sinkt es, | Infinite One! How it sinks |

*Text from Schütz's play *Lacrimas*

Wenn's auf sich herunterschaut!	When it gazes down upon itself!
Elend schaut's wehklagend dann und Nacht und Tod.	Lamenting, it sees but misery, night and death.
Allein du rufst mich aus meiner Nacht, der im Elend, der im Tode hilft!	You alone call me from my night, You alone help me in misery and death!
Dann denk' ich es ganz, dass du ewig mich schufst,	Then I know that you created me for eternity,
Herrlicher, den kein Preis, unten am Grab, oben am Thron,	Lord of Glory, for whom no praise is sufficient, in the grave below or by Your throne above;
Herr Gott, den, dankend entflammt, kein Jubel genug besingt!	Lord God, no paeans of thanks are worthy of You.
Weht, Bäume des Lebens, ins Harfengetön!	Sway, trees of life, to the music of the harps!
Rausche mit ihnen ins Harfengetön, kristallner Strom!	Murmur with them to the harps' music, crystal streams!
Ihr lispelt und rauscht, und, Harfen, ihr tönt	You whisper and murmur, and, harps, you play,
Nie es ganz! Gott ist es, den ihr preist!	But never fully; it is God whom you praise!
Welten, donnert,	Thunder, you spheres,
In feierlichem Gang, in der Posaunen Chor!	In solemn motion, to the choir of trumpets!
Tönt, all ihr Sonnen auf der Strasse voll Glanz,	Resound, all you suns, on your shining course,
In der Posaunen Chor!	To the choir of trumpets!
Ihr Welten, donnert,	You thunder, spheres,
Du, der Posaunen Chor, hallest	Choir of trumpets, you blaze forth,
Nie es ganz: Gott — nie es ganz: Gott,	But never fully:
Gott, Gott ist es, den ihr preist!	It is God, God whom you praise.

Der Abend / *The Evening*

LUDWIG KOSEGARTEN

D 221 (1815)

Der Abend blüht,	The evening blossoms,
Temora glüht	Temora glows
Im Glanz der tiefgesunknen Sonne.	In the light of the setting sun.
Es küsst die See	As it sinks
Die Sinkende,	It kisses the sea,
Von Ehrfurcht schaudernd und von Wonne.	Which trembles in awe and ecstasy.
Ein grauer Duft	A grey haze
Durchwebt die Luft,	Pervades the air,
Umschleiert Daura's güldne Auen.	Veiling Daura's golden meadows.
Es rauscht umher	Round about
Das düstre Meer,	The sombre ocean roars,
Und rings herrscht ahndungsreiches Grauen.	And grey foreboding hangs over all.

O trautes Land! \
O heil'ger Strand! \
O Flur, die jede Flur verdunkelt. \
Flur, deren Schoss die Blum' entspross, \
Die alle Blumen überfunkelt.

Paart nicht den Schnee \
Der Lilie \
Die Holde mit der Glut der Rosen? \
Die Au, ein Kranz voll Duft und \
    Glanz, \
Reicht ihr den Preis, der \
    Tadellosen. \
Ihr Ambraduft \
Durchweht die Luft, \
Und würzet rings die Näh' und Ferne. \
Und stirbt das Licht des Liedes nicht, \
So reicht ihr Nam' einst an die Sterne.

O trautes Land, \
O hehrer Strand, \
Sei stolz auf deiner Blumen Blume. \
Das heil'ge Meer und rings umher \
Die Inseln huld'gen deinem Ruhme.

Nacht hüllt den Strand, \
Temora schwand, \
Verlodert sind des Spätrots Gluthen. \
Das Weltmeer grollt, und glutrot rollt \
Der Vollmond aus den düstern Fluten.

Beloved land! \
Sacred shore! \
Meadows which eclipse all other meadows, \
And from which the flower sprang \
Which outshines all other flowers.

Does not the lovely flower \
With the fiery glow of roses \
Match the snow-white lily? \
The meadow, garlanded with fragrance \
    and splendour, \
Awards that flower, which is without \
    blemish, the prize. \
Its fragrance \
Pervades the air, \
Its spicy scent is wafted near and far. \
And if this song does not die \
One day its fame will extend to the stars.

Beloved land, \
Noble shore, \
Be proud of your fairest flower. \
The sacred sea and the surrounding islands \
Pay homage to your glory.

Night shrouds the shore, \
Temora has vanished, \
The sunset's last glow has faded. \
The ocean roars and, gleaming red, \
The full moon rolls from the dark waves.

Der Abend / The Evening

FRIEDRICH VON MATTHISSON

D 108 (1814)

Purpur malt die \
    Tannenhügel \
Nach der Sonne Scheideblick, \
Lieblich strahlt des Baches Spiegel \
Hespers Fackelglanz zurück.

Wie in Totenhallen düster \
Wird's im Pappelweidenhain, \
Unter leisem Blattgeflüster \
Schlummern alle Vögel ein.

Nur dein Abendlied, o Grille! \
Tönt noch aus betautem Grün, \
Durch der Dämmrung Zauberhülle \
Süße Trauermelodien.

Tönst du einst im Abendhauche, \
Grillchen, auf mein frühes \
    Grab, \
Aus der Freundschaft Rosenstrauche, \
Deinen Klaggesang herab:

The pine-covered hills are painted with \
    purple \
After the sun's parting glance, \
The brook's mirror reflects \
The lovely gleaming torch of Hesperus.

In the poplar grove \
It grows dark, as in the vaults of death. \
Beneath softly whispering leaves \
All the birds fall asleep.

Only your evening song, o cricket, \
Echoes from the dewy grass, \
Wafting sweet, mournful melodies \
Through the enchanted cloak of dusk.

Cricket, if one day \
You sound your lament in the evening \
    breeze \
Over my early grave, \
From the rose-bush planted by friends:

Wird mein Geist noch stets dir lauschen,
Horchend wie er jetzt dir lauscht,
Durch des Hügels Blumen
rauschen,
Wie dies Sommerlüftchen
rauscht!

My spirit will always listen to you
As it listens to you now,
And murmur through the flowers on the
hillside
As this summer breeze
murmurs.

Der Alpenjäger / The Alpine Huntsman

JOHANN MAYRHOFER

D 524 (1817)

Auf hohem Bergesrücken,
Wo frischer alles grünt,
Ins Land hinabzublicken,
Das nebelleicht zerrinnt,
Erfreut den Alpenjäger.

High on the mountain ridge
Where everything is greener and fresher,
The huntsman delights
In gazing down at the landscape
Veiled in mist.

Je steiler und je schräger
Die Pfade sich verwinden,
Je mehr Gefahr aus Schlünden,
So freier schlägt die Brust.
Er ist der fernen Lieben,
Die ihm daheimgeblieben,
Sich seliger bewusst.

The more steeply the paths
Wind upwards,
The more dangerous the precipices,
The more freely his heart beats,
The more fondly he thinks
Of his distant beloved
Who remains at home.

Und ist er nun am Ziele,
So drängt sich in der Stille
Ein süsses Bild ihm vor;
Der Sonne goldne Strahlen,
Sie weben und sie malen,
Die er im Tal erkor.

And when he reaches his goal
A sweet image fills his mind
In the stillness;
The sun's golden beams
Weave and paint a portrait of her
Whom he has chosen in the valley.

Der Alpenjäger / The Alpine Huntsman

FRIEDRICH VON SCHILLER

D 588 (1817)

Willst du nicht das Lämmlein hüten?
Lämmlein ist so fromm und sanft,
Nährt sich von des Grases Blüten,
Spielend an des Baches Ranft.
»Mutter, Mutter, lass mich gehen,
Jagen nach des Berges Höhen!«

Will you not tend the lamb,
So meek and mild?
It feeds on flowers in the grass,
Gambolling beside the brook.
'Mother, let me go
Hunting on the high mountains.'

Willst du nicht die Herde locken
Mit des Hornes munterm Klang?
Lieblich tönt der Schall der Glocken
In des Waldes Lustgesang.
»Mutter, Mutter, lass mich gehen,
Schweifen auf den wilden Höhen!«

Will you not call the herd
With the merry sound of your horn?
The bells mingle sweetly
With the joyful song of the forest.
'Mother, let me go
And roam the wild heights.'

Willst du nicht die Blümlein warten,
Die im Beete freundlich stehn?
Draussen ladet dich kein Garten,
Wild ists auf den wilden Höhn!
»Lass die Blümlein, lass sie blühen!
Mutter, Mutter, lass mich ziehen!«

Will you not tend the flowers
That grow so charmingly in their beds?
Out there no garden invites you;
It is harsh on those wild mountains.
'Let the flowers bloom;
Mother, let me go!'

Und der Knabe ging zu jagen,
Und es treibt und reisst ihn fort,
Rastlos fort mit blindem Wagen
An des Berges finstern Ort,
Vor ihm her mit Windesschnelle
Flieht die zitternde Gazelle.

Auf der Felsen nackte Rippen
Klettert sie mit leichtem Schwung,
Durch den Riss gespaltener Klippen
Trägt sie der gewagte Sprung,
Aber hinter ihr verwogen
Folgt er mit dem Todesbogen.

Jetzo auf den schroffen Zinken
Hängt sie, auf dem höchsten Grat,
Wo die Felsen jäh versinken
Und verschwunden ist der Pfad.
Unter sich die steile Höhe,
Hinter sich des Feindes Nähe.

Mit der Jammers stummen Blicken
Fleht sie zu dem harten Mann,
Fleht umsonst, denn loszudrücken
Legt er schon den Bogen an.
Plötzlich aus der Felsenspalte
Tritt der Geist, der Bergesalte.

Und mit seinen Götterhänden
Schützt er das gequälte Tier.
»Musst du Tod und Jammer senden«,
Ruft er, »bis herauf zu mir?
Raum für alle hat die Erde,
Was verfolgst du meine Herde?«

And the boy went hunting,
Driven relentlessly onwards,
With blind daring,
To the bleak parts of the mountain.
Before him, swift as the wind,
Flees the trembling gazelle.

On the bare rock face
She bounds effortlessly;
Bravely she leaps
Across chasms in the rocks;
But he pursues her boldly
With his deadly bow.

Now she clings to the jagged spur
On the top of the ridge,
Where the cliff falls sheer,
And the path vanishes.
Beneath her is the steep drop,
Behind her the approaching enemy.

Gazing in mute distress
She implores the pitiless man;
But in vain, for already he draws his bow
And prepares to shoot.
Suddenly, from a rocky cleft,
The spirit of the mountain steps forth.

With his godlike hands
He protects the tormented beast.
'Must you even bring death and woe,'
He cries, 'Up here to me?
The earth has room for all;
Why do you persecute my herd?'

Der Atlas / Atlas

HEINRICH HEINE

see Schwanengesang no. 8

Der blinde Knabe / The Blind Boy

COLLEY CIBBER, translated by JACOB NICOLAUS CRAIGHER

D 833 (1825)
A literal translation of the German is given here. Cibber's original poem is printed
below in italics.

O sagt, ihr Lieben, mir einmal,
Welch Ding ist's, Licht genannt?
Was sind des Sehens Freuden all',
Die niemals ich gekannt?

Die Sonne, die so hell ihr seht,
Mir Armen scheint sie nie;
Ihr sagt, sie auf- und niedergeht,
Ich weiss nicht, wann noch wie.

Now tell me, dear friends,
What is this thing called Light?
What are all these joys of seeing
That I have never known?

The sun that you see so bright
Never shines for me, poor boy;
You tell me it rises and sets,
Yet I know not when nor how.

Ich mach' mir selbst so Tag und Nacht,	I myself make my day and night
Dieweil ich schlaf' und spiel',	Whilst I sleep or play;
Mein inn'res Leben schön mir lacht,	My inner life smiles brightly,
Ich hab' der Freuden viel.	And many are my joys.

Zwar kenn' ich nicht, was euch erfreut,	Though I do not know what gladdens you
Doch drückt mich keine Schuld,	No guilt weighs me down.
Drum freu' ich mich in meinem Leid	Therefore I rejoice in my sorrow,
Und trag' es mit Geduld.	And bear it patiently.

Ich bin so glücklich, bin so reich	I am so happy and so rich
Mit dem, was Gott mir gab,	With that which God gave me.
Bin wie ein König froh, obgleich	I am as joyful as a king,
Ein armer, blinder Knab'.	Though but a poor, blind boy.

O say! what is that thing call'd Light,
Which I must ne'er enjoy;
What are the blessings of the sight,
O tell your poor blind boy!

You talk of wondrous things you see,
You say the sun shines bright;
I feel him warm, but how can he
Or make it day or night?

My day or night myself I make
When e'er I sleep or play;
And could I ever keep awake
With me 'twere always day.

With heavy sighs I often hear
You mourn my hapless woe;
But sure with patience I can bear
A loss I ne'er can know.

Then let not what I cannot have
My cheer of mind destroy:
Whilst thus I sing, I am a king,
Although a poor blind boy.

Der Blumen Schmerz / The Flowers' Pain

JOHANN, COUNT MAJLÁTH

D731 (1821)

Wie tönt es mir so schaurig	With what dread do I hear
Des Lenzes erstes Weh'n,	The first breezes of spring;
Wie dünkt es mir so traurig,	How sad it is to me
Dass Blumen auferstehn.	That flowers rise up again.

In ihrer Mutter Armen	They lay so quietly
Da ruhten sie so still,	In their mother's arms,
Nun müssen, ach, die Armen	And now the poor things
Hervor ans Weltgewühl.	Must come out into the teeming world.

Die zarten Kinder heben	The delicate children shyly
Die Häupter scheu empor:	Raise their heads:
»Wer rufet uns ins Leben	'Who summons us into life
Aus stiller Nacht hervor?«	From the peaceful night?'

Der Lenz mit Zauberworten,
Mit Hauchen süsser Lust,
Lockt aus den dunkeln Pforten
Sie von der Mutter Brust.

Spring, with magic words,
Breathing sweet delight,
Lures them through the dark portals
From their mother's breast.

In bräutlich heller Feier
Erscheint der Blumen Pracht,
Doch fern ist schon der Freier,
Wild glüht der Sonne Macht.

In a lustrous bridal ceremony
The flowers appear in their glory;
But the groom is already far away,
And the mighty sun glows harshly.

Nun künden ihre Düfte,
Dass sie voll Sehnsucht sind;
Was labend würzt die
  Lüfte,
Es ist der Schmerzen Kind.

Now their fragrance reveals
That they are full of longing;
The refreshing scent that spices
  the air
Is the child of sorrow.

Die Kelche sinken nieder,
Sie schauen erdenwärts:
»O Mutter, nimm uns wieder,
Das Leben gibt nur Schmerz.«

The chalices droop,
Gazing earthwards:
'O mother, receive us again,
For life gives only pain.'

Die welken Blätter fallen,
Mild deckt der Schnee sie zu —
Ach Gott! So geht's mit allen,
Im Grabe nur ist Ruh.

The withered leaves fall,
The snow gently covers them.
O God, so it is with all;
Only in the grave is there peace.

Der Blumenbrief / The Message of Flowers

ALOIS SCHREIBER

D622 (1818)

Euch Blümlein will ich senden
Zur schönen Jungfrau dort,
Fleht sie mein Leid zu enden
Mit einem guten Wort.

Flowers, I will send you
To that fair lady;
Implore her to end my suffering
With one kind word.

Du Rose kannst ihr sagen,
Wie ich in Lieb' erglühn',
Wie ich um sie muss klagen
Und weinen spät und früh.

You, rose, can tell her
How I burn with love,
And how I pine for her,
Weeping night and day.

Du, Myrte, flüstre leise
Ihr meine Hoffnung zu,
Sag': »Auf des Lebens Reise
Glänzt ihm kein Stern als du.«

You, myrtle, softly whisper
My hopes to her;
Tell her: 'On life's journey
You are the only star that shines for him.'

Du Ringelblume deute
Ihr der Verzweiflung Schmerz;
Sag' ihr: «Des Grabes Beute
Wird ohne dich sein Herz.«

You marigold, reveal to her
The pain of despair;
Tell her: 'Without you
His heart will fall prey to the grave.'

Der Doppelgänger / The Wraith

HEINRICH HEINE

see Schwanengesang no. 13

Der Einsame / The Solitary

KARL LAPPE

D800 (1825?)

Wenn meine Grillen schwirren,	When my crickets chirp
Bei Nacht, am spät erwärmten Herd,	At night, by the late-glowing hearth,
Dann sitz' ich mit vergnügtem Sinn	I sit contentedly,
Vertraulich zu der Flamme hin,	Confiding to the flame,
So leicht, so unbeschwert.	So light-hearted and untroubled.

Ein trautes, stilles Stündchen	For one cosy, peaceful hour
Bleibt man noch gern am Feuer wach,	It is pleasant to stay awake by the fire,
Man schürt, wenn sich die Lohe senkt,	Kindling the sparks when the blaze dies down,
Die Funken auf und sinnt und denkt:	Musing and thinking,
»Nun abermal ein Tag!«	'Well, yet another day!'

Was Liebes oder Leides	What joy or grief
Sein Lauf für uns dahergebracht,	Its course has brought us
Es geht noch einmal durch den Sinn;	We run once again through our mind.
Allein das Böse wirft man hin,	But the bad is discarded
Es störe nicht die Nacht.	Lest it disturb the night.

Zu einem frohen Traume,	We gently prepare ourselves
Bereitet man gemach sich zu,	For pleasant dreams.
Wann sorgenlos ein holdes Bild	When a sweet image
Mit sanfter Lust die Seele füllt,	Fills our carefree soul with gentle pleasure
Ergibt man sich der Ruh.	We succumb to rest.

Oh, wie ich mir gefalle	Oh, how happy I am
In meiner stillen Ländlichkeit!	With my quiet rustic life.
Was in dem Schwarm der lauten Welt	What in the bustle of the noisy world
Das irre Herz gefesselt hält,	Keeps the heart fettered
Gibt nicht Zufriedenheit.	Does not bring contentment.

Zirpt immer, liebe Heimchen,	Chirp on, dear crickets
In meiner Klause eng und klein.	In my narrow little room.
Ich duld' euch gern: ihr stört mich nicht,	I like to hear you: you don't disturb me.
Wenn euer Lied das Schweigen bricht,	When your song breaks the silence
Bin ich nicht ganz allein.	I am not completely alone.

Der Entfernten / To the Distant Beloved

JOHANN GAUDENZ VON SALIS-SEEWIS

D350 (1816?)

Wohl denk' ich allenthalben,	Everywhere I think of you,
O du Entfernte, dein!	Beloved, so far away!
Früh, wenn die Wolken falben,	Early in the morning, when the clouds grow pale,
Und spät im Sternenschein.	And late at night, by starlight.
Im Grund des Morgengoldes	On the earth, gilded by the light of dawn,
Im roten Abendlicht,	And in the red glow of evening,
Umschwebst du mich, o holdes,	You haunt me,
Geliebtes Traumgesicht!	Sweet, beloved vision.

Wo rauschender und	Where the river, darker and more
trüber	turbulent,
Der Strom Gebirge trennt,	Cleaves the mountains,
Weht oft sein Laut herüber,	Its sound often drifts across to me,
Den meine Seele kennt;	And is recognized by my soul;
Wenn ich den Fels erklimme,	When I climb the rock
Den noch kein Fuß erreicht,	That no foot has yet reached,
Lausch' ich nach jener Stimme;	I listen for that voice;
Doch Echo schweigt.	But the echo is silent.

Wo durch die Nacht der Fichten	Where the twilight gleam of the pines
Ein Dämmrungs-Flimmer wallt,	Flickers through the night,
Seh' ich dich zögernd flüchten,	I see your beloved, ethereal form
Geliebte Luftgestalt!	Skimming hesitantly through the air.
Wenn sanft dir nachzulangen,	When my longing arms are raised
Der Sehnsucht Arm sich hebt,	To touch you gently,
Ist dein Fantom zergangen,	Your phantom image has dissolved,
Wie Taugedüft verschwebt.	Dispelled like the dewy mist.

Der entsühnte Orest / Orestes Purified

JOHANN MAYRHOFER

D699 (1817?)

Zu meinen Füssen brichst du dich,	You break at my feet,
O heimatliches Meer,	Sea of my homeland,
Und murmelst sanft. »Triumph,	And softly murmur: 'Triumph!
Triumph!«	Triumph!'
Ich schwinge Schwert und Speer.	I wield my sword and spear.

Mykene ehrt als König mich,	Mycenae honours me as King,
Beut meinem Wirken Raum,	Offers me freedom for my actions;
Und über meinem Scheitel saust	And above my head rustles
Des Lebens goldner Baum.	The golden tree of life.

Mit morgendlichen Rosen schmückt	Spring adorns my path
Der Frühling meine Bahn,	With fresh roses,
Und auf der Liebe Wellen schwebt	And my boat glides lightly along
Dahin mein leichter Kahn.	On waves of love.

Diana naht; o Retterin,	Diana approaches; my saviour,
Erhöre du mein Fleh'n!	Hear my prayer!
Lass mich, das Höchste wurde mir,	Let me know the highest joy:
Zu meinen Vätern geh'n!	Let me return to my fathers.

Der Fischer / The Fisherman

JOHANN WOLFGANG VON GOETHE

D225 (1815)

Das Wasser rauscht', das Wasser schwoll,	The waters murmured, the waters swelled,
Ein Fischer sass daran,	A fisherman sat on the bank;
Sah nach dem Angel ruhevoll,	Calmly he gazed at his rod,
Kühl bis ans Herz hinan.	His heart was cold.
Und wie er sitzt und wie er lauscht,	And as he sat and listened
Teilt sich die Flut empor;	The waters surged up and divided;

Aus dem bewegten Wasser rauscht
Ein feuchtes Weib hervor.

Sie sang zu ihm, sie sprach zu ihm:
»Was lockst du meine Brut
Mit Menschenwitz und Menschenlist
Hinauf in Todesglut?
Ach wüsstest du, wie's Fischlein ist
So wohlig auf dem Grund,
Du stiegst herunter, wie du bist,
Und würdest erst gesund.

»Labt sich die liebe Sonne nicht,
Der Mond sich nicht im Meer?
Kehrt wellenatmend ihr
    Gesicht
Nicht doppelt schöner her?
Lockt dich der tiefe Himmel nicht,
Das feuchtverklärte Blau?
Lockt dich dein eigen Angesicht
Nicht her in ewgen Tau?«

Das Wasser rauscht', das Wasser schwoll,
Netzt' ihm den nackten Fuss;
Sein Herz wuchs ihm so sehnsuchtsvoll,
Wie bei der Liebsten Gruss.
Sie sprach zu ihm, sie sang zu ihm;
Da wars um ihn geschehn:
Halb zog sie ihn, halb sank er hin,
Und ward nicht mehr gesehn.

From the turbulent flood
A water nymph arose.

She sang to him, she spoke to him:
'Why do you lure my brood
With human wit and guile
Up into the fatal heat?
Ah, if you only knew how contented
The fish are in the depths,
You would descend, just as you are,
And at last be made whole.

'Do not the dear sun and moon
Refresh themselves in the ocean?
Do not their countenances emerge doubly
    fair
From breathing the waters?
Are you not enticed by the heavenly deep,
The transfigured, watery blue?
Are you not lured by your own face
Into this eternal dew?'

The waters murmured, the waters swelled,
Moistening his bare foot;
His heart surged with such yearning,
As if his sweetheart had called him.
She spoke to him, she sang to him,
Then it was all over;
She half dragged him, he half sank down
And was never seen again.

Der Flüchtling / *The Fugitive*

FRIEDRICH VON SCHILLER

D 402 (1816)

Frisch atmet des Morgens lebendiger
    Hauch;
Purpurisch zuckt durch düst'rer Tannen
    Ritzen
Das junge Licht und äugelt aus dem
    Strauch;
In gold'nen Flammen blitzen
Der Berge Wolkenspitzen.
Mit freudig melodisch gewirbeltem
    Lied
Begrüssen erwachende Lerchen die
    Sonne,
Die schon in lachender Wonne
Jugendlich schön in Auroras Umarmungen
    glüht.

Sei, Licht, mir gesegnet!
Dein Strahlenguss regnet
Erwärmend hernieder auf Anger
    und Au.
Wie flittern die Wiesen,
Wie silberfarb zittern
Tausend Sonnen im perlenden Tau!

The lively morning breeze blows
    fresh;
The young light flickers between the dark
    pines
And glints from the
    bushes;
The cloud-capped mountain peaks
Blaze with golden flames.
Warbling their happy, melodious
    song
The awakening larks greet the
    sun
Which, with joyful laughter,
Glows young and fair in the dawn's
    embrace.

I bless you, light!
Your rays stream down
To warm meadow and
    pasture.
See how the fields glitter,
And a thousand silvery suns
Glisten in the pearly dew!

In säuselnder Kühle
Beginnen die Spiele
Der jungen Natur.
Die Zephyre kosen
Und schmeicheln um Rosen,
Und Düfte beströmen die lachende
    Flur.
	In the whispering coolness
	Young nature
	Begins her games.
	The zephyrs caress
	And fondle the roses,
	And sweet scents pervade the smiling
	    meadows.

In säuselnder Kühle
Beginnen die Spiele
Der jungen Natur.
Die Zephyre kosen
Und schmeicheln um Rosen,
Und Düfte beströmen die lachende
    Flur.

Wie hoch aus den Städten die Rauchwolken
    dampfen!
Laut wiehern und schnauben und
    knirschen und strampfen
Die Rosse, die Farren;
Die Wagen erknarren
Ins ächzende Tal.
Die Waldungen leben,
Und Adler und Falken und Habichte
    schweben
Und wiegen die Flügel im blendenden
    Strahl.

Den Frieden zu finden,
Wohin soll ich wenden
Am elenden Stab?
Die lachende Erde
Mit Jünglingsgebärde,
Für mich nur ein Grab!

Steig empor, o Morgenrot, und röte
Mit purpurnem Kusse Hain und
    Feld!
Säusle nieder, o Abendrot, und flöte
In sanften Schlummer die tote Welt!
Morgen, ach, du rötest
Eine Totenflur;
Ach! und du, o Abendrot! umflötest
Meinen langen Schlummer nur.

In the whispering coolness
Young nature
Begins her games.
The zephyrs caress
And fondle the roses,
And sweet scents pervade the smiling
    meadows.

How high the clouds of smoke rise from the
    town!
Horses and bulls neigh loudly,
    snort,
Stamp and gnash their teeth;
Creaking carts
Roll along the valley,
The woods are alive,
Eagles, falcons and hawks
    hover
And move their wings in the dazzling
    light.

To find peace
Where shall I turn
With my wretched staff?
The smiling earth,
With youthful countenance,
Is but a grave for me!

Rise up, o dawn,
And with your crimson kiss tinge grove and
    field!
Descend with a whisper, o sunset,
And lull the dead world to gentle sleep.
Morning, you tinge with red
A land of death;
Ah, and you, o sunset,
Merely warble around my long sleep.

Der Flug der Zeit / *The Flight of Time*

LUDWIG VON SZÉCHÉNYI

D 515 (1821?)

Es floh die Zeit im Wirbelfluge
Und trug des Lebens Plan mit sich.
Wohl stürmisch war es auf dem Zuge,
Beschwerlich oft und widerlich.

Time flew past like a whirlwind,
And bore with it the plan of life.
It was stormy on the journey,
Often arduous and unpleasant.

So ging es fort durch alle Zonen,
Durch Kinderjahre, durch
    Jugendglück,
Durch Täler, wo die Freuden wohnen,
Die sinnend sucht der Sehnsucht Blick.

Thus it went through each age,
Through childhood years and youthful
    happiness;
Through valleys wherein joys dwell,
Sought by longing's reflective gaze.

Bis an der Freundschaft lichten Hügel
Die Zeit nun sanfter, stiller flog,
Und endlich da die raschen Flügel
In süsser Ruh' zusammenbog.

Until, flying more gently and calmly,
Time came to the shining hill of friendship,
And there at last folded its fleet wings
In sweet repose.

Der Fluß / The River

FRIEDRICH VON SCHLEGEL

D693 (1820)

Wie rein Gesang sich windet
Durch wunderbarer Saitenspiele
  Rauschen,
Er selbst sich wiederfindet,
Wie auch die Weisen tauschen,
Daß neu entzückt die Hörer ewig
  lauschen.

As pure song curls
Through the murmuring of the wondrous
  strings,
Finding itself again,
However much the melodies change,
That, captivated anew, the audience listens
  for ever.

So fließet mir gediegen
Die Silbermasse schlangengleich
  gewunden,
Durch Büsche, die sich wiegen,
Vom Zauber süß gebunden,
Weil sie im Spiegel neu sich selbst
  gefunden.

So flows, steadfast,
The silver band, twisting snake-
  like
Through swaying bushes,
Sweetly spellbound
Because they have found themselves anew
  in the mirror.

Wo Hügel sich so gerne
Und helle Wolken leise schwankend
  zeigen,
Wenn fern schon matte Sterne
Aus blauer Tiefe steigen,
Der Sonne trunk'ne Augen abwärts
  neigen.

Where hills and bright clouds
Gladly reveal themselves, gently
  rolling,
When in the distance faint stars
Already rise from the blue depths
And the sun's drunken eyes sink
  downwards.

So schimmern alle Wesen
Den Umriß nach im kindlichen Gemüte,
Das, zur Schönheit erlesen,
Durch milder Götter Güte,
In dem Kristall bewahrt die flücht'ge
  Blüte.

So all things shimmer
In outline in the childlike mind,
Which, chosen for beauty
By the goodness of the kindly gods,
Preserves the fleeting blossom in the crystal
  waters.

Der Geistertanz / Ghost Dance

FRIEDRICH VON MATTHISSON

D116 (1814)

Die bretterne Kammer
Der Toten erbebt,
Wenn zwölfmal den Hammer
Die Mitternacht hebt.

The boarded chamber
Of the dead trembles
When midnight twelve times
Raises the hammer.

Rasch tanzen um Gräber
Und morsches Gebein
Wir luftigen Schweber
Den sausenden Reih'n.

Quickly we airy spirits
Strike up a whirling dance
Around graves
And rotting bones.

Was winseln die Hunde
Beim schlafenden Herrn?
Sie wittern die Runde
Der Geister von fern.

Why do the dogs whine
As their masters sleep?
They scent from afar
The spirits' dance.

Die Raben entflattern	Ravens flutter up
Der wüsten Abtei,	From the ruined abbey,
Und flieh'n an den Gattern	And fly past
Des Kirchhofs vorbei.	The graveyard gates.

Wir gaukeln und scherzen
Hinab und empor
Gleich irrenden Kerzen
Im dunstigen Moor.

Jesting, we flit
Up and down,
Like will o' the wisps
Over the misty moor.

O Herz, dessen Zauber
Zur Marter uns ward,
Du ruhst nun in tauber
Verdumpfung erstarrt;

O heart, whose spell
Was our torment,
You rest now,
Frozen in a numb stupor.

Tief bargst du im düstern
Gemach unser Weh;
Wir Glücklichen flüstern
Dir fröhlich: Ade!

You have buried our grief
Deep in the gloomy chamber;
Happy we, who whisper you
A cheerful farewell!

Der Goldschmiedsgesell / *The Goldsmith's Apprentice*

JOHANN WOLFGANG VON GOETHE

D 560 (1817)

Es ist doch meine Nachbarin
Ein allerliebstes Mädchen!
Wie früh ich in der Werkstatt bin,
Blick ich nach ihrem Lädchen.

My neighbour is
An enchanting girl.
In the morning, at my work-bench,
I gaze at her little shop.

Ich feile; wohl zerfeil ich dann
Auch manches goldne Drähtchen.
Der Meister brummt, der harte Mann!
Er merkt, es war das Lädchen.

I file away, and at times I file right through
Many a golden thread.
My master grumbles, unfeeling man!
He sees it was that little shop.

Und flugs, wie nur der Handel still,
Gleich greift sie nach dem Rädchen.
Ich weiss wohl, was sie spinnen will:
Es hofft das liebe Mädchen.

And as soon as her work is finished
She reaches for her spinning wheel.
I well know what she intends to spin.
She has her hopes, the darling girl.

Das kleine Füsschen tritt und tritt;
Da denk ich mir das Wädchen,
Das Strumpfband denk ich auch
 wohl mit,
Ich schenkt's dem lieben Mädchen.

As her little foot keeps on working
I think of her dainty calves
And of her
 garter;
I gave it to the darling girl.

Und nach den Lippen führt der Schatz
Das allerfeinste Fädchen.
O wär ich doch an seinem Platz,
Wie küsst ich mir das Mädchen!

My sweetheart takes
The finest thread to her lips.
Ah, if only I could be in its place,
How I should kiss her!

Der Gott und die Bajadere / *The God and the Dancing-girl*

JOHANN WOLFGANG VON GOETHE

D 254 (1815)

Mahadöh, der Herr der Erde,
Kommt herab zum sechstenmal,

Mahadeva, Lord of the Earth,
Descends a sixth time

Daß er unsers gleichen werde,
Mit zu fühlen Freud' und Qual.
Er bequemt sich hier zu wohnen,
Läßt sich alles selbst geschehn.
Soll er strafen oder schonen,
Muß er Menschen menschlich sehn.
Und hat er die Stadt sich als Wandrer
betrachtet,
Die Großen belauert, auf Kleine
geachtet,
Verläßt er sie Abends, um weiter zu
gehn.

Als er nun hinaus gegangen,
Wo die letzten Häuser sind,
Sieht er, mit gemalten Wangen,
Ein verlornes schönes Kind.
»Grüß' dich, Jungfrau!« — »Dank
der Ehre!
Wart', ich komme gleich hinaus — «
»Und wer bist du?« — »Bajadere,
Und dies ist der Liebe Haus.«
Sie rührt sich, die Cymbeln zum Tanze du
schlagen;
Sie weiß sich so lieblich im Kreise zu
tragen,
Sie neigt sich und biegt sich, und reicht
ihm den Strauß.

Schmeichelnd zieht sie ihn zur
Schwelle,
Lebhaft ihn ins Haus hinein.
»Schöner Fremdling, lampenhelle
Soll sogleich die Hütte sein.
Bist du müd', ich will dich laben,
Lindern deiner Füße Schmerz.
Was du willst, das sollst du haben,
Ruhe, Freuden oder Scherz.«
Sie lindert geschäftig geheuchelte
Leiden.
Der Göttliche lächelt; er siehet mit
Freuden,
Durch tiefes Verderben, ein menschliches
Herz.

Und er fordert
Sklavendienste;
Immer heitrer wird sie nur,
Und des Mädchens frühe Künste
Werden nach und nach Natur.
Und so stellet auf die Blüte
Bald und bald die Frucht sich ein;
Ist Gehorsam im Gemüte,
Wird nicht fern die Liebe sein.
Aber, sie schärfer und schärfer zu
prüfen,
Wählet der Kenner der Höhen und
Tiefen
Lust und Entsetzen und grimmige
Pein.

That he might become one of us
And with us feel joy and sorrow.
He deigns to dwell here
And experience all things himself.
If he is to punish or forgive
He must see mortals as a mortal.
And having viewed the town in the guise of
a traveller,
Watching the great, observing
the lowly,
He leaves it in the evening to journey
onwards.

When he had walked out
To where the last houses are,
He encounters a lovely, forlorn girl
With painted cheeks.
'Greetings to you, maiden!' 'I thank you for
this honour!
Wait, I shall come straight out.'
'And who are you?' 'A dancing-girl,
And this is the house of love.'
She hastens to begin the dance with a clash
of cymbals.
She knows how to circle round so
charmingly;
She dips and turns, and hands him a
posy.

She coaxes him to the
threshold
And vivaciously draws him into the house.
'Fair stranger, this humble abode
Shall at once be bright with lamplight.
If you are weary, I shall refresh you,
And soothe your sore feet.
You shall have whatever you desire:
Rest, pleasure or play.'
Assiduously she soothes his feigned
pains.
The immortal smiles; joyfully he
beholds,
Through her deep corruption, a human
heart.

And he demands that she serves him like
a slave;
But this only makes her happier.
And the girl's early-acquired arts
Gradually become nature.
And thus the fruit appears
Quickly after the blossom;
If the heart is obedient,
Love will not be far off.
But, in order to test her ever more
keenly,
He who knows both the heights and the
depths
Chooses pleasure, but also horror and cruel
pain.

Und er küßt die bunten Wangen,
Und sie fühlt der Liebe Qual,
Und das Mädchen steht gefangen,
Und sie weint zum erstenmal;
Sinkt zu seinen Füßen nieder,
Nicht um Wollust noch Gewinnst,
Ach! und die gelenken Glieder,
Sie versagen allen Dienst.
Und so zu des Lagers vergnüglicher
Feier
Bereiten den dunklen behaglichen
Schleier
Die nächtlichen Stunden das schöne
Gespinnst.

Spät entschlummert, unter Scherzen,
Früh erwacht, nach kurzer Rast,
Findet sie an ihrem Herzen
Todt den vielgeliebten Gast.
Schreiend stürzt sie auf ihn nieder;
Aber nicht erweckt sie ihn,
Und man trägt die starren Glieder
Bald zur Flammengrube hin.
Sie höret die Priester, die
Totengesänge,
Sie raset und rennet, und teilet die
Menge.
»Wer bist du? was drängt zu der Grube
dich hin?«

Bei der Bahre stürzt sie nieder,
Ihr Geschrei durchdringt die Luft:
«Meinen Gatten will ich wieder!
Und ich such' ihn in der Gruft.
Soll zu Asche mir zerfallen
Dieser Glieder Götterpracht?
Mein! er war es, mein vor allen!
Ach, nur Eine süße Nacht!«
Es singen die Priester: »Wir tragen die
Alten,
Nach langem Ermatten und spätem
Erkalten,
Wir tragen die Jugend, noch eh' sie's
gedacht.

»Höre deiner Priester Lehre:
Dieser war dein Gatte nicht.
Lebst du doch als Bajadere,
Und so hast du keine Pflicht.
Nur dem Körper folgt der Schatten
In das stille Totenreich;
Nur die Gattin folgt dem Gatten:
Das ist Pflicht und Ruhm zugleich.
Ertöne, Drommete, zu heiliger Klage!
O, nehmet, ihr Götter! die Zierde der
Tage,
O, nehmet den Jüngling in Flammen zu
euch!«

So das Chor, das ohn' Erbarmen
Mehret ihres Herzens Not;

And he kisses her brightly painted cheeks,
And she feels love's anguish;
And the girl stands captive,
And weeps for the first time.
She sinks down at his feet,
Desiring neither pleasure nor gain.
And, alas, her supple limbs
Deny all service.
And thus, for the bed's pleasurable
ceremony,
The night hours fashion from lovely
gossamer
A dark, comforting
veil.

Falling asleep late while dallying,
Waking early after brief rest,
She finds the beloved guest
Dead at her side.
Screaming, she falls upon him,
But she cannot revive him.
And soon his rigid limbs
Are borne to the funeral pyre.
She hears the priests and the funeral
chants;
In her frenzy she rushes and pierces the
crowd.
'Who are you? What drives you to this
grave?'

By the bier she throws herself down,
And her cries echo through the air:
'I want my husband back!
And I shall seek him in the tomb.
Shall these limbs in their divine glory
Fall to ashes before me?
He was mine, mine alone,
Alas, for but one sweet night!'
The priests chant: 'We bear away
the old,
For long exhausted, lately grown
cold;
We bear away the young sooner than they
imagine.

'Hear the teaching of your priests:
This man was not your husband.
For you live as a dancing-girl,
And thus you know no duty.
The body is followed only by its shadow
Into the silent kingdom of death.
Only the wife follows the husband;
That is at once her duty and her glory.
Sound, trumpet, in sacred mourning!
Take, o gods, the flower of his
days,
Take the youth to you in
flames!'

Thus chants the choir, mercilessly
Deepening the pain within her heart.

Und mit ausgestreckten Armen
Springt sie in den heißen Tod.
Doch der Götter-Jüngling hebet
Aus der Flamme sich empor,
Und in seinen Armen schwebet
Die Geliebte mit hervor.
Es freut sich die Gottheit der reuigen
    Sünder;
Unsterbliche heben verlorene Kinder
Mit feurigen Armen zum Himmel empor.

And with outstretched arms
She leaps into the burning death.
But the divine youth rises up
From the pyre,
And his beloved soars aloft
In his arms.
The godhead rejoices in penitent
    sinners;
With arms of fire immortals raise
Lost children up to heaven.

Der gute Hirt / The Good Shepherd

JOHANN PETER UZ

D 449 (1816)

Was sorgest du? Sei stille, meine Seele!
Denn Gott ist ein guter Hirt,
Der mir, auch wenn ich mich nicht quäle,
Nichts mangeln lassen wird.

Why are you troubled? Be calm, my soul!
For God is a good shepherd;
Even if I am not suffering
He will let me want for nothing.

Er weidet mich auf blumenreicher Aue,
Er führt mich frischen Wassern zu,
Und bringet mich im kühlen Taue
Zur sichern Abendruh'.

He feeds me in flower-filled meadows,
He leads me to fresh waters,
And in the cool dew
Brings me to safe evening rest.

Er hört nicht auf, mich liebreich zu
    beschirmen,
Im Schatten vor des Tages Glut,
In seinem Schosse vor den Stürmen
Und schwarzer Bosheit Wut.

He does not cease to protect me
    lovingly,
In shade from the heat of day,
In his bosom from tempests
And from the rage of black evil.

Auch wenn er mich durch finstre Täler
    Leiten,
Mich durch die Wüste führen wird,
Will ich nichts fürchten; mir zur Seiten
Geht dieser treue Hirt.

Even when he leads me through dark
    vales,
Or through the wilderness,
I shall fear nothing; at my side
Walks the faithful shepherd.

Ich aber will ihn preisen und ihm
    danken!
Ich halt an meinem Hirten fest;
Und mein Vertrauen soll nicht wanken,
Wenn alles mich verlässt.

But I will praise Him and thank
    Him!
I shall hold fast to my shepherd,
And my faith shall never waver
When all else forsakes me.

Der Herbstabend / Autumn Evening

JOHANN GAUDENZ VON SALIS-SEEWIS

D 405 (1816)

Abendglockenhalle zittern
Dumpf durch Moorgedüfte hin;
Hinter jenes Kirchhofs Gittern
Blasst des Dämmerlichts Karmin.

Evening bells chime, dull and tremulous,
In the marshland breeze;
Behind those churchyard railings
The crimson glow of twilight fades.

Aus umstürmten Lindenzweigen	From storm-tossed linden branches
Rieselt welkes Laub herab,	Withered leaves stream down,
Und gebleichte Gräser beugen	And blanched grasses bend
Sich auf ihr bestimmtes Grab.	Over their appointed graves.
Freundin! wankt, im Abendwinde,	Beloved, soon, too, the grass will flutter
Bald auch Gras auf meiner Gruft,	In the evening breeze upon my grave;
Schwärmt das Laub um ihre Linde	The leaves will swirl around the linden-tree
Ruhelos in feuchter Luft,	Restlessly in the moist air.
Wann schon meine	When only your withered wreath still
Rasenstelle	adorns
Nur dein welker Kranz noch ziert,	The grass where I lie,
Und auf Lethes leiser Welle	And my misty image is lost
Sich mein Nebelbild verliert:	On Lethe's gentle waves:
Lausche dann! Im Blütenschauer	Listen then! In the shower of blossom
Wird es dir vernehmlich wehn:	This message shall be wafted to you:
Jenseits schwindet jede Trauer;	In the world beyond all sorrow shall vanish;
Treue wird sich wiedersehn!	Constant lovers shall be reunited!

Der Hirt / The Shepherd

JOHANN MAYRHOFER

D 490 (1816)

Du Turm! zu meinem Leide	Bell-tower, to my grief
Ragst du so hoch empor,	You soar so high,
Und mahnest grausam immer	And forever remind me cruelly
An das, was ich verlor.	Of what I have lost.
Sie hängt an einem Andern,	She is devoted to another,
Und wohnt im Weiler dort.	And lives in the hamlet there.
Mein armes Herz verblutet,	My poor heart bleeds,
Vom schärfsten Pfeil durchbohrt.	Pierced by the sharpest arrow.
In ihren schönen Augen	In her beautiful eyes
War keiner Untreu Spur;	There was no trace of faithlessness,
Ich sah der Liebe Himmel,	I saw in them only heavenly love,
Der Anmut Spiegel nur.	The mirror of grace.
Wohin ich mich nun wende—	Now wherever I turn
Der Turm, er folget mir;	The bell-tower follows me;
O sagt' er, statt der Stunden,	Would that, instead of telling the hours,
Was mich vernichtet, ihr!	It told her what is destroying me.

Der Hirt auf dem Felsen / The Shepherd on the Rock

WILHELM MÜLLER (the authorship of verses 5 and 6 is generally attributed to
HELMINA VON CHÉZY)

D 965 (1828)

Wenn auf dem höchsten Fels ich steh',	When I stand on the highest rock,
In's tiefe Tal hernieder seh',	Look down into the deep valley
Und singe,	And sing,

Fern aus dem tiefen dunkeln Tal	The echo from the ravines rises up
Schwingt sich empor der Wiederhall	From the dark depths
Der Klüfte.	Of the distant valley.
Je weiter meine Stimme dringt,	The further my voice carries,
Je heller sie mir wieder klingt	The clearer it echoes back to me
Von unten.	From below.
Mein Liebchen wohnt so weit von mir,	My sweetheart dwells so far from me,
Drum sehn' ich mich so heiß nach ihr	And thus I long so ardently
Hinüber.	For her.
In tiefem Gram verzehr ich mich,	I am consumed by deep sorrow;
Mir ist die Freude hin,	My joy has gone.
Auf Erden mir die Hoffnung wich,	My hope on this earth has vanished;
Ich hier so einsam bin.	I am so alone here.
So sehnend klang im Wald das	So fervently the song resounded through
Lied,	the forest,
So sehnend klang es durch die	So fervently it resounded through the
Nacht;	night;
Die Herzen es zum Himmel zieht	It drew hearts heavenwards
Mit wunderbarer Macht.	With its wondrous power.
Der Frühling will kommen,	Spring will come,
Der Frühling, meine Freud',	Spring, my delight;
Nun mach' ich mich fertig	Now I shall prepare
Zum Wandern bereit.	To go a-wandering.

Der Jüngling am Bache / The Youth by the Brook

FRIEDRICH VON SCHILLER

First version: D 30 (1812)
Second version: D 192 (1815)
Third version: D 638 (1819)

An der Quelle sass der Knabe,	By the stream sat a youth,
Blumen wand er sich zum Kranz,	Weaving flowers into a wreath;
Und er sah sie fortgerissen,	He saw them carried off
Treiben in der Wellen Tanz.	And swept along in the dancing waves.
»Und so fliehen meine Tage	'Thus my days speed by,
Wie die Quelle rastlos hin!	Relentlessly, like the stream!
Und so bleichet meine Jugend,	And my youth grows pale,
Wie die Kränze schnell verblühn!	As quickly as the wreaths wilt!
Fraget nicht, warum ich traure	'Do not ask why I mourn
In des Lebens Blütenzeit!	In life's fullest bloom!
Alles freuet sich und hoffet,	All is filled with joy and hope
Wenn der Frühling sich erneut.	When spring returns.
Aber tausend Stimmen	But a thousand voices
Der erwachenden Natur	Of burgeoning nature
Wecken in dem tiefen Busen	Awaken deep in my heart
Mir den schweren Kummer nur.	Only heavy grief.
Was soll mir die Freude frommen,	'What good to me is the joy
Die der schöne Lenz mir beut?	Which the fair spring offers me?
Eine nur ist's, die ich suche,	There is only one I seek,
Sie ist nah und ewig weit.	She is near and yet eternally distant.

Sehnend breit' ich meine Arme
Nach dem teuren Schattenbild,
Ach, ich kann es nicht erreichen,
Und das Herz ist ungestillt!

Komm herab, du schöne Holde,
Und verlass dein stolzes Schloss!
Blumen, die der Lenz geboren,
Streu ich dir in deinen Schoss.
Horch, der Hain erschallt von Liedern,
Und die Quelle rieselt klar!
Raum ist in der kleinsten Hütte
Für ein glücklich liebend Paar.«

Yearningly I stretch out my arms
Towards that beloved shadowy image,
Ah, I cannot reach it,
And my heart is unquiet.

'Come down, gracious beauty,
And leave your proud castle!
Flowers, which the spring has borne,
I shall strew on your lap.
Listen! The grove echoes with song
And the brook ripples limpidly.
There is room in the tiniest cottage
For a happy, loving couple.'

Der Jüngling an der Quelle / The Youth by the Spring

JOHANN GAUDENZ VON SALIS-SEEWIS

D 300 (1821?)

Leise, rieselnder Quell!
Ihr wallenden, flispernden Pappeln!
Euer Schlummergeräusch
Wecket die Liebe nur auf,
Linderung sucht ich bei euch,
Und sie zu vergessen, die Spröde,
Ach, und Blätter und Bach
Seufzen, Luise, dir zu.

Softly rippling brook,
Swaying, whispering poplars,
Your slumbrous murmur
Awakens only love.
I sought consolation in you,
Wishing to forget her, who is so aloof.
But alas, the leaves and the brook
Sigh for you, Louise!

Der Jüngling auf dem Hügel / The Youth on the Hill

HEINRICH HÜTTENBRENNER

D 702 (1820)

Ein Jüngling auf dem Hügel
Mit seinem Kummer sass,
Wohl ward der Augen Spiegel
Ihm trüb' und tränennass.

Sah frohe Lämmer spielen
Am grünen Felsenhang,
Sah frohe Bächlein quillen
Das bunte Tal entlang;

Die Schmetterlinge sogen
Am roten Blütenmund,
Wie Morgenträume flogen
Die Wolken in dem Rund;

Und Alles war so munter,
Und Alles schwamm in Glück,
Nur in sein Herz hinunter
Sah nicht der Freude Blick.

Ach, dumpfes Grabgeläute
Im Dorfe nun erklang,
Schon tönte aus der Weite
Ein klagender Gesang;

A youth sat on the hill
With his sorrow;
His eyes grew dim
And moist with tears.

He watched lambs gambolling happily
On the green hillside,
And brooks rippling merrily
Through the bright valley.

Butterflies sipped
At the red mouth of the flowers;
Clouds scudded about
Like morning dreams.

And everything was so cheerful,
Bathed in happiness;
His heart alone
Was untouched by the light of joy.

Ah, just now the muffled death-knell
Sounded in the village,
And in the distance
A mournful song echoed.

Sah nun die Lichter scheinen,	Then he saw the lights shining,
Den schwarzen Leichenzug,	And the black cortège;
Fing bitter an zu weinen,	He began to weep bitterly,
Weil man sein Röschen trug.	For they were bearing his Rosie.
Jetzt liess den Sarg man nieder,	Then they lowered the coffin;
Der Totengräber kam,	The gravedigger came
Und gab der Erde wieder,	And restored to the earth
Was Gott aus selber nahm.	What God once took from it.
Da schwieg des Jünglings Klage,	Then the youth ceased lamenting,
Und betend ward sein Blick,	And his eyes were fixed in prayer;
Sah schon am schönern Tage	Already he saw that fair day
Des Wiedersehens Glück.	When they would be reunited in joy.
Und wie die Sterne kamen,	And as the stars came out
Der Mond heraufgeschifft,	And the moon sailed heavenwards,
Da las er in den Sternen	He read in those stars high above
Der Hoffnung hohe Schrift.	A message of hope.

Der Jüngling und der Tod / The Youth and Death

JOSEF VON SPAUN

D 545 (1817)

Der Jüngling:	*The Youth:*
Die Sonne sinkt, o könnt ich mit ihr scheiden,	The sun is sinking; O that I might depart with it,
Mit ihrem letzten Strahl entfliehen!	Flee with its last ray:
Ach diese namenlosen Qualen meiden	Escape these nameless torments,
Und weit in schön're Welten ziehn!	And journey far away to fairer worlds!
O komme, Tod, und löse diese Bande!	O come, death, and loose these bonds!
Ich lächle dir, o Knochenmann,	I smile upon you, skeleton;
Entführe mich leicht in geträumte Lande!	Lead me gently to the land of dreams!
O komm und rühre mich doch an!	O come and touch me, Come!
Der Tod:	*Death:*
Es ruht sich kühl und sanft in meinen Armen,	In my arms you will find cool, gentle rest;
Du rufst, ich will mich deiner Qual erbarmen.	You call. I will take pity on your suffering.

Der Kampf / The Battle

FRIEDRICH VON SCHILLER

D 594 (1817)

Nein, länger, länger werd' ich diesen Kampf nicht kämpfen,	No! I shall fight this battle no longer,
Den Riesenkampf der Pflicht.	This mighty battle of duty.
Kannst du des Herzens Flammentrieb nicht dämpfen	If you cannot cool the fierce ardour within my heart
So fordre, Tugend, dieses Opfer nicht.	Then, Virtue, do not demand this sacrifice.

Geschworen hab ich's, ja, ich hab's
geschworen,
Mich selbst zu bändigen.
Hier ist dein Kranz. Er sei auf ewig mir
verloren,
Nimm ihn zurück, und lass mich
sündigen.

I took a vow, yes, I took a
vow
To master myself.
Here is your crown; let it be lost to me for
ever,
Take it back and let me
sin.

Zerrissen sei, was wir bedungen haben,
Sie liebt mich — deine Krone sei
verscherzt.
Glückselig, wer, in Wonnetrunkenheit
begraben,
So leicht wie ich den tiefen Fall
verschmerzt.

Let us tear up the bond we have made
She loves me — your crown shall be
forfeit.
Happy he who, drunk with
ecstasy,
Takes his precipitous fall as lightly
as I.

Sie sieht den Wurm an meiner Jugend
Blume nagen
Und meinen Lenz entfloh'n;
Bewundert still mein heldenmütiges Ent-
sagen,
Und grossmutvoll beschliesst sie meinen
Lohn.

She sees the worm gnawing at the flower of
my youth,
She sees the spring of my life slip by;
She silently admires my heroic renunciation,
And generously decides on my
reward.

Misstraue, schöne Seele, dieser
Engelgüte!
Dein Mitleid waffnet zum Verbrechen
mich,
Gibt's in des Lebens unermesslichem
Gebiete,
Gibt's einen andern schönern Lohn —
als dich?

Fair soul, distrust this angelic
kindness!
Your compassion steels me for my
crime.
Is there in life's vast
realm
A fairer reward than
you?

Als das Verbrechen, das ich ewig fliehen
wollte?
Tyrannisches Geschick!
Der einz'ge Lohn, der meine Tugend
krönen sollte,
Ist meiner Tugend letzter Augenblick.

Than the crime which I sought to flee for
ever?
Tyrannical fate!
The sole reward which was to crown my
virtue
Is my virtue's final moment.

Der Knabe / The Boy

FRIEDRICH VON SCHLEGEL

D 692 (1820)

Wenn ich nur ein Vöglein wäre,
Ach, wie wollt' ich lustig fliegen,
Alle Vögel weit besiegen.

If only I were a bird,
Ah, how joyfully I would fly,
Far outstripping all other birds.

Wenn ich so ein Vogel bin,
Darf ich alles haschen
Und die höchsten Kirschen naschen.
Fliege dann zur Mutter hin.
Ist sie bös in ihrem Sinn,
Kann ich lieb mich an sie schmiegen,
Ihren Ernst gar bald besiegen.

If I were a bird
I could get everything
And nibble the highest cherries.
Then I'd fly back to mother.
If she were angry
I could nestle sweetly up to her
And soon overcome her sternness.

Bunte Federn, leichte Flügel	Coloured feathers, light wings,
Dürft' ich in der Sonne schwingen,	I could flap them in the sunlight,
Daß die Lüfte laut erklingen,	So that the air resounded loudly,
Weiß nichts mehr von Band und Zügel.	I would no longer be curbed and shackled.

Wär' ich über jene Hügel,	If I were beyond those hills,
Ach, dann wollt' ich lustig fliegen,	Ah, how joyfully I would fly,
Alle Vögel weit besiegen.	Far outstripping all other birds.

Der Knabe in der Wiege / The Infant in the Cradle

ANTON OTTENWALT

D 579 (1817)

Er schläft so süß, der Mutter Blicke hangen	He sleeps so sweetly. His mother's gaze
An ihres Lieblings leisem Atemzug,	Hangs on the soft breathing of her darling,
Den sie mit stillem sehnsuchtsvollem Bangen	Whom, with silent, anxious yearning,
So lange unterm Herzen trug.	She carried for so long beneath her heart.

Sie sieht so froh die vollen Wangen glühen	With joy she sees his full cheeks glowing,
In gelbe Ringellocken halb versteckt,	Half-hidden in yellow curls,
Und will das Ärmchen sanft herunter ziehen,	And gently tucks in the little arm
Das sich im Schlummer ausgestreckt.	That lies stretched out in sleep.

Und leis' und leiser schaukelt sie die Wiege	Ever more gently she rocks the cradle,
Und singt den kleinen Schläfer leis' in Ruh;	And softly sings the infant to sleep;
Ein Lächeln spielet um die holden Züge,	A smile plays around his fair features,
Doch bleibt das Auge friedlich zu.	But his eyes stay peacefully closed.

Erwachst du Kleiner, o so lächle wieder,	When you awake, little one, smile once more,
Und schau ihr hell ins Mutterangesicht:	And look brightly into your mother's face.
So lauter Liebe schaut es auf dich nieder,	With pure love she looks down upon you,
Noch kennest du die Liebe nicht.	Though you do not yet know what love is.

Der König in Thule / The King of Thule

JOHANN WOLFGANG VON GOETHE

D 367 (1816)

Es war ein König in Thule	There was a king in Thule,
Gar treu bis an das Grab,	Faithful unto the grave,
Dem sterbend seine Buhle	Whose dying mistress
Einen goldnen Becher gab.	Gave him a golden goblet.

Es ging ihm nichts darüber,	Nothing was more precious to him,
Er leert ihn jeden Schmaus;	He drained it at every feast;
Die Augen gingen ihm über,	His eyes filled with tears
So oft er trank daraus.	Whenever he drank from it.

Und als er kam zu sterben,	And when he came to die
Zählt' er seine Städt' im Reich,	He counted the towns in his realm,
Gönnt alles seinen Erben,	Bequeathed all to his heirs,
Den Becher nicht zugleich.	Except for that goblet.

Er sass beim Königsmahle,	He sat at the royal banquet,
Die Ritter um ihn her,	His knights around him,
Auf hohem Vätersaale,	In the lofty ancestral hall
Dort auf dem Schloss am Meer.	In his castle by the sea.

Dort stand der alte Zecher,	The old toper stood there,
Trank letzte Lebensglut,	Drank life's last glowing draught,
Und warf den heilgen Becher	And hurled the sacred goblet
Hinunter in die Flut.	Into the waves below.

Er sah ihn stürzen, trinken	He watched it fall and drink
Und sinken tief ins Meer.	And sink deep into the sea.
Die Augen täten ihm sinken;	His eyes, too, sank;
Trank nie einen Tropfen mehr.	He drank not one drop more.

Der Kreuzzug / The Crusade

KARL GOTTFRIED VON LEITNER

D 932 (1827)

Ein Münich steht in seiner Zell	A monk stands in his cell
Am Fenstergitter grau,	At the grey window grating,
Viel Rittersleut in Waffen hell	A band of knights in shining armour
Die reiten durch die Au.	Comes riding through the meadows.

Sie singen Lieder frommer Art	They sing holy songs
In schönem ernstem Chor,	In fine, solemn chorus,
Inmitten fliegt, von Seide zart,	In their midst the banner of the Cross,
Die Kreuzesfahn empor.	Made of delicate silk, flies aloft.

Sie steigen an dem Seegestad	At the shore they climb
Das hohe Schiff hinan,	Aboard the tall ship.
Es läuft hinweg auf grünem Pfad,	It sails away over the green waters,
Ist bald nur wie ein Schwan.	And soon seems but a swan.

Der Münich steht am Fenster noch,	The monk still stands at the window,
Schaut ihnen nach hinaus:	Gazing out after them:
»Ich bin, wie ihr, ein Pilger doch,	'I am, after all, a pilgrim like you,
Und bleib ich gleich zu Haus.	Although I remain at home.

»Des Lebens Fahrt durch Wellentrug	'Life's journey through the treacherous waves
Und heissen Wüstensand,	And the burning desert sands,
Es ist ja auch ein Kreuzeszug	Is also a crusade
In das gelobte Land.«	Into the Promised Land.'

Der Leidende / The Sufferer

POET UNKNOWN

D 432 (1816)

| Nimmer trag' ich länger | No longer can I bear |
| Dieser Leiden Last; | The burden of this suffering; |

Nimm den müden Pilger	Take this weary pilgrim
Bald hinauf zu dir.	To you soon.
Immer, immer enger	Ever more oppressed
Wird's in meinem Busen,	Grows my heart,
Immer, immer trüber	Ever dimmer
Wird der Augen Blick.	Grows my gaze.
Nimmer trag' ich länger	No longer can I bear
Dieser Leiden Last.	The burden of this suffering.
Öffne mir den Himmel,	Open your heaven for me,
Milder, güt'ger Gott!	Kind and merciful God!
Lass mich meine Schmerzen	Let me bury my sorrows
Senken in das Grab!	In the grave.
Allzu viele Qualen	All too many torments
Wüten mir im Innern,	Rage within me;
Hin ist jede Hoffnung,	Gone is all hope,
Hin des Herzens Glut.	Gone my heart's ardour.
Öffne mir den Himmel,	Open your heaven for me,
Milder, güt'ger Gott!	Kind and merciful God!

Der Liebende / The Lover

LUDWIG HEINRICH CHRISTOPH HÖLTY

D 207 (1815)

Beglückt, beglückt,	Blessed is he
Wer dich erblickt,	Who beholds you,
Und deinen Himmel trinket;	And drinks your heavenly beauty
Wenn dein Gesicht	When your face,
Voll Engellicht	Bathed in angelic light,
Den Gruß des Friedens winket.	Bestows the greeting of peace.
Ein süßer Blick,	One sweet glance,
Ein Wink, ein Nick,	A sign, a nod,
Glänzt mir wie Frühlingssonnen;	Shines upon me like the spring sun.
Den ganzen Tag	The whole day long
Sinn' ich ihm nach,	I think of it,
Und schweb' in Himmelswonnen.	And float in heavenly bliss.
Dein holdes Bild	Your sweet image
Führt mich so mild	Leads me so tenderly along
An sanfter Blumenkette;	By a gentle chain of flowers.
In meinem Arm	In my arms
Erwacht es warm,	It awakens warm,
Und geht mit mir zu Bette.	And goes with me to bed.
Beglückt, beglückt,	Blessed is he
Wer dich erblickt,	Who beholds you,
Und deinen Himmel trinket;	And drinks your heavenly beauty,
Wem süßer Blick	Who is lured to sweeter kisses
Und Wink und Nick	By a sweet glance,
Zum süßern Kusse winket.	A sign, a nod.

Der liebliche Stern / The Lovely Star

ERNST SCHULZE

D 861 (1825)

Ihr Sternlein, still in der Höhe,	Little stars, so silent in the heavens,
Ihr Sternlein, spielend im Meer,	Little stars, playing upon the sea,

Wenn ich von ferne daher
So freundlich euch leuchten sehe,
So wird mir von Wohl und Wehe
Der Busen so bang und so schwer.

When from afar
I see you sparkling so delightfully,
Then, for weal or woe,
My heart grows troubled and heavy.

Es zittert von Frühlingswinden
Der Himmel im flüssigen Grüne,
Manch' Sternlein sah ich entblüh'n,
Manch Sternlein sah ich entschwinden;
Doch kann ich das schönste nicht finden,
Das früher dem Liebenden schien.

The sky trembles in the spring breezes
Above the watered meadows;
I saw many a star blossom,
I saw many a star vanish.
But I cannot find the fairest star,
That once shone for this lover.

Nicht kann ich zum Himmel mich
    schwingen,
Zu suchen den freundlichen Stern;
Stets hält ihn die Wolke mir fern.
Tief unten, da möcht' es gelingen,
Das friedliche Ziel zu erringen,
Tief unten, da ruht' ich so gern!

I cannot soar to the
    heavens
To seek that kindly star;
Clouds forever conceal it from me.
Deep below, there I might succeed
In reaching the peaceful refuge;
Deep below I would gladly find rest.

Was wiegt ihr im laulichen Spiele,
Ihr Lüftchen, den schwankenden
    Kahn?
O treibt ihn auf rauherer Bahn
Hernieder ins Wogengewühle!
Lasst tief in der wallenden Kühle
Dem lieblichen Sterne mich nah'n!

Breezes, why do you lull the rocking boat
In gentle
    play?
Drive it along a rougher course,
Down into the whirlpool!
Deep in the cool, turbulent waters
Let me draw near to that lovely star.

Der Liedler / The Minstrel

JOSEF KENNER

D 209 (1815)

Gib, Schwester, mir die Harf' herab,
Gib mir Biret und Wanderstab,
Kann hier nicht fürder weilen!
Bin ahnenlos, bin nur ein Knecht,
Bin für die edle Maid zu schlecht,
Muss stracks von hinnen eilen.

Sister, pass down my harp,
Hand me my hat and staff,
I can no longer tarry here.
I am but a servant, without forebears,
I am too humble for the noble maiden
And must at once hasten from here.

»Still, Schwester, bist gottlob nun
    Braut,
Wirst morgen Wilhelm angetraut,
Soll mich nichts weiter halten.
Nun küsse mich, leb, Trude, wohl!
Dies Herze, schmerz- und liebevoll,
Lass Gott den Herrn bewalten.«

'Be calm, sister, you are now, praise God,
    a bride.
Tomorrow you will wed Wilhelm.
There is nothing more to keep me here.
So kiss me, Trude, farewell!
This heart of mine, so full of pain and love
Let the Lord God guide it.'

Der Liedler zog durch manches
    Land
Am alten Rhein- und Donaustrand,
Wohl über Berg und Flüsse.
Wie weit er flieht, wohin er
    zieht,
Er trägt den Wurm im Herzen mit
Und singt nur sie, die Süsse.

The minstrel travelled through many a
    land,
On the banks of the old Rhine and Danube,
Across mountains and rivers,
However far he journeyed, wherever he
    wandered,
He carried the worm in his heart,
And sang only of her, his sweet love.

Und er's nicht länger tragen kann,
Tät sich mit Schwert und Panzer an,
Den Tod sich zu erstreiten.
Im Tod ist Ruh, im Grab ist Ruh,
Das Grab deckt Herz und Wünsche zu;
Ein Grab will er erreiten.

Der Tod ihn floh, und Ruh ihn floh!
Des Herzogs Banner flattert froh
Der Heimat Gruss entgegen,
Entgegen wallt, entgegen schallt
Der Freunde Gruss durch Saat und
　　Wald
Auf allen Weg' und Stegen.

Da ward ihm unterm Panzer weh!
Im Frührot glüht der ferne Schnee
Der heimischen Gebirge;
Ihm war, als zög's mit Hünenkraft
Dahin sein Herz, der Brust
　　entrafft,
Als ob's ihn hier erwürge.

Da konnt er's fürder nicht bestehn:
»Muss meine Heimat wiedersehn,
Muss sie noch einmal schauen!«
Die mit der Minne
　　Rosenhand
Sein Herz an jene Berge band,
Die herrlichen, die blauen!

Da warf er Wehr und Waffe weg,
Sein Rüstzeug weg ins Dorngeheg;
Die liederreichen Saiten,
Die Harfe nur, der Süssen Ruhm,
Sein Klagepsalm, sein Heiligtum,
Soll ihn zurück-
　　begleiten.

Und als der Winter trat ins Land,
Der Frost im Lauf die Ströme band,
Betrat er seine Berge.
Da lag's, ein Leichentuch von Eis,
Lag's vorn und neben totenweiss,
Wie tausend Hünensärge!

Lag's unter ihm, sein Muttertal,
Das gräflich Schloss im
　　Abendstrahl,
Wo Milla drin geborgen.
Glück auf, der Alpe Pilgerruh
Winkt heute Ruh dir Ärmster zu;
Zur Feste, Liedler, morgen!

Ich hab nicht Rast, ich hab nicht Ruh,
Muss heute noch der Feste zu,
Wo Milla drin geborgen.
»Bist starr, bist blass!« Bin
　　totenkrank,
Heut ist noch mein! Tot, Gott sei Dank,
Tot find't mich wohl der Morgen.

And when he could bear it no longer
He girded on sword and armour,
To seek death in battle.
In death is peace, in the grave is peace,
The grave buries the heart and its desires,
On horseback he sought a grave.

Death eluded him, peace eluded him!
The duke's banner gaily waved
A greeting from the homeland;
His friends' greetings resounded
Through field and
　　wood,
On every road and bridge.

Then he grew melancholy in his armour.
The distant snow on his native mountains
Glistened in the dawn.
It seemed as if, with titanic force,
His heart were being drawn there,
　　wrenched from his breast;
It was as if he were suffocating here.

Then he could no longer resist:
'I must see my homeland again,
I must behold it once more!'
With the rosy hand of love it bound his
　　heart
To those mountains,
Blue and glorious!

He threw away his weapons,
Cast his armour into the thorny hedge;
His melodious strings,
His harp, his sweetheart's eulogy,
His threnody and his sacred hymn —
His harp lone would accompany him
　　home.

When winter came to the country,
And frost congealed the flowing rivers,
He reached his mountains.
There lay his homeland, a shroud of ice,
Deathly white all around,
Like a thousand Titans' coffins!

Beneath him lay his native valley,
And, in the sun's dying rays, the count's
　　castle
In which Milla was sheltered.
Good luck! The Alpine pilgrim's rest
Bids you pause today, poor boy;
Tomorrow, minstrel, to the castle!

I know no peace, I know no repose,
This very day I must reach the castle
Where Milla is sheltered.
'You are frozen, you are pale.' I am sick
　　unto death,
Today is still mine! Death, thank the Lord,
Death will strike me tomorrow!

Horch Maulgetrab, horch Schellen-
  klang!
Vom Schloss herab der Alp'
  entlang
Zog's unter Fackelhelle.
Ein Ritter führt ihm angetraut,
Führt Milla heim als seine Braut.
Bist Liedler schon zur Stelle!

Hark mules' hooves, hark the jingling of
  bells!
Down from the castle, along the
  mountainside
Rode a torchlit procession.
A knight led his bride,
Led Milla home as his wife.
You are already here, minstrel!

Der Liedler schaut und sank in
  sich.
Da bricht und schnaubet wütiglich
Ein Werwolf durchs Gehege,
Die Maule fliehn, kein Saum sie zwingt,
Der Schecke stürzt. Weh! Milla sinkt
Ohnmächtig hin am Wege.

The minstrel watched, overcome with
  gloom.
Then a werewolf broke through the wood,
Snorting with rage.
The mules fled from the path,
The dappled pony fell. Alas! Milla
Fainted by the wayside.

Da riss er sich, ein Blitz, empor,
Zum Hort der Heissgeminnten vor,
Hoch auf des Untiers Nacken
Schwang er sein teures Harfenspiel,
Dass es zersplittert niederfiel,
Und Nick und Rachen knacken.

Then, like lightning, he leapt forward
To his beloved's aid;
High against the monster's neck
He hurled his cherished harp,
That it shattered,
And neck and throat were crushed.

Und wenn er stark wie Simson wär',
Erschöpft mag er und sonder Wehr
Den Grimmen nicht bestehen.
Vom Busen, vom zerfleischten Arm
Quillt's Herzblut nieder,
  liebewarm,
Schier denkt er zu vergehen.

Had he been as strong as Samson
He could not, exhausted and unarmed,
Have resisted the raging beast.
From his breast, from his lacerated arm
His heart's blood gushed down, hot with
  love;
He thought he was near to death.

Ein Blick auf sie, und alle Kraft
Mit einmal er zusammenrafft,
Die noch verborgen schliefe!
Ringt um den Werwolf Arm und
  Hand,
Und stürzt sich von der Felsenwand
Mit ihm in schwindle Tiefe.

One glance at her, and at once
He summoned all the strength
Which lay hidden within him.
He gripped the werewolf with arms and
  hands,
And plunges with it from the rock face
Into the giddy depths.

Fahr, Liedler, fahr auf ewig wohl!
Dein Herze schmerz- und liebevoll
Hat Ruh im Grab gefunden!
Das Grab ist aller Pilger Ruh,
Das Grab deckt Herz und Wünsche zu,
Macht alles Leids gesunden.

Farewell, minstrel, farewell for ever!
Your heart, so full of pain and love,
Has found rest in the grave!
The grave brings rest to all pilgrims;
The grave buries the heart and its desires,
And heals all sorrows.

Der Mondabend / *The Moonlit Evening*

JOHANN GOTTFRIED KUMPF

D 141 (1815)

Rein und freundlich lacht der Himmel
Nieder auf die dunkle Erde;
Tausend goldne Augen blinken
Lieblich in die Brust der Menschen,
Und des Mondes lichte Scheibe
Segelt heiter durch die Bläue.

The heavens smile, pure and kindly,
Upon the dark earth below,
A thousand golden eyes shine
Fondly into men's hearts,
And the moon's bright disc
Sails serenely through the blue.

Auf den goldnen Strahlen zittern
Süßer Wehmut Silbertropfen,
Dringen sanft mit leisem Hauche
In das stille Herz voll Liebe,
Und befeuchten mir das Auge
Mit der Sehnsucht zartem Taue.

On the golden beams tremble
The silver drops of sweet melancholy,
Gently, with soft breath,
They penetrate the silent, loving heart,
And moisten my eyes
With the tender dew of longing.

Funkelnd prangt der Stern des
    Abends
In den lichtbesä'ten Räumen,
Spielt mit seinem Demantblitzen
Durch der Lichte Duftgewebe,
Und viel holde Engelsknaben
Streuen Lilien um die Sterne.

The evening star sparkles
    resplendently
In the light-strewn expanses of space,
And with diamond flashes plays
Through the hazy web of light;
And many a sweet cherub
Strews lilies around the stars.

Schön und hehr ist wohl der Himmel
In des Abends Wunderglanze,
Aber meines Lebens Sterne
Wohnen in dem kleinsten Kreise:
In das Auge meiner Silli
Sind sie alle hingezaubert.

Fair and exalted are the heavens
In the wondrous light of evening;
But the stars of my life
Dwell within the smallest circle:
They have all been charmed
Into the eyes of my Silli.

Der Morgenkuss / The Morning Kiss

GABRIELE VON BAUMBERG

D 264 (1815)

Durch eine ganze Nacht sich nah zu sein,
So Hand in Hand, so Arm im Arme
    weilen,
So viel empfinden, ohne
    mitzuteilen,
Ist eine wonnevolle Pein.

To be close the whole night long,
To linger hand in hand, arm in
    arm,
To feel so much, without revealing it in
    words,
Is blissful torment.

So immer Seelenblick im Seelenblick
Auch den geheimsten Wunsch des
    Herzens sehen,
So wenig sprechen, und sich doch
    verstehen —
Ist hohes martervolles Glück!

To gaze constantly into each other's soul,
To see into the heart's most secret
    desire,
To speak so little, and yet to understand
    each other,
Is sublime, anguished happiness.

Zum Lohn für die im Zwang
    verschwundne Zeit
Dann bei dem Morgenstrahl, warm, mit
    Entzücken
Sich Mund an Mund, und Herz an Herz
    sich drücken —
O dies ist — Engelseligkeit!

Then, in the morning light, as a
    reward
For time of necessity wasted, warmly,
    rapturously
To press mouth to mouth and heart to
    heart —
Oh, that is angelic bliss!

Der Musensohn / The Son of the Muses

JOHANN WOLFGANG VON GOETHE

D 764 (1822)

Durch Feld und Wald zu schweifen,
Mein Liedchen weg zu pfeifen,

Roaming through field and wood,
Whistling my song,

So geht's von Ort zu Ort!
Und nach dem Takte reget
Und nach dem Mass beweget
Sich alles an mir fort.

Ich kann sie kaum erwarten,
Die erste Blum' im Garten,
Die erste Blüt' am Baum.
Sie grüssen meine Lieder,
Und kommt der Winter wieder,
Sing ich noch jenen Traum.

Ich sing ihn in der Weite,
Auf Eises Läng' und Breite, ·
Da blüht der Winter schön!
Auch diese Blüte schwindet,
Und neue Freude findet
Sich auf bebauten Höhn.

Denn wie ich bei der Linde
Das junge Völkchen finde,
Sogleich erreg ich sie.
Der stumpfe Bursche bläht sich,
Das steife Mädchen dreht sich
Nach meiner Melodie.

Ihr gebt den Sohlen Flügel
Und treibt durch Tal und Hügel
Den Liebling weit vom Haus.
Ihr lieben, holden Musen,
Wann ruh ich ihr am Busen
Auch endlich wieder aus?

Thus I go from place to place!
And all keep time with me,
And all move
In measure with me.

I can scarcely wait for them,
The first flower in the garden,
The first blossom on the tree.
They greet my songs,
And when winter returns
I am still singing my dream of them.

I sing it far and wide,
The length and breadth of the ice.
Then winter blooms in beauty!
This blossom, too, vanishes,
And new joys are found
On the cultivated hillsides.

For when, by the linden tree,
I come upon young folk,
I at once stir them.
The dull lad puffs himself up,
The demure girl whirls
In time to my tune.

You give my feet wings,
And drive your favourite over hill and dale,
Far from home.
Dear, gracious Muses,
When shall I at last find rest again
On her bosom?

Der Pilgrim / The Pilgrim

FRIEDRICH VON SCHILLER

D 794 (1823)

Noch in meines Lebens Lenze
War ich, und ich wandert' aus,
Und der Jugend frohe Tänze
Liess ich in des Vaters Haus.

All mein Erbteil, all mein Habe
Warf ich fröhlich glaubend hin,
Und am leichten Pilgerstabe
Zog ich fort mit Kindersinn.

Denn mich trieb ein mächtig Hoffen
Und ein dunkles Glaubenswort,
»Wandle,« rief's »der Weg ist
    offen,
Immer nach dem Aufgang fort.

»Bis zu einer goldnen Pforten
Du gelangst, da gehst du ein,
Denn das Irdische wird dorten
Himmlisch, unvergänglich sein.«

I was still in the springtime of my life
When I journeyed forth,
And left the merry dances of youth
In my father's house.

All my inheritance, all my possessions
I cast away in cheerful faith,
And with childlike heart
Set off with my light pilgrim's staff.

For a mighty hope drove me on,
And a dark word of faith.
'Journey onwards,' came the cry, 'the way is
    open,
Ever onwards toward the east.

'Until you reach a golden gate;
There you will enter,
For there earthly things.
Become celestial, immortal.'

Abend ward's und wurde Morgen,	Evening came, and morning,
Nimmer, nimmer stand ich still,	Never, never did I stop;
Aber immer blieb's verborgen,	Yet what I seek, what I long for,
Was ich suche, was ich will.	Always remained hidden.
Berge lagen mir im Wege,	Mountains loomed in my path,
Ströme hemmten meinen Fuss,	Rivers checked my step;
Über Schlünde baut ich Stege,	I built bridges over the abyss
Brücken durch den wilden Fluss.	And across the turbulent river.
Und zu eines Stroms Gestaden	And I came to the bank of a river
Kam ich, der nach Morgen floss;	That flowed eastwards;
Froh vertrauend seinem Faden,	Joyfully trusting to its current
Warf ich mich in seinen Schoss.	I threw myself upon its bosom.
Hin zu einem grossen Meere	The play of its waves
Trieb mich seiner Wellen Spiel;	Bore me to a great ocean;
Vor mir liegt's in weiter Leere,	It lies before me in its vast emptiness.
Näher bin ich nicht dem Ziel.	I am no nearer my goal.
Ach, kein Steg will dahin führen,	Ah, no bridge will take me there;
Ach, der Himmel über mir	Ah, the sky above me
Will die Erde nicht berühren,	Will not touch the earth,
Und das Dort ist niemals hier!	And the There is never here!

Der Rattenfänger / The Rat-catcher

JOHANN WOLFGANG VON GOETHE

D 255 (1815)

Ich bin der wohlbekannte Sänger,	I am the well-known singer,
Der vielgereiste Rattenfänger,	The much-travelled rat-catcher,
Den diese altberühmte Stadt	Of whom this famous old city
Gewiss besonders nötig hat.	Certainly has special need.
Und wären's Ratten noch so viele,	However many rats there are,
Und wären Wiesel mit im Spiele,	And even if there are weasels too,
Von allen säubr' ich diesen Ort,	I'll clear the place of them all,
Sie müssen miteinander fort.	They must go, every single one.
Dann ist der gut gelaunte Sänger	Now, this good-humoured singer
Mitunter auch ein Kinderfänger,	Is also occasionally a child-catcher,
Der selbst die wildesten bezwingt,	Who can tame even the most unruly,
Wenn er die goldnen Märchen singt.	When he sings his golden tales.
Und wären Knaben noch so trutzig,	However defiant the boys,
Und wären Mädchen noch so stutzig,	However suspicious the girls,
In meine Saiten greif ich ein,	When I pluck my strings
Sie müssen alle hinterdrein.	They must all follow me.
Dann ist der vielgewandte Sänger	Now, this versatile singer
Gelegentlich ein Mädchenfänger;	Is occasionally a catcher of girls.
In keinem Städtchen langt er an,	He never enters a town
Wo er's nicht mancher angetan.	Without captivating many.
Und wären Mädchen noch so blöde,	However shy the girls,
Und wären Weiber noch so spröde,	And however aloof the ladies,
Doch allen wird so liebebang	They all become lovesick
Bei Zaubersaiten und	At the sound of his magic lute and his
Gesang.	singing.

Der Sänger / The Minstrel

JOHANN WOLFGANG VON GOETHE

D 149 (1815)

»Was hör' ich draussen vor dem Tor,
Was auf der Brücke schallen?
Lass den Gesang vor unserm Ohr
Im Saale widerhallen!«
Der König sprach's, der Page lief,
Der Page kam, der König rief:
»Lasst mir herein den Alten!«

»Gegrüsset seid mir, edle Herrn,
Gegrüsst ihr schönen Damen!
Welch' reicher Himmel! Stern bei
Stern!
Wer kennet ihre Namen?
Im Saal voll Pracht und Herrlichkeit
Schliesst, Augen, euch, hier ist nicht
Zeit,
Sich staunend zu ergötzen.«

Der Sänger drückt' die Augen ein
Und schlug in vollen Tönen;
Die Ritter schauten mutig drein,
Und in den Schoss die
Schönen.
Der König, dem das Lied gefiel,
Liess, ihn zu lohnen für sein Spiel,
Eine goldne Kette holen.

»Die goldne Kette gib mir nicht,
Die Kette gib den Rittern,
Vor deren kühnem Angesicht
Der Feinde Lanzen splittern.
Gib sie dem Kanzler, den du hast,
Und lass ihn noch die goldne Last
Zu andern Lasten tragen.

»Ich singe, wie der Vogel singt,
Der in den Zweigen wohnet;
Das Lied, das aus der Kehle dringt,
Ist Lohn, der reichlich lohnet.
Doch darf ich bitten, bitt' ich eins:
Lass mir den besten Becher Weins
In purem Golde reichen.«

Er setzt' ihn an, er trank ihn aus:
»O Trank voll süsser Labe!
O, wohl dem hochbeglückten Haus,
Wo das ist kleine Gabe!
Ergeht's euch wohl, so denkt an mich
Und danket Gott so warm, als ich
Für diesen Trunk euch danke.«

'What do I hear outside the gate,
What sounds are those on the bridge?
Let that song echo in our ears
Throughout the hall!'
Thus spake the king, the page ran out;
The page returned, the king cried:
'Let the old man enter!'

'Greetings, noble lords,
Greetings, fair ladies!
How rich is this galaxy! Star upon
star!
Who can know their names?
In this hall of pomp and splendour
Close, eyes; now is not the
time
To feast yourselves in wonder.'

The minstrel closed his eyes
And sang in resonant tones;
Resolutely the knights looked on,
While the fair ladies looked down into their
laps.
The king, pleased with the song,
Sent for a gold chain
To reward him for his singing.

'Do not give the golden chain to me
But to your knights,
Before whose bold countenance
Enemy lances shatter.
Give it to your chancellor
And let him bear its golden burden
With his other burdens.

'I sing as the bird sings
Who lives among the branches;
The song that pours from my throat
Is its own rich reward.
But if I may, I will ask one thing:
Bring me your best wine
In a chalice of pure gold.'

He raised it to his lips and drained it:
'O draught of sweet refreshment!
Happy the blessed house
Where that is but a trifling gift!
If you fare well, think of me,
And thank God as warmly as I
Thank you for this drink.'

Der Sänger am Felsen / The Singer on the Rock

KAROLINE PICHLER

D 482 (1816)

Klage, meine Flöte, klage
Die entschwundnen schönen Tage,
Und des Frühlings schnelle Flucht,
Hier auf den verwelkten Fluren,
Wo mein Geist umsonst die Spuren
Süss gewohnter Freuden sucht.

Klage, meine Flöte, klage!
Einsam rufest du dem Tage,
Der dem Schmerz zu spät erwacht.
Einsam schallen meine Lieder;
Nur das Echo hallt sie wieder
Durch die Schatten stiller Nacht.

Mourn, my flute, mourn
The beautiful, vanished days,
And the swift flight of spring
Here on the faded meadows,
Where in vain my spirit seeks the traces
Of sweet, familiar pleasures.

Mourn, my flute, mourn!
All alone you cry out to the day
Which too late awakes to pain.
My lonely songs ring out;
Only the echo carries them back
Through the shades of the silent night.

Der Schäfer und der Reiter / The Shepherd and the Horseman

FRIEDRICH DE LA MOTTE FOUQUÉ

D 517 (1817)

Ein Schäfer sass im Grünen,
Sein Liebchen süss im Arm,
Durch Buchenwipfel schienen
Der Sonne Strahlen warm.

Sie kosten froh und heiter
Von Liebeständelei.
Da ritt, bewehrt, ein Reiter
Den Glücklichen vorbei.

»Sitz ab und suche Kühles,«
Rief ihm der Schäfer zu,
»Des Mittags nahe Schwüle
Gebietet stille Ruh'.

»Noch lacht im Morgenglanze
So Strauch als Blume hier,
Und Liebchen pflückt zum
    Kranze
Die schönsten Blüten dir.«

Da sprach der finstre Reiter;
»Nie hält mich Wald und Flur;
Mich treibt mein Schicksal weiter,
Und ach, mein ernster Schwur.

»Ich gab mein junges Leben
Dahin um schnöden Sold,
Glück kann ich nicht erstreben
Nur höchstens Ruhm und Gold.

»Drum schnell, mein Ross, und trabe
Vorbei wo Blumen blühn,
Einst lohnt wohl Ruh im Grabe
Des Kämpfenden Bemühn.«

A shepherd sat amid the greenery,
His sweetheart in his arms;
Through the tops of the beech-trees
Shone the sun's warm rays.

Joyfully, blithely,
They dallied and caressed.
Then a horseman, armed,
Rode by the happy pair.

'Dismount and come to the cool shade,'
The shepherd called to him.
'The sultry midday heat approaches
And bids us rest quietly.

'Here bush and flower
Still smile in the radiant morning,
And my sweetheart will pick the loveliest
    flowers
To make you a garland.'

Then the gloomy rider spoke;
'Woods and meadows can never keep me:
My fate drives me onwards,
And, ah, my solemn vow.

'I gave up my young life
For vile money;
I can never aspire to happiness,
At best only to gold and glory.

'Make haste then, my steed, and trot
Past the flowers in bloom.
One day the peace of the grave
May reward the warrior's toil.'

Der Schatzgräber / The Treasure-seeker

JOHANN WOLFGANG VON GOETHE

D 256 (1815)

Arm am Beutel, krank am Herzen,
Schleppt ich meine langen Tage.
Armut ist die grösste Plage,
Reichtum ist das höchste Gut!
Und, zu enden meine Schmerzen,
Ging ich, einen Schatz zu graben.
»Meine Seele sollst du haben!«
Schrieb ich hin mit eignem Blut.

Und so zog ich Kreis um Kreise,
Stellte wunderbare Flammen,
Kraut und Knochenwerk zusammen:
Die Beschwörung war vollbracht.
Und auf die gelernte Weise
Grub ich nach dem alten Schatze
Auf dem angezeigten Platze;
Schwarz und stürmisch war die Nacht.

Und ich sah ein Licht von weiten,
Und es kam gleich einem Sterne
Hinten aus der fernsten Ferne,
Eben als es Zwölfe schlug.
Und da galt kein Vorbereiten:
Heller wards mit einem Male
Von dem Glanz der vollen Schale,
Die ein schöner Knabe trug.

Holde Augen sah ich blinken
Unter dichtem Blumenkranze;
In des Trankes Himmelsglanze
Trat er in den Kreis herein.
Und er hiess mich freundlich trinken;
Und ich dacht: es kann der Knabe
Mit der schönen lichten Gabe
Wahrlich nicht der Böse sein.

»Trinke Mut des reinen Lebens!
Dann verstehst du die Belehrung,
Kommst, mit ängstlicher Beschwörung,
Nicht zurück an diesen Ort.
Grabe hier nicht mehr vergebens:
Tages Arbeit! Abends Gäste!
Saure Wochen! Frohe Feste!
Sei dein künftig Zauberwort.«

Empty of purse, sick of heart,
I dragged out my long days.
Poverty is the greatest ill,
Wealth the highest good.
And to end my suffering
I went to dig for treasure.
'You shall have my soul!'
I wrote in my own blood.

I drew circle upon circle,
And mixed herbs and bones
In magic flames:
The spell was cast.
In the decreed manner
And in the appointed place
I dug for the old treasure;
The night was black and stormy.

I saw a far-off light,
It came like a star
From the remote distance
On the stroke of twelve.
Then, without warning,
It suddenly grew brighter
From the radiance of the filled cup
Borne by a fair youth.

I saw his kindly eyes sparkling
Beneath a close-woven garland of flowers;
In the potion's celestial glow
He stepped into the circle.
Graciously he bade me drink;
And I thought: that boy
With his fair, shining gift
Can surely not be the Devil.

'Drink the courage of pure life!
Then you will understand my words,
And never, with anxious incantation,
Return to this place.
Dig here no more in vain;
Work by day, conviviality in the evening,
Weeks of toil and joyous holidays!
Let this from now on be your magic spell.'

Der Schiffer / The Boatman

JOHANN MAYRHOFER

D 536 (1817?)

Im Winde, im Sturme befahr' ich den
   Fluss,
Die Kleider durchweichet der Regen
   im Guss;

In wind and storm I row on the
   river,
My clothes are soaked by the pouring
   rain;

Ich peitsche die Wellen mit mächtigem
   Schlag,
Erhoffend mir heiteren Tag.

Die Wellen, sie jagen das ächzende Schiff,
Es drohet der Strudel, es drohet der Riff,
Gesteine entkollern den felsigen Höh'n,
Und Tannen erseufzen wie
   Geistergestöh'n.

So musste es kommen, ich hab' es gewollt,
Ich hasse ein Leben behaglich entrollt;
Und schlängen die Wellen den ächzenden
   Kahn,
Ich priese doch immer die eigene Bahn.

Drum tose des Wassers ohnmächtiger
   Zorn,
Dem Herzen entquillet ein seliger Born,
Die Nerven erfrischend, o himmlische
   Lust,
Dem Sturme zu trotzen mit männlicher
   Brust!

I lash the waves with powerful
   strokes,
Hoping for a fine day.

The waves drive the creaking boat,
Whirlpool and reef threaten;
Rocks roll down from the craggy heights,
And fir-trees sigh like moaning
   ghosts.

It had to come to this, I wished it so;
I hate a life that unfolds comfortably.
And if the waves devoured the creaking
   boat,
I would still extol my chosen course.

So let the waters roar with impotent
   rage;
A fountain of bliss gushes from my heart,
Refreshing my nerves. O celestial
   joy,
To defy the storm with a manly
   heart!

Der Schiffer / The Boatman

FRIEDRICH VON SCHLEGEL

D694 (1820)

Friedlich lieg' ich hingegossen,
Lenke hin und her das Ruder,
Atme kühl im Licht des Mondes,
Träume süss im stillen Mute;
Gleiten lass ich auch den Kahn,
Schaue in die blanken Fluten,
Wo die Sterne lieblich schimmern,
Spiele wieder mit dem Ruder.

Sässe doch das blonde Mägdlein
Vor mir auf dem Bänkchen ruhend,
Sänge schmachtend zarte Lieder.
Himmlisch wär' mir dann zu Mute,
Liess mich necken von dem Kinde,
Wieder tändelnd mit der Guten.

Friedlich lieg' ich hingegossen,
Träume süss im stillen Mute,
Atme kühl im Licht des Mondes,
Führe hin und her das Ruder.

Peacefully I lie stretched out,
Turning the rudder this way and that,
Breathing the cool air in the moonlight,
Tranquil in spirit, dreaming sweetly.
And I let the boat drift,
Gazing into the shining waters,
Where the stars shimmer enchantingly;
And again I play with the rudder.

If only that fair-haired girl
Were reclining on the seat before me,
Singing tenderly soulful songs,
Then I should feel blissfully happy.
I should let the child tease me
And flirt again with the sweet girl.

Peacefully I lie stretched out,
Tranquil in spirit, dreaming sweetly,
Breathing the cool air in the moonlight,
Moving the rudder this way and that.

Der Schmetterling / The Butterfly

FRIEDRICH VON SCHLEGEL

D 633 (1820?)

Wie soll ich nicht tanzen,
Es macht keine Mühe,

Why should I not dance?
It costs me no effort,

Und reizende Farben
Schimmern hier im Grünen.

Immer schöner glänzen
Meine bunten Flügel,
Immer süsser hauchen
Alle kleinen Blüten.

Ich nasche die Blüten,
Ihr könnt sie nicht hüten.

Wie gross ist die Freude.
Sei's spät oder frühe,
Leichtsinnig zu schweben
Über Tal und Hügel.

Wenn der Abend säuselt,
Seht ihr Wolken glühen;
Wenn die Lüfte golden,
Scheint die Wiese grüner.

Ich nasche die Blüten,
Ihr könnt sie nicht hüten.

And enchanting colours
Shimmer here amid the verdure.

Ever lovelier
My brightly coloured wings glisten,
Ever sweeter is the scent
From each tiny blossom.

I sip from the blossoms,
You cannot protect them.

How great my joy,
Be it early or late,
To flit so blithely
Over hill and dale.

When the evening murmurs
You see the clouds glow,
When the air is golden
The meadows are more radiantly green.

I sip from the blossoms,
You cannot protect them.

Der Sieg / The Victory

JOHANN MAYRHOFER

D805 (1824)

O unbewölktes Leben!
So rein und tief und klar!
Uralte Träume schweben
Auf Blumen wunderbar.

Der Geist zerbrach die Schranken,
Des Körpers träges Blei;
Er waltet gross und frei.

Es laben die Gedanken
An Edens Früchten sich;
Der alte Fluch entwich.

Was ich auch je gelitten,
Die Palme ist erstritten,
Gestillet mein Verlangen.

Die Musen selber sangen
Die Sphinx in Todesschlaf,
Und meine Hand, sie traf.

O unbewölktes Leben!
So rein und tief und klar.
Uralte Träume schweben
Auf Blumen wunderbar.

O unclouded life!
So pure, so deep and clear!
Age-old dreams float
Miraculously over the flowers.

The spirit broke the fetters
Of the body's inert leaden mass;
It roams great and free.

The mind is refreshed
By the fruits of Paradise;
The ancient curse is no more.

Whatever I may have suffered
The palm is now won,
And my longing stilled.

The Muses themselves sang
The sphinx to the sleep of death,
And my hand struck the blow.

O unclouded life!
So pure, so deep and clear!
Age-old dreams float
Miraculously over the flowers.

Der Strom / The River

POET UNKNOWN

D 565 (1817?)

Mein Leben wälzt sich murrend fort,
Es steigt und fällt in krausen Wogen,
Hier bäumt es sich, jagt nieder dort
In wilden Zügen, hohen Bogen.

Das stille Tal, das grüne Feld
Durchrauscht es nun mit leisem Beben,
Sich Ruh' ersehnend, ruhigen Welt,
Ergötzt es sich am ruhigen Leben.

Doch nimmer findend, was es sucht,
Und immer sehnend tost es weiter,
Unmutig rollt's auf steter Flucht,
Wird nimmer froh, wird nimmer heiter.

My life rolls grumbling onwards,
Rising and falling in curling waves;
Here it rears up, there it plunges down,
With wild spurts and soaring curves.

Now, gently quivering, it ripples through
Silent valleys and green fields,
Yearning for peace, a tranquil world,
And delighting in a life of calm.

Yet never finding what it seeks,
Forever longing, it surges onwards;
Discontented, it rolls on in ceaseless flight,
Never joyful, never serene.

Der Taucher / The Diver

FRIEDRICH VON SCHILLER

D 77 (1813–1815)

»Wer wagt es, Rittersmann oder Knapp,
Zu tauchen in diesen Schlund?
Einen goldnen Becher werf' ich hinab.
Verschlungen schon hat ihn der schwarze
     Mund.
Wer mir den Becher kann wieder zeigen,
Er mag ihn behalten, er ist sein eigen.«

Der König spricht es und wirft von der
     Höh'
Der Klippe, die schroff und steil
Hinaushängt in die unendliche See,
Den Becher in der Charybde
     Geheul.
»Wer ist der Beherzte, ich frage
     wieder,
Zu tauchen in diese Tiefe nieder?«

Und die Ritter, die Knappen um ihn her
Vernehmen's und schweigen still,
Sehen hinab in das wilde Meer,
Und keiner den Becher gewinnen will.
Und der König zum drittenmal wieder
     fraget:
»Ist keiner, der sich hinunter waget?«

Doch alles noch stumm bleibt wie zuvor,
Und ein Edelknecht, sanft und keck,
Tritt aus der Knappen zagendem Chor,
Und den Gürtel wirft er, den Mantel
     weg,
Und alle die Männer umher und Frauen
Auf den herrlichen Jüngling verwundert
     schauen.

'Who will dare, knight or squire
To dive into this abyss?
I hurl this golden goblet down,
The black mouth has already devoured
     it.
He who can show me the goblet again
May keep it, it is his.'

Thus the king speaks, and from the
     top
Of the cliff, which juts abruptly and steeply
Into the infinite sea,
He hurls the goblet into the howling
     Charybdis.
'Who is there brave enough, I ask once
     more,
To dive down into the depths?'

And the knights and squires around him
Listen, and keep silent,
Looking down into the turbulent sea,
And none desires to win the goblet.
And the king asks a third
     time:
'Is there no one who will dare the depths?'

Yet all remain as silent as before;
Then a young squire, gentle and bold,
Steps from the hesitant throng,
Throws off his belt and his
     cloak,
And all the men and women around him
Gaze in astonishment at the fine
     youth.

Und wie er tritt an des Felsen Hang
Und blickt in den Schlund hinab,
Die Wasser, die sie hinunterschlang,
Die Charybde jetzt brüllend wiedergab,
Und wie mit des fernen Donners
    Getose
Entstürzen sie schäumend dem finstern
    Schosse.

Und es wallet und siedet und brauset und
    zischt,
Wie wenn Wasser mit Feuer sich mengt,
Bis zum Himmel spritzet der dampfende
    Gischt,
Und Flut auf Flut sich ohn' Ende drängt,
Und will sich nimmer erschöpfen und
    leeren,
Als wollte das Meer noch ein Meer
    gebären.

Doch endlich, da legt sich die wilde
    Gewalt,
Und schwarz aus dem weissen Schaum
Klafft hinunter ein gähnender Spalt,
Grundlos, als ging's in den Höllenraum,
Und reissend sieht man die brandenden
    Wogen
Hinab in den strudelnden Trichter
    gezogen.

Jetzt schnell, eh' die Brandung
    wiederkehrt,
Der Jüngling sich Gott befiehlt,
Und — ein Schrei des Entsetzens wird
    rings gehört,
Und schon hat ihn der Wirbel
    hinweggespült,
Und geheimnisvoll über dem kühnen
    Schwimmer
Schliesst sich der Rachen, er zeigt sich
    nimmer.

Und stille wird's über dem
    Wasserschlund.
In der Tiefe nur brauset es hohl,
Und bebend hört man von Mund zu
    Mund:
»Hochherziger Jüngling, fahre wohl!«
Und hohler und hohler hört man's heulen,
Und es harrt noch mit bangem, mit
    schrecklichem Weilen.

Und wärfst du die Krone selber hinein
Und sprächst: wer mir bringet die Kron',
Er soll sie tragen und König sein —
Mich gelüstete nicht nach dem teuren
    Lohn.
Was die heulende Tiefe da unten
    verhehle,
Das erzählt keine lebende glückliche
    Seele.

And as he steps to the cliff's edge
And looks down into the abyss,
The waters which Charybdis devoured
She now regurgitates, roaring,
And, as if with the rumbling of distant
    thunder,
They rush foaming from the black
    womb.

The waters seethe and boil, rage and
    hiss
As if they were mixed with fire,
The steaming spray gushes up to the
    heavens,
And flood piles on flood, ceaselessly,
Never exhausting itself, never
    emptying,
As if the sea would beget another
    sea.

But at length the turbulent force
    abates,
And black from the white foam
A yawning rift gapes deep down,
Bottomless, as if it led to hell's domain,
And you see the tumultuous foaming
    waves,
Sucked down into the seething
    crater.

Now swiftly, before the surge
    returns,
The youth commends himself to God,
And — a cry of horror is heard all
    around —
The whirlpool has already borne him
    away,
And over the bold swimmer,
    mysteriously,
The gaping abyss closes; he will never be
    seen again.

Calm descends over the watery
    abyss.
Only in the depths is there a hollow roar,
And the words falter from mouth to
    mouth:
'Valiant youth, farewell!'
The roar grows ever more hollow,
And they wait, anxious and
    fearful.

Even if you threw in the crown itself,
And said: 'Whoever brings me this crown
Shall wear it and be king' —
I would not covet the precious
    reward.
What the howling depths may
    conceal
No living soul will ever
    tell.

Wohl manches Fahrzeug, vom Strudel
   gefasst,
Schoss gäh in die Tiefe hinab,
Doch zerschmettert nur rangen sich Kiel
   und Mast
Hervor aus dem alles verschlingenden
   Grab —
Und heller und heller, wie Sturmes
   Sausen,
Hört man's näher und immer näher
   brausen.

Und es wallet und siedet und brauset und
   zischt,
Wie wenn Wasser mit Feuer sich mengt,
Bis zum Himmel spritzet der dampfende
   Gischt,
Und Well' auf Well' sich ohn' Ende drängt,
Und wie mit des fernen Donners
   Getose
Entstürzt es brüllend dem finstren
   Schosse.

Und sieh! aus dem finster flutenden
   Schoss
Da hebet sich's schwanenweiss,
Und ein Arm und ein glänzender Nacken
   wird bloss,
Und es rudert mit Kraft und mit emsigem
   Fleiss,
Und er ist's, und hoch in seiner Linken
Schwingt er den Becher mit freudigem
   Winken.

Und atmete lang' und atmete tief
Und begrüsste das himmlische Licht.
Mit Frohlocken es einer dem andern rief:
»Er lebt! Er ist da! Es behielt ihn
   nicht!
Aus dem Grab, aus der strudelnden
   Wasserhöhle
Hat der Brave gerettet die lebende Seele.«

Und er kommt, es umringt ihn die jubelnde
   Schar,
Zu des Königs Füssen er sinkt,
Den Becher reicht er ihm knieend dar,
Und der König der lieblichen Tochter
   winkt,
Die füllt ihn mit funkelndem Wein bis zum
   Rande,
Und der Jüngling sich also zum König
   wandte:

»Lange lebe der König! Es freue sich,
Wer da atmet im rosigen Licht!
Da unten aber ist's fürchterlich,
Und der Mensch versuche die Götter
   nicht
Und begehre nimmer und nimmer zu
   schauen,
Was sie gnädig bedecken mit Nacht und
   Grauen.

Many a vessel, caught by the
   whirlpool,
Has plunged sheer into the depths,
Yet only wrecked keels and
   masts
Have struggled out of the all-consuming
   grave.
Like the rushing of a
   storm,
The roaring grows ever closer and more
   vivid.

The waters seethe and boil, rage and
   hiss,
As if they were mixed with fire;
The steaming spray gushes up to the
   heavens
And flood piles on flood, ceaselessly,
And, as if with the rumbling of distant
   thunder,
The waters rush foaming from the black
   womb.

But look! From the black watery
   womb
A form rises, as white as a swan,
An arm and a glistening neck are
   revealed,
Rowing powerfully, and with energetic
   zeal,
It is he! And high in his left hand
He joyfully waves the
   goblet.

He breathes long, he breathes deeply,
And greets the heavenly light.
Rejoicing they call to each other:
'He's alive! He's here! The abyss did not
   keep him!
From the grave, the swirling watery
   cavern,
The brave man has saved his living soul.'

He approaches, the joyous throng surround
   him,
And he falls down at the king's feet,
Kneeling, he hands him the goblet,
And the king signals to his charming
   daughter,
Who fills it to the brim with sparkling
   wine;
Then the youth turned to the
   king:

'Long live the king! Rejoice,
Whoever breathes this rosy light!
But down below it is terrible,
And man should never tempt the
   gods
Nor ever desire to
   see
What they graciously conceal in night and
   horror.

»Es riss mich hinunter blitzesschnell —
Da stürzt' mir aus felsigem Schacht
Entgegen ein reissender Quell:
Mich packte des Doppelstroms wütende
    Macht,
Und wie einen Kreisel mit schwindelndem
    Drehen
Trieb mich's um, ich konnte nicht
    widerstehen.

»Da zeigte mir Gott, zu dem ich rief
In der höchsten schrecklichen
    Not,
Aus der Tiefe ragend ein Felsenriff,
Das erfasst' ich behend und entrann dem
    Tod —
Und da hing auch der Becher an spitzen
    Korallen,
Sonst wär' er ins Bodenlose
    gefallen.

»Denn unter mir lag's noch,
    bergetief,
In purpurner Finsternis da,
Und ob's hier dem Ohre gleich ewig
    schlief,
Das Auge mit Schaudern hinuntersah,
Wie's von Salamandern und Molchen
    und Drachen
Sich regte in dem furchtbaren
    Höllenrachen.

»Schwarz wimmelten da, in grausem
    Gemisch,
Zu scheusslichen Klumpen geballt,
Der stachligte Roche, der
    Klippenfisch,
Des Hammers greuliche Ungestalt,
Und dräuend wies mir die grimmigen
    Zähne
Der entsetzliche Hai, des Meeres Hyäne.

»Und da hing ich und war's mir mit
    Grausen bewusst
Von der menschlichen Hilfe so weit,
Unter Larven die einzige fühlende Brust,
Allein in der grässlichen Einsamkeit,
Tief unter dem Schall der menschlichen
    Rede
Bei den Ungeheuern der traurigen
    Öde.

»Und schaudernd dacht' ich's, da kroch's
    heran,
Regte hundert Gelenke zugleich,
Will schnappen nach mir — in des
    Schreckens Wahn
Lass' ich los der Koralle umklammerten
    Zweig;
Gleich fasst mich der Strudel mit rasendem
    Toben,

'It tore me down as fast as lightning —
Then, from a rocky shaft
A torrential flood poured towards me:
I was seized by the double current's raging
    force,
And, like the giddy whirling of a
    top,
It hurled me round; I could not
    resist.

'Then God, to whom I cried,
Showed me, at the height of my dire
    distress,
A rocky reef, rising from the depths,
I swiftly gripped it and escaped
    death —
And there, too, the goblet hung on coral
    lips,
Or else it would have fallen into the bottom-
    less ocean.

'For below me still it lay, fathomlessly
    deep,
There in purple darkness,
And even if, for the ear, there was eternal
    calm here,
The eye looked down with dread,
At the salamanders and
    dragons
Swarming in the terrifying caverns
    of hell.

'Black, in a ghastly
    mêlée,
Massed in horrifying clumps,
Teemed the stinging roach, the fish of
    the cliffs,
The hammer-head, hideously misshapen,
And, threatening me with his wrathful
    teeth,
The gruesome shark, the hyena of the sea.

'And there I hung, terrifyingly
    conscious
How far I was from human help,
Among larvae the only living heart,
Alone in terrible solitude,
Deep beneath the sound of human
    speech
With the monsters of that dismal
    wilderness.

'And, with a shudder, I thought it was
    creeping along,
Moving hundreds of limbs at once,
It wanted to grab me — in a terrifying
    frenzy
I let go of the coral's clinging
    branch;
At once the whirlpool seized me with raging
    force,

Doch es war mir zum Heil, er riss mich
nach oben.«

Der König darob sich verwundert schier
Und spricht:»Der Becher ist dein,
Und diesen Ring noch bestimm' ich dir,
Geschmückt mit dem köstlichsten
Edelgestein,
Versuchst du's noch einmal und bringst
mir Kunde,
Was du sahst auf des Meers tiefunterstem
Grunde.«

Das hörte die Tochter mit weichem
Gefühl,
Und mit schmeichelndem Munde sie
fleht:
»Lasst, Vater, genug sein das grausame
Spiel!
Er hat Euch bestanden, was keiner
besteht,
Und könnt Ihr des Herzens Gelüsten nicht
zähmen,
So mögen die Ritter den Knappen
beschämen.«

Drauf der König greift nach dem Becher
schnell,
In den Strudel ihn schleudert hinein:
»Und schaffst du den Becher mir wieder
zur Stell',
So sollst du der trefflichste Ritter mir sein
Und sollst sie als Ehgemahl heut' noch
umarmen,
Die jetzt für dich bittet mit zartem Erbar-
men.«

Da ergreift's ihm die Seele mit Himmels-
gewalt,
Und es blitzt aus den Augen
ihm kühn,
Und er siehet erröten die schöne Gestalt
Und sieht sie erbleichen und sinken hin —
Da treibt's ihn, den köstlichen Preis zu
erwerben,
Und stürzt hinunter auf Leben und
Sterben.

Wohl hört man die Brandung, wohl kehrt
sie zurück,
Sie verkündigt der donnernde Schall —
Da bückt sich's hinunter mit liebendem
Blick:
Es kommen, es kommen die Wasser all,
Sie rauschen herauf, sie rauschen nieder,
Doch den Jüngling bringt keines wieder.

But it was my salvation, pulling me
upwards.'

At this the king is greatly amazed,
And says: 'The goblet is yours,
And the ring, too, I will give you,
Adorned with the most precious
stone
If you try once more, and bring me
news
Of what you have seen on the sea's deepest
bed.'

His daughter hears this with
tenderness,
And implores with coaxing
words:
'Father, let the cruel game
cease!
He has endured for you what no other
can endure,
And if you cannot tame the desires of your
heart,
Then let the knights put the squire
to shame.'

Thereupon the king quickly seizes the
goblet,
And hurls it into the whirlpool:
'If you return the goblet to this
spot,
You shall be my noblest knight,
And you shall embrace as a bride this very
day
The one who now pleads for you with
tender pity.'

Now his soul is seized with heavenly
power,
And his eyes flash
boldly,
And he sees the fair creature blush,
Then grow pale and swoon —
This impels him to gain the precious
prize,
And he plunges down, to life or
death.

The foaming waves are heard, they
return,
Heralded by the thunderous roar —
She leans over with loving
gaze:
The waves keep on returning,
Surging, they rise and fall;
Yet not one will bring back the youth.

Der Tod Oscars / The Death of Oscar

JAMES MACPHERSON (OSSIAN), translated by EDMUND VON HAROLD

D 375 (1816)

Warum öffnest du wieder, Erzeugter von Alpin, die Quelle meiner Wehmut, da du mich fragst, wie Oscar erlag? Meine Augen sind von Tränen erblindet. Aber Erinnerung strahlt aus meinem Herzen. Wie kann ich den traurigen Tod des Führers der Krieger erzählen! Führer der Helden, o Oscar, soll ich dich nicht mehr erblicken! er fiel wie der Mond in einem Sturm, wie die Sonne in der Mitte ihres Laufs; wenn Wolken vom Schoose der Wogen sich heben; wenn das Dunkel des Sturms Ardanniders Felsen einhüllt. Wie eine alte Eiche von Morven, vermodre ich einsam auf meiner Stelle. Der Windstoß hat mir die Äste entrissen; mich schrecken die Flügel des Nordes. Führer der Helden, o Oscar, mein Sohn, soll ich dich nicht mehr erblicken!

Der Held, o Alpins Erzeugter, fiel nicht friedlich, wie Gras auf dem Feld, der Mächtigen Blut befärbte sein Schwert, er riß sich, mit Tod, durch die Reihen ihres Stolzes, aber Oscar, Erzeugter von Caruth, du bist unrühmlich gefallen! deine Rechte erschlug keinen Feind. Deinen Speer befleckte das Blut deines Freunds. Eins war Dermid und Oscar: sie mähten die Schlacht zusammen. Ihre Freundschaft war stark, wie ihr Eisen; und im Felde wandelte der Tod zwischen ihnen. Sie fuhren gegen den Feind, wie zwei Felsen, die von Ardvens Stirne sich stürzen. Ihr Schwert war vom Blute der Tapfern befärbt: Krieger erbebten bei ihrem Namen. Wer glich Oscarn, als Dermid? und wer Dermid als Oscar!

Sie erlegten den mächtigen Dargo im Feld, Dargo, der nie aus dem entfloh. Seine Tochter war schön, wie der Morgen; sanft, wie der Strahl des Abends. Ihre Augen glichen zween Sternen im Regen: ihr Athem dem Hauche des Frühlings. Ihr Busen, wie neugefallener Schnee, der auf der wiegenden Heide sich wälzt. Sie ward von den Helden gesehn, und geliebt; ihre Seelen wurden ans Mädchen geheftet. Jeder liebte sie, gleich seinem Ruhm; sie wollte jeder besitzen, oder sterben. Aber ihr Herz wählte Oscarn; Caruths Erzeugter war der Jüngling ihrer Liebe. Sie vergaß das Blut ihres Vaters. Und liebte die Rechte, die ihn erschlug.

»Caruths Sohn,« sprach Dermid, »ich liebe, o Oscar! ich liebe dies Mädchen. Aber ihre Seele hängt an dir; und nichts

Why openest thou afresh the spring of my grief, O son of Alpin, inquiring how Oscar fell? My eyes are blind with tears; but memory beams on my heart. How can I relate the mournful death of the head of the people! Chief of the warriors, Oscar, my son, shall I see thee no more!

He fell as the moon in a storm; as the sun from the midst of his course, when clouds rise from the waste of the waves, when the blackness of the storm wraps the rocks of Ardannider. I, like an ancient oak on Morven, I moulder alone in my place. The blast hath lopped my branches away; and I tremble at the wings of the north. Chief of the warriors, Oscar, my son! shall I see thee no more!

But, son of Alpin, the hero fell not harmless as the grass of the field; the blood of the mighty was on his sword, and he travelled with death through the ranks of their pride. But Oscar, thou son of Caruth, thou hast fallen low! No enemy fell by thy hand. Thy spear was stained with the blood of thy friend.

Dermid and Oscar were one: They reaped the battle together. Their friendship was strong as their steel; and death walked between them to the field. They came on the foe like to rocks falling from the brows of Ardven. Their swords were stained with the blood of the valiant: warriors fainted at their names. Who was equal to Oscar, but Dermid? and who to Dermid, but Oscar!

They killed mighty Dargo in the field: Dargo who never fled in war. His daughter was fair as the morn; mild as the beam of night. Her eyes, like two stars in a shower: her breath, the gale of spring: her breasts, as the new-fallen snow floating on the moving heath. The warriors saw her, and loved; their souls were fixed on the maid. Each loved her as his fame; each must possess her or die. But her soul was fixed on Oscar; the son of Caruth was the youth of her love. She forgot the blood of her father; and loved the hand that slew him.

Son of Caruth, said Dermid, I love; O Oscar, I love that maid. But her soul cleaveth unto thee; and nothing can heal Dermid. Here, pierce this bosom, Oscar; relieve me, my friend, with thy sword.

My sword, son of Diaran, shall never be stained with the blood of Dermid.

127

kann Dermiden heilen. Hier durchdring diesen Busen, o Oscar; hilf deinem Freund mit deinem Schwert.«

»Nie soll mein Schwert, Diarans Sohn! nie soll es mit Dermids Blute befleckt sein.« »Wer ist dann würdig mich zu erlegen, o Oscar, Caruths Sohn! laß nicht mein Leben unrühmlich vergehen, laß niemand, als Oscar, mich töten. Schick mich mit Ehre zum Grab, und Ruhm begleite meinen Tod.«

»Dermid brauch deine Klinge; Diarans Erzeugter schwing deinen Stahl. O fiel ich mit dir! daß mein Tod von Dermids Rechte herrühre!« Sie fochten beim Bache des Bergs, bei Brannos Strom. Blut färbte die fließenden Fluten, und ronn um die be- moosten Steine. Dermid der Stattliche fiel, er fiel, und lächelte im Tod!

»Und fällst du, Erzeugter Diarans, fällst du durch die Rechte von Oscar! Dermid, der nie im Kriege gewichen, seh ich dich also erliegen?« — er ging, und kehrte zum Mädchen seiner Liebe. Er kehrte, aber sie vernahm seinen Jammer.

Warum dies Dunkel, Sohn von Caruth! was überschattet deine mächtige Seele?

Einst war ich, o Mädchen, im Bogen berühmt, aber meinen Ruhm hab ich itzo verloren. Am Baum, beim Bache des Hügels, hängt der Schild des muthigen Gormurs, Gormurs, den ich im Kampfe erschlug. Ich hab den Tag vergebens ver- zehrt, und konnte ihn nicht mit meinem Pfeil durchdringen. Laß mich, Erzeuger von Caruth, die Kunst der Tochter von Dargo versuchen. Meine Rechte lernte den Bogen zu spannen, in meiner Kunst frohlockte mein Vater.

Sie ging, er stand hinter dem Schild. Es zischte ihr Pfeil, er durchdrang seine Brust.

Heil der schneeweißen Rechten; auch Heil diesem eibenen Bogen; wer, als Dargos Tochter war wert, Caruths Erzeugten zu töten? Leg mich ins Grab, meine Schönste; leg mich an Dermids Seite.

Oscar, versetzte das Mädchen, mein Seel ist die Seele des mächtigen Dargo. Ich kann dem Tode mit Freude begegnen. Ich kann meine Traurigkeit enden. — Sie durch- stieß ihren weißen Busen mit Stahl. Sie fiel, bebte, und starb!

Ihre Gräber liegen beim Bache des Hügels; ihr Grabmal bedeckt der ungleiche Schatten einer Birke. Oft grasen die astigen Söhne des Bergs an ihren grünenden Gräbern. Wenn der Mittag seine glühenden Flammen ausstreut, und Schweigen alle die Hügel beherrscht.

Who then is worthy to slay me, O Oscar son of Caruth? Let not my life pass away unknown. Let none but Oscar slay me. Send me with honour to the grave, and let my death be renowned.

Dermid, make use of thy sword; son of Diaran, wield thy steel. Would that I fell with thee! that my death came from the hand of Dermid!

They fought by the brook of the mountain, by the streams of Branno. Blood tinged the running water, and curled round the mossy stones. The stately Dermid fell; he fell, and smiled in death.

And fallest thou, son of Diaran, fallest thou by Oscar's hand! Dermid who never yielded in war, thus do I see thee fall! — He went, and returned to the maid of his love; he returned, but she perceived his grief.

Why that gloom, son of Caruth? What shades thy mighty soul?

Though once renowned for the bow, O maid, I have lost my fame. Fixed on the tree by the brook of the hill, is the shield of the valiant Gormur, whom I slew in battle. I have wasted the day in vain, nor could my arrow pierce it.

Let me try, son of Caruth, the skill of Dargo's daughter. My hands were taught the bow: my father delighted in my skill.

She went. He stood behind the shield. Her arrow flew, and pierced his breast.

Blessed be that hand of snow; and bles- sed that bow of yew! Who but the daughter of Dargo was worthy to slay the son of Caruth? Lay me in the earth, my fair one; lay me by the side of Dermid.

Oscar! the maid replied, I have the soul of the mighty Dargo. Well pleased I can meet death. My sorrow I can end — She pierced her white bosom with the steel. She fell; she trembled; and died.

By the brook of the hill their graves are laid; a birch's unequal shade covers their tomb. Often on their green earthen tombs the branchy sons of the mountain feed, when mid-day is all in flames, and silence over all the hills.

Der Tod und das Mädchen / Death and the Maiden

MATTHIAS CLAUDIUS

D 531 (1817)

Das Mädchen:
Vorüber, ach, vorüber!
Geh, wilder Knochenmann!
Ich bin noch jung, geh, Lieber!
Und rühre mich nicht an.

Der Tod:
Gib deine Hand, du schön und zart
  Gebild!
Bin Freund und komme nicht zu strafen.
Sei gutes Muts! Ich bin nicht wild,
Sollst sanft in meinen Armen schlafen!

The Maiden:
Pass by, ah, pass by!
Away, cruel Death!
I am still young, leave me, dear one,
And do not touch me.

Death:
Give me your hand, you lovely, tender
  creature.
I am your friend, and come not to chastise.
Be of good courage. I am not cruel;
You shall sleep softly in my arms.

Der Traum / The Dream

LUDWIG HEINRICH CHRISTOPH HÖLTY

D 213 (1815)

Mir träumt', ich war ein Vögelein,
Und flog auf ihren Schoß,
Und zupft' ihr, um nicht laß zu sein,
Die Busenschleifen los.
Und flog, mit gaukelhaftem Flug,
Dann auf die weiße Hand,
Dann wieder auf das Busentuch,
Und pickt' am roten Band.

I dreamt I was a little bird,
And flew on to her lap,
And, so as not to be idle,
Loosened the bows around her breast.
Then I flitted playfully
On to her white hand,
Then back on to her bodice,
And pecked at its red ribbon.

Dann schwebt' ich auf ihr blondes Haar,
Und zwitscherte vor Lust,
Und ruhte, wann ich müde war,
Auf ihrer weißen Brust.
Kein Veilchenbett' im Paradies
Geht diesem Lager vor.
Wie schlief sich's da so süß, so süß
Auf ihres Busens Flor!

Then I glided on to her fair hair
And twittered with pleasure,
And when I grew weary
I rested on her white breast.
There is no violet bed in paradise
Which can surpass that resting place.
How sweetly I would sleep
On her beauteous breast.

Sie spielte, wie ich tiefer sank,
Mit leisem Fingerschlag,
Der mir durch Leib und Leben drang,
Mich frohen Schlummrer wach.
Sah mich so wunderfreundlich
  an,
Und bot den Mund mir dar,
Daß ich es nicht beschreiben kann,
Wie froh, wie froh ich war.

As I sank deeper she fondled me
With a gentle touch of her fingers
That ran through my body and soul,
Awakening me from my happy slumber.
She gazed at me with such wondrous
  kindness,
And offered me her lips,
That I cannot describe
How happy I was.

Da trippelt' ich auf einem Bein
Und hatte so mein Spiel,
Und spielt' ihr mit dem Flügelein
Die rote Wange kühl.
Doch, ach, kein Erdenglück besteht,
Tag sei es oder Nacht!
Schnell war mein süßer Traum verweht,
Und ich war aufgewacht.

Then I tripped about on one leg
As a game,
And with my little wings
Playfully cooled her red cheeks.
But, alas, no earthly happiness endures,
Whether it be day or night!
Swiftly my dream vanished,
And I awoke.

Der Unglückliche / The Unhappy One

KAROLINE PICHLER

D 713 (1821)

Die Nacht bricht an, mit leisen Lüften sinket
Sie auf die müden Sterblichen herab;
Der sanfte Schlaf, des Todes Bruder, winket,
Und legt sie freundlich in ihr täglich Grab.

Night falls, descending with light breezes
Upon weary mortals;
Gentle sleep, death's brother, beckons,
And lays them fondly in their daily graves.

Jetzt wachet auf der lichtberaubten Erde
Vielleicht nur noch die Arglist und der Schmerz,
Und jetzt, da ich durch nichts gestöret werde,
Lass deine Wunden bluten, armes Herz.

Now only malice and pain
Perchance watch over the earth, robbed of light;
And now, since nothing may disturb me,
Let your wounds bleed, poor heart.

Versenke dich in deines Kummers Tiefen,
Und wenn vielleicht in der zerrissnen Brust
Halb verjährte Leiden schliefen,
So wecke sie mit grausam süsser Lust.

Plunge to the depths of your grief,
And if perchance half-forgotten sorrows
Have slept in your anguished heart,
Awaken them with cruelly sweet delight.

Berechne die verlornen Seligkeiten,
Zähl' alle, alle Blumen in dem Paradies,
Woraus in deiner Jugend goldnen Zeiten
Die harte Hand des Schicksals dich verstiess.

Consider your lost happiness,
Count all the flowers in paradise,
From which, in the golden days of your youth,
The harsh hand of fate banished you.

Du hast geliebt, du hast das Glück empfunden,
Dem jede Seligkeit der Erde weicht.
Du hast ein Herz, das dich verstand, gefunden,
Der kühnsten Hoffnung schönes Ziel erreicht.

You have loved, you have experienced a happiness
Which eclipses all earthly bliss.
You have found a heart that understands you,
Your wildest hopes have attained their fair goal.

Da stürzte dich ein grausam Machtwort nieder,
Aus deinen Himmeln nieder, und dein stilles Glück,
Dein allzu schönes Traumbild kehrte wieder
Zur besser'n Welt, aus der es kam, zurück.

Then the cruel decree of authority dashed you down
From your heaven, and your tranquil happiness,
Your all-too-lovely dream vision, returned
To the better world from which it came.

Zerrissen sind nun alle süssen Bande,
Mir schlägt kein Herz mehr auf der weiten Welt.

Now all the sweet bonds are torn asunder;
No heart now beats for me in the whole world.

Der Vater mit dem Kind / The Father with his Child

EDUARD VON BAUERNFELD

D906 (1827)

Dem Vater liegt das Kind im Arm,
Es ruht so wohl, es ruht so warm,

The child lies in its father's arms,
Resting so snug, resting so warm.

Es lächelt süss: lieb' Vater mein!
Und mit dem Lächeln schläft es ein.

It smiles sweetly: 'Dear father!'
And with the smile falls asleep.

Der Vater beugt sich, atmet kaum,
Und lauscht auf seines Kindes Traum;
Er denkt an die entschwund'ne Zeit
Mit wehmutsvoller Seligkeit.

The father stoops, scarcely breathing,
Listening to his child's dream;
He thinks of times past
With wistful happiness.

Und eine Trän' aus Herzensgrund
Fällt ihm auf seines Kindes Mund;
Schnell küsst er ihm die Träne ab,
Und wiegt es leise auf und ab.

And a tear from deep in his heart
Falls on the child's mouth;
Quickly he kisses the tear away,
And rocks the child gently to and fro.

Um einer ganzen Welt Gewinn
Gäb er das Herzenskind nicht hin.
Du Seliger schon in der Welt,
Der so sein Glück in Armen
    hält!

He would not give up his beloved child
For all the world.
Happy are you in this world,
Who hold thus your happiness in your
    arms.

Der Vatermörder / *The Parricide*

GOTTLIEB CONRAD PFEFFEL

D 10 (1811)

Ein Vater starb von des Sohnes Hand.
Kein Wolf, kein Tiger, nein,
Der Mensch allein, der Tiere Fürst,
Erfand den Vatermord allein.

A father died by his son's hand.
No wolf, no tiger,
But man alone, the prince of beasts,
He alone invented parricide.

Der Täter floh, um dem Gericht
Sein Opfer zu entziehn,
In einen Wald, doch konnt er nicht
Den innern Richter fliehn.

To cheat the law of its victim,
The murderer fled
Into a wood, yet he could not
Escape the inner judge.

Verzehrt und hager, stumm und bleich
Mit Lumpen angetan,
Dem Dämon der Verzweiflung gleich,
Traf ihn ein Häscher an.

Consumed and haggard, silent and pale,
Dressed in rags,
Like the demon of despair,
He was found by a henchman.

Voll Grimm zerstörte der Barbar
Ein Nest mit einem Stein
Und mordete die kleine Schar
Der armen Vögelein.

Filled with rage, the savage man
Destroyed a nest with a stone
And murdered the little brood
Of poor fledglings.

»Halt ein!« rief ihm der Scherge zu,
»Verruchter Bösewicht,
Mit welchem Rechte marterst du
Die frommen Tierchen so?«

'Stop,' cried the henchman,
'Accursed murderer,
What right do you have
To torture these harmless creatures?'

»Was fromm«, sprach jener, den die Wut
Kaum hörbar stammeln liess,
»Ich tat es, weil die Höllenbrut
Mich Vatermörder hiess.«

'Harmless?' he replied, stammering,
Barely audible in his fury,
'I did it because this hellish brood
Called me a parricide'.

Der Mann beschaut ihn, seine Tat
Verrät sein irrer Blick.
Er fasst den Mörder, und das Rad
Bestraft das Bubenstück.

The henchman looked at him
Whose crazed look betrayed his deed.
He seized the murderer, and the rack
Punished the evil man.

Du, heiliges Gewissen, bist
Der Tugend letzter Freund;
Ein schreckliches Triumphlied ist
Dein Donner ihrem Feind.

You, sacred conscience, are
Virtue's last friend;
To her enemy your thunder
In an awesome song of triumph.

Der Wachtelschlag / Song of the Quail

SAMUEL FRIEDRICH SAUTER

D 742 (1822?)

Ach! mir schallt's dorten so lieblich
    hervor:
»Fürchte Gott, fürchte Gott!«
Ruft mir die Wachtel ins Ohr.
Sitzend im Grünen, von Halmen
    umhüllt,
Mahnt sie den Horcher am Saatengefild:
»Liebe Gott, liebe Gott!«
Er ist so gütig, so mild.

Ah, how sweet that sound from
    yonder:
'Fear God! Fear God!'
The quail cries into my ear
Sitting amid the greenery, hidden by the
    corn,
It exhorts the listener in the field:
'Love God! Love God!'
He is so gracious and so kind.

Wieder bedeutet ihr hüpfender Schlag:
»Lobe Gott, lobe Gott!«
Der dich zu loben vermag.
Siehst du die herrlichen Früchte im Feld?
Nimm es zu Herzen, Bewohner
    der Welt:
»Danke Gott, danke Gott!«
Der dich ernährt und erhält.

Again its leaping call echoes:
'Praise God! Praise God!'
For He can praise you.
Do you see the wonderful fruits of the field?
Reflect on them in your hearts, dwellers on
    this earth:
'Give thanks to God! Give thanks to God!'
For He nourishes and sustains you.

Schreckt dich im Wetter der Herr der
    Natur:
»Bitte Gott, bitte Gott!«
Ruft sie, er schonet die Flur.
Machen Gefahren der Krieger dir bang:
»Traue Gott, traue Gott!«
Sieh', er verziehet nicht lang.

If the Lord of Nature terrifies you in the
    storm,
'Pray to God! Pray to God!'
He spares the fields when they call to Him.
If the perils of warriors make you fearful,
'Trust in God! Trust in God!'
See, He does not tarry long.

Der Wallensteiner Lanzknecht beim Trunk / Wallenstein's Lancer Drinking

KARL GOTTFRIED VON LEITNER

D 931 (1827)

He! schenket mir im Helme ein,
Der ist des Knappen Becher,
Er ist nicht seicht, und traun, nicht klein,
Das freut den wackern Zecher.

Here, pour it into my helmet;
That's the squire's cup!
It's not shallow or, indeed, small,
Which pleases the lusty drinker.

Er schützte mich zu tausendmal
Vor Kolben, Schwert und Spiessen,
Er dient mir jetzt als Trinkpokal
Und in der Nacht als Kissen.

It has protected me a thousand times
From club, sword and spear;
Now it serves me as a drinking cup,
And at night as a pillow.

Vor Lützen traf ihn jüngst ein Speer,
Bin fast ins Gras gesunken,
Ja, wär' er durch, hätt' nimmermehr
Ein Tröpfelchen getrunken;

At Lützen lately it was hit by a spear;
I almost sank to the ground.
Yes, had it gone through
I would never have drunk another drop.

132

Doch kam's nicht so, ich danke dir,
Du brave Pickelhaube!
Der Schwede büsste bald dafür
Und röchelte im Staube.

Nu, tröst' ihn Gott! Schenkt ein, schenkt
ein!
Mein Krug hat tiefe Wunden,
Doch hält er noch den deutschen Wein
Und soll mir oft noch munden.

But it was not so, thanks to you,
My good helmet!
The Swede soon paid the price
And bit the dust.

Well, God comfort him! Pour,
pour!
My tankard has deep wounds,
But it can still hold German wine,
And I shall often relish it.

Der Wanderer / The Wanderer

FRIEDRICH VON SCHLEGEL

D 649 (1819?)

Wie deutlich des Mondes Licht
Zu mir spricht,
Mich beseelend zu der Reise:
»Folge treu dem alten Gleise,
Wähle keine Heimat nicht.
Ew'ge Plage
Bringen sonst die schweren Tage.
Fort zu andern
Sollst du wechseln, sollst du wandern,
Leicht entfliehend jeder Klage.«

How clearly the moon's light
Speaks to me,
Inspiring me on my journey:
'Follow faithfully the old track,
Choose nowhere as your home,
Lest bad times
Bring endless cares.
You will move on, and go forth
To other places,
Lightly casting off all grief.'

Sanfte Ebb' und hohe Flut,
Tief im Mut,
Wandr' ich so im Dunkeln weiter,
Steige mutig, singe heiter,
Und die Welt erscheint mir gut.
Alles reine
Seh' ich mild im Widerscheine,
Nichts verworren
In des Tages Glut verdorren:
Froh umgeben, doch alleine.

Thus, with gentle ebb and swelling flow
Deep within my soul,
I walk on in the darkness;
I climb boldly, singing merrily,
And the world seems good to me.
I see all things clearly
In their gentle reflection;
Nothing is blurred
Or withered in the heat of day:
There is joy all around, yet I am alone.

Der Wanderer / The Wanderer

GEORG PHILIPP SCHMIDT VON LÜBECK

D 493 (1816)

Ich komme vom Gebirge her,
Es dampft das Tal, es braust das Meer.
Ich wandle still, bin wenig froh,
Und immer fragt der Seufzer: wo?

I come from the mountains,
The valley steams, the ocean roars,
I wander, silent and joyless,
And my sighs forever ask: Where?

Die Sonne dünkt mich hier so kalt,
Die Blüte welk, das Leben alt,
Und was sie reden, leerer Schall,
Ich bin ein Fremdling überall.

Here the sun seems so cold,
The blossom faded, life old,
And men's words mere hollow noise;
I am a stranger everywhere.

Wo bist du, mein geliebtes Land?
Gesucht, geahnt und nie gekannt!
Das Land, das Land, so hoffnungsgrün,
Das Land, wo meine Rosen blühn,

Where are you, my beloved land?
Sought, dreamt of, yet never known!
The land so green with hope,
The land where my roses bloom,

Wo meine Freunde wandeln gehn,	Where my friends walk,
Wo meine Toten auferstehn,	Where my dead ones rise again,
Das Land, das meine Sprache spricht,	The land that speaks my tongue,
O Land, wo bist du?	O land, where are you?
Ich wandle still, bin wenig froh,	I wander, silent and joyless,
Und immer fragt der Seufzer: wo?	And my sighs forever ask: Where?
Im Geisterhauch tönt's mir zurück:	In a ghostly whisper the answer comes:
»Dort, wo du nicht bist, dort ist das	'There, where you are not, is
Glück!«	happiness!'

Der Wanderer an den Mond / The Wanderer's Address to the Moon

JOHANN GABRIEL SEIDL

D870 (1826?)

Ich auf der Erd', am Himmel du,	I on earth, you in the sky,
Wir wandern beide rüstig zu:	Both of us travel briskly on;
Ich ernst und trüb, du mild und rein,	I solemn and gloomy, you gentle and pure,
Was mag der Unterschied wohl sein?	What can be the difference between us?
Ich wandre fremd von Land zu Land,	I wander, a stranger, from land to land,
So heimatlos, so unbekannt;	So homeless, so unknown;
Bergauf, bergab, Wald ein, Wald	Up and down mountains, in and out of
aus,	forests,
Doch bin ich nirgend, ach! zu Haus.	Yet, alas, nowhere am I at home.
Du aber wanderst auf und ab	But you wander up and down,
Aus Ostens Wieg' in Westens	From the east's cradle to the west's
Grab,	grave,
Wallst Länder ein und Länder aus,	Travel from country to country
Und bist doch, wo du bist, zu Haus.	And yet are at home wherever you are.
Der Himmel, endlos ausgespannt,	The sky, infinitely extended,
Ist dein geliebtes Heimatland:	Is your beloved homeland;
O glücklich, wer, wohin er geht,	O happy he who, wherever he goes,
Doch auf der Heimat Boden steht!	Still stands on his native soil!

Der Weiberfreund / The Philanderer

ABRAHAM COWLEY, translated by JOSEF VON RATSCHKY

D271 (1815)
A literal rendering of Ratschky's free version is given here. The first three
verses of Cowley's original poem, entitled 'The Inconstant', are printed below
in italics.

Noch fand von Evens Töchterschaaren	Among the daughters of Eve
Ich keine, die mir nicht	I have never yet found one that
gefiel.	displeased me.
Von fünfzehn bis zu fünfzig Jahren	From fifteen years to fifty
Ist jede meiner Wünsche Ziel.	Each one is the object of my desires.
Durch Farb' und Form, durch Witz und	Everything about them delights
Güte,	me—
Durch alles fühl' ich mich entzückt;	Colour and shape, wit and goodness;
Ein Ebenbild der Aphrodite	Each one that my eyes behold
Ist jede, die mein Aug' erblickt.	Is an image of Aphrodite.

Selbst die vermag mein Herz zu
  angeln,
Bei der man jeden Reiz vermißt:
Mag immerhin ihr alles mangeln,
Wenn's nur ein weiblich Wesen ist!

Even she in whom all charms are deemed
  lacking
Has the power to win my heart:
It matters not that she lacks everything,
As long as she is a female creature!

I never yet could see that face
Which had no dart for me;
From fifteen years, to fifties space,
They all victorious be.
Love thou'rt a Devil: if I may call thee One,
For sure in Me thy name is Legion.

Colour, or Shape, good Limbs, or Face,
Goodness, or Wit in all I find.
In Motion or in Speech a grace,
If all fail, yet 'tis Woman-kind;
And I'm so weak, the Pistol need not be
Double, or treble charg'd to murder Me.

If Tall, the Name of Proper slays;
If Fair, she's pleasant as the Light;
If Low, her Prettiness does please:
If Black, what Lover loves not Night?
If Yellow-hair'd, I Love, lest it should be
Th' excuse to others for not loving Me.

Der Winterabend / The Winter Evening

KARL GOTTFRIED VON LEITNER

D 938 (1828)

Es ist so still, so heimlich um mich,
Die Sonne ist unter, der Tag entwich.
Wie schnell nun heran der Abend graut!
Mir ist es recht, sonst ist mir's zu laut.

It is so silent and secret all around me,
The sun has set, the day has vanished.
How swiftly now the evening grows grey!
It suits me well; day is too loud for me.

Jetzt aber ist's ruhig, es hämmert kein
  Schmied,
Kein Klempner, das Volk verlief und ist
  müd.
Und selbst, dass nicht rass'le der Wagen
  Lauf,
Zog Decken der Schnee durch die Gassen
  auf.
Wie tut mir so wohl der selige Frieden!
Da sitz ich im Dunkeln, ganz
  abgeschieden,
So ganz für mich; nur der Mondenschein
Kommt leise zu mir ins Gemach.
Er kennt mich schon und lässt mich
  schweigen,
Nimmt nur seine Arbeit, die Spindel, das
  Gold,
Und spinnet stille, webt und lächelt
  hold,
Und hängt dann sein schimmerndes
  Schleiertuch

But now it is peaceful, no blacksmith
  hammers,
And no plumber. The people have
  dispersed, tired.
And, lest carts should rattle on their
  way,
The snow has even draped blankets
  through the streets.
How welcome to me is this blissful peace!
Here I sit in the darkness, quite
  secluded,
Quite self-contained; only the moonlight
Comes softly into my room.
It knows me and lets me be
  silent,
And just takes up its work, the spindle, the
  gold,
And spins and weeps silently, smiling
  sweetly,
And then hangs its shimmering
  veil

Ringsum an Gerät und Wänden aus.
Ist gar ein stiller, ein lieber Besuch,
Macht mir gar keine Unruh' im Haus.
Will er bleiben, so hat er Ort,
Freut's ihn nimmer, so geht er fort.

Ich sitze dann stumm im Fenster gern
Und schaue hinauf in Gewölk und Stern.
Denke zurück, ach weit, gar weit
In eine schöne verschwundne Zeit.
Denk an sie, an das Glück der Minne,
Seufze still und sinne und sinne.

Over the furniture and walls all around.
It is a silent and beloved visitor
That causes no disturbance in my house.
If it wishes to stay, there is room,
If it is not happy, then it goes away.

Then I like to sit silently at the window,
Gazing up at the clouds and stars,
Thinking back to long, long ago,
To a beautiful, vanished past.
I think of her, of love's happiness,
And sigh softly, and muse.

Der Zufriedene / The Contented Man

CHRISTIAN LUDWIG REISSIG

D 320 (1815)

Zwar schuf das Glück hienieden
Mich weder reich noch groß,
Allein ich bin zufrieden
Wie mit dem schönsten Los.

So ganz nach meinem Herzen
Ward mir ein Freund vergönnt,
Denn küssen, trinken, scherzen,
Ist auch sein Element.

Mit ihm wird froh und weise
Manch Fläschchen ausgeleert!
Denn auf der Lebensreise
Ist Wein das beste Pferd.

Wenn mir bei diesem Lose
Nun auch ein trüb'res fällt,
So denk' ich, keine Rose
Blüht dornlos in der Welt.

Fortune here on earth
Has made me neither rich nor great,
But I am contented
As if with the finest of lots.

A friend quite after my own heart
Has been granted me.
For with kissing, drinking and jesting
He too is in his element.

With him, cheerfully and wisely,
Many a bottle is emptied!
For on life's journey
Wine is the best of steeds.

If, amid this lot of mine,
A gloomier fate should overtake me,
I shall reflect that no rose
Blooms without thorns in this world.

Der zürnende Barde / The Indignant Bard

FRANZ VON BRUCHMANN

D 785 (1823)

Wer wagt's, wer wagt's, wer wagt's,
Wer will mir die Leier zerbrechen,
Noch tagt's, noch tagt's, noch tagt's,
Noch glühet die Kraft, mich zu
    rächen.

Heran, heran, ihr alle,
Wer immer sich erkühnt,
Aus dunkler Felsenhalle
Ist mir die Leier ergrünt.

Who dares, who dares, who dares,
Who wishes to shatter my lyre?
It is still day, still day, still day,
The strength to avenge myself still burns
    within me.

Draw near, draw near, all of you,
Whoever will make so bold;
My lyre burgeoned
From dark rocky vaults.

Ich habe das Holz gespalten
Aus riesigem Eichenbaum,
Worunter einst die Alten
Umtanzten Wodans Saum.

I split the wood
From the giant oak-tree,
Beneath which our ancestors
Once danced around Wotan's grove.

Die Saiten raubt ich der Sonne,
Den purpurnen, glühenden Strahl,
Als einst sie in seliger Wonne
Versank in das blühende Tal.

As strings I stole from the sun
Its glowing, crimson rays,
As once it sank in blissful ecstasy
Into the flowering valley.

Aus alter Ahnen Eichen,
Aus rotem Abendgold,
Wirst Leier du nimmer weichen,
Solang' die Götter mir hold.

My lyre, you will never desert
The oaks of our ancient forebears,
The red gold of evening,
So long as the gods smile upon me.

Der zürnenden Diana / To Diana in her Wrath

JOHANN MAYRHOFER

D707 (1820)

Ja, spanne nur den Bogen, mich zu töten,
Du himmlisch Weib! im zürnenden
  Erröten
Noch reizender. Ich werd' es nie
  bereuen,
Dass ich dich sah am blühenden Gestade
Die Nymphen überragen in dem Bade,
Der Schönheit Funken in die Wildnis
  streuen.
Den Sterbenden wird noch dein Bild
  erfreuen.
Er atmet reiner, er atmet freier,
Wem du gestrahlet ohne Schleier.
Dein Pfeil, er traf, doch linde rinnen
Die warmen Wellen aus der Wunde;
Noch zittert vor den matten Sinnen
Des Schauens süsse letzte Stunde.

Yes, draw your bow to slay me,
Divine lady! In the flush of
  wrath
You are still more enchanting. I shall never
  regret
That I saw you on the flowering bank,
Outshining the nymphs as they bathed,
Spreading rays of beauty through the
  wilderness.
Your image will gladden me even as
  I die.
He who has beheld your unveiled radiance
Will breathe more purely and more freely.
Your arrow hit its mark, yet warm waves
Flow gently from the wound.
My failing senses still tremble
In contemplation of this last sweet hour.

Der Zwerg / The Dwarf

MATTHÄUS VON COLLIN

D771 (1822?)

Im trüben Licht verschwinden schon die
  Berge,
Es schwebt das Schiff auf glatten
  Meereswogen,
Worauf die Königin mit ihrem Zwerge.

In the dim light the mountains already
  fade;
The ship drifts on the sea's smooth
  swell,
With the queen and her dwarf on board.

Sie schaut empor zum hochgewölbten
  Bogen,
Hinauf zur lichtdurchwirkten blauen
  Ferne,
Die mit der Milch des Himmels blass
  durchzogen.

She gazes up at the high arching
  vault,
At the blue distance, interwoven with
  light,
Streaked with the pale milky
  way.

Nie, nie habt ihr mir gelogen noch, ihr Sterne,
So ruft sie aus, bald werd' ich nun entschwinden,
Ihr sagt es mir, doch sterb' ich wahrlich gerne.

'Stars, never yet have you lied to me,'
She cries out. 'Soon now I shall be no more.
You tell me so; yet in truth I shall die gladly.'

Da tritt der Zwerg zur Königin, mag binden
Um ihren Hals die Schnur von roter Seide,
Und weint, als wollt' er schnell vor Gram erblinden.

Then the dwarf comes up to the queen, begins
To tie the cord of red silk about her neck,
And weeps, as if he would soon go blind with grief.

Er spricht: Du selbst bist schuld an diesem Leide,
Weil um den König du mich hast verlassen,
Jetzt weckt dein Sterben einzig mir noch Freude.

He speaks: 'You are yourself to blame for this suffering,
Because you have forsaken me for the king;
Now your death alone can revive joy within me.

Zwar werd' ich ewiglich mich selber hassen,
Der dir mit dieser Hand den Tod gegeben,
Doch musst zum frühen Grab du nun erblassen.

'Though I shall forever hate myself
For having brought you death by this hand,
Yet now you must grow pale for an early grave.'

Sie legt die Hand aufs Herz voll jungem Leben,
Und aus dem Aug' die schweren Tränen rinnen,
Das sie zum Himmel betend will erheben.

She lays her hand on her heart, so full of youthful life,
And heavy tears flow from her eyes
Which she would raise to heaven in prayer.

Mögst du nicht Schmerz durch meinen Tod gewinnen!
Sie sagt's, da küsst der Zwerg die bleichen Wangen,
D'rauf alsobald vergehen ihr die Sinnen.

'May you reap no sorrow from my death!'
She says; then the dwarf kisses her pale cheeks,
Whereupon her senses fade.

Der Zwerg schaut an die Frau, vom Tod befangen,
Er senkt sie tief ins Meer mit eig'nen Händen.
Ihm brennt nach ihr das Herz so voll Verlangen,
An keiner Küste wird er je mehr landen.

The dwarf looks upon the lady in the grip of death;
He lowers her with his own hands deep into the sea.
His heart burns with such longing for her,
He will never again land on any shore.

Des Fischers Liebesglück / The Fisherman's Luck in Love

KARL GOTTFRIED VON LEITNER

D933 (1827)

Dort blinket
Durch Weiden,
Und winket
Ein Schimmer
Blaßstrahlig
Vom Zimmer
Der Holden mir zu.

Yonder light gleams
Through the willows,
And a pale
Glimmer
Beckons to me
From the bedroom
Of my sweetheart.

Es gaukelt	It flickers
Wie Irrlicht,	Like a will o' the wisp,
Und schaukelt	And its reflection
Sich leise	Sways
Sein Abglanz	Gently
Im Kreise	In the circle
Des schwankenden Sees.	Of the undulating lake.
Ich schaue	I gaze
Mit Sehnen	Longingly
In's Blaue	Into the blue
Der Wellen,	Of the waves,
Und grüße	And greet
Den hellen,	The bright
Gespiegelten Strahl.	Reflected beam.
Und springe	And spring
Zum Ruder,	To the oar,
Und schwinge	And swing
Den Nachen	The boat
Dahin auf	Away on
Den flachen,	Its smooth,
Krystallenen Weg.	Crystal course.
Fein-Liebchen	My sweetheart
Schleicht traulich	Slips lovingly
Vom Stübchen	Down
Herunter,	From her little room,
Und sputet	And joyfully
Sich munter	Hastens to me
Zu mir in das Boot.	In the boat.
Gelinde	Then the breezes
Dann treiben	Gently
Die Winde	Blow us
Uns wieder	Again
See-einwärts	Out into the lake
Vom Flieder	From the elder tree
Des Ufers hindann.	On the shore.
Die blassen	The pale
Nachtnebel	Evening mists
Umfassen	Envelop
Mit Hüllen	And veil
Vor Spähern	Our silent,
Den stillen,	Innocent dallying
Unschuldigen Scherz.	From prying onlookers.
Und tauschen	And as we exchange
Wir Küsse,	Kisses,
So rauschen	The waves
Die Wellen	Lap,
Im Sinken	Rising
Und Schwellen,	And falling,
Den Horchern zum Trotz	To foil eavesdroppers.
Nur Sterne	Only stars
Belauschen	In the far distance
Uns ferne,	Overhear us,
Und baden	And bathe
Tief unter	Deep down

Den Pfaden Des gleitenden Kahns.	Below the course Of the gliding boat.
So schweben Wir selig, Umgeben Vom Dunkel, Hoch überm Gefunkel Der Sterne einher.	So we drift on Blissfully, In the midst Of darkness, High above The twinkling Stars.
Und weinen Und lächeln, Und meinen, Enthoben Der Erde, Schon oben, Schon d'rüben zu sein.	Weeping, Smiling, We think We have soared free Of the earth, And are already up above, On another shore.

Des Mädchens Klage / The Maiden's Lament

FRIEDRICH VON SCHILLER

First version: D6 (1811?)
Second version: D 191 (1815)
Third version: D 389 (1816)

Der Eichwald braust, die Wolken ziehn, Das Mägdlein sitzt an Ufers Grün, Es bricht sich die Welle mit Macht, mit Macht, Und sie seufzt hinaus in die finstere Nacht, Das Auge von Weinen getrübet.	The oak-wood roars, the clouds scud by, The maiden sits on the verdant shore; The waves break with mighty force, And she sighs into the dark night, Her eyes dimmed with weeping.
»Das Herz ist gestorben, die Welt ist leer, Und weiter gibt sie dem Wunsche nichts mehr, Du Heilige, rufe dein Kind zurück, Ich habe genossen das irdische Glück, Ich habe gelebt und geliebet!«	'My heart is dead, the world is empty, And no longer yields to my desire; Holy one, call back your child. I have enjoyed earthly happiness, I have lived and loved!'
Es rinnet der Tränen vergeblicher Lauf, Die Klage, sie wecket die Toten nicht auf; Doch nenne, was tröstet und heilet die Brust Nach der süßen Liebe verschwund'ner Lust, Ich, die Himmlische, will's nicht versagen.	Her tears run their vain course, Her lament does not awaken the dead; But say, what can comfort and heal the heart When the joys of sweet love have vanished? I, the heavenly maiden, shall not be denied it.
»Laß rinnen der Tränen vergeblichen Lauf, Es wecke die Klage den Toten nicht auf! Das süßeste Glück für die trauernde Brust, Nach der schönen Liebe verschwund'ner Lust, Sind der Liebe Schmerzen und Klagen.«	'Let my tears run their vain course, Let my lament not awaken the dead! For the grieving heart the sweetest happiness, When the joys of fair love have vanished, Is the sorrow and lament of love.'

Des Sängers Habe / The Minstrel's Possessions

FRANZ XAVER VON SCHLECHTA

D 832 (1825)

Schlagt mein ganzes Glück in Splitter,
Nehmt mir alle Habe gleich,
Lasset mir nur meine Zither,
Und ich bleibe froh und reich.

Break my happiness in pieces,
Take from me all I possess;
Leave me only my zither,
And I shall remain glad and rich.

Wenn des Grames Wolken ziehen,
Haucht sie Trost in meine Brust,
Und aus ihrem Golde blühen
Alle Blumen meiner Lust.

When clouds of sorrow approach
It breathes comfort into my heart,
And from its golden strings
Bloom all the flowers of my joy.

Will die Liebe nicht gewähren,
Freundschaft brechen ihre Pflicht,
Kann ich beide stolz entbehren,
Aber meine Zither nicht.

If love is not forthcoming,
And friendship fails in its duty,
Then I can proudly forgo them both,
But not my zither.

Reisset meines Lebens Sehne,
Wird sie mir ein Kissen sein,
Lullen mich die süssen Töne
In den letzten Schlummer ein.

When the sinews of my life are torn
It will be as a pillow for me;
Its sweet tones will lull me
To my last sleep.

In den Grund des Tannenhaines
Senkt mich leise dann hinab;
Und statt eines Leichensteines
Stellt die Zither auf mein Grab,

Then in the grove of fir-trees
Lower me gently into the earth;
And instead of a tombstone
Place my zither upon my grave.

Dass ich, wenn zum stillen Reigen,
Aus des Todes dunklem Bann,
Mitternachts die Geister Steigen,
Ihre Saiten rühren kann.

So that when at midnight
The spirits rise from death's dark spell
For their silent dance,
I may touch its strings.

Didone Abbandonata / Dido Abandoned

PIETRO METASTASIO

D 510 (1816)

Vedi quanto t'adoro ancora
  ingrato.
Con un tuo sguardo solo
Mi togli ogni difesa, e mi
  disarmi.
Ed hai cor di tradirmi? E puoi
  lasciarmi?

See how much I still love you, ungrateful
  man!
With a single glance
You remove all my defences, and disarm
  me.
Do you have the heart to betray me? And
  then to leave me?

Ah! non lasciarmi, no,
Bell' idol mio:
Di chi mi fiderò
Se tu m'inganni?
Di vita mancherei
Nel dirti addio;
Chè viver non potrei
Fra tanti affanni.

Ah, do not leave me,
My beloved.
Whom shall I trust
If you deceive me?
My life would fail me
As I said farewell to you.
I could not live
With such grief.

Die abgeblühte Linde / The Faded Linden Tree

LUDWIG VON SZÉCHÉNYI

D 514 (1821?)

Wirst du halten, was du schwurst,
Wenn mir die Zeit die Locken bleicht?
Wie du über Berge fuhrst,
Eilt das Wiedersehn nicht leicht.

Ändrung ist das Kind der Zeit,
Wo mit Trennung uns bedroht,
Und was die Zukunft beut,
Ist ein blässer's Lebensrot.

Sieh, die Linde blühet noch,
Als du heute von ihr gehst;
Wirst sie wieder finden, doch
Ihre Blüten stiehlt der West.

Einsam steht sie dann, vorbei
Geht man kalt, bemerkt sie kaum.
Nur der Gärtner bleibt ihr treu,
Denn er liebt in ihr den Baum.

Will you abide by what you pledged to me
When time has made my hair white?
Since you went away over the mountains
Reunions are not easy.

Change is the child of time
With which parting threatens us;
And what the future offers us
Is a paler gleam of life.

See, the linden tree is still blooming
As you leave here today;
You will find it again,
Though the west wind steals its blossoms.

Then it will stand alone, people will
Pass by, indifferent, scarcely noticing it.
Only the gardener will remain true,
Since he loves the tree for itself.

Die Allmacht / Omnipotence

JOHANN LADISLAUS PYRKER

D852 (1825)

Gross ist Jehova, der Herr! Denn
    Himmel
Und Erde verkünden seine Macht.
Du hörst sie im brausenden Sturm,
In des Waldstroms laut aufrauschendem
    Ruf;
Du hörst sie in des grünen Waldes
    Gesäusel,
Siehst sie in wogender Saaten Gold,
In lieblicher Blumen glühendem Schmelz,
Im Glanz des sternebesäten Himmels;
Furchtbar tönt sie im Donnergeroll
Und flammt in des Blitzes schnell hinzuck-
    endem Flug.
Doch kündet das pochende Herz dir
    fühlbarer noch
Jehovas Macht, des ewigen Gottes,
Blickst du flehend empor und hoffst auf
    Huld und Erbarmen.

Great is Jehovah, the Lord! For
    heaven
And earth proclaim His might.
You hear it in the roaring storm,
In the loud, surging cry of the forest
    stream;
You hear it in the rustling of the
    greenwood,
You see it in the golden, waving corn,
In the glowing lustre of the lovely flowers,
In the sparkling, star-strewn heavens;
It echoes terrifyingly in the rolling thunder,
And flames in the lightning's swiftly flick-
    ering flight.
But your beating heart will reveal still more
    palpably
The power of Jehovah, the eternal God,
If you gaze up in prayer and hope for grace
    and mercy.

Die Befreier Europas in Paris / The Liberators of Europe in Paris

JOHANN CHRISTIAN MIKAN

D 104 (1814)

Sie sind in Paris!
Die Helden! Europa's Befreier!

They are in Paris!
The heroes, Europe's liberators!

Der Vater von Östreich, der Herrscher der
  Reußen,
Der Wiedererwecker der tapferen
  Preußen.
Das Glück Ihrer Völker — es war ihnen
  teuer.
Sie sind in Paris!
Nun ist uns der Friede gewiß!

The father of Austria, the ruler of the
  Russians,
He who aroused once more the brave
  Prussians.
The happiness of their nations was dear to
  them.
They are in Paris!
Now we are assured of peace.

Die Berge / The Mountains

FRIEDRICH VON SCHLEGEL

D 634 (1820?)

Sieht uns der Blick gehoben,
So glaubt das Herz, die Schwere zu
  besiegen,
Zu den Himmlischen oben
Will es dringen und fliegen;
Der Mensch emporgeschwungen,
Glaubt schon, er sei durch die Wolken
  gedrungen.

When we gaze upwards,
Our hearts believe they can overcome
  gravity,
They desire to fly up
And reach the gods above;
Soaring aloft, man imagines
He has already passed through the
  clouds.

Bald muss er staunend merken,
Wie ewig fest wir auf uns selbst
  begründet;
Dann strebt in sichern Werken
Sein ganzes Tun, verbündet,
Vom Grunde nie zu wanken,
Und baut wie Felsen den Bau der
  Gedanken.

Soon he must realize with astonishment
That we are for ever firmly rooted in
  ourselves;
Then, with concentrated effort,
He strives to create lasting achievements,
Endeavouring never to stray from his roots,
And builds, as of rock, an edifice of
  thoughts.

Und dann in neuen Freuden
Sieht er die kühnen Klippen spottend
  hangen;
Vergessend aller Leiden,
Fühlt er einzig Verlangen
An dem Abgrund zu scherzen,
Denn hoher Mut schwillt ihm in hohem
  Herzen.

And then, with new joy,
He sees the bold cliffs hang in
  mockery;
Forgetting all his sorrows
He feels only the craving
To jest on the edge of the abyss,
For noble courage swells in his noble
  heart.

Die Betende / The Maiden at Prayer

FRIEDRICH VON MATTHISSON

D 102 (1814)

Laura betet! Engelharfen hallen
Frieden Gottes in ihr krankes Herz,
Und, wie Abels Opferdüfte, wallen
Ihre Seufzer himmelwärts.

Laura is praying! Angels' harps sound,
Filling her sick heart with God's peace,
And, like the scents of Abel's sacrifice,
Her sighs waft heavenwards.

Wie sie kniet, in Andacht hingegossen,
Schön, wie Raphael die Unschuld malt;
Vom Verklärungsglanze schon
  umflossen,
Der um Himmelswohner
  strahlt.

Kneeling, lost in prayer, she is
As lovely as Innocence painted by Raphael,
Already bathed in that transfigured
  radiance
Which shines around those who dwell in
  heaven.

So von Andacht, so von Gottvertrauen
Ihre engelreine Brust geschwellt,
Betend diese Heilige zu schauen,
Ist ein Blick in jene Welt.

Her angelically pure breast swells
With devotion, with trust in God;
To behold this saintly maiden at prayer
Is to look into the world beyond.

Die Blumensprache / The Language of Flowers

(?) ANTON PLATNER

D 519 (1817?)

Es deuten die Blumen des Herzens
  Gefühle,
Sie sprechen manch' heimliches Wort,
Sie neigen sich traulich am schwankenden
  Stiele,
Als zöge die Liebe sie fort.
Sie bergen verschämt sich im deckenden
  Laube,
Als hätte verraten der Wunsch sie dem
  Raube.

Flowers reveal the feelings of the
  heart,
They speak many a secret word;
They incline confidingly on their swaying
  stems,
As though drawn by love.
They hide shyly amid concealing
  foliage,
As though desire had betrayed them to
  seduction.

Sie deuten im leise bezaubernden
  Bilde
Der Frauen, der Mädchen Sinn;
Sie deuten das Schöne, die Anmut, die
  Milde,
Sie deuten des Lebens Gewinn:
Es hat mit der Knospe, so heimlich
  verschlungen,
Der Jüngling die Perle der Hoffnung
  gefunden.

They reveal, in a delicate, enchanting
  image,
The nature of women and maidens;
They signify beauty, grace,
  gentleness,
They embody life's rewards:
In the bud, so secretly
  concealed,
The youth has found the pearl of
  hope.

Sie weben der Sehnsucht, des Harmes
  Gedanken
Aus Farben ins duftige Kleid,
Nichts frommen der Trennung gehässige
  Schranken,
Die Blumen verkünden das Leid.
Was laut nicht der Mund, der bewachte,
  darf sagen,
Das waget die Huld sich in Blumen zu
  klagen.

With coloured strands they weave into their
  fragrant dress
Thoughts of yearning and sorrow;
The hateful barriers of separation are of no
  importance,
Flowers proclaim our suffering.
What guarded lips may not speak
  aloud,
Kindness will dare to lament through
  flowers.

Die Bürgschaft / The Bond

FRIEDRICH VON SCHILLER

D 246 (1815)

Zu Dionys, dem Tyrannen, schlich
Möros, den Dolch im Gewande;
Ihn schlugen die Häscher in Bande.
»Was wolltest du mit dem Dolche,
  sprich!«
Entgegnet ihm finster der Wüterich.
»Die Stadt vom Tyrannen befreien!«
»Das sollst du am Kreuze bereuen.«

Moros, his dagger concealed in his cloak,
Stealthily approached the tyrant Dionysos.
The henchmen clapped him in irons.
'What did you intend with your dagger,
  speak!'
The evil tyrant asked menacingly.
'To free this city from the tyrant.'
'You shall rue this on the cross.'

»Ich bin,« spricht jener, »zu sterben
  bereit
Und bitte nicht um mein Leben;
Doch willst du Gnade mir geben,
Ich flehe dich um drei Tage Zeit,
Bis ich die Schwester dem Gatten gefreit;
Ich lasse den Freund dir als Bürgen —
Ihn magst du, entrinn' ich, erwürgen.«

Da lächelt der König mit arger List
Und spricht nach kurzem Bedenken:
»Drei Tage will ich dir schenken.
Doch wisse: wenn sie verstrichen, die
  Frist,
Eh' du zurück mir gegeben bist,
So muss er statt deiner erblassen,
Doch dir ist die Strafe erlassen.«

Und er kommt zum Freunde: »Der
  König gebeut,
Dass ich am Kreuz mit dem Leben
Bezahle das frevelnde Streben;
Doch will er mir gönnen drei Tage
  Zeit,
Bis ich die Schwester dem Gatten
  gefreit.
So bleib du dem König zum Pfande,
Bis ich komme, zu lösen die Bande.«

Und schweigend umarmt ihn der treue
  Freund
Und liefert sich aus dem Tyrannen,
Der andere zieht von dannen.
Und eh' noch das dritte Morgenrot
  erscheint,
Hat er schnell mit dem Gatten die Schwes-
  ter vereint
Eilt heim mit sorgender Seele,
Damit er die Frist nicht
  verfehle.

Da giesst unendlicher Regen herab,
Von den Bergen stürzen die Quellen
  herab,
Und die Bäche, die Ströme schwellen.
Und er kommt ans Ufer mit wanderndem
  Stab —
Da reisset die Brücke der Strudel
  hinab
Und donnernd sprengen die Wogen
Des Gewölbes krachenden Bogen.

Und trostlos irrt er an Ufers Rand:
Wie weit er auch spähet und blicket
Und die Stimme, die rufende, schicket —
Da stösset kein Nachen vom sichern
  Strand,
Der ihn setze an das gewünschte Land,
Kein Schiffer lenket die Fähre,
Und der wilde Strom wird zum Meere.

'I am,' he said, 'ready to
  die.
And do not beg for my life.
But if you will show me clemency
I ask from you three days' grace
Until I have given my sister in marriage
As surety I will leave you my friend —
If I fail, then hang him.'

The king smiled with evil cunning,
And after reflecting awhile spoke:
'I will grant you three days
But know this: if the time runs
  out
Before you are returned to me,
He must die instead of you,
But you will be spared punishment.'

He went to his friend. 'The king
  decrees
That I am to pay on the cross with my life
For my attempted crime.
But he is willing to grant me three days'
  grace
Until I have married my sister to her
  spouse.
Stand surety with the king
Until I return to redeem the bond.'

Silently his faithful friend embraced
  him,
And gave himself up to the tyrant.
Moros departed.
Before the third day
  dawned
He had quickly married his sister to her
  betrothed.
He now hastened home with troubled soul
Lest he should fail to meet the appointed
  time.

Then rain poured down ceaselessly
Torrents streamed down the
  mountains,
Brooks and rivers swelled.
When he came to the bank, staff in
  hand,
The bridge was swept down by the
  whirlpool,
And the thundering waves destroyed
Its crashing arches.

Disconsolate, he trudged along the bank.
However far his eyes travelled,
And his shouts resounded,
No boat left the safety of the
  banks
To carry him to the shore he sought.
No boatman steered his ferry,
And the turbulent river became a sea.

Da sinkt er ans Ufer und weint und
    fleht,
Die Hände zum Zeus erhoben:
»O hemme des Stromes Toben!
Es eilen die Stunden, im Mittag steht
Die Sonne, und wenn sie niedergeht
Und ich kann die Stadt nicht erreichen,
So muss der Freund mir erbleichen.«

Doch wachsend erneut sich des Stromes
    Wut,
Und Welle auf Welle zerrinnet,
Und Stunde an Stunde entrinnet.
Da treibt ihn die Angst, da fasst er sich
    Mut
Und wirft sich hinein in die brausende
    Flut
Und teilt mit gewaltigen Armen
Den Strom, und ein Gott hat Erbarmen.

Und gewinnt das Ufer und eilet fort
Und danket dem rettenden Gotte;
Da stürzet die raubende Rotte
Hervor aus des Waldes nächtlichem
    Ort,
Den Pfad ihm sperrend, und schnaubet
    Mord
Und hemmet des Wanderers Eile
Mit drohend geschwungener Keule.

»Was wollt ihr?« ruft er für Schrecken
    bleich,
»Ich habe nichts als mein Leben,
Das muss ich dem Könige geben!«
Und entreisst die Keule dem nächsten
    gleich:
»Um des Freundes willen erbarmet euch!«
Und drei, mit gewaltigen
    Streichen,
Erlegt er, die andern entweichen.

Und die Sonne versendet glühenden
    Brand,
Und von der unendlichen Mühe
Ermattet sinken die Knie:
»O hast du mich gnädig aus
    Räubershand,
Aus dem Strom mich gerettet ans heilige
    Land,
Und soll hier verschmachtend verderben,
Und der Freund mir, der liebende,
    sterben!«

Und horch! da sprudelt es silberhell
Ganz nahe, wie rieselndes Rauschen,
Und stille hält er zu lauschen;
Und sieh, aus dem Felsen, geschwätzig,
    schnell,
Springt murmelnd hervor ein lebendiger
    Quell,

He fell on to the bank, sobbing and
    imploring,
His hands raised to Zeus:
'O curb the raging torrent!
The hours speed by, the sun stands
At its zenith, and when it sets
And I cannot reach the city,
My friend will die for me.

But the river grew ever more
    angry,
Wave upon wave broke,
And hour upon hour flew by.
Gripped by fear, he took
    courage
And flung himself into the seething
    flood;
With powerful arms he clove
The waters, and a god had mercy on him.

He reached the bank and hastened on,
Thanking the god that saved him.
Then a band of robbers
Stormed from the dark recesses of the
    forest,
Blocking his path and threatening
    death.
They halted the traveller's swift course
With their menacing clubs.

'What do you want?' he cried, pale with
    terror,
'I have nothing but my life,
And that I must give to the king!'
He seized the club of the one nearest
    him:
'For the sake of my friend, have mercy!'
Then with mighty blows he felled three of
    them,
And the others escaped.

The sun shed its glowing
    fire,
And from their ceaseless exertion
His weary knees gave way.
'You have mercifully saved me from the
    hands of robbers,
You have saved me from the river and
    brought me to sacred land.
Am I to die of thirst here,
And is my devoted friend to
    perish?'

But hark, a silvery bubbling sound
Close by, like rippling water.
He stopped and listened quietly;
And lo, bubbling from the
    rock,
A living spring gushed
    forth.

Und freudig bückt er sich nieder
Und erfrischet die brennenden Glieder.

Und die Sonne blickt durch der Zweige
    Grün
Und malt auf glänzenden Matten
Der Bäume gigantische Schatten;
Und zwei Wandrer sieht er die Strasse
    ziehn,
Will eilenden Laufes vorüber
    fliehn,
Da hört er die Worte sie sagen:
»Jetzt wird er ans Kreuz geschlagen.«

Und die Angst beflügelt den eilenden
    Fuss,
Ihn jagen der Sorge Qualen;
Da schimmern in Abendrots Strahlen
Von Ferne die Zinnen von Syrakus,
Und entgegen kommt ihm
    Philostratus,
Des Hauses redlicher Hüter,
Der erkennet entsetzt den Gebieter:

»Zurück! du rettest den Freund nicht
    mehr,
So rette das eigene Leben!
Den Tod erleidet er eben.
Von Stunde zu Stunde gewartet' er
Mit hoffender Seele der Wiederkehr,
Ihm konnte den mutigen Glauben
Der Hohn des Tyrannen nicht rauben.«

»Und ist es zu spät und kann ich ihm nicht
Ein Retter wilkommen erscheinen,
So soll mich der Tod ihm vereinen.
Des rühmte der blut'ge Tyrann sich nicht,
Dass der Freund dem Freunde gebrochen
    die Pflicht —
Er schlachte der Opfer zweie
Und glaube an Liebe und Treue.«

Und die Sonne geht unter, da steht er
    am Tor
Und sieht das Kreuz schon erhöh't,
Das die Menge gaffend umstehet;
Und an dem Seile schon zieht man den
    Freund empor,
Da zertrennt er gewaltig den dichten
    Chor:
»Mich, Henker!« ruft er, »erwürget!
Da bin ich, für den er gebürget!«

Und Erstaunen ergreift das Volk
    umher,
In den Armen liegen sich beide
Und weinen vor Schmerzen und Freude.
Da sieht man kein Auge tränenleer,
Und zum König bringt man die
    Wundermär';
Der fühlt ein menschlich Rühren,

Joyfully he stopped
To refresh his burning body.

Now the sun shone through green
    branches
And upon the radiant fields
The trees' gigantic shadows.
He saw two travellers on the
    road,
And with rapid steps was about to overtake
    them
When he heard them speak these words:
'Now he is being bound to the cross.'

Fear quickened his
    steps,
He was driven on by torments of anxiety;
Then, in the sun's dying rays,
The towers of Syracuse glinted from afar,
And Philostratus, his household's faithful
    steward,
Came towards him.
With horror he recognized his master.

'Turn back! You will not save your friend
    now,
So save your own life!
At this moment he meets his death.
From hour to hour he awaited
Your return with hope in his soul,
The tyrant's derision could not weaken
His courageous faith.'

'If it is too late, if I cannot
Appear before him as his welcome saviour,
Then let death unite us.
The bloodthirsty tyrant shall never gloat
That one friend broke his pledge to
    another —
Let him slaughter two victims
And believe in love and loyalty.'

The sun set as he reached the
    gate
And saw the cross already raised,
Surrounded by a gaping throng.
His friend was already being hoisted up by
    the ropes,
When he forced his way through the dense
    crowd.
'Kill me, hangman!' he cried,
It is I, for whom he stood surety.'

The people standing by were seized with
    astonishment;
The two friends were in each other's arms,
Weeping with grief and joy.
No eye was without tears;
The wondrous tidings reached the
    king;
He was stirred by humane feelings,

Lässt schnell vor den Thron sie führen.	And at once summoned the friends before his throne.

Und blickt sie lange verwundert an;	He looked at them long, amazed,
Drauf spricht er: »Es ist euch gelungen,	Then he spoke: 'You have succeeded,
Ihr habt das Herz mir bezwungen,	You have conquered this heart of mine.
Und die Treue ist doch kein leerer Wahn —	Loyalty is no vain delusion —
So nehmt auch mich zum Genossen an.	Then take me, too, as a friend.
Ich sei, gewährt mir die Bitte,	Grant me this request: Admit me
In eurem Bunde der Dritte.«	As the third in your fellowship.'

Die Einsiedelei / The Hermitage

JOHANN GAUDENZ VON SALIS-SEEWIS

First version: D 393 (1816?)
Second version: D 563 (1817)

Es rieselt, klar und wehend,	In the oak wood flows a stream,
Ein Quell im Eichenwald;	Clean and rippling.
Da wähl' ich, einsam gehend,	Wandering alone, I choose there
Mir meinen Aufenthalt.	My resting place.
Mir dienet zur Kapelle	A grotto, cool and fragrant.
Ein Gröttchen, duftig, frisch;	Serves as my chapel;
Zu meiner Klausnerzelle	Entwined bushes
Verschlungenes Gebüsch.	Are my hermit's cell.

Wie sich das Herz erweitert	How the heart is elated
Im engen, dichten Wald!	In the thick, dense forest!
Dem öden Trübsinn heitert	Gloomy melancholy is soon cheered
Der traute Schatten bald.	By its friendly shade.
Kein überleg'ner Späher	Here no disdainful eye
Erforscht hier meine Spur;	Spies on my steps;
Ich bin hier frei und näher	Here I am free, and closer
Der Einfalt und Natur.	To simplicity and to nature.

Die Entzückung an Laura / Delight in Laura

FRIEDRICH VON SCHILLER

First version: D 390 (1816)
Second version: D 577 (1817)

Laura, über diese Welt zu flüchten	Laura, when your shimmering eyes are reflected in mine,
Wähn' ich, mich in Himmelsmaienglanz zu lichten,	I imagine I am fleeing this world
Wenn dein Blick in meinem Blicke flimmt;	To bathe in the light of some heavenly May.
Ätherlüfte träum' ich, einzusaugen,	I dream I am breathing ethereal air
Wenn mein Bild in deiner sanften Augen	When my image floats
Himmelblauem Spiegel schwimmt.	In the sky-blue mirror of your gentle eyes.

Leierklang aus Paradieses Fernen,	I burn to draw to my intoxicated ear
Harfenschwung aus angenehmern Sternen	The sound of lyres from distant Paradise,
Ras' ich, in mein trunknes Ohr zu ziehn;	The flourish of harps from more pleasurable stars;
Meine Muse fühlt die Schäferstunde,	My muse senses the hour of love
Wenn von deinem wollustheissen Munde	When from your warm, sensual lips
Silbertöne ungern fliehn.	Silvery notes reluctantly escape.

Die Erde / The Earth

FRIEDRICH VON MATTHISSON

D989 (1817)

Wenn sanft entzückt mein Auge sieht,
Wie schön im Lenz die Erde blüht;
Wie jedes Wesen angeschmiegt
An ihren Segensbrüsten liegt;

Und wie sie jeden Säugling liebt,
Ihm gern die milde Nahrung gibt,
Und so in steter Jugendkraft
Hervor bringt, nährt und Wachstum
    schafft:

Dann fühl' ich hohen Busendrang,
Zu rühmen den mit Tat und Sang,
Deß wundervoller Allmachtstruf
Die weite Welt so schön erschuf.

When with tender rapture my eyes behold
How fair the earth blooms in spring,
How every creature nestles
At her bountiful breasts;

And how she loves each infant,
And gladly gives it gentle nourishment,
And thus, with constant youthful strength,
Brings forth, nurtures and creates
    growth:

Then I have an ardent, heartfelt longing
To praise in deed and song Him
Whose wondrous omnipotence
Made this vast world so beautiful.

Die Erscheinung / The Apparition

LUDWIG KOSEGARTEN

see Erinnerung: Die Erscheinung

Die erste Liebe / First Love

JOHANN GEORG FELLINGER

D 182 (1815)

Die erste Liebe füllt das Herz mit Sehnen
Nach einem unbekannten Geisterlande,
Die Seele gaukelt an dem Lebensrande,
Und süsse Wehmut letzet sich in Tränen.

Da wacht es auf, das Vorgefühl des
    Schönen,
Du schaust die Göttin in dem
    Lichtgewande,
Geschlungen sind des Glaubens leise
    Bande,
Und Tage rieseln hin auf Liebestönen.

Du siehst nur sie allein im Widerscheine,
Die Holde, der du ganz dich
    hingegeben,
Nur sie durchwebt deines Daseins Räume.
Sie lächelt dir herab vom
    Goldgesäume,
Wenn stille Lichter an den Himmeln
    schweben,
Der Erde jubelst du: Sie ist die Meine!

First love fills the heart with longing
For an unknown enchanted land.
The soul flutters on the edge of life,
And sweet melancholy dissolves in tears.

Now dawns the intimation of
    beauty,
You behold the goddess in her robe of
    light,
The gentle bonds of faith are
    sealed,
And the days flow by in songs of love.

Her alone you see reflected,
The fair one to whom you have surrendered
    yourself.
She alone pervades your whole being,
She smiles down on you from heaven's
    golden fringes
When silent lights hover in the
    sky.
Joyfully you cry to the world: She is mine!

Die Erwartung / Anticipation

FRIEDRICH VON SCHILLER

D 159 (1816)

Hör' ich das Pförtchen nicht gehen?
Hat nicht der Riegel geklirrt?
Nein, es war des Windes Wehen,
Der durch die Pappeln schwirrt.

Did I not hear the gate?
Was that not the bolt creaking?
No, it was the wind
Blowing through the poplars.

O schmücke dich, du grünbelaubtes
  Dach,
Du sollst die Anmutstrahlende
  empfangen!
Ihr Zweige, baut ein schattendes Gemach,
Mit holder Nacht sie heimlich zu
  umfangen,
Und all' ihr Schmeichellüfte, werdet wach
Und scherzt und spielt um ihre
  Rosenwangen,
Wenn seine schöne Bürde, leicht bewegt,
Der zarte Fuss zum Sitz der Liebe trägt.

Adorn yourself, leaf-clad
  roof,
You are to receive her in all her radiant
  beauty!
Branches, build a shady bower
To envelop her secretly in sweet
  night,
And all you caressing breezes, be awake,
Play and dally about her rosy
  cheeks
When her delicate foot lightly bears
Its fair burden to the seat of love.

Stille, was schlüpft durch die
  Hecken
Raschelnd mit eilendem Lauf?
Nein, es scheuchte nur der Schrecken
Aus dem Busch den Vogel auf.

Hush, what is that darting through the
  hedge,
Rustling and scurrying?
No, it was only a startled bird
Frightened from the hedge.

O lösche deine Fackel, Tag!
Hervor, du geist'ge Nacht, mit deinem
  holden Schweigen!
Breit' um uns her den purpurroten Flor,
Umspinne uns mit geheimnisvollen
  Zweigen!
Der Liebe Wonne flieht des Lauschers
  Ohr,
Sie flieht des Strahles unbescheid'nen
  Zeugen!
Nur Hesper, der Verschwiegene, allein
Darf still herblickend ihr Vertrauter sein.

Extinguish your torch, day!
Draw on, contemplative night, with your
  sweet silence!
Spread your purple veil around us,
Enfold us with secret
  boughs!
The rapture of love shuns both the listening
  ear
And the immodest witness of the sun's
  rays!
Hesperus alone, the silent one,
Looking calmly on, may be its confidant.

Rief es von ferne nicht leise,
Flüsternden Stimmen gleich?
Nein, der Schwan ist's, der die Kreise
Zieht durch den Silberteich.

Was that not a faint, distant call,
Like whispering voices?
No, it is the swan, tracing circles
Over the silvery lake.

Mein Ohr umtönt ein Harmonienfluss,
Der Springquell fällt mit angenehmem
  Rauschen,
Die Blume neigt sich bei des Westes Kuss,
Und alle Wesen seh' ich Wonne tauschen,
Die Traube winkt, die Pfirsche zum
  Genuss,
Die üppig schwellend hinter Blättern
  lauschen,
Die Luft, getaucht in der Gewürze Flut,
Trinkt von der heissen Wange mir die
  Glut.

Flowing harmonies fill my ears,
The spring murmurs
  sweetly,
The flower bows at the west wind's kiss,
And I see all creatures united in bliss.
The grape beckons, the peach is ripe to be
  relished,
Swelling lusciously, hidden among
  leaves.
The air, bathed in spicy scents,
Drinks the glow from my burning cheeks.

Hör' ich nicht Tritte erschallen?	Do I not hear footsteps,
Rauscht's nicht den Laubgang daher?	Something rustling in the leafy walk?
Die Frucht ist dort gefallen,	A fruit has fallen there,
Von der eig'nen Fülle schwer.	Heavy with its own ripeness.
Des Tages Flammenauge selber bricht	The flaming eye of day perishes
In süssem Tod, und seine Farben blassen;	In sweet death, and its colours fade.
Kühn öffnen sich im holden Dämmerlicht	In the beauteous dusk the flower-bells,
Die Kelche schon, die seine Gluten	Which loathe day's fire, open
hassen.	boldly.
Still hebt der Mond sein strahlend	Silently the moon raises its radiant
Angesicht,	countenance,
Die Welt zerschmilzt in ruhig grosse	The world dissolves in vast, calm
Massen.	shapes,
Der Gürtel ist von jedem Reiz gelöst,	The girdle is released by each magic spell,
Und alles Schöne zeigt sich mir entblösst.	And all beauty is revealed to me.
Seh' ich nichts Weisses dort schimmern?	Do I not see a shimmer of white,
Glänzt's nicht wie seid'nes Gewand?	The glistening of a silver garment?
Nein, es ist der Säule Flimmern	No, it is the column gleaming
An der dunkeln Taxuswand.	Against the row of dark yew trees.
O! sehnend Herz, ergötze dich nicht	Yearning heart, delight no
mehr,	longer
Mit süssen Bildern wesenlos zu spielen,	In toying with sweet, airy images.
Der Arm, der sie umfassen will, ist	The arms that desire to embrace them are
leer;	empty.
Kein Schattenglück kann diesen Busen	No joy in shadows can cool this
kühlen,	breast.
O! führe mir die Liebende daher,	O, bring my beloved to me,
Lass ihre Hand, die zärtliche, mich	Let me feel her delicate
fühlen,	hand,
Den Schatten nur von ihres Mantels	The bare shadow of her mantle's
Saum!	hem,
Und in das Leben tritt der hohle Traum.	And the hollow dream will come to life!
Und leis', wie aus himmlischen Höhen	And softly, as if from celestial heights,
Die Stunde des Glückes erscheint,	The hour of bliss arrives,
So war sie genaht, ungesehen,	Thus she had come, unseen,
Und weckte mit Küssen den Freund.	Waking her beloved with kisses.

Die Forelle / The Trout

CHRISTIAN FRIEDRICH DANIEL SCHUBART

D 550 (1817?)

In einem Bächlein helle,	In a limpid brook
Da schoß in froher Eil'	The capricious trout
Die launische Forelle	In joyous haste
Vorüber wie ein Pfeil.	Darted by like an arrow.
Ich stand an dem Gestade	I stood on the bank
Und sah in süßer Ruh'	In blissful peace, watching
Des muntern Fischleins Bade	The lively fish swim
Im klaren Bächlein zu.	In the clear brook.
Ein Fischer mit der Rute	An angler with his rod
Wohl an dem Ufer stand,	Stood on the bank,
Und sah's mit kaltem Blute,	Cold-bloodedly watching
Wie sich das Fischlein wand.	The fish's contortions.

Solang dem Wasser Helle,
So dacht' ich, nicht gebricht,
So fängt er die Forelle
Mit seiner Angel nicht.

Doch endlich ward dem Diebe
Die Zeit zu lang. Er macht
Das Bächlein tückisch trübe,
Und eh ich es gedacht,
So zuckte seine Rute,
Das Fischlein zappelt dran,
Und ich mit regem Blute
Sah die Betrog'ne an.

As long as the water
Is clear, I thought,
He won't catch the trout
With his rod.

But at length the thief
Grew impatient. Cunningly
He made the brook cloudy,
And in an instant
His rod quivered,
And the fish struggled on it.
And I, my blood boiling,
Looked at the cheated creature.

Die Fröhlichkeit / *Gaiety*

MARTIN JOSEF PRANDSTETTER

D 262 (1815)

Weß Adern leichtes Blut durchspringt,
Der ist ein reicher Mann;
Auch keine goldnen Ketten zwingt
Ihm Furcht und Hoffnung an.

The man whose blood flows lightly
Through his veins is rich.
He is not fettered by the golden chains
Of fear and hope.

Denn Fröhlichkeit geleitet ihn
Bis an ein sanftes Grab
Wohl durch ein langes Leben hin
An ihrem Zauberstab.

For gaiety guides him
With its magic wand
Through a long life
To a gentle death.

Mit allen Menschen ausgesöhnt
Liebt er als Brüder sie:
Der Rache helle Flamme brennt
In seinem Herzen nie.

Reconciled with all men,
He loves them as brothers;
The bright flame of vengeance
Never burns in his heart.

Denn Freundschaft ist', die das umflicht
Mit Armen ohne Zahl:
Drum haßt er seine Feinde nicht
Und kennt sie nicht einmal.

For it is friendship that embraces his heart
With countless arms;
Therefore he does not hate his enemies,
Nor does he even know them.

Wohin sein muntrer Blick sich kehrt,
Ist alles schön und gut,
Ist alles heil und liebenswert
Und fröhlich wie sein Mut.

Wherever he turns his cheerful gaze
All is fair and good;
All is well, worthy of love
And as blithe as his heart.

Für ihn nur wird bei Sonnenschein
Die Welt zum Paradies,
Ist klar der Bach, die Quelle rein,
Und ihr Gemurmel süß.

For him alone sunshine
Makes the world a paradise;
The brook is clear, the spring pure,
And its murmur sweet.

In ewig wechselnder Gestalt
Labt ihn die Blumenflur,
Und nur für ihn wird nimmer alt
Die heilige Natur.

The flowery meadows refresh him
With their ever-changing aspect;
And for him alone holy nature
Never grows old.

Drum wär' ich reich, wie Krösus war,
Und mächtig obendrein,
Und wären Klumpen Goldes gar,
So groß wie Berge, mein;

Therefore if I were as rich as Croesus,
And mighty too,
And if gold nuggets,
As big as mountains, were mine,

Und wär' ich noch von allem Herr
Was von der Nordsee an
Bis tief hinab ans Schwarze Meer
Je Menschenaugen sahn;

Und hätte frohes Mutes nicht,
So senkt' ich trüb den Blick;
Ich dünkte mir ein armer Wicht,
Und spräche zu dem Glück:

O Göttin, ist mein Wohl dir lieb,
So höre mich! nimm hier
Zurück dies alles, aber gib
Mir leichtes Blut dafür!

Denn Fröhlichkeit macht reich und frei,
Und nur der seltne Mann
Ist glücklich, sei er, wer er sei,
Der sie erhalten kann.

And if I were master of all
That men's eyes have ever seen,
From the North Sea
Right down to the Black Sea,

If I did not have a glad heart,
I should lower my gaze gloomily;
I should deem myself a poor wretch,
And speak to Fortune thus:

O goddess, if my well-being is dear to you,
Hear me! Take all this back,
But give me in return
A light heart!

For gaiety makes us rich and free,
And only rarely is a man fortunate enough,
Whoever he may be,
To know how to preserve it.

Die frühe Liebe / Early Love

LUDWIG HEINRICH CHRISTOPH HÖLTY

D 430 (1816)

Schon im bunten Knabenkleide,
Pflegten hübsche Mägdelein
Meine liebste Augenweide,
Mehr als Pupp' und Ball zu sein.

Ich vergass der Vogelnester,
Warf mein Steckenpferd ins Gras,
Wenn am Baum bei meiner Schwester
Eine schöne Dirne sass.

Freute mich der muntern Dirne,
Ihres roten Wangenpaars,
Ihres Mundes, ihrer Stirne,
Ihres blonden Lockenhaars;

Blickt' auf Busentuch und Mieder,
Hinterwärts gelehnt am Baum;
Streckte dann ins Gras mich nieder,
Dicht an ihres Kleides Saum.

When I was still a lad in bright clothes
I would rather feast my eyes
On pretty girls
Than on a doll or ball.

I forgot about birds' nests,
And threw my hobby-horse on the grass,
When a pretty girl sat beside my sister
Under a tree.

I delighted in the lively girl,
Her red cheeks,
Her mouth, her brow,
Her blond curly hair.

I would gaze at her shawl and bodice
As she leant against a tree,
Then I would stretch out in the grass
Close to the hem of her dress.

Die frühen Gräber / The Early Graves

FRIEDRICH GOTTLIEB KLOPSTOCK

D 290 (1815)

Willkommen, o silberner Mond,
Schöner, stiller Gefährt' der Nacht!
Du entfliehst? Eile nicht, bleib',
     Gedankenfreund!
Sehet, er bleibt, das Gewölk wallte nur
     hin.

Welcome, silvery moon,
Fair, silent companion of the night!
You flee? Do not hasten away, stay, friend
     of contemplation.
See, she stays; it was only the clouds
     passing.

Des Maies Erwachen ist nur
Schöner noch, wie die Sommernacht,
Wenn ihm Tau, hell wie Licht, aus der
 Locke träuft,
Und zu dem Hügel herauf rötlich er
 kömmt.

May's awakening
Is lovelier even than the summer's night,
When dew, glistening brightly, drips from
 his locks,
And he rises red
 above the hills.

Ihr Edleren, ach, es bewächst
Eure Male schon ernstes Moos!
O, wie war glücklich ich, als ich noch mit
 euch
Sahe sich röten den Tag, schimmern die
 Nacht!

Nobler spirits, alas, your tombstones
Are already overgrown with gloomy moss.
Ah, how happy I was then, when with
 you
I watched the day dawn and the night sky
 glitter.

Die Gebüsche / The Bushes

FRIEDRICH VON SCHLEGEL

D 646 (1819)

Es wehet kühl und leise
Die Luft durch dunkle Auen,
Und nur der Himmel lächelt
Aus tausend hellen Augen.

The breeze blows cool and soft
Through dark meadows,
And only the heavens smile
From a thousand bright eyes.

Es regt nur eine Seele
Sich in des Meeres Brausen,
Und in den leisen Worten,
Die durch die Blätter rauschen.

Only one soul stirs
Amid the roaring ocean,
And in the soft words
That whisper through the leaves.

So tönt in Welle Welle,
Wo Geister heimlich trauren;
So folgen Worte Worten,
Wo Geister Leben hauchen.

Thus wave echoes wave
Where spirits secretly mourn;
Thus words follow words
Where spirits breathe life.

Durch alle Töne tönet
Im bunten Erdentraume
Ein leiser Ton gezogen,
Für den, der heimlich lauschet.

Through all the sounds
In the earth's many-coloured dream,
One faint sound echoes
For him who secretly listens.

Die gefangenen Sänger / The Captive Singers

AUGUST WILHELM VON SCHLEGEL

D 712 (1821)

Hörst du von den Nachtigallen
Die Gebüsche widerhallen?
Sieh, es kam der holde Mai.
Jedes buhlt um seine Traute,
Schmelzend sagen alle Laute,
Welche Wonn' im Lieben sei.

Do you hear the bushes echoing
With the nightingales' song?
See, fair May is here.
Every creature woos his sweetheart;
Every sound sweetly declares
What bliss there is in love.

Andre, die im Käfig leben,
Hinter ihren Gitterstäben,
Hören draussen den Gesang;
Möchten in die Freiheit
 eilen,

Others, who live in cages,
Behind bars,
Hear the song outside;
They would dearly like to fly to their
 freedom,

Frühlingslust und Liebe teilen:
Ach, da hemmt sie enger
 Zwang.

Und nun drängt sich in die
 Kehle
Aus der gramzerrissnen Seele
Schmetternd ihres Lieds Gewalt,
Wo es, statt im Weh'n der
 Haine
Mit zu wallen, an der Steine
Hartem Bau zurücke prallt.

So, im Erdental gefangen,
Hört der Menschen Geist mit Bangen
Hehrer Brüder Melodie;
Sucht umsonst zu Himmelsheitern
Dieses Dasein zu erweitern,
Und das nennt er Poesie.

Aber scheint er ihre Rhythmen
Jubelhymnen auch zu widmen,
Wie aus lebenstrunkner Brust:
Dennoch fühlen's zarte Herzen,
Aus der Wurzel tiefer Schmerzen
Stammt die Blüte seiner Lust.

To share in love and the joys of spring:
But, alas, force keeps them closely
 confined.

And now, bursting from their grief-stricken
 souls,
The power of their song
Wells up in their throats;
But, instead of soaring amid the swaying
 trees,
It rebounds from the hard stone
Of the walls.

Thus, captive in this vale of earth,
Man's spirit hears with longing
The songs of his noble brothers;
He seeks in vain to expand this earthly life,
To embrace the serene joys of heaven.
And he calls this Poetry.

But, if he appears to dedicate its rhythms
To hymns of praise,
As from a heart intoxicated with life,
Yet do tender hearts feel
That the flower of his joy
Springs from the root of deep suffering.

Die Gestirne / The Constellations

FRIEDRICH GOTTLIEB KLOPSTOCK

D 444 (1816)

Es tönet sein Lob Feld und Wald, Tal und
 Gebirg,
Das Gestad hallet, es donnert das Meer
 dumpfbrausend
Des Unendlichen Lob, siehe des
 Herrlichen,
Unerreichten von dem Danklied der
 Natur!

Field and forest, valley and mountain
 sound his praise,
The shore resounds, the sea thunders with
 a dull roar
The praise of the Infinite Being, the
 Glorious One
With whom nature's song of thanksgiving
 cannot compare.

Die Götter Griechenlands / The Gods of Greece

FRIEDRICH VON SCHILLER

D677 (1819)

Schöne Welt, wo bist du? Kehre wieder,
Holdes Blütenalter der Natur!
Ach, nur in dem Feenland der Lieder
Lebt noch deine fabelhafte Spur.
Ausgestorben trauert das Gefilde,
Keine Gottheit zeigt sich meinem Blick,
Ach, von jenem lebenwarmen Bilde
Blieb der Schatten nur zurück.

Fair world, where are you? Return again,
Sweet springtime of nature!
Alas, only in the magic land of song
Does your fabled memory live on.
The deserted fields mourn,
No god reveals himself to me;
Of that warm, living image
Only a shadow has remained.

Die Herbstnacht / Autumn Night

JOHANN GAUDENZ VON SALIS-SEEWIS

D 404 (1816)

Mit leisen Harfentönen
Sei, Wehmut, mir gegrüsst!
O Nymphe, die der Tränen
Geweihten Quell verschiesst!
Mich weht an deiner Schwelle
Ein linder Schauer an,
Und deines Zwielichts Helle
Glimmt auf des Schicksals Bahn.

To the soft strains of a harp
I greet you, Melancholy!
O nymph, you who lock
The hallowed source of tears.
On your threshold
I feel a gentle shudder,
And your dusky light
Glimmers on the path of destiny.

Du, so die Freude weinen,
Die Schwermut lächeln heisst,
Kannst Wonn' und Schmerz vereinen,
Dass Harm in Lust verfleusst;
Du hellst bewölkte Lüfte
Mit Abendsonnenschein,
Hängst Lampen in die Grüfte
Und krönst den Leichenstein.

You, who bid joy weep
And sorrow smile,
Can unite grief and happiness,
So that pain mingles with pleasure;
You brighten the clouded air
With evening sunlight;
You hang lamps in tombs,
And crown gravestones.

Die junge Nonne / The Young Nun

JACOB NICOLAUS CRAIGHER

D828 (1824–25)

Wie braust durch die Wipfel der heulende
   Sturm!
Es klirren die Balken, es zittert das Haus!
Es rollet der Donner, es leuchtet der Blitz,
Und finster die Nacht, wie das Grab!

How the raging storm roars through the
   treetops!
The rafters rattle, the house shudders!
The thunder rolls, the lightning flashes,
And the night is as dark as the grave.

Immerhin, immerhin, so tobt' es auch
   jüngst noch in mir!
Es brauste das Leben, wie jetzo der Sturm,
Es bebten die Glieder, wie jetzo das Haus,
Es flammte die Liebe, wie jetzo der Blitz,
Und finster die Brust, wie das Grab.

So be it, so be it, not long ago a storm still
   raged in me.
My life roared like the storm now,
My limbs trembled like the house now,
Love flashed like the lightning now,
And my heart was as dark as the grave.

Nun tobe, du wilder, gewalt'ger Sturm,
Im Herzen ist Friede, im Herzen ist Ruh,
Des Bräutigams harret die liebende Braut,
Gereinigt in prüfender Glut,
Der ewigen Liebe getraut.

Now rage, wild, mighty storm,
In my heart is peace, in my heart is calm,
The loving bride awaits the bridegroom,
Purified in the testing flames,
Betrothed to eternal love.

Ich harre, mein Heiland, mit sehnendem
   Blick!
Komm, himmlischer Bräutigam, hole die
   Braut,
Erlöse die Seele von irdischer Haft.
Horch, friedlich ertönet das Glöcklein vom
   Turm!
Es lockt mich das süsse Getön
Allmächtig zu ewigen Höh'n.
Alleluja!

I wait, my Saviour, with longing
   gaze!
Come, heavenly bridegroom, take your
   bride,
Free the soul from earthly bonds,
Listen, the bell sounds peacefully from the
   tower!
Its sweet pealing invites me
All-powerfully to eternal heights.
Alleluia!

Die Knabenzeit / Boyhood

LUDWIG HÖLTY

D 400 (1816)

Wie glücklich, wem das Knabenkleid Noch um die Schultern fliegt! Nie lästert er der bösen Zeit, Stets munter und vergnügt.	Happy he, from whose shoulders A boy's coat still hangs. He never curses the bad times, He is always cheerful and content.
Das hölzerne Husarenschwert Belustiget ihn jetzt, Der Kreisel und das Steckenpferd, Auf dem er herrisch sitzt.	The wooden hussar's sword Delights him now, The top and the hobby-horse, On which he sits proudly.
O Knabe, spiel und laufe nur, Den lieben langen Tag, Durch Garten und durch grüne Flur Den Schmetterlingen nach.	Play, child, and run about The whole day long Through garden and green meadow, Chasing butterflies.
Bald schwitzest du, nicht immer froh, Im engen Kämmerlein, Und lernst vom dicken Cicero Verschimmeltes Latein!	Soon you will be sweating, not always happily, In the cramped classroom, Learning fusty Latin From a fat tome of Cicero.

Die Laube / The Arbour

LUDWIG HEINRICH CHRISTOPH HÖLTY

D 214 (1815)

Nimmer werd ich, nimmer dein vergessen, Kühle grüne Dunkelheit, Wo mein liebes Mädchen oft gesessen, Und des Frühlings sich gefreut.	Never shall I forget you, Cool, green darkness, Where my beloved often sat And delighted in the spring.
Schauer wird durch meine Nerven beben, Werd ich deine Blüten sehn, Und ihr Bildnis mir entgegenschweben, Ihre Gottheit mich umwehn.	My nerves will quiver When I see your blossoms, See her image float towards me, And her divine radiance envelop me.
Tränenvoll, werd ich, beim Mondenlichte, In der Geisterstunde Graun, Dir entgegenzittern, und Gesichte Auf Gesichte werd ich schaun.	Tearfully, by moon- light, At the dread hour of the spirits, I shall walk hesitantly towards you, And behold spectre upon spectre.
Mich in manchen Göttertraum verirren, Bis Entzückung mich durchbebt, Und nach meinem süßen Täubchen girren, Dessen Abschied vor mir schwebt.	I shall lose myself in many a heavenly dream Until rapture thrills my being, I shall coo for my sweet dove Whose parting haunts me.
Wenn ich auf der Bahn der Tugend wanke, Weltvergnügen mich bestrickt; Dann durchglühe mich der Feu'rgedanke, Was in dir ich einst erblickt.	When I totter on the path of virtue, Lured by earthly pleasures, Then let the thought burn through me Of what I once beheld in you.

Und, als strömt' aus Gottes offnem
   Himmel
Tugendkraft auf mich herab,
Werd' ich fliehen, und vom Erdgewimmel
Fernen meinen Pilgerstab.

And when virtue streams down upon
   me
From God's open heaven,
I shall flee, and with my pilgrim's staff
Leave this earthly throng.

Die Liebe (Clärchen's Lied) / Love (Clärchen's Song)

JOHANN WOLFGANG VON GOETHE

D 210 (1815)
From the play Egmont

Freudvoll
Und leidvoll,
Gedankenvoll sein;
Langen
Und bangen
In schwebender Pein;
Himmelhoch jauchzend,
Zum Tode betrübt;
Glücklich allein
Ist die Seele, die liebt.

Joyful,
Sorrowful,
Thoughtful;
Yearning
And grieving
In lingering pain;
Touching the heavens in joy,
Despairing unto death;
Happy alone
Is the soul that loves.

Die Liebe / Love

GOTTLIEB VON LEON

D 522 (1817)

Wo weht der Liebe hoher Geist?
Er weht in Blum' und Baum,
Im weiten Erdenraum,
Er weht, wo sich die Knospen spalten
Und wo die Blümlein sich entfalten.

Where does love's noble spirit breathe?
It breathes in flower and tree,
In the wide world,
It breathes wherever the buds burst open
And the flowers unfold.

Wo weht der Liebe hoher Geist?
Er weht im Abendglanz,
Er weht im Sternenkranz,
Wo Bien' und Maienkäfer schwirren
Und zart die Turteltauben girren.

Where does love's noble spirit breathe?
It breathes in the glow of evening,
It breathes in the circle of stars;
Wherever bees and cockchafers hum,
And turtle doves coo tenderly.

Wo weht der Liebe hoher Geist?
Er weht bei Freud' und Schmerz
In aller Mütter Herz,
Er weht in jungen Nachtigallen,
Wenn lieblich ihre Lieder schallen.

Where does love's noble spirit breathe?
It breathes in joy and sorrow
In every mother's heart,
It breathes in young nightingales
When their sweet songs sound forth.

Wo weht der Liebe hoher Geist?
In Wasser, Feuer, Luft,
Und in des Morgens Duft,
Er weht, wo sich ein Leben reget,
Und wo sich nur ein Herz beweget.

Where does love's noble spirit breathe?
In water, fire and air,
And in the morning fragrance;
It breathes wherever life stirs
And wherever even a single heart beats.

Die Liebe hat gelogen / Love has Lied

AUGUST GRAF VON PLATEN

D751 (1822)

Die Liebe hat gelogen,	Love has lied,
Die Sorge lastet schwer,	Care weighs heavily upon me.
Betrogen, ach! betrogen	Alas, I am deceived, deceived
Hat alles mich umher!	By all around me!
Es fliessen heisse Tropfen	Hot tears flow
Die Wange stets herab,	Ceaselessly down my cheek.
Lass ab, mein Herz, zu klopfen,	Heart, beat no more,
Du armes Herz, lass ab!	Poor heart, beat no more!
Die Liebe hat gelogen,	Love has lied,
Die Sorge lastet schwer,	Care weighs heavily upon me.
Betrogen, ach! betrogen	Alas, I am deceived, deceived
Hat alles mich umher!	By all around me!

Die Liebende schreibt / Letter from a Girl in Love

JOHANN WOLFGANG VON GOETHE

D 673 (1819)

Ein Blick von deinen Augen in die meinen,	One glance from your eyes into mine,
Ein Kuß von deinem Mund auf meinem Munde,	One kiss from your lips upon mine;
Wer davon hat, wie ich, gewisse Kunde,	Can he who has certain knowledge of these, as I do,
Mag dem was anders wohl erfreulich scheinen?	Take pleasure in anything else?
Entfernt von dir, entfremdet von den Meinen,	Far from you, estranged from my loved ones,
Führ' ich stets die Gedanken in die Runde,	I let my thoughts rove constantly,
Und immer treffen sie auf jene Stunde,	And always they fix upon that one
Die einzige; da fang' ich an zu weinen.	And only hour; then I begin to weep.
Die Träne trocknet wieder unversehens:	Suddenly my tears are dried:
Er liebt ja, denk' ich, her in diese Stille,	He loves indeed, I reflect, here in this stillness;
O solltest du nicht in die Ferne reichen?	O, should you not reach out to me in the far distance?
Vernimm das Lispeln dieses Liebewehens;	Hear these whispered words of love;
Mein einzig Glück auf Erden ist dein Wille,	Your goodwill towards me is my sole happiness on earth;
Dein freundlicher zu mir; gib mir ein Zeichen!	Give me a sign!

Die Liebesgötter / The Gods of Love

JOHANN PETER UZ

D 446 (1816)

Cypris, meiner Phyllis gleich,
Sass von Grazien umgeben;
Denn ich sah ihr frohes Reich;
Mich berauschten Cyperns Reben.
Ein geweihter Myrthenwald,
Den geheime Schatten schwärzten,
War der Göttin Aufenthalt,
Wo die Liebesgötter scherzten.

Unter grüner Büsche Nacht,
Unter abgelegnen Sträuchen,
Wo so manche Nymphe lacht,
Sah ich sie am liebsten schleichen.
Viele flohn mit leichtem Fuss
Allen Zwang beträter Ketten,
Flatterten von Kuss zu Kuss
Und von Blonden zu Brünetten.

Cypris, like my Phyllis,
Sat surrounded by Graces;
For I saw her happy realm,
Cypris' grapes made me euphoric.
A consecrated myrtle grove,
Darkened by mysterious shadows,
Was the goddess's abode;
Here the gods of love frolicked.

Under cover of the green bushes
In the far-off thicket,
Where many a nymph laughed,
I saw them steal most gladly.
Many shunned with light step
All restraints of tear-soaked fetters,
Flitted from kiss to kiss
And from blondes to brunettes.

Die Macht der Liebe / The Power of Love

JOHANN VON KALCHBERG

D 308 (1815)

Überall wohin mein Auge blicket,
Herrschet Liebe, find' ich ihre Spur;
Jedem Strauch und Blümchen auf der Flur
Hat sie tief ihr Siegel eingedrücket.

Sie erfüllt, durchglüht, verjüngt und
  schmücket
Alles Lebende in der Natur:
Erd' und Himmel, jede Kreatur,
Leben nur durch sie, von ihr
  beglücket.

Wherever my eyes turn
Love reigns; everywhere I find its trace.
On every bush and flower in the meadows
It has deeply imprinted its seal.

It pervades, warms, rejuvenates and
  adorns
All that lives in nature.
Heaven, earth and all creatures
Live and find happiness through love
  alone.

Die Mainacht / May Night

LUDWIG HEINRICH CHRISTOPH HÖLTY

D 194 (1815)

Wann der silberne Mond durch die
  Gesträuche blinkt,
Und sein schlummerndes Licht über den
  Rasen streut,
Und die Nachtigall flötet,
Wandl' ich traurig von Busch zu Busch.

When the silver moon shines through the
  shrubbery,
And casts its drowsy light over the
  grass;
When the nightingale warbles,
I wander mournfully from bush to bush.

Selig preis ich dich dann, flötende Nachtigall,	Then I deem you blessed, fluting nightingale,
Weil dein Weibchen mit dir wohnet in einem Nest,	Because your sweetheart dwells with you in a single nest,
Ihrem singenden Gatten	And gives a thousand loving kisses
Tausend trauliche Küsse gibt.	To her warbling mate.
Überhüllet von Laub, girret ein Taubenpaar	Concealed in foliage, a pair of doves
Sein Entzücken mir vor; aber ich wende mich,	Coo to me in delight; but I turn away
Suche dunklere Schatten,	In search of deeper shadows,
Und die einsame Träne rinnt.	And shed a solitary tear.
Wann, o lächelndes Bild, welches wie Morgenrot	O smiling image, that shines like the dawn,
Durch die Seele mir strahlt, find' ich auf Erden dich?	Through my soul, when shall I find you on this earth?
Und die einsame Träne	And the solitary tear, glistening,
Bebt mir heißer die Wang' herab.	Flows more warmly down my cheek.

Die Männer sind méchant / Men are Faithless

JOHANN GABRIEL SEIDL

D 866 no. 3 (1828?)

Du sagtest mir es, Mutter:	You told me, mother:
Er ist ein Springinsfeld!	He's a young rogue!
Ich würd' es dir nicht glauben,	I would not believe you
Bis ich mich krank gequält!	Until I had tormented myself sick.
Ja, ja, nun ist er's wirklich;	Yes, I now know he really is;
Ich hatt' ihn nur verkannt!	I had simply misjudged him.
Du sagtest mir's, o Mutter:	You told me, mother:
»Die Männer sind méchant!«	'Men are faithless!'
Vor'm Dorf im Busch, als gestern	Yesterday, as dusk fell silently,
Die stille Dämm'rung sank,	In the copse outside the village,
Da rauscht' es: »Guten Abend!«	I heard a whispered 'Good evening!'
Da rauscht' es: »Schönen Dank!«	And then a whispered 'Many thanks!'
Ich schlich hinzu, ich horchte;	I crept up and listened;
Ich stand wie festgebannt:	I stood as if transfixed:
Er war's mit einer Andern —	It was he, with someone else —
»Die Männer sind méchant!«	'Men are faithless!'
O Mutter, welche Qualen!	O mother, what torture!
Es muß heraus, es muß! —	I must be out with it, I must!
Es blieb nicht bloß bei'm Rauschen,	It didn't just stop at whispering,
Es blieb nicht bloß bei'm Gruß!	It didn't just stop at greetings!
Vom Gruße kam's zum Kusse,	It went from greetings to kisses,
Vom Kuß zum Druck der Hand,	From kisses to holding hands,
Vom Druck, ach liebe Mutter! —	From holding hands . . . ah, dear mother,
»Die Männer sind méchant!«	'Men are faithless!'

Die Mondnacht / The Moonlit Night

LUDWIG KOSEGARTEN

D 238 (1815)

Siehe, wie die Mondenstrahlen
Busch und Flur in Silber malen!
Wie das Bächlein rollt und flimmt!
Strahlen regnen, Funken schmettern
Von den sanftgeregten Blättern,·
Und die Tauflur glänzt und
glimmt.
Glänzend erdämmern der Berge Gipfel,
Glänzend der Pappeln wogende Wipfel.

Durch die glanzumrauschten Räume
Flüstern Stimmen, gaukeln Träume,
Sprechen mir vertraulich zu.
Seligkeit, die mich gemahnet,
Höchste Lust, die süß mich
schwanet,
Sprich, wo blühst, wo zeitigst
du?
Sprenge die Brust nicht, mächtiges
Sehnen!
Löschet die Wehmut, labende Tränen!

Wie, ach, wie der Qual
genesen?
Wo, ach, wo ein liebend Wesen,
Das die süßen Qualen stillt?
Eins ins andre gar versunken,
Gar verloren, gar ertrunken,
Bis sich jede Öde füllt . . .
Solches, ach, wähnt' ich, kühlte das
Sehnen,
Löschte die Wehmut mit köstlichen
Tränen.

Eine weiß ich, ach, nur Eine,
Dich nur weiß ich, dich o Reine,
Die des Herzens Wehmut meint.
Dich umringend, von dir umrungen,
Dich umschlingend, von dir
umschlungen,
Gar in Eins mit dir geeint . . .
Schon', ach schone des Wonnever-
sunk'nen!
Himmel und Erde verschwinden dem
Trunk'nen.

See how the moonbeams
Paint bush and meadow silver,
And how the brook ripples and sparkles.
Rays of light pour down, sparks rain
From the gently stirring leaves,
And the dewy countryside glistens and
shimmers.
The darkening mountain peaks glimmer,
The swaying tops of the poplars gleam.

Through the luminous spaces,
Voices whisper, dreams hover,
Speaking confidingly to me.
Remembered bliss,
Great joy that fills me with sweet
intimations,
Tell me, where do you bloom, where do
you bear fruit?
Mighty longing, do not shatter my
heart!
Soothing tears, ease my melancholy!

How, how shall I recover from my
torment?
Where, o where is there a loving soul
To calm my sweet anguish?
One absorbed in the other,
Quite lost, quite enraptured,
Until every wasteland is filled . . .
I sense that such a soul would cool my
longing,
And ease my sorrow with exquisite
tears.

I know one, ah, only one;
I know only you, purest one,
Who understands the heart's sorrow.
Enfolding you, enfolded by you,
Embracing you, embraced by
you,
Joined in unity with you . . .
Spare, oh spare me, sunk in
bliss!
For me, in my rapture, heaven and earth
vanish.

Die Mutter Erde / Mother Earth

FRIEDRICH LEOPOLD, GRAF ZU STOLBERG-STOLBERG

D 788 (1823)

Des Lebens Tag ist schwer und schwül,
Des Todes Atem leicht und kühl,
Er wehet freundlich uns hinab
Wie welkes Laub ins stille Grab.

Life's day is heavy and sultry,
The breath of death is light and cool;
Fondly it wafts us down,
Like withered leaves, into the silent grave.

Es scheint der Mond, es fällt der Tau
Auf's Grab wie auf die Blumenau;
Auch fällt der Freunde Trän hinein
Erhellt von sanfter Hoffnung Schein.

Uns sammelt alle, klein und
    gross,
Die Mutter Erd' in ihren Schoss;
O sähn wir ihr ins Angesicht,
Wir scheuten ihren Busen nicht!

The moon shines, the dew falls
On the grave as on the flowery meadow;
The tears of friends also fall,
Lit by the gleam of gentle hope.

Mother earth gathers us all, great and
    small,
In her lap;
If we would only look upon her face
We should not fear her bosom.

Die Nacht / *The Night*

JAMES MACPHERSON (OSSIAN), translated by EDMUND VON HAROLD

D 534 (1817)

Erster Barde
Die Nacht ist dumpfig und finster. An den Hügeln ruhn die Wolken. Kein Stern mit grünzitterndem Strahl; kein Mond schaut durch die Luft. Im Walde hör ich den Hauch; aber ich hör ihn weit in der Ferne. Der Strom des Tals erbraust; aber sein Brausen ist stürmisch und trüb. Vom Baum beim Grabe der Toten, hört man die lang, die krächzende Eul. An der Ebne erblick ich eine dämmernde Bildung! es ist ein Geist! er schwindet, er flieht. Durch diesen Weg wird eine Leiche getragen: ihren Pfad bezeichnet das Luftbild. Die fernere Dogge heult von der Hütte des Hügels. Der Hirsch liegt im Moose des Bergs: neben ihm ruht die Hündin. In seinem astigten Geweihe hört sie den Wind; fährt auf, und legt sich zur Ruhe wieder nieder.
Düster und keuchend, zitternd und traurig, verlor der Wandrer den Weg. Er irrt durch Gebüsche, durch Dornen längs der sprudelnden Quelle. Er fürchtet die Klippe und den Sumpf. Er fürchtet den Geist der Nacht. Der alte Baum ächzt zu dem Windstoß; der fallende Ast erschallt. Die verwelkte zusammen verworrene Klette, treibt der Wind über das Gras. Es ist der leichte Tritt eines Geists! er bebt in der Mitte der Nacht.
Die Nacht ist düster, dunkel, und heulend; wolkigt, stürmisch und schwanger mit Geistern! Die Toten streifen umher! Empfangt mich von der Nacht, meine Freunde.

Der Gebieter
Laß Wolken an Hügeln ruhn; Geister fliegen und Wandrer beben. Laß die Winde der Wälder sich heben, brausende Stürme herabsteigen. Ströme brüllen, Fenster klirren, grünbeflügelte Dämpfe fliegen; den

First bard
Night is dull and dark. The clouds rest on the hills. No star with green trembling beam; no moon looks from the sky. I hear the blast in the wood; but I hear it distant far. The stream of the valley murmurs; but its murmur is sullen and sad. From the tree at the grave of the dead the long-howling owl is heard. I see a dim form on the plain! It is a ghost! it fades, it flies. Some funeral shall pass this way: the meteor marks the path.
The distant dog is howling from the hut of the hill. The stag lies on the mountain moss: the hind is at his side. She hears the wind in his branchy horns. She starts, but lies again.
Dark, panting, trembling, sad, the traveller has lost his way. Through shrubs, through thorns, he goes, along the gurgling rill. He fears the rock and the fen. He fears the ghost of night. The old tree groans to the blast; the falling branch resounds. The wind drives the withered burs, clung together, along the grass. It is the light tread of a ghost! He trembles amidst the night.
Dark, dusty, howling is night, cloudy, windy, and full of ghosts! The dead are abroad! my friends, receive me from the night.

The chief
Let clouds rest on the hills: spirits fly, and travellers fear. Let the winds of the woods arise, the sounding storms descend. Roar streams and windows flap, and green-winged meteors fly! Rise the pale moon

bleichen Mond sich hinter seinen Hügeln erheben, oder sein Haupt in Wolken einhüllen; die Nacht gilt mir gleich; die Luft sei blau, stürmisch, oder dunkel. Die Nacht flieht vorm Strahl, wenn er am Hügel sich giest. Der junge Tag kehrt von seinen Wolken, aber wir kehren nimmer zurück.

Wo sind uns're Führer der Vorwelt; wo sind uns're weit berühmten. Gebieter? Schweigend sind die Felder ihrer Schlachten. Kaum sind ihre moosigten Gräber noch übrig. Man wird auch unser vergessen. Dies erhabene Gebäu wird zerfallen. Unsere Söhne werden die Trümmer im Grase nicht erblicken. Sie werden die Greisen befragen, »Wo standen die Mauern unsrer Väter?«

Ertönet das Lied und schlaget die Harfen; sendet die fröhlichen Muscheln herum. Stellt hundert Kerzen in die Höhe. Jünglinge, Mädchen beginnet den Tanz. Nah sei ein grau die lockiger Barde, mir Taten der Vorwelt zu singen; von Königen berühmt in unserm Land, von Gebietern, die wir nicht mehr sehn. Laß die Nacht also vergehen, bis der Morgen in unsern Hallen erscheine. Dann seien nicht ferne, der Bogen, die Doggen, die Jünglinge der Jagd. Wir werden die Hügel mit dem Morgen besteigen, und die Hirsche erwecken.

from behind her hills, or enclose her head in clouds! night is alike to me, blue, stormy, or gloomy the sky. Night flies before the beam, when it is poured on the hill. The young day returns from his clouds, but we return no more.

Where are our chiefs of old? Where our kings of mighty name? The fields of their battles are silent. Scarce their mossy tombs remain. We shall also be forgot. This lofty house shall fall. Our sons shall not behold the ruins in grass. They shall ask of the aged, 'where stood the walls of our fathers?'

Raise the song, and strike the harp; send round the shells of joy. Suspend a hundred tapers on high. Youth and maids begin the dance. Let some grey bard be near me to tell the deeds of other times; of kings renowned in our land, of chiefs we behold no more. Thus let the night pass until morning shall appear in our halls. Then let the bow be at hand, the dogs, the youths of the chase. We shall ascend the hill with day, and awake the deer.

Die Nacht / The Night

JOHANN PETER UZ

D 358 (1816?)

Du verstörst uns nicht, o Nacht!
Sieh! wir trinken im Gebüsche;
Und ein kühler Wind erwacht,
Daß er unsern Wein erfrische.

You do not disturb us, O night.
See, we are drinking in the grove
And a refreshing breeze arises
To cool our wine.

Mutter holder Dunkelheit,
Nacht! Vertraute süßer Sorgen,
Die betrogner Wachsamkeit
Viele Küsse schon verborgen!

Mother of gentle darkness,
Night, confidant of our sweet cares,
You have already concealed many a kiss
From cheated vigilance.

Dir allein sei mitbewußt,
Welch Vergnügen mich berausche,
Wenn ich an geliebter Brust
Unter Tau und Blumen lausche!

You alone shall know
What rapture overcomes me
When, on my beloved's breast,
I listen amid the dew and the flowers.

Murmelt ihr, wenn alles ruht,
Murmelt, sanftbewegte Bäume,
Bei dem Sprudeln heisser Flut,
Mich in wollustvolle Träume!

Murmur to her, gently swaying trees,
Murmur when all is at rest;
As the hot flood foams
Murmur me into dreams of ecstasy.

Die Nonne / The Nun

LUDWIG HEINRICH CHRISTOPH HÖLTY

First version: D 208 (1815)
Second version: D 212 (1815)

Es liebt' in Welschland irgendwo
Ein schöner junger Ritter
Ein Mädchen, das der Welt enfloh,
Troz Klostertor und
    Gitter;
Sprach viel von seiner Liebespein,
Und schwur, auf seinen Knieen,
Sie aus dem Kerker zu befreien,
Und stets für sie zu glühen.

»Bei diesem Muttergottesbild,
Bei diesem Jesuskinde,
Das ihre Mutterarme füllt,
Schwör' ich's dir, o Belinde!
Dir ist mein ganzes Herz geweiht,
So lang ich Odem habe,
Bei meiner Seelen Seligkeit!
Dich lieb' ich bis zum Grabe.«

Was glaubt ein armes Mädchen nicht,
Zumal in einer Zelle?
Ach! sie vergaß der Nonnenpflicht,
Des Himmels und der Hölle.
Die, von den Engeln angeschaut,
Sich ihrem Jesu weihte,
Die reine, schöne Gottesbraut.
Ward eines Frevlers Beute.

Drauf wurde, wie die Männer sind,
Sein Herz von Stund' an lauer,
Er überließ das arme Kind
Auf ewig ihrer Trauer.
Vergaß der alten Zärtlichkeit,
Und aller seiner Eide,
Und floh, im bunten
    Galakleid,
Nach neuer Augenweide.

Begann mit andern Weibern Reihn,
Im kerzenhellen Saale,
Gab andern Weibern Schmeichelein,
Beim lauten Traubenmahle,
Und rühmte sich des Minneglücks
Bei seiner schönen Nonne,
Und jedes Kusses, jedes Blicks,
Und jeder andern Wonne.

Die Nonne, voll von welscher Wut,
Entglüht' in ihrem Mute,
Und sann auf nichts als Dolch und
    Blut,
Und träumte nur von Blute.
Sie dingte plötzlich eine
    Schaar
Von wilden Meuchelmördern,

Once upon a time, somewhere in Italy,
A fair young knight loved
A maiden who shunned this world,
Loved her despite convent gate and iron
    bars;
He spoke much of his anguish in love
And vowed, upon his knees,
To free her from her prison,
And to love her ardently for ever.

'By this image of the Virgin,
By this child Jesus
That fills her maternal arms,
I swear to you, Belinda:
My whole heart is consecrated to you
As long as I draw breath;
By my soul's salvation
I will love you unto the grave.'

What will a poor maiden not believe,
Especially in a convent cell?
Alas, she forgot her duty as a nun,
Forgot heaven and hell.
She who, watched by the angels,
Had dedicated herself to Jesus,
The fair, spotless bride of God,
Fell prey to a sinner.

From this moment, as is the way of men,
His heart grew more tepid;
He abandoned the poor child
Forever to her sorrow.
Forgetting his former tenderness
And all his vows,
He went off, in resplendent ceremonial
    dress,
To feast his eyes on new delights.

He danced with other women
In the candlelit ballroom,
Complimented other women
At the noisy, drunken banquet,
And boasted to his fair nun
Of his luck in love,
Boasted of every kiss, every glance,
And every other delight.

The nun, filled with Italian fury,
Blazed within her heart,
And thought of nothing but dagger and
    blood,
And dreamed only of blood.
Then, with sudden resolve, she hired a
    band
Of rough assassins,

165

Den Mann, der treulos worden war,	To dispatch to the realm of the dead
Ins Totenreich zu fördern.	The man who had turned faithless.

Die bohren manches Mörderschwert	They plunged many a murderous sword
In seine schwarze Seele.	Into his black soul.
Sein schwarzer, falscher Geist entfährt,	His black, treacherous spirit escaped,
Wie Schwefeldampf der Höhle.	Like a sulphurous mist from hell.
Er wimmert durch die Luft, wo sein	It moaned through the air
Ein Krallenteufel harret.	To a devil's awaiting claws.
Drauf ward sein blutendes Gebein	Then his bleeding corpse
In eine Gruft verscharret.	Was buried in a vault.

Die Nonne flog, wie Nacht begann,	As night fell the nun fled
Zur kleinen Dorfkapelle,	To the little village chapel,
Und riß den wunden Rittersmann	And seized the dead knight
Aus seiner Ruhestelle.	From his resting place.
Riß ihm das Bubenherz heraus,	She tore out his wicked heart,
Und warf's, den Zorn zu büßen,	And, to vent her fury, hurled it,
Daß dumpf erscholl das Gotteshaus,	So that the house of God resounded with a muffled thud,
Und trat es mit den Füßen.	And trampled it under foot.

Ihr Geist soll, wie die Sagen gehn,	As legend has it, her spirit
In dieser Kirche weilen,	Lingers in this church,
Und, bis im Dorf die Hähne krähn,	Now whimpering, now wailing
Bald wimmern, und bald heulen.	Until the cocks crow in the village.
Sobald der Hammer zwölfe schlägt,	As soon as the hammer strikes twelve
Rauscht sie, an Grabsteinwänden,	She rises up from a vault,
Aus einer Gruft empor, und trägt	Past tombstones, bearing
Ein blutend Herz in Händen.	In her hands a bleeding heart.

Die tiefen, hohlen Augen sprühn	Her sunken, hollow eyes flash
Ein düsterrotes Feuer,	With sombre red fire,
Und glühn, wie Schwefelflammen glühn,	Glowing like sulphurous flames
Durch ihren weißen Schleier.	Through her white veil.
Sie gafft auf das zerrißne Herz,	She stares at the mutilated heart
Mit wilder Rachgebärde,	With a gesture of wild revenge,
Und hebt es dreimal himmelwärts,	Raises it three times towards heaven,
Und wirft es auf die Erde;	And hurls it to the ground.

Und rollt die Augen voller Wut,	Filled with rage, she rolls her eyes
Die eine Hölle blicken,	In which hell blazes,
Und schüttelt aus dem Schleier Blut,	Shakes blood from her veil,
Und stampft das Herz in Stücken.	And tramples the heart into pieces.
Ein bleicher Totenflimmer macht	Meanwhile a pallid, deathly gleam
Indeß die Fenster helle.	Lights the windows.
Der Wächter, der das Dorf bewacht,	The watchman who guards the village
Sah's oft in der Kapelle.	Has often seen her in the chapel.

Die Perle / *The Pearl*

JOHANN GEORG JACOBI

D 466 (1816)

Es ging ein Mann zur Frühlingszeit	A man wandered in the springtime
Durch Busch und Felder weit und breit	Through bush and field, far and wide,
Um Birke, Buch' und Erle;	Past birch, beech and alder;
Der Bäume Grün im Maienlicht,	He did not see the green trees in the May sunlight,

Die Blumen drunter sah er nicht;
Er suchte seine Perle.

Der arme Pilger! So wie er,
Geh' ich zur Frühlingszeit umher
Um Birke, Buch' und Erle;
Des Maien Wunder seh' ich nicht;
Was aber, ach! was mir gebricht,
Ist mehr als eine Perle.

Was mir gebricht, was ich verlor,
Was ich zum höchsten Gut
  erkor,
Ist Lieb' in treuem Herzen.
Vergebens wall' ich auf und ab;
Doch find' ich einst ein kühles Grab,
Das endet alle Schmerzen.

Nor the flowers below;
He was looking for his pearl.

Poor pilgrim! Like him
I wander at springtime
Past birch, beech and alder;
I do not see May's splendour;
But, alas, what I lack
Is more than a pearl.

What I lack, what I have lost,
What I counted as my most treasured
  possession,
Is love from a faithful heart.
In vain I roam hither and thither;
But one day I shall find a cool grave
To end all my suffering.

Die Rose / The Rose

FRIEDRICH VON SCHLEGEL

D 745 (1820?)

Es lockte schöne Wärme,
Mich an das Licht zu wagen,
Da brannten wilde Gluten;
Das muß ich ewig klagen.
Ich konnte lange blühen
In milden, heitern Tagen;
Nun muß ich frühe welken,
Dem Leben schon entsagen.

Es kam die Morgenröte,
Da ließ ich alles Zagen
Und öffnete die Knospe,
Wo alle Reize lagen.
Ich konnte freundlich duften
Und meine Krone tragen,
Da ward zu heiß die Sonne,
Die muß ich drum verklagen.

Was soll der milde Abend?
Muß ich nun traurig fragen.
Er kann mich nicht mehr retten,
Die Schmerzen nicht verjagen.
Die Röte ist verblichen,
Bald wird mich Kälte nagen.
Mein kurzes junges Leben
Wollt' ich noch sterbend sagen.

Lovely warmth tempted me
To venture into the light.
There fires burned furiously;
I must for ever bemoan that.
I could have bloomed for long
In mild, bright days.
Now I must wither early,
Renounce life prematurely.

The red dawn came,
I abandoned all timidity
And opened the bud
In which lay all my charms.
I could have spread sweet fragrance
And worn my crown . . .
Then the sun grew too hot —
Of this I must accuse it.

Of what avail is the mild evening?
I must now ask sadly.
It can no longer save me,
Or banish my sorrows.
My red colouring is faded,
Soon cold will gnaw me.
As I die I wished to tell once more
Of my brief young life.

Die Schatten / The Shades

FRIEDRICH VON MATTHISSON

D 50 (1813)

Freunde, deren Grüfte sich schon
  bemoosten!
Wann der Vollmond über dem Walde
  dämmert,

Friends, whose graves are already
  mossy!
When the full moon rises over the
  forest,

Schweben eure Schatten empor
Vom stillen Ufer des Lethe.

Seid mir, Unvergessliche, froh gesegnet!
Du vor allen, welcher im Buch der
Menschheit
Mir der Hieroglyphen so viel gedeutet,
Redlicher Bonnet!

Längst verschlürft im Strudel der
Brandung
Wäre wohl mein Fahrzeug,
Oder am Riff zerschmettert, hättet ihr
nicht,
Genien gleich, im Sturme schirmend
gewaltet!

Wiederseh'n, Wiederseh'n der Liebenden!
Wo der Heimat goldne Sterne
leuchten,
O du der armen Psyche, die gebunden
Im Grabtal schmachtet, himmlische
Sehnsucht!

Your shades float up
From the silent banks of Lethe.

With joy I bless you, unforgotten creatures,
And you above all, who in the book of
life
Explained so many secrets to me,
Honest Bonnet.

Long ago my vessel would have
sunk
In the swirling surf,
Or been wrecked on the reef, had you
not,
Like guardian spirits, protected me in the
storm.

To see again those we love,
Where the golden stars of the homeland
shine!
O celestial longing of the poor soul
Which languishes, captive, in the
grave.

Die schöne Müllerin / *The Fair Maid of the Mill*

WILHELM MÜLLER

D795 (1823)

1 *Das Wandern*
Das Wandern ist des Müllers Lust,
Das Wandern!
Das muß ein schlechter Müller sein,
Dem niemals fiel das Wandern ein,
Das Wandern.

Vom Wasser haben wir's gelernt,
Vom Wasser!
Das hat nicht Rast bei Tag und Nacht,
Ist stets auf Wanderschaft bedacht,
Das Wasser.

Das sehn wir auch den Rädern ab,
Den Rädern!
Die gar nicht gerne stille stehn,
Die sich mein Tag nicht müde drehn,
Die Räder.

Die Steine selbst, so schwer sie sind,
Die Steine!
Sie tanzen mit den muntern Reihn
Und wollen gar noch schneller sein,
Die Steine.

O Wandern, Wandern, meine Lust,
O Wandern!
Herr Meister und Frau Meisterin,
Laßt mich in Frieden weiter ziehn
Und wandern.

1 *Wandering*
To wander is the miller's delight,
To wander!
A poor miller he must be
Who never thought of wandering,
Of wandering.

We have learnt it from the water,
From the water!
It never rests, by day or night,
But is always intent on wandering,
The water.

We can see it in the wheels too,
The wheels!
They never care to stand still
But turn tirelessly the whole day long,
The wheels.

The stones themselves, heavy as they are,
The stones!
They join in the merry dance
And seek to move still faster,
The stones.

O wandering, my delight,
O wandering!
Master and mistress,
Let me go my way in peace,
And wander.

2 Wohin?

Ich hört' ein Bächlein rauschen
Wohl aus dem Felsenquell,
Hinab zum Tale rauschen
So frisch und wunderhell.

Ich weiß nicht, wie mir wurde,
Nicht, wer den Rat mir gab,
Ich mußte auch hinunter
Mit meinem Wanderstab.

Hinunter und immer weiter
Und immer dem Bache nach,
Und immer heller rauschte,
Und immer heller der Bach.

Ist das denn meine Straße?
O Bächlein, sprich, wohin?
Du hast mit deinem Rauschen
Mir ganz berauscht den Sinn.

Was sag' ich denn vom Rauschen?
Das kann kein Rauschen sein:
Es singen wohl die Nixen
Tief unten ihren Reihn.

Laß singen, Gesell, laß
    rauschen,
Und wandre fröhlich nach!
Es gehn ja Mühlenräder
In jedem klaren Bach.

3 Halt!

Eine Mühle seh' ich blinken
Aus den Erlen heraus,
Durch Rauschen und Singen
Bricht Rädergebraus.

Ei willkommen, ei willkommen,
Süßer Mühlengesang!
Und das Haus, wie so traulich!
Und die Fenster, wie blank!

Und die Sonne, wie helle
Vom Himmel sie scheint!
Ei, Bächlein, liebes Bächlein,
War es also gemeint?

4 Dankgesang an den Bach

War es also gemeint,
Mein rauschender Freund,
Dein Singen, dein Klingen,
War es also gemeint?
»Zur Müllerin hin!«
So lautet der Sinn.
Gelt, hab' ich's verstanden?
»Zur Müllerin hin!«

Hat sie dich geschickt?
Oder hast mich berückt?
Das möcht' ich noch wissen,
Ob sie dich geschickt.

2 Where to?

I heard a little brook babbling
From its rocky source,
Babbling down to the valley,
So bright, so wondrously clear.

I know not what came over me,
Nor who prompted me;
But I too had to go down
With my wanderer's staff.

Down and ever onwards,
Always following the brook,
As it babbled ever brighter
And ever clearer.

Is this, then, my path?
O brook, say where it leads.
With your babbling
You have quite befuddled my mind.

Why do I speak of babbling?
That is no babbling,
It is the water nymphs singing
As they dance their round far below.

Let them sing, my friend, let the brook
    babble,
And follow it cheerfully.
For mill-wheels turn
In every clear brook.

3 Halt!

I see a mill gleaming
Amid the alders;
The roar of mill-wheels
Cuts through the babbling and singing.

Welcome, welcome,
Sweet song of the mill!
How inviting the house looks,
How sparkling its windows!

And how brightly the sun
Shines from the sky.
Now, dear little brook,
Is this what you meant?

4 Thanksgiving to the Brook

Is this what you meant,
My babbling friend?
Your singing, your murmuring,
Is this what you meant?
'To the maid of the mill!'
This is your meaning;
Have I understood you?
'To the maid of the mill!'

Did she send you,
Or have you entranced me?
I should like to know this, too:
Did she send you?

Nun wie's auch mag sein,
Ich gebe mich drein:
Was ich such', hab' ich funden,
Wie's immer mag sein.

Nach Arbeit ich frug,
Nun hab' ich genug,
Für die Hände, für's Herze
Vollauf genug!

5 *Am Feierabend*
Hätt' ich tausend
Arme zu rühren!
Könnt' ich brausend
Die Räder führen!
Könnt' ich wehen
Durch alle Haine!
Könnt' ich drehen
Alle Steine!
Daß die schöne Müllerin
Merkte meinen treuen Sinn!

Ach, wie ist mein Arm so schwach!
Was ich hebe, was ich trage,
Was ich schneide, was ich schlage,
Jeder Knappe tut mir's nach.
Und da sitz' ich in der großen Runde,
In der stillen kühlen Feierstunde,
Und der Meister spricht zu Allen:
»Euer Werk hat mir gefallen;«
Und das liebe Mädchen sagt
Allen eine gute Nacht.

6 *Der Neugierige*
Ich frage keine Blume,
Ich frage keinen Stern,
Sie können mir alle nicht sagen,
Was ich erführ' so gern.

Ich bin ja auch kein Gärtner,
Die Sterne stehn zu hoch;
Mein Bächlein will ich fragen,
Ob mich mein Herz belog.

O Bächlein meiner Liebe,
Wie bist du heut' so stumm!
Will ja nur Eines wissen,
Ein Wörtchen um und um.

»Ja«, heißt das eine Wörtchen,
Das andre heißet »Nein«,
Die beiden Wörtchen schließen
Die ganze Welt mir ein.

O Bächlein meiner Liebe,
Was bist du wunderlich!
Will's ja nicht weiter sagen,
Sag', Bächlein, liebt sie mich?

7 *Ungeduld*
Ich schnitt' es gern in alle Rinden ein,

However it may be,
I yield to my fate:
What I sought, I have found,
However it may be.

I asked for work,
Now I have enough
For hands and heart;
Enough, and more besides.

5 *After Work*
If only I had a thousand
Arms to wield!
If only I could drive
The rushing wheels!
If only I could blow like the wind
Through every wood,
And turn
Every millstone,
So that the fair maid of the mill
Would see my true love.

Ah, how weak my arm is!
What I lift and carry,
What I cut and hammer —
Any apprentice could do the same.
And there I sit with them, in a circle,
In the quiet, cool hour after work,
And the master says to us all:
'I am pleased with your work.'
And the sweet maid bids us all
Goodnight.

6 *The Inquisitive One*
I ask no flower,
I ask no star;
None of them can tell me
What I would so dearly like to hear.

For I am no gardener,
And the stars are too high;
I will ask my little brook
If my heart has lied to me.

O brook of my love,
How silent you are today!
I wish to know just one thing,
One small word, over and over again.

One word is 'yes';
The other is 'no';
These two words contain for me
The whole world.

O brook of my love,
How strange you are.
I will tell no one else:
Say, brook, does she love me?

7 *Impatience*
I should like to carve it in the bark of every tree,

Ich grüb' es gern in jeden Kieselstein,
Ich möcht' es sä'n auf jedes frische Beet
Mit Kressensamen, der es schnell
    verrät,
Auf jeden weißen Zettel möcht' ich's
    schreiben:
Dein ist mein Herz, und soll es ewig
    bleiben.

Ich möcht' mir ziehen einen jungen Star,
Bis daß er spräch' die Worte rein und klar,
Bis er sie spräch' mit meines Mundes
    Klang,
Mit meines Herzens vollem, heißem
    Drang;
Dann säng' er hell durch ihre
    Fensterscheiben:
Dein ist mein Herz, und soll es ewig
    bleiben.

Den Morgenwinden möcht' ich's hauchen
    ein,
Ich möcht' es säuseln durch den regen
    Hain;
O, leuchtet' es aus jedem Blumenstern!
Trüg' es der Duft zu ihr von nah und
    fern!
Ihr Wogen, könnt ihr nichts als Räder
    treiben?
Dein ist mein Herz, und soll es ewig
    bleiben.

Ich meint', es müßt' in meinen Augen
    stehn,
Auf meinen Wangen müßt' man's brennen
    sehn,
Zu lesen wär's auf meinem stummen
    Mund,
Ein jeder Atemzug gäb's laut ihr
    kund;
Und sie merkt nichts von all' dem bangen
    Treiben:
Dein ist mein Herz, und soll es ewig
    bleiben!

8 *Morgengruß*
Guten Morgen, schöne Müllerin!
Wo steckst du gleich das Köpfchen hin,
Als wär' dir was geschehen?
Verdrießt dich denn mein Gruß so
    schwer?
Verstört dich denn mein Blick so sehr?
So muß ich wieder gehen.

O laß mich nur von ferne stehn,
Nach deinem lieben Fenster sehn,
Von ferne, ganz von ferne!
Du blondes Köpfchen, komm hervor!
Hervor aus eurem runden Tor,
Ihr blauen Morgensterne!

I should like to inscribe it on every pebble,
Sow it in every fresh plot
With cress seed that would quickly reveal
    it;
I should like to write it on every scrap of
    white paper:
My heart is yours, and shall ever remain
    so.

I should like to train a young starling
Until it spoke the words, pure and clear,
Until it spoke with the sound of my
    voice,
With my heart's full, ardent
    yearning:
Then it would sing brightly at her
    window:
My heart is yours, and shall ever remain
    so.

I should like to breathe it to the morning
    winds,
And whisper it through the rustling
    grove;
If only it shone from every flower,
If only fragrant scents could bear it to her
    from near and far.
Waves, can you drive only mill-
    wheels?
My heart is yours, and shall ever remain
    so.

I should have thought it would show in my
    eyes,
Could be seen burning on my
    cheeks,
Could be read on my silent
    lips;
I should have thought my every breath
    would proclaim it to her;
But she notices none of these anxious
    signs:
My heart is yours, and shall ever remain
    so.

8 *Morning Greeting*
Good morning, fair maid of the mill!
Why do you quickly turn your head away
As if something was wrong?
Does my greeting annoy you so
    deeply,
Does my glance upset you so much?
If so, I must go away again.

O, just let me stand far off
And gaze at your beloved window,
From the far distance!
Little blonde head, come out!
Come forth from your round gates,
Blue morning stars.

Ihr schlummertrunknen Äugelein,
Ihr taubetrübten Blümelein,
Was scheuet ihr die Sonne?
Hat es die Nacht so gut gemeint,
Daß ihr euch schließt und bückt und weint
Nach ihrer stillen Wonne?

Nun schüttelt ab der Träume Flor,
Und hebt euch frisch und frei empor
In Gottes hellen Morgen!
Die Lerche wirbelt in der Luft,
Und aus dem tiefen Herzen ruft
Die Liebe Leid und Sorgen.

9 *Des Müllers Blumen*
Am Bach viel kleine Blumen stehn,
Aus hellen blauen Augen sehn;
Der Bach, der ist der Müllers Freund,
Und hellblau Liebchens Auge scheint;
Drum sind es meine Blumen.

Dicht unter ihrem Fensterlein
Da will ich pflanzen die Blumen ein,
Da ruft ihr zu, wenn alles schweigt,
Wenn sich ihr Haupt zum Schlummer
    neigt,
Ihr wißt ja, was ich meine.

Und wenn sie tät die Äuglein zu,
Und schläft in süßer, süßer Ruh',
Dann lispelt als ein Traumgesicht
Ihr zu: «Vergiß, vergiß mein nicht!»
Das ist es, was ich meine.

Und schließt sie früh die Laden
    auf,
Dann schaut mit Liebesblick hinauf:
Der Tau in euren Äugelein,
Das sollen meine Tränen sein,
Die will ich auf euch weinen.

10 *Tränenregen*
Wir saßen so traulich beisammen
Im kühlen Erlendach,
Wir schauten so traulich zusammen
Hinab in den rieselnden Bach.

Der Mond war auch gekommen,
Die Sternlein hinterdrein,
Und schauten so traulich zusammen
In den silbernen Spiegel hinein.

Ich sah nach keinem Monde,
Nach keinem Sternenschein,
Ich schaute nach ihrem Bilde,
Nach ihren Augen allein.

Und sahe sie nicken und blicken
Herauf aus dem seligen Bach,
Die Blümlein am Ufer, die blauen,
Sie nickten und blickten ihr nach.

Little eyes, drunk with slumber,
Little flowers, saddened by the dew,
Why do you fear the sun?
Has night been so good to you
That you close and droop, and weep
For its silent bliss?

Shake off now the veil of dreams
And rise up, refreshed and free,
To God's bright morning!
The lark is trilling in the sky
And from the depths of the heart
Love draws grief and care.

9 *The Miller's Flowers*
Many small flowers grow by the brook,
Gazing from bright blue eyes;
The brook is the miller's friend,
And my sweetheart's eyes are bright blue;
Therefore they are my flowers.

Right under her window
I will plant the flowers;
There you shall call to her when all is silent,
When she lays down her head to
    sleep;
For you know what I wish to say.

And when she closes her eyes
And sleeps in sweet repose,
Then whisper to her as a dream:
'Forget me not!'
That is what I wish to say.

And when, early in the morning, she opens
    the shutters,
Then gaze up lovingly;
The dew in your eyes
Shall be the tears
That I will weep upon you.

10 *Shower of Tears*
We sat together in such harmony
Beneath the cool canopy of alders,
And in harmony gazed down
Into the rippling brook.

The moon had appeared too,
And then the stars;
They gazed down in harmony
Into the silvery mirror.

I did not look at the moon,
I did not look at the stars;
I gazed only at her reflection
And her eyes.

I saw them nod and gaze up
From the happy brook;
The little blue flowers on the bank
Nodded and glanced at her.

Und in den Bach versunken Der ganze Himmel schien, Und wollte mich mit hinunter In seine Tiefe ziehn.	The whole sky seemed Immersed in the brook, And sought to drag me down Into its depths.
Und über den Wolken und Sternen Da rieselte munter der Bach, Und rief mit Singen und Klingen: »Geselle, Geselle, mir nach!«	Above the clouds and stars The brook rippled merrily, And called me with its singing and ringing: 'Friend, follow me!'
Da gingen die Augen mir über, Da ward es im Spiegel so kraus; Sie sprach:»Es kommt ein Regen, Ade, ich geh' nach Haus.«	Then my eyes filled with tears And the mirror became blurred; She said:'It's about to rain, Goodbye, I'm going home.'

11 Mein / 11 Mine

Bächlein, laß dein Rauschen sein! Räder, stellt eur Brausen ein! All' ihr muntern Waldvögelein, Groß und klein, Endet eure Melodein! Durch den Hain Aus und ein Schalle heut' ein Reim allein: Die geliebte Müllerin ist mein! Mein! Frühling, sind das alle deine Blümelein? Sonne, hast du keinen hellern Schein? Ach, so muß ich ganz allein, Mit dem seligen Worte mein, Unverstanden in der weiten Schöpfung sein.	Brook, cease your babbling, Wheels, stop your roaring! All you merry woodbirds Great and small, End your warbling! Throughout the wood, Within it and beyond, Let one rhyme alone ring out today: My beloved, the maid of the mill, is mine! Mine! Spring, are these all of your flowers? Sun, do you have no brighter light? Ah, then I must remain all alone With that blissful word of mine, Understood nowhere in the whole of creation.

12 Pause / 12 Pause

Meine Laute hab' ich gehängt an die Wand, Hab' sie umschlungen mit einem grünen Band — Ich kann nicht mehr singen, mein Herz ist zu voll, Weiß nicht, wie ich's in Reime zwingen soll. Meiner Sehnsucht allerheißesten Schmerz Durft' ich aushauchen in Liederscherz, Und wie ich klagte so süß und fein, Glaubt' ich doch, mein Leiden wär' nicht klein. Ei, wie groß ist wohl meines Glückes Last, Daß kein Klang auf Erden es in sich faßt?	I have hung my lute on the wall, And tied a green ribbon around it. I can sing no more, my heart is too full, I do not know how to force it into rhyme. The most ardent pangs of my longing I could express in playful song, And as I lamented, so sweetly and tenderly, I believed my sorrows were not trifling. Ah, how great can my burden of joy be That no song on earth will contain it?
Nun, liebe Laute, ruh' an dem Nagel hier! Und weht ein Lüftchen über die Saiten dir, Und streift eine Biene mit ihren Flügeln dich, Da wird mir so bange und es durchschauert mich. Warum ließ ich das Band auch hängen so lang'? Oft fliegt's um die Saiten mit seufzendem Klang. Ist es der Nachklang meiner Liebespein? Soll es das Vorspiel neuer Lieder sein?	Rest now, dear lute, here on this nail, And if a breath of air wafts over your strings, Or a bee touches you with its wings, I shall feel afraid, and shudder. Why have I let this ribbon hang down so far? Often it flutters across the strings with a sighing sound. Is this the echo of my love's sorrow, Or could it be the prelude to new songs?

13 *Mit dem grünen Lautenbande*
»Schad' um das schöne grüne Band,
Daß es verbleicht hier an der Wand,
Ich hab' das Grün so gern!«
So sprachst du, Liebchen, heut' zu mir;
Gleich knüpf' ich's ab und send' es dir:
Nun hab' das Grüne gern!

Ist auch dein ganzer Liebster weiß,
Soll Grün doch haben seinen Preis,
Und ich auch hab' es gern.
Weil unsre Lieb' ist immergrün,
Weil grün der Hoffnung Fernen blühn,
Drum haben wir es gern.

Nun schlinge in die Locken dein
Das grüne Band gefällig ein,
Du hast ja 's Grün so gern.
Dann weiß ich, wo die Hoffnung wohnt,
Dann weiß ich, wo die Liebe thront,
Dann hab' ich 's Grün erst gern.

14 *Der Jäger*
Was sucht denn der Jäger am Mühlbach
hier?
Bleib', trotziger Jäger, in deinem Revier!
Hier gibt es kein Wild zu jagen für dich,
Hier wohnt nur ein Rehlein, ein zahmes,
für mich.
Und willst du das zärtliche Rehlein
sehn,
So laß deine Büchsen im Walde stehn,
Und laß deine klaffenden Hunde zu Haus,
Und laß auf dem Horne den Saus und
Braus,
Und scheere vom Kinne das struppige
Haar,
Sonst scheut sich im Garten das Rehlein
fürwahr.

Doch besser, du bliebest im Walde
dazu,
Und ließest die Mühlen und Müller
in Ruh'.
Was taugen die Fischlein im grünen
Gezweig?
Was will denn das Eichhorn im bläulichen
Teich?
Drum bleibe, du trotziger Jäger, im Hain,
Und laß mich mit meinen drei Rädern
allein;
Und willst meinem Schätzchen dich
machen beliebt,
So wisse, mein Freund, was ihr Herzchen
betrübt:
Die Eber, die kommen zur Nacht aus dem
Hain,
Und brechen in ihren Kohlgarten ein,
Und treten und wühlen herum in dem
Feld:
Die Eber die schieße, du Jägerheld!

13 *To Accompany the Lute's Green Ribbon*
'What a pity that the lovely green ribbon,
Should fade on the wall here;
I am so fond of green!'
That is what you said to me today, my love;
I untied it at once and sent it to you:
Now delight in green!

Though your sweetheart is all in white
Green shall have its reward,
And I, too, am fond of it.
For our love is evergreen,
For distant hope blossoms green,
That is why we are fond of it.

Now plait the green ribbon
Prettily into your hair,
For you are so fond of green.
Then I shall know where hope dwells,
Then I shall know where love reigns,
Then I shall truly delight in green.

14 *The Huntsman*
What does the huntsman seek here by the
millstream?
Stay in your own territory, defiant hunter!
Here is no game for you to hunt,
Here dwells only a tame fawn for
me.
And should you wish to see that gentle
fawn,
Leave your guns in the forest,
Leave your baying hounds at home,
Stop that pealing din on your
horn,
And shave that unkempt beard from your
chin,
Or the fawn will take fright in the
garden.

But it would be better if you stayed in the
forest,
And left mills and millers in
peace.
How can fish thrive among green
branches?
What can the squirrel want in the blue
pond?
Stay in the wood, then, defiant hunter,
And leave me alone with my three mill-
wheels;
And if you wish to make yourself popular
with my sweetheart,
Then, my friend, you should know what
distresses her heart:
Wild boars come out of the wood at
night,
And break into her cabbage patch,
Rooting about and trampling over the
field;
Shoot the wild boars, heroic huntsman!

15 Eifersucht und Stolz

Wohin so schnell, so kraus und wild, mein
lieber Bach?
Eilst du voll Zorn dem frechen Bruder
Jäger nach?
Kehr' um, kehr' um, und schilt erst deine
Müllerin
Für ihren leichten, losen, kleinen
Flattersinn.
Sahst du sie gestern abend nicht am
Tore stehn,
Mit langem Halse nach der großen Straße
sehn?
Wenn von dem Fang der Jäger lustig zieht
nach Haus,
Da steckt kein sittsam Kind den Kopf zum
Fenster 'naus.
Geh', Bächlein, hin und sag' ihr das, doch
sag' ihr nicht,
Hörst du, kein Wort, von meinem
traurigen Gesicht;
Sag' ihr: Er schnitzt bei mir sich eine Pfeif'
aus Rohr,
Und bläst den Kindern schöne Tänz' und
Lieder vor.

16 Die liebe Farbe

In Grün will ich mich kleiden,
In grüne Tränenweiden,
Mein Schatz hat's Grün so gern.
Will suchen einen Zypressenhain,
Eine Heide von grünem Rosmarein,
Mein Schatz hat's Grün so gern.

Wohlauf zum fröhlichen Jagen!
Wohlauf durch Heid' und Hagen!
Mein Schatz hat's Jagen so gern.
Das Wild, das ich jage, das ist der Tod,
Die Heide, die heiß ich die Liebesnot,
Mein Schatz hat's Jagen so gern.

Grabt mir ein Grab im Wasen,
Deckt mich mit grünem Rasen,
Mein Schatz hat's Grün so gern.
Kein Kreuzlein schwarz, kein Blümlein
bunt,
Grün, alles grün so rings und rund!
Mein Schatz hat's Grün so gern.

17 Die böse Farbe

Ich möchte ziehn in die Welt hinaus,
Hinaus in die weite Welt,
Wenn's nur so grün, so grün nicht wär'
Da draußen in Wald und Feld!

Ich möchte die grünen Blätter all'
Pflücken von jedem Zweig,
Ich möchte die grünen Gräser all'
Weinen ganz totenbleich.

15 Jealousy and Pride

Whither so fast, so ruffled and fierce, my
beloved brook?
Do you hurry full of anger after our insolent
huntsman friend?
Turn back, and first reproach your maid of
the mill
For her frivolous, wanton
inconstancy.
Did you not see her standing by the gate
last night,
Craning her neck as she looked towards the
high road?
When the huntsman returns home merrily
after the kill
A nice girl does not put her head out of the
window.
Go, brook, and tell her this; but breathe not
a word—
Do you hear?— about my unhappy
face;
Tell her: he has cut himself a reed pipe on
my banks,
And is piping pretty songs and dances for
the children.

16 The Beloved Colour

I shall dress in green,
In green weeping willows:
My love is so fond of green.
I shall seek out a cypress grove,
A heath full of green rosemary;
My love is so fond of green.

Up, away to the merry hunt!
Away over heath and hedge!
My love is so fond of hunting.
The game I hunt is death;
The heath I call Love's Torment;
My love is so fond of green.

Dig me a grave in the grass,
Cover me with green turf;
My love is so fond of green.
No black cross, no colourful
flowers,
Green, everything green, all around.
My love is so fond of green.

17 The Loathsome Colour

I should like to go out into the world,
Into the wide world.
If only it were not so green
Out there in field and forest!

I should like to pluck the green leaves
From every branch,
I should like to make the green grass
Deathly pale with my weeping.

Ach Grün, du böse Farbe du,	O green, you loathsome colour,
Was siehst mich immer an,	Why do you look at me,
So stolz, so keck, so schadenfroh,	So proud, so insolent, so gloating;
Mich armen, armen weißen Mann?	At me, a poor white miller.
Ich möchte liegen vor ihrer Tür,	I should like to lie at her door
Im Sturm und Regen und Schnee,	In storm and rain and snow,
Und singen ganz leise bei Tag und Nacht	And sing softly, day and night,
Das eine Wörtchen Ade!	One single word: Farewell!
Horch, wenn im Walde ein Jagdhorn	Hark: when a hunting horn sounds in the
schallt,	wood,
So klingt ihr Fensterlein,	I can hear her window.
Und schaut sie auch nach mir nicht aus,	And though she does not look out to see me,
Darf ich doch schauen hinein.	Yet I can look in.
O binde von der Stirn dir ab	O untie the green ribbon
Das grüne, grüne Band,	From your brow;
Ade, Ade! und reiche mir	Farewell! And in parting
Zum Abschied deine Hand!	Give me your hand.

18 *Trockne Blumen*	18 *Withered Flowers*
Ihr Blümlein alle,	All you flowers
Die sie mir gab,	That she gave to me,
Euch soll man legen	You shall be laid
Mit mir ins Grab.	With me in the grave.
Wie seht ihr alle	How sorrowfully
Mich an so weh,	You all look at me,
Als ob ihr wüßtet,	As though you knew
Wie mir gescheh'?	What was happening to me!
Ihr Blümlein alle,	All you flowers,
Wie welk, wie blaß?	How faded and pale you are!
Ihr Blümlein alle	All you flowers,
Wovon so naß?	Why are you so moist?
Ach, Tränen machen	Alas, tears will not create
Nicht maiengrün,	The green of May,
Machen tote Liebe	Nor make dead love
Nicht wieder blühn.	Bloom anew.
Und Lenz wird kommen	Spring will come,
Und Winter wird gehn,	And winter will pass,
Und Blümlein werden	And flowers
Im Grase stehn.	Will grow in the grass.
Und Blümlein liegen	And flowers will lie
In meinem Grab,	On my grave,
Die Blümlein alle,	All the flowers
Die sie mir gab.	That she gave me.
Und wenn sie wandelt	And when she walks
Am Hügel vorbei,	Past that mound
Und denkt im Herzen:	And ponders in her heart:
»Der meint' es treu!«	'His love was true.'
Dann Blümlein alle,	Then, all you flowers,
Heraus, heraus!	Come forth, come forth!
Der Mai ist kommen,	May is here,
Der Winter ist aus.	Winter is over!

19 Der Müller und der Bach

Der Müller:
Wo ein treues Herze
In Liebe vergeht,
Da welken die Lilien
Auf jedem Beet.

Da muß in die Wolken
Der Vollmond gehn,
Damit seine Tränen
Die Menschen nicht sehn.

Da halten die Englein
Die Augen sich zu,
Und schluchzen und singen
Die Seele zur Ruh'.

Der Bach:
Und wenn sich die Liebe
Dem Schmerz entringt,
Ein Sternlein, ein neues
Am Himmel erblinkt.

Da springen drei Rosen,
Halb rot und halb weiß,
Die welken nicht wieder,
Aus Dornenreis.

Und die Engelein schneiden
Die Flügel sich ab,
Und gehn alle Morgen
Zur Erde hinab.

Der Müller:
Ach, Bächlein, liebes Bächlein,
Du meinst es so gut:
Ach, Bächlein, aber weißt du,
Wie Liebe tut?

Ach, unten, da unten,
Die kühle Ruh'!
Ach, Bächlein, liebes Bächlein,
So singe nur zu.

20 Des Baches Wiegenlied
Gute Ruh', gute Ruh'!
Tu' die Augen zu!
Wandrer, du müder, du bist zu Haus.
Die Treu' ist hier,
Sollst liegen bei mir,
Bis das Meer will trinken die Bächlein aus.

Will betten dich kühl,
Auf weichen Pfühl,
In dem blauen krystallenen Kämmerlein.
Heran, heran,
Was wiegen kann,
Woget und wieget den Knaben mir ein!

19 The Miller and the Brook

The Miller:
Where a true heart
Dies of love,
The lilies wilt
In their beds.

There the full moon
Must disappear behind clouds,
So that mankind
Does not see its tears.

There angels
Cover their eyes,
And, sobbing, sing
The soul to rest.

The Brook:
And when love
Struggles free of sorrow,
A new star
Shines in the sky;

Three roses,
Half-red, half-white,
Spring from thorny stems,
And will never wither.

And the angels
Cut off their wings,
And every morning
Descend to earth.

The Miller:
Ah, brook, beloved brook,
You mean so well:
Ah, brook, but do you know,
What love can do?

Ah, below, down below
Is cool rest!
Brook, beloved brook,
Sing on!

20 The Brook's Lullaby
Rest well, rest well!
Close your eyes!
Weary wanderer, this is your home.
Here is constancy,
You shall lie with me,
Until the sea drinks up all brooks.

I shall make you a cool bed
On a soft pillow
In this blue crystal chamber.
Come, come,
All you who can lull,
Rock and lull this boy for me!

Wenn ein Jagdhorn schallt
Aus dem grünen Wald,
Will ich sausen und brausen wohl um
dich her.
Blickt nicht herein,
Blaue Blümelein!
Ihr macht meinem Schläfer die Träume so
schwer.

When a hunting-horn echoes
From the green forest,
I shall surge and roar about
you.
Do not peep in,
Little blue flowers!
You will give my slumberer such bad
dreams.

Hinweg, hinweg
Von dem Mühlensteg,
Böses Mägdelein, daß ihn dein Schatten
nicht weckt!
Wirf mir herein
Dein Tüchlein fein,
Daß ich die Augen ihm halte bedeckt!

Away, away
From the mill-path,
Wicked girl, lest your shadow should wake
him!
Throw me
Your fine shawl,
That I may keep his eyes covered!

Gute Nacht, gute Nacht!
Bis alles wacht,
Schlaf aus deine Freude, schlaf aus dein
Leid!
Der Vollmond steigt,
Der Nebel weicht,
Und der Himmel da oben, wie ist er so
weit!

Good night, good night,
Until all awaken,
Sleep away your joy, sleep away your
sorrow!
The full moon rises,
The mist vanishes,
And the sky above, how vast
it is!

Die Sommernacht / The Summer Night

FRIEDRICH GOTTLIEB KLOPSTOCK

D 289 (1815)

Wenn der Schimmer von dem Monde nun
herab
In die Wälder sich ergiesst, und Gerüche
Mit den Düften von der Linde
In den Kühlungen wehn:

When the moon's soft
light
Shines into the woods,
And the scent of the lime-tree
Is wafted in the cool breezes:

So umschatten mich Gedanken an das
Grab
Meiner Geliebten, und ich seh' im Walde
Nur es dämmern, und es weht
mir
Von der Blüte nicht her.

Then my mind is darkened by
thoughts
Of my beloved's grave; this alone
Do I see growing dusky in the woods; and
the blossom's fragrance
Does not reach me.

Ich genoss einst, o ihr Toten, es mit
euch!
Wie umwehten uns der Duft und die
Kühlung,
Wie verschönt warst du von dem Monde,
Du, o schöne
Natur!

Spirits of the dead, with you I once enjoyed
it!
How the fragrance and the cool breezes
caressed us!
Beautiful nature,
How you were transfigured in the
moonlight!

Die Spinnerin / The Spinner

JOHANN WOLFGANG VON GOETHE

D 247 (1815)

Als ich still und ruhig spann,
Ohne nur zu stocken,
Trat ein schöner junger Mann
Nahe mir zum Rocken.

As I span, silently and calmly,
Without stopping,
A fair young man
Approached me at my distaff.

Lobte, was zu loben war:
Sollte das was schaden?
Mein dem Flachse gleiches Haar,
Und den gleichen Faden.

He duly complimented me —
What harm could that do? —
On my flaxen hair
And on the flaxen thread.

Ruhig war er nicht dabei,
Ließ es nicht beim Alten;
Und der Faden riß entzwei,
Den ich lang' erhalten.

But he was not content with that,
And would not let things be.
And the thread which I had long held
Snapped in two.

Und des Flachses Stein-Gewicht
Gab noch viele Zahlen;
Aber, ach! ich konnte nicht
Mehr mit ihnen prahlen.

And the flax's stone-weight
Still produced many a thread;
But, alas, I could no longer
Boast about them.

Als ich sie zum Weber trug,
Fühlt' ich was sich regen,
Und mein armes Herze schlug
Mit geschwindern Schlägen.

When I took them to the weaver
I felt something stir,
And my poor heart beat
More quickly.

Nun, beim heißen Sonnenstich,
Bring' ich's auf die Bleiche,
Und mit Mühe bück' ich mich
Nach dem nächsten Teiche.

Now, in the scorching sun,
I take my work out to be bleached,
And with great effort
I bend over the nearest pool.

Was ich in dem Kämmerlein
Still und fein gesponnen,
Kommt — wie kann es anders
    sein? —
Endlich an die Sonnen.

What I span so quietly and finely
In my little room
Will at length — how can it be
    otherwise? —
Come out into the light of day.

Die Stadt / The Town

HEINRICH HEINE

see Schwanengesang no. 11

Die Sterbende / The Dying Girl

FRIEDRICH VON MATTHISSON

D 186 (1815)

Heil! dies ist die lezte Zähre,
Die der Müden Aug' entfällt!
Schon entschattet sich die Sphäre
Ihrer heimatlichen Welt.
Leicht, wie Frühlingsnebel schwinden,

Hail! This is the last tear
To fall from the weary girl's eyes.
Already the sphere of her familiar world
Is shadowed.
The dream of life has fled

Ist des Lebens Traum entflohn,
Paradiesesblumen
  winden
Seraphim zum Kranze schon!

As lightly as spring mists vanish;
Already seraphim are weaving flowers of
  paradise
Into a wreath.

Die Sterne / The Stars

JOHANN GEORG FELLINGER

D 176 (1815)

Was funkelt ihr so mild mich an?
Ihr Sterne, hold und hehr!
Was treibet euch auf dunkler Bahn
Im ätherblauen Meer?
Wie Gottes Augen schaut ihr dort,
Aus Ost und West, aus Süd und Nord,
So freundlich auf mich her.

Why do you sparkle so gently at me,
You stars, so noble and so fair,
What drives you on your dark course
Through the blue ocean of the ether?
Like the eyes of God,
From east and west, north and south,
You gaze kindly down on me.

Und überall umblinkt ihr mich
Mit sanftem Dämmerlicht,
Die Sonne hebt in Morgen sich,
Doch ihr verlaßt mich nicht,
Wenn kaum der Abend wieder graut,
So blickt ihr mir, so fromm und traut,
Schon wieder ins Gesicht.

Everywhere you bathe me
In soft, dusky light.
The run rises in the morning,
But you never forsake me.
Evening hardly darkens
Before you shine, so pure and tender,
Once more upon my face.

Wilkommen denn, wilkommen mir!
Ihr Freunde, still und bleich!
Wie lichte Geister wandelt ihr
Durch euer weites Reich,
Und ach! vielleicht begrüßet mich
Ein edler, der zu früh verblich,
Ein treuer Freund aus euch!

Welcome then, welcome
Friends, pale and silent!
Like shining spirits you wander
Through your vast realm.
And ah, perhaps a noble, faithful friend,
Who perished too soon,
Greets me from among you!

Vielleicht wird einst mein Aufenthalt
Im hellen Sirius,
Wenn diese kleine Wurmgestalt
Die Hülle wechseln muß;
Vielleicht erhebt der Funke
  Geist,
Wenn diese schwache Form zerreißt,
Sich auf zum Uranus!

Perhaps one day my abode
Will be upon bright Sirius,
When this small, wormlike frame
Must change its skin;
Perhaps, when this feeble form is torn
  apart,
The spirit will rise like a spark
Up to Olympus.

O lächelt nur, o winket nur,
Mir still zu euch hinan!
Mich führet Mutter Allnatur
Nach ihrem großen Plan;
Mich kümmert nicht der Welten Fall,
Wenn ich nur dort die Lieben all'
Vereinet finden kann.

O smile! O beckon me silently
Towards you!
Mother Nature guides me
According to her great plan;
The end of the world does not trouble me,
If only I can find all my loved ones
United there.

Die Sterne / The Stars

LUDWIG KOSEGARTEN

D 313 (1815)

Wie wohl ist mir im Dunkeln!
Wie weht die laue Nacht!

How happy I am in the darkness!
How warm the night breeze!

Die Sterne Gottes funkeln
In feierlicher Pracht!

Komm, Ida, komm ins Freie,
Und lass in jene Bläue
Und lass zu jenen Höhn
Uns staunend aufwärts sehn.

O Sterne Gottes, Zeugen
Und Boten bess'rer Welt,
Ihr heisst den Aufruhr schweigen,
Der unsern Busen schwellt.

Ich seh' hinauf, ihr Hehren,
Zu euren lichten Sphären,
Und Ahndung bess'rer Lust
Stillt die empörte Brust.

God's stars glitter
In their solemn splendour.

Come, Ida, into the open air
And let us gaze up in wonder
At the blue sky
And at those peaks.

God's stars, witnesses
And harbingers of a better world,
You silence the tumult
Which fills our breast.

I gaze up, lofty stars,
To your shining spheres,
And a presentiment of higher bliss
Calms my incensed heart.

Die Sterne / The Stars

KARL GOTTFRIED VON LEITNER

D939 (1828)

Wie blitzen die Sterne so hell durch die
  Nacht!
Bin oft schon darüber vom Schlummer
  erwacht.
Doch schelt' ich die lichten Gebilde drum
  nicht,
Sie üben im Stillen manch heilsame
  Pflicht.

Sie wallen hoch oben in
  Engelgestalt,
Sie leuchten dem Pilger durch Heiden und
  Wald.
Sie schweben als Boten der Liebe umher,
Und tragen oft Küsse weit über das Meer.

Sie blicken dem Dulder recht mild ins
  Gesicht,
Und säumen die Tränen mit silbernem
  Licht.
Und weisen von Gräbern gar tröstlich und
  hold
Uns hinter das Blaue mit Fingern von
  Gold.

So sei denn gesegnet, du strahlige Schar!
Und leuchte mir lange noch freundlich und
  klar!
Und wenn ich einst liebe, seid hold dem
  Verein,
Und euer Geflimmer lasst Segen uns
  sein!

How brightly the stars glitter through the
  night!
I have often been aroused by them from
  slumber.
But I do not chide the shining beings for
  that,
For they secretly perform many a
  benevolent task.

They wander high above in the form of
  angels,
They light the pilgrim's way through heath
  and wood.
They hover like harbingers of love,
And often bear kisses far across the sea.

They gaze tenderly into the sufferer's
  face,
And fringe his tears with silver
  light;
And comfortingly, gently, direct us away
  from the grave,
Beyond the azure with fingers of
  gold.

I bless you, radiant throng!
Long may you shine upon me with your
  clear, pleasing light!
And if one day I fall in love, then smile
  upon the bond,
And let your twinkling be a blessing upon
  us.

Die Sterne / The Stars

D 684 (1820?)

Du staunest, o Mensch, was heilig wir
strahlen?
O folgest du nur den himmlischen Winken,
Vernähmest du besser, was freundlich wir
blinken,
Wie wären verschwunden die irdischen
Qualen!
Dann flösse die Liebe aus ewigen Schalen,
Es atmeten alle die reinen Azuren,
Das lichtblaue Meer umschwebte die
Fluren,
Und funkelten Sterne auf den heimischen
Talen.

Aus göttlicher Quelle sind alle genommen,
Ist jegliches Wesen nicht eines im Chore?
Nun sind ja geöffnet die himmlischen
Tore,
Was soll denn das bange Verzagen noch
frommen?
O wäret ihr schon zur Tiefe geklommen,
So sähet das Haupt ihr von Sternen
umflogen
Und spielend um's Herz die kindlichen
Wogen,
Zu denen die Stürme des Lebens nicht
kommen.

You marvel, o man, at our sacred
radiance?
If only you followed the heavenly signs
You would understand better how benignly
we twinkle,
How earthly suffering would
vanish!
Then love would flow from eternal vessels,
All would breathe the pure azure,
The light-blue sea would lap about the
meadows,
And stars would sparkle in our native
valleys.

All spring from a divine source;
Is not all creation united in the choir?
Now the heavenly gates are
open;
Of what avail is timorous
despair?
If you had already climbed to the depths
You would see the stars circling around
your head,
And the childlike waves, unruffled by life's
storms,
Playing about your
heart.

Die Sternennächte / The Starry Nights

JOHANN MAYRHOFER

D 670 (1819)

In monderhellten Nächten
Mit dem Geschick zu rechten,
Hat diese Brust verlernt.
Der Himmel, reich besternt,
Umwoget mich mit Frieden;
Da denk' ich, auch hienieden
Gedeihet manche Blume;
Und frischer schaut der stumme,
Sonst trübe Blick hinauf
Zu ew'ger Sterne Lauf.

Auf ihnen bluten Herzen,
Auf ihnen quälen Schmerzen,
Sie aber strahlen heiter,
So schliess' ich selig weiter:
Auch unsre kleine Erde,
Voll Misston und Gefährde,
Sich als ein heiter Licht
Ins Diadem verflicht;

On moonlit nights
My heart has learnt
Not to quarrel with fate.
The heavens, rich with stars,
Leave me in peace,
And I think: even here on earth
Many a flower blooms;
And my silent, troubled gaze
Brightens as it contemplates
The stars' eternal course.

On them, too, hearts bleed,
On them pain torments,
But they shine serenely on.
And so I happily conclude:
Even our little earth,
Full of discord and danger,
Is a bright light
Woven into this diadem;

So werden Sterne
Durch die Ferne!

Stars are made thus
By distance!

Die Sternenwelten / The Starry Worlds

JOHANN GUSTAV FELLINGER

D 307 (1815)

Oben drehen sich die großen
Unbekannten Welten dort,
Von dem Sonnenlicht umflossen,
Kreisen sie die Bahnen fort;
Traulich reihet sich der Sterne
Zahlenloses Heer ringsum,
Sieht sich lächelnd durch die Ferne,
Und verbreitet Gottes Ruhm.

High above, the great
Unknown worlds revolve;
Bathed in the sun's light
They circle in their course.
Around them, in harmonious array,
Spreads the numberless host of stars;
Smiling, they gaze at each other from afar,
And proclaim widely the glory of God.

Eine lichte Straße gleitet
Durch das weite Blau herauf,
Und die Macht der Gottheit leitet
Schwebend hier den Sternenlauf;
Alles hat sich zugeründet,
Alles wogt in Glanz und Brand,
Und dies große All verkündet
Eine hohe Bildnerhand.

A path of light glides up
Through the vast blue firmament,
And the power of God gently guides
The course of the stars;
Everything has attained perfection,
Everything swirls in light and fire,
And this great universe proclaims
The hand of the sublime Architect.

Jene Sternenheere weisen
Schöpfer! deine Majestät!
Selig kann nur der sich preisen,
Dessen Geist zu dir entweht;
Nur dein Loblied wird er singen,
Wohnen ob dem Sphärengang,
Freudig sich durch Welten schwingen
Trinkend reinen Engelsang.

Creator, those starry hosts
Reveal your majesty!
Only he whose spirit wafts towards you,
Can consider himself blessed;
He will sing in praise of you alone,
Who dwell beyond the spheres,
Soaring joyfully through the worlds,
Drinking the pure song of angels.

Die Taubenpost / Pigeon Post

JOHANN GABRIEL SEIDL

see Schwanengesang no. 14

Die Täuschung / Deception

LUDWIG KOSEGARTEN

D 230 (1815)

Im Erlenbusch, im Tannenhain,
In Sonn- und Mond- und Sternenschein
Umlächelt mich ein Bildnis;
Vor seinem Lächeln klärt sich schnell
Die Dämmerung in
    Himmelhell,
In Paradies die Wildnis.

In the alder grove, in the pine wood,
By the light of sun, moon and stars,
An image smiles upon me.
At that smile
Dusk quickly changes to celestial
    brightness,
And the wilderness turns to paradise.

Es säuselt in der Abendluft,
Es dämmert in dem Morgenduft,
Es tanzet auf der Aue.
Es flötet in der Wachtel Schlag,
Und spiegelt sich im klaren Bach,
Und badet sich im Taue.

It whispers in the evening air,
It drowses in the morning fragrance,
It dances in the meadow,
It sings like the quail,
It is reflected in the clear brook,
And bathes in the dew.

Ich öffn' ihm sehnend meinen Arm,
Und streb', es traut und liebewarm
An meine Brust zu drücken.
Ich hasch', und hasche leere Luft,
Und nichtig, wie ein Nebelduft,
Entwallt es meinen Blicken.

I open my arms to it longingly,
And strive to press it
Tenderly, ardently, to my breast.
I snatch at it, and snatch empty air,
And it drifts from my sight,
As insubstantial as mist.

Wer bist du, holdes Luftgebild,
Das engelhold und engelmild
Mit Schmerz und Lust mich tränket?
Bist du ein Bote bess'rer Welt,
Der mich aus diesem öden Feld
In seine Heimat winket?

Who are you, sweet etheral creature
Who with angelic grace and tenderness,
Flood me with pain and joy?
Are you a messenger from a better world,
Calling me from this desolate land
To your own country?

O, fleuch voran! Ich folge dir.
Bei dir ist Seligkeit, nicht hier!
Sprich, wo ich dich erfasse,
Und ewig aller Pein entrückt,
Umstrickend dich, von dir umstrickt!
Dich nimmer, nimmer lasse!

O flee hence! I shall follow you.
Bliss is with you, not here!
Tell me where I may hold you,
And never, ever leave you,
Eternally freed from all pain,
Embracing and embraced by you!

Die Unterscheidung / The Distinction

JOHANN GABRIEL SEIDL

D 866 no. 1 (1828?)

Die Mutter hat mich jüngst gescholten
Und vor der Liebe streng gewarnt.
»Noch jede,« sprach sie, »hat's entgolten:
Verloren ist, wen sie umgarnt.«
D'rum ist es besser, wie ich meine,
Wenn keins von uns davon mehr spricht:
Ich bin zwar immer noch die Deine—
Doch lieben, Hans!— kann ich dich nicht!

Mother recently scolded me,
And warned me sternly against love.
'Every woman,' she said, 'has paid its price;
She who is ensnared by love is lost.'
And so I think it better
If neither of us speaks of it again.
I am in truth still yours for ever,
But *love* you, Hans— this I cannot do!

Vor allem, Hans, vergiß mir nimmer,
Daß du nur mich zu lieben hast.
Mein Lächeln sei dir Lust nur immer,
Und jeder Andern Lächeln
Last!
Ja, um der Mutter nachzugeben,
Will ich mich, treu der Doppelpflicht,
Dir zu gefallen stets bestreben,
Doch lieben, Hans!— kann ich dich nicht.

Above all, Hans, never forget
That you must love only me.
My smile alone shall always be your delight,
And the smiles of other girls shall be
irksome to you.
Yes, in order to give in to mother
I shall, true to my twofold duty,
Strive always to please you;
But *love* you, Hans— this I cannot do!

Bei jedem Feste, das wir haben,
Soll's meine größte Wonne sein,
Flicht deine Hand des Frühlings Gaben
Zum Schmucke mir in's Mieder ein.
Beginnt der Tanz, dann ist, wie
billig,

Whenever we have a holiday,
It will be my greatest joy
If your hands twine the gifts of springtime
To adorn my bodice.
When the dancing begins, then— as is only
fair—

Ein Tanz mit Gretchen deine
  Pflicht;
Selbst eifersüchtig werden will ich,
Doch lieben, Hans! kann ich dich nicht.

Und sinkt der Abend kühl hernieder,
Und ruh'n wir dann recht mild bewegt,
Halt' immer mir die Hand an's Mieder,
Und fühle, wie mein Herzchen schlägt!
Und willst du mich durch Küsse lehren,
Was stumm dein Auge zu mir spricht,
Selbst das will ich dir nicht verwehren,
Doch lieben, Hans! kann ich dich nicht.

It will be your duty to dance with
  Gretchen;
I shall even be jealous.
But *love* you, Hans — this I cannot do!

And when cool evening descends,
And we rest, filled with tender emotion,
Keep your hand on my bodice,
And feel how my heart beats!
And if you wish to teach me with kisses
What your eyes silently tell me,
Even that I shall not deny you.
But *love* you, Hans — this I cannot do!

Die verfehlte Stunde / The Unsuccessful Hour

AUGUST WILHELM VON SCHLEGEL

D 409 (1816)

Quälend ungestilltes Sehnen
Pocht mir in empörter Brust.
Liebe, die mir Seel' und Sinnen
Schmeichelnd wußte zu gewinnen,
Wiegt dein zauberisches Wähnen
Nur in Träume kurzer Lust,
Und erweckt zu Tränen?
Süß berauscht in Tränen
An des Lieben Brust mich lehnen,
Arm um Arm gestrickt,
Mund auf Mund gedrückt,
Das nur stillt mein Sehnen!

Ach, ich gab ihm keine Kunde,
Wußt' es selber nicht zuvor;
Und nun beb' ich so beklommen:
Wird der Traute, wird er kommen?
Still und günstig ist die Stunde,
Nirgends droht ein horchend Ohr
Dem geheimen Bunde.
Treu im sel'gen Bunde
An des Lieben Brust mich lehnen,
Arm um Arm gestrickt,
Mund auf Mund gedrückt,
Das nur stillt mein Sehnen.

Hor' ich leise Tritte rauschen,
Denk' ich: ah, da ist er schon!
Ahndung hat ihm wohl verkündet,
Daß die schöne Zeit sich findet,
Wonn' um Wonne frei zu tauschen —
Doch sie ist schon halb entflohn
Bei vergebnem Lauschen.
Mit entzücktem Lauschen
An des Lieben Brust mich lehnen,
Arm um Arm gestrickt,
Mund auf Mund gedrückt,
Das nur stillt mein Sehnen.

The torment of unquiet longing
Beats within my raging breast.
Love, you knew how to win
My soul and my senses with your flattery;
Does your magic illusion lull me
To dreams of fleeting pleasure,
Only to awaken me to tears?
O to be drunk with sweet tears,
Leaning on my beloved's breast,
My arms entwined in his arms,
My lips pressed to his lips —
This alone will still my longing!

Ah, I gave him no indication,
I myself did not know beforehand;
And now I tremble so anxiously:
Will my beloved come?
The hour is silent and favourable;
Nowhere does an eavesdropper threaten
Our secret bond.
O to lean on my beloved's breast
In true, blissful union,
My arms entwined in his arms,
My lips pressed to his lips —
This alone will still my longing!

When I hear soft footsteps
I think: ah, here it is!
A presentiment must have told him
That the fair hour is at hand,
The hour to exchange joy freely.
But already it is half gone,
Passed in vain waiting.
O to lean on my beloved's breast
In rapturous communion,
My arms entwined in his arms,
My lips pressed to his lips —
This alone will still my longing!

Täuschen wird vielleicht mein Sehnen,
Hofft' ich, des Gesanges Lust.
Ungestümer Wünsche Glühen
Lindern sanfte Melodien —
Doch das Lied enthob mit Stöhnen
Tief eratmend sich der Brust,
Und erstarb in Tränen.
Süß berauscht in Tränen
An des Lieben Brust mich lehnen,
Arm um Arm gestrickt,
Mund auf Mund gedrückt,
Das nur stillt mein Sehnen.

I had hoped that the joy of song
Might perhaps delude my longing,
And that gentle melodies might quench
The fire of impetuous desire.
But the song escaped from my heart,
Groaning and panting,
And died in tears.
O to be drunk with sweet tears,
Leaning on my beloved's breast,
My arms entwined in his arms,
My lips pressed to his lips —
This alone will still my longing!

Die vier Weltalter / The Four Ages of the World

FRIEDRICH VON SCHILLER

D 391 (1816?)

Wohl perlet im Glase der purpurne Wein,
Wohl glänzen die Augen der Gäste,
Es zeigt sich der Sänger, er tritt herein,
Zu dem Guten bringt er das Beste;
Denn ohne die Leier im himmlischen
  Saal
Ist die Freude gemein auch beim
  Nektarmahl.

The crimson wine sparkles in the glass,
The guests' eyes shine;
The minstrel appears and enters,
To the good things he brings the best;
For without the lyre joy is
  vulgar,
Even at a nectar banquet in the hall of the
  gods.

Erst regierte Saturnus schlicht und
  gerecht,
Da war es heute wie morgen,
Da lebten die Hirten, ein harmlos
  Geschlecht,
Und brauchten für gar nichts zu
  sorgen;
Sie liebten, und taten weiter nichts mehr,
Die Erde gab alles freiwillig
  her.

First Saturn ruled, simply and
  justly,
Then one day was like the next;
Then shepherds lived, a harmless
  race;
They did not need to worry about
  anything;
They loved, and did nothing else,
The earth yielded everything of its own
  accord.

Drauf kam die Arbeit, der Kampf begann
Mit Ungeheuern und Drachen,
Die Helden fingen, die Herrscher an,
Und den Mächtigen suchten die
  Schwachen;
Und der Streit zog in des Skamanders
  Feld,
Doch die Schönheit war immer der Gott
  der Welt.

Then came work, and the struggle began
With monsters and dragons;
Heroes emerged, and rulers,
And the weak sought the man of
  might;
And the battle came to Scamander's
  fields,
But Beauty was always the god of the
  world.

Aus dem Kampf ging endlich der Sieg
  hervor,
Und der Kraft entblühte die Milde,
Da sangen die Musen im himmlischen
  Chor,
Da erhuben sich Göttergebilde;
Das Alter der göttlichen Phantasie,
Es ist verschwunden, es kehret nie.

At last the struggle yielded
  victory,
And from force gentleness blossomed,
Then the muses sang in celestial
  choir,
Then images of gods arose;
The age of divine imagination
Has vanished; it will never return.

Die Vögel / The Birds

FRIEDRICH VON SCHLEGEL

D 691 (1820)

Wie lieblich und fröhlich,
Zu schweben, zu singen,
Von glänzender Höhe
Zur Erde zu blicken!

How delightful and exhilarating it is
To soar and to sing,
To look down on the earth
From the radiant heights!

Die Menschen sind töricht,
Sie können nicht fliegen.
Sie jammern in Nöten,
Wir flattern gen Himmel.

Men are foolish:
They cannot fly.
They lament in their distress;
We fly up to the heavens.

Der Jäger will töten,
Dem Früchte wir pickten;
Wir müssen ihn höhnen,
Und Beute gewinnen.

The huntsman whose fruit we pecked
Wants to kill us;
But we should mock him
And snatch our spoils.

Die Wallfahrt / The Pilgrimage

FRIEDRICH RÜCKERT

D2 778A (1822–3?)

Meine Tränen im Bussgewand
Die Wallfahrt haben
Zur Aula der Schönheit angetreten;
In der Wüste brennendem Sand
Sind sie begraben,
Nicht hingelangten sie anzubeten.

My tears initiated the pilgrimage
In penitential robes
To the hall of beauty;
They are buried
In the desert's burning sand,
For they did not arrive to worship.

Die Wehmut / Melancholy

SALIS-SEEWIS

see Die Herbstnacht

Dithyrambe / Dithyramb

FRIEDRICH VON SCHILLER

D801 (1824?)

Nimmer, das glaubt mir, erscheinen die
    Götter,
Nimmer allein.
Kaum dass ich Bacchus, den lustigen,
    habe,
Kommt auch schon Amor, der lächelnde
    Knabe,
Phöbus der Herrliche findet sich ein.
Sie nahen, sie kommen, die Himmlischen
    alle,
Mit Göttern erfüllt sich die irdische Halle.

Never, believe me, do the
    gods
Appear alone.
No sooner is jolly Bacchus with
    me,
Than Cupid comes too, the smiling
    boy,
And glorious Phoebus arrives.
They approach, they are here, all the
    deities;
This earthly abode is filled with gods.

Sagt, wie bewirt ich, der Erdegeborne,
Himmlischen Chor?
Schenket mir euer unsterbliches Leben,
Götter! Was kann euch der Sterbliche
geben?
Hebet zu eurem Olymp mich empor!
Die Freude, sie wohnt nur in Jupiters
Saale,
O füllet mit Nektar, o reich mir die Schale!

Reich ihm die Schale! O schenke dem
Dichter,
Hebe, nur ein.
Netz ihm die Augen mit himmlischem
Taue,
Dass er den Styx, den verhassten, nicht
schaue,
Einer der Unsern sich dünke zu sein.
Sie rauschet, sie perlet, die himmlische
Quelle,
Der Busen wird ruhig, das Auge wird
helle.

Tell me, how shall I, earth-born,
Entertain the heavenly choir?
Bestow on me your immortal life,
O gods! What can a mortal give
you?
Raise me up to your Olympus!
Joy dwells only in the hall of
Jupiter;
Fill the cup with nectar and pass it to me!

Pass him the cup!
Hebe,
Give the poet to drink!
Moisten his eyes with celestial
dew,
That he may not behold the hateful
Styx,
That he may deem himself one of us.
It murmurs, it bubbles, the heavenly
spring.
The heart grows calm, the eye grows
bright.

Don Gayseros I / Don Gayseros I

FRIEDRICH DE LA MOTTE FOUQUÉ

D93 no. 1 (1815?)

»Don Gayseros, Don Gayseros,
Wunderlicher, schöner Ritter,
Hast mich aus der Burg beschworen,
Lieblicher, mit Deinen Bitten.

Don Gayseros, Dir im
Bündnis,
Lockten Wald und Abendlichter.
Sieh mich hier nun, sag' nun weiter,
Wohin wandeln wir, du Lieber?«

»Donna Clara, Donna Clara,
Du bist Herrin, ich der Diener,
Du bist Lenk'rin, ich Planet nur,
Süße Macht, o wollst gebieten!«

»Gut, so wandeln wir den
Berghang
Dort zum Kruzifixe nieder;
Wenden drauf an der Kapelle
Heimwärts uns, entlängst den
Wiesen.«

»Ach, warum an der Kapelle,
Ach, warum bei'm Kruzifixe?« —
»Sprich, was hast Du nun zu streiten?
Meint ich ja, Du wärst mein Diener.«

»Ja, ich wandle, ja ich schreite,
Herrin ganz nach Deinem Willen.« —
Und sie wandelten zusammen,
Sprachen viel von süßer Minne.

'Don Gayseros, Don Gayseros,
Strange, fair knight,
Have you lured me from my castle
With your entreaties?

Don Gayseros, the forest and the evening
light,
In league with you, enticed me.
Behold me here now, and tell me,
Dearest, where we are to go.'

'Donna Clara, Donna Clara,
You are the mistress, I the servant;
You guide my course, I am but your planet.
Sweet ruler, give your command!'

'Good, then let us walk down the
mountainside
To yonder crucifix;
When we come to the chapel
Let us turn homewards, crossing the
meadows.'

'Ah, why to the chapel,
Why to the crucifix?'
'Tell me, why do you argue now?
I thought you were my servant.'

'Yes, mistress, I shall walk there,
Just as you wish.'
And they strolled together,
Talking much of sweet love.

»Don Gayseros, Don Gayseros,
Sieh, wir sind am Kruzifixe,
Hast Du nicht Dein Haupt gebogen
Vor dem Herrn, wie andre Christen?«

»Donna Clara, Donna Clara,
Konnt' ich auf was anders blicken,
Als auf Deine zarten Hände,
Wie sie mit den Blumen spielten?«

»Don Gayseros, Don Gayseros,
Konntest Du denn nichts erwidern,
Als der fromme Mönch Dich grüßte,
Sprechend: Christus geb' Dir
    Frieden?«

»Donna Clara, Donna Clara,
Durft' ins Ohr ein Laut mir dringen,
Irgend noch ein Laut auf Erden,
Da Du flüsternd sprachst: Ich liebe?«

»Don Gayseros, Don Gayseros,
Sieh' vor der Kapelle blinket
Des geweihten Wassers Schale!
Komm und tu' wie ich, Geliebter.«

»Donna Clara, Donna Clara,
Gänzlich mußt' ich jetzt erblinden,
Denn ich schaut' in Deine Augen,
Konnt' mich selbst nicht wiederfinden.«

»Don Gayseros, Don Gayseros,
Tu mir's nach, bist Du mein Diener,
Tauch' ins Wasser Deine Rechte,
Zeichn' ein Kreuz auf Deine
    Stirne.«

Don Gayseros schwieg erschrocken,
Don Gayseros floh von hinnen;
Donna Clara lenkte bebend
Zu der Burg die scheuen Tritte.

'Don Gayseros, Don Gayseros,
See, we have reached the crucifix;
Have you not bowed your head
Before the Lord, like other Christians?'

'Donna Clara, Donna Clara,
How could I look at anything
But your delicate hands,
Playing with the flowers?'

'Don Gayseros, Don Gayseros,
Could you not reply then
When the holy monk greeted you
With the words: "May Christ bring you
    peace"?'

'Donna Clara, Donna Clara,
How could any other sound on earth
Penetrate my ears,
As you whispered: "I love you"?'

'Don Gayseros, Don Gayseros,
Look, the basin of holy water
Glistens in front of the chapel!
Come and do as I do, beloved.'

'Donna Clara, Donna Clara,
I must now be completely blind,
For I gazed into your eyes,
And could not find myself again.'

'Don Gayseros, Don Gayseros,
Do as I do, you are my servant;
Dip your right hand into the water,
And make the sign of the cross on your
    brow.'

Don Gayseros, in horror, kept silent,
Don Gayseros fled from there;
And Donna Clara, trembling,
Turned her timid steps back to the castle.

Don Gayseros II / Don Gayseros II

FRIEDRICH DE LA MOTTE FOUQUÉ

D93 no. 2 (1815?)

Nächtens klang die süße Laute
Wo sie oft zu Nacht geklungen,
Nächtens sang der schöne Ritter,
Wo er oft zu Nacht gesungen.

Und das Fenster klirrte wieder,
Donna Clara schaut' herunter,
Aber furchtsam ihre Blicke
Schweiften durch das tau'ge Dunkel.

By night the sweet sound echoed,
Where it had so often echoed,
By night the fair knight sang,
As he had so often sung.

The window rattled once more,
And Donna Clara looked down;
But her fearful gaze
Swept through the dewy darkness.

Und statt süßer Minnelieder,
Statt der Schmeichelworte Kunde
Hub sie an ein streng Beschwören:
»Sag, wer bist Du, finstrer Buhle?

»Sag, bei Dein' und meiner Liebe,
Sag, bei Deiner Seelenruhe,
Bist ein Christ Du, bist ein Spanier?
Stehst Du in der Kirche
    Bunde?«

»Herrin, hoch hast Du beschworen,
Herrin, ja, Du sollst's erkunden.
Herrin, ach, ich bin kein Spanier,
Nicht in Deiner Kirche Bunde.

»Herrin, bin ein Mohrenkönig,
Glüh'nd in Deiner Liebe Gluten,
Groß an Macht und reich an Schätzen,
Sonder gleich an tapferm Mut.

»Rötlich blühn Granadas Gärten,
Golden stehn Alhambras Burgen,
Mohren harren ihrer Königin —
Fleuch mit mir durch's tau'ge Dunkel.«

«Fort, Du falscher Seelenräuber,
Fort, Du Feind!« — Sie wollt' es rufen,
Doch bevor sie Feind
    gesprochen,
Losch das Wort ihr aus im Munde.

Ohnmacht hielt in dunkeln Netzen,
Ihren schönen Leib umschlungen.
Er alsbald trug sie zu Rosse,
Rasch dann fort im mächt'gen Fluge.

And instead of sweet songs of love,
Instead of coaxing words,
She solemnly conjured him:
'Say, who are you, dark lover?

'Say, by your love and mine,
Say, upon the peace of your soul,
Are you a Christian, are you a Spaniard?
Do you stand within the family of the
    church?'

'Mistress, you have conjured nobly;
Mistress, you shall indeed discover.
Alas, mistress, I am no Spaniard,
Nor do I belong to your church.

'Mistress, I am a Moorish king,
Glowing with the fires of love for you;
I am great in power, rich in treasures,
And equally courageous.

'The gardens of Granada bloom red,
The turrets of the Alhambra are golden,
The Moors await their queen —
Fly with me through the dewy darkness.'

'Away with you, false plunderer of souls,
Away, Evil One!' — She tried to call out,
But before she had uttered the words 'Evil
    One',
They died on her lips.

Powerless, her fair body,
Was held in his dark clutches.
At once he bore her to his horse,
And then swiftly away in powerful flight.

Don Gayseros III / Don Gayseros III

FRIEDRICH DE LA MOTTE FOUQUÉ

D93 no. 3 (1815?)

An dem jungen Morgenhimmel
Steht die reine Sonne klar,
Aber Blut quillt auf der Wiese,
Und ein Roß, des Reiters baar,
Trabt verschüchtert in der Runde,
Starr steht eine reis'ge
    Schaar.
Mohrenkönig, bist erschlagen
Von dem tapfern Brüderpaar,
Das Dein kühnes Räuberwagnis
Nahm im grünen Forste wahr!
Donna Clara kniet bei'm Leichnam
Aufgelöst ihr goldnes Haar,
Sonder Scheue nun bekennend,
Wie ihr lieb der Tote war,
Brüder bitten, Priester lehren,

The sun shines pure and brightly
In the youthful morning sky;
But blood flows in the meadow,
And a horse without its rider,
Trots, frightened, in a circle.
A band of mounted mercenaries stands
    motionless;
Moorish king, you have been slain
By the two brave brothers
Who observed your bold abduction
In the green forest.
Donna Clara kneels by the corpse,
Her golden hair undone,
Now confessing freely
How dear the dead man was to her.
Her brothers plead, the priests exhort;

Eins nur bleibt ihr offenbar.
Sonne geht, und Sterne kommen,
Auf und nieder schwebt der Aar,
Alles auf der Welt ist Wandel
Sie allein unwandelbar.
Endlich bau'n die treuen Brüder
Dort Kapell' ihr und Altar,
Betend nun verrinnt ihr Leben,
Tag für Tag und Jahr für Jahr,
Bringt verhauchend sich als
   Opfer
Für des Liebsten Seele dar.

Only one thing is apparent to her.
The sun disappears, the stars come out,
The eagle soars up and down.
Everything in this world is in flux;
She alone is unchanging.
At length the faithful brothers
Build a chapel and an altar for her there;
Now her life passes in prayer;
Day after day, year after year,
She pines away, offering herself as a
   sacrifice
To the soul of her beloved.

Drang in die Ferne / *Longing to Escape*

KARL GOTTFRIED VON LEITNER

D770 (1823?)

Vater, du glaubst es nicht,
Wie's mir zum Herzen spricht,
Wenn ich die Wolken seh',
Oder am Strome steh';

Father, you do not believe
That my heart quickens
When I see the clouds
Or stand beside the stream?

Wolkengold, Wellengrün
Ziehen so leicht dahin,
Weilen im Sonnenlicht,
Aber bei Blumen nicht;

Golden clouds, green waves
Drift along so effortlessly,
Lingering in the sunshine,
But not by the flowers.

Zögern und rasten nie,
Eilen, als wüssten sie,
Ferne und ungekannt,
Irgend ein schönres Land.

They never tarry or rest,
Hastening as if they knew
Of some fairer land,
Distant and undiscovered.

Ach! von Gewölk und Flut
Hat auch mein wildes Blut
Heimlich geerbt den Drang,
Stürmet die Welt entlang!

Ah, from clouds and streams
My hot blood, too,
Has secretly caught the urge
To storm through the world.

Vaterlands Felsental
Wird mir zu eng, zu schmal,
Denn meiner Sehnsucht Traum
Findet darin nicht Raum.

The rocky valley of my native land
Is too narrow and confined,
For my yearning dreams
Cannot be contained there.

Lasst mich! ich muss
Fordern den Scheidekuss.
Vater und Mutter mein,
Müsset nicht böse sein!

Let me go! I must
Ask for the parting kiss.
Father and mother,
You must not be angry!

Hab euch ja herzlich lieb;
Aber ein wilder Trieb
Jagt mich waldein, waldaus,
Weit von dem Vaterhaus.

I love you dearly,
But a wild urge
Drives me to the forest and beyond,
Far from home.

Sorgt nicht, durch welches Land
Einsam mein Weg sich wand;
Monden- und Sternenschein
Leuchtet auch dort hinein.

Do not worry about where
My lonely, tortuous path may lead;
There too
The moon and stars will shine.

Überall wölbt's Gefild	Over all the earth
Sich den azur'nen Schild,	Arches the azure shield
Den um die ganze Welt	Which the Creator holds
Schirmend der Schöpfer hält.	To protect the whole world.
Ach! und wenn nimmermehr	Ah, and if I never
Ich zu euch wiederkehr',	Return to you, my loved ones,
Lieben, so denkt, er fand	Then you must think that I have found
Glücklich das schönre Land.	Happiness in a fairer land.

Du bist die Ruh / *You are Repose*

FRIEDRICH RÜCKERT

D776 (1823)

Du bist die Ruh,	You are repose
Der Friede mild,	And gentle peace;
Die Sehnsucht du,	You are longing
Und was sie stillt.	And what stills it.
Ich weihe dir	Full of joy and grief,
Voll Lust und Schmerz	I consecrate to you
Zur Wohnung hier	My eyes and my heart
Mein Aug'und Herz.	As a dwelling place.
Kehr ein bei mir	Come in to me,
Und schliesse du	And softly close
Still hinter dir	The gate
Die Pforte zu.	Behind you.
Treib andern Schmerz	Drive all other grief
Aus dieser Brust!	From my breast!
Voll sei dies Herz	Let my heart
Von deiner Lust.	Be full of your joy.
Dies Augenzelt,	The temple of my eyes
Von deinem Glanz	Is lit
Allein erhellt,	By your radiance alone:
O füll es ganz!	O, fill it wholly!

Du liebst mich nicht / *You do not Love me*

AUGUST GRAF VON PLATEN

D756 (1822)

Mein Herz ist zerrissen, du liebst mich nicht!	My heart is broken; you do not love me.
Du liessest mich's wissen, du liebst mich nicht!	You gave me to know that you do not love me.
Wiewohl ich dir flehend und werbend erschien,	Though I appeared before you, entreating, wooing,
Und liebebeflissen, du liebst mich nicht!	Zealously loving, you do not love me.
Du hast es gesprochen, mit Worten gesagt,	You told me so, you said it in words,
Mit allzu gewissen, du liebst mich nicht!	All too explicitly: you do not love me.
So soll ich die Sterne, so soll ich den Mond,	Then I must forgo the stars, the moon
Die Sonne vermissen, du liebst mich nicht!	And the sun. You do not love me.

Was blüht mir die Rose, was blüht der
    Jasmin,
Was blühn die Narzissen, du liebst mich
    nicht!

What is it to me that the rose
    blooms,
The jasmine and the narcissus? You do not
    love me.

Edone / Edone

FRIEDRICH GOTTLIEB KLOPSTOCK

D 445 (1816)

Dein süßes Bild, Edone,
Schwebt stets vor meinem Blick;
Allein ihn trüben Zähren,
Daß du es selbst nicht bist.

Your sweet image, Edone,
Forever hovers before my eyes;
But they are clouded by tears,
For it is not you.

Ich seh' es, wenn der Abend
Mir dämmert, wenn der Mond
Mir glänzt, seh' ich's, und weine,
Daß du es selbst nicht bist.

I see it when evening falls,
I see it when the moon shines,
And I weep,
For it is not you.

Bei jenes Tales Blumen,
Die ich ihr lesen will,
Bei jenen Myrtenzweigen,
Die ich ihr flechten will,

By the flowers in yonder valley,
Which I would gather for her,
By those myrtle stems,
Which I would plait for her,

Beschwör' ich dich, Erscheinung,
Auf, und verwandle dich!
Verwandle dich, Erscheinung,
Und werd' Edone selbst!

I call you up, apparition;
Arise, and transform yourself!
Transform yourself, apparition,
And become Edone herself!

Eine altschottische Ballade / An Old Scottish Ballad

PERCY'S 'RELIQUES', translated by J. G. HERDER

D 923 (1827)

»Dein Schwert, wie ist's von Blut so rot?
Eduard, Eduard!
Dein Schwert, wie ist's von Blut so rot
Und gehst so traurig da! — O!«
»Ich hab geschlagen meinen Geier tot,
Mutter, Mutter!
Ich hab geschlagen meinen Geier tot,
Und das, das geht mir nah! — O!«

'Why does your brand so drop wi' blood,
Edward, Edward?
Why does your brand so drop wi' blood,
And why so sad gang ye, O?'
'O, I have killed my hawk so good,
Mother, mother,
O I have killed my hawk so good,
And I had no more but he, O.'

»Dein's Geiers Blut ist nicht so rot!
Eduard, Eduard!
Dein's Geiers Blut ist nicht so rot,
Mein Sohn, bekenn mir frei! — O!«
»Ich hab geschlagen mein Rotroß tot!
Mutter, Mutter!
Ich hab geschlagen mein Rotroß tot!
Und's war so stolz und treu! O!«

'Your hawk's blood was never so red,
Edward, Edward:
Your hawk's blood was never so red,
My dear son I tell thee, O.'
'O, I have killed my red-roan steed,
Mother, mother!
O, I have killed my red-roan steed,
That erst was so fair and free, O.'

»Dein Roß war alt und hast's nicht not!
Eduard, Eduard,
Dein Roß war alt und hast's nicht not,

'Your steed was old, and ye have got more,
Edward, Edward:
Your steed was old, and ye have got more,

Dich drückt ein and'rer Schmerz! O!«	Some other dole ye dree, O!'
»Ich hab geschlagen meinen Vater tot,	'O, I have killed my father dear,
Mutter, Mutter!	Mother, mother;
Ich hab geschlagen meinen Vater tot,	O, I have killed my father dear,
Und das, das quält mein Herz! O!«	Alas, and woe is me, O!'

»Und was wirst du nun an dir tun?	'And what penance will ye dree for that,
Eduard, Eduard!	Edward, Edward?
Und was wirst du nun an dir tun?	And what penance will ye dree for that,
Mein Sohn, bekenn mir mehr! O!«	My dear son, now tell me, O.'
»Auf Erden soll mein Fuß nicht ruhn!	'I'll set my feet in yonder boat,
Mutter, Mutter,	Mother, mother:
Auf Erden soll mein Fuß nicht ruhn!	I'll set my feet in yonder boat,
Will wandern über's Meer! O!«	And I'll fare over the sea, O.'

»Und was soll werden dein Hof und Hall,	'And what will ye do with your towers and your hall,
Eduard, Eduard,	Edward, Edward?
Und was soll werden dein Hof und Hall?	And what will ye do with your towers and your hall,
So herrlich sonst und schön! O!«	That were so fair to see, O?'
»Ach! immer steh's und sink' und fall,	'I'll let them stand till they down fall,
Mutter, Mutter,	Mother, mother:
Ach immer steh's und sink' und fall,	I'll let them stand till they down fall,
Ich werd' es nimmer sehn! O!«	For here never more may I be, O.'

»Und was soll werden dein Weib und Kind,	'And what will ye leave to your bairns and your wife,
Eduard, Eduard?	Edward, Edward?
Und was soll werden dein Weib und Kind,	And what will ye leave to your bairns and your wife,
Wenn du gehst über's Meer — O!«	When ye gang o'er the sea, O?'
»Die Welt ist groß! laß sie betteln drinn,	'The world's room, let them beg thro' life,
Mutter, Mutter!	Mother, mother:
Die Welt ist groß! laß sie betteln drinn,	The world's room, let them beg thro' life,
Ich seh sie nimmer mehr! — O!«	For them never more will I see, O.'

»Und was soll deine Mutter tun?	'And what will ye leave to your own mother dear,
Eduard, Eduard!	Edward, Edward?
Und was soll deine Mutter tun?	And what will ye leave to your own mother dear,
Mein Sohn, das sage mir! O!«	My dear son, now tell me, O.'
»Der Fluch der Hölle soll auf Euch ruhn,	'The curse of hell from me shall she bear,
Mutter, Mutter!	Mother, mother!
Der Fluch der Hölle soll auf Euch ruhn,	The curse of hell from me shall she bear,
Denn ihr, ihr rietet's mit! O.«	Such counsels she gave to me, O.'

Eine Leichenphantasie / *A Funereal Fantasy*

FRIEDRICH VON SCHILLER

D7 *(1811)*

Mit erstorb'nem Scheinen	With dim light
Steht der Mond auf totenstillen Hainen,	The moon shines over the death-still groves,
Seufzend streift der Nachtgeist durch die Luft —	Sighing, the night spirit skims through the air —

Nebelwolken schauern,
Sterne trauern
Bleich herab, wie Lampen in der Gruft.
Gleich Gespenstern, stumm und hohl
    und hager,
Zieht in schwarzem Totenpompe dort
Ein Gewimmel nach dem Leichenlager
Unterm Schauerflor der Grabnacht fort.

Zitternd an der Krücke,
Wer mit düsterm, rückgesunknem Blicke,
Ausgegossen in ein heulend Ach,
Schwer geneckt vom eisernen Geschicke,
Schwankt dem stummgetragnen Sarge
    nach?
Floss es »Vater« von des Jünglings Lippe?
Nasse Schauer schauern fürchterlich
Durch sein gramgeschmolzenes Gerippe,
Seine Silberhaare bäumen sich.

Aufgerissen seine Feuerwunde!
Durch die Seele Höllenschmerz!
»Vater« floss es von des Jünglings Munde.
»Sohn« gelispelt hat das Vaterherz.
Eiskalt, eiskalt liegt er hier im Tuche,
Und dein Traum, so golden einst, so süss,
Süss und golden, Vater, dir zum
    Fluche!
Eiskalt, eiskalt liegt er hier im Tuche,
Deine Wonne und dein Paradies!

Mild, wie umweht von Elysiumslüften,
Wie, aus Auroras Umarmung geschlüpft,
Himmlisch umgürtet mit rosigten
    Düften,
Florens Sohn über das Blumenfeld
    hüpft,
Flog er einher auf den lachenden Wiesen,
Nachgespiegelt von silberner Flut,
Wollustflammen entsprühten den Küssen,
Jagten die Mädchen in liebende Glut.

Mutig sprang er im Gewühle der
    Menschen,
Wie ein jugendlich Reh;
Himmel um flog er in schweifenden
    Wünschen,
Hoch wie der Adler in wolkiger Höh':
Stolz wie die Rosse sich sträuben und
    schäumen,
Werfen im Sturme die Mähnen umher,
Königlich wider den Zügel sich bäumen,
Trat er vor Sklaven und Fürsten daher.

Heiter wie Frühlingstag schwand ihm das
    Leben,
Flog ihm vorüber in Hesperus' Glanz,
Klagen ertränkt' er im Golde der Reben,
Schmerzen verhüpft' er im wirbelnden
    Tanz.

Mist-clouds are shivering,
Pale stars shine down mournfully
Like lamps in a vault.
Like ghosts, silent, hollow,
    gaunt,
In black funeral pomp
A procession moves towards the graveyard
Beneath the dread veil of the burial night.

Who is he, who, trembling on crutches,
With sombre, sunken gaze,
Pouring out his misery in a cry of pain,
And harshly tormented by an iron fate,
Totters behind the silently borne
    coffin?
Did the boy's lips say 'Father'?
Damp, fearful shudders run through
His frame, racked with grief;
His silver hair stands on end.

His burning wound is torn open
By the hellish pain of his soul!
'Father', uttered the boy's lips,
'Son', whispered the father's heart.
Ice-cold, he lies here in his shroud,
And your dream, once so golden, so sweet,
Sweet and golden, now a curse on you,
    father!
Ice-cold he lies here in his shroud,
Your joy and your paradise!

Gentle, as if stroked by Elysian breezes,
As if, slipping from Aurora's embrace,
Wreathed in the heavenly fragrance of
    roses,
It were Flora's son dancing over the flowery
    fields,
He flew across the smiling meadows,
Mirrored by the silver waters;
Flames of desire sprang from his kisses,
Driving maidens to burning passion.

Bravely he leapt amid the swarm of
    humanity,
Like a young deer;
With his restless longings he flew around
    the heavens.
As high as an eagle, soaring in the clouds;
Proud as the steeds as they rear,
    foaming,
Tossing their manes in the storm,
And regally resisting the reins,
Did he walk before slaves and princes.

His life slipped by, as bright as a spring
    day,
Flying past him in the glow of Hesperus;
He drowned his sorrows in the golden vine,
He tripped away his grief in the whirling
    dance.

Welten schliefen im herrlichen
    Jungen,
Ha! wenn er einsten zum Manne gereift —
Freue dich, Vater, im herrlichen Jungen,
Wenn einst die schlafenden Keime
    gereift!

Nein doch, Vater — Horch! die
    Kirchhoftüre brauset,
Und die ehrnen Angel klirren auf —
Wie's hinein ins Grabgewölbe grauset!
Nein doch, lass den Tränen ihren Lauf!
Geh, du Holder, geh im Pfade der Sonne
Freudig weiter der Vollendung zu,
Lösche nun den edlen Durst nach Wonne,
Gramentbundner, in Walhallas
    Ruh!

Wiedersehen — himmlischer Gedanke!
Wiedersehen dort an Edens Tor!
Horch! der Sarg versinkt mit dumpfigem
    Geschwanke,
Wimmernd schnurrt das Totenseil empor!
Da wir trunken um einander
    rollten,
Lippen schwiegen und das Auge sprach
»Haltet! Haltet!« da wir boshaft grollten —
Aber Tränen stürzten wärmer nach.

Mit erstorb'nem Scheinen
Steht der Mond auf totenstillen Hainen,
Seufzend streift der Nachtgeist durch die
    Luft —
Nebelwolken schauern,
Sterne trauern
Bleich herab, wie Lampen in der Gruft.
Dumpfig schollert's überm Sarg zum
    Hügel,
O um Erdballs Schätze nur noch einen
    Blick!
Starr und ewig schliesst des Grabes Riegel,
Dumpfer schollert's überm Sarg zum
    Hügel,
Nimmer gibt das Grab zurück.

Whole worlds lay dormant in the fine
    youth,
Ah! When he matures into a man —
Rejoice, father, in the fine boy,
When, one day, the latent seeds are
    ripened!

But no, father — hark! the churchyard gate
    is rattling,
And the iron hinges are creaking open —
How terrifying it is to peer into the grave!
But no, let the tears flow!
So, gracious youth, in the sun's path,
Joyfully onwards to perfection,
Quench your noble thirst for joy,
Released from pain, in the peace of
    Valhalla!

To see him again — heavenly thought!
To see him again at the gates of Eden!
Hark! the coffin sways and falls with dull
    thud,
The ropes whirr upwards with a whine!
When we rolled drunkenly among one
    another
Our lips were silent, but our eyes spoke:
'Stop! Stop!' When we grew angry —
But afterwards tears fell more warmly.

With dim light
The moon shines over the death-still groves
Sighing, the night spirit skims through the
    air —
Mist-clouds are shivering,
Pale stars shine down mournfully,
Like lamps in a vault.
With a thud clods pile over the
    coffin,
Oh, for just one more glimpse of the earth's
    treasure!
The grave's bolts close, rigid and eternal,
The thud of the clods grows duller as they
    pile over the coffin,
The grave will never yield up!

Einsamkeit / Solitude

JOHANN MAYRHOFER

D 620 (1818)

»Gib mir die Fülle der Einsamkeit.«
Im Tal, von Blüten
    überschneit,
Da ragt ein Dom, und nebenbei
In hohem Stile die Abtei:
Wie ihr Begründer, fromm und still,
Der Müden Hafen und Asyl,
Hier kühlt mit heiliger Betauung,

'Give me my fill of solitude.'
In the valley, bedecked with snowy
    blossom,
A cathedral soars up, and nearby
The abbey in the gothic style,
Devout and calm, like its founder,
Haven and refuge of the weary.
Here unending contemplation

Die nie versiegende Beschauung.
Doch den frischen Jüngling quälen
Selbst in gottgeweihten Zellen
Bilder, feuriger verjüngt;
Und ein wilder Strom entspringt
Aus der Brust, die er umdämmt,
Und in einem Augenblick
Ist der Ruhe zartes Glück
Von den Wellen weggeschwemmt.

»Gib mir die Fülle der Tätigkeit.«
Menschen wimmeln weit und breit,
Wagen kreuzen sich und stäuben,
Käufer sich um Läden treiben,
Rotes Gold und heller Stein
Lockt die Zögernden hinein,
Und Ersatz für Landesgrüne
Bieten Maskenball und Bühne.
Doch in prangenden Palästen,
Bei der Freude lauten Festen,
Spriesst empor der Schwermut Blume,
Senkt ihr Haupt zum Heiligtume
Seiner Jugend Unschuldlust,
Zu dem blauen Hirtenland
Und der Lichten Quelle Rand.
Ach, dass er hinweggemusst!

»Gib mir das Glück der Geselligkeit.«
Gefährten, freundlich angereiht
Der Tafel, stimmen Chorus an
Und ebenen die Felsenbahn!
So geht's zum schönen Hügelkranz
Und abwärts zu des Stromes Tanz,
Und immer mehr befestiget sich Neigung
Mit treuer, kräftiger
    Verzweigung.
Doch, wenn ihm die Freunde schieden,
Ist's getan um seinen Frieden.
Ihn bewegt der Sehnsucht Schmerz,
Und er schauet himmelwärts:
Das Gestirn der Liebe strahlt.
Liebe, Liebe ruft die laue Luft,
Liebe, Liebe atmet Blumenduft,
Und sein Inn'res Liebe hallt.

»Gib mir die Fülle der Seligkeit.«
Nun wandelt er in Trunkenheit
An ihrer Hand in schweigenden
    Gesprächen,
Im Buchengang, an weissen
    Bächen,
Und muss er auch durch Wüstenein,
Ihm leuchtet süsser Augen Schein;
Und in der feindlichsten Verwirrung
Vertrauet er der holden Führung.
Doch die Särge grosser Ahnen,
Siegerkronen, Sturmes-
    fahnen
Lassen ihn nicht fürder ruh'n:
Und er muss ein Gleiches tun,
Und wie sie unsterblich sein.

Brings sacred refreshment to the spirit.
But the young man,
Even in his consecrated cell, is tortured
By ever more ardent longings.
A wild torrent pours forth
From his breast; he seeks to stem it,
But in a single moment
His fragile, tranquil happiness
Is swept away by the flood.

'Give me my fill of activity.'
Everywhere there are throngs of people;
Coaches pass each other, throwing up dust,
Customers crowd around shops,
Red gold and dazzling stones
Tempt the hesitant inside.
Masked balls and plays
Are a substitute for the green countryside.
But in the magnificent palaces,
Amid noisy, joyful banquets,
The flower of melancholy springs up,
And lowers her head towards the sanctuary
Of his happy, innocent youth,
To the blue land of shepherds
And the edge of the sparkling stream.
Alas, that he had to depart!

'Give me the pleasure of good company!'
Friends, cheerfully seated
At table, strike up a song
To smoothe life's rocky path.
Up we go to the fair hills,
And down to the dancing river;
Our affection grows ever stronger,
And other firm, devoted attachments are
    formed.
But when friends have parted
His peace is gone.
Pierced by the pain of longing
He gazes heavenwards;
There the star of love shines.
Love calls in the balmy air,
Love wafts from the fragrant flowers,
And his inmost being is vibrant with love.

'Give me my fill of bliss!'
Now he walks, enraptured,
Holding her hand in silent
    communion,
Along the avenue of beech-trees, beside the
    clear brook;
And even if he has to walk through deserts,
Her sweet eyes will shine for him.
Amid the most hostile confusion
He trusts his fair guide.
But the tombs of his great forebears,
The crowns of conquerors, the ensigns of
    war,
Allow him no further peace.
He must do as they,
And like them become immortal.

Sieh, er steigt aufs hohe Pferd,	See, he mounts his noble steed,
Schwingt und prüft das blanke Schwert,	Tests his shining sword with a flourish,
Reitet in die Schlacht hinein.	And rides into battle.

»Gib mir die Fülle der Düsterkeit.«	'Give me my fill of gloom!'
Da liegen sie im Blute	There they lie, stretched out in their own
hingestreut,	blood,
Die Lippe starr, das Auge wild gebrochen,	Who first defied terror,
Die erst dem Schrecken Trotz gesprochen.	Their lips rigid, their eyes wild with death.
Kein Vater kehrt den Seinen mehr,	No father comes back to his family,
Und heimwärts kehrt ein ander Heer,	A quite different army returns home;
Und denen Krieg das Teuerste	And those who have lost their dearest in the
genommen,	war
Begrüssen nun mit schmerzlichem	Now bid that army a sorrowful
Willkommen!	welcome.
So deucht ihm des Vaterlandes Wächter	His fatherland's guardians
Ein ergrimmter Bruderschlächter,	Now appear to him as incensed murderers,
Der der Freiheit edel Gut	Nurturing noble freedom
Düngt mit rotem Menschenblut.	With the red blood of mankind.
Und er flucht dem tollen Ruhm	And he curses giddy fame,
Und tauschet lärmendes Gewühl	Exchanging noisy tumult
Mit dem Forste, grün und kühl,	For the cool, green forest,
Mit dem Waldesleben um.	For life amid the woodland

»Gib mir die Weihe der Einsamkeit.«	'Give me the consecration of solitude!'
Durch dichte Tannendunkelheit	Through the darkness of dense pines
Dringt Sonnenblick nur halb und halb,	The sun only half penetrates,
Und färbet Nadelschichten	And paints the beds of needles with a dusky
falb.	hue.
Der Kuckuck ruft aus Zweiggeflecht,	The cuckoo calls from the thicket
An grauer Rinde pickt der Specht,	The woodpecker pecks at the grey bark,
Und donnernd über Klippenhemmung	And the bold torrent
Ergeht des Giessbachs kühne Strömung.	Thunders over the barrier of rocks.
Was er wünschte, was er liebte,	Whatever he desired, whatever he loved,
Ihn erfreute, ihn betrübte,	Whatever brought him joy and pain
Schwebt mit sanfter Schwärmerei	Floats past with gentle rapture,
Wie im Abendrot vorbei.	As if in the glow of evening.
Jünglings Sehnsucht, Einsamkeit,	Solitude, the young man's longing,
Wird dem Greisen nun zuteil,	Is now the old man's lot,
Und ein Leben rauh und steil	And a harsh, arduous life
Führte doch zur Seligkeit.	Has finally led to happiness.

Ellens Gesang I / *Ellen's Song I*

SIR WALTER SCOTT, translated by ADAM STORCK

D837 (1825)
The texts of Ellen's three songs come from Scott's narrative poem 'The Lady of the Lake'. A literal rendering of Storck's translation is followed by Scott's original verses, in italics.

Raste Krieger! Krieg ist aus,	Rest, warrior! Your war is over,
Schlaf den Schlaf, nichts wird dich	Sleep the sleep, nothing shall wake
wecken,	you;
Träume nicht vom wilden Strauß,	Do not dream of the fierce battle,
Nicht von Tag und Nacht voll Schrecken.	Of days and nights filled with terrors.

In der Insel Zauberhallen	In the island's enchanted halls
Wird ein weicher Schlafgesang	A soft lullaby

Um das müde Haupt dir wallen
Zu der Zauberharfe Klang.

Feen mit unsichtbaren Händen
Werden auf dein Lager hin
Holde Schlummerblumen senden,
Die im Zauberlande blühn.

Raste Krieger, Krieg ist aus,
Schlaf den Schlaf, nichts wird dich
    wecken.
Träume nicht vom wilden Strauß,
Nicht von Tag und Nacht voll Schrecken.

Nicht der Trommel wildes Rasen,
Nicht des Kriegs Kommandowort,
Nicht der Todeshörner Blasen
Scheuchen deinen Schlummer fort.

Nicht das Stampfen wilder Pferde,
Nicht der Schreckensruf der Wacht,
Nicht das Bild von Tagsbeschwerde
Stören deine stille Nacht.

Doch der Lerche Morgensänge
Wecken sanft dein schlummernd Ohr,
Und des Sumpfgefieders Klänge
Steigend aus Geschilf und Rohr.

Raste Krieger! Krieg ist aus,
Schlaf den Schlaf, nichts wird dich
    wecken,
Träume nicht vom wilden Strauß,
Nicht von Tag und Nacht voll Schrecken.

Shall caress your weary head
To the strains of a magic harp.

Fairies with unseen hands
Shall strew upon your bed
Sweet flowers of sleep
That bloom in the enchanted land.

Rest, warrior! Your war is over,
Sleep the sleep, nothing shall wake
    you;
Do not dream of the fierce battle,
Of days and nights filled with terrors.

Neither the wild crash of drums,
Nor the summons to battle,
Nor the blaring of death's horns
Shall frighten away your sleep.

Neither the stomping of frenzied horses,
Nor the sentry's fearful cry,
Nor a vision of the day's cares
Shall disturb your tranquil night.

Yet the lark's morning song
Shall gently awaken your slumbering ear,
And the sounds of marsh birds
Soaring from reeds and rushes.

Rest, warrior! Your war is over,
Sleep the sleep, nothing shall wake
    you;
Do not dream of the fierce battle,
Of days and nights filled with terrors.

Soldier rest! thy warfare o'er,
Sleep the sleep that knows not breaking;
Dream of battled fields no more,
Days of danger, nights of waking.

In our isle's enchanted hall,
Hands unseen thy couch are strewing,
Fairy strains of music fall,
Every sense in slumber dewing,

Soldier rest! thy warfare o'er,
Dream of fighting fields no more:
Sleep the sleep that knows not breaking,
Morn of toil, nor night of waking.

No rude sound shall reach thine ear,
Armour's clang, or war-steed champing,
Trump nor pibroch summon here
Mustering clan, or squadron tramping.

Yet the lark's shrill fife may come
At the day-break from the fallow,
And the bittern sound his drum.
Booming from the sedgy shallow.

Ruder sounds shall none be near
Guards nor warders challenge here,
Here's no war-steeds neigh and champing,
Shouting clans, or squadrons stamping.

Ellens Gesang II / Ellen's Song II

SIR WALTER SCOTT, translated by ADAM STORCK

D 838 (1825)

Jäger, ruhe von der Jagd!	Huntsman, rest from the chase!
Weicher Schlummer soll dich decken,	Gentle slumber shall cover you;
Träume nicht, wenn Sonn' erwacht,	Do not dream that when the sun rises
Daß Jagdhörner dich aufwecken.	Hunting horns shall wake you.

Schlaf! der Hirsch ruht in der Höhle,	Sleep! The stag rests in his den,
Bei dir sind die Hunde wach,	Your hounds lie awake beside you;
Schlaf, nicht quäl' es deine Seele,	Sleep! Let it not torment your soul
Daß dein edles Roß erlag.	That your noble steed has perished.

Jäger, ruhe von der Jagd!	Huntsman, rest from the chase!
Weicher Schlummer soll dich decken;	Gentle slumber shall cover you;
Wenn der junge Tag erwacht,	When the new day dawns
Wird kein Jägerhorn dich wecken.	No hunting horn shall wake you.

'Huntsman, rest! thy chase is done,
While our slumbrous spells assail ye,
Dream not, with the rising sun,
Bugles here shall sound reveillé.
Sleep! the deer is in his den;
Sleep! Thy hounds are by thee lying;
Sleep! nor dream in yonder glen,
How thy gallant steed lay dying.
Huntsman, rest! thy chase is done,
Think not of the rising sun,
For at dawning to assail ye,
Here no bugles sound reveillé.'

Ellens Gesang III / Ellen's Song III

SIR WALTER SCOTT, translated by ADAM STORCK

D839 (1825)

Ave Maria! Jungfrau mild,	Ave Maria! Maiden mild!
Erhöre einer Jungfrau Flehen,	Listen to a maiden's entreaty;
Aus diesem Felsen starr und wild	From this wild, unyielding rock
Soll mein Gebet zu dir hinwehen.	My prayer shall be wafted to you.
Wir schlafen sicher bis zum Morgen,	We shall sleep safely until morning,
Ob Menschen noch so grausam sind.	However cruel men may be.
O Jungfrau, sieh der Jungfrau Sorgen,	O Maiden, behold a maiden's cares,
O Mutter, hör ein bittend Kind!	O Mother, hear a suppliant child!
Ave Maria!	Ave Maria!

Ave Maria! Unbefleckt!	Ave Maria! Undefiled!
Wenn wir auf diesen Fels hinsinken	When we sink down upon this rock
Zum Schlaf, und uns dein Schutz	To sleep, and your protection hovers over
bedeckt,	us,
Wird weich der harte Fels uns dünken.	The hard rock shall seem soft to us.
Du lächelst, Rosendüfte wehen	You smile, and the fragrance of roses
In dieser dumpfen Felsenkluft,	Wafts through this musty cavern.
O Mutter, höre Kindes Flehen,	O Mother, hear a suppliant child,
O Jungfrau, eine Jungfrau ruft!	O Maiden, a maiden cries to you!
Ave Maria!	Ave Maria!

Ave Maria! Reine Magd!
Der Erde und der Luft Dämonen,
Von deines Auges Huld verjagt,
Sie können hier nicht bei uns wohnen.
Wir woll'n uns still dem Schicksal beugen,
Da uns dein heil'ger Trost anweht;
Der Jungfrau wolle hold dich neigen,
Dem Kind, das für den Vater fleht.
Ave Maria!

Ave Maria! Purest Maiden!
Demons of the earth and air,
Banished by the grace of your gaze,
Cannot dwell with us here.
Let us silently bow to our fate,
Since your holy comfort touches us;
Incline in grace to a maiden,
To a child that prays for its father.
Ave Maria!

Ave Maria! maiden mild!
Listen to a maiden's prayer!
Thou canst hear though from the wild,
Thou canst save amid despair.
Safe may we sleep beneath thy care,
Though banish'd, outcast, and reviled —
Maiden! hear a maiden's prayer;
Mother, hear a suppliant child!
Ave Maria!

Ave Maria! undefiled!
The flinty couch we now must share
Shall seem this down of eider piled,
If thy protection hover there.
The murky cavern's heavy air
Shall breathe of balm if thou hast smiled;
Then, maiden! hear a maiden's prayer;
Mother, list a suppliant child!
Ave Maria!

Ave Maria! stainless styled!
Foul demons of the earth and air,
From this their wonted haunt exiled,
Shall flee before thy presence fair.
We bow us to our lot of care,
Beneath thy guidance reconciled;
Hear for a maid a maiden's prayer,
And for a father hear a child!
Ave Maria!

Elysium / Elysium

FRIEDRICH VON SCHILLER

D 584 (1817)

Vorüber die stöhnende Klage!
Elysium's Freudengelage
Ersäufen jegliches Ach.
Elysium's Leben
Ewige Wonne, ewiges Schweben,
Durch lachende Fluren ein flötender
   Bach.

Cease all plaintive moaning!
Elysian banquets
Drown all suffering.
Elysian life
Is eternal bliss, eternal lightness,
A melodious stream flowing through
   smiling meadows.

Jugendlich milde
Beschwebt die Gefilde
Ewiger Mai;
Die Stunden entfliehen in goldenen
   Träumen,

Eternal May,
Young and tender,
Hovers over the landscape;
The hours fly past in golden
   dreams,

Die Seele schwillt aus in unendlichen Räumen.	The soul expands in infinite space.
Wahrheit reisst hier den Schleier entzwei.	Here truth rends the veil.

Unendliche Freude
Durchwallet das Herz.
Hier mangelt der Name dem trauernden Leide,
Sanftes Entzücken nur heisset man Schmerz.

Endless joy
Fills the heart.
Here grieving sorrow has no name;
And rapture that is but gentle seems like pain.

Hier strecket der wallende Pilger die matten
Brennenden Glieder in säuselnden Schatten,
Leget die Bürde auf ewig dahin—
Seine Sichel entfällt hier dem Schnitter,
Eingesungen von Harfengezitter
Träumt er, geschnittene Halme zu sehn.

Here the pilgrim stretches his weary,
Burning limbs in the murmuring shade,
And lays down his burden for ever.
The reaper's sickle falls from his hand;
Lulled to sleep by quivering harps
He dreams he sees blades of mown grass.

Dessen Fahne Donnerstürme wallte,
Dessen Ohren Mordgebrüll umhallte,
Berge bebten unter dessen Donnergang,
Schläft hier linde bei des Baches Rieseln,
Der wie Silber spielet über Kieseln;
Ihm verhallet wilder Speere Klang.

He whose standard raged with violent storms,
Whose ears rang with murderous cries
And beneath whose thunderous steps mountains quaked,
Sleeps gently here by the babbling stream
That plays like silver over the pebbles.
For him the violent clash of spears grows faint.

Hier umarmen sich getreue Gatten,
Küssen sich auf grünen samtnen Matten,
Liebgekost vom Balsamwest;
Ihre Krone findet hier die Liebe,
Sicher vor des Todes strengem Hiebe
Feiert sie ein ewig Hochzeitsfest.

Here faithful couples embrace
And kiss on the green velvet sward,
Caressed by the balmy west wind.
Here love finds its crown;
Safe from the cruel stroke of death
It celebrates an eternal wedding feast.

Entzückung / *Rapture*

FRIEDRICH VON MATTHISSON

D 413 (1816)

Tag voll Himmel! da aus Lauras Blicken
Mir der Liebe heiligstes Entzücken
In die wonnetrunk'ne Seele drang!
Und, von ihrem Zauber hingerissen,
Ich der Holden, unter Feuerküssen,
An den süssbeklommnen Busen sank!

Heavenly day! When from Laura's gaze
Love's most sacred rapture
Pierced my soul in its ecstasy!
And, carried away by her magic,
I sank, amid ardent kisses,
On my fair one's sweetly trembling breast!

Goldner sah ich Wolken sich besäumen,
Jedes Blättchen auf den Frühlingsbäumen
Schien zu flüstern: »Ewig, ewig dein!«
Glücklicher, in solcher Taumelfülle,
Werd' ich, nach verstäubter Erdenhülle,
Kaum in Edens Myrthenlauben sein.

I saw the clouds fringed with a richer gold;
Every tiny leaf on the trees of springtime
Seemed to whisper: 'For ever yours!'
I shall scarcely be happier, or in such joyful delirium,
In the myrtle groves of Eden,
When this mortal frame has turned to dust.

Tag voll Himmel! da aus Lauras Blicken
Mir der Liebe heiligstes Entzücken
In die wonnetrunk'ne Seele drang!

Day of heaven! When from Laura's gaze
Love's most sacred rapture
Pierced my soul in its ecstasy!

Epistel: Musikalischer Schwank / Epistle: A Musical Farce

MATTHÄUS VON COLLIN

D749 (1822)

Recitativo:
Und nimmer schreibst du?
Bleibest uns verloren,
Ein starr Verstummter,
Nun für ewige Zeit?
Vielleicht, weil neue Freunde du
  erkoren?
Wardst du Assessor denn am Tisch so
  breit,
Woran beim Aktenstoss seufzt Langeweile,
Um abzusterben aller Freudigkeit?
Doch nein, nur wir sind's.
Nur uns ward zuteile
Dies Schweigen, dies Verstummen und
  Vergessen.
Armut und Not selbst an der kleinsten
  Zeile!
Für jeden bist du schriftkarg nicht
  gesessen;
Für manchen kamen Briefe angeflogen,
Und nach der Elle hast du sie
  gemessen;
Doch uns, Barbar, hast du dein Herz
  entzogen!

Recitative:
And do you never write?
Are you lost to us
For all time,
Struck dumb?
Perhaps because you have found new
  friends?
Or have you become a judge, sitting at a
  vast desk,
Sighing with boredom at your heap of files,
In order to forgo all joy?
Of course not, it's just us.
Only we have been granted
This silence, this muteness, this forgetful-
  ness.
Not even the smallest line for the poor and
  needy!
Not for everyone have you been miserly
  with your pen;
For some, letters have streamed in,
And you have surely measured them by the
  yard.
But from us, barbarian, you have with-
  drawn your heart!

Aria:
Schwingt euch kühn, zu bange Klagen,
Aus empörter Brust hervor,
Und, von Melodien getragen,
Wagt euch an des Fernen Ohr!
Was er immer mag erwidern,
Dieses hier saget doch:
»Zwar vergessen, jenes Biedern
Denken wir in Liebe noch!«

Aria:
Anxious plaints, soar boldly
From our incensed hearts
And, borne aloft by melodies,
Dare to approach his distant ear.
Whatever he may retort
Tell him this:
'Though we are forgotten,
We still think lovingly of the good fellow!'

Erinnerung: Die Erscheinung / Remembrance: Apparition

LUDWIG KOSEGARTEN

D229 (1815)

Ich lag auf grünen Matten,
An klarer Quellen Rand.
Mir kühlten Erlenschatten
Der Wangen heißen Brand.
Ich dachte dies und jenes,
Und träumte, sanftbetrübt,
Viel Süßes mir und Schönes,
Was diese Welt nicht gibt.

I lay in green meadows
By the edge of the clear spring;
The shade of alders
Cooled the fire of my cheeks.
I thought of this and that,
And dreamed with gentle sorrows
Of many a good and lovely thing
Which this world does not yield.

Und sieh, dem Hain entschwebte	And lo, from the grove there arose
Ein Mägdlein sonnenklar.	A maiden, as bright as the sun.
Ein weißer Schleier webte	A white veil flowed
Um ihr nußbraunes Haar.	Around her nut-brown hair.
Ihr Auge, feucht und schimmernd,	Her moist, shining eyes
Umfloß ätherisch Blau,	Were flooded with heavenly blue,
Die Wimper näßte flimmernd	And on her eyelashes glistened
Der Wehmut Perlentau.	Dewy pearls of sadness.
Ein traurend Lächeln schwebte	A mournful smile hovered
Um ihren süßen Mund.	Around her sweet lips.
Sie schauerte! Sie bebte!	She shuddered, she trembled!
Ihr Auge, tränenwund,	I thought her tearful eyes
Ihr Hinschau'n liebesehnend,	And her lovelorn gaze
So wähnt' ich, suchte mich.	Were seeking me.
Wer war, wie ich, so wähnend,	Who was so deluded,
So selig, wer, wie ich?	Who was so blissfully happy as I?
Ich auf, sie zu umfassen!	I stood up to embrace her,
Und ach, sie trat zurück.	And, alas, she receded;
Ich sah sie schnell erblassen,	I saw her quickly pale,
Und trüber ward ihr Blick.	And her gaze grew more sorrowful.
Sie sah mich an so innig,	She looked upon me so fervently,
Sie wies mit ihrer Hand,	And with her hand she gestured
Erhaben und tiefsinnig,	Solemnly and pensively towards heaven,
Gen Himmel und verschwand.	And vanished.
Fahr wohl, fahr wohl, Erscheinung!	Farewell, farewell, vision!
Fahr wohl, dich kenn' ich wohl!	Farewell, I know you well,
Und deines Winkes Meinung	And understand as I should
Versteh' ich, wie ich soll . . .	The meaning of your sign.
»Wohl für die Zeit geschieden	'Though we are parted for a time,
Eint uns ein schön'res Band.	A fairer bond unites us;
Hoch droben, nicht hinieden	High above, not here below,
Hat Lieb' ihr Vaterland!	Love has its home!'

Errinerungen / Memories

FRIEDRICH VON MATTHISSON

D98 (1814)

Am Seegestad', in lauen Vollmond- nächten,	By the shores of the lake, on warm nights with full moon,
Denk' ich nur dich!	I think only of you,
Zu deines Namens goldnem Zug verflechten	The stars intertwine
Die Sterne sich.	To spell your name in gold.
Die Wildnis glänzt in ungewohnter Helle,	The wilderness gleams with unwonted brightness,
Von dir erfüllt;	Filled with you;
Auf jedes Blatt, in jede Schattenquelle	On every leaf, in every shady spring
Malt sich dein Bild.	Your image is painted.
Gern weil' ich, Grazie, wo du den Hügel Hinabgeschwebt,	I gladly linger, fair one, as you glide down The hillside
Leicht, wie ein Rosenblatt auf Zephyrs Flügel	Light as a passing roseleaf
Vorüberbebt.	Quivering on the zephyr's wings.

Am Hüttchen dort bekränzt' ich dir,
umflossen
Von Abendglut,
Mit Immergrün und jungen
Blütensprossen
Den Halmenhut.

Bei jedem Lichtwurm in den
Felsenstücken,
Als ob die Feen
Da Tänze webten, riefst du voll
Entzücken:
»Wie schön! wie schön!«

Wohin ich blick' und geh', erblick' ich
immer
Den Wiesenplan,
Wo wir der Berge Schnee mit Purpur-
schimmer
Beleuchtet sahn.

Ihr schmelzend Mailied weinte Philomele
Im Uferhain;
Da fleht' ich dir, im Blick die ganze
Seele:
Gedenke mein!

There, by the little
hut,
Bathed in evening light,
I garlanded your straw
hat
With evergreens and fresh blossoms.

Watching the glow-
worms
Dance among the rocks like fairies,
You would cry out with
delight:
'How lovely!'

Wherever I look, wherever I
go,
I always see the meadows,
Where we once saw the mountain
snow
Tinged with crimson.

Philomel sighed her melting May song
In the grove by the shore;
There I implored you, with my whole soul
in my gaze:
Remember me!

Erlafsee / Lake Erlaf

JOHANN MAYRHOFER

D 586 (1817)

Mir ist so wohl, so weh'
Am stillen Erlafsee:
Heilig Schweigen
In Fichtenzweigen,
Regungslos
Der blaue Schoss,
Nur der Wolken Schatten flieh'n
Überm glatten Spiegel hin,
Frische Winde
Kräuseln linde
Das Gewässer
Und der Sonne
Güld'ne Krone
Flimmert blässer.
Mir ist so wohl, so weh'
Am stillen Erlafsee.

I am so happy, and yet so sad,
By the calm waters of Lake Erlaf.
A solemn silence
Amid the pine-branches;
Motionless
The blue depths.
Only the clouds' shadows flit
Across the glassy surface.
Cool breezes
Gently ruffle
The water,
And the sun's
Golden corona
Grows paler.
I am so happy, and yet so sad,
By the calm waters of Lake Erlaf.

Erlkönig / The Erlking

JOHANN WOLFGANG VON GOETHE

D 328 (1815)

Wer reitet so spät durch Nacht und Wind?
Es ist der Vater mit seinem Kind;

Who rides so late through night and wind?
It is the father with his child.

Er hat den Knaben wohl in dem Arm,
Er fasst ihn sicher, er hält ihn warm.

»Mein Sohn, was birgst du so bang dein
        Gesicht?«
»Siehst, Vater, du den Erlkönig nicht?
Den Erlenkönig mit Kron und Schweif?«
»Mein Sohn, es ist ein Nebelstreif.«

»Du liebes Kind, komm, geh mit mir!
Gar schöne Spiele spiel ich mit dir;
Manch bunte Blumen sind an dem Strand,
Meine Mutter hat manch gülden Gewand.«

»Mein Vater, mein Vater, und hörest du
        nicht,
Was Erlenkönig mir leise verspricht?«
»Sei ruhig, bleibe ruhig, mein Kind:
In dürren Blättern säuselt der Wind.«

»Willst, feiner Knabe, du mit mir gehn?
Meine Töchter sollen dich warten schön;
Meine Töchter führen den nächtlichen
        Reihn
Und wiegen und tanzen und singen dich
        ein.«

»Mein Vater, mein Vater, und siehst du
        nicht dort
Erlkönigs Töchter am düstern Ort?«
»Mein Sohn, mein Sohn, ich seh es genau:
Es scheinen die alten Weiden so grau.«

»Ich liebe dich, mich reizt deine schöne
        Gestalt;
Und bist du nicht willig, so brauch ich
        Gewalt.«
«Mein Vater, mein Vater, jetzt fasst er
        mich an!
Erlkönig hat mir ein Leids getan!«

Dem Vater grausets, er reitet geschwind,
Er hält in Armen das ächzende Kind,
Erreicht den Hof mit Mühe und Not:
In seinen Armen das Kind war tot.

He has the boy in his arms,
He holds him safely, he keeps him warm.

'My son, why do you hide your face in
        fear?'
'Father, can you not see the Erlking?
The Erlking with his crown and tail?'
'My son, it is a streak of mist.'

'Sweet child, come with me,
I'll play wonderful games with you;
Many a pretty flower grows on the shore,
My mother has many a golden robe.'

'Father, father, do you not
        hear
What the Erlking softly promises me?'
'Calm, be calm my child:
The wind is rustling in the withered leaves.'

'Won't you come with me, my fine lad?
My daughters shall wait upon you;
My daughters lead the nightly
        dance,
And will rock, and dance, and sing you to
        sleep.'

'Father, father, can you not
        see
Erlking's daughters there in the darkness?'
'My son, I can see clearly:
It is the old grey willows gleaming.'

'I love you, your fair form allures
        me,
And if you don't come willingly, I'll use
        force.'
'Father, father, now he's seizing
        me!
The Erlking has hurt me!'

The father shudders, he rides swiftly,
Holding the moaning child in his arms;
With one last effort he reaches home;
The child lay dead in his arms.

Erntelied / Harvest Song

LUDWIG HEINRICH CHRISTOPH HÖLTY

D 434 (1816)

Sicheln schallen,
Ähren fallen
Unter Sichelschall;
Auf den Mädchenhüten
Zittern blaue Blüten,
Freud ist überall.

Sickles echo,
Ears of corn fall
To the sound of the sickles,
On the girls' bonnets
Blue flowers quiver;
Joy is everywhere.

Sicheln klingen,	Sickles resound,
Mädchen singen	Girls sing
Unter Sichelklang,	To the sound of the sickles;
Bis vom Mond beschimmert,	Until, bathed in moonlight,
Rings die Stoppel flimmert,	The stubble shimmers all around,
Tönt der Erntesang.	And the harvest song rings out.

Alles springet,	All leap about,
Alles singet,	All who can utter a sound
Was nur lallen kann.	Sing out.
Bei dem Erntemahle	At the harvest feast
Ißt aus einer Schale	The farmer and his labourer
Knecht und Bauersmann.	Eat from the same bowl.

Jeder scherzet,	Then every man teases
Jeder herzet	And hugs
Dann sein Liebelein.	His sweetheart.
Nach geleerten Kannen,	When the tankards are empty
Gehen sie von dannen,	They go off
Singen und juchhein!	Singing and shouting with joy.

Erster Verlust / First Loss

JOHANN WOLFGANG VON GOETHE

D 226 (1815)

Ach, wer bringt die schönen Tage,	Ah, who will bring back those fair days,
Jene Tage der ersten Liebe,	Those days of first love?
Ach, wer bringt nur eine Stunde	Ah, who will bring back but one hour
Jener holden Zeit zurück!	Of that sweet time?
Einsam nähr ich meine Wunde,	Alone I nurture my wound
Und mit stets erneuter Klage	And, forever renewing my lament,
Traur ich ums verlorne Glück.	Mourn my lost happiness.
Ach, wer bringt die schönen Tage,	Ah, who will bring back those fair days,
Jene holde Zeit zurück!	That sweet time?

Fahrt zum Hades / Journey to Hades

JOHANN MAYRHOFER

D 526 (1817)

Der Nachen dröhnt, Cypressen flüstern,	The boat moans, the cypresses whisper;
Horch, Geister reden schaurig drein;	Hark, the spirits add their gruesome cries.
Bald werd' ich am Gestad', dem düstern,	Soon I shall reach the shore, so gloomy,
Weit von der schönen Erde sein.	Far from the fair earth.

Da leuchten Sonne nicht, noch Sterne,	There neither sun nor stars shine,
Da tönt kein Lied, da ist kein Freund.	No song echoes, no friend is nigh.
Empfang die letzte Träne, o Ferne,	Distant earth, accept the last tear
Die dieses müde Auge weint.	That these tired eyes will weep.

Schon schau' ich die blassen Danaiden,	Already I see the pale Danaids,
Den fluchbeladnen Tantalus;	And curse-laden Tantalus.
Es murmelt todesschwangern Frieden,	Your ancient river, Oblivion,
Vergessenheit, dein alter Fluss.	Breathes a peace heavy with death.

Vergessen nenn' ich zwiefach Sterben,
Was ich mit höchster Kraft
  gewann,
Verlieren, wieder es erwerben —
Wann enden diese Qualen? Wann?

Oblivion I deem a twofold death;
To lose that which I won with all my
  strength,
To strive for it once more —
When will these torments cease? O When?

Fischerlied / Fisherman's Song

JOHANN GAUDENZ VON SALIS-SEEWIS

First version: D 351 (1816?)
Second version: D 562 (1817)

Das Fischergewerbe
Gibt rüstigen Mut!
Wir haben zum Erbe
Die Güter der Flut.
Wir graben nicht Schätze,
Wir pflügen kein Feld;
Wir ernten im Netze,
Wir angeln uns Geld.

The fisherman's trade
Give us a cheerful heart.
Our inheritance
Is the wealth of the waters.
We dig for no treasure,
We plough no fields;
We harvest with our nets,
We fish for money.

Wir heben die Reusen
Den Schilfbach entlang,
Und ruhn bei den Schleusen,
Zu sondern den Fang;
Goldweiden beschatten
Das moosige Dach,
Wir schlummern auf Matten
Im kühlen Gemach.

We lay the fish traps
Along the reed-covered stream,
And rest at the locks
To sort our catch.
Golden willows shade
The mossy roof;
We sleep on mats
In the cool chamber.

Der Herr, der in Stürmen
Der Mitternacht blitzt,
Vermag uns zu schirmen,
Und kennt, was uns nützt.
Gleich unter dem Flügel
Des Ewigen ruht
Der Rasengruft Hügel,
Das Grab in der Flut.

The Lord, whose thunderbolts flash
In midnight storms,
Can protect us
And knows what we need.
Beneath the wings
Of the Eternal One
Rest the mound of the grassy tomb,
And the grave beneath the waters.

Fischerweise / Fisherman's Song

FRANZ XAVER VON SCHLECHTA

D 881 (1826?)

Den Fischer fechten Sorgen
Und Gram und Leid nicht an;
Er löst am frühen Morgen
Mit leichtem Sinn den Kahn.

The fisherman is not plagued
By cares, grief or sorrow.
In the early morning he casts off
His boat with a light heart.

Da lagert rings noch Friede
Auf Wald und Flur und Bach,
Er ruft mit seinem Liede
Die gold'ne Sonne wach.

Round about, peace still lies
Over forest, meadow and stream,
With his song the fisherman
Bids the golden sun awake.

Er singt zu seinem Werke	He sings at his work
Aus voller frischer Brust,	From a full, vigorous heart.
Die Arbeit gibt ihm Stärke,	His work gives him strength,
Die Stärke Lebenslust.	His strength exhilarates him.
Bald wird ein bunt' Gewimmel	Soon a bright multitude
In allen Tiefen laut	Will resound in the depths,
Und plätschert durch den Himmel,	And splash
Der sich im Wasser baut.	Through the watery heavens.
Doch wer ein Netz will stellen,	But whoever wishes to set a net
Braucht Augen klar und gut,	Needs good, clear eyes,
Muß heiter gleich den Wellen	Must be as cheerful as the waves,
Und frei sein wie die Flut.	And as free as the tide.
Dort angelt auf der Brücke	There, on the bridge, the shepherdess
Die Hirtin. Schlauer Wicht,	Is fishing. Cunning wench,
Entsage deiner Tücke,	Leave off your tricks!
Den Fisch betrügst du nicht!	You won't deceive *this* fish!

Florio / Florio*

CHRISTIAN WILHELM VON SCHÜTZ

D857 no. 1 (1825)

Florio (vortretend)	*Florio (stepping forward)*
Nun, da Schatten niedergleiten,	Now that the shadows glide down,
Und die Lüfte zärtlich wehen,	And the breezes blow gently,
Dringet Seufzen aus der Seele,	Call forth sighs from the soul
Und umgirrt die treuen Saiten.	And caress the faithful strings.
Klaget, daß ihr mit mir sterbet	Lament that you die with me
Bittern Tod, wenn die nicht heilet,	A bitter death, unless she
Die den Becher mir gereicht,	Who handed me the cup,
Voller Gift in süßem	Filled with sweet, poisoned sherbet, cures
Scherbet.	me.
Erst mit Tönen, sanft wie Flöten,	First with sounds as soft as flutes
Goß sie Schmerz in meine Adern;	She poured pain into my veins;
Sehen wollte sie der Kranke,	The invalid desired to see her,
Und nun wird ihr Reiz ihn töten.	But now her charms will kill him.
Nacht, komm her, mich zu umwinden	Come, o night, and envelop me
Mit dem farbenlosen Dunkel!	In your colourless darkness!
Ruhe will ich bei dir suchen,	With you I will seek the rest
Die mir not tut bald zu finden.	Which I need to find quickly.

Fragment aus dem Aeschylus / Fragment from Aeschylus

JOHANN MAYRHOFER

D450 (1816)

So wird der Mann, der sonder Zwang	Thus the man who is by nature
gerecht ist,	just
Nicht unglücklich sein, versinken ganz in	Will not be unhappy; he can never sink
Elend kann er nimmer;	completely into misery.

*Text from Schütz's play *Lacrimas*.

Indes der frevelnde Verbrecher im Strome
der Zeit
Gewaltsam untergeht, wenn am zer-
schmetterten Maste
Das Wetter die Segel ergreift.
Er ruft, von keinem Ohr vernommen,
Kämpft in des Strudels Mitte,
hoffnungslos.
Des Frevlers lacht die Gottheit nun,
Sieht ihn, nun nicht mehr stolz,
In Banden der Not verstrickt,
Umsonst die Felsbank fliehn;
An der Vergeltung Fels scheitert sein
Glück,
Und unbeweint versinkt er.

Whereas in the river of time the wicked
criminal
Is swept under violently when the storm
tears the sails
From the shattered mast.
He cries out, but no ear hears him,
He struggles hopelessly in the midst of the
maelstrom.
Now the gods mock the evildoer,
And behold him, no longer proud,
Enmeshed in the toils of distress,
Fleeing in vain the rocky reef;
On the cliffs of vengeance his fortune is
wrecked,
And unmourned he sinks.

Freiwilliges Versinken / Voluntary Oblivion

JOHANN MAYRHOFER

D700 (1817?)

Wohin, o Helios? Wohin? In kühlen
Fluten
Will ich den Flammenleib versenken,
Gewiss im Innern, neue Gluten
Der Erde Feuerreich zu schenken.

Whither, o Helios? In cool
waters
I will immerse my burning body,
Inwardly certain that I can bestow
New warmth upon the earth's fires.

Ich nehme nicht, ich pflege nur zu geben;
Und wie verschwenderisch mein Leben,
Umhüllt mein Scheiden gold'ne Pracht,
Ich scheide herrlich, naht die Nacht.

I do not take; I am wont only to give.
As prodigal as my life,
My parting is bathed in golden splendour;
I depart in glory when night draws near.

Wie blass der Mond, wie matt die Sterne!
Solang ich kräftig mich bewege;
Erst wenn ich auf die Berge meine Krone
lege,
Gewinnen sie an Mut und Kraft in weiter
Ferne.

How pale the moon, how faint the stars,
As long as I move on my powerful course;
Only when I lay down my crown upon the
mountains
Do they gain strength and courage in the far
distance.

Freude der Kinderjahre / Joy of Childhood

FRIEDRICH VON KÖPKEN

D455 (1816)

Freude, die im frühen Lenze
Meinem Haupte Blumen wand,
Sieh, noch duften deine Kränze,
Noch geh' ich an deiner Hand;
Selbst der Kindheit Knospen blühen
Auf in meiner Phantasie;
Und mit frischem Reize glühen
Noch in meinem Herbste sie.

Joy which in early spring
Wove flowers around my head,
See, your garlands are still fragrant,
And I still walk holding your hand.
Even the buds of childhood bloom
In my imagination,
And still shine with fresh charm
In my autumn.

Früh schon kannt' ich dich! du
wehtest
Froh bei jedem Spiel um mich,

From early childhood I knew you! You
fluttered
Happily around me whenever I played,

Sprangst in meinem Balle, drehtest
Leicht in meinem Kreisel dich:
Liefst mit mir durch Gras und
    Hecken
Flüchtig Schmetterlingen nach,
Rittest mit auf bunten
    Stecken,
Wirbeltest im Trommelschlag.

Kamen auch zuweilen Sorgen:
Kindersorgen sind nicht gross!
Früh hüpft' ich am andern Morgen,
Schaukelte die Sorgen los;
Kletterte dir nach auf Bäume,
Wälzte müd' im Grase mich;
Und entschlief ich: süsse Träume
Zeigten mir im Bilde dich!

You bounced with my ball, spun
Easily in my top;
You ran swiftly with me through grass and
    hedgerow,
Chasing butterflies.
You rode with me on bright-painted hobby
    horses,
And rolled when I played the drum.

At times, too, there were cares;
A child's cares are not great.
Early the next morning I would skip about,
And swing away my cares.
I would climb trees, following you,
And roll in the grass when tired;
And when I fell asleep sweet dreams
Would reveal your image.

Frohsinn / Cheerfulness

IGNAZ FRANZ CASTELLI

D 520 (1817)

Ich bin von lockrem Schlage,
Geniess ohne Trübsinn die Welt,
Mich drückt kein Schmerz, keine Plage,
Mein Frohsinn würzt mir die Tage,
Ihn hab ich zum Schild mir gewählt.

I'm a happy-go-lucky fellow,
And enjoy the world without melancholy;
No sorrow, no care worries me,
My cheerfulness adds spice to my days;
I have chosen it as my shield.

Frühlingsglaube / Faith in Spring

LUDWIG UHLAND

D 686 (1820)

Die linden Lüfte sind erwacht,
Sie säuseln und weben Tag und Nacht,
Sie schaffen an allen Enden.
O frischer Duft, o neuer Klang!
Nun, armes Herze, sei nicht bang!
Nun muss sich alles, alles wenden.

Die Welt wird schöner mit jedem Tag,
Man weiss nicht, was noch werden mag,
Das Blühen will nicht enden;
Es blüht das fernste, tiefste
    Tal:
Nun, armes Herz, vergiss der Qual!
Nun muss sich alles, alles wenden.

Balmy breezes are awakened,
They stir and whisper day and night,
Everywhere creative.
O fresh scents, o new sounds!
Now, poor heart, do not be afraid.
Now all must change.

The world grows fairer each day,
We cannot know what is still to come,
The flowering knows no end.
The deepest, most distant valley is in
    flower.
Now, poor heart, forget your torment.
Now all must change.

Frühlingslied / Spring Song

LUDWIG HEINRICH CHRISTOPH HÖLTY

D 398 (1816)

Die Luft ist blau, das Tal ist grün,
Die kleinen Maienglocken blühn,
Und Schlüsselblumen drunter;
Der Wiesengrund
Ist schon so bunt
Und malt sich täglich bunter.

Drum komme, wem der Mai gefällt,
Und schaue froh die schöne Welt
Und Gottes Vatergüte,
Die solche Pracht
Hervorgebracht,
Den Baum und seine Blüte.

The sky is blue, the valley green,
The lilies of the valley are in bloom,
With cowslips among them;
The meadows
Are already so colourful,
And grow more so each day.

Come, then, if you love May,
Behold with joy the beautiful world
And God's fatherly kindness,
That brought forth
Such splendour,
The tree and its blossom.

Frühlingslied / Spring Song

AARON POLLAK

D 919 (1827?)

Geöffnet sind des Winters Riegel,
Entschwunden ist sein Silberflor;
Hell blinken der Gewässer Spiegel,
Die Lerche schwingt sich hoch empor;
Wie durch des greisen Königs Siegel
Geweckt ertönt der Freude Chor.

Der Frühling schwebt auf das Gefilde
Und lieblich wehet Zephyr nur,
Der Blumenfülle süße Milde
Erhebt sich in der Luft Azur,
In der Verklärung Wunderbilde
Empfängt uns lächelnd die Natur.

Schon prangen goldgeschmückt
Sylphiden
Und Florens Reich erblüht
verschönt,
Rings waltet Lust und stiller Frieden,
Der Hain ist nun mit Laub bekrönt,
Wer fühlet, ihm ist Glück
beschieden,
Weil Eros' süßer Ruf ertönt.

Empfanget denn mit trautem Gruße
Den holden Lenz, den Schmuck der Welt,
Der weihend uns mit leisem Kusse
Des Daseins Rosenbahn
erhellt,
Der hold uns winkt zum
Hochgenusse
Und jedes Herz mit Wonne schwellt.

Winter's bolts are opened,
His silver veil has vanished;
The mirrors of the water sparkle brightly,
The lark soars aloft;
As if awakened by the old king's seal,
The chorus of joy resounds.

Spring hovers over the fields,
And zephyrs blow softly;
The gentle sweetness of abundant flowers
Rises into the azure air.
In its magical transfiguration
Smiling nature receives us.

Already sylphs are resplendent in gold
array,
And Flora's realm blooms with enhanced
beauty;
All around there is joy and tranquil peace;
The grove is now crowned with leaves,
And happiness is granted to all who have
feelings,
Since the sweet call of Eros resounds.

So receive with a heartfelt greeting
Fair spring, the jewel of the world,
Who with a soft kiss consecrates
And brightens the rosy path of our
existence,
Sweetly beckons us to the highest
pleasures,
And fills ever heart with bliss.

Frühlingssehnsucht / Spring Longing

LUDWIG RELLSTAB

see Schwanengesang no. 3

Fülle der Liebe / Love's Abundance

FRIEDRICH VON SCHLEGEL

D854 (1825)

Ein sehnend' Streben
Teilt mir das Herz,
Bis alles Leben
Sich löst in Schmerz.

A yearning desire
Pierces my heart,
Till all life
Is dissolved in sorrow.

In Leid erwachte
Der junge Sinn,
Und Liebe brachte
Zum Ziel mich hin.

The youthful spirit
Awoke in suffering
And love brought me
To my goal.

Ihr, edle Flammen,
Wecktet mich auf,
Es ging mitsammen
Zu Gott der Lauf.

You, noble flames,
Aroused me,
Everything surged
To God.

Ein Feuer war es,
Das alles treibt,
Ein starkes, klares,
Das ewig bleibt.

It was a fire
Driving it all,
A strong, clear fire
That remains for ever.

Was wir anstrebten,
War treu gemeint;
Was wir durchlebten,
Bleibt tief vereint.

What we strove for
Was truly meant;
What we lived through
Remains profoundly united.

Da trat ein Scheiden
Mir in die Brust,
Das tiefe Leiden
Der Liebeslust.

Then a parting
Entered my heart;
The deep sorrow
Of love's joy.

Im Seelengrunde
Wohnt mir ein Bild,
Die Todeswunde
Ward nie gestillt.

In the depths of my soul
Dwells an image.
The fatal wound
Was never healed.

Viel tausend Tränen
Flossen hinab,
Ein ewig Sehnen
Zu ihr ins Grab.

Many thousand tears
Flowed down,
An eternal longing
For her in the grave.

In Liebeswogen
Wallet der Geist,
Bis fortgezogen
Die Brust zerreißt.

The spirit surges
In waves of love
Until, when it has departed,
The heart breaks.

Ein Stern erschien
Mir vom Paradies,
Und dahin fliehn
Wir vereint gewiß.

A star appeared
To me from Paradise;
And there, united,
We shall assuredly escape.

Hier noch befeuchtet	Here my gaze is still moist
Der Blick sich lind,	With gentle tears
Wenn mich umleuchtet	When around me shines
Dies Himmelskind.	This heavenly child.
Ein Zauber waltet	A magic spell
Jetzt über mich,	Now holds me in thrall,
Und der gestaltet	Fashioning all this
Dies all' nach sich,	In its own way,
Als ob uns vermähle	As if a spiritual power
Geistesgewalt,	United us
Wo Seel' in Seele	Where soul surges
Hinüber wallt.	Into soul.
Ob auch zerspalten	Although my heart
Mir ist das Herz,	Is torn in two
Selig doch halten	I will consider
Will ich den Schmerz.	My sorrow a blessing.

Furcht der Geliebten / The Beloved's Fear

FRIEDRICH GOTTLIEB KLOPSTOCK

D 285 (1815)

Cidli, du weinest, und ich schlummre sicher,	Cidli, you weep, and I slumber safely
Wo im Sande der Weg verzogen fortschleicht;	Where the path winds through the sand,
Auch wenn stille Nacht ihn umschattend decket,	Even when the silent night shrouds that path in shadow
Schlummr' ich ihn sicher.	I shall slumber safely.
Wo er sich endet, wo ein Strom das Meer wird,	Where it ends, where river becomes sea,
Gleit ich über den Strom, der sanfter aufschwillt;	I shall glide upon the current which flows more gently,
Denn der mich begleitet, der Gott gebot's ihm.	For God, who accompanies me, bids it flow thus.
Weine nicht, Cidli!	Do not weep, Cidli.

Ganymed / Ganymede

JOHANN WOLFGANG VON GOETHE

D 544 (1817)

Wie im Morgenglanze	How your glow envelops me
Du rings mich anglühst,	In the morning radiance,
Frühling, Geliebter!	Spring, my beloved!
Mit tausendfacher Liebeswonne	With love's thousandfold joy
Sich an mein Herz drängt	The hallowed sensation
Deiner ewigen Wärme	Of your eternal warmth
Heilig Gefühl,	Floods my heart,
Unendliche Schöne!	Infinite beauty!
Dass ich dich fassen möcht	O that I might clasp you
In diesen Arm!	In my arms!

Ach, an deinem Busen
Lieg ich, schmachte,
Und deine Blumen, dein Gras
Drängen sich an mein Herz.
Du kühlst den brennenden
Durst meines Busens,
Lieblicher Morgenwind!
Ruft drein die Nachtigall
Liebend nach mir aus dem Nebeltal.

Ich komm, ich komme!
Wohin? Ach, wohin?

Hinauf! Hinauf strebt's.
Es schweben die Wolken
Abwärts, die Wolken
Neigen sich der sehnenden Liebe.
Mir! Mir!
In euerm Schosse
Aufwärts!
Umfangend umfangen!
Aufwärts an deinen Busen,
Alliebender Vater!

Ah, on your breast
I lie languishing,
And your flowers, your grass
Press close to my heart.
You cool the burning
Thirst within my breast,
Sweet morning breeze,
As the nightingale calls
Tenderly to me from the misty valley.

I come, I come!
But whither? Ah whither?

Upwards! strive upwards!
The clouds drift
Down, yielding
To yearning love,
To me, to me!
In your lap,
Upwards,
Embracing and embraced!
Upwards to your bosom,
All-loving Father!

Gebet während der Schlacht / *Prayer during Battle*

THEODOR KÖRNER

D 171 (1815)

Vater, ich rufe dich!
Brüllend umwölkt mich der Dampf der
    Geschütze,
Sprühend umzucken mich rasselnde
    Blitze.
Lenker der Schlachten, ich rufe dich!
Vater du, führe mich!

Vater du, führe mich!
Führ' mich zum Siege, führ' mich zum
    Tode:
O Herr, ich erkenne deine Gebote;
Herr, wie du willst, so führe mich.
Gott, ich erkenne dich!

Gott, ich erkenne dich!
So im herbstlichen Rauschen der
    Blätter,
Als im Schlachtendonnerwetter,
Urquell der Gnade, erkenn' ich dich!
Vater du, segne mich!

Vater du, segne mich!
In deine Hand befehl' ich mein Leben,
Du kannst es nehmen, du hast es gegeben;
Zum Leben, zum Sterben segne
    mich!
Vater, ich preise dich!

Father, I cry unto You!
The smoke of roaring guns envelops
    me,
Explosive flashes dart all around
    me.
Lord of battles, I cry unto You!
Father, guide me!

Father, guide me!
Lead me to victory, lead me to
    death.
Lord, I acknowledge Your commands;
Lead me, Lord, where You will.
God, I acknowledge You!

God, I acknowledge You!
In the autumnal rustling of
    leaves,
As in the thunder of battle;
Source of grace, I acknowledge You!
Father, grant me Your blessing!

Father, grant me Your blessing!
Into Your hands I commend my life;
You may take it, for You gave it.
Whether for life or death, grant me Your
    blessing!
Father, I praise You!

Vater, ich preise dich!	Father, I praise You!
'S ist ja kein Kampf für die Güter der Erde;	This is no battle for the riches of this earth;
Das Heiligste schützen wir mit dem Schwerte:	With the sword we defend that which is most sacred;
Drum, fallend, und siegend, preis' ich dich.	Therefore, whether dying or victorious, I praise you.
Gott, dir ergeb' ich mich!	God, I surrender myself to You!
Gott, dir ergeb' ich mich!	God, I surrender myself to You!
Wenn mich die Donner des Todes begrüßen,	If the thunder of death greets me,
Wenn meine Adern geöffnet fließen:	If my open veins flow,
Dir, mein Gott, dir ergeb' ich mich!	To You, my God, I surrender myself!
Vater, ich rufe dich!	Father, I cry unto You!

Geheimes / A Secret

JOHANN WOLFGANG VON GOETHE

D 719 (1821)

Über meines Liebchens Äugeln	Everyone is astonished
Stehn verwundert alle Leute;	At the eyes my sweetheart makes;
Ich, der Wissende, dagegen,	But I, who understand,
Weiss recht gut, was das bedeute.	Know very well what they mean.
Denn es heisst: ich liebe diesen,	For they are saying: *he* is the one I love,
Und nicht etwa den und jenen.	Not this one or that one.
Lasset nur, ihr guten Leute,	So, good people,
Euer Wundern, euer Sehnen!	Cease your wondering and your longing!
Ja, mit ungeheuren Mächten	Indeed, she may well look about her
Blicket sie wohl in die Runde;	With a mightily powerful eye,
Doch sie sucht nur zu verkünden	But she seeks only to give him a foretaste
Ihm die nächste süsse Stunde.	Of the next sweet hour.

Geheimnis (An Franz Schubert) / Secret (To Franz Schubert)

JOHANN MAYRHOFER

D 491 (1816)

Sag an, wer lehrt dich Lieder,	Tell us, who teaches you
So schmeichelnd und so zart?	Such tender, flattering songs?
Sie rufen einen Himmel	They evoke a heaven
Aus trüber Gegenwart.	From these cheerless times.
Erst lag das Land, verschleiert,	First the land lay veiled
Im Nebel vor uns da —	In mist before us —
Du singst — und Sonnen leuchten,	Then you sing, and the sun shines,
Und Frühling ist uns nah.	And spring is near.
Den Alten schilfbekränzten,	You do not see
Der seine Urne gießt,	The old man, crowned with reeds,
Erblickst du nicht, nur Wasser,	Emptying his urn;
Wie's durch die Wiesen fließt.	You see only water flowing through the meadows.
So geht es auch dem Sänger,	So, too, it is with the singer.
Er singt, er staunt in sich;	He sings, he marvels inwardly;
Was still ein Gott bereitet,	He wonders, as you do,
Befremdet ihn, wie dich.	At God's silent creation.

Geist der Liebe / Spirit of Love

LUDWIG KOSEGARTEN

D 233 (1815)

Wer bist du, Geist der Liebe,
Der durch das Weltall webt,
Den Schoss der Erde schwängert
Und den Atom belebt?
Der Elemente bindet,
Der Weltenkugeln ballt,
Aus Engelharfen jubelt,
Und aus dem Säugling lallt?

Nur der ist gut und edel,
Dem du den Bogen spannst.
Nur der ist gross und göttlich,
Den du zum Mann ermannst.
Sein Werk ist Pyramide,
Sein Wort ist Machtgebot,
Ein Spott ist ihm die Hölle,
Ein Hohn ist ihm der Tod.

Who are you, spirit of love,
Who are at work throughout the universe,
Sowing the seed in the earth's womb,
And giving life to the atom?
Who are you, who bind the elements,
Fashion the spheres,
Rejoice with angels' harps,
And lisp from the infant's mouth.

He alone is good and noble
Whose bow is drawn by you,
He alone is great and godlike
Who through you attains true manhood.
His work is a pyramid,
His word is a mighty command.
He mocks hell,
And scorns death.

Geist der Liebe / Spirit of Love

FRIEDRICH VON MATTHISSON

D 414 (1816)

Der Abend schleiert Flur und Hain
In traulichholde Dämmrung ein;
Hell flimmt, wo goldne Wölkchen ziehn,
Der Stern der Liebeskönigin.

Die Wogenflut hallt Schlummerklang,
Die Bäume lispeln Abendsang,
Der Wiese Gras umgaukelt lind
Mit Sylphenkuß der Frühlingswind.

Der Geist der Liebe wirkt und strebt,
Wo nur ein Puls der Schöpfung bebt;
Im Strom, wo Wog' in Woge fließt,
Im Hain, wo Blatt an Blatt sich schließt.

O Geist der Liebe! führe du
Dem Jüngling die Erkorne zu!
Ein Minneblick der Trauten hellt
Mit Himmelsglanz die Erdenwelt!

Evening veils meadow and grove
In sweet, friendly dusk;
Brightly, amid passing golden clouds,
The star of Venus shines.

The waves murmur lullabies,
The trees whisper evensong,
With delicate kisses the spring breeze
Plays gently in the meadow grass.

The spirit of love is busy at work
Wherever the pulse of creation beats;
In the torrent, where wave flows into wave,
In the grove, where leaf clings to leaf.

O spirit of love, lead the youth
To his chosen one!
One tender glance from his beloved
Will fill this world with heavenly radiance!

Geisternähe / Nearby Spirits

FRIEDRICH VON MATTHISSON

D 100 (1814)

Der Dämm'rung Schein
Durchblinkt den Hain;
Hier, beim Geräusch des Wasserfalles,
Denk' ich nur dich, o du mein
  Alles!

The light of dusk
Glimmers through the grove;
Here, by the murmur of the waterfall
I think only of you, who are everything to
  me!

Dein Zauberbild	Your magical image
Erscheint, so mild	Appears, so gentle,
Wie Hesperus im Abendgolde,	Like Hesperus in the gold of evening,
Dem fernen Freund, geliebte Holde!	To your distant friend, my beloved!

Er sehnt wie hier	He yearns for you always,
Sich stets nach dir;	As he does here;
Fest, wie den Stamm die Efeuranke	His loving thoughts embrace you
Umschlingt dich liebend sein	As tightly as the ivy embraces the tree-
Gedanke.	trunk.

Durchbebt dich auch	Do you, too, quiver
Im Abendhauch	In the evening breeze
Des Brudergeistes leises Weh'n	With the faint breath of a kindred spirit,
Mit Vorgefühl von Wiederseh'n?	A presentiment of our reunion?

Er ist's, der lind	It is this, sweet child,
Dir, süsses Kind,	Which gently
Des Schleiers Silbernebel kräuselt,	Weaves a silver veil of mist
Und in der Locken Fülle säuselt.	And ruffles your abundant curls.

Oft hörst du ihn,	Often you hear it,
Wie Melodien	Like wistful melodies
Der Wehmut aus gedämpften Saiten	From muted strings,
In stiller Nacht vorübergleiten.	Wafting past in the silent night.

Auch fesselfrei	Although unfettered,
Wird er getreu,	This spirit will faithfully
Dir ganz und einzig hingegeben,	Devote himself to you alone,
In allen Welten dich	And hover over you throughout the
umschweben.	universe.

Geistes-Gruss / A Spirit's Greeting

JOHANN WOLFGANG VON GOETHE

D 142 (1815?)

Hoch auf dem alten Turme steht	High on the ancient tower
Des Helden edler Geist,	Stands the hero's noble spirit;
Der, wie das Schiff vorübergeht,	As the ship passes
Es wohl zu fahren heisst.	He bids it a safe voyage.

»Sieh, diese Sehne war so stark,	'See, these sinews were so strong,
Dies Herz so fest und wild,	This heart so steadfast and bold,
Die Knochen voll von Rittermark,	These bones full of knightly valour;
Der Becher angefüllt;	My cup was overflowing.

»Mein halbes Leben stürmt' ich fort,	'Half my life I sallied forth,
Verdehnt' die Hälft' in Ruh,	Half I spent in tranquillity;
Und du, du Menschenschifflein dort,	And you, little boat of mankind,
Fahr' immer, immer zu!«	Sail ever onward!'

Genügsamkeit / Simple Needs

FRANZ VON SCHOBER

D 143 (1815?)

»Dort raget ein Berg aus den Wolken	'There a mountain rises nobly above the
hehr,	clouds,
Ihn erreicht wohl mein eilender Schritt.	My rapid steps approach it.

Doch ragen neue und immer mehr, Fort, da mich der Drang noch durchglüht.«	But new peaks, more and more, tower up, As I am inspired to press onwards.'
Es treibt ihn vom schwebenden Rosenlicht Aus dem ruhigen, heitern Azur. Und endlich waren's die Berge nicht, Es war seine Sehnsucht nur.	He is urged on by the shimmering rosy light From the calm, serene azure. But in the end there were no mountains; It was only his longing.
Doch nun wird es ringsum öd' und flach, Und doch kann er nimmer zurück. »O Götter, gebt mir ein Hüttendach Im Tal und ein friedliches Glück.«	All around it is desolate and flat And yet he can never turn back. 'Gods, give me a hut In the valley, and tranquil good fortune.'

Gesang der Norna / Norna's Song

SIR WALTER SCOTT, translated by S. H. SPIKER

D831 (1825)
A literal rendering of Spiker's translation is given here. Scott's original poem
is printed below in italics.

Mich führt mein Weg wohl meilenlang Durch Gold und Strom und Wassergrab. Die Welle kennt den Runensang Und glättet sich zum Spiegel ab.	My course leads me for many a mile Through gulf and stream and moat; The waves know the Runic lay And grow mirror-smooth.
Die Welle kennt den Runensang, Der Golf wird glatt, der Strom ist still; Doch Menschenherz, im wilden Drang, Es weiß nicht, was es selber will.	The waves know the Runic lay, The gulf grows smooth, the stream is still; But the heart of man, in its wild impulse, Does not know its own desires.
Nur eine Stund' ist mir vergönnt, In Jahresfrist, zum Klageton, Sie schlägt, wenn diese Lampe brennt — Ihr Schein erlischt — sie ist entflohn.	I am granted only one hour in the year To sing of my woes; It strikes when this lamp burns — When its gleam dies the hour has fled!
Heil, Magnus Töchter, fort und fort! Die Lampe brennt in tiefer Ruh'; Euch gönn' ich dieser Stunde Wort, Erwacht, erhebt Euch, hört mir zu!	Hail, daughters of Magnus, forever hail! The lamp burns in deep peace; To you, at this hour, I tell my tale. Awake, arise, hear me!

For leagues along the watery way,
Through gulf and stream my course has been;
The hillows know my Runic lay,
And smooth their crests to silent green.

The hillows know my Runic lay —
The gulf grows smooth, the stream is still;
The human hearts, more wild than they,
Know but the rule of wayward will.

One hour is mine, in all the year,
To tell my woes — and one alone;
When gleams this magic lamp, 'tis here —
When dies the mystic light, 'tis gone.

Daughters of northern Magnus, hail!
The lamp is lit, the flame is clear —
To you I come to tell my tale,
Awake, arise, my tale to hear!

Gesänge des Harfners / The Harper's Songs

JOHANN WOLFGANG VON GOETHE

see Harfenspieler

Glaube, Hoffnung und Liebe / Faith, Hope and Love

CHRISTOPH KUFFNER

D 955 (1828)

Glaube, hoffe, liebe!	Have faith, hope and love!
Hältst du treu an diesen Dreien,	If you hold constantly to these three
Wirst du nie dich selbst entzweien,	You will never be divided within yourself,
Wird dein Himmel nimmer trübe.	And your skies will never be darkened.
Glaube fest an Gott und	Have steadfast faith in God and in your
Herz!	heart!
Glaube schwebet himmelwärts.	Faith soars heavenwards.
Mehr noch als im Sternrevier,	The Lord dwells within your breast
Lebt der Gott im Busen dir.	Still more than among the stars.
Wenn auch Welt und Menschen lügen,	Though this world and mankind may lie,
Kann das Herz doch nimmer trügen.	The heart can never deceive.
Hoffe dir Unsterblichkeit,	Hope for immortality,
Und hienieden bess're Zeit!	And for better days here on earth!
Hoffnung ist ein schönes Licht,	Hope is a fair light
Und erhellt den Weg der Pflicht.	Illuminating the path of duty.
Hoffe, aber fordre nimmer!	Hope, but never make demands!
Tag wird mählig, was erst	Gradually the first glimmer becomes
Schimmer.	daylight.
Edel liebe, fest und rein!	May your love be noble, strong and pure!
Ohne Liebe bist du Stein.	Without love you are as stone.
Liebe läutre dein Gefühl,	Let love purify your feelings,
Liebe leite dich ans Ziel!	Let love lead you to your goal!
Soll das Leben glücklich blühen,	If life is to flower in happiness
Muss der Liebe Sonne glühen.	The sun of love must glow warmly.
Willst du nie dich selbst	If you would never be divided within
entzweien,	yourself,
Halte treu an diesen Dreien!	Hold constantly to these three!
Dass nichts deinen Himmel trübe:	Lest anything should darken your skies,
Glaube, hoffe, liebe!	Have faith, hope and love!

Gondelfahrer / The Gondolier

JOHANN MAYRHOFER

D 808 (1824)

Es tanzen Mond und Sterne	Moon and stars dance
Den flücht'gen Geisterreih'n:	The fleeting round of the spirits:
Wer wird von Erdensorgen	Who would be forever fettered
Befangen immer sein!	By earthly cares!
Mondesstrahlen	Now, my boat, you can drift
arke, wallen;	In the moonlight;
anken los,	Free from all restraints
Meeres Schoss.	You are rocked on the bosom of the sea.

Vom Markusturme tönte
Der Spruch der Mitternacht:
Sie schlummern friedlich alle,
Und nur der Schiffer wacht.

From the tower of St Mark's
Midnight's decree tolled forth:
All sleep peacefully;
Only the boatman wakes.

Gott im Frühling / God in Spring

JOHANN PETER UZ

D 448 (1816)

In seinem schimmernden Gewand
Hast du den Frühling uns gesandt,
Und Rosen um sein Haupt gewunden.
Holdlächelnd kömmt er schon!
Es führen ihn die Stunden,
O Gott, auf seinen Blumenthron.

You have sent us Spring
In his shimmering robes,
And entwined roses about his head.
Already he comes, sweetly smiling,
The hours lead him
To his throne of flowers, O Lord.

Er geht in Büschen, und sie blühen;
Den Fluren kommt ihr frisches Grün,
Und Wäldern wächst ihr Schatten wieder,
Der West liebkosend schwingt
Sein tauendes Gefieder,
Und jeder frohe Vogel singt.

He walks among bushes, and they bloom;
The meadows acquire their fresh green,
And shade returns to the woods;
Caressingly the west wind
Waves its dewy wings,
And every happy bird sings.

Mit eurer Lieder süssem Klang,
Ihr Vögel, soll auch mein Gesang
Zum Vater der Natur sich schwingen.
Entzückung reisst mich hin!
Ich will dem Herrn lobsingen,
Durch den ich wurde, was ich bin!

Birds, with the sweet notes of your songs
Let my song also
Soar up to the Father of Nature.
I am filled with rapture!
I will sing praises to the Lord,
Who made me what I am.

Grablied / Song of the Grave

JOSEF KENNER

D 218 (1815)

Er fiel den Tod für's Vaterland,
Den süssen der Befreiungsschlacht,
Wir graben ihn mit treuer Hand,
Tief, tief, den schwarzen Ruheschacht.

He met his death for the fatherland,
A sweet death in the battle for freedom.
With loyal hands we bury him
Deep in the dark tomb of peace.

Da schlaf' gestillt, zerriss'nes Herz,
So wunschreich einst, auf Blumen
ein,
Die wir im veilchenvollen März
Dir in die stille Grube streu'n.

Shattered heart, once so rich in hopes,
There may you sleep peacefully upon the
flowers,
Which we scatter on your silent grave
In March, with its abundant violets.

Ein Hügel hebt sich über dir,
Den drückt kein Mal von Marmorstein,
Von Rosmarin nur pflanzen wir
Ein Pflänzchen auf dem Hügel ein.

A mound rises above you,
Weighed down by no marble monument.
We plant only a sprig of rosemary
Upon that mound.

Grablied auf einen Soldaten / Dirge for a Soldier

CHRISTIAN FRIEDRICH SCHUBART

D 454 (1816)

Zieh hin, du braver Krieger, du!
Wir gleiten dich zur Grabesruh,
Und schreiten mit gesunkner Wehr,
Von Wehmut schwer
Und stumm vor deinem Sarge her.

Depart hence, brave warrior!
We accompany you to a peaceful grave,
And with lowered weapons,
Heavy with sorrow,
Walk silently before your coffin.

Du warst ein biedrer, deutscher Mann.
Hast immerhin so brav getan.
Dein Herz, voll edler Tapferkeit,
Hat nie im Streit
Geschoß und Säbelhieb gescheut.

You were an upright German.
You fought so bravely.
Your heart, full of noble courage,
Never in battle
Feared the bullet and the sword.

Warst auch ein christlicher Soldat,
Der wenig sprach und vieles tat,
Dem Fürsten und dem Lande treu,
Und fromm dabei
Von Herzen, ohne Heuchelei.

You were a Christian soldier, too;
You said little and did much,
True to your prince and country,
And pious in heart,
Without cant.

Du standst in grauser Mitternacht,
In Frost und Hitze auf der Wacht,
Ertrugst so standhaft manche Not
Und danktest Gott
Für Wasser und für's liebe Brot.

You kept watch at dread midnight,
In frost and heat;
You steadfastly endured many hardships,
And gave thanks to God
For water and for bread.

Wie du gelebt, so starbst auch du,
Schlossest deine Augen freudig zu.
Und dachtest: Aus ist nun der Streit
Und Kampf der Zeit.
Jetzt kommt die ew'ge Seligkeit.

You died as you lived,
Willingly closing your eyes,
And reflecting: The battle
And struggle of Time is past.
Now comes eternal bliss.

Grablied für die Mutter / A Mother's Funeral Song

POET UNKNOWN

D 616 (1818)

Hauche milder, Abendluft,
Klage sanfter, Philomele;
Eine schöne, engelreine Seele
Schläft in dieser Gruft.

Breathe more gently, evening breeze,
Lament more softly, Philomel;
A beautiful, pure, angelic soul
Sleeps in this grave.

Bleich und stumm, am düstern Rand,
Steht der Vater mit dem Sohne,
Denen ihres Lebens schönste Krone
Schnell mit ihr verschwand.

The father stands, pale and silent,
With his son at the gloomy graveside;
With her the fairest crown of their lives
Has suddenly vanished.

Und sie weinen in die Gruft,
Aber ihrer Liebe Zähren
Werden sich zum Perlenkranz
   verklären,
Wenn der Engel ruft.

And they weep upon the grave;
But their tears of love
Shall be transfigured to a wreath of
   pearls
When the angel calls.

Greisengesang / Song of Old Age

FRIEDRICH RÜCKERT

D778 (1822?)

Der Frost hat mir bereifet des Hauses
  Dach;
Doch warm ist mir's geblieben im
  Wohngemach.
Der Winter hat die Scheitel mir weiss
  gedeckt;
Doch fliesst das Blut, das rote, durchs
  Herzgemach.

The frost has covered the roof of my
  house;
But I have kept warm in my living-
  room.
Winter has whitened the top of my
  head,
But the blood flows red in my
  heart.

Der Jugendflor der Wangen, die Rosen
  sind
Gegangen, all gegangen einander nach—
Wo sind sie hingegangen? ins Herz
  hinab:
Da blühn sie nach Verlangen, wie vor so
  nach.

The youthful flush of my cheeks, the
  roses
Have gone, one by one.
Where have they gone? Down into my
  heart;
There, as before, they bloom as
  desired.

Sind alle Freudenströme der Welt
  versiegt?
Noch fliesst mir durch den Busen ein stiller
  Bach.
Sind alle Nachtigallen der Flur
  verstummt?
Noch ist bei mir im Stillen hier eine wach.

Have all the rivers of joy in this world run
  dry?
A silent stream still flows through my
  breast.
Have all the nightingales in the meadows
  fallen silent?
Within me, secretly, one still stirs.

Sie singet:»Herr des Hauses! verschleuss
  dein Tor,
Dass nicht die Welt, die kalte, dring ins
  Gemach.
Schleuss aus den rauhen Odem der
  Wirklichkeit,
Und nur dem Duft der Träume gib Dach
  und Fach!«

She sings: 'Master of the house, bolt your
  door,
Lest the cold world should penetrate the
  parlour.
Shut out the harsh breath of
  reality,
And give shelter only to the fragrance of
  dreams!'

Grenzen der Menschheit / Man's Limitations

JOHANN WOLFGANG VON GOETHE

D716 (1821)

Wenn der uralte
Heilige Vater
Mit gelassener Hand
Aus rollenden Wolken
Segnende Blitze
Über die Erde sät,
Küss' ich den letzten
Saum seines Kleides,
Kindliche Schauer
Tief in der Brust.

When the age-old
Holy Father,
With a calm hand,
Scatters beneficent thunderbolts
Over the earth
From the rolling clouds,
I kiss the extreme hem
Of his garment,
With childlike awe
Deep in my heart.

Denn mit Göttern	For no mortal
Soll sich nicht messen	Shall measure himself
Irgendein Mensch.	Against the gods.
Hebt er sich aufwärts	If he reaches upwards
Und berührt	And touches the stars
Mit dem Scheitel die Sterne,	With his head,
Nirgends haften dann	Then his unsure feet
Die unsichern Sohlen,	Have no hold,
Und mit ihm spielen	And clouds and winds
Wolken und Winde.	Sport with him.

Steht er mit festen	If he stands firm
Markigen Knochen	With vigorous limbs
Auf der wohlgegründeten	On the solid,
Dauernden Erde,	Enduring earth,
Reicht er nicht auf,	He cannot even reach up
Nur mit der Eiche	To compare himself
Oder der Rebe	With the oak-tree
Sich zu vergleichen.	Or the vine.

Was unterscheidet	What distinguishes
Götter von Menschen?	Gods from men?
Dass viele Wellen	Before them many waves
Vor jenen wandeln,	Roll onwards,
Ein ewiger Strom:	An eternal river;
Uns hebt die Welle,	But the wave lifts us up,
Verschlingt die Welle,	The wave swallows us,
Und wir versinken.	And we sink.

Ein kleiner Ring	A narrow ring
Begrenzt unser Leben,	Bounds our life,
Und viele Geschlechter	And generations
Reihen sich dauernd	Forever succeed one another
An ihres Daseins	In the infinite chain
Unendliche Kette.	Of their existence.

Gretchen am Spinnrade / Gretchen at the Spinning-wheel

JOHANN WOLFGANG VON GOETHE

D 118 (1814)

From *Faust*

Meine Ruh' ist hin,	My peace is gone,
Mein Herz ist schwer,	My heart is heavy,
Ich finde sie nimmer	I shall never, never again
Und nimmermehr.	Find peace.

Wo ich ihn nicht hab',	Wherever he is not with me
Ist mir das Grab,	Is my grave,
Die ganze Welt	The whole world
Ist mir vergällt.	Is turned to gall.

Mein armer Kopf	My poor head
Ist mir verrückt,	Is crazed,
Mein armer Sinn	My poor mind
Ist mir zerstückt.	Is shattered.

Nach ihm nur schau' ich	I look out of the window
Zum Fenster hinaus,	Only to seek him,
Nach ihm nur geh' ich	I leave the house
Aus dem Haus.	Only to seek him.
Sein hoher Gang,	His fine gait,
Sein' edle Gestalt,	His noble form,
Seines Mundes Lächeln,	The smile of his lips,
Seiner Augen Gewalt.	The power of his eyes.
Und seiner Rede	And the magic flow
Zauberfluß.	Of his words,
Sein Händedruck,	The pressure of his hand
Und ach, sein Kuß!	And, ah, his kiss!
Mein Busen drängt sich	My bosom yearns
Nach ihm hin.	For him.
Ach dürft' ich fassen	Ah, if only I could grasp him
Und halten ihn.	And hold him.
Und küssen ihn,	And kiss him
So wie ich wollt',	As I would like,
An seinen Küssen	I should die
Vergehen sollt'!	From his kisses!

Gretchens Bitte / Gretchen's Plea

JOHANN WOLFGANG VON GOETHE

D 564 (1817)

From *Faust*

Ach neige,	You who are laden with sorrow,
Du Schmerzenreiche,	Incline your face graciously
Dein Antlitz gnädig meiner Not!	To my distress.
Das Schwert im Herzen,	With the sword in your heart,
Mit tausend Schmerzen	And a thousand sorrows,
Blickst auf zu deines Sohnes Tod.	You look up at your dying son.
Zum Vater blickst du,	You gaze up to the Father,
Und Seufzer schickst du	And let a sigh rise up
Hinauf um sein' und deine Not.	For His affliction and your own.
Wer fühlet,	Who can feel
Wie wühlet	How the pain
Der Schmerz mir im Gebein?	Gnaws away in my bones?
Was mein armes Herz hier banget,	What my poor heart fears,
Was es zittert, was verlanget,	What it dreads, what it craves,
Weißt nur du, nur du allein!	Only you can know!
Wohin ich immer gehe,	Wherever I go,
Wie weh, wie weh, wie wehe	How it hurts, how it hurts
Wird mir im Busen hier!	Here in my breast!
Ich bin, ach, kaum alleine,	Alas, no sooner am I alone
Ich wein', ich wein', ich weine,	Than I weep, I weep,
Das Herz zerbricht in mir.	And my heart breaks within me.

Gruppe aus dem Tartarus / Group from Hades

FRIEDRICH VON SCHILLER

D 583 (1817)

Horch — wie Murmeln des empörten
  Meeres,
Wie durch hohler Felsen Becken weint ein
  Bach,
Stöhnt dort dumpfigtief ein schweres —
  leeres,
Qualerpresstes Ach!

Hark! Like the angry murmuring of the
  sea,
Or a brook sobbing through pools in hollow
  rocks,
From the depths arises a muffled
  groan,
Heavy, empty and tormented!

Schmerz verzerret
Ihr Gesicht — Verzweiflung sperret
Ihren Rachen fluchend auf.
Hohl sind ihre Augen — ihre
  Blicke
Spähen bang nach des Cocytus Brücke,
Folgen tränend seinem
  Trauerlauf.

Pain distorts
Their faces — in despair
Their mouths open wide, cursing.
Their eyes are hollow — their frightened
  gaze
Strains towards Cocytus' bridge,
Following as they weep that river's
  mournful course.

Fragen sich einander ängstlich leise,
Ob noch nicht Vollendung sei?
Ewigkeit schwingt über ihnen Kreise,
Bricht die Sense des Saturns entzwei.

Anxiously, softly, they ask one another
If the end is yet nigh.
Eternity sweeps in circles above them,
Breaking Saturn's scythe in two.

Hagars Klage / Hagar's Lament

CLEMENS AUGUST SCHÜCKING

D 5 (1811)

Hier am Hügel heißen Sandes
Sitz' ich, und mir gegenüber
Liegt mein sterbend Kind!

Here I sit, on a mound of burning sand,
And before me
Lies my dying child!

Lechzt nach einem Tropfen Wasser,
Lechzt und ringt schon mit dem
  Tode,
Weint, und blickt mit stieren Augen
Mich bedrängte Mutter an!

He thirsts for a drop of water,
He thirsts, and already struggles with
  death,
He weeps, and with vacant eyes
Looks upon me, his distressed mother.

Du mußt sterben, armes Würmchen,
Ach, nicht eine Träne
Hab' ich in den trocknen Augen,
Wo ich dich mit stillen kann!

You must die, poor mite;
Alas, not a single tear do I have
In my dry eyes
To soothe you.

Ha! säh' ich eine Löwenmutter
Ich wollte mit ihr kämpfen,
Kämpfen mit ihr um die Eiter.

If I saw a lioness
I would fight with her,
Fight with her for her milk.

Könnt' ich aus dem dürren Sande
Nur ein Tröpfchen Wasser
  saugen!
Aber ach, ich muß dich sterben sehn!

If I could only suck
But one drop of water from the parched
  sand!
But alas, I must watch you die!

Kaum ein schwacher Strahl des Lebens
Dämmert auf der bleichen Wange,
Dämmert in den matten Augen,
Deine Brust erhebt sich kaum.

Scarcely a feeble ray of life
Glimmers on your pale cheeks
And in your dull eyes;
Your little chest scarcely rises.

Hier am Busen kom und welke!
Kömmt ein Mensch dann durch die Wüste,
So wird er in den Sand uns scharren,
Sagen: »Das ist Weib und Kind!«

Come to my breast and perish there!
If a man then comes through the wilderness
He will bury us in the sand,
Saying: 'Here is a woman and her child!'

Ich will mich von dir wenden,
Daß ich dich nicht sterben seh',
Und im Taumel der Verzweiflung
Murre wider Gott!

No, I shall turn away from you
Lest I see you die,
And in the frenzy of despair
Cry out against God!

Ferne von dir will ich gehen,
Und ein rührend Klaglied singen,
Daß du noch im Todeskampfe
Tröstung einer Stimme hörst.

I shall go far away from you
And sing a touching lament,
So that in your struggle with death
You will still hear a comforting voice.

Noch zum letzten Klaggebete
Öffn' ich meine dürren Lippen,
Und dann schließ' ich sie auf immer,
Und dann komme bald, o Tod!

I shall open my parched lips
In one last grieving prayer;
Then I shall close them for ever,
Then death soon will come.

Jehova! Blick auf uns herab,
Jehova, erbarme dich des Knaben!
Send' aus einem Taugewölke
Labung uns herab!

Look down upon us, Jehovah!
Take pity on the child!
From dewy clouds
Send us refreshing rain!

Ist er nicht von Abrams Samen?
Er weinte Freudentränen,
Als ich ihm das Kind geboren,
Und nun wird er ihm zum
       Fluch!

Is he not of Abraham's seed?
Ah, he wept tears of joy
When I bore him this child,
And now the child has become a curse to
       him!

Rette deines Lieblings Samen!
Selbst sein Vater bat um Segen,
Und du sprachst: »Es komme Segen
Über dieses Kindes Haupt.«

Save the seed of Your chosen one!
His father asked for Your blessing,
And You spoke: 'Let this child's head
Be blessed.'

Hab' ich wider dich gesündigt,
Ha so treffe mich die Rache,
Aber, ach, was tat der Knabe,
Daß er mit mir leiden muß?

If I have sinned against You
May vengeance strike me!
But what has the boy done
That he must suffer with me?

Wär' ich doch in Sir gestorben,
Als ich in der Wüste irrte,
Und das Kind noch ungeboren
Unter meinem Herzen lag!

Would that I had died in Syria
When I was walking in the wilderness,
And the child lay unborn
Under my heart!

Nein; da kam ein holder Fremdling,
Hieß mich rück zu Abram gehen,
Und des Mannes Haus betreten,
Der uns grausam jetzt verstieß.

No! A fair stranger came to me,
Bade me return to Abraham
And enter the house of the man
Who now cruelly rejects us.

War der Fremdling nicht ein Engel?
Denn er sprach mit holder Miene:
»Ismael wird groß auf Erden,
Sein Samen zahlreich sein!«

Was the stranger not your angel?
For he spoke with gracious mien:
'Ishmael will be great on earth,
And his seed will multiply!'

Nun liegen wir und welken,
Unsre Leichen werden modern
Wie die Leichen der Verfluchten,
Die der Erde Schoß nicht birgt.

Schrei zum Himmel armer Knabe!
Öffne deine welken Lippen!
Gott, sein Herr! verschmäh' das Flehen
Des unschuld'gen Knaben nicht.

Now we lie dying,
And our bodies will rot
Like the corpses of the accursed
Which the earth's womb does not conceal.

Cry unto heaven, my poor boy!
Open your parched lips!
God, his Lord, do not scorn
The pleas of this innocent boy.

Hänflings Liebeswerbung / The Linnet's Wooing

JOHANN FRIEDRICH KIND

D 552 (1817)

Ahidi! ich liebe.
Mild lächelt die Sonne,
Mild wehen die Weste,
Sanft rieselt die Quelle,
Süß duften die Blumen.
Ich liebe, Ahidi!

Chirp, chirp, I am in love!
The sun smiles gently,
The west wind blows mild,
The stream murmurs softly,
The flowers' scent is sweet!
I am in love, chirp, chirp!

Ahidi! ich liebe.
Dich lieb' ich, du Sanfte,
Mit seidnem Gefieder,
Mit strahlenden Äuglein,
Dich, Schönste der Schwestern!
Ich liebe, Ahidi!

Chirp, chirp, I am in love!
I love you, my tender one,
With your silken feathers
And your radiant little eyes.
Fairest among your sisters!
I am in love, chirp, chirp!

Ahidi! ich liebe.
O sieh, wie die Blumen
Sich liebevoll grüßen,
Sich liebevoll nicken!
O liebe mich wieder!
Ich liebe, Ahidi!

Chirp, chirp, I am in love!
See how the flowers
Lovingly greet one another,
Lovingly nod to each other!
Love me in return!
I am in love, chirp, chirp!

Ahidi! ich liebe.
O sieh, wie der Epheu
Mit liebenden Armen
Die Eiche umschlinget.
O liebe mich wieder!
Ich liebe, Ahidi!

Chirp, chirp, I am in love!
See how the ivy
Embraces the oak tree
With loving arms.
Love me in return!
I am in love, chirp, chirp!

Harfenspieler: I / The Harper's Songs: I

JOHANN WOLFGANG VON GOETHE

First version: D 325 (1815)
Second version: D 478 (1816)

The texts of the three Harper songs are taken from the novel *Wilhelm Meister*.

Wer sich der Einsamkeit ergibt,
Ach! der ist bald allein;
Ein jeder lebt, ein jeder liebt
Und lässt ihn seiner Pein.

He who gives himself up to solitude,
Ah, he is soon alone;
Each man lives, each man loves
And leaves him to his suffering.

Ja! lasst mich meiner Qual!
Und kann ich nur einmal
Recht einsam sein,
Dann bin ich nicht allein.

Yes, leave me to my suffering!
And if I can just once
Be truly lonely,
Then I shall not be alone.

Es schleicht ein Liebender lauschend
  sacht,
Ob seine Freundin allein?
So überschleicht bei Tag und Nacht
Mich Einsamen die Pein,
Mich Einsamen die Qual.
Ach, werd ich erst einmal
Einsam im Grabe sein,
Da lässt sie mich allein!

A lover steals softly,
  listening:
Is his sweetheart alone?
Thus, day and night,
Suffering steals upon me,
Torment steals upon me in my solitude.
Ah, when I lie lonely
In the grave,
Then they will leave me alone.

Harfenspieler: II / The Harper's Songs: II

JOHANN WOLFGANG VON GOETHE

First version: D 480/1 (1816)
Second version: D 480/2 (1816)
Third version: D 480/3 (1822)

Wer nie sein Brot mit Tränen ass,
Wer nie die kummervollen Nächte
Auf seinem Bette weinend sass,
Der kennt euch nicht, ihr himmlischen
  Mächte.

Who has never eaten his bread with tears,
Who, through nights of grief,
Has never sat weeping on his bed,
Knows you not, heavenly
  powers.

Ihr führt ins Leben uns hinein,
Ihr lasst den Armen schuldig werden,
Dann überlasst ihr ihn der Pein:
Denn alle Schuld rächt sich auf Erden.

You bring us into life,
You let the poor wretch fall into guilt,
Then you abandon him to his agony:
For all guilt is avenged on earth.

Harfenspieler: III / The Harper's Songs: III

JOHANN WOLFGANG VON GOETHE

D 479 (1816)

An die Türen will ich schleichen,
Still und sittsam will ich stehn,
Fromme Hand wird Nahrung reichen,
Und ich werde weitergehn.
Jeder wird sich glücklich scheinen,
Wenn mein Bild vor ihm erscheint,
Eine Träne wird er weinen,
Und ich weiss nicht, was er weint.

I shall steal from door to door
And stand there, silent and humble;
A kind hand will offer food
And I shall go on my way.
Each will deem himself happy
When he sees me before him,
He will shed a tear;
And yet I know not why he should weep.

Heidenröslein / Wild Rose

JOHANN WOLFGANG VON GOETHE

D 257 (1815)

Sah ein Knab ein Röslein stehn,
Röslein auf der Heiden,
War so jung und morgen-
  schön,

A boy saw a wild rose
Growing in the heather,
It was so young, and as lovely as the
  morning.

Lief er schnell, es nah zu sehn,
Sahs mit vielen Freuden.
Röslein, Röslein, Röslein rot,
Röslein auf der Heiden.

Knabe sprach: Ich breche dich,
Röslein auf der Heiden!
Röslein sprach: Ich steche dich,
Dass du ewig denkst an mich,
Und ich wills nicht leiden.
Röslein, Röslein, Röslein rot,
Röslein auf der Heiden.

Und der wilde Knabe brach
's Röslein auf der Heiden;
Röslein wehrte sich und stach,
Half ihm doch kein Weh und Ach,
Musst es eben leiden.
Röslein, Röslein, Röslein rot,
Röslein auf der Heiden.

He ran swiftly to look more closely,
Looked on it with great joy.
Wild rose, wild rose, wild rose red,
Wild rose in the heather.

Said the boy: I shall pluck you,
Wild rose in the heather!
Said the rose: I shall prick you,
So that you will always remember me,
And I will not suffer it.
Wild rose, wild rose, wild rose red,
Wild rose in the heather.

And the impetuous boy plucked
The wild rose in the heather;
The rose defended herself and pricked him,
But her cries of pain were to no avail,
She simply had to suffer.
Wild rose, wild rose, wild rose red,
Wild rose in the heather.

Heimliches Lieben / Secret Love

KAROLINE LOUISE VON KLENKE

D922 (1827)

O du, wenn deine Lippen mich berühren,
Dann will die Lust die Seele mir
    entführen;
Ich fühle tief ein namenloses Beben
Den Busen heben.

Mein Auge flammt, Glut schwebt auf
    meinen Wangen;
Es schlägt mein Herz ein unbekannt
    Verlangen;
Mein Geist, verirrt in trunkner Lippen
    Stammeln,
Kann kaum sich sammeln.

Mein Leben hängt in einer solchen Stunde
An deinem süßen, rosenweichen Munde,
Und will, bei deinem trauten
    Armumfassen,
Mich fast verlassen.

O! daß es doch nicht außer sich kann
    fliehen,
Die Seele ganz in deiner Seele glühen!
Daß doch die Lippen, die voll Sehnsucht
    brennen,
Sich müssen trennen!

Daß doch im Kuß' mein Wesen nicht
    zerfließet,
Wenn es so fest an deinen Mund sich
    schließet,
Und an dein Herz, das niemals laut darf
    wagen,
Für mich zu schlagen!

When your lips touch me,
Desire all but bears away my
    soul;
I feel a nameless trembling
Deep within my breast.

My eyes flame, a glow tinges my
    cheeks;
My heart beats with a strange
    longing;
My mind, lost in the stammering of my
    drunken lips,
Can scarcely compose itself.

At such a time my life hangs
On your sweet lips, soft as roses,
And, in your beloved
    embrace,
Life almost deserts me.

Oh that my life cannot escape from
    itself,
With my soul aflame in yours!
Oh that lips ardent with
    longing
Must part!

Oh that my being may not dissolve in
    kisses
When my lips are pressed so tightly to
    yours,
And to your heart, which may never
    dare
To beat aloud for me!

Heiß mich nicht reden (Mignons Gesang) | Do not Bid me Speak (Mignon's Song)

JOHANN WOLFGANG VON GOETHE

First version: D726 (1821)
Second version: D877 no. 2 (1826?)

From *Wilhelm Meister*

Heiß mich nicht reden, heiß mich
    schweigen,
Denn mein Geheimnis ist mir Pflicht;
Ich möchte dir mein ganzes Innre zeigen,
Allein das Schicksal will es nicht.

Zur rechten Zeit vertreibt der Sonne Lauf
Die finstre Nacht, und sie muß sich
    erhellen;
Der harte Fels schließt seinen Busen auf,
Mißgönnt der Erde nicht die
    tiefverborgnen Quellen.

Ein jeder sucht im Arm des Freundes
    Ruh,
Dort kann die Brust in Klagen sich
    ergießen;
Allein ein Schwur drückt mir die Lippen zu,
Und nur ein Gott vermag sie
    aufzuschließen.

Do not bid me speak, bid me be
    silent,
For my duty is to keep my secret;
I long to reveal my whole soul to you,
But fate does not permit it.

At the appointed time the sun in its course
Drives away the dark night, and day must
    break;
The hard rock opens its bosom,
And ungrudgingly bestows on the earth its
    deep-hidden springs.

Every man seeks peace in the arms of a
    friend;
There the heart can pour out its
    sorrows.
But an oath seals my lips,
And only a god can open
    them.

Hektors Abschied | Hector's Farewell

FRIEDRICH VON SCHILLER

D312 (1815)

Andromache:
Will sich Hektor ewig von mir wenden,
Wo Achill mit den unnahbaren Händen
Dem Patroklus schrecklich Opfer bringt?
Wer wird künftig deinen Kleinen lehren
Speere werfen und die Götter ehren,
Wenn der finstre Orkus dich verschlingt?

Hektor:
Teures Weib, gebiete deinen Tränen!
Nach der Feldschlacht ist mein feurig
    Sehnen,
Diese Arme schützen Pergamus.
Kämpfend für den heil'gen Herd der
    Götter
Fall ich, und des Vaterlandes
    Retter
Steig' ich nieder zu dem styg'schen Fluß.

Andromache:
Nimmer lausch' ich deiner Waffen
    Schalle,
Müßig liegt dein Eisen in der Halle,
Priams großer Heldenstamm verdirbt.

Andromache:
Will Hector for ever turn away from me,
While Achilles, with proud hands,
Makes a terrible sacrifice for Patroclus?
Who, in the future, will teach your son
To hurl the javelin and revere the gods,
When black Hades engulfs you?

Hector:
Dear wife, stem your tears!
I long ardently for
    battle;
These arms shall protect Troy.
I shall fall fighting for the sacred
    home
Of the gods, and descend to the Stygian
    river
As the saviour of my fatherland.

Andromache:
Never again shall I hear the clang of your
    arms,
Your sword will lie idle in the hall.
Priam's great heroic race will perish.

Du wirst hingeh'n, wo kein Tag mehr
  scheinet,
Der Cocytus durch die Wüsten
  weinet,
Deine Lieb' im Lethe stirbt.

Hektor:
All mein Sehnen will ich, all mein
  Denken,
In des Lethe stillen Strom versenken,
Aber meine Liebe nicht.
Horch! der Wilde tobt schon an den
  Mauern,
Gürte mir das Schwert um, laß das
  Trauern!
Hektors Liebe stirbt im Lethe nicht.

You will go where no daylight
  shines,
Where Cocytus weeps through the
  wastelands;
Your love will die in the waters of Lethe.

Hector:
I would drown all my longing, all my
  thoughts
In the silent waters of Lethe,
But not my love.
Hark! The wild mob already rages at the
  walls;
Gird on my sword, cease your
  grieving.
Hector's love will not perish in Lethe.

Herbst / Autumn

LUDWIG RELLSTAB

D 945 (1828)

Es rauschen die Winde
So herbstlich und kalt;
Verödet die Fluren,
Entblättert der Wald.

Ihr blumigen Auen!
Du sonniges Grün!
So welken die Blüten
Des Lebens dahin.

Es ziehen die Wolken
So finster und grau;
Verschwunden die Sterne
Am himmlischen Blau!

Ach, wie die Gestirne
Am Himmel entflieh'n,
So sinket die Hoffnung
Des Lebens dahin!

Ihr Tage des Lenzes
Mit Rosen geschmückt,
Wo ich die Geliebte
Ans Herze gedrückt!

Kalt über den Hügel
Rauscht, Winde, dahin!
So sterben die Rosen
Der Liebe dahin!

The winds blow
With an autumnal chill,
The meadows are bare,
The woods leafless.

Flowering meadows!
Sunlit green!
Thus do life's blossoms
Wilt.

The clouds drift by,
So sombre and grey;
The stars have vanished
In the blue heavens!

Ah, as the stars disappear
In the sky,
So does life's hope
Fade away!

You days of spring,
Adorned with roses,
When I pressed
My beloved to my heart!

Winds, blow cold
Over the hillside!
So do the roses
Of love die!

Herbstlied / Autumn Song

JOHANN GAUDENZ VON SALIS-SEEWIS

D 502 (1816)

Bunt sind schon die Wälder,
Gelb die Stoppelfelder,
Und der Herbst beginnt.
Rote Blätter fallen,
Graue Nebel wallen,
Kühler weht der Wind.

Wie die volle Traube
Aus dem Rebenlaube
Purpurfarbig strahlt!
Am Geländer reifen
Pfirsiche mit Streifen
Rot und weiß bemahlt.

Sieh! Wie hier die Dirne
Emsig Pflaum' und Birne
In ihr Körbchen legt;
Dort, mit leichten Schritten,
Jene, goldne Quitten
In den Landhof
 trägt!

Flinke Träger springen,
Und die Mädchen singen,
Alles jubelt froh!
Bunte Bänder schweben
Zwischen hohen Reben
Auf dem Hut von Stroh!

Geige tönt und Flöte
Bei der Abendröte
Und im Mondenglanz;
Junge Winzerinnen
Winken und beginnen
Deutschen Ringeltanz.

The woods are already brightly coloured,
The fields of stubble yellow,
And autumn is here.
Red leaves fall,
Grey mists surge,
The wind blows colder.

How purple shines
The plump grape
From the vine leaves!
On the espalier
Peaches ripen,
Painted with red and white streaks.

Look how busily the maiden here
Gathers plums and pears
In her basket;
Look how that one there,
With light steps,
Carries golden quinces
 to the house.

The lads dance nimbly
And the girls sing;
All shout for joy.
Amid the tall vines
Coloured ribbons flutter
On hats of straw.

Fiddles and flutes play
In the glow of evening
And by the moon's light.
The girls who gather grapes
Wave, and begin
A German round-dance.

Hermann und Thusnelda / Hermann and Thusnelda

FRIEDRICH GOTTLIEB KLOPSTOCK

D 322 (1815)

Ha, dort kommt er mit Schweiß, mit
 Römerblute,
Mit dem Staube der Schlacht bedeckt! So
 schön war
Hermann niemals! So hat's ihm
Nie von dem Auge geflammt!

Komm! ich bebe vor Lust! reich mir den
 Adler
Und das triefende Schwert! komm, atm',
 und ruh hier
Aus in meiner Umarmung,
Von der zu schrecklichen Schlacht!

Ah, there he comes, covered with sweat,
 with Roman blood,
And with the dust of battle.
 Never
Was Hermann so fair!
Never did his eyes flame so!

Come! I tremble with desire! Hand me the
 eagle
And the dripping sword! Come, breathe,
 and rest here
In my embrace
From the dread battle!

Ruh hier, daß ich den Schweiß von der
  Stirn abtrockne,
Und der Wange das Blut! Wie glüht die
  Wange!
Hermann! Hermann! so hat dich
Niemals Thusnelda geliebt!

Selbst nicht, als du zuerst im
  Eichenschatten
Mit dem kraftvollen Arm mich wilder
  umfaßtest.
Fliehend blieb ich und sah dir
Schon die Unsterblichkeit an,

Die nun dein ist! Erzählt's in allen
  Hainen,
Daß Augustus nun bang mit seinen
  Göttern
Nektar trinket! daß Hermann
Hermann unsterblicher ist!

»Warum lockst du mein Haar? Liegt nicht
  der stumme
Tote Vater vor uns! O hätt'
  Augustus
Seine Heere geführt; er
Läge noch blutiger da!«

Laß dein sinkendes Haar mich, Hermann,
  heben,
Daß es über dem Kranz' in Locken
  drohe!
Siegmar ist bei den Göttern!
Folg du, und wein' ihm nicht
  nach!

Rest here, that I may wipe the sweat from
  your brow,
And the blood from your cheeks! How your
  cheeks glow!
Hermann! Hermann! Never has Thusnelda
Loved you so!

Not even when, in the shade of the
  oak-tree,
Your powerful arms first embraced me
  wildly!
As I fled I remained there, already
Glimpsing the immortality

Which is now yours! Proclaim it in every
  grove,
That Augustus is now uneasy as he
  drinks
Nectar with his gods! That Hermann
Is more immortal than he!

'Why do you coil my hair? Does not my
  father
Lie dead and silent before us? Oh, if only
Augustus had led his armies; he would be
  lying there
Still more bloodied!'

Let me gather up your lank hair,
  Hermann,
That it may fall in menacing locks over the
  laurel wreath!
Siegmar is with the gods!
You shall be his successor, and not mourn
  him!

Himmelsfunken / Intimations of Heaven

JOHANN PETER SILBERT

D 651 (1819)

Der Odem Gottes weht!
Still wird die Sehnsucht wach;
Das trunkne Herz vergeht
In wundersüßem Ach!

Wie löst sich äthermild
Der Erde schweres Band,
Die heil'ge Träne quillt,
Ach! nach des Himmels Land.

Wie mächtig hebt das Herz
Sich zu den blauen Höh'n!
Was macht vor süßem Schmerz
Es ach! so zart vergehn? —

God's breath is felt,
Silently longing awakens.
The ecstatic heart
Swoons in sweet suffering.

The earth's oppressive bonds
Dissolve in the mild air.
Sacred tears flow
As we yearn for the heavenly land.

How the heart soars
To the azure heights.
Ah, why does it
Swoon so tenderly with sweet sorrow?

O süßer Hochgenuß!
Mild, wie des Himmels Tau,
Winkt Gottes Feiergruß
Hoch aus dem stillen Blau!

Und das verwaiste Herz
Vernimmt den stillen Ruf,
Und sehnt sich heimatwärts
Zum Vater, der es schuf!

Sweet bliss!
Gentle as the heavenly dew,
With solemn greeting God beckons
From high in the silent azure.

And the orphaned heart
Hears the soft call,
And longs to return home
To the Father, its creator.

Hin und wieder fliegen die Pfeile / To and fro the Arrows fly

JOHANN WOLFGANG VON GOETHE

see Ariette der Lucinde

Hippolits Lied / Song of Hippolytus

FRIEDRICH VON GERSTENBERG

D 890 (1826)

Laßt mich, ob ich auch still verglüh',
Laßt mich nur stille geh'n,
Sie seh' ich spät, sie seh' ich
    früh',
Und ewig vor mir steh'n.

Was ladet ihr zur Ruh' mich ein?
Sie nahm die Ruh' mir fort,
Und wo sie ist, da muß ich sein,
Hier sei es, oder dort.

Zürnt diesem armen Herzen nicht,
Es hat nur einen Fehl,
Treu muß es schlagen, bis es bricht,
Und hat dess' nimmer Hehl.

Laßt mich, ich denke doch nur sie,
In ihr nur denke ich;
Ja, ohne sie wär' ich einst nie
Bei Engeln ewiglich.

Im Leben denn und auch im Tod,
Im Himmel, so wie hier,
Im Glück und in der Trennung Not
Gehör' ich einzig ihr.

Let me be, though I waste silently,
Let me go quietly;
I see her in the evening, I see her in the
    morning,
Forever standing before me.

Why do you bid me find repose?
She took away all my repose,
And wherever she is, there must I be,
Either here, or there.

Do not be angry with this poor heart,
It has only one failing:
It must beat faithfully until it breaks,
And has never concealed that.

Let me be, I think only of her,
And in her;
Without her I should not one day
Hope to be with the angels for evermore.

In life and in death,
In heaven, as here below,
In joy and in the grief of parting,
I belong to her alone.

Hochzeitlied / Wedding Song

JOHANN GEORG JACOBI

D 463 (1816)

Will singen euch im alten Ton
Ein Lied von alter Treu;
Es sangen's unsre Väter schon;
Doch bleibt's der Liebe neu.

I will sing you a song in the old style,
A song of age-old constancy.
Our fathers once sang it,
But it remains ever new for lovers.

Im Glücke macht es freudenvoll,
Kann trösten in der Not:
»Daß nichts die Herzen scheiden soll,
Nichts scheiden, als der Tod:

In good times it brings joy,
In times of distress it can comfort:
'Let nothing part these hearts,
Nothing, save death.

»Daß immerdar mit frischem Mut
Der Mann die Traute schützt,
Und alles opfert, Gut und
    Blut,
Wenn's seinem Weibchen nützt;.

'Let the man protect his bride
Evermore with new heart,
And sacrifice everything, his wealth and his
    blood,
For the good of his wife.

»Daß er auf weiter Erde nichts
Als sie allein begehrt,
Sie gern im Schweiß des Angesichts
Für ihren Kuß ernährt;

'Let him desire nothing on earth
Save her alone,
Let him keep her with the sweat of his brow
For the sake of her kiss.

»Daß, wenn die Lerch' im Felde schlägt,
Sein Weib ihm Wonne lacht,
Ihm, wenn der Acker Dornen trägt,
Zum Spiel die Arbeit macht,

'When the lark sings in the field
Let his wife's laughter bring him joy;
When the land is strewn with thorns
May she lighten his work.

»Und doppelt süß der Ruhe Lust,
Erquickend jedes Brot,
Den Kummer leicht an ihrer Brust,
Gelinder seinen Tod.

'The delights of rest shall be doubly sweet,
Every meal shall refresh;
His cares shall be eased on her breast,
His death shall be gentler.

»Dann fühlt er noch die kalte Hand
Von ihrer Hand gedrückt,
Und sich in's neue Vaterland
Aus ihrem Arm entrückt.«

'Then he shall feel his cold hand
Pressed by her hand;
He shall be borne from her arms
To his new homeland.'

Hoffnung / Hope

JOHANN WOLFGANG VON GOETHE

D 295 (1819?)

Schaff', das Tagwerk meiner Hände,
Hohes Glück, dass ich's vollende!
Lass, o lass mich nicht ermatten!
Nein, es sind nicht leere Träume:
Jetzt nur Stangen, diese Bäume
Geben einst noch Frucht und Schatten.

O fortune, let me complete
My hands' daily task!
Let me not, O let me not grow weary!
No, these are not vain dreams;
Though now but shoots, these trees
Will one day yield fruit and shade.

Hoffnung / Hope

FRIEDRICH VON SCHILLER

First version: D 251 (1815)
Second version: D 637 (1817?)

Es reden und träumen die Menschen viel
Von bessern künftigen Tagen;
Nach einem glücklichen, goldenen Ziel
Sieht man sie rennen und jagen.
Die Welt wird alt und wird wieder jung,
Doch der Mensch hofft immer
    Verbesserung.

Men talk and dream
Of better days to come;
You see them running and chasing
After a happy, golden goal.
The world grows old, and young again,
But man forever hopes for better
    things.

Die Hoffnung führt ihn ins Leben ein,
Sie umflattert den fröhlichen Knaben,
Den Jüngling begeistert ihr
   Zauberschein,
Sie wird mit dem Greis nicht begraben;
Denn beschliesst er im Grabe den müden
   Lauf,
Noch am Grabe pflanzt er die Hoffnung
   auf.

Hope leads man into life,
It hovers around the happy boy;
Its magic radiance inspires the
   youth,
Nor is it buried with the old man.
For though he ends his weary life in the
   grave,
Yet on that grave he plants his
   hope.

Es ist kein leerer, schmeichelnder Wahn,
Erzeugt im Gehirne des Toren.
Im Herzen kündet es laut sich an:
Zu was Besserm sind wir geboren!
Und was die innere Stimme spricht,
Das täuscht die hoffende Seele nicht.

It is no vain, flattering illusion,
Born in the mind of a fool.
Loudly it proclaims itself in men's hearts:
We are born for better things.
And what the inner voice tells us
Does not deceive the hopeful soul.

Huldigung / Homage

LUDWIG KOSEGARTEN

D 240 (1815)

Gar verloren, ganz versunken,
In dein Anschau'n, Lieblingin,
Wonnebebend, liebetrunken
Schwingt zu dir der Geist sich hin.
Nichts vermag ich zu beginnen,
Nichts zu denken, dichten, sinnen,
Nichts ist, was das Herz mir füllt,
Huldin, als dein holdes Bild.

Lost and absorbed
In contemplation of you, my darling,
Trembling with ecstasy, drunk with love,
My spirit flies to you.
I can do nothing,
I cannot think, or write or plan.
Nothing fills my heart, beloved lady,
But your sweet image.

Süße, Reine, Makellose,
Kalt und keusch wie Jennerschnee,
Ungeschminkte rote Rose,
Ungesonnte Lilie,
Ammutreiche Anemone,
Aller Schönheit Preis und Krone,
Weißt du auch, Gebieterin,
Wie ich ganz dein eigen bin?

You are sweet, pure and spotless,
Noble, beloved and sublime,
Unadorned red rose,
Unblemished lily,
Gracious anemone,
Prize and crown of all beauty.
Do you know, fair lady,
That I am utterly yours?

Hymne I / Hymn I

NOVALIS

D 659 (1819)

Wenige wissen
Das Geheimnis der Liebe,
Fühlen Unersättlichkeit
Und ewigen Durst.
Des Abendmahls
Göttliche Bedeutung
Ist den irdischen Sinnen Rätsel;
Aber wer jemals
Von heissen, geliebten Lippen
Atem des Lebens sog,
Wem heilige
   Glut

Few know
The secret of love,
Few feel its insatiability,
Its endless thirst.
The divine meaning
Of the Last Supper
Is a riddle to earthly minds.
But he who has drawn
The breath of life
From ardent, beloved lips,
He whose heart has melted in trembling
   waves

237

In zitternden Wellen das Herz schmolz,
Wem das Auge aufging,
Dass er des Himmels
Unergründliche Tiefe mass,
Wird essen von seinem Leibe
Und trinken von seinem Blute
Ewiglich.

Wer hat des irdischen Leibes
Hohen Sinn erraten?
Wer kann sagen,
Dass er das Blut versteht?
Einst ist alles Leib,
Ein Leib,
In himmlischem Blute
Schwimmt das selige Paar —

O! dass das Weltmeer
Schon errötete,
Und in duftiges Fleisch
Aufquölle der Fels!
Nie endet das süsse Mahl,
Nie sättigt die Liebe sich;
Nicht innig, nicht eigen genug
Kann sie haben den Geliebten.
Von immer zärteren Lippen
Verwandelt wird das Genossene
Inniglicher und näher.

Heissere Wollust
Durchbebt die Seele,
Durstiger und hungriger
Wird das Herz:
Und so währt der Liebe Genuss
Von Ewigkeit zu Ewigkeit.
Hätten die Nüchternen
Einmal nur gekostet,
Alles verliessen sie,
Und setzten sich zu uns
An den Tisch der Sehnsucht,
Der nie leer wird.
Sie erkennten der Liebe
Unendliche Fülle,
Und priesen die Nahrung
Von Leib und Blut.

Of sacred passion,
He who has opened his eyes
To measure the fathomless depths
Of heaven,
Will eat of his body
And drink of his blood
Eternally.

Who has guessed the lofty meaning
Of that earthly body?
Who can say
That he understands the blood?
One day all will be body,
One single body;
The blessed pair
Shall swim in heavenly blood.

O that the world's oceans
Might now turn red,
And the rock spring up
As fragrant flesh!
The sweet meal never ends,
Love is never satisfied;
It can never possess the beloved
Profoundly and exclusively.
With ever more tender kisses
The beloved is transformed,
Possessed more inwardly and more closely.

Desire still more ardent
Pierces the soul;
Thirstier, hungrier
Grows the heart;
Thus the pleasure of love
Endures throughout eternity.
If only the sober
Once tasted it,
They would abandon all else
And sit with us
At the table of longing,
Which is never empty
They would see love's
Infinite richness,
And extol the nourishment
Of body and blood.

Hymne II / Hymn II

NOVALIS

D 660 (1819)

Wenn ich ihn nur habe,
Wenn er mein nur ist,
Wenn mein Herz bis hin zum Grabe
Seine Treue nie vergisst:
Weiss ich nichts von Leide,
Fühle nichts als Andacht, Lieb' und
  Freude.

If only I have him,
If he is mine alone,
If my heart never forsakes its trust
Unto the grave:
Then shall I know no suffering,
Feel nothing but devotion, love and
  joy.

Wenn ich ihn nur habe,
Laß ich alles gern,
Folg an meinem Wanderstabe
Treugesinnt nur meinem Herrn;
Lasse still die Andern
Breite, lichte, volle Straßen
  wandern.

If only I have him
I shall gladly forgo all else,
And with my pilgrim's staff
Follow my Lord, true to him alone,
Quietly letting others
Walk through the wide, bright, crowded
  streets.

Wenn ich ihn nur habe,
Schlaf ich fröhlich ein,
Ewig wird zu süßer Labe
Seines Herzens Flut mir sein,
Die mit sanftem Zwingen
Alles wird erweichen und durchdringen.

If only I have him,
I shall fall joyfully asleep;
His heart's flow
Will forever be my sweet comfort;
With gentle force
It will soften and pervade all things.

Wenn ich ihn nur habe,
Hab ich auch die Welt;
Selig, wie ein Himmelsknabe,
Der der Jungfrau Schleier hält.
Hingesenkt im Schauen
Kann mir vor dem Irdischen nicht
  grauen.

If only I have him
I have the whole world.
Blissful as a cherub
Holding the Virgin's veil,
Deep in contemplation,
Nothing in this earthly life can make me
  afraid.

Wo ich ihn nur habe,
Ist mein Vaterland,
Und es fällt mir jede Gabe
Wie ein Erbteil in die Hand;
Längst vermißte Brüder
Find ich nun in seinen Jüngern wieder.

Wherever I have him
There is my homeland;
And every gift falls into my hand
As an inheritance:
In his disciples I find again
My long-lost brothers.

Hymne III / Hymn III

NOVALIS

D 661 (1819)

Wenn alle untreu werden,
So bleib ich dir doch treu;
Daß Dankbarkeit auf Erden
Nicht ausgestorben sei.
Für mich umfing dich Leiden,
Vergingst für mich in Schmerz;
Drum geb ich dir mit Freuden
Auf ewig dieses Herz.

If all men should prove faithless
Yet will I remain true to you,
Lest gratitude should die out
On this earth.
For my sake suffering enveloped you,
For my sake you died in pain.
Therefore I joyfully give you
My heart for ever.

Oft muß ich bitter weinen,
Daß du gestorben bist,
Und mancher von den Deinen
Dich lebenslang vergißt.
Von Liebe nur durchdrungen
Hast du so viel getan,
Und doch bist du verklungen,
Und keiner denkt daran.

Often I must weep bitterly
That you are dead,
And that many of your loved ones
Forget you throughout their lives.
Inspired by love alone
You have done so much,
And yet, now you have departed,
No one thinks about it.

Du stehst voll treuer Liebe
Noch immer jedem bei,
Und wenn dir keiner bliebe,
So bleibst du dennoch treu;

Filled with true love
You stand by every man,
And if no one stayed true to you,
Yet would you remain true;

Die treuste Liebe sieget,
Am Ende fühlt man sie,
Weint bitterlich und schmieget
Sich kindlich an dein Knie.

Ich habe dich empfunden,
O! lasse nicht von mir;
Laß innig mich verbunden
Auf ewig sein mit dir.
Einst schauen meine Brüder   .
Auch wieder himmelwärts,
Und sinken liebend nieder,
Und fallen dir ans Herz.

The truest love triumphs,
In the end men feel it,
And weep bitterly, nestling
Like children at your knee.

I have known you,
O do not forsake me!
Let me be inwardly
United with you for ever.
One day my brothers will look
Once more towards heaven,
And swoon with love,
And sink down upon your heart.

Hymne IV / Hymn IV

NOVALIS

D 662 (1819)

Ich sag es jedem, daß er lebt
Und auferstanden ist,
Daß er in unsrer Mitte schwebt
Und ewig bei uns ist.

I tell everyone that he lives
And is risen,
That he hovers in our midst
And is forever with us.

Ich sag es jedem, jeder sagt
Es seinen Freunden gleich,
Daß bald an allen Orten tagt
Das neue Himmelreich.

I tell everyone, and everyone
At once tells his friends
That the new kingdom of heaven
Will soon dawn.

Jetzt scheint die Welt dem neuen Sinn
Erst wie ein Vaterland;
Ein neues Leben nimmt man hin
Entzückt aus seiner Hand.

Only now, with our new understanding,
Does the world seem like home;
Joyfully we receive a new life
From his hand.

Hinunter in das tiefe Meer
Versank des Todes Graun,
Und jeder kann nun leicht und hehr
In seine Zukunft schaun.

The fear of death has sunk
Into the deep ocean,
And everyone can now look to his future,
Elated and carefree.

Der dunkle Weg, den er betrat,
Geht in den Himmel aus,
Und wer nur hört auf seinen Rat,
Kommt auch in Vaters Haus.

The dark path he trod
Leads to heaven,
And all those who heed his counsel
Shall also enter the Father's house.

Nun weint auch keiner mehr allhie,
Wenn Eins die Augen schließt;
Vom Wiedersehn, spät oder früh,
Wird dieser Schmerz versüßt.

Now no one shall weep here on earth
When eyes are closed;
This sorrow will be sweetened,
Soon or late, by heavenly reunion.

Es kann zu jeder guten Tat
Ein jeder frischer glühn,
Denn herrlich wird ihm diese Saat
In schönern Fluren blühn.

For every good deed
Another can burn still more brightly;
For this seed will flower gloriously
In fairer fields.

Er lebt, und wird nun bei uns sein,
Wenn alles uns verläßt!
Und so soll dieser Tag uns sein
Ein Weltverjüngungs-Fest.

He lives, and will be with us
When all else forsakes us!
Therefore let this day be
A celebration of the reborn world.

Idens Nachtgesang / Ida's Song to the Night

LUDWIG KOSEGARTEN

D 227 (1815)

Vernimm es Nacht, was Ida dir vertrauet,
Die satt des Tags in deine Arme flieht.
Ihr Sterne, die ihr hold und liebend auf
  mich schauet,
Vernehmt süßlauschend Idens Lied.

Den ich geahnt in liebevollen Stunden,
Dem sehnsuchtsvoll mein Herz
  entgegenschlug,
O Nacht, o Sterne, hört's, ich habe ihn
  gefunden,
Des Bild ich längst im Innern
  trug.

Hear, night, what Ida confides to you;
Sated with the day, I fly to your arms.
Stars, gazing down sweetly and lovingly
  upon me,
Listen fondly to Ida's song.

O night, o stars, hear me: I have found him,
Whom I dreamed of in hours of
  bliss,
For whom my yearning heart
  beat,
And whose image I have long carried within
  me.

Idens Schwanenlied / Ida's Swan Song

LUDWIG KOSEGARTEN

D 317 (1815)

Wie schaust du aus dem Nebelflor
O Sonne, bleich und müde!
Es schwirrt der Heimchen heis'rer Chor
Zu meinem Schwanenliede.

Es girrt die scheidende Natur
Ihr Lebewohl so traurig.
Es stehen Busch und Wald und Flur
So trostlos und so schaurig.

Entblättert steht der Erlenhain,
Entlaubt der graue Garten,
Wo Er und ich im
  Mondenschein
Einander bang' erharrten;

Wo Er und ich im Mondenblitz
Im Schirm der Linden saßen,
Und auf des Rasens weichem Sitz
Der öden Welt vergaßen;

Wo ich, gelehnt an seine Brust,
In süße Träume nickte,
Und holder Wahn und Edens
  Lust
Die Träumende durchzückte.

O sun, how pale and weary
You gaze from your misty veil!
The hoarse chorus of crickets
Chirrups to my swan song.

Departing nature coos
Its sad farewell.
Bushes, woods and meadows
Stand so desolate, so eerie.

The alder grove,
The bleak garden stand leafless,
Where he and I anxiously awaited one
  another
In the moonlight.

Where, in the moon's rays, he and I
Sat beneath the canopy of the linden tree,
And on the soft lawn
Forgot this dismal world.

Where, leaning against his breast,
I drifted into sweet reverie,
Where blissful delirium and the pleasures
  of Eden
Thrilled through me as I dreamed.

Ihr Bild / Her Picture

HEINRICH HEINE

see Schwanengesang no. 9

Ihr Grab / Her Grave

KARL AUGUST ENGELHARDT

D736 (1822?)

Dort ist ihr Grab,
Die einst im Schmelz der Jugend glühte,
Dort fiel sie, dort, die schönste Blüte,
Vom Baum des Lebens ab.

There is her grave,
Who once glowed with the lustre of youth;
There she fell down, the fairest blossom,
From the tree of life.

Dort ist ihr Grab,
Dort schläft sie unter jener Linde;
Ach, nimmer ich ihn wiederfinde,
Den Trost, den sie mir gab.

There is her grave;
There she sleeps beneath that linden tree.
Ah, never again shall I find
The consolation she gave me.

Dort ist ihr Grab;
Vom Himmel kam sie, dass die Erde
Mir Glücklichen zum Himmel
  werde,
Und dort stieg sie hinab.

There is her grave;
She came from heaven, that the earth
Might turn to heaven for me in my
  happiness.
And there she sank down.

Dort ist ihr Grab,
Und dort in jenen stillen Hallen,
Bei ihr, lass ich mit Freuden fallen
Auch meinen Pilgerstab.

There is her grave,
And there in those silent vaults,
At her side, I too shall joyfully
Lay down my pilgrim's staff.

Il modo di prender moglie / How to Choose a Wife

POET UNKNOWN (formerly attributed to METASTASIO)

D902 no. 3 (1827)

Or sù! non ci pensiamo,
Corraggio e concludiamo,
Al fin s'io prendo moglie,
Sò ben perchè lo fò.
Lo fò per pagar i debiti,
La prendo per contanti,
Di dirlo, e di repeterlo,
Difficoltà non ho.
Fra tanti modi e tanti
Di prender moglie al mondo,
Un modo più giocondo
Del mio trovar non sò.
Si prende per affetto,
Si prende per rispetto,
Si prende per consiglio,
Si prende per puntiglio,
Si prende per capriccio,
È vero, si o nò?
Ed io per medicina
Di tutti i mali miei
Un poco di sposina
Prendere non potrò?
Ho detto e'l ridico,
Lo fò per li contanti,
Lo fanno tanti e tanti
Anch' io lo farò.

Now then, let's not think about it,
Courage, let's get it over with.
If in the end I have to take a wife
I know very well why I do it.
I do it to pay my debts.
I take her for the money.
I have no compunction telling you,
And repeating it.
Of all the ways of choosing a wife
In the world,
I know of no happier way
Than mine.
One chooses a wife for love,
Another out of respect,
Another because he is advised to,
Another out of propriety,
Another for a whim.
Is it true or not?
And I, why can't I take a little wife
As remedy
For all my ills?
I've said it,
  and I'll say it again:
I do it for the money.
So many do it.
I do it too.

Il traditor deluso / The Traitor Deceived

PIETRO METASTASIO

D 902 no. 2 (1827)

Recit:
Aimè, io tremo!
Io sento tutto in ondarmi
Il seno di gelido sudor!
Fuga si, ah quale?
Qual' è la via?
Chi me l'addita?
Oh Dio! che ascoltai?
Che m'avvenne?
Oh Dio! che ascoltai?
Ove son io?

Recit:
Alas, I tremble!
I feel a cold sweat
Upon my brow!
I must flee, but whither?
Where is the way?
Who will show it to me?
O God, what do I hear?
What is happening to me?
O God, what do I hear?
Where am I?

Aria:
Ah l'aria d'intorno lampeggia, sfavilla;
Ondeggia, vacilla l'infido terren!
Qual notte profonda
D'orror mi circonda!
Che larve funeste,
Che smanie son queste!
Che fiero spavento
Mi sento nel sen!

Aria:
The air around me flashes and sparkles;
The perfidious earth quakes and trembles!
The deep night
Surrounds me with horror!
What baleful creatures,
What furies are these?
What raging terror
I feel in my breast!

Im Abendrot / In the Glow of Evening

KARL LAPPE

D 799 (1825?)

O wie schön ist deine Welt,
Vater, wenn sie golden strahlet!
Wenn dein Glanz herniederfällt,
Und den Staub mit Schimmer malet,
Wenn das Rot, das in der Wolke
  blinkt,
In mein stilles Fenster sinkt!

How lovely is your world,
Father, in its golden radiance!
When your glory descends,
And paints the dust with glitter;
When the red light that shines from the
  clouds
Falls silently upon my window.

Könnt ich klagen, könnt ich
  zagen?
Irre sein an dir und mir?
Nein, ich will im Busen tragen
Deinen Himmel schon allhier.
Und dies Herz, eh es zusammenbricht,
Trinkt noch Glut und schlürft noch
  Licht.

Could I complain, could I be
  apprehensive?
Could I lose faith in you and in myself?
No, already I bear your heaven
Here within my heart.
And this heart, before it breaks,
Still drinks in the fire and savours the
  light.

Im Freien / In the Open

JOHANN GABRIEL SEIDL

D 880 (1826)

Draussen in der weiten Nacht
Steh ich wieder nun,
Ihre helle Sternenpracht
Lässt mein Herz nicht ruhn!

Now once more I stand outside
In the vast night;
Its bright, starry splendour
Gives my heart no peace.

Tausend Arme winken mir	A thousand arms beckon to me
Süss begehrend zu,	With sweet longing;
Tausend Stimmen rufen hier,	A thousand voices call:
»Grüss dich, Trauter, du!«	'Greetings, dear friend!'
O ich weiss auch, was mich zieht,	Oh, I know what draws me,
Weiss auch, was mich ruft,	What calls me,
Was wie Freundes Gruss und Lied	Like a friend's greeting, a song,
Locket, locket durch die Luft.	Floating enticingly through the air.
Siehst du dort das Hüttchen stehn,	Do you see the cottage there
Drauf der Mondschein ruht?	On which the moonlight lingers?
Durch die blanken Scheiben sehn	From its shining windows
Augen, die mir gut!	Fond eyes gaze out.
Siehst du dort das Haus am Bach,	Do you see the house there by the brook,
Das der Mond bescheint?	Lit by the moon?
Unter seinem trauten Dach	Beneath its cosy roof
Schläft mein liebster Freund.	Sleeps my dearest friend.
Siehst du jenen Baum,	Do you see that tree,
Der voll Silberflocken flimmt?	Glittering with silver flakes?
O wie oft mein Busen schwoll,	Oh, how often did my heart swell
Froher dort gestimmt!	With joy there!
Jedes Plätzchen, das mir winkt,	Every little place that beckons
Ist ein lieber Platz,	Is dear to me,
Und wohin ein Strahl nur sinkt,	And wherever a moonbeam falls,
Lockt ein teurer Schatz.	Cherished treasure entices.
Drum auch winkt mir's überall	So everything here beckons to me
So begehrend hier,	With longing,
Drum auch ruft es, wie der Schall	And calls to me with the sounds
Trauter Liebe mir.	Of true love.

Im Frühling / In Spring

ERNEST SCHULZE

D882 (1826)

Still sitz ich an des Hügels Hang,	I sit silently on the hillside,
Der Himmel ist so klar,	The sky is so clear,
Das Lüftchen spielt im grünen Tal,	The breezes play in the green valley
Wo ich beim ersten Frülingsstrahl	Where once, in the first rays of spring,
Einst, ach so glücklich war.	I was, oh, so happy.
Wo ich an ihrer Seite ging	Where I walked by her side,
So traulich und so nah,	So tender, so close,
Und tief im dunklen Felsenquell	And saw deep in the dark rocky stream
Den schönen Himmel blau und hell	The fair sky, blue and bright,
Und sie im Himmel sah.	And her reflected in that sky.
Sieh, wie der bunte Frühling schon	See how the colourful spring
Aus Knosp' und Blüte blickt!	Already peeps from bud and blossom.
Nicht alle Blüten sind mir gleich,	Not all the blossoms are the same to me:
Am liebsten pflück ich von dem Zweig,	I like most of all to pluck them from the branch
Von welchem sie gepflückt!	From which she has plucked.

Denn alles ist wie damals noch,
Die Blumen, das Gefild;
Die Sonne scheint nicht minder hell,
Nicht minder freundlich schwimmt im
    Quell
Das blaue Himmelsbild.

For all is still as it was then,
The flowers, the fields;
The sun shines no less brightly,
And no less cheer-
    fully
The sky's blue image bathes in the stream.

Es wandeln nur sich Will und Wahn,
Es wechseln Lust und Streit,
Vorüber flieht der Liebe Glück,
Und nur die Liebe bleibt zurück,
Die Lieb und ach, das Leid!

Only will and whim change,
And joy alternates with strife;
The happiness of love flies past,
And only love remains,
Love and, alas, sorrow.

O wär ich doch ein Vöglein nur
Dort an dem Wiesenhang!
Dann blieb ich auf den Zweigen hier,
Und säng ein süsses Lied von ihr,
Den ganzen Sommer lang.

Oh, if only I were a bird,
There on the sloping meadow!
Then I would stay on these branches here,
And sing a sweet song about her
All summer long.

Im Haine / In the Wood

FRANZ VON BRUCHMANN

D 738 (1822?)

Sonnenstrahlen
Durch die Tannen,
Wie sie fallen;
Ziehn von dannen
Alle Schmerzen,
Und im Herzen
Wohnet reiner Friede nur.

As rays of sunlight,
Fall
Through the fir-trees,
All sorrow
Drifts away,
And in our hearts
Dwells only peace.

Stilles Sausen
Lauer Lüfte,
Und im Brausen
Zarte Düfte,
Die sich neigen
Aus den Zweigen,
Atmet aus die ganze Flur.

Balmy breezes
Murmuring softly,
And the whispering,
Delicate scents
That float down
From the branches,
Caress every meadow.

Wenn nur immer
Dunkle Bäume,
Sonnenschimmer,
Grüne Säume
Uns umblühten
Und umglühten,
Tilgend aller Qualen Spur!

If only
Dark trees,
Shimmering sunlight
And the edge of green woods
Were to flower
And glow about us for ever,
Wiping away all traces of pain!

Im Walde / In the Forest

FRIEDRICH VON SCHLEGEL

D 708 (1820)
This song was originally published as 'Waldesnacht', and appears under this title
in the Peters edition.

Windes Rauschen, Gottes Flügel,
Tief in kühler Waldesnacht,

The rushing of the wind, God's own wings,
Deep in the cool night of the forest,

Wie der Held in Rosses Bügel,
Schwingt sich des Gedankens Macht.
Wie die alten Tannen sausen,
Hört man Geistes Wogen brausen.

As the hero leaps on to his horse,
So does the power of thought soar.
As the old pine-trees rustle,
So we hear the surging waves of the spirit.

Herrlich ist der Flamme Leuchten
In des Morgenglanzes Rot,
Oder die das Feld beleuchten,
Blitze, schwanger oft von Tod.
Rasch die Flamme zuckt und lodert,
Wie zu Gott hinauf gefordert.

Glorious is the flame's glow
In the red light of morning,
Or the flashes that light up the fields,
Often pregnant with death.
Swiftly the flame flickers and blazes,
As if summoned upward to God.

Ewig's Rauschen sanfter Quellen
Zaubert Blumen aus dem Schmerz,
Trauer doch in linden
   Wellen
Schlägt uns lockend an das Herz;
Fernab hin der Geist gezogen,
Die uns locken, durch die Wogen.

The eternal murmuring of gentle springs
Conjures flowers from sorrow;
Yet sadness beats alluringly against our
   hearts
In gentle waves.
The spirit is borne far away
By those waves that allure us.

Drang des Lebens aus der Hülle,
Kampf der starken Triebe wild,
Wird zur schönsten Liebesfülle
Durch des Geistes Hauch gestillt.
Schöpferischer Lüfte Wehen
Fühlt man durch die Seele gehen.

Life's urge to be free of its fetters,
The struggle of strong, wild impulses,
Are turned to love's fair fulfilment,
Stilled by the breath of the spirit.
We feel the creative breath
Pervade our souls.

Windes Rauschen, Gottes Flügel,
Tief in dunkler Waldesnacht,
Freigegeben alle Zügel
Schwingt sich des Gedankens Macht,
Hört in Lüften ohne Grausen
Den Gesang der Geister brausen.

The rushing of the wind, God's own wings,
Deep in the dark night of the forest;
Free from all restraints
The power of thought soars;
Without fear we hear the song of the spirits
Echoing in the breezes.

Im Walde / In the Forest

ERNST SCHULZE

D834 (1825?)

Ich wandre über Berg und Tal
Und über grüne Heiden,
Und mit mir wandert meine Qual,
Will nimmer von mir scheiden.
Und schifft' ich auch durch's weite
   Meer,
Sie käm' auch dort wohl hinterher.

I wander over hill and dale,
And over green heather,
And my suffering wanders with me,
Never leaving me.
And were I to sail across the wide
   sea,
It would still follow me there.

Wohl blühn viel Blumen auf der
   Flur,
Die hab' ich nicht gesehen.
Denn eine Blume seh' ich nur
Auf allen Wegen stehen.
Nach ihr hab' ich mich oft gebückt
Und doch sie nimmer abgepflückt.

Though many flowers bloom in the
   meadow,
I have not seen them,
For I see but one flower
On every path I tread.
I have often stooped down towards it,
But have never plucked it.

Die Bienen summen durch das Gras
Und hängen an den Blüten;
Das macht mein Auge trüb' und naß,
Ich kann mir's nicht verbieten.

The bees hum through the grass
And linger on the blossoms;
At this my eyes grow clouded and moist,
I cannot help it.

| Ihr süßen Lippen, rot und weich, | Sweet lips, so red and soft, |
| Wohl hing ich nimmer so an euch! | Never did I linger so on you. |

Gar lieblich singen nah und fern	Far and near the birds sing sweetly
Die Vögel auf den Zweigen;	On the branches;
Wohl säng' ich mit den Vögeln gern,	I should dearly love to sing with the birds,
Doch muß ich traurig schweigen.	But I must keep a mournful silence.
Denn Liebeslust und Liebespein,	For the joy and the pain of love
Die bleiben jedes gern allein.	Prefer to remain alone.

Am Himmel seh' ich flügelschnell	I watch the clouds wing their way
Die Wolken weiter ziehen,	Swiftly across the sky;
Die Welle rieselt leicht und hell,	The waves ripple softly and brightly,
Muß immer nahn und fliehen.	They must ever come and go.
Doch haschen, wenn's vom Winde ruht,	Yet when the wind dies down,
Sich Wolk' und Wolke, Flut und	In play cloud catches cloud, and wave
Flut.	catches wave.

Ich wandre hin, ich wandre her,	I wander here and there,
Bei Sturm und heitern Tagen,	Through storm and fine weather,
Und doch erschau' ich's nimmermehr	Yet I shall never again behold it,
Und kann es nicht erjagen.	Shall never find it.
O Liebessehnen, Liebesqual,	O longing and torment of love,
Wann ruht der Wanderer einmal?	When will the wanderer find rest?

In der Ferne / Far Away

LUDWIG RELLSTAB

see Schwanengesang no. 6

In der Mitternacht / At Midnight

JOHANN GEORG JACOBI

D 464 (1816)

Todesstille deckt das Tal	Deathly silence lies over the valley
Bei des Mondes halbem Strahl;	Beneath the moon's half-light;
Winde flüstern, dumpf und bang,	Winds whisper, dull and troubled,
In des Wächters Nachtgesang.	Mingling with the watchman's night song.

Leiser, dumpfer tönt es hier	Softer, duller, are the sounds
In der bangen Seele mir,	Within my troubled soul;
Nimmt den Strahl der Hoffnung fort,	They eclipse my ray of hope
Wie den Mond die Wolke dort.	As the clouds eclipse the moon.

Hüllt, ihr Wolken, hüllt den Schein	Clouds, conceal the light
Immer tiefer, tiefer ein!	Ever more deeply!
Vor ihm bergen will mein Herz	My heart would hide from him
Seinen tiefen, tiefen Schmerz.	Its deep, deep pain.

Nennen soll ihn nicht mein Mund;	My lips shall not name him;
Keine Träne mach' ihn kund;	No tear shall make him known;
Senken soll man ihn hinab	One day they shall lower him
Einst mit mir in's kühle Grab.	Into the cool grave, to lie with me.

Ins stille Land / To the Land of Rest!

SALIS-SEEWIS

see Lied

Iphigenia / Iphigenia

JOHANN MAYRHOFER

D573 (1817)

Blüht denn hier an Tauris Strande
Keine Blum' aus Hellas Lande,
Weht kein milder Segenshauch
Aus den lieblichen Gefilden,
Wo Geschwister mit mir
    spielten? —
Ach, mein Leben ist ein Rauch!

Trauernd wank' ich durch die Haine, —
Keine Hoffnung nähr' ich — keine,
Meine Heimat zu erseh'n,
Und die See mit hohen Wellen,
Die an Klippen kalt zerschellen,
Übertäubt mein leises Fleh'n.

Göttin, welche mich gerettet,
An die Wildnis mich gekettet, —
Rette mich zum zweitenmal;
Gnädig lasse mich den Meinen,
Laß' o Göttin! mich erscheinen
In des großen Königs Saal!

Does no flower from my beloved homeland
Bloom here on the shore of Tauris?
Does no breeze blow
From the blessed fields
Where my brothers and sisters played
    with me?
Ah, my life is but smoke!

Sadly, hesitantly, I walk through the grove;
I cherish no hope — none —
Of ever seeing my homeland.
And the sea, with its mighty waves
Crashing against the cold cliffs,
Drowns my soft pleas.

Goddess who rescued me
And chained me in this wilderness,
Rescue me a second time;
Mercifully grant, o goddess,
That I may appear before my own people
In the hall of the great king!

Irdisches Glück / Earthly Happiness

JOHANN GABRIEL SEIDL

D866 no. 4 (1828?)

So mancher sieht mit finst'rer Miene
Die weite Welt sich grollend an,
Des Lebens wunderbare Bühne
Liegt ihm vergebens aufgetan.
Da weiss ich besser mich zu nehmen,
Und fern, der Freude mich zu schämen,
Geniess' ich froh den Augenblick:
Das ist denn doch gewiss ein Glück.

Um manches Herz hab ich geworben,
Doch währte mein Triumph nicht lang,
Denn Blödheit hat mir oft verdorben,
Was kaum mein Frohsinn mir errang.
D'rum bin ich auch dem Netz entgangen:
Denn, weil kein Wahn mich hielt
    umfangen,
Kam ich von keinem auch zurück:
Und das ist doch gewiss ein Glück!

So many people look with grim faces
And resentment on the wide world;
Life's wondrous stage
Lies open to them, though in vain.
But I know better what to do,
And far from being ashamed of joy,
I gladly delight in the moment:
That, for sure, is happiness.

I have wooed many a heart,
Though my triumph did not last long,
For my stupidity often ruined
What my cheerful spirit had only just won.
And so I escaped the net;
For since no illusion held me
    captive,
I had none to escape from:
And that, for sure, is happiness.

Kein Lorbeer grünte meinem Scheitel,
Mein Haupt umstrahlt' kein Ehrenkranz;
Doch ist darum mein Tun nicht eitel;
Ein stiller Dank ist auch ein Kranz!
Wem, weit entfernt von kecken Flügen,
Des Tales stille Freuden
   g'nügen,
Dem bangt auch nie für sein Genick:
Und das ist doch gewiss ein Glück!

Und ruft der Bot' aus jenen
   Reichen
Mir einst, wie allen, ernst und
   hohl,
Dann sag ich willig, im Entweichen,
Der schönen Erde » Lebe wohl!«
Sei's denn, so drücken doch am Ende
Die Hand mir treue Freundeshände,
So segnet doch mich Freundesblick:
Und das ist, Brüder, doch wohl Glück!

No laurels have adorned my locks,
No halo of glory has shone about my head.
Yet my life is not in vain;
Quiet thanks are also a halo!
He who, far from bold flights,
Is content with the peaceful pleasures of the
   valley,
Need never fear for his neck:
And that, for sure, is happiness.

And when one day the messenger from the
   world beyond
Calls me, as he does all, with grave, hollow
   voice,
Then, in parting, I shall gladly
Bid this lovely world farewell.
Maybe, after all, the hands of true friends
Will at the end press my hand,
And friendly eyes will bless me:
And that, brothers, is surely happiness!

Jagdlied / Hunting Song

ZACHARIAS WERNER

D 521 (1817)

Trarah, trarah! Wir kehren daheim —
Wir bringen die Beute der Jagd! —
Es sinket die Nacht, drum halten wir
   Wacht;
Das Licht hat über das Dunkel Macht!
Trarah, trarah! Auf, auf!
Das Feuer angefacht!

Trarah, trarah! Wir zechen im Kreis!
Wir spotten des Dunkels der Nacht!
Des Menschen Macht,
In freudiger Pracht,
Die Qual verhöhnt, des Todes lacht! —
Trarah, trarah! Auf, auf!
Die Glut ist angefacht!

Tara, tara! We are returning home,
Bringing the spoils of the chase!
Night is falling, so we keep
   watch;
Light has power over darkness!
Tara, tara! Up, up!
Fan the flames!

Tara, tara! We drink in a circle!
We mock the darkness of the night!
The might of man,
Joyous and glorious,
Scorns pain and laughs at death!
Tara, tara! Up, up!
The fire is ablaze!

Jäger, ruhe von der Jagd / Huntsman, Rest from the Chase!

SIR WALTER SCOTT

see Ellens Gesang II

Jägers Abendlied / Huntsman's Evening Song

JOHANN WOLFGANG VON GOETHE

First version: D 215 (1815)
Second version: D 368 (1816)

Im Felde schleich ich, still und wild,
Gespannt mein Feuerrohr.
Da schwebt so licht dein liebes Bild,
Dein süsses Bild mir
vor.

I stalk through the fields, grim and silent,
My gun at the ready.
Then your beloved image,
Your sweet image hovers brightly before
me.

Du wandelst jetzt wohl still und mild	Perhaps you are now wandering, silent and gentle,
Durch Feld und liebes Tal,	Through field and beloved valley;
Und ach, mein schnell verrauschet Bild,	Ah, does my fleeting image
Stellt sich dir's nicht einmal?	Not even appear before you?
Mir ist es, denk' ich nur an dich,	Whenever I think of you
Als in den Mond zu sehn;	It is as if I were gazing at the moon;
Ein stiller Friede kommt auf mich,	A silent peace descends upon me,
Weiss nicht wie mir geschehn.	I know not how.

Jägers Liebeslied / *Huntsman's Love Song*

FRANZ VON SCHOBER

D909 (1827)

Ich schieß' den Hirsch im dunklen Forst,	I shoot the stag in the green forest,
Im stillen Tal das Reh,	And the roe in the silent valley;
Den Adler in dem Klippenhorst,	The eagle in its eyrie on the cliffs,
Die Ente auf dem See.	The duck on the lake.
Kein Ort, der Schutz gewähren kann,	No place can give protection
Wenn meine Flinte zielt;	When my gun is aimed,
Und dennoch hab' ich harter Mann	And yet I, though a hard man,
Die Liebe auch gefühlt! —	Have also felt love.
Hab' oft hantiert in rauher Zeit,	I have often worked in harsh conditions,
In Sturm und Winternacht,	In storms and winter nights,
Und übereist und eingeschneit	And, covered with ice and snow,
Zum Bett den Stein gemacht.	Have made a bed of stones.
Auf Dornen schlief ich wie auf Flaum,	I have slept on thorns as on down,
Vom Nordwind ungerührt,	Untroubled by the north wind.
Doch hat der Liebe zarten Traum	Yet my rough breast has also felt
Die rauhe Brust gespürt.	Love's tender dream.
Der wilde Falk war mein Gesell,	The fierce hawk was my companion,
Der Wolf mein Kampfgespann;	The wolf my adversary in battle;
Mir es fing der Tag mit Hundgebell,	My day began with the baying of hounds,
Die Nacht mit Hussa an.	My night with the cry of tally-ho.
Ein Tannreis war die Blumenzier	A sprig of fir was the flower
Auf schweißbeflecktem Hut,	That adorned my sweaty hat;
Und dennoch schlug die Liebe mir	And yet love penetrated
Ins wilde Jägerblut.	My wild huntsman's blood.
O Schäfer auf dem weichen Moos,	O shepherd on the soft moss,
Der du mit Blüten spielst,	Playing with flowers,
Wer weiß, ob du so heiß, so groß	Who knows if you feel love
Wie ich die Liebe fühlst.	As much and as ardently as I do?
Allnächtlich überm schwarzen Wald,	Every night, above the dark forest,
Vom Mondenschein umstrahlt,	Its radiance hovers, bathed in moonlight,
Schwebt königsgroß die Lichtgestalt,	With a regal splendour
Wie sie kein Meister malt.	That no master could paint.
Wenn sie dann auf mich niedersieht,	When she looks down upon me,
Wenn mich der Blick durchglüht,	When her gaze burns through me,
Dann fühl' ich, wie dem Wild geschieht,	Then I know how the wild animals feel
Das vor dem Rohre flieht.	When they flee from my gun.
Ich fühl's mit allem Glück vereint	And yet that feeling is united
Das nur auf Erden ist;	With all the happiness on earth,
Wie wenn der allerbeste Freund	As if my dearest friend
Mich in die Arme schließt!	Held me in his arms.

Julius an Theone / Julius to Theone

FRIEDRICH VON MATTHISSON

D 419 (1816)

Nimmer, nimmer darf ich dir gestehen,	Never, never can I confess to you
Was beim ersten Drucke deiner Hand,	What my heart felt, sweet enchantress,
Süsse Zauberin, mein Herz empfand!	When I first pressed your hand.
Meiner Einsamkeit verborg'nes Flehen,	My sighs, the hidden entreaties of my loneliness,
Meine Seufzer wird der Sturm verwehen,	Will be blown away by the storm,
Meine Tränen werden ungesehen	My tears will flow unseen
Deinem Bilde rinnen, bis die Gruft	For the image of you, until the grave
Mich in ihr verschwieg'nes Dunkel ruft.	Calls me to its secret darkness.
Ach! du schautest mir so unbefangen,	Ah! You gazed into my face so candidly,
So voll Engelunschuld ins Gesicht,	So full of angelic innocence,
Wähntest den Triumph der Schönheit nicht!	Not suspecting the triumph of your beauty.
O Theone! sahst du nicht den bangen	O Theone! Did you not see the anxious
Blick der Liebe an deinen Blicken hangen?	Loving glance hanging on your glances?
Schimmerte die Röte meiner Wangen	Did not my flushed cheeks give
Dir nicht Ahnung der verlornen Ruh'	A hint of the lost peace
Meines hoffnungslosen Herzens zu?	Of my hopeless heart?
Dass uns Meere doch geschieden hätten	Would that oceans had separated us
Nach dem ersten leisen Druck der Hand!	After that first soft touch of hands!
Schaudernd wank' ich nun am Rand	Shuddering, I now totter on the brink
Eines Abgrunds, wo auf Dornenbetten,	Of an abyss where, on beds of thorns,
Tränenlos, mit diamantmen Ketten,	With diamond chains and without tears,
Die Verzweiflung lauscht! Mich zu retten,	Despair lies in wait. To save me,
Holde Feindin meines Friedens,	Fair enemy of my inner peace,
Beut mir die Schale der Vergessenheit!	Hand me the cup of forgetfulness.

Kennst du das Land? (Mignon's Gesang) / Do You Know the Land? (Mignon's Song)

JOHANN WOLFGANG VON GOETHE

D 321 (1815)
from *Wilhelm Meister*

Kennst du das Land, wo die Zitronen blühn,	Do you know the land where lemon trees blossom,
Im dunklen Laub die Gold-Orangen glühn,	Where golden oranges glow amid dark leaves?
Ein sanfter Wind vom blauen Himmel weht,	A gentle wind blows from the blue sky,
Die Myrte still und hoch der Lorbeer steht,	The myrtle stands silent, the laurel tall:
Kennst du es wohl?	Do you know it?
Dahin! Dahin	There, o there
Möcht' ich mit dir, o mein Geliebter, ziehn.	I desire to go with you, my beloved!

Kennst du das Haus? Auf Säulen ruht sein Dach,
Es glänzt der Saal, es schimmert das Gemach,
Und Mamorbilder stehn und sehn mich an:
Was hat man dir, du armes Kind, getan?
Kennst du es wohl?
Dahin! Dahin
Möcht' ich mit dir, o mein Beschützer, ziehn.

Do you know the house? Its roof rests on pillars,
The hall gleams, the chamber shimmers,
And marble statues stand and gaze at me:
What have they done to you, poor child?
Do you know it?
There, o there
I desire to go with you, my protector!

Kennst du den Berg und seinen Wolkensteg?
Das Maultier sucht im Nebel seinen Weg;
In Höhlen wohnt der Drachen alte Brut;
Es stürzt der Fels und über ihn die Flut,
Kennst du ihn wohl?
Dahin! Dahin
Geht unser Weg! o Vater, laß uns ziehn!

Do you know the mountain and its clouded path?
The mule seeks its way through the mist,
In caves the ancient brood of dragons dwells;
The rock falls steeply, and over it the torrent.
Do you know it?
There, o there
Lies our way! O father, let us go!

Klage / Lament

FRIEDRICH VON MATTHISSON

D 415 (1816)

Die Sonne steigt, die Sonne sinkt,
Des Mondes Wechselscheibe blinkt,
Des Äthers Blau durchwebt mit Glanz
Der Sterne goldner Reihentanz:
Doch es durchströmt der Sonne Licht
Des Mondes lächelndes Gesicht.
Der Sterne Reigen, still und hehr,
Mit Hochgefühl dies Herz nicht mehr!

The sun rises, the sun sinks,
The moon's ever-changing disc gleams,
The blue ether is shot through
With the brilliant, golden dance of the stars.
But the sun's light,
The moon's smiling countenance,
The dance of the stars, silent and sublime,
No longer flood this heart with elation.

Die Wiese blüht, der Büsche Grün
Ertönt von Frühlingsmelodien,
Es wallt der Bach im Abendstrahl
Hinab ins hainumkränzte Tal:
Doch es erhebt der Haine Lied,
Die Au, die tausendfarbig blüht,
Der Erlenbach im Abendlicht
Wie vormals meine Seele nicht!

The meadow blooms, the green bushes
Echo with spring melodies;
In the evening sunlight the brook
Gushes down into the wooded valley.
But the song of the woods,
The meadow, blooming with a thousand colours,
The alders by the brook in the twilight
Do not uplift my soul as they once did.

Klage / Lament

POET UNKNOWN

D 371 (1816?)

Trauer umfliesst mein Leben,
Hoffnungslos mein Streben,
Stets in Glut und Beben
Schleicht mir hin das Leben;
O nimmer trag ich's länger!

Sorrow floods my life,
My endeavours are in vain,
In unremitting ardour and trembling
My life slips by;
I can endure it no longer!

Leiden, Schmerzen wühlen	Grief and suffering gnaw away
Mir in den Gefühlen,	At my feelings;
Keine Lüfte kühlen	No breezes cool
Banger Ahnung Schwülen;	My feverish, anxious foreboding.
O nimmer trag ich's länger!	I can endure it no longer!

Nur ferner Tod kann heilen	Only distant death can cure
Solcher Schmerzen Weilen;	The presence of such suffering;
Wo sich die Pforten teilen,	When the gates open
Werd' ich wieder heilen;	I shall be cured;
O nimmer trag ich's länger!	I can endure it no longer!

Klage an den Mond / Lament to the Moon

LUDWIG HEINRICH CHRISTOPH HÖLTY

D 436 (1816)

Dein Silber schien	Your silver
Durch Eichengrün,	Shone down on me
Das Kühlung gab,	Through the green oaks
Auf mich herab,	That gave cool shade,
O Mond, und lachte Ruh'	O moon, and, smiling, shed peace
Mir frohem Knaben zu.	On me, a happy youth.

Wenn jetzt dein Licht	When now your light
Durch's Fenster bricht,	Breaks through the window,
Lacht's keine Ruh'	No peace smiles on me,
Mir Jüngling zu,	Now a young man;
Sieht's meine Wange blass,	It sees my cheeks pale,
Mein Auge tränennass.	My eyes moist with tears.

Bald, lieber Freund,	Soon, dear friend,
Ach bald bescheint	Soon your silver light
Dein Silberschein	Will shine
Den Leichenstein,	On the tombstone
Der meine Asche birgt,	That hides my ashes,
Des Jünglings Asche birgt!	The young man's ashes.

Klage der Ceres / Ceres' Lament

FRIEDRICH VON SCHILLER

D 323 (1815–16)

Ist der holde Lenz erschienen?	Has fair spring appeared?
Hat die Erde sich verjüngt?	Has the earth grown young again?
Die besonnten Hügel grünen,	The sunny hills turn green,
Und des Eises Rinde springt.	The ice's crust cracks.
Aus der Ströme blauem Spiegel	From the blue mirror of the rivers
Lacht der unbewölkte Zeus,	Cloudless Zeus laughs;
Milder wehen Zephyrs Flügel,	The Zephyrs' wings beat more gently,
Augen treibt das junge Reis.	The young shoots push forth buds.
In dem Hain erwachen Lieder,	Song awakens in the grove,
Und die Oreade spricht:	And the Oread speaks:
Deine Blumen kehren wieder,	Your flowers return,
Deine Tochter kehret nicht.	But your daughter does not.

Ach, wie lang' ist's, daß ich walle
Suchend durch der Erde Flur!
Titan, deiner Strahlen alle
Sandt' ich nach der teuren Spur;
Keiner hat mir noch verkündet
Von dem lieben Angesicht,
Und der Tag, der alles findet,
Die Verlorne fand er nicht.
Hast du, Zeus, sie mir entrissen?
Hat, von ihrem Reiz gerührt,
Zu des Orkus schwarzen Flüssen
Pluto sie hinabgeführt?

Wer wird nach dem düstern Strande
Meines Grames Bote sein?
Ewig stößt der Kahn vom Lande,
Doch nur Schatten nimmt er ein.
Jedem sel'gen Aug' verschlossen
Bleibt das nächtliche Gefild,
Und so lang der Styx geflossen,
Trug er kein lebendig Bild.
Nieder führen tausend Steige,
Keiner führt zum Tag zurück,
Ihre Tränen bringt kein Zeuge
Vor der bangen Mutter Blick.

Mütter, die aus Pyrrhas Stamme
Sterbliche geboren sind,
Dürfen durch des Grabes Flamme
Folgen dem geliebten Kind;
Nur was Jovis Haus bewohnet,
Nahet nicht dem dunkeln Strand,
Nur die Seligen verschonet,
Parzen, eure strenge Hand.
Stürzt mich in die Nacht der Nächte
Aus des Himmels goldnem Saal!
Ehret nicht der Göttin Rechte.
Ach! sie sind der Mutter Qual!

Wo sie mit dem finstern Gatten
Freudlos thronet, stieg' ich hin,
Und träte mit den leisen Schatten
Leise vor die Herrscherin.
Ach, ihr Auge, feucht von Zähren,
Sucht umsonst das goldne Licht,
Irret nach entfernten Sphären,
Auf die Mutter fällt es nicht —
Bis die Freude sie entdecket,
Bis sich Brust mit Brust vereint,
Und, zum Mitgefühl erwecket,
Selbst der rauhe Orkus weint.

Eitler Wunsch! Verlorne Klagen!
Ruhig in dem gleichen Gleis
Rollt des Tages sichrer Wagen,
Ewig steht der Schluß des Zeus.
Weg von jenen Finsternissen
Wandt' er sein beglücktes Haupt;
Einmal in die Nacht gerissen,
Bleibt sie ewig mir geraubt,
Bis des dunkeln Stromes Welle

Ah, how long have I been wandering
Through the earth's meadows, searching!
Titan, I sent all your rays of light
To seek out my dear one;
No one has yet brought me word
Of her beloved countenance,
And day, that finds all things,
Has not found my lost daughter.
Have you, Zeus, snatched her from me?
Has Pluto, touched by her charms,
Carried her
Down to the black rivers of Orcus?

Who will convey the tidings of my grief
To the sombre shore?
The boat forever pulls away from land,
But it takes only shades on board.
The fields of night remain closed
To the eyes of every immortal,
And as long as the Styx has flowed
It has borne no living creature.
A thousand paths lead downwards,
But none leads back to the light.
No witness evokes the daughter's tears
Before the eyes of the anxious mother.

Mothers, born immortal
Of Pyrrha's race,
May follow their beloved children
Through the flames of the grave.
Only they that dwell in the house of Jove
May not approach the dark shore.
Your stern hand, O Fates,
Spares only the immortals.
Plunge me from the golden halls of heaven
Into the night of nights!
Do not respect the rights of the goddess;
Alas, they are a mother's torment!

Where she is joylessly enthroned
With her gloomy spouse, I would descend,
And with the soft shadows
Tread softly before the queen.
Ah, here eyes, moist with tears,
Seek in vain the golden light;
They stray to far-off spheres,
But do not alight on her mother —
Until, to her joy, she discovers her,
Until their bosoms are united,
And even harsh Orcus,
Aroused to pity, weeps.

Vain wish! Forlorn laments!
The trusty chariot of day
Rolls calmly on its even course;
The decree of Zeus stands for ever.
He has turned his august head
Away from those black realms.
Snatched into the night,
She remains forever lost to me,
Until the waves of the dark river

Von Aurorens Farben glüht,
Iris mitten durch die Hölle
Ihren schönen Bogen zieht.

Ist mir nichts von ihr geblieben?
Nicht ein süß erinnernd Pfand,
Daß die Fernen sich noch
  lieben,
Keine Spur der teuren Hand?
Knüpfet sich kein Liebesknoten
Zwischen Kind und Mutter an?
Zwischen Lebenden und Toten
Ist kein Bündnis aufgetan?
Nein, nicht ganz ist sie enflohen!
Wir sind nicht ganz getrennt!
Haben uns die ewig Hohen
Eine Sprache doch vergönnt!

Wenn des Frühlings Kinder sterben,
Wenn von Nordes kaltem Hauch
Blatt und Blumen sich entfärben,
Traurig steht der nackte Strauch,
Nehm ich mir das höchste Leben
Aus Vertumnus' reichem Horn,
Opfernd es dem Styx zu geben,
Mir des Samens goldnes Korn.
Trauernd senk' ich's in die Erde,
Leg' es an des Kindes Herz,
Daß es eine Sprache werde
Meiner Liebe, meinem Schmerz.

Führt der gleiche Tanz der
  Horen
Freudig nun den Lenz zurück,
Wird das Tote neu geboren
Von der Sonne Lebensblick;
Keime, die dem Auge starben
In der Erde kaltem Schoß,
In das heitre Reich der Farben
Ringen sie sich freudig los.
Wenn der Stamm zum Himmel eilet,
Sucht die Wurzel scheu die Nacht,
Gleich in ihre Pflege
  teilet
Sich des Styx, des Äthers Macht.

Halb berühren sie der Toten,
Halb der Lebenden Gebiet —
Ach, sie sind mir teure Boten,
Süße Stimmen vom Cocyt!
Hält er gleich sie selbst verschlossen
In dem schauervollen Schlund,
Aus des Frühlings jungen Sprossen
Redet mir der holde Mund;
Daß auch fern vom goldnen
  Tage,
Wo die Schatten traurig ziehn,
Liebend noch der Busen schlage,
Zärtlich noch die Herzen glühn.

O, so laßt euch froh begrüßen,
Kinder der verjüngten Au,

Glow with the colours of the dawn,
And Iris draws her fair bow
Through the midst of hell.

Is nothing of her left to me?
No sweet pledge to remind me
That, though far distant, we still love one
  another?
No trace of her beloved hand?
Is there no bond of love
Between mother and child?
Is there no alliance
Between the living and the dead?
No, she is not completely lost to me!
We are not completely separated!
For the eternal gods
Have granted us a language!

When the children of spring die,
When leaves and flowers fade
At the north wind's cold breath,
And the bare bushes stand mournful,
I take the highest life
From Vertumnus's cornucopia,
And sacrifice the seed's golden corn
To the Styx.
Lamenting, I plant it in the earth,
Laying it on the heart of my child,
That it may become a language
Of my love and my sorrow.

Then, when the unchanging dance of the
  hours
Brings back joyous spring,
What was dead is born anew
Under the sun's life-giving gaze.
Seeds which the eye took for dead
In the earth's cold womb,
Struggle joyfully free
Into the bright realm of colours.
As stems surge towards the sky,
Roots shyly seek the night.
The powers of the Styx and those of the
  ether
Are equally divided in their cultivation.

They exist half in the regions of the dead
And half in those of the living —
Ah, to me they are dear messengers,
Sweet voices from Cocytus!
Though it holds her captive
In the gruesome abyss,
Her beloved mouth speaks to me
Through spring's young shoots,
It tells me that, though far from the golden
  day,
Where the shades wander mournfully,
Her breast still beats lovingly,
And hearts still glow tenderly.

O, let me greet you joyfully,
Children of the reborn meadows;

Euer Kelch soll überfließen
Von des Nektars reinstem Tau.
Tauchen will ich euch in Strahlen,
Mit der Iris schönstem Licht
Will ich eure Blätter malen
Gleich Aurorens Angesicht.
In des Lenzes heiterm Glanze
Lese jede zarte Brust,
In des Herbstes welkem Kranze
Meinen Schmerz und meine Lust.

Your cup shall overflow
With the purest dew of nectar.
I shall bathe you in sunbeams,
I shall paint your leaves
With the rainbow's fairest light,
Like Aurora's countenance.
In the serene radiance of spring
In the faded wreath of autumn,
Every tender heart may discern
My sorrow and my joy.

Klage um Ali Bey / Lament for Ali Bey

MATTHIAS CLAUDIUS

D 2 496A (1816?)

Laßt mich! laßt mich! ich will klagen,
Fröhlich sein nicht mehr!
Aboudahab hat geschlagen
Aly und sein Heer.

Leave me! Leave me! I wish to lament,
And never again be joyful!
Abu Dahab has slain
Ali and his army!

So ein muntrer kühner Krieger
Wird nicht wieder sein;
Über alles ward er Sieger,
Haut' es kurz und klein.

Such a bold and cheerful warrior
There will never be again;
He vanquished all,
Hacking them to pieces.

Er verschmähte Wein und Weiber,
Ging nur Kriegesbahn,
Und war für die Zeitungsschreiber
Gar ein lieber Mann.

He scorned wine and women,
Pursuing only the path of war,
And was beloved
By the newspapers.

Aber, nun ist er gefallen,
Daß er's doch nicht wär!
Ach, von allen Bey's, von allen
War kein Bey wie er.

But now he is fallen.
Would that he had not!
Ah, among all the Beys
There was no Bey like him.

Jedermann in Sirus saget:
»Schade, daß er fiel!«
Und in ganz Ägypten klaget
Mensch und Krokodil.

Everyone in Syria is saying:
'What a pity that he has fallen!'
And throughout all Egypt
Men and crocodiles lament.

Daher sieht im Geist, wie's scheinet,
Am Serail mit Graus
Seines Freundes Kopf, und weinet
Sich die Augen aus.

With horror Daher pictures
His friend's head
In the harem,
And cries his eyes out.

Klaglied / Lament

JOHANN FRIEDRICH ROCHLITZ

D 23 (1812)

Meine Ruh' ist dahin,
Meine Freud' ist entfloh'n,
In dem Säuseln der Lüfte,
In dem Murmeln des Bach's
Hör' ich bebend nur Klageton.

My peace is gone,
My joy has fled;
In the rustling of the breezes,
In the murmuring of the brook
I hear only the quivering plaint.

Seinem schmeichelnden Wort,
Und dem Druck seiner Hand,
Seinem heißen Verlangen,
Seinem glühenden Kuß,
Weh' mir, daß ich nicht widerstand!

His flattering words
And the press of his hand,
His ardent desire,
His burning kisses —
Alas, that I did not resist!

Wenn ich von fern ihn seh',
Will ich ihn zu mir zieh'n,
Kaum entdeckt mich sein Auge,
Kaum tritt näher er mir,
Möcht' ich gern in mein Grab entflieh'n.

When I see him from afar
I long to draw him to me;
No sooner does his eye discern me,
No sooner does he approach me
Than I desire to escape to my grave.

Einmal, ach einmal nur
Möcht' ich ihn glücklich seh'n
Hier am klopfenden Herzen,
An der sehnenden Brust:
Wollte dann lächelnd untergehn!

Ah, if once, but once
I might see him happy
Here upon my beating heart,
Upon my yearning breast,
I could then die with a smile!

Klärchens Lied / Klärchen's Song

JOHANN WOLFGANG VON GOETHE

see Die Liebe

Kolmas Klage / Colma's Lament

JAMES MACPHERSON (OSSIAN), translator unknown

D 217 (1815)
The anonymous translation is a free verse adaptation of Macpherson's prose original. A literal rendering of the German is given here.

Rund um mich Nacht,
Ich irr' allein,
Verloren am stürmischen Hügel;
Der Sturm braust vom Gebirg,
Der Strom die Felsen hinab,
Mich schützt kein Dach vor Regen,
Verloren am stürmischen Hügel,
Irr' ich allein.

Around me is night,
I wander alone,
Lost on the stormy hill;
The storm roars from the mountains,
The torrent pours down the rocks;
No roof shelters me from the rain.
Lost on the stormy hill,
I wander alone.

Erschein', o Mond,
Dring' durch's Gewölk;
Erscheinet, ihr nächtlichen Sterne,
Geleitet freundlich mich,
Wo mein Geliebter ruht.
Mit ihm flieh' ich den Vater,
Mit ihm meinen herrischen Bruder,
Erschein', o Mond.

Appear, o moon!
Pierce through the clouds!
Appear, stars of the night!
Lead me kindly
To the place where my love rests.
With him I would flee from my father,
With him, from my overbearing brother.
Appear, o moon!

Ihr Stürme, schweigt,
O schweige, Strom,
Mich höre, mein liebender Wanderer,
Salgar! ich bin's, die ruft.
Hier ist der Baum, hier der Fels,
Warum verweilst du länger?
Wie, hör' ich den Ruf seiner Stimme?
Ihr Stürme, schweigt!

Be silent, storms,
Be silent, stream!
Let my loving wanderer hear me!
Salgar! It is I who call.
Here is the tree, here the rock.
Why do you tarry longer?
Do I hear the cry of his voice
Be silent, storms!

Doch, sieh, der Mond erscheint,	But lo, the moon appears,
Der Hügel Haupt erhellet,	The tips of the hills are bright,
Die Flut im Tale glänzt,	The flood sparkles in the valley,
Im Mondlicht wallt die Heide.	The heath is bathed in moonlight.
Ihn seh' ich nicht im Tale,	I do not see him in the valley,
Ihn nicht am hellen Hügel,	Nor on the bright hillside;
Kein Laut verkündet ihn,	No sound announces his approach,
Ich wand'le einsam hier.	Here I walk alone.
Doch wer sind jene dort,	But who are they,
Gestreckt auf dürrer Heide?	Stretched out there on the barren heath?
Ist's mein Geliebter, Er!	It is he, my love,
Und neben ihm mein Bruder!	And beside him my brother!
Ach, beid' in ihrem Blute,	Ah, both lie in their blood,
Entblößt die wilden Schwerter!	Their fierce swords drawn!
Warum erschlugst du ihn?	Why have you slain him?
Und du, Salgar, warum?	And you, Salgar, why?
Geister meiner Toten,	Ghosts of my dead,
Sprecht vom Felsenhügel,	Speak from the rocky hillside,
Von des Berges Gipfel,	From the mountain top;
Nimmer schreckt ihr mich!	You will never frighten me!
Wo gingt ihr zur Ruhe,	Where are you gone to rest?
Ach, in welcher Höhle	Ah, in what cave
Soll ich euch nun finden?	Shall I find you now?
Doch es tönt kein Hauch.	But there is no sound.
Hier in tiefem Grame	Here, in deep grief,
Wein' ich bis am Morgen,	I shall weep until morning;
Baut das Grab, ihr Freunde,	Build the tomb, friends,
Schließt's nicht ohne mich.	Do not close it without me.
Wie sollt' ich hier weilen?	Why should I remain here?
An des Bergstroms Ufer	On the banks of the mountain stream,
Mit den lieben Freunden	With my dear friends,
Will ich ewig ruh'n.	I shall rest for ever.

Kriegers Ahnung / Warrior's Foreboding

LUDWIG RELLSTAB

see Schwanengesang no. 2

Labetrank der Liebe / Love's Reviving Potion

JOSEPH LUDWIG STOLL

D 302 (1815)

Wenn im Spiele leiser Töne	When, amid the strains of soft music,
Meine kranke Seele schwebt,	My suffering soul hovers,
Und der Wehmut süsse Träne	And sweet tears of sadness
Deinem warmen Blick entschwebt:	Flow from your warm gaze:
Sink' ich dir bei sanftem Wallen	I sink down silently
Deines Busens sprachlos hin;	On your gently heaving breast.
Engelmelodien schallen,	Angelic melodies sound
Und der Erde Schatten fliehn.	And the earth's shadows take flight.

So in Eden hingesunken,
Lieb' mit Liebe umgetauscht,
Küsse lispelnd wonnetrunken,
Wie von Seraphim umrauscht:

Reichst du mir im Engelbilde
Liebewarmen Labetrank,
Wenn im schnöden Staubgefilde
Schmachtend meine Seele sank.

Thus, immersed in paradise,
Exchanging love with love,
Whispering kisses, drunk with ecstasy,
As if seraphim played about us:

You gave me, in the form of an angel,
A reviving potion, warm with love,
As my languishing soul
Sank in the hateful, dusty wastes.

Lachen und Weinen / Laughter and Tears

FRIEDRICH RÜCKERT

D777 (1822–3?)

Lachen und Weinen zu jeglicher Stunde
Ruht bei der Lieb auf so mancherlei
    Grunde.
Morgens lacht ich vor Lust,
Und warum ich nun weine
Bei des Abends Scheine,
Ist mir selb' nicht bewusst.

Laughter and tears, at whatever hour,
Arise, in love, from so many different
    causes.
In the morning I laughed for joy,
And why, in the glow of evening,
I am now weeping,
I myself do not know.

Weinen und Lachen zu jeglicher Stunde
Ruht bei der Lieb auf so mancherlei
    Grunde.
Abends weint ich vor Schmerz;
Und warum du erwachen
Kannst am Morgen mit Lachen,
Muss ich dich fragen, o Herz.

Tears and laughter, at whatever hour,
Arise, in love, from so many different
    causes.
In the evening I wept with grief;
And how you can awake
In the morning laughing,
I must ask you, my heart.

Lambertine / Lambertine

JOSEF LUDWIG STOLL

D301 (1815)

O Liebe, die mein Herz erfüllet,
Wie wonnevoll ist deine Seligkeit!
Doch ach! wie grausam peinigend
    durchwühlet
Mich Hoffnungslosigkeit.

O love, that fills my heart,
How sweet is your bliss!
But ah, how cruelly, how
    painfully
I am consumed by despair.

Er liebt mich nicht, er liebt mich nicht,
    verloren
Ist ohne ihn des Lebens süße
    Lust.
Ich bin zu bittern Leiden nur geboren,
Nur Schmerz drückt meine Brust.

He does not love me, he does not love
    me;
Without him life's sweet pleasure has
    vanished.
I am born only to bitter suffering;
Sorrow alone oppresses my heart.

Doch nein, ich will nicht länger trostlos
    klagen!
Zu sehen ihn gönnt mir das Schicksal
    noch;
Darf ich ihm auch nicht meine Liebe
    sagen,
G'nügt mir sein Anblick doch.

But no, I shall no longer lament
    inconsolably!
Fate still permits me to see
    him.
Though I may not declare my love to
    him,
Yet the very sight of him is enough for me.

Sein Bild ist Trost in meinem stillen
  Kummer,
Hier hab' ich's mir zur Wonne aufgestellt;
Dies soll mich laben, bis daß ew'ger
  Schlummer
Mein mattes Herz befällt.

His image is a comfort in my silent
  grief,
I have set it up here to bring me joy;
This will console me until eternal
  slumber
Overcomes my weary heart.

La Pastorella al Prato / The Shepherdess in the Meadow

CARLO GOLDONI

D 528 (1817)

La pastorella al prato
Contenta se ne va,
Coll' agnelline a lato
Cantando in libertà.
Se l'innocente amore
Grandisce il suo pastore
La bella pastorella
Contenta ognor sarà.

The shepherdess in the meadow
Wanders happily,
The little lambs at her side,
And sings blithely.
If her innocent love
Pleases her shepherd,
The fair shepherdess
Will always be happy.

Laura am Klavier / Laura at the Piano

FRIEDRICH VON SCHILLER

D 388 (1816)

Wenn dein Finger durch die Saiten
  meistert,
Laura, jetzt zur Statue
  entgeistert,
Jetzt entkörpert steh' ich da.
Du gebiestest über Tod und Leben,
Mächtig, wie von tausend Nervgeweben
Seelen fordert
  Philadelphia!

When your fingers hold sway over the
  strings,
Laura, I stand there, now dumbfounded,
  as if turned into a statue,
Now disembodied.
You have command over life and death,
As mighty as Philadelphia,
Drawing the souls from a thousand
  sensitive beings.

Ehrerbietig leiser
  rauschen
Dann die Lüfte, dir zu lauschen;
Hingeschmiedet zum Gesang
Stehn im ew'gen Wirbelgang,
Einzuzieh'n die Wonnefülle,
Lauschende Naturenstille.
Zauberin! mit Tönen, wie
Mich mit Blicken, zwingst du sie.

In reverence the breezes whisper more
  softly,
So as to listen to you;
Riveted by the music,
Nature, listening silently,
Stops in her whirling course
To take in the abundant delights.
Enchantress! With sounds you enthral her,
As you enthral me with your eyes.

Seelenvolle Harmonien wimmeln,
Ein wollüstig Ungestüm,
Aus ihren Saiten, wie aus ihren
  Himmeln
Neugebor'ne Seraphim;

Soulful harmonies,
Sensual and impetuous,
Teem from her strings, like new-born
  seraphim
From their heaven.

Wie, des Chaos Riesenarm entronnen,
Aufgejagt vom Schöpfungssturm, die
  Sonnen
Funkelnd fuhren aus der Nacht,
Strömt der Töne Zaubermacht.

As the flashing suns shot from the night,
Escaping the giant arm of
  Chaos,
Driven away by the storm of creation,
So the magic power of music pours forth.

Lieblich jetzt, wie über glatten Kieseln
Silberhelle Fluten rieseln,
Majestätisch prächtig nun,
Wie des Donners Orgelton,
Stürmend von hinnen jetzt, wie sich von
    Felsen
Rauschende, schäumende Giessbäche
    wälzen,
Holdes Gesäusel bald,
Schmeichlerisch linde, wie durch den
    Espenwald
Buhlende Winde —

Schwerer nun und melancholisch düster,
Wie durch tote Wüsten Schauernacht-
    geflüster,
Wo verlornes Heulen
    schweift,
Tränenwellen der Cocytus schleift.

Mädchen, sprich! Ich frage, gib mir
    Kunde:
Stehst mit höhern Geistern du im Bunde?
Ist's die Sprache, lüg' mir nicht,
Die man in Elysen spricht?

Sweetly now, as clear, silvery water
Ripples over smooth pebbles;
Now with majestic splendour,
Like the thunder's organ-tones;
Now raging forth, like rushing, foaming
    torrents
Surging from
    rocks;
Now sweetly murmuring,
Gently coaxing, like wooing
    breezes
Wafting through the aspen woods.

Now heavier, dark with melancholy,
Like fearful nocturnal whisperings through
    dead wastes,
Where the howls of lost, wandering souls
    echo,
And Cocytus drags waves of tears.

Maiden, speak! I beg you, tell
    me:
Are you in league with divine spirits?
Do not lie to me: is this the language
They speak in Elysium?

Lebenslied / *Song of Life*

FRIEDRICH VON MATTHISSON

D 508 (1816)

Kommen und Scheiden,
Suchen und Meiden,
Fürchten und Sehnen,
Zweifeln und Wähnen,
Armut und Fülle, Verödung und
    Pracht
Wechseln auf Erden, wie Dämmrung und
    Nacht!

Fruchtlos hinieden
Ringst du nach Frieden!
Täuschende Schimmer
Winken dir immer;
Doch, wie die Furchen des gleitenden
    Kahns,
Schwinden die Zaubergebilde des Wahns!

Auf zu der Sterne
Leuchtender Ferne
Blicke vom Staube
Mutig der Glaube:
Dort nur verknüpft ein unsterbliches
    Band
Wahrheit und Frieden, Verein und
    Bestand!

Arriving and departing,
Seeking and shunning,
Fearing and yearning,
Doubting and guessing,
Poverty and abundance, desolation and
    splendour,
Alternate on earth like dusk and
    night.

In vain you strive
For peace here below.
Will-o'-the-wisps
Forever beckon to you;
But, like the furrows ploughed by the
    gliding boat,
These magic creations of illusion vanish.

Let faith bravely
Gaze up from the dust
To the stars
Shining in the distance;
Only there does an undying
    bond
Unite truth and peace, fellowship and
    permanence.

Männlich zu leiden,	To suffer manfully,
Kraftvoll zu meiden,	To avoid resolutely,
Kühn zu verachten,	To despise boldly:
Bleib' unser Trachten!	Let us make this our endeavour
Bleib' unser Kämpfen! in eherner Brust	And our striving,
Uns des unsträflichen Willens	Conscious of a spotless will within our iron
bewußt!	breast.

Lebensmelodien / Melodies of Life

AUGUST WILHELM VON SCHLEGEL

D 395 (1816)

Der Schwan:
Auf den Wassern wohnt mein stilles Leben,
Zieht nur gleiche Kreise, die
   verschweben,
Und mir schwindet nie im feuchten Spiegel
Der gebogne Hals und die Gestalt.

The Swan:
My tranquil life is on the waters,
Drawing equal circles that ripple away to
   nothing;
And in the damp mirror my curved neck
And my figure never disappear.

Der Adler:
Ich haus' in den felsigen Klüften,
Ich braus' in den stürmenden Lüften,
Vertrauend dem schlagenden Flügel
Bei Jagd und Kampf und Gewalt.

The Eagle:
I dwell in the rocky crevasses,
I race in the stormy winds,
Trusting my beating wings
In the hunt, in battle and in attack.

Der Schwan:
Ahndevoll betracht' ich oft die
   Sterne
In der Flut die tiefgewölbte Ferne,
Und mich zieht ein innig rührend Sehnen
Aus der Heimat in ein himmlisch Land.

The Swan:
Often, filled with intuition, I behold the
   stars
In the deep-vaulted, distant flood,
And I am drawn by a fervent longing
From my home to a heavenly land.

Der Adler:
Ich wandte die Flügel mit Wonne
Schon früh zur unsterblichen Sonne,
Kann nie an dem Staub mich gewöhnen,
Ich bin mit den Göttern verwandt.

The Eagle:
In early youth I turned my wings
With joy towards the immortal sun;
I can never accustom myself to the dust;
I am related to the gods.

Die Tauben:
In der Myrten Schatten
Gatte treu dem Gatten
Flattern wir und tauschen
Manchen langen Kuß.
Suchen und irren,
Finden und girren,
Schmachten und lauschen,
Wunsch und Genuß.

The Doves:
In the shade of the myrtles,
Spouse true to spouse,
We flutter, and exchange
Many a long kiss.
We seek and rove,
Find and coo,
Languish and listen,
With desire and pleasure.

Venus Wagen ziehen
Schnäbelnd wir im Fliehen,
Unsre blauen Schwingen
Säumt der Sonne Gold.
O wie es fächelt,
Wenn sie uns lächelt!
Leichtes Gelingen!
Lieblicher Sold!

We draw the chariot of Venus,
Billing in our flight;
Our blue wings
Are fringed by the gold of the sun.
How we stir
When she smiles upon us!
Easy success,
A charming reward!

Wende denn die Stürme,	Then avert your storms,
Schöne Göttin! schirme	Fair goddess! Shield
Bei bescheidner Freude	Your pair of doves
Deiner Tauben Paar!	In their modest pleasure!
Laß uns beisammen!	Let us be together,
Oder in Flammen	Or sacrifice us both
Opfre uns beide	In flames
Deinem Altar.	Upon your altar!

Lebensmut / Courage for Living

LUDWIG RELLSTAB

D 937 (1827?)

Fröhlicher Lebensmut	Joyful courage for living
Braust in dem raschen Blut;	Surges in the quick blood;
Sprudelnd und silberhell	The fountain of life flows,
Rauschet der Lebensquell.	Bubbling and silver-bright.
Doch eh' die Stunde flieht,	But before the hour flies,
Ehe der Geist verglüht,	Before the spirit's ardour fades,
Schöpft aus der klaren Flut	Draw joyful courage for living
Fröhlichen Lebensmut!	From the clear waters.
Mutigen Sprung gewagt;	Dare the bold leap;
Nimmer gewinnt, wer zagt;	He who hesitates never wins;
Schnell ist das Wechselglück,	Fortune changes rapidly,
Dein ist der Augenblick.	The moment is yours.
Wer keinen Sprung versucht,	He who does not venture the leap
Bricht keine süße Frucht,	Will reap no sweet fruit.
Auf! Wer das Glück erjagt,	Come! He who chases fortune
Mutigen Sprung gewagt.	Must dare the bold leap.
Mutig umarmt den Tod!	Bravely embrace death
Trifft Euch sein Machtgebot.	When his mighty decree touches you.
Nehmt Euer volles Glas,	Take your full glass,
Stoßt an sein Stundenglas;	Knock it against his hour-glass;
Des Todes Brüderschaft	The brotherhood of death
Öffnet des Lebens Haft.	Opens the prison of life.
Neu glänzt ein Morgenrot:	A new dawn shines;
Mutig umarmt den Tod!	Bravely embrace death!

Lebensmut / Courage for Living

ERNST SCHULZE

D 883 (1826)

O wie dringt das junge Leben	How vigorously young life
Kräftig mir durch Sinn und Herz!	Pulses through my mind and heart!
Alles fühl' ich glühn und streben,	I feel everything is glowing, aspiring,
Fühle doppelt Lust und Schmerz.	I feel pleasure and pain doubly.
Fruchtlos such' ich euch zu halten,	In vain I seek to restrain you,
Geister meiner regen Brust!	Spirits of my quickened breast!
Nach Gefallen mögt ihr walten,	You rule at will,
Sei's zum Leide, sei's zur Lust.	For sorrow or for pleasure.

Lodre nur, gewalt'ge Liebe,
Höher lodre nur empor!
Brecht, ihr vollen Blütentriebe,
Mächtig schwellend nur hervor!
Mag das Herz sich blutig färben,
Mag's vergehn in rascher Pein;
Lieber will ich ganz verderben,
Als nur halb lebendig sein.

Dieses Zagen, dieses Sehnen,
Das die Brust vergeblich schwellt,
Diese Seufzer, diese Tränen,
Die der Stolz gefangen hält,
Dieses schmerzlich eitle Ringen,
Dieses Kämpfen ohne Kraft,
Ohne Hoffnung und Vollbringen
Hat mein bestes Mark erschlafft.

Lieber wecke rasch und mutig,
Schlachtruf, den entschlafnen Sinn!
Lange träumt' ich, lange ruht' ich,
Gab der Kette lang mich hin;
Hier ist Hölle nicht, noch Himmel,
Weder Frost ist hier, noch Glut;
Auf in's feindliche Getümmel,
Rüstig weiter durch die Flut!

Daß noch einmal Wunsch und Wagen,
Zorn und Liebe, Wohl und Weh
Ihre Wellen um mich schlagen
Auf des Lebens wilder See,
Und ich kühn im tapfern Streite
Mit dem Strom, der mich entrafft,
Selber meinen Nachen leite,
Freudig in geprüfter Kraft.

Blaze on, mighty love,
Blaze higher!
Burst open, ripe, blossoming desires,
Swelling abundantly!
Let my heart be tinged with blood,
Let it perish swiftly in pain;
I would rather be completely ruined
Than be only half alive.

This hesitation, this longing
That swells my breast in vain,
These sighs, these tears
Which pride holds captive,
This painful, futile struggle,
This fighting without strength,
Without hope, without fulfilment,
Has sapped my whole being.

Rather let the quick, bold battle-cry
Awaken my sleeping mind!
Long have I dreamt, long have I rested,
Long have I yielded to the chain;
Here there is neither hell nor heaven,
Neither frost nor warmth;
Up, into the hostile tumult,
Briskly beyond it through the flood!

So that once more desire and daring,
Anger and love, weal and woe
Pound me with their waves
On life's stormy sea,
And I, boldly, bravely struggling,
Steer my boat with the current
That sweeps me along,
Happy in my well-tried strength.

Leiden der Trennung / The Sorrow of Separation

HEINRICH VON COLLIN

D 509 (1816)

Vom Meere trennt sich die Welle,
Und seufzet durch Blumen im Tal,
Und fühlet, gewiegt in der Quelle,
Gebannt in dem Brunnen,
    nur Qual!

Es sehnt sich die Welle
In lispelnder Quelle,
Im murmelnden Bache,
Im Brunnengemache,

Zum Meer, zum Meer,
Von dem sie kam,
Von dem sie Leben nahm,
Von dem, des Irrens matt und
    müde,
Sie süsse Ruh' verhofft und Friede.

The wave is separated from the sea,
And sighs amid the flowers in the valley;
Cradled in the spring,
Captive in the well, it feels
    nothing but torment.

In the whispering spring,
In the murmuring brook,
In the well-chamber,
The wave longs

For the sea
From which it came,
From which it drew life,
From which, faint and weary with
    wandering,
It hopes for peace and sweet repose.

Liane / Liane

JOHANN MAYRHOFER

D 298 (1815)

»Hast du Lianen nicht gesehen?«
»Ich sah sie zu dem Teiche gehn.«
Durch Busch und Hecken rennt er fort,
Und kommt an ihren Lieblingsort.

Die Linde spannt ihr grünes Netz,
Aus Rosen tönt des Bachs Geschwätz;
Die Blätter rötet Sonnengold,
Und alles ist der Freude hold.

Liane fährt auf einem Kahn,
Vertraute Schwäne nebenan.
Sie spielt die Laute, singt ein Lied,
Wie Liebe in ihr selig
    blüht.

Das Schifflein schwanket, wie es will,
Sie senkt das Haupt und denket still
An ihn, der an dem Ufer ist,
Sie bald in seine Arme schliesst.

'Have you seen Liane?'
'I saw her walking to the pond.'
He runs off, through bush and hedgerow,
Until he reaches her favourite spot.

The lime tree stretches its green net,
The brook babbles among the roses;
Golden sunlight tinges the leaves,
And everything is touched with joy.

Liane glides along in a boat,
Her beloved swans accompany her.
She plays her lute, and sings
Of the blissful love that blossoms within
    her.

The boat rocks as it pleases,
She lets her head sink, and thinks silently
Of him who is in the bushes,
And who will soon enfold her in his arms.

Lieb Minna / Darling Minna

ALBERT STADLER

D 222 (1815)

»Schwüler Hauch weht mir herüber,
Welkt die Blum' an meiner Brust.
Ach, wo weilst du, Wilhelm, Lieber?
Meiner Seele süße Lust!
Ewig Weinen,
Nie Erscheinen!
Schläfst wohl schon im kühlen
    Schoße,
Denkst auch mein noch unterm Moose?«

Minna weinet, es verflogen
Mählig Wang- und Lippenrot.
Wilhelm war hinweggezogen
Mit den Reihn zum Schlachtentod.
Von der Stunde
Keine Kunde!
Schläfst wohl längst im kühlen
    Schoße,
Denkt dein Minna unterm Moose.

Liebchen sitzt im stillen Harme,
Sieht die gold'nen Sternlein ziehn,
Und der Mond schaut auf die Arme
Mitleidsvollen Blickes hin.
Horch, da wehen
Aus den Höhen
Abendlüftchen ihr herüber:
Dort am Felsen harrt dein Lieber.

'A sultry breeze wafts across to me,
The flower at my breast withers.
Ah, where do you linger, Wilhelm dearest,
My soul's sweet delight?
I weep eternally,
You never appear!
Perhaps you already sleep in the earth's cool
    womb;
Do you still think of me beneath the moss?'

Minna wept; gradually the crimson drained
From her cheeks and lips.
Wilhelm had departed
With the ranks to death in battle.
From that hour
There was no news.
Your Minna thinks: perhaps you have long
    been sleeping
Beneath the cool moss.

The sweet maiden sits in silent grief,
Watching the motion of the golden stars,
And the moon looks upon the poor creature
With compassionate gaze.
Hark, evening breezes
Waft across to her
From the heights:
Your beloved is waiting there by the cliff.

Minna eilt im
  Mondenflimmer
Bleich und ahnend durch die
  Flur,
Findet ihren Wilhelm nimmer,
Findet seinen Hügel nur.
»Bin bald drüben
Bei dir Lieben,
Sagst mir aus dem kühlen Schoße:
'Denk' dein, Minna, unterm
  Moose.'«
	Pale and filled with foreboding, Minna
	  hastens
	Across the meadows in the shimmering
	  moonlight.
	But she does not find her Wilhelm;
	She finds only his grave.
	'Soon I shall be there
	With you, beloved,
	If from the cool womb you tell me:
	"I am thinking of you, Minna, beneath the
	  moss."'

Und viel tausen Blümchen steigen Freundlich aus dem Grab herauf. Minna kennt die Liebeszeugen, Bettet sich ein Plätzchen drauf. »Bin gleich drüben Bei dir Lieben!« Legt sich auf die Blümchen nieder, Findet ihren Wilhelm wieder.	And many thousands of flowers spring Tenderly from the grave. Minna understands this testimony of love, And makes a little bed upon them. 'Very soon I shall be there With you, beloved!' She lies down upon the flowers And finds her Wilhelm again.

Liebe schwärmt auf allen Wegen / *Love Roves Everywhere*

JOHANN WOLFGANG VON GOETHE

see Ariette der Claudine

Liebesbotschaft / *Love's Message*

LUDWIG RELLSTAB

see Schwanengesang no. 1

Liebeslauschen / *Serenade*

FRANZ XAVER VON SCHLECHTA

D 698 (1820)

Hier unten steht ein Ritter Im hellen Mondenstrahl, Und singt zu seiner Zither Ein Lied von süsser Qual:	A knight stands down below In the bright moonlight, And sings to his zither A song of sweet suffering:
»Lüfte, spannt die blauen Schwingen Sanft für meine Botschaft aus, Rufet sie mit leisem Klingen An dies Fensterlein heraus.	'Breezes, gently spread your blue wings And bear my message; With soft strains call her To this window.
»Sagt ihr, dass im Blätterdache Seufz' ein wohlbekannter Laut, Sagt ihr, dass noch einer wache, Und die Nacht sei kühl und traut.	'Tell her that beneath the canopy of leaves A familiar voice is sighing; Tell her that someone is still awake, And that the night is cool and intimate.
»Sagt ihr, wie des Mondes Welle Sich an ihrem Fenster bricht, Sagt ihr, wie der Wald, die Quelle Heimlich und von Liebe spricht!	'Tell her how the wave of moonlight Breaks upon her window; Tell her how the grove and the fountain Speak secretly of love.

»Lass ihn leuchten durch die Bäume,	'Let the sweet light of your image
Deines Bildes süssen Schein,	Shine through the trees,
Das sich hold in meine Träume	Your image which is gently woven
Und mein Wachen webet ein.«	Into my dreams and my waking hours.
Doch drang die zarte	'But the tender melody could not have
Weise	reached
Wohl nicht zu Liebchens Ohr,	His sweetheart's ear,
Der Sänger schwang sich leise	For the singer swung himself softly
Zum Fensterlein empor.	Up to her window.
Und oben zog der Ritter	And once up there the knight
Ein Kränzchen aus der Brust;	Drew a garland from his breast
Das band er fest am Gitter	And bound it fast to the grille,
Und seufzte: »Blüht in Lust!	Sighing: 'Bloom in joy.
Und fragt sie, wer euch brachte,	And if she asks who brought you,
Dann, Blumen, tut ihr kund.«	Then flowers, tell her.'
Ein Stimmchen unten lachte:	A voice below laughed:
»Dein Ritter Liebemund.«	'Your knight, Liebemund!'

Liebesrausch / Love's Intoxication

THEODOR KÖRNER

D 179 (1815)

Dir, Mädchen, schlägt mit leisem Beben	For you, maiden, my heart beats,
Mein Herz voll Treu' und Liebe	Gently trembling, filled with love and
zu.	devotion.
In dir, in dir versinkt mein Streben,	In you, in you, my striving ceases,
Mein schönstes Ziel bist du!	You are my life's fairest goal.
Dein Name nur in heil'gen Tönen	Your name alone has filled my bold heart
Hat meine kühne Brust gefüllt;	With sacred tones.
Im Glanz des Guten und des Schönen	In the radiance of goodness and beauty
Strahlt mir dein hohes Bild.	Your noble image shines for me.
Die Liebe sproßt aus zarten Keimen,	Love burgeons from tender seeds,
Und ihre Blüten welken nie!	And its blossoms never wither.
Du, Mädchen, lebst in meinen Träumen	You, maiden, live in my dreams
Mit süßer Harmonie.	With sweet harmonies.
Begeist'rung rauscht auf mich hernieder,	I am fired with the rapture of inspiration,
Kühn greif' ich in die Saiten ein,	Boldly I pluck the strings,
Und alle meine schönsten Lieder,	And all my loveliest songs
Sie nennen dich allein.	Utter your name alone.
Mein Himmel glüht in deinen Blicken,	My heaven glows in your eyes,
An deiner Brust mein Paradies.	My paradise is upon your breast.
Ach! alle Reize, die dich schmücken,	Ah, all the charms that adorn you
Sie sind so hold, so süß.	Are so fair, so sweet.
Es wogt die Brust in Freud' und	My breast surges with joy and
Schmerzen,	pain;
Nur eine Sehnsucht lebt in mir,	One desire alone dwells within me,
Nur ein Gedanke hier im Herzen:	One thought alone lies here in my heart:
Der ew'ge Drang nach dir.	Eternal yearning for you!

Liebeständelei / Flirtation

THEODOR KÖRNER

D 206 (1815)

Süßes Liebchen! Komm' zu mir!	My sweet love! Come to me!
Tausend Küsse geb' ich dir.	I will give you a thousand kisses.
Sieh' mich hier zu deinen Füßen.	You behold me here at your feet.
Mädchen, deiner Lippen Glut	Fair maiden, the ardour of your lips
Gibt mir Kraft und Lebensmut.	Gives me strength and the courage for life.
Laß dich küssen!	Let me kiss you!
Mädchen, werde doch nicht rot!	Fair maiden, do not blush!
Wenn's die Mutter auch verbot,	Even though your mother has forbidden it,
Sollst du alle Freuden missen?	Are you to forgo all pleasures?
Nur an des Geliebten Brust	Only on your lover's breast
Blüht des Lebens schönste Lust.	Does life's fairest joy flower.
Laß dich küssen!	Let me kiss you!
Liebchen, warum zierst du dich?	My love, why are you so coy?
Höre doch und küsse mich.	Listen, and kiss me.
Willst du nichts von Liebe wissen?	Do you wish to know nothing of love?
Wogt dir nicht dein kleines Herz	Does your little heart not surge,
Bald in Freuden, bald in Schmerz?	Now with pleasure, now with pain?
Laß dich küssen!	Let me kiss you!
Sieh', dein Sträuben hilft dir nicht;	See, your reluctance is to no avail;
Schon hab' ich nach Sängers Pflicht	Already, my duty as a singer done,
Dir den ersten Kuß entrissen! —	I have snatched the first kiss from you!
Und nun sinkst du, liebewarm,	And now, warm with love, you sink
Willig selbst in meinen Arm.	Willingly into my arms.
Läßt dich küssen!	Let me kiss you!

Liebhaber in allen Gestalten / A Lover in All Guises

JOHANN WOLFGANG VON GOETHE

D 558 (1817)

Ich wollt' ich wär' ein Fisch,	I wish I were a fish,
So hurtig und frisch;	So agile and fresh;
Und kämst Du zu anglen,	And if you came to catch me,
Ich würde nicht manglen.	I would not fail you.
Ich wollt' ich wär' ein Fisch,	I wish I were a fish,
So hurtig und frisch.	So agile and fresh.
Ich wollt' ich wär' ein Pferd,	I wish I were a horse,
Da wär' ich Dir wert.	Then you would esteem me.
O wär' ich ein Wagen!	Would that I were a coach!
Bequem Dich zu tragen.	I should carry you in comfort.
Ich wollt' ich wär' ein Pferd!	I wish I were a horse!
Da wär' ich Dir wert.	Then you would esteem me.
Ich wollt' ich wäre Gold!	I wish I were gold,
Dir immer im Sold;	Always at your service.
Und tätst Du was kaufen,	And if you bought something,
Käm' ich wieder gelaufen.	I would come running back again.
Ich wollt' ich wäre Gold!	I wish I were gold,
Dir immer im Sold.	Always at your service!

Doch bin ich wie ich bin,	But I am as I am;
Und nimm mich nur hin!	Just accept me like this.
Willst Du bess're besitzen,	If you want a better man,
So laß Dir sie schnitzen.	Then have him made for you.
Ich bin nun wie ich bin;	I am as I am;
So nimm mich nur hin!	Just accept me like this.

Lied / Song

MATTHIAS CLAUDIUS

D 362 (1816?)
A setting of the first 2 verses of Claudius's poem 'Zufriedenheit'. Some months later
Schubert composed a different setting, including all 5 verses. For text and
translation see page 373.

Lied / Song

FRIEDRICH DE LA MOTTE FOUQUÉ

D 373 (1816)

Mutter geht durch ihre Kammern	Mother goes through her rooms,
Räumt die Schränke ein und aus,	Filling and emptying the cupboards,
Sucht, und weiß nicht was, mit Jammern,	Seeking she knows not what, and with sorrow
Findet nichts, als leeres Haus.	Finding nothing but an empty house.
Leeres Haus! O Wort der Klage,	Empty house! O words of grief
Dem, der einst ein holdes Kind	For one who once cosseted there
Drin gegängelt hat am Tage,	A sweet child in the daytime,
Drin gewiegt in Nächten lind.	And gently rocked it to sleep at night.
Wieder grünen wohl die Buchen,	The beech-trees will grow green again,
Wieder kommt der Sonne Licht,	The light of the sun will return,
Aber, Mutter, laß' dein Suchen,	But, mother, cease your searching;
Wieder kommt dein Liebes nicht.	Your beloved child will not return.
Und wenn Abendlüfte fächeln,	And when the evening breezes stir
Vater heim zum Herde kehrt,	And the father returns home to the fireside,
Regt sich's fast in ihm, wie Lächeln	There is a flicker of a smile within him
Dran doch gleich die Träne zehrt.	Which at once turns to tears.
Vater weiß, in seinen Zimmern	Father knows that in his rooms
Findet er die Todesruh,	He will find a deathly peace;
Hört nur bleicher Mutter Wimmern,	He will hear only the whimpering of the pale mother,
Und kein Kindlein lacht ihm zu.	And no little child will gurgle at him.

Lied / Song

KAROLINE PICHLER

D 483 (1816)

Ferne von der großen Stadt,	Far from the great city,
Nimm mich auf in deine Stille,	Receive me into your stillness,

Tal, das mit der Frühlingsfülle
Die Natur geschmücket hat!
Wo kein Lärmen, kein Getümmel
Meinen Schlummer kürzer macht,
Und ein ewig heitrer Himmel
Über sel'gen Fluren lacht!

Freuden, die die Ruhe beut,
Will ich ungestört hier schmecken,
Hier, wo Bäume mich bedecken,
Und die Linde Duft verstreut,
Diese Quelle sei mein Spiegel,
Mein Parkett der junge Klee,
Und der frischberaste Hügel
Sei mein grünes Kanapeh.

O valley, which nature has adorned
With spring's abundance;
Where no din, no turmoil
Shortens my slumber,
And a serene sky smiles eternally
Upon happy meadows.

Here I shall savour undisturbed
The joys that tranquillity offers;
Here, where trees cover me
And the linden scatters its sweet scent;
Let this spring be my mirror,
And the young clover my floor,
And the hill, fresh with grass,
My green couch.

Lied / Song

JOHANN GAUDENZ VON SALIS-SEEWIS

D 403 (1816)

Ins stille Land!
Wer leitet uns hinüber?
Schon wölkt sich uns der Abendhimmel
    trüber,
Und immer trümmervoller wird der
    Strand.
Wer leitet uns mit sanfter Hand
Hinüber! ach! hinüber,
Ins stille Land?

Ins stille Land!
Zu euch, ihr freien Räume
Für die Veredlung! zarte Morgenträume
Der schönen Seelen! künft'gen Daseins
    Pfand.
Wer treu des Lebens Kampf
    bestand,
Trägt seiner Hoffnung Keime
Ins stille Land.

Ach Land! ach Land!
Für alle Sturmbedrohten.
Der mildeste von unsers Schicksals Boten
Winkt uns, die Fackel umgewandt,
Und leitet uns mit sanfter Hand
Ins Land der großen Toten,
Ins stille Land.

To the land of rest!
Who will lead us there?
Already the evening sky grows darker
    with cloud,
And the shore is ever more strewn with
    flotsam.
Who will lead us gently by the hand
Across, ah, across
To the land of rest?

To the land of rest!
To the free, ennobling spaces!
Tender morning dreams
Of fine souls! Pledge of a future
    life!
He who faithfully won life's
    battle
Carries the seeds of his hopes
To the land of rest.

O land
For all those threatened by storms.
The gentlest harbinger of our fate
Beckons us, brandishing a torch,
And leads us gently by the hand
To the land of the great dead,
The land of rest.

Lied / Song

FRIEDRICH VON SCHILLER (?)

D 284 (1815)

Es ist so angenehm, so süß,
Um einen lieben Mann zu spielen,
Entzückend, wie ein Paradies,
Des Mannes Feuerkuß zu fühlen.

It is so pleasant and so sweet
To dally with a man you love,
And as delightful as paradise
To feel the man's fiery kisses.

Jetzt weiß ich, was mein Taubenpaar Mit seinem sanften Girren sagte, Und was der Nachtigallen Schar So zärtlich sich in Liedern klagte;	Now I know what my pair of doves Were saying with their soft cooing, And what the host of nightingales Were lamenting so tenderly in their songs.
Jetzt weiß ich, was mein volles Herz In ewig langen Nächten engte; Jetzt weiß ich, welcher süße Schmerz Oft seufzend meinen Busen drängte;	Now I know what weighed upon my full heart In long, never-ending nights; Now I know what sweet sorrow so often Oppressed my breast with its sighs.
Warum kein Blümchen mir gefiel, Warum der Mai mir nimmer lachte, Warum der Vögel Liederspiel Mich nimmermehr zur Freude fachte.	And why no flower pleased me, Why May never smiled upon me, Why the song of the birds Never aroused me to joy.
Mir trauerte die ganze Welt, Ich kannte nicht die schönsten Triebe. Nun hab' ich, was mir längst gefehlt, Beneide mich, Natur — ich liebe!	To me the whole world seemed in mourning, I did not know fair desire. Now I have what I lacked for so long; Envy me, Nature: I am in love!

Lied aus der Ferne / Song from Afar

FRIEDRICH VON MATTHISSON

D 107 (1814)

Wenn, in des Abends letztem Scheine, Dir eine lächelnde Gestalt, Am Rasensitz im Eichenhaine, Mit Wink und Gruß vorüber wallt, Das ist des Freundes treuer Geist, Der Freud' und Frieden dir verheißt.	When in the dying light of evening, As you sit on the sward in the oak grove, A smiling figure passes you, Waving a greeting, That is the faithful spirit of your friend, Promising you joy and peace.
Wenn in des Mondes Dämmerlichte Sich deiner Liebe Traum verschönt, Durch Cytisus und Weimutsfichte Melodisches Gesäusel tönt, Und Ahnung dir den Busen hebt: Das ist mein Geist, der dich umschwebt.	When in the moon's dusky light Your dream of love grows fairer, And a melodious rustling echoes Through laburnum and pine, And your breast swells with a presentiment, It is my spirit which hovers about you.
Fühlst du, beim seligen Verlieren In des Vergangnen Zauberland, Ein lindes, geistiges Berühren, Wie Zephyrs Kuß an Lipp' und Hand, Und wankt der Kerze flatternd Licht: Das ist mein Geist, o zweifle nicht!	If, lost in blissful contemplation Of the magic realm of the past, You feel a gentle, unearthly touch, Like the kiss of Zephyr on your lips and hands, And if the wavering candlelight flickers: That is my spirit, do not doubt it!
Hörst du, beim Silberglanz der Sterne, Leis' im verschwiegnen Kämmerlein, Gleich Aeolsharfen aus der Ferne, Das Bundeswort: Auf ewig dein! Dann schlummre sanft; es ist mein Geist, Der Freud' und Frieden dir verheißt.	If, by the silver light of the stars, In your secret chamber, You hear, like soft, distant aeolian harps, The words of our bond: For ever yours! Then sleep sweetly; it is my spirit That promises you joy and peace.

Lied der Anne Lyle / Anne Lyle's Song

Original lines from *Love and Loyalty* by ANDREW MACDONALD, quoted by
SIR WALTER SCOTT in *The Legend of Montrose* (translator unknown)

D 830 (1825?)
A literal translation of the German is given here. Macdonald's original is printed
below in italics.

Wärst du bei mir im Lebenstal,
Gern wollt' ich alles mit dir teilen;
Mit dir zu flieh'n wär' leichte Wahl,
Bei mildem Wind, bei Sturmes Heulen.
Doch trennt uns harte Schicksalsmacht,
Uns ist nicht gleiches Los geschrieben,
Mein Glück ist, wenn dir Freude
  lacht,
Ich wein' und bete für den Lieben.

If you were with me in life's valley,
I would gladly share everything with you;
It would be an easy choice to fly with you
In gentle breezes, or in the howling storm.
But the harsh power of fate separates us;
We are not granted the same destiny.
Happiness is mine when joy smiles upon
  you;
I weep and pray for my beloved.

Es wird mein töricht' Herz vergeh'n,
Wenn's alle Hoffnung sieht verschwinden,
Doch soll's nie seinen Gram gesteh'n,
Nie mürrisch klagend ihn verkünden.
Und drückt des Lebens Last das Herz,
Soll nie den matten Blick sie trüben,
So lange mein geheimer Schmerz
Ein Kummer wäre für den Lieben

My foolish heart will beat no more
If it sees all hope vanish.
But it shall never admit its grief,
Nor proclaim it with sullen lament.
And if life's burden oppresses my heart,
It shall never cloud my weary eyes
While my secret sorrow
May distress my beloved.

Wert thou, like me, in life's low vale,
With thee how blest, that lot I share;
With thee I'd fly wherever gale
Could waft, or bounding galley bear.
But parted by severe decree,
Far different must our fortunes prove;
May thine be joy — enough for me
To weep and pray for him I love.

The pangs this foolish heart must feel,
When hope shall be for ever flown,
No sullen murmur shall reveal,
No selfish murmurs ever own.
Nor will I through life's weary years,
Like a pale drooping mourner move,
While I can think my secret tears
May wound the heart of him I love.

Lied der Liebe / Song of Love

FRIEDRICH VON MATTHISSON

D 109 (1814)

Durch Fichten am Hügel, durch Erlen am
  Bach,
Folgt immer dein Bildnis, du Traute!
  mir nach;
Es lächelt bald Wehmut, es lächelt bald
  Ruh',
Im freundlichen Schimmer des Mondes,
  mir zu.

Past spruces on hillsides, through alders by
  the brook,
Your image, beloved, follows me
  always.
To me it smiles now love, now
  peace
In the kindly glimmer of the
  moon.

Den Rosengesträuchen des Gartens entwallt	In the brightness of early morning your fair form
Im Glanze der Frühe die holde Gestalt;	Arises from the rose bushes in the garden;
Sie schwebt aus der Berge bepurpurtem Flor	It floats from the crimson-flowering mountains
Gleich einem elysischen Schatten hervor.	Like an Elysian shadow.

Oft hab' ich, im Traum, als die schönste der Feen,
Auf goldenem Throne dich strahlen gesehn;
Oft hab' ich, zum hohen Olympus entzückt,
Als Hebe dich unter den Göttern erblickt.

Often in dreams I have seen you,
The loveliest of fairies, radiant on your golden throne;
Often I have glimpsed you, spirited to lofty Olympus,
As Hebe among the gods.

Mir hallt aus den Tiefen, mir hallt von den Höhn,
Dein himmlischer Name wie Sphärengetön.
Ich wähne den Hauch, der die Blüten umwebt,
Von deiner melodischen Stimme durchbebt.

From the depths, from the heights
I hear your heavenly name echo like music of the spheres,
I imagine the scent enveloping the blossom,
Shot through with your melodious voice.

In heiliger Mitternachtstunde durchkreist
Des Äthers Gefilde mein ahnender Geist,
Geliebte! dort winkt uns ein Land, wo der Freund
Auf ewig der Freundin sich wieder vereint.

At midnight's holy hour my prescient mind
Floats through the realms of the ether.
Beloved! There a land beckons
Where lover and beloved are forever reunited.

Die Freude, sie schwindet, es dauert kein Leid;
Die Jahre verrauschen im Strome der Zeit;
Die Sonne wird sterben, die Erde vergehn:
Doch Liebe muß ewig und ewig bestehn.

Joy vanishes, no sorrow endures;
The years flow away in the river of time;
The sun will die, the earth perish:
But love must last for ever and ever.

Lied des gefangenen Jägers / *Song of the Imprisoned Huntsman*

SIR WALTER SCOTT, translated by ADAM STORCK

D843 (1825)
A literal rendering of Storck's translation is given here. Scott's original poem is printed below in italics.

Mein Ross so müd' in dem Stalle sich steht,
Mein Falk ist der Kapp' und der Stange so leid,
Mein müssiges Windspiel sein Futter verschmäht,
Und mich kränkt des Turmes Einsamkeit.

My horse is so weary of his stall,
My hawk is so tired of perch and hood;
My idle greyhound spurns his food,
And I am sick of this tower's solitude.

Ach' wär ich nur, wo ich zuvor bin gewesen,
Die Hirschjagd wäre so recht mein Wesen,
Den Bluthund los, gespannt den Bogen,
Ja, solchem Leben bin ich gewogen.

I wish I were as I have been before;
Hunting the hart is truly in my nature,
With bloodhound free and bow drawn,
Yes, I favour such a life.

Ich hasse der Turmuhr schläfrigen Klang,
Ich mag nicht seh'n, wie die Zeit verstreicht,
Wenn Zoll um Zoll die Mauer entlang
Der Sonnenstrahl so langsam schleicht.

Sonst pflegte die Lerche den Morgen zu bringen,
Die dunkle Dohle zur Ruh' mich zu singen,
In dieses Schlosses Königshallen,
Da kann kein Ort mir je gefallen.

Früh, wenn der Lerche Lied erschallt,
Sonn' ich mich nicht in Ellens Blick,
Nicht folg' ich dem flüchtigen Hirsch durch den Wald,
Und kehre, wenn Abend taut, zurück.

Nicht schallt mir ihr frohes Willkommen entgegen,
Nicht kann ich das Wild ihr zu Füssen mehr legen,
Nicht mehr wird der Abend uns selig entschweben,
Dahin ist Lieben und Leben.

I hate the drowsy chime of the steeple clock,
I do not wish to see how time passes,
As, inch by inch along the wall,
The sunbeams crawl so slowly.

Once the lark would herald the morning,
And the dark rook sing me to rest.
In the kingly halls of this castle
I can find nowhere that pleases me.

At early morning, when the lark's song echoes,
I do not sun myself in Ellen's eyes;
Nor do I pursue the fleet deer through the forest,
And return home with the evening dew.

No joyful welcome rings in my ears,
I cannot lay my catch at her feet;
No more will evening float past in bliss.
Love and life are lost.

My hawk is tired of perch and hood,
My idle greyhound loathes his food,
My horse is weary of his stall,
And I am sick of captive thrall.

I wish I were, as I have been,
Hunting the hart in forest green,
With bended bow and bloodhound free,
For that's the life is meet for me.

I hate to learn the ebb of time
From yon dull steeple's drowsy chime,
Or mark it as the sunbeams crawl,
Inch after inch, along the wall.

The lark was wont my matins ring,
The sable rook my vespers sing;
These towers, although a king's they be,
Have not a hall of joy for me.

No more at dawning morn I rise,
And sun myself in Ellen's eyes,
Drive the fleet deer the forest through,
And homeward wend with evening dew;

A blithesome welcome blithely meet,
And lay my trophies at her feet,
While fled the eve on wing of glee:
That life is lost to love and me!

Lied des Orpheus, als er in die Hölle ging | Song of Orpheus as he entered Hell

JOHANN GEORG JACOBI

D 474 (1816)

Wälze dich hinweg, du wildes Feuer!
Diese Saiten hat ein Gott gekrönt;
Er, mit welchem jedes Ungeheuer,
Und vielleicht die Hölle sich versöhnt.

Roll back, savage fire!
These strings have been crowned by a god;
With whom every monster
And perhaps hell itself is reconciled.

Diese Saiten stimmte seine Rechte:
Fürchterliche Schatten, flieht!
Und ihr winselnden Bewohner dieser
    Nächte,
Horchet auf mein Lied!

His right hand tunes these strings;
Flee, dread shadows!
And you, whimpering inhabitants of this
    darkness,
Listen to my song!

Von der Erde, wo die Sonne leuchtet
Und der stille Mond,
Wo der Tau das junge Moos befeuchtet,
Wo Gesang im grünen Felde wohnt;

From earth, where the sun
And the silent moon shine,
Where dew moistens fresh moss,
Where song dwells in green fields;

Aus der Menschen süssem Vaterlande,
Wo der Himmel euch so frohe Blicke
    gab,
Ziehen mich die schönsten Bande,
Ziehet mich die Liebe selbst herab.

From the sweet country of mankind,
Where the heavens once looked upon you
    with joyful gaze,
I am drawn by the fairest of ties,
I am drawn down by love itself.

Meine Klage tönt in eure Klage;
Weit von hier geflohen ist das Glück;
Aber denkt an jene Tage,
Schaut in jene Welt zurück!

My lament mingles with yours,
Happiness has fled far from here;
But remember those days,
Look back into that world!

Wenn ihr da nur einen Leidenden
    umarmt,
O, so fühlt die Wollust noch einmal,
Und der Augenblick, in dem ihr euch
    erbarmt,
Lindre diese lange Qual.

If there you embraced but one
    sufferer,
Then feel desire once more,
And may that moment when you took
    pity
Soothe my long torment.

O, ich sehe Tränen fliessen!
Durch die Finsternisse bricht
Ein Strahl von Hoffnung; ewig
    büssen
Lassen euch die guten Götter nicht.

O, I see tears flowing!
Through the darkness
A ray of hope breaks through; the good
    gods
Will not let you atone for ever.

Götter, die für euch die Erde schufen,
Werden aus der tiefen Nacht
Euch in selige Gefilde rufen,
Wo die Tugend unter Rosen lacht.

The gods who created the earth for you
Will call you from deep night
Into the Elysian fields
Where virtue smiles amid roses.

Lied eines Schiffers an die Dioskuren | Sailor's Song to the Dioscuri

JOHANN MAYRHOFER

D 360 (1822?)

Dioskuren, Zwillingssterne,
Die ihr leuchtet meinem Nachen,
Mich beruhigt auf dem Meere
Eure Milde, euer Wachen.

Dioscuri, twin stars,
Shining on my boat,
Your gentleness and vigilance
Comfort me on the ocean.

Wer auch fest in sich begründet,
Unverzagt dem Sturm begegnet,
Fühlt sich doch in euren Strahlen
Doppelt mutig und gesegnet.

Dieses Ruder, das ich schwinge,
Meeresfluten zu zerteilen,
Hänge ich, so ich geborgen,
Auf an eures Tempels Säulen.

However firmly a man believes in himself,
However fearlessly he meets the storm,
He feels doubly valiant and blessed
In your light.

This oar which I ply
To cleave the ocean's waves,
I shall hang, once I have landed safely,
On the pillars of your temple.

Lied in der Abwesenheit / Song of Absence

FRIEDRICH LEOPOLD, GRAF ZU STOLBERG-STOLBERG

D 416 (1816)

Ach, mir ist das Herz so schwer!
Traurig irr' ich hin und her.
Suche Ruhe und finde keine,
Geh' an's Fenster hin, und weine!

Säßest du auf meinem Schoß,
Würd' ich aller Sorgen los,
Und aus deinen blauen Augen
Würd' ich Lieb' und Wonne saugen!

Könnt' ich gleich, du süßes Kind,
Fliegen hin zu dir geschwind!
Könnt' ich ewig dich umfangen,
Und an deinen Lippen hangen!

Ah, my heart is so heavy!
Sadly I wander to and fro.
I seek peace, but find none,
I go to the window and weep.

If you were sitting on my lap,
All my cares would vanish;
And from your blue eyes
I would draw love and bliss.

Sweet child, if only I could at once
Fly swiftly to you!
If only I could embrace you for ever,
And hang on your lips!

Liedesend / Song's End

JOHANN MAYRHOFER

D 473 (1816)

Auf seinem goldnen Throne
Der graue König sitzt,
Und starret in die Sonne,
Die rot im Westen blitzt.

Der Sänger rührt die Harfe,
Es rauschet Siegessang;
Der Ernst jedoch, der scharfe,
Er trotzt dem vollen Klang.

Nun stimmt er süsse Weisen,
An's Herz sich klammernd, an;
Ob er ihn nicht mit leisen
Versuchen mildern kann.

Vergeblich ist sein Mühen,
Erschöpft des Liedes Reich,
Und auf der Stirne ziehen
Die Sorgen wettergleich.

On his golden throne
The grey king sits,
Staring into the sun
That glows red in the west.

The minstrel strokes his harp,
A song of victory resounds;
But austere solemnity
Defies the swelling tones.

Now he plays sweet tunes
Which touch the heart;
To see if he can soothe the king
With gentle strains.

His efforts are in vain,
The realm of song is exhausted,
And, like stormclouds,
Cares form upon the king's brow.

Der Barde, tief erbittert,	The bard, sorely embittered,
Schlägt die Harf' entzwei,	Breaks his harp in two,
Und durch die Lüfte zittert	And through the air vibrates
Der Silbersaiten Schrei.	The cry of the silver strings.

Und wie auch alle beben,	But, though all tremble,
Der Herrscher zürnet nicht;	The ruler is not enraged;
Der Gnade Strahlen schweben	The light of mercy
Auf seinem Angesicht.	Lingers on his countenance.

»Du wollest mich nicht zeihen	'Do not reproach me
Der Unempfindlichkeit;	With insensitivity;
In lang verblühten Maien	In months of May long past
Wie hast du mich erfreut!	How you have gladdened me!

»Wie jede Lust gesteigert,	'How you enhanced every joy
Die aus der Urne fiel!	Which fell from fate's urn!
Was mir ein Gott verweigert,	What a god denied me
Erstattete dein Spiel.	Your playing restored to me.

»Vom kalten Herzen gleitet	'From a cold heart
Nun Liedeszauber ab,	The magic of song now steals away,
Und immer näher schreitet	And ever closer step
Nun Vergänglichkeit und Grab.«	Transience and the grave.'

Lilla an die Morgenröte / *Lilla to the Dawn*

POET UNKNOWN

D 273 (1815)

Wie schön bist du, du güldne Morgenröte,	How beautiful you are, golden dawn,
Wie feierlich bist du!	How majestic!
Dir jauchzt im festlichen Gesang der Flöte	With his flute's festive song
Der Schäfer dankbar zu.	The shepherd offers you joyful thanks.

Dich grüßt des Waldes Chor, melodisch singet	The chorus of the woods greets you,
Die Lerch' und Nachtigall,	Lark and nightingale sing sweetly,
Und rings umher von Berg und Tal erklinget	And round about joy's echo
Der Freude Wiederhall.	Resounds from mountain and valley.

L'incanto degli occhi / *The Magic of Eyes*

PIETRO METASTASIO

D 902 no. 1 (1827)

Da voi, cari lumi,	On you, beloved eyes,
Di pende il mio stato;	Depends my life;
Voi siete i miei Numi,	You are my gods,
Voi siete il mio fato.	You are my destiny.

A vostro talento	At your bidding
Mi sento cangiar,	My mood changes.

Ardir m'inspirate,
Se liete splendete;
Se torbidi siete,
Mi fate tremar.

You inspire me with daring
If you shine joyfully;
If you are overcast,
You make me tremble.

Litanei auf das Fest Allerseelen / Litany for the Feast of All Souls

JOHANN GEORG JACOBI

D 343 (1816)

Ruhn in Frieden alle Seelen,
Die vollbracht ein banges Quälen,
Die vollendet süßen Traum,
Lebenssatt, geboren kaum,
Aus der Welt hinüber schieden:
Alle Seelen ruhn in Frieden!

May all souls rest in peace,
Those whose fearful torment is past,
Those whose sweet dreams are over,
Those sated with life, those barely born
Who have left this world:
May all souls rest in peace!

Liebevoller Mädchen Seelen,
Deren Tränen nicht zu zählen,
Die ein falscher Freund verließ,
Und die blinde Welt verstieß:
Alle, die von hinnen schieden,
Alle Seelen ruhn in Frieden!

The souls of girls in love
Whose tears are without number,
Who, abandoned by a faithless lover,
Rejected the blind world.
May all who have departed hence,
May all souls rest in peace!

Und die nie der Sonne lachten,
Unterm Mond auf Dornen
  wachten,
Gott, im reinen Himmels-
  licht,
Einst zu sehn von Angesicht:
Alle, die von hinnen schieden,
Alle Seelen ruhn in Frieden!

And those who never smiled at the sun,
Who lay awake beneath the moon on beds of
  thorns,
So that they might one day see God face to
  face
In the pure light of heaven:
May all who have departed hence,
May all souls rest in peace!

Lob der Tränen / In Praise of Tears

AUGUST WILHELM VON SCHLEGEL

D 711 (1818?)

Laue Lüfte,
Blumendüfte,
Alle Lenz- und Jugendlust;
Frischer Lippen
Küsse nippen,
Sanft gewiegt an zarter Brust;
Dann der Trauben
Nektar rauben,
Reihentanz und Spiel und Scherz:
Was die Sinnen
Nur gewinnen:
Ach, erfüllt es je das Herz?

Warm breezes,
Fragrant flowers,
All the pleasures of spring and youth;
Sipping kisses
From fresh lips,
Lulled gently on a tender breast;
Then stealing nectar
From the grapes,
Dancing, games and banter:
Whatever the senses
Can obtain:
Ah, does it ever satisfy the heart?

Wenn die feuchten
Augen leuchten
Von der Wehmut lindem Tau,
Dann entsiegelt,
Drin gespiegelt,

When moist eyes
Glisten
With the gentle dew of sadness,
Then, reflected in them,
The fields of heaven

Sich dem Blick die Himmelsau.	Are revealed to the gaze.
Wie erquicklich	How refreshingly,
Augenblicklich	How swiftly
Löscht es jede wilde Glut;	Every fierce passion is quelled;
Wie vom Regen	As flowers are revived
Blumen pflegen,	By the rain,
Hebet sich der matte Mut.	So do our weary spirits revive.

Lob des Tokayers / *In Praise of Tokay*

GABRIELE VON BAUMBERG

D 248 (1815)

O köstlicher Tokayer, o königlicher Wein,	Exquisite Tokay, prince among wines!
Du stimmest meine Leier zu seltnen Reimerei'n.	You inspire my lute to rare flights of poetry.
Mit langentbehrter Wonne	With long-desired bliss,
Und neu erwachtem Scherz	And newly awakened gaiety,
Erwärmst du, gleich der Sonne,	You warm my half-frozen heart
Mein halberstorbnes Herz.	Like the sun.
Du stimmest meine Leier zu seltnen Reimerei'n,	You inspire my lute to rare flights of poetry.
O köstlicher Tokayer, o königlicher Wein!	Exquisite Tokay, prince among wines!

O köstlicher Tokayer, du königlicher Wein!	Exquisite Tokay, prince among wines!
Du giessest Kraft und Feuer durch Mark und durch Gebein.	You pour strength and ardour through my whole being.
Ich fühle neues Leben	I feel new life
Durch meine Adern sprühn,	Sparkling in my veins,
Und deine Nektarreben	I feel your nectar grapes
In meinem Busen glühn.	Glowing in my breast.
Du giessest Kraft und Feuer durch Mark und durch Gebein.	You pour strength and ardour through my whole being.
O köstlicher Tokayer, du königlicher Wein!	Exquisite Tokay, prince among wines!

O köstlicher Tokayer, du königlicher Wein!	Exquisite Tokay, prince among wines!
Dir soll, als Gramzerstreuer, dies Lied geweihet sein!	To you who allay sorrow this song is dedicated.
In schwermutsvollen Launen	In melancholy moods
Beflügelst du das Blut,	You fire the blood;
Bei Blonden und bei Braunen	You give courage to the bashful,
Gibst du dem Blödsinn Mut.	To blonde and brunette alike.
Dir soll, als Gramzerstreuer, dies Lied gewidmet sein,	To you who allay sorrow this song is dedicated,
O köstlicher Tokayer, du königlicher Wein!	Exquisite Tokay, prince of wines!

Lodas Gespenst / *Loda's Ghost*

JAMES MACPHERSON (OSSIAN), translated by EDMUND VON HAROLD

D 150 (1816)

| Der bleiche, kalte Mond erhob sich in Osten. Der Schlaf stieg auf die Jünglinge | The wan, cold moon rose, in the east. Sleep descended on the youths. Their blue |

nieder! ihre blauen Helme schimmern zum Strahl; das sterbende Feuer vergeht. Der Schlaf aber ruhte nicht auf dem König: er hob sich mitten in seinen Waffen, und stieg langsam den Hügel hinauf, die Flamme des Thurns von Sarno zu sehn.

Die Flamme war düster und fern; der Mond verbarg in Osten sein rotes Gesicht, es stieg ein Windstoß vom Hügel herab, auf seinen Schwingen war Lodas Gespenst. Es kam zu seiner Heimat, umringt von seinen Schrecken; und schüttelt seinen düstern Speer. In seinem dunkeln Gesicht glühn seine Augen wie Flammen; seine Stimme gleicht entferntem Donner. Fingal stieß seinen Speer in die Nacht, und hob seine mächtige Stimme.

Zieh dich zurück, du Nachtsohn: ruf deine Winde und fleuch! Warum erscheinst du, vor mir, mit deinen schattigten Waffen? Fürcht ich deine düstre Bildung, du Geist des leidigen Loda? Schwach ist dein Schild dein: kraftlos Luftbild und dein Schwert. Der Windstoß rollt sie zusammen; und du selber bist verloren; fleuch von meinen Augen, du Nachtsohn! ruf deine Winde und fleuch!

Mit hohler Stimme versetzte der Geist, Willst du aus meiner Heimat mich treiben? Vor mir beugt sich das Volk. Ich dreh die Schlacht im Felde der Tapfern. Auf Völker werf ich den Blick, und sie verschwinden: mein Odem verbreitet den Tod. Auf den Rücken der Winde schreit ich voran: vor meinem Gesichte brausen Orkane. Aber mein Sitz ist über den Wolken; angenehm die Gefilde meiner Ruh.

Bewohn deine angenehmen Gefilde, sagte der König: denk nicht an Comhals Erzeugten. Steigen meine Schritte aus meinen Hügeln in deine friedliche Ebne hinauf? Begegnet ich dir mit einem Speer, auf deiner Wolke, du Geist des leidigen Loda? Warum runzelst du denn deine Stirn auf mich? Warum schüttelst du deinen luftigen Speer? Du runzelst deine Stirn vergebens: nie floh ich vor den Mächtigen im Krieg. Und sollen die Söhne des Winds, den König von Morven erschrecken? Nein nein; er kennt die Schwäche ihrer Waffen! Fleuch zu deinem Land, versetzte die Bildung: Faß die Wunde, und fleuch! Ich halte die Winde in der Höhle meiner Hand: ich bestimm den Lauf des Sturms. Der König von Sora ist mein Sohn; er neigt sich vor dem Stein meiner Kraft. Sein Heer umringt Carric-Thura; und er wird siegen! Fleuch zu deinem Land, Erzeuger von Comhal, oder spüre meine Wut, meine flammende Wut! Er hob seinen schattigen Speer in die Höhe! er neigte vorwärts seine

helmets glitter to the beam; the fading fire decays. But sleep did not rest on the king: he rose in the midst of his arms, and slowly ascended the hill, to behold the flame of Sarno's tower.

The flame was dim and distant; the moon hid her red face in the east. A blast came from the mountain, on its wings was the spirit of Loda. He came to his place in his terrors, and shook his dusky spear. His eyes appear like flames in his dark face; his voice is like distant thunder. Fingal advanced his spear in night and raised his voice on high.

Son of night, retire: call thy winds, and fly! Why dost thou come to my presence, with thy shadowy arms? Do I fear thy gloomy form, spirit of dismal Loda? Weak is thy shield of clouds: feeble is that meteor, thy sword! The blast rolls them together; and thou thyself art lost. Fly from my presence, son of night! call thy winds and fly!

Dost thou force me from my place? replied the hollow voice. The people bend before me. I turn the battle in the field of the brave. I look on the nations, and they vanish: my nostrils pour the blast of death. I come abroad on the winds: the tempests are before my face. But my dwelling is calm, above the clouds; the fields of my rest are pleasant.

Dwell in thy pleasant fields, said the king: Let Comhal's son be forgot. Do my steps ascend from my hills, into the peaceful plains? Do I meet thee, with a spear, on thy cloud, spirit of dismal Loda? Why then dost thou frown on me? Why shake thine airy spear? Thou frownest in vain. I never fled from the mighty in war. And shall the sons of the wind frighten the king of Morven? No; he knows the weakness of their arms!

Fly to thy land, replied the form: receive the wind, and fly! The blasts are in the hollow of my hand: the course of the storm is mine. The king of Sora is my son, he bends at the stone of my power. His battle is around Carric-Thura; and he will prevail! Fly to thy land, son of Comhal, or feel my flaming wrath!

He lifted high his shadowy spear! He bent forward his dreadful height. Fingal, advancing, drew his sword. The gleaming path of the steel winds through the gloomy ghost. The form fell shapeless into air, like a column of smoke, which the staff of the boy disturbs, as it rises from the half-extinguished furnace.

The spirit of Loda shrieked, as, rolled into himself, he rose on the wind. Inistore shook at the sound. The waves heard it on

schreckbare Länge. Fingal ging ihm entgegen, und zuckte sein Schwert. Der blitzende Pfad des Stahls durchdrang den düstern Geist. Die Bildung zerfloss, gestaltlos, in Luft, wie eine Säule von Rauch, welche der Stab des Jünglings berührt, wie er aus der sterbenden Schmiede aufsteigt. Laut schrie Lodas Gespenst, als es, in sich selber gerollt, auf dem Winde sich hob. Inistore bebte beim Klang. Auf dem Abgrund hörtens die Wellen. Sie standen, vor Schrecken, in der Mitte ihres Laufs! die Freunde von Fingal sprangen plötzlich empor. Sie griffen ihre gewichtigen Speere. Sie mißten den König: zornig fuhren sie auf; all ihre Waffen erschollen! Der Mond rückte in Osten voran. Fingal kehrt im Klang seiner Waffen zurück. Groß war der Jünglinge Freude, ihre Seelen ruhig, wie das Meer nach dem Sturm. Ullin hob den Freudengesang. Die Hügel Inistores frohlockten. Hoch stieg die Flamme der Eiche; Heldengeschichten wurden erzählt.

the deep. The waves stopped in their course, with fear: the friends of Fingal started, at once; and took their heavy spears. They missed the king: they rose in rage; all their arms resound! The moon came forth in the east. Fingal returned in the gleam of his arms. The joy of his youth was great, their souls settled, as a sea from the storm. Ullin raised the song of gladness. The hills of Inistore rejoiced. The flame of the oak arose; and the tales of heroes are told.

Luisens Antwort / Louisa's Answer

LUDWIG KOSEGARTEN

D 319 (1815)

Wohl weinen Gottes Engel,	God's angels weep
Wenn Liebende sich trennen.	When lovers part.
Wie werd' ich leben können,	How shall I be able to live
Geliebter, ohne dich!	Without you, beloved?
Gestorben allen Freuden,	Dead to all joys
Leb' ich fortan den Leiden,	I shall henceforth live for sorrow,
Und nimmer, Wilhelm, nimmer	And never, William, never
Vergißt Luisa dich.	Shall Louisa forget you.
Wie könnt ich dein vergessen!	How could I forget you?
Wohin ich, Freund, mich wende,	Wherever I turn, beloved,
Wohin den Blick nur sende,	Wherever I cast my eyes,
Umstrahlt dein Bildnis mich.	Your image shines around me.
Mit trunkenem Entzücken	With heady rapture
Seh' ich es auf mich blicken.	I see it gaze upon me.
Nein, nimmer, Wilhelm, nimmer	No, never, William, never
Vergißt Luisa dich.	Shall Louisa forget you.
Wie könnt' ich dein vergessen!	How could I forget you?
Gerötet von Verlangen,	How your cheeks burned,
Wie flammten deine Wangen,	Flushed with desire,
Von Inbrunst naß, um mich!	Perspiring with ardour for me!
Im Widerschein der deinen,	How my cheeks glowed
Wie leuchteten die meinen!	In the reflection of yours!
Nein, nimmer, Wilhelm, nimmer	No, never, William, never
Vergißt Luisa dich.	Shall Louisa forget you.

In mildem Engelglanze
Würd' ich dein Bett' umschimmern
Und zärtlich dich umwimmern:
»Ich bin Luisa, ich:
Luisa kann nicht hassen,
Luisa dich nicht lassen,
Luisa kommt zu segnen,
Und liebt auch droben dich.«

I would bathe your bed
In a gentle, angelic radiance,
And murmur tenderly into your ear:
'I am Louisa:
Louisa cannot hate you,
Louisa cannot leave you.
Louisa comes to bless you,
And still loves you up above.'

Mailied / May Song

LUDWIG HEINRICH CHRISTOPH HÖLTY

D 503 (1816)

Grüner wird die Au,
Und der Himmel blau;
Schwalben kehren wieder,
Und die Erstlingslieder
Kleiner Vögelein
Zwitschern durch den Hain.

The meadow grows greener,
And the sky is blue;
Swallows return
And the little birds
Warble their first songs
Throughout the grove.

Aus dem Blütenstrauch
Weht der Liebe Hauch:
Seit der Lenz erschienen,
Waltet sie im Grünen,
Malt die Blumen bunt,
Rot des Mädchens Mund.

The breath of love wafts;
From the blossoming bushes
Since spring has appeared
Love reigns over the verdant landscape,
Painting the flowers bright colours,
And the lips of maidens red.

Brüder, küsst ihn!
Denn die Jahre fliehn!
Einen Kuß in Ehren
Kann euch Niemand wehren!
Küßt ihn, Brüder, küßt,
Weil er küßlich ist!

Brothers, kiss them,
For the years fly past!
No one can forbid you
One honourable kiss!
Kiss them, brothers, kiss them,
Since they are kissable!

Seht, der Tauber girrt,
Seht, der Tauber schwirrt
Um sein liebes Täubchen!
Nehmt euch auch ein Weibchen,
Wie der Tauber tut,
Und seid wohlgemut!

See, the dove is cooing,
See, the dove is billing
Around his beloved mate!
Like the dove,
You, too, should take a wife
And be happy!

Marie / Mary

NOVALIS

D658 (1819?)

Ich sehe dich in tausend Bildern,
Maria, lieblich ausgedrückt,
Doch keins von allen kann dich schildern,
Wie meine Seele dich erblickt.

I see you in a thousand pictures,
Mary, sweetly portrayed;
Yet none of them can depict you
As my soul has seen you.

Ich weiss nur, dass der Welt Getümmel
Seitdem mir wie ein Traum
    verweht;
Und ein unnennbar süsser Himmel
Mir ewig im Gemüte steht.

I only know that since then
The world's tumult has drifted away from
    me like a dream,
And an ineffably sweet heaven
Is forever in my heart.

Meeres Stille / Calm at Sea

JOHANN WOLFGANG VON GOETHE

First version: D 2 215A (1815)
Second version: D 216 (1815)

Tiefe Stille herrscht im Wasser,
Ohne Regung ruht das Meer,
Und bekümmert sieht der Schiffer
Glatte Fläche rings umher.
Keine Luft von keiner Seite!
Todesstille fürchterlich!
In der ungeheuern Weite
Reget keine Welle sich.

Profound calm reigns over the waters,
The sea lies motionless;
Anxiously the sailor beholds
The glassy surface all around.
No breeze from any quarter!
A fearful, deathly calm!
In the vast expanse
No wave stirs.

Mein Gruß an den Mai / My Greeting To May

JOHANN GOTTFRIED KUMPF

D 305 (1815)

Sei mir gegrüßt, o Mai! mit deinem
Blütenhimmel,
Mit deinem Lenz, mit deinem
Freudenmeer;
Sei mir gegrüßt, du fröhliches Gewimmel
Der neubelebten Wesen um mich her.

Welcome, May, with your canopy of blossom,
With your spring, with your ocean of joy.
Welcome, with your happy swarm
Of newly awakened creatures around me.

Dein Götterhauch durchströmt das düstre
Grau der Lüfte,
Und schnell begrünt sich Berg und Tal und
Au,
Es wehen schmeichelnd linde
Balsamdüfte,
Es lachet hell des Äthers klares Blau.

Your divine breath streams through the
gloomy grey air,
And mountain, valley and meadow swiftly
grow green;
Gentle, fragrant breezes blow
caressingly,
The clear blue ether rings with laughter.

An deine Brust, Natur! laß mich ver-
trauend sinken,
Erhalte mir den reinen Lebensmut;
In vollen Zügen will ich Frohsinn trinken,
Und neu durchströme mich der Freude
Glut.

Nature, let me sink trustingly upon your
breast;
Sustain my sheer courage for life.
I would drink happiness in full draughts;
May the glow of joy fill me
anew.

Sei mir gegrüßt, o Mai! mit deinem
Freudenmeere,
Mit deiner Lust, mit deiner
Blumenpracht;
Du schöner Jüngling, trockne jede Zähre,
Erhelle jede dunkle Schicksalsnacht!

Welcome, May, with your ocean of
joys,
With your pleasures, with your flowery
splendour;
Fair youth, dry every tear,
And brighten every dark night of fate!

Memnon / Memnon

JOHANN MAYRHOFER

D 541 (1817)

Den Tag hindurch nur einmal mag ich
sprechen,
Gewohnt zu schweigen immer und zu
trauern:

Constant silence and grieving are my
wont;
The whole day long I may speak but
once:

Wenn durch die nachtgebor'nen Nebelmauern
Aurorens Purpurstrahlen liebend brechen.

Für Menschenohren sind es Harmonien.
Weil ich die Klage selbst melodisch künde
Und durch der Dichtung Glut das Rauhe rinde,
Vermuten sie in mir ein selig Blühen.

In mir, nach dem des Todes Arme langen,
In dessen tiefstem Herzen Schlangen wühlen;
Genährt von meinen schmerzlichen Gefühlen
Fast wütend durch ein ungestillt Verlangen:

Mit dir, des Morgens Göttin, mich zu einen,
Und weit von diesem nichtigen Getriebe,
Aus Sphären edler Freiheit, aus Sphären reiner Liebe,
Ein stiller, bleicher Stern herab zu scheinen.

When Aurora's tender crimson rays
Break through the night-begotten walls of mist.

To men's ears this music.
Since I proclaim my very grief in song
And transfigure its harshness in the fire of poetry,
They imagine that joy flowers within me.

Within me, to whom the arms of death stretch out,
As serpents writhe deep in my heart;
I am nourished by my anguished thoughts,
And almost frenzied with unquiet longing.

Oh to be united with you, goddess of morning,
And, far from this vain bustle,
To shine down as a pale, silent star
From spheres of noble freedom and pure love.

Minnelied / Love Song

LUDWIG HEINRICH CHRISTOPH HÖLTY

D 429 (1816)

Holder klingt der Vogelsang,
Wenn die Engelreine,
Die mein Jünglingsherz bezwang.
Wandelt durch die Haine.

Röter blühet Tal und Au,
Grüner wird der Rasen,
Wo mir Blumen rot und blau
Ihre Hände lasen.

Ohne sie ist alles tot,
Welk sind Blüt' und Kräuter;
Und kein Frühlingsabendrot
Dünkt mir schön und heiter.

Traute, minnigliche Frau,
Wollest nimmer fliehen;
Dass mein Herz, gleich dieser Au,
Mög' in Wonne blühen!

The birdsong sounds sweeter
When the pure angel
Who has conquered my youthful heart
Walks through the woods.

Valley and meadow bloom with a redder hue,
The grass grows greener
Where her hands have gathered
Red and blue flowers.

Without her all is dead,
Flowers and herbs wilt;
And no spring sunset
Seems beautiful or serene to me.

Dear, lovely lady,
Never leave me;
For then my heart, like this meadow,
Will bloom in joy!

Minona oder die Kunde der Dogge / Minona, or the Mastiff's Tidings

FRIEDRICH ANTON FRANZ BERTRAND

D 152 (1815)

Wie treiben die Wolken so finster und
  schwer
Über die liebliche Leuchte daher!
Wie rasseln die Tropfen auf Fenster und
  Dach!
Wie treibet's da draußen so wütig und
  jach,
Als trieben sich Geister in Schlachten!

Und Wunder! Wie plötzlich die Kämp-
  fenden ruhn,
Als bannten jetzt Gräber ihr Treiben und
  Tun!
Und über die Heide, und über den
  Wald —
Wie weht es so öde, wie weht es so kalt!
So schaurig vom schimmernden Felsen!

O Edgar! wo schwirret dein
  Bogengeschoß?
Wo flattert dein Haarbusch? wo tummelt
  dein Roß?
Wo schnauben die schwärzlichen Doggen
  um dich?
Wo spähst du am Felsen Beute
  für mich?
Dein harret das liebende Mädchen!

Dein harret, o Jüngling! im jeglichen
  Laut,
Dein harret so schmachtend die zagende
  Braut;
Es dünkt ihr zerrissen das liebliche Band,
Es dünkt ihr so blutig dein
  Jägergewand —
Wohl minnen die Toten uns nimmer!

Noch hallet den moosigen Hügel
  entlang
Wie Harfengelispel ihr Minnegesang.
Was frommt es? Schon blicken die Sterne
  der Nacht
Hinunter zum Bette von Erde gemacht,
Wo eisern die Minnenden schlafen!

So klagt sie; und leise tappt's draußen
  umher,
Es winselt so innig, so schaudernd und
  schwer;
Es fasst sie Ensetzen, sie wanket zur Tür,
Bald schmiegt sich die schönste der
  Doggen vor ihr,
Der Liebling des harrenden Mädchens;

Nicht, wie sie noch gestern mit kosendem
  Drang,

How the clouds, so dark and
  heavy,
Scud across the sweet sun!
How the raindrops rattle on window and
  roof!
How furious is the storm out
  there,
As if spirits were locked in battle.

And strange to tell! How suddenly the
  combatants cease,
As if the grave now put an end to their
  conflict!
And over the heath and the
  forest
How desolate, how cold is the wind,
Blowing eerily from the shimmering rock!

O Edgar! Where is your whirring
  arrow?
Where is your flowing mane of hair? Where
  is your steed?
Where are the black mastiffs romping
  around you?
Where among the rocks are you seeking
  game for me?
Your loving maiden awaits you!

Your anxious bride awaits you, young man,
  with every sound;
She awaits you with such
  yearning.
She imagines the bonds of love broken,
She imagines your huntsman's clothes
  covered with blood.
For the dead never love us!

Their love song echoes like whispering
  harps
Over the mossy hillside.
To what avail? Already the night
  stars
Gaze down upon the bed of earth
Where the lovers sleep unshakeably.

Thus she laments; outside there is a soft
  tapping,
And a low whine, urgent and
  fearful.
Seized with horror she staggers to the door;
The finest of the mastiffs, her
  favourite,
Nuzzles against the awaiting maiden.

Not a messenger of love, as
  yesterday

Ein Bote des Lieben, zum Busen ihr sprang —	When it leapt at her breast with eager affection.
Kaum hebt sie vom Boden den trauernden Blick,	It barely lifts its mournful eyes from the ground,
Schleicht nieder zum Pförtchen, und kehret zurück,	Creeps down to the door, and back again,
Die schreckliche Kunde zu deuten.	To indicate its terrible tidings.
Minona folgt schweigend mit bleichem Gesicht,	Minona follows, pale-faced and silent,
Als ruft es die Arme vor's hohe Gericht —	As if, poor girl, she were summoned before the high court.
Es leuchtet so düster der nächtliche Strahl —	The night sky shines with sombre gleam.
Sie folgt ihr durch Moore, durch Heiden und Tal	She follows the mastiff through bog, heath and valley
Zum Fuße des schimmernden Felsen.	To the foot of the shimmering rock.
»Wo weilet, o schimmernder Felsen, der Tod?	'O shimmering rock, where does death lurk?
Wo schlummert der Schläfer, vom Blute noch rot?«	Where does the sleeper slumber, still red with blood?'
Wohl war es zerrissen das liebliche Band,	The bonds of love were indeed broken;
Wohl hatt' ihm, geschleudert von tückischer Hand,	A fatal arrow, unleashed by an evil hand,
Ein Mordpfeil den Busen durchschnitten.	Had pierced his breast.
Und als sie nun nahet mit ängstlichem Schrei,	And now, as she draws near with a fearful cry,
Gewahrt sie den Bogen des Vaters dabei.	She sees her father's bow nearby.
»O Vater, o Vater, verzeih es dir Gott!	'O father, father, may God forgive you!
Wohl hast du mir heute mit frevelndem Spott	Today you have fulfilled your vow of vengeance
So schrecklich den Dräuschwur erfüllet!	So terribly, and with such cruel mockery!
»Doch soll ich zermalmet von hinnen nun gehn?	'But am I now to leave here, crushed?
Er schläft ja so lockend, so wonnig, so schön!	He sleeps, so alluring, so happy, so handsome.
Geknüpft ist auf ewig das eherne Band;	The iron bond is tied for ever;
Und Geister der Väter im Nebelgewand	In misty garments the spirits of our fathers
Ergreifen die silbernen Harfen.«	Strike the silver harps.'
Und plötzlich entreißt sie mit sehnender Eil	And suddenly, with passionate haste, she rips
Der Wunde des Lieben den tötenden Pfeil;	The deathly arrow from her beloved's wound;
Und stößt ihn, ergriffen von innigem Weh,	Overcome by intense grief, she plunges it
Mit Hast in den Busen so blendend als Schnee,	Swiftly into her breast, as dazzling white as snow,
Und sinkt am schimmernden Felsen.	And sinks down upon the shimmering rock.

Misero pargoletto / Unhappy Child

PIETRO METASTASIO

D 42 (1812/13)

Misero pargoletto,	Unhappy child,
Il tuo destino non sai.	You do not know your fate.

Ah! non gli dite mai
Qual era il genitor.

Ah, never tell him
Who his father was.

Come in un punto, oh Dio,
Tutto cambiò d'aspetto!
Voi foste il mio diletto,
Voi siete il mio terror.

O God, how in one moment
Everything changed its aspect!
You were my delight,
Now you make me afraid.

Morgenlied / Morning Song

FRIEDRICH LEOPOLD, GRAF ZU STOLBERG-STOLBERG

D 266 (1815)

Willkommen, rotes Morgenlicht!
Es grüsset dich mein Geist,
Der durch des Schlafes Hülle bricht,
Und seinen Schöpfer preist.

Welcome, rosy light of morning!
My spirit greets you,
Breaking through the veil of sleep
To praise its Creator.

Wilkommen, goldner Morgenstrahl,
Der schon den Berg begrüsst,
Und bald im stillen Quellental
Die kleine Blume küsst.

Welcome, golden ray of morning,
Which already greets the mountains,
And in the silent valley, by the stream,
Will soon kiss the little flowers.

O Sonne, sei mir Gottes Bild,
Der täglich dich erneut,
Der immer hehr, und immer mild,
Die ganz Welt erfreut!

O sun, be for me the image of God,
Who renews you each day,
Who, ever noble and gentle,
Brings joy to the whole world!

Der, wie die Blum' im Quellental,
O Sonne, dich erschuf,
Als deine Schwestern allzumal
Entflammten seinem Ruf.

Who created you, o sun,
As He did the flowers in the watered valley,
When all your sisters
Were kindled at His command.

Ihr wandelt auf bestimmter Bahn
Einher und strauchelt nicht;
Denn Gottes Odem haucht euch an,
Sein Aug' ist euer Licht.

You each move on your appointed course,
And do not falter;
For God's breath touches you,
His eye is your light.

Morgenlied / Morning Song

ZACHARIAS WERNER

D 685 (1820)

Eh' die Sonne früh aufersteht,
Wenn aus dem dampfenden Meer,
Herauf und herunter das Morgenrot weht,
Voranfährt mit dem leuchtenden Speer:
Flattern Vöglein dahin und daher,
Singen fröhlich die Kreuz und die Quer
Ein Lied, ein jubelndes Lied.

Before the sun rises early,
When from the misty sea
The dawn flutters up and down,
Surging ahead with shining spear;
Little birds flit to and fro,
Singing merrily here and there
A song, a jubilant song.

»Was freut ihr Vöglein euch
   allzumal
So herzig im wärmenden Sonnenstrahl?«
»Wir freu'n uns, dass wir leben und sind,
Und dass wir luft'ge Gesellen sind,

'Why are you all so delightfully happy, little
   birds,
In the sun's warming rays?'
'We are happy to be alive,
And to be companions of the air;

Nach löblichem Brauch
Durchflattern wir fröhlich den Strauch,
Umweht vom lieblichen Morgenwind
Ergötzet die Sonne sich auch. «

»Was sitzt ihr Vöglein so stumm und
    geduckt
Am Dach im moosigen Nest? «
»Wir sitzen, weil uns die Sonn' nicht
    beguckt,
Schon hat sie die Nacht in die Wellen
    geduckt,
Der Mond allein, der liebliche Schein,
Der Sonne lieblicher Widerschein
Uns in der Dunkelheit nie verlässt,
Darob wir im Stillen uns freu'n. «

O Jugend, kühlige Morgenzeit,
Wo wir die Herzen geöffnet und weit,
Mit raschem und erwachenden Sinn,
Der Lebensfrische uns erfreut,
Wohl flohst du dahin!
Wir Alten sitzen geduckt im Nest,
Allein der liebliche Widerschein der
    Jugendzeit,
Wo wir im Frührot uns erfreut,
Uns auch im Alter nie verlässt,
Die stille, sinnige Fröhlichkeit.

In the time-honoured tradition
We flutter merrily through the bushes,
Fanned by the sweet morning breeze;
And the sun, too, rejoices.'

'Why do you little birds sit so dumb and
    hunched up
In your mossy nests on the roof?'
'We sit here because the sun is not looking
    at us;
Night has already dipped it in the
    waves;
The moon alone, that sweet light,
The sun's sweet reflection,
Never forsakes us in the dark:
Therefore we quietly rejoice.'

O youth, cool morning hour,
When, with hearts wide open,
With quickened, awakening senses,
We delighted in life's freshness,
You have fled, alas.
We old ones sit huddled in our nests;
But the sweet reflection of our
    youth,
When we rejoiced in the dawn,
Never forsakes us, even in old age:
That calm, pensive happiness.

Morgenlied / Morning Song

POET UNKNOWN

D 381 (1816)

Die frohe neubelebte Flur
Singt ihrem Schöpfer Dank.
O Herr und Vater der Natur,
Dir tön' auch mein Gesang!

Der Lebensfreuden schenkst du viel
Dem, der sich weislich freut.
Dies sei, o Vater, stets das Ziel
Bei meiner Fröhlichkeit.

Ich kann mich noch des Lebens freun
In dieser schönen Welt;
Mein Herz soll dem geheiligt sein
Der weislich sie erhält.

Wenn dann mir Müden winkt der Tod,
Zur bessern Welt zu gehn,
So bricht ein schön'res Morgenrot
Mir an beim Auferstehen.

The newly awakened fields
Sing joyful thanks to their Creator.
O Lord and Father of nature,
Let my song also resound for You!

You bestow many of life's pleasures
On him who can enjoy them wisely.
Let this, O Father, always be my aim
In my happiness.

I can still enjoy life
In this beautiful world;
My heart shall be consecrated to Him
Who in His wisdom sustains the world.

Then, when I am weary and death bids me
Depart for a better world,
A fairer day will dawn for me
At the resurrection.

Nach einem Gewitter / After a Thunderstorm

JOHANN MAYRHOFER

D 561 (1817)

Auf den Blumen flimmern Perlen,
Philomelens Klagen fliessen,
Mutiger nun dunkle Erlen
In die reinen Lüfte spriessen.

Und dem Tale, so erblichen,
Kehret holde Röte wieder,
In der Blüten Wohlgerüchen
Baden Vögel ihr Gefieder.

Hat die Brust sich
    ausgewittert,
Seitwärts lehnt der Gott den Bogen,
Und sein golden Antlitz zittert
Reiner auf versöhnten Wogen.

Pearls glisten on the flowers,
Philomel's lament pours forth;
More boldly now dark alders
Shoot up into the pure air.

And to the valley, grown so pale,
A fair flush returns.
In the fragrance of the flowers
Birds bathe their plumage.

When the storm has ceased within the
    heart,
God tilts his bow sideways
And his golden countenance glitters
More clearly upon the stilled waves.

Nacht und Träume / Night and Dreams

MATTHÄUS VON COLLIN

D 827 (1822?)

Heil'ge Nacht, du sinkest nieder;
Nieder wallen auch die Träume,
Wie dein Mondlicht durch die Räume,
Durch der Menschen stille Brust.
Die belauschen sie mit Lust;
Rufen, wenn der Tag erwacht:
Kehre wieder, heil'ge Nacht!
Holde Träume, kehret wieder!

Holy night, you sink down;
Dreams, too, float down,
Like your moonlight through space,
Through the silent hearts of men.
They listen with delight,
Crying out when day awakes:
Come back, holy night!
Fair dreams, return!

Nachtgesang / Night Song

JOHANN WOLFGANG VON GOETHE

D 119 (1814)

O gib, vom weichen Pfühle,
Träumend, ein halb Gehör!
Bei meinem Saitenspiele
Schlafe! was willst du mehr?

Bei meinem Saitenspiele
Segnet der Sterne Heer
Die ewigen Gefühle;
Schlafe! was willst du mehr?

Die ewigen Gefühle
Heben mich, hoch und hehr,
Aus irdischem Gewühle;
Schlafe! was willst du mehr?

O lend, from your soft pillow,
Dreaming, but half an ear!
To the music of my strings
Sleep! What more can you wish?

To the music of my strings
The host of stars
Blesses eternal feelings;
Sleep! What more can you wish?

These eternal feelings
Raise me high and glorious
Above the earthly throng;
Sleep! What more can you wish?

Vom irdischen Gewühle	From this earthly throng
Trennst du mich nur zu sehr,	You separate me only too well,
Bannst mich in deine Kühle;	You spellbind me to this coolness,
Schlafe! was willst du mehr?	What more can you wish?
Bannst mich in diese Kühle,	You spellbind me to this coolness,
Gibst nur im Traum Gehör.	Giving ear only in your dream,
Ach, auf dem weichen Pfühle	Ah, on your soft pillow
Schlafe! was willst du mehr?	Sleep! What more can you wish?

Nachtgesang / Night Song

LUDWIG KOSEGARTEN

D 314 (1815)

Tiefe Feier	Deep peace
Schauert um die Welt.	Hovers over the world.
Braune Schleier	A brown veil
Hüllen Wald und Feld.	Shrouds wood and field.
Trüb und matt und müde	Unhappy, listless and weary
Nickt jedes Leben ein,	All living creatures drowse off to sleep,
Und namenloser Friede	And ineffable peace
Umsäuselt alles Sein!	Envelops every being.
Wacher Kummer,	Wakeful sorrow,
Lass ein Weilchen mich!	Leave me a while.
Goldner Schlummer,	Golden slumber,
Komm, umflügle mich!	Come, enfold me in your wings.
Trockne meine Tränen	Dry my tears
Mit deines Schleiers Saum,	With the hem of your veil,
Und täusche, Freund, mein Sehnen	And delude my longing, friend,
Mit deinem schönsten Traum!	With your loveliest dream.

Nachthymne / Hymn to the Night

NOVALIS

D687 (1820)

Hinüber wall' ich,	I shall pass over,
Und jede Pein	And all pain
Wird einst ein Stachel	Will be a stab
Der Wollust sein.	Of pleasure.
Noch wenig Zeiten,	In a short while
So bin ich los,	I shall be freed
Und liege trunken	And lie enraptured
Der Lieb' im Schoss.	In the bosom of love.
Unendliches Leben	Eternal life
Wogt mächtig in mir;	Will surge powerfully within me,
Ich schaue von oben	I shall gaze down on you
Herunter nach dir,	From above.
An jenem Hügel	Your radiance will fade
Verlischt dein Glanz,	On yonder hill,
Ein Schatten bringet	Shadow will bring
Den kühlenden Kranz.	A cooling wreath.
O sauge, Geliebter,	Beloved, draw me
Gewaltig mich an,	Powerfully in,

Das ich entschlummern	That I may fall asleep
Und lieben kann!	And love.
Ich fühle des Todes	I feel the rejuvenating
Verjüngende Flut,	Tide of death,
Zu Balsam und Äther	My blood is changed
Verwandelt mein Blut —	To balm and ether.
Ich lebe bei Tage	By day I live
Voll Glauben und Mut,	Full of faith and courage;
Und sterbe die Nächte	At night I die
In heiliger Glut.	In the sacred fire.

Nachtstück / Nocturne

JOHANN MAYRHOFER

D672 (1819)

Wenn über Berge sich der Nebel breitet,	When the mists spread over the mountains,
Und Luna mit Gewölken kämpft,	And the moon battles with the clouds,
So nimmt der Alte seine Harfe, und schreitet,	The old man takes his harp, and walks
Und singt waldeinwärts und gedämpft:	Towards the wood, quietly singing:

»Du heilge Nacht:	'Holy night,
Bald ist's vollbracht,	Soon it will be done.
Bald schlaf ich ihn, den langen Schlummer,	Soon I shall sleep the long sleep
Der mich erlöst von allem Kummer.«	Which will free me from all grief.'

Die grünen Bäume rauschen dann:	Then the green trees rustle:
»Schlaf süss, du guter, alter Mann;«	'Sleep sweetly, good old man;'
Die Gräser lispeln wankend fort:	And the swaying grasses whisper:
»Wir decken seinen Ruheort;«	'We shall cover his resting place.'

Und mancher liebe Vogel ruft:	And many a sweet bird calls:
»O lasst ihn ruhn in Rasengruft!«	'Let him rest in his grassy grave!'
Der Alte horcht, der Alte schweigt,	The old man listens, the old man is silent.
Der Tod hat sich zu ihm geneigt.	Death has inclined towards him.

Nachtviolen / Dame's Violets

JOHANN MAYRHOFER

D752 (1822)

Nachtviolen, Nachtviolen,	Dame's violets,
Dunkle Augen, seelenvolle,	Dark, soulful eyes,
Selig ist es, sich versenken	It is blissful to immerse myself
In dem samtnen Blau.	In your velvety blue.

Grüne Blätter streben freudig,	Green leaves strive joyously
Euch zu hellen, euch zu schmücken;	To brighten you, to adorn you;
Doch ihr blicket ernst und schweigend	But you gaze, solemn and silent,
In die laue Frühlingsluft.	Into the mild spring air.

Mit erhabnen Wehmutsstrahlen	With sublime shafts of melancholy
Trafet ihr mein treues Herz,	You have pierced my faithful heart,
Und nun blüht in stummen Nächten,	And now, in silent nights,
Fort die heilige Verbindung.	Our sacred union blossoms.

Nähe des Geliebten / The Beloved Nearby

JOHANN WOLFGANG VON GOETHE

D 162 (1815)

Ich denke dein, wenn mir der Sonne Schimmer
Vom Meere strahlt;
Ich denke dein, wenn sich des Mondes Flimmer
In Quellen malt.

Ich sehe dich, wenn auf dem fernen Wege
Der Staub sich hebt;
In tiefer Nacht, wenn auf dem schmalen Stege
Der Wandrer bebt.

Ich höre dich, wenn dort mit dumpfem Rauschen
Die Welle steigt.
Im stillen Hain da geh ich oft zu lauschen,
Wenn alles schweigt.

Ich bin bei dir, du seist auch noch so ferne.
Du bist mir nah!
Die Sonne sinkt, bald leuchten mir die Sterne.
O wärst du da!

I think of you when sunlight
Glints from the sea.
I think of you when the moon's glimmer
Is reflected in streams.

I think of you when, on distant roads,
Dust rises;
In the depths of night, when on the narrow bridge
The traveller trembles.

I hear you when, with a dull roar,
The waves surge up.
I often go to listen in the tranquil grove
When all is silent.

I am with you, however far away you are.
You are close to me!
The sun sets, soon the stars will shine for me.
Would that you were here!

Namenstaglied / Name-day Song

ALBERT STADLER

D 695 (1820)

Vater, schenk' mir diese Stunde,
Hör' ein Lied aus meinem Munde!
Dir verdank' ich das Gelingen
Meine Wünsche heut' zu singen,
Denn du hast mit güt'ger Hand
Mir den Weg dazu gebahnt.

O, laß diese Hand mich küssen!
Sieh' des Dankes Tränen fließen!
Denn sie hat mir mehr gegeben
Als Gesang: ein schönes Leben;
Und mit kindlich frohem Blick
Dank' ich ihr des Lebens Glück.

Himmel, sende deinen Segen
Dem verehrten Mann entgegen!
Strahle ihm, des Glückes Sonne!
Schäum' ihm über, Kelch der Wonne!
Und von Blumen voller Pracht
Sei ein Kranz ihm dargebracht.

Father, grant me this hour,
Hear a song from my lips!
I thank you that my wish
To sing today is fulfilled,
For with a kindly hand
You have prepared the way for me.

Oh, let me kiss this hand!
See how my tears of thanks flow!
For your hand has given me more
Than song: a fine life;
And with a look of childlike joy
I thank you for life's happiness.

Heaven, bestow your blessing
On this revered man!
Shine upon him, sun of happiness!
Overflow for him, cup of joy!
And let a garland of flowers in their full glory
Be offered him.

Diesen Kranz in deinen Haaren
Möge Gott uns stets bewahren,
Und ich fleh's mit nassen Blicken:
Noch ein zweiter soll dich schmücken,
Blau und golden, denn dir spricht
Jeder Mund: Vergiß mein nicht!

May God always preserve for us
This garland in your hair:
Thus I pray with moist eyes.
A second garland, blue and gold,
Shall adorn you; for all lips
Say to you: Forget me not!

Naturgenuss / Delight in Nature

FRIEDRICH VON MATTHISSON

D 188 (1815?)

Im Abendschimmer wallt der Quell
Durch Wiesenblumen
  purpurhell,
Der Pappelweide wechselnd
  Grün
Weht ruhelispelnd drüber hin.

In the soft light of evening the brook flows
Through meadows of bright, purple
  flowers,
The poplar, with its changing shades of
  green,
Whispers gently above them.

Im Lenzhauch webt der Geist des Herr'n!
Sieh! Auferstehung nah' und fern,
Sieh! Jugendfülle, Schönheitsmeer,
Und Wonnetaumel ringsumher!

God's spirit stirs in the spring breeze;
Behold life's resurrection, near and far,
See, youth's abundance, a sea of beauty
And teeming joys lie all around.

Ich blicke her, ich blicke hin,
Und immer höher schwebt mein Sinn.
Nur Tand sind Pracht und Gold und
  Ruhm,
Natur, in deinem Heiligtum!

I look about me, close and far away,
And my soul soars ever higher.
Pomp, gold and fame are but
  dross
In your sanctuary, Nature!

Des Himmels Ahnung den umweht,
Der deinen Liebeston versteht;
Doch, an dein Mutterherz gedrückt,
Wird er zum Himmel selbst entzückt!

Intimations of heaven envelop him
Who understands your music of love;
For he, pressed to your maternal breast,
Will know the delights of heaven itself!

Normans Gesang / Norman's Song

SIR WALTER SCOTT, translated by ADAM STORCK

D 846 (1825)
A literal rendering of Storck's translation is given here. Scott's original poem
is printed below in italics.

Die Nacht bricht bald herein, dann leg' ich
  mich zur Ruh,
Die Heide ist mein Lager, das Farnkraut
  deckt mich zu,
Mich lullt der Wache Tritt wohl in den
  Schlaf hinein.
Ach, muss so weit von dir, Maria, Holde,
  sein.

Soon night will fall. Then I shall lie down to
  rest;
The heath shall be my bed, the bracken
  shall cover me.
The sentry's tread shall lull me to
  sleep.
Alas, I must be so far from you,
  Mary.

Und wird es morgen Abend, und kommt
  die trübe Zeit,
Dann ist vielleicht mein Lager der blutig
  rote Plaid,
Mein Abendlied verstummet, du
  schleichst dann trüb und bang,

Come tomorrow evening, come the bleak
  hour,
My bed may be the blood-red
  plaid;
My vesper song will cease, and you,
  Mary,

Maria, mich wecken kann nicht dein Tot-
ensang.

So musst ich von dir scheiden, du holde,
süsse Braut,
Wie magst du nach mir rufen, wie magst
du weinen laut,
Ach, denken darf ich nicht an deinen
herben Schmerz,
Ach, denken darf ich nicht an dein getreues
Herz.

Nein, zärtlich treues Sehnen darf hegen
Norman nicht,
Wenn in den Feind Clan Alpin wie Sturm
und Hagel bricht,
Wie ein gespannter Bogen sein mutig Herz
dann sei,
Sein Fuss, Maria, wie der Pfeil so rasch und
frei.

Wohl wird die Stunde kommen, wo nicht
die Sonne scheint,
Du wankst zu deinem Norman, dein holdes
Auge weint,
Doch fall ich in der Schlacht, hüllt
Todesschauer mich,
O glaub, mein letzter Seufzer, Maria, ist
für dich.

Doch kehr' ich siegreich wieder aus kühner
Männerschlacht,
Dann grüssen wir so freudig das Nah'n der
stillen Nacht,
Das Lager ist bereitet, uns winkt die süsse
Ruh
Der Hänfling singt Brautlieder, Maria,
bald uns zu.

Will creep about, gloomy and troubled;
your threnody will not waken me.

Thus I had to leave you, fair, sweet
bride.
Though you may call out for me, though
you may weep aloud,
I cannot, alas, think of your bitter suffering,
I cannot, alas, think of your faithful
heart.

No, Norman cannot feel tender, devoted
longing,
When Clan-Alpine bursts like hail and
tempest on the foe;
His bold heart must be then like a drawn
bow,
His foot, Mary, as swift and free as an
arrow.

A time will come when the sun does not
shine,
You will totter towards your Norman, your
fair eyes will weep;
But if I fall in battle, if grim death shrouds
me,
Believe this, Mary: my last sigh shall be for
you.

But if I return victorious from the brave
battle,
How joyfully we shall greet the approach of
the silent night.
The bed is prepared, sweet repose beckons
to us;
Soon, Mary, the linnet will sing us wedding
songs.

The heath this night must be my bed,
The bracken curtain for my head,
My lullaby the warder's tread,
Far, far from love and thee, Mary.

To-morrow eve, more stilly laid,
My couch may be my bloody plaid,
My vesper song, thy wail, sweet maid!
It will not waken me, Mary!

I may not, dare not, fancy now
The grief that clouds thy lovely brow,
I dare not think upon thy vow,
And all it promised me, Mary.

No fond regret must Norman know;
When bursts Clan-Alpine on the foe,
His heart must be like bended bow,
His foot like arrow free, Mary.

A time will come with feeling fraught,
For, if I fall in battle fought,

Thy hapless lover's dying thought
Shall be a thought on thee, Mary.

And if returned from conquered foes,
How blithely will the evening close,
How sweet the linnet sing repose,
To my young bride and me, Mary!

Nur wer die Sehnsucht kennt (Mignons Gesang) | Only He Who Knows Longing (Mignon's Song)

JOHANN WOLFGANG VON GOETHE
from *Wilhelm Meister*

First version: D 310 (1815)
Second version: D 359 (1816)
Third version: D 481 (1816)
Fourth version: D 877 no. 4 (1826)
Fifth version: D 877 no. 1 (1826)

Nur wer die Sehnsucht kennt
Weiß, was ich leide!
Allein und abgetrennt
Von aller Freude,
Seh' ich an's Firmament
Nach jener Seite.
Ach! der mich liebt und kennt
Ist in der Weite.
Es schwindelt mir, es brennt
Mein Eingeweide.
Nur wer die Sehnsucht kennt
Weiß, was ich leide!

Only he who knows longing
Knows what I suffer.
Alone, cut off
From all joy,
I gaze at the firmament
In that direction.
Ah, he who loves and knows me
Is far away.
I feel giddy,
My inmost being is aflame.
Only he who knows longing
Knows what I suffer.

Orest auf Tauris | Orestes on Tauris

JOHANN MAYRHOFER

D 548 (1817)

Ist dies Tauris, wo der Eumeniden
Wut zu stillen Pythia versprach?
Weh! die Schwestern mit den
    Schlangenhaaren
Folgen mir vom Land der Griechen nach.

Is this Tauris, where Pythia promised
To appease the anger of the Eumenides?
Alas, the snake-haired
    sisters
Pursue me from the land of the Greeks.

Rauhes Eiland, kündest keinen Segen:
Nirgends sprosst der Ceres milde Frucht;
Keine Reben blüh'n, der Lüfte Sänger,
Wie die Schiffe, meiden diese Bucht.

Bleak island, you announce no blessing:
Nowhere does Ceres' tender fruit grow;
No vines bloom; the singers of the air,
Like the ships, shun this bay.

Steine fügt die Kunst nicht zu
    Gebäuden,
Zelte spannt des Skythen Armut
    sich;
Unter starren Felsen, rauhen Wäldern
Ist das Leben einsam, schauerlich!

Art does not fashion these stones into
    buildings;
In their poverty the Scythians erect only
    tents.
Amid harsh rocks and wild forests
Life is lonely and frightening.

Und hier soll, so ist ja doch ergangen	'And here,' according to the sacred decree
An den Flehenden der heilige Spruch,	Revealed to the suppliant,
Eine hohe Priesterin Dianens	'A high priestess of Diana
Lösen meinen und der Väter Fluch.	Is to lift the curse on me and my fathers.'

Ossians Lied nach dem Falle Nathos | Ossian's Song after the Death of Nathos

JAMES MACPHERSON (OSSIAN), translated by EDMUND VON HAROLD

D 278 (1815)

»Beugt euch aus euren Wolken nieder, ihr Geister meiner Väter! beugt euch, legt ab das rote Schrecken eures Laufs. Empfangt den fallenden Führer! Er komme aus einem entfernten Land, oder steig aus dem tobenden Meer! Sein Kleid von Nebel sei nah, sein Speer aus einer Wolke gestaltet. Stell ein halb erloschenes Luftbild an seine Seite, in Gestalt des Helden-Schwerts. Und ach sein Gesicht sei lieblich, daß seine Freunde frohlocken in seiner Gegenwart! Beugt euch aus euren Wolken nieder! ihr Geister meiner Väter, beugt euch.«

'Bend forward from your clouds, ghosts of my fathers! bend. Lay by the red terror of your course. Receive the falling chief; whether he comes from a distant land, or rises from the rolling sea. Let his robe of mist be near; his spear that is formed of a cloud. Place an half extinguished meteor by his side, in the form of the hero's sword. And oh! let his countenance be lovely, that his friends may delight in his presence. Bend from your clouds,' I said, 'ghosts of my fathers! bend!'

Pax Vobiscum / Peace be with you

FRANZ VON SCHOBER

D 551 (1817)

»Der Friede sei mit euch!«
Das war dein Abschiedssegen.
Und so vom Kreis der Gläubigen umkniet,
Vom Siegesstrahl der Gottheit angeglüht,
Flogst du dem ew'gen Heimatland entgegen.
Und Friede kam in ihre treuen Herzen,
Und lohnte sie in ihren grössten Schmerzen,
Und stärkte sie in ihrem Martertod.
Ich glaube dich, du grosser Gott!

'Peace be with you!'
That was your parting blessing.
And so, surrounded by the kneeling faithful,
Lit by the rays of the triumphant godhead,
You soared to the eternal homeland.
Peace entered their devoted hearts,
Rewarded them in their greatest sorrow,
And strengthened them in their martyrs' death.
I believe in You, Almighty God!

Pensa, che questo istante / Consider that this Moment

PIETRO METASTASIO

D 76 (1813)

Pensa, che questo istante
Del tuo destin decide,
Ch'oggi rinasce Alcide
Per la futura età.

Consider that this moment
In your destiny will decide
Whether Alcides is today reborn
For future ages.

Pensa che a dulto sei,
Che sei di Giove un figlio,
Che merto e non consiglio
La scelta tua sarà.

Consider that you are an adult,
That you are a son of Jove,
And that your reward
Will depend on your merit, not on advice.

Pflicht und Liebe / Duty and Love

FRIEDRICH WILHELM GOTTER

D 467 (1816)

Du, der ewig um mich trauert,
Nicht allein, nicht unbedauert,
Jüngling, seufzest du;
Wenn vor Schmerz die Seele schauert,
Lüget meine Stirne Ruh.

O youth, who always mourn for me,
You do not sigh
Alone and unpitied;
When your soul is racked with pain
My brow's calm is feigned.

Deines nassen Blickes Flehen
Will ich, darf ich nicht verstehen;
Aber zürne nicht!
Was ich fühle, zu gestehen,
Untersagt mir meine Pflicht.

I will not, should not understand
The entreaty of your moist eyes;
But do not be angry!
What I feel, my duty
Forbids me to confess.

Freund, schweif' aus mit deinen Blicken!
Laß dich die Natur entzücken,
Die dir sonst gelacht!
Ach, sie wird auch mich beglücken,
Wenn sie dich erst glücklich macht.

Friend, avert your eyes!
Take pleasure in nature,
Which has always smiled on you.
Ah, it will make me happy
If only it makes you happy.

Trauter Jüngling, lächle wieder!
Sieh, beim Gruße froher Lieder,
Steigt die Sonn' empor!
Trüber sank sie gestern nieder;
Herrlich geht sie heut' hervor.

Dearest youth, smile once more!
See, the sun rises,
Greeted by joyous songs!
Yesterday it set bedimmed;
Today it emerges in splendour.

Pflügerlied / Ploughman's Song

JOHANN GAUDENZ VON SALIS-SEEWIS

D 392 (1816)

Arbeitsam und wacker,
Pflügen wir den Acker,
Singend auf und ab.
Sorgsam trennen wollen
Wir die lockern Schollen.
Unsrer Saaten Grab.

Hard-working and stout-hearted
We plough the fields,
Singing as we go.
Carefully we separate
The loose clods,
The grave for our seeds.

Auf- und abwärts ziehend
Furchen wir, stets fliehend
Das erreichte Ziel.
Wühl', o Pflugschar, wühle!
Aussen drückt die Schwüle,
Tief im Grund ist's kühl.

Moving up and down
We make the furrows, always turning back
From our achieved goal.
Dig, o ploughshare, dig!
Outside the sultriness is oppressive,
Deep in the earth it is cool.

Neigt den Blick zur Erde,
Lieb und heimlich werde
Uns ihr dunkler Schoss:

Turn your eyes to the earth;
May its dark womb
Become dear and welcoming to us:

Hier ist doch kein Bleiben,
Ausgesät zerstäuben
Ist auch unser Los.

From here there is no resting place;
To be scattered, as the dust,
Is also our own lot.

Phidele / Phidele

MATTHIAS CLAUDIUS

D 500 (1816)

Ich war erst sechzehn Sommer alt,
Unschuldig und nichts weiter,
Und kannte nichts als unsern Wald,
Als Blumen, Gras und Kräuter.

I was only sixteen summers old,
Nothing more than an innocent,
And knew nothing but our woods,
Flowers, grass and herbs.

Da kam ein fremder Jüngling her;
Ich hatt' ihn nicht verschrieben,
Und wußte nicht, wohin noch her;
Der kam und sprach von Lieben.

Then a youthful stranger came along;
I had not bid him come,
And knew not whence he came.
He came and spoke of love.

Er hatte schönes langes Haar
Um seinen Nacken wehen;
Und einen Nacken, als das war,
Hab ich noch nie gesehen.

He had beautiful long hair
That flowed about his neck;
And such a neck as that
I have never seen.

Sein Auge, himmelblau und klar!
Schien freundlich was zu flehen;
So blau und freundlich, als das war,
Hab ich noch kein's gesehen.

His clear, sky-blue eyes
Seemed to plead fondly for something;
Such clear, sky-blue eyes
I have never seen.

Und sein Gesicht, wie Milch und Blut!
Ich hab's nie so gesehen,
Auch was er sagte, war sehr gut,
Nur konnt' ichs nicht verstehen.

And his face, like milk and blood!
I have never seen such a face,
And what he said was also very fine,
Only I could understand none of it.

Er ging mir allenthalben nach,
Und drückte mir die Hände,
Und sagte immer O und Ach,
Und küßte sie behende.

He followed me everywhere,
And pressed my hands,
And kept saying 'oh' and 'alas',
And kissed them quickly.

Ich sah' ihn einmal freundlich an,
Und fragte, was er meinte;
Da fiel der junge schöne Mann
Mir um den Hals und weinte.

One day I looked at him kindly
And asked what he meant;
Then the fair young man
Fell upon my neck and wept.

Das hatte niemand noch getan;
Doch war's mir nicht zuwider
Und meine beiden Augen sahn
In meinen Busen nieder.

No one had ever done that;
But I did not find it unpleasant,
And my two eyes
Looked down at my bosom.

Ich sagt' ihm nicht ein einzig Wort,
Als ob ich's übel nähme,
Kein einzigs, und — er flohe fort;
Wenn er doch wieder käme!

I did not say a single word to him
To indicate that I took it amiss,
Not a single word — and he fled;
If only he would come back again!

Philoktet / Philoctetes

JOHANN MAYRHOFER

D 540 (1817)

Da sitz ich ohne Bogen und starre in den Sand.	I sit here without my bow, staring at the sand.
Was tat ich dir Ulysses, dass du sie mir entwandt?	What did I do to you, Ulysses, that you took from me
Die Waffe, die den Trojern des Todes Bote war,	The weapon that was the harbinger of death to the Trojans,
Die auf der wüsten Insel mir Unterhalt gebar.	That gave me sustenance on this desolate island?
Es rauschen Vogelschwärme mir über'm greisen Haupt;	Flocks of birds sweep over my grey head;
Ich greife nach dem Bogen, umsonst, er ist geraubt!	I reach for my bow: in vain, it has been stolen.
Aus dichtem Busche raschelt der braune Hirsch hervor:	The brown stag rushes from the dense thicket;
Ich strecke leere Arme zur Nemesis empor.	I stretch bare arms up to Nemesis.
Du schlauer König, scheue der Göttin Rächerblick!	Cunning king, beware the vengeful goddess's gaze!
Erbarme dich und stelle den Bogen mir zurück.	Take pity and restore to me my bow.

Pilgerweise / Pilgrim's Song

FRANZ VON SCHOBER

D 789 (1823)

Ich bin ein Waller auf der Erde	I am a pilgrim on this earth
Und gehe still von Haus zu Haus,	And go silently from house to house.
O reicht mit freundlicher Gebärde	O bestow on me the gifts of love
Der Liebe Gaben mir heraus!	With a friendly gesture!
Mit offnen, teilnahmsvollen Blicken,	With open, sympathetic glances,
Mit einem warmen Händedruck	With a warm grasp of the hand
Könnt ihr dies arme Herz erquicken	You can refresh this poor heart,
Und es befrein von langem Druck.	And free it from long oppression.
Doch rechnet nicht, dass ich euch's lohnen,	But do not count on me rewarding you,
Mit Gegendienst vergelten soll:	Or repaying you with service in return;
Ich streue nur mit Blumenkronen,	I shall only strew your thresholds
Mit blauen, eure Schwellen voll.	With wreaths of blue flowers.
Und geb' ein Lied euch noch zur Zither,	And I shall give you a song, to my zither,
Mit Fleiss gesungen und gespielt,	Sung and played with vigour,
Das euch vielleicht nur leichter Flitter,	Which will seem to you, perhaps, like flimsy tinsel,
Ein leicht entbehrlich Gut euch gilt —	Something easily done without.
Mir gilt es viel, ich kann's nicht missen,	To me it means much, I cannot do without it,
Und allen Pilgern ist es wert;	And it is valued by every pilgrim;
Doch freilich ihr, ihr könnt nicht wissen,	But you, of course, cannot know
Was den beseligt, der entbehrt.	What makes him happy who does without.

Vom Überfluss seid ihr erfreuet,
Und findet tausendfach Ersatz;
Ein Tag dem andern angereihet
Vergrössert euren Liebesschatz.

Doch mir, so wie ich weiter strebe
An meinem harten Wanderstab,
Reisst in des Glückes Lustgewebe
Ein Faden nach dem andern ab.

Drum kann ich nur von Gaben leben,
Von Augenblick zu Augenblick,
O wollet vorwurfslos sie geben,
Zu eurer Lust, zu meinem Glück.

Ich bin ein Waller auf der Erde
Und gehe still von Haus zu Haus,
O reicht mit freundlicher Gebärde
Der Liebe Gaben mir heraus!

You rejoice in abundance,
Which can be replenished a thousandfold;
Each successive day
Increases the treasury of your love.

But for me, as I strive onwards
With my hardy pilgrim's staff,
One thread after another is torn
In the tissue of my happiness.

So I can only live on gifts,
From moment to moment.
O, give them without reproach,
For your pleasure, for my happiness.

I am a pilgrim on this earth
And go silently from house to house.
O bestow on me the gifts of love
With a friendly gesture!

Prometheus / *Prometheus*

JOHANN WOLFGANG VON GOETHE

D 674 (1819)

Bedecke deinen Himmel, Zeus,
Mit Wolkendunst
Und übe, dem Knaben gleich,
Der Disteln köpft,
An Eichen dich und Bergeshöhn;
Musst mir meine Erde
Doch lassen stehn
Und meine Hütte, die du nicht gebaut,
Und meinen Herd,
Um dessen Glut
Du mich beneidest.

Ich kenne nichts Ärmeres
Unter der Sonn', als euch, Götter!
Ihr nähret kümmerlich
Von Opfersteuern
Und Gebetshauch
Euere Majestät
Und darbtet, wären
Nicht Kinder und Bettler
Hoffnungsvolle Toren.

Da ich ein Kind war,
Nicht wusste, wo aus noch ein,
Kehrt' ich mein verirrtes Auge
Zur Sonne, als wenn drüber wär'
Ein Ohr, zu hören meine Klage,
Ein Herz wie meins,
Sich des Bedrängten zu erbarmen.

Wer half mir
Wider der Titanen
    Übermut?
Wer rettete vom Tode mich,

Cover your heaven, Zeus,
With a gauze of cloud.
And, like a boy beheading thistles,
Practise on oak-trees
And mountain peaks;
But you will have to leave
My world standing,
And my hut, which you did not build,
And my fireside,
Whose glow
You envy me.

I know nothing more wretched
Beneath the sun than you gods!
Meagrely you nourish
Your majesty
With offerings
And the breath of prayer,
And would starve,
If children and beggars were not
Ever-hopeful fools.

When I was a child
And did not know a thing,
I turned my perplexed gaze
To the sun, as if beyond it
There were an ear to listen to my lament
And a heart like mine
To pity the distressed.

Who helped me
Against the overweening pride of the
    Titans?
Who saved me from death

Von Sklaverei?
Hast du nicht alles selbst vollendet
Heilig glühend Herz?
Und glühtest jung und gut,
Betrogen,
    Rettungsdank
Dem Schlafenden da droben?

Ich dich ehren? Wofür?
Hast du die Schmerzen gelindert
Je des Beladenen?
Hast du die Tränen gestillet
Je des Geängsteten?
Hat nicht mich zum Manne geschmiedet
Die allmächtige Zeit
Und das ewige Schicksal,
Meine Herrn und deine?

Wähntest du etwa,
Ich sollte das Leben hassen,
In Wüsten fliehen,
Weil nicht alle
Blütenträume reiften?

Hier sitz' ich, forme Menschen
Nach meinem Bilde,
Ein Geschlecht, das mir gleich sei,
Zu leiden, zu weinen,
Zu geniessen und zu freuen sich
Und dein nicht zu achten,
Wie ich!

And from slavery?
Did you not accomplish it all yourself,
Sacred, ardent heart?
And, deceived in your youthful goodness,
Were you not fired with gratitude for your
    deliverance
To the sleeper up above?

I honour you? What for?
Have you ever eased the suffering
Of him who is oppressed?
Have you ever dried the tears
Of him who is troubled?
Did not almighty Time
And eternal Fate,
My masters and yours,
Forge me into a man?

Did you perhaps imagine
That I would hate life,
Flee into the wilderness,
Because not all
My blossoming dreams bore fruit?

Here I sit, forming men
In my own image,
A race that shall be like me,
That shall suffer, weep,
Enjoy and rejoice,
And ignore you,
As I do!

Punschlied (Im Norden zu singen)   On Drinking Punch (To be Sung in the North)

FRIEDRICH VON SCHILLER

D 253 (1815)

Auf der Berge freien Höhen,
In der Mittagssonne Schein,
An des warmen Strahles Kräften
Zeugt Natur den goldnen Wein.

On the free heights of the mountains,
In the light of the midday sun,
And by the power of its warm beams,
Nature produces the golden vine.

Funkelnd wie ein Sohn der Sonne,
Wie des Lichtes Feuerquell,
Springt er perlend aus der Tonne,
Purpurn und kristallenhell.

Sparkling like a child of the sun,
Like the fiery source of light,
It spurts, bubbling, from the barrel,
Crimson and crystal-bright.

Und erfreuet alle Sinnen,
Und in jede bange Brust
Gießt er ein balsamisch Hoffen
Und des Lebens neue Lust.

It delights all the senses,
And pours into every troubled breast
Soothing hope
And renewed joy in life.

Quell'innocente figlio / The Innocent Son

PIETRO METASTASIO

D 17 no. 1 (1812?)

Quell'innocente figlio,
Dono del Ciel si raro,
Quel figlio a te si caro
Quello vuol Dio da te.
Vuol che rimanga esangue
Sotto al paterno ciglio,
Vuol che ne sparga il sangue
Chi vita già gli diè.

This innocent son,
Such a rare gift from heaven,
This son, so dear to you,
God demands from you.
He demands that he bleeds
Before his father's eyes;
He demands that he who once gave him life
Should shed his blood.

Raste Krieger! Krieg ist aus / Rest, Warrior! Your War is over

SIR WALTER SCOTT

see Ellens Gesang I

Rastlose Liebe / Restless Love

JOHANN WOLFGANG VON GOETHE

D 222 (1815)

Dem Schnee, dem Regen,
Dem Wind entgegen,
Im Dampf der Klüfte,
Durch Nebeldüfte,
Immer zu! Immer zu!
Ohne Rast und Ruh!

Into the snow, the rain
And the wind,
Through steamy ravines,
Through mists,
Onwards, ever onwards!
Without respite!

Lieber durch Leiden
Wollt ich mich schlagen,
Als so viel Freuden
Des Lebens ertragen.

I would sooner fight my way
Through suffering,
Than endure so much
Of life's joy.

Alle das Neigen
Von Herzen zu Herzen,
Ach, wie so eigen
Schaffet das Schmerzen!

This affection
Of one heart for another,
Ah, how strangely
It creates pain!

Wie soll ich fliehen?
Wälderwärts ziehen?
Alles vergebens!
Krone des Lebens,
Glück ohne Ruh,
Liebe, bist du!

How shall I flee?
Into the forest?
It is all in vain!
Crown of life,
Happiness without peace —
This, o Love, is you.

Ritter Toggenburg / The Knight of Toggenburg

FRIEDRICH VON SCHILLER

D 397 (1816)

»Ritter, treue Schwesterliebe
Widmet euch dies Herz,

'Knight, this heart dedicates to you
True sisterly love;

Fordert keine andre Liebe,
Denn es macht mir Schmerz.
Ruhig mag ich euch erscheinen,
Ruhig gehen sehn;
Eurer Augen stilles Weinen
Kann ich nicht verstehn.»

Und er hört's mit stummem Harme,
Reißt sich blutend los,
Preßt sie heftig in die Arme,
Schwingt sich auf sein Roß,
Schickt zu seinen Mannen allen
In dem Lande Schweiz;
Nach dem heil'gen Grab sie
    wallen,
Auf der Brust das Kreuz.

Große Taten dort geschehen
Durch der Helden Arm,
Ihres Helmes Büsche wehen
In der Feinde Schwarm,
Und des Toggenburgers Name
Schreckt den Muselmann;
Doch das Herz von seinem Grame
Nicht genesen kann.

Und ein Jahr hat er's getragen,
Trägt's nicht länger mehr,
Ruhe kann er nicht erjagen
Und verläßt das Heer,
Sieht ein Schiff an Joppes Strande,
Das die Segel bläht,
Schiffet heim zum teuren Lande,
Wo ihr Atem weht.

Und an ihres Schlosses Pforte
Klopft der Pilger an,
Ach! und mit dem Donnerworte
Wird sie aufgetan:
»Die ihr suchet, trägt den Schleier,
Ist des Himmels Braut,
Gestern war des Tages Feier,
Der sie Gott getraut.«

Da verlässet er auf immer
Seiner Väter Schloß,
Seine Waffen sieht er nimmer,
Noch sein treues Roß,
Von der Toggenburg hernieder
Steigt er unbekannt,
Denn es deckt die edeln Glieder
Härenes Gewand.

Und erbaut ich eine Hütte
Jener Gegend nah,
Wo das Kloster aus der Mitte
Düstrer Linden sah;
Harrend von des Morgens Lichte
Bis zu Abends Schein,
Stille Hoffnung im Gesichte,
Saß er da allein.

Demand no other love,
For that grieves me.
Calmly I should like to see you appear
And leave again;
I cannot understand
The silent tears in your eyes.'

And he listened with silent sorrow,
Tore himself away in anguish,
Pressed her violently in his arms,
Jumped on his horse
And sent word to all his men
In the country of Switzerland;
They made a pilgrimage to the holy
    sepulchre,
The cross on their breasts.

Great deeds were accomplished there
By the heroes' might;
The plumes on their helmets
Fluttered amid the teeming foe,
And the name of Toggenburg
Terrified the Mussulman;
But his heart could not be cured
Of its grief.

When he had endured it for one year
He could endure it no longer;
He could gain no peace,
And left his army.
He saw a ship on the shore at Joppa,
Its sails billowing,
And sailed home to the beloved land
Where she breathed.

And the pilgrim knocked
At the gate of her castle;
Alas, it was opened
With these shattering words:
'She whom you seek wears the veil;
She is a bride of heaven.
Yesterday was the day of the ceremony
That wedded her to God.'

Thereupon he left
The castle of his fathers for ever;
He never again saw his weapons
Or his trusty steed.
He descended from Toggenburg
Unrecognized,
For a hair shirt
Covered his noble limbs.

And he built himself a hut
Near to the place
Where the convent looked out
From amid sombre linden-trees;
Waiting from the light of dawn
To the glow of evening,
With silent hope on his face,
He sat there alone.

Blickte nach dem Kloster drüben,	He gazed across at the convent,
Blickte stundenlang	Gazed for hours on end
Nach dem Fenster seiner Lieben,	At his beloved's window,
Bis das Fenster klang,	Until the window rattled,
Bis die Liebliche sich zeigte,	Until his sweetheart appeared,
Bis das teure Bild	Until her dear form
Sich ins Tal herunter neigte,	Bent down towards the valley,
Ruhig, engelmild.	Tranquil and as gentle as an angel.
Und dann legt' er froh sich nieder,	And then he lay down happily
Schlief getröstet ein,	And fell asleep, comforted,
Still sich freuend, wenn es wieder	Silently looking forward to when
Morgen würde sein.	It would be morning again.
Und so saß er viele Tage,	Thus he sat for many days,
Saß viel Jahre lang,	For many long years,
Harrend ohne Schmerz und Klage	Waiting without sorrow or complaint
Bis das Fenster klang.	Until the window rattled.
Bis die Liebliche sich zeigte,	Until his sweetheart appeared,
Bis das teure Bild	Until the dear form
Sich ins Tal herunter neigte,	Bent down towards the valley,
Ruhig, engelmild,	Tranquil and as gentle as an angel.
Und so saß er, eine Leiche,	And thus he sat there one morning,
Eines Morgens da,	A corpse,
Nach dem Fenster noch das bleiche	His pale, silent face
Stille Antlitz sah.	Still gazing at the window.

Romanze / Romance

FRIEDRICH VON MATTHISSON

D 114 (1814)

Ein Fräulein klagt' im finstern Turm,	A maiden wept in a dark tower
Am Seegestad erbaut.	Built on the sea shore.
Es rauscht' und heulte Wog und Sturm	Waves and storm rushed and howled,
In ihres Jammers Laut.	Through her cries of grief.
Rosalie von Montanvert	Rosalia of Montanvert
Hiess manchem Troubadour	Was, for many a troubadour
Und einem ganzen Ritterheer	And a whole host of knights,
Die Krone der Natur.	The crown of nature.
Doch ehe noch ihr Herz die Macht	But before her heart
Der süssen Minn' empfand,	Had felt the power of sweet love,
Erlag der Vater in der Schlacht	Her father died in battle
Am Sarazenenstrand.	On the Saracen shore.
Der Ohm, ein Ritter Manfry, ward	Her uncle, a knight named Manfry,
Zum Schirmvogt ihr bestellt;	Was appointed her guardian;
Dem lacht' ins Herz, wie Felsen hart,	In his rock-hard heart he rejoiced
Des Fräuleins Gut und Geld.	At the maiden's gold and wealth.
Bald überall im Lande ging	Soon the sorrowful news
Die Trauerkund' umher:	Spread throughout the land:
»Des Todes kalte Nacht umfing	'The cold night of death has enveloped
Die Rose Montanvert.«	Rose Montanvert.'

Ein schwarzes Totenfähnlein wallt'	A black flag of death flew
Hoch auf des Fräuleins Burg;	High over the maiden's castle;
Die dumpfe Leichenglocke schallt	The muffled death-knell sounded
Drei Tag' und Nächt' hindurch.	For three days and three nights.

Auf ewig hin, auf ewig tot,	Gone for ever, dead for ever,
O Rose Montanvert!	O Rose Montanvert,
Nun milderst du der Witwe	No longer will you soothe the widow's
Not,	distress,
Der Waise Schmerz nicht mehr!	The orphan's sorrow.

So klagt einmütig alt und jung,	Thus, from dawn till dusk,
Den Blick von Träumen schwer,	Their eyes heavy with tears,
Vom Frührot bis zur Dämmerung,	Young and old with one voice
Die Rose Montanvert.	Mourned Rose Montanvert.

Der Ohm in einem Turm sie barg,	Her uncle hid her in a tower,
Erfüllt mit Moderduft!	Filled with the stench of decay!
Drauf senkte man den leeren Sarg	Then the empty coffin was lowered
Wohl in der Väter Gruft.	Into her ancestors' vault.

Das Fräulein horchte still und bang	In fear and silence the maiden heard
Der Priester Litanei'n,	The priests' litanies,
Trüb in des Kerkers Gitter drang	The red gleam of the torches
Der Fackeln roter Schein.	Penetrated dimly through the prison bars.

Sie ahnte schaudernd ihr Geschick;	With foreboding she guessed her fate;
Ihr ward so dumpf, ihr ward so schwer,	Her senses grew dull and heavy,
In Todesnacht entstarb ihr Blick;	Her eyes faded in the darkness of death,
Sie sank und war nicht mehr.	She sank down, and was no more.

Des Turms Ruinen an der See	The ruins of the tower by the sea
Sind heute noch zu schaun;	Are still to be seen today;
Den Wandrer fasst in ihrer Näh'	As he draws near
Ein wundersames Graun.	The traveller is gripped by a strange dread.

Auch mancher Hirt verkündet euch,	And many a shepherd will tell you
Dass er bei Nacht allda	How, at night,
Oft, einer Silberwolke gleich,	He has often seen the maiden
Das Fräulein schweben sah.	Hovering there like a silver cloud.

Romanze des Richard Löwenherz / Romance of Richard the Lionheart

SIR WALTER SCOTT, translated by KARL LUDWIG MILLER

D907 (1826?)
A literal rendering of Miller's translation is given here. Scott's original poem, entitled 'The Crusader's Return', is printed below in italics.

Grosse Taten tat der Ritter	The knight achieved great deeds
Fern im heil'gen Lande viel;	Far away in the holy land;
Und das Kreuz auf seiner Schulter	The cross on his shoulder
Bleicht' im rauhen Schlachtgewühl;	Had dimmed in the fierce tumult of battle;
Manche Narb' auf seinem Schilde	Many a dint on his shield
Trug er aus dem Kampfgefilde;	He bore from the battlefield;
An der Dame Fenster dicht,	Thus, close by his lady's window,
Sang er so im Mondenlicht:	He sang in the moonlight:

»Heil der Schönen! aus der Ferne
Ist der Ritter heimgekehrt,
Doch nichts durft' er mit sich nehmen,
Als sein treues Ross und Schwert.
Seine Lanze, seine Sporen
Sind allein ihm unverloren,
Dies ist all sein irdisch Glück,
Dies und Theklas Liebesblick.

»Heil der Schönen! was der Ritter
   tat,
Verdankt' er ihrer Gunst,
Darum soll ihr Lob verkünden
Stets des Sängers süsse Kunst.
»Seht, da ist sie«, wird es heissen,
Wenn sie ihre Schöne preisen,
»Deren Augen Himmelsglanz
Gab bei Askalon den Kranz.«

»Schaut ihr Lächeln, eh'rne Männer
Streckt es leblos in den Staub,
Und Iconium, ob sein Sultan
Mutig stritt, ward ihm zum Raub.
Diese Locken, wie sie golden
Schwimmen um die Brust der Holden,
Legten manchem Muselmann
Fesseln unzerreissbar an.

»Heil der Schönen, dir gehöret,
Holde, was dein Ritter tat,
Darum öffne ihm die Pforte,
Nachtwind streift, die Stunde
   naht;
Dort in Syriens heissen Zonen,
Musst' er leicht des Nords entwohnen,
Lieb' ersticke nun die Scham,
Weil von ihm der Ruhm dir kam.«

'Joy to the fair! Your knight
Has returned from distant lands,
But he could bring nothing with him
Save his trusty steed and sword;
His lance, his spurs
Are all he has;
This is all his earthly wealth,
This — and Tekla's loving gaze.

'Joy to the fair! What your knight has
   achieved,
He owes to your favour;
Therefore the minstrel's sweet art
Shall always be to sing her praises.
"See, it is she," they will proclaim
When they extol the fair beauty,
"Whose celestial eyes
Won the garland at Askalon."

'Behold her smile — it laid men of iron
Lifeless in the dust,
And Iconium, though his Sultan
Fought bravely, became its victim.
These golden locks,
Flowing around the fair maid's breast,
Cast many a Moslem
In unbreakable chains.

'Joy to the fair! To you, my beloved,
Belongs all that your knight has achieved;
Then open the gate to him,
The night wind blows, the hour
   approaches;
There, in Syria's torrid clime,
He became a stranger to the cold north.
Let love stifle modesty,
Since your glory came from him.'

High deeds achieved of knightly fame,
From Palestine the champion came;
The cross upon his shoulders borne,
Battle and blast had dimm'd and torn.
Each dint upon his batter'd shield
Was token of a foughten field;
And thus, beneath his lady's bower,
He sung, as fell the twilight-hour —

Joy to the fair! — thy knight behold,
Return'd from yonder land of gold;
No wealth he brings, nor wealth can need,
Save his good arms and battle-steed;
His spurs, to dash against a foe,
His lance and sword to lay him low;
Such all the trophies of his toil,
Such — and the hope of Tekla's smile!

Joy to the fair! whose constant knight
Her favour fired to feats of might;
Unnoted shall she not remain,
Where meet the bright and noble train,
Minstrel shall sing and herald tell —

"Mark yonder maid of beauty well,
'Tis she for whose bright eyes was won
The listed field of Askalon!"

'Note well her smile! — it edged the blade
Which fifty wives to widows made,
When, vain his strength and Mahound's spell,
Iconium's turban'd Soldan fell.
Seest thou her locks, whose sunny glow
Half shows, half shades, her neck of snow?
Twines not of them one golden thread,
But for its sake a Paynim bled.'

'Joy to the fair! — my name unknown,
Each deed, and all its praise thine own;
Then, oh, unbar this churlish gate,
The night dew falls, the hour is late.
Inured to Syria's glowing breath,
I feel the north breeze chill as death;
Let grateful love quell maiden shame,
And grant him bliss who brings thee fame.'

Rückweg / The Way Back

JOHANN MAYRHOFER

D 476 (1816)

Zum Donaustrom, zur Kaiserstadt
Geh' ich in Bangigkeit:
Denn was das Leben Schönes hat,
Entweichet weit und weit.

To the river Danube, to the imperial city
I go with apprehension;
For all that is beautiful in life
Recedes further and further behind me.

Die Berge schwinden allgemach,
Mit ihnen Wald und Fluß;
Der Kühe Glocken läuten nach,
Und Hütten nicken Gruß.

The mountains gradually disappear,
And with them forests and rivers;
The tinkling of cowbells lingers in the air,
And the huts nod their greeting.

Was starrt dein Auge tränenfeucht
Hinaus in blaue Fern'?
Ach, dorten weilt ich, unerreicht,
Frei unter Freien gern!

Why do your eyes, moist with tears,
Stare out into the blue distance?
Ah, there I dwelt happily, in seclusion,
A free man among free men.

Wo Liebe noch und Treue gilt,
Da öffnet sich das Herz;
Die Frucht an ihren Strahlen schwillt,
Und strebet himmelwärts.

Where love and faith are still cherished
The heart will open;
The fruit will ripen in their light,
And aspire towards heaven.

Sängers Morgenlied / The Minstrel's Morning Song

THEODOR KÖRNER

First version: D 163 (1815)
Second version: D 165 (1815)

Süßes Licht! Aus goldnen Pforten
Brichst du siegend durch die Nacht.
Schöner Tag! Du bist erwacht.

Sweet light! Through golden portals
You break victoriously through the night.
Fairest day! You are awakened.

Mit geheimnisvollen Worten,	With mysterious words,
In melodischen Akkorden	And melodious strains
Grüß' ich deine Rosenpracht!	I greet your roseate splendour!
Ach! der Liebe sanftes Wehen	Ah, the soft breath of love
Schwellt mir das bewegte Herz,	Swells my full heart,
Sanft, wie ein geliebter Schmerz.	As softly as a beloved pain.
Dürft' ich nur auf goldnen	If only I could wander on those golden
Höhen	heights
Mich im Morgenduft ergehen!	In the fragrant morning!
Sehnsucht zieht mich himmelwärts.	A yearning draws me heavenwards.

Schäfers Klagelied / Shepherd's Lament

JOHANN WOLFGANG VON GOETHE

D 121 (1814)

Da droben auf jenem Berge,	On yonder hill
Da steh ich tausendmal,	I have stood a thousand times,
An meinem Stabe hingebogen,	Leaning on my staff
Und schaue hinab in das Tal.	And looking down into the valley.
Dann folg ich der weidenden Herde,	I have followed the grazing flocks,
Mein Hündchen bewahret mir sie.	Watched over by my dog,
Ich bin herunter gekommen	I have come down here
Und weiss doch selber nicht wie.	And do not know how.
Da stehet von schönen Blumen	The whole meadow is so full
Die ganze Wiese so voll.	Of lovely flowers;
Ich breche sie, ohne zu wissen,	I pluck them, without knowing
Wem ich sie geben soll.	To whom I shall give them.
Und Regen, Sturm und Gewitter	From rain, storm and tempest
Verpass ich unter dem Baum.	I shelter under a tree.
Die Türe dort bleibet verschlossen;	The door there remains locked;
Doch alles ist leider ein Traum.	For, alas, it is all a dream.
Es stehet ein Regenbogen	There is a rainbow
Wohl über jenem Haus!	Above that house!
Sie aber ist fortgezogen,	But she has moved away,
Und weit in das Land hinaus.	To distant regions.
Hinaus in das Land und weiter,	To distant regions and beyond,
Vielleicht gar über die See.	Perhaps even over the sea.
Vorüber, ihr Schafe, nur vorüber!	Move on, sheep, move on!
Dem Schäfer ist gar so weh.	Your shepherd is so wretched.

Schatzgräbers Begehr / The Treasure-Hunter's Desire

FRANZ VON SCHOBER

D 761 (1822)

In tiefster Erde ruht ein alt Gesetz,	Deep in the earth sleeps an old law.
Dem treibt's mich rastlos immer	I feel a restless, ceaseless urge to seek it
nachzuspüren;	out,
Und grabend kann ich Andres nicht	And as I dig I can accomplish nothing
vollführen.	else.

Wohl spannt auch mir die Welt ihr goldnes Netz,	Let the world spread its golden net to lure me, too;
Wohl tönt auch mir der Klugheit seicht Geschwätz: »Du wirst die Müh und Zeit umsonst verlieren!« Das soll mich nicht in meiner Arbeit irren, Ich grabe glühend fort, so nun, wie stets.	Let wisdom's shallow prattle ring in my ears: 'You are wasting your time and efforts to no avail!' That shall not turn me aside from my labour; I go on digging ardently, now as ever.
Und soll mich nie des Findens Wonne laben, Sollt' ich mein Grab mit dieser Hoffnung graben, Ich steige gern hinab, gestillt ist dann mein Sehnen.	And even if the joy of discovery never rewards me, If I am digging my own grave with this hope, Yet will I gladly climb down, for then my longing will be stilled.
Drum lasset Ruhe mir in meinem Streben, Ein Grab mag man wohl jedem gerne geben, Wollt ihr es denn nicht mir, ihr Lieben, gönnen?	So leave me in peace with my endeavour. Surely a grave is gladly given to every man; Will you then not grant me one, friends?

Schiffers Scheidelied / The Sailor's Song of Farewell

FRANZ VON SCHOBER

D910 (1827)

Die Wogen am Gestade schwellen, Es klatscht der Wind das Segeltuch Und murmelt in den weissen Wellen, Ich höre seinen wilden Spruch. Es ruft mich fort, es winkt der Kahn, Vor Ungeduld schaukelnd, auf weite Bahn.	The waves surge on the shore, The wind beats against the canvas And murmurs amid the white waves; I hear its wild voice. It calls me away, and the boat, Rocking impatiently, bids me embark on a distant course.
Dort streckt sie sich in öder Ferne, Du kannst nicht mit, siehst du, mein Kind; Wie leicht versinken meine Sterne, Wie leicht erwächst zum Sturm der Wind, Dann droht in tausend Gestalten der Tod, Wie trotzt' ich ihm, wüsst' ich dich in Not?	That course stretches far across the empty wastes; You cannot come with me, my child, do you not see? How easily my stars may sink, How easily the wind may grow to a tempest; Then death will threaten in a thousand forms. How could I defy it if I knew you were in peril?
O löse deiner Arme Schlinge Und löse auch von mir dein Herz! Weiss ich es denn, ob ich's vollbringe Und siegreich kehre heimatwärts? Die Welle, die jetzt so lockend singt, Vielleicht ist's dieselbe, die mich verschlingt.	O loose your arms' embrace, And free your heart of me. How do I know if I shall triumph, And return home victorious? The very wave that now sings so enticingly May be the one that engulfs me.

Noch ist's in deine Hand gegeben,
Noch gingst du nichts unlösbar ein,
O trenne schnell dein junges Leben
Von meinem ungewissen Sein,
O wolle, o wolle, bevor du
  mußt,
Entsagung ist leichter als Verlust!

It still lies in your hands;
You have still not embarked irrevocably.
O sever your young life quickly
From my uncertain existence.
Do it of your own free will, before you have
  to;
Renunciation is easier than loss.

O laß mich im Bewußtsein steuern,
Daß ich allein auf Erden bin,
Dann beugt sich vor dem Ungeheuern,
Vorm Unerhörten nicht mein Sinn.
Ich treibe mit dem Entsetzen Spiel
Und stehe plötzlich vielleicht am
  Ziel.

Let me navigate in the knowledge
That I am alone on this earth,
Then my mind will not flinch
Before terrors, before the unknown.
I shall sport with horrors,
And shall perhaps stand suddenly at my
  goal.

Denn hoch auf meiner Maste Spitzen
Wird stets dein Bild begeisternd stehn,
Und, angeflammet von den Blitzen,
Mit seinem Glanz den Mut erhöhn;
Und der Winde Heulen auch noch so bang,
Übertäubet nicht deiner Stimme
  Klang.

For your image will always be
High on my mast, inspiring me,
And, illuminated by lightning,
Will raise my spirits with its radiance.
And however fearfully the winds howl,
They will never drown the sound of your
  voice.

Und kann ich dich nur sehn und hören,
Dann hat's mit mir noch keine Not,
Das Leben will ich nicht entbehren,
Und kämpfen werd ich mit dem Tod.
Wie würde mir eine Welt zur
  Last,
Die Engel so schön, wie dich umfaßt?

And if I can but see and hear you,
I have no other needs;
I shall not be without life,
And shall fight with death.
How could a world ever become a burden to
  me
Which contains angels as fair as you?

Auch du sollst nicht mein Bild
  zerschlagen,
Mit Freundschaftstränen weih es ein,
Es soll in Schmerz- und
  Freudetagen
Dein Trost und dein Vertrauter sein.
Ja bleibe, wenn mich auch alles verließ,
Mein Freund im heimischen
  Paradies.

You, too, must not destroy my
  image;
Consecrate it with tears of friendship!
May it be your comfort and close
  companion
In times of sorrow and joy.
If all else has deserted me,
You shall remain my friend in this paradise
  of home.

Und spült dann auch die falsche Welle
Mich tot zurück zum
  Blumenstrand,
So weiß ich doch an lieber Stelle
Noch eine, eine treue Hand,
Der weder Verachtung noch Schmerz es
  wehrt,
Daß sie meinen Resten ein Grab beschert.

And if a treacherous wave should then
Wash my dead body back upon the flowery
  shore,
Then I shall know that at the beloved spot
There will still be one hand
Which neither disdain nor sorrow will
  prevent
From granting my remains a grave.

Schlaflied / Lullaby

JOHANN MAYRHOFER

D 527 (1817)

Es mahnt der Wald, es ruft der Strom:
»Du liebes Bübchen, zu uns komm!«
Der Knabe kommt, und staunt, und weilt,
Und ist von jedem Schmerz geheilt.

The woods exhort, the river cries out:
'Sweet boy, come to us!'
The boy approaches, marvels and tarries,
And is healed of all pain.

Aus Büschen flötet Wachtelschlag,	The quail's song echoes from the bushes,
Mit irren Farben spielt der	The day makes play with shimmering
Tag;	colours;
Auf Blümchen rot, auf Blümchen blau	On flowers red and blue
Erglänzt des Himmels feuchter Tau.	The moist dew of heaven glistens.

Ins frische Gras legt er sich hin,
Lässt über sich die Wolken ziehn,
An seine Mutter angeschmiegt,
Hat ihn der Traumgott eingewiegt.

He lies down in the cool grass
And lets the clouds drift above him;
Nestling close to his mother,
He is lulled to sleep by the god of dreams.

Schwanengesang / Swan Song

LUDWIG KOSEGARTEN

D318 (1815)

Endlich steh'n die Pforten offen,
Endlich winkt das kühle Grab,
Und nach langem Fürchten, Hoffen,
Neigt sich mir die Nacht hinab.
Durchgewacht sind nun die Tage
Meines Lebens, süsse Ruh'
Drückt nach ausgeweinter Klage
Mir die müden Wimpern zu.

At last the gates are open,
At last the cool grave beckons,
And after long fears and hopes
Night descends over me.
I have watched through the days of my life;
After weeping in lamentation, sweet peace
Closes my weary
eyelids.

Ewig wird die Nacht nicht dauern,
Ewig dieser Schlummer nicht.
Hinter jenen Gräberschauern
Dämmert unauslöschlich Licht.
Aber bis das Licht mir funkle,
Bis ein schön'rer Tag mir lacht,
Sink' ich ruhig in die dunkle,
Stille, kühle Schlummernacht.

The night will not last for ever,
Nor will this sleep.
Beyond the terror of the grave
An eternal light dawns.
But until that light shines for me,
Until a fairer day smiles upon me,
I will sink peacefully
Into the cool, silent night of sleep.

Schwanengesang / Swan Song

1–7 LUDWIG RELLSTAB
8–13 HEINRICH HEINE
14 JOHANN GABRIEL SEIDL

D957 (1827–8)

1 *Liebesbotschaft*
Rauschendes Bächlein, so silbern und hell,
Eilst zur Geliebten so munter und
schnell?
Ach, trautes Bächlein, mein Bote sei du;
Bringe die Grüße des Fernen ihr zu.

1 *Love's Message*
Murmuring brook, so silver and bright,
Do you hasten, so lively and swift, to my
beloved?
Ah, sweet brook, be my messenger;
Bring her greetings from her distant lover.

All ihre Blumen im Garten gepflegt,
Die sie so lieblich am Busen
trägt,
Und ihre Rosen in purpurner Glut,
Bächlein, erquicke mit kühlender
Flut.

All the flowers, tended in her garden,
Which she wears so charmingly on her
breast,
And her roses with their crimson glow:
Refresh them, brooklet, with your cooling
waters.

Wenn sie am Ufer, in Träume versenkt,
Meiner gedenkend, das Köpfchen hängt,
Tröste die Süße mit freundlichem
　Blick,
Denn der Geliebte kehrt bald zurück.

Neigt sich die Sonne mit rötlichem
　Schein,
Wiege das Liebchen in Schlummer ein.
Rausche sie murmelnd in süße
　Ruh,
Flüstre ihr Träume der Liebe zu.

When on your banks she inclines her head,
Lost in dreams, thinking of me,
Comfort my sweetheart with a kindly
　glance,
For her beloved will soon return.

When the sun sinks in a red
　flush,
Lull my sweetheart to sleep.
With your soft murmurings bring her sweet
　repose,
And whisper dreams of love.

2 Kriegers Ahnung

In tiefer Ruh liegt um mich her
Der Waffenbrüder Kreis;
Mir ist das Herz so bang und schwer,
Von Sehnsucht mir so heiß.

Wie hab' ich oft so süß geruht
An ihrem Busen warm!
Wie freundlich schien des Herdes Glut,
Lag sie in meinem Arm!

Hier, wo der Flamme düstrer
　Schein
Ach! nur auf Waffen spielt,
Hier fühlt die Brust sich ganz allein,
Der Wehmut Träne quillt.

Herz! Daß der Trost Dich nicht verläßt!
Es ruft noch manche Schlacht —
Bald ruh' ich wohl und schlafe fest,
Herzliebste — Gute Nacht!

2 Warrior's Foreboding

In deep repose my comrades-in arms
Lie in a circle around me;
My heart is so anxious and heavy,
So ardent with longing.

How often I have dreamt sweetly
Upon her warm breast!
How cheerful the fireside glow seemed
When she lay in my arms.

Here, where the sombre glimmer of the
　flames,
Alas, plays only on weapons,
Here the heart feels utterly alone;
A tear of sadness wells up.

Heart, may comfort not forsake you;
Many a battle still calls.
Soon I shall rest well and sleep deeply.
Beloved, goodnight!

3 Frühlingssehnsucht

Säuselnde Lüfte wehend so mild,
Blumiger Düfte atmend erfüllt!
Wie haucht ihr mich wonnig begrüßend
　an!
Wie habt ihr dem pochenden Herzen
　getan?
Es möchte euch folgen auf luftiger Bahn,
Wohin? Wohin?

Bächlein, so munter rauschend zumal,
Wollen hinunter silbern ins Tal.
Die schwebende Welle, dort eilt sie dahin!
Tief spiegeln sich Fluren und Himmel
　darin.
Was ziehst du mich, sehnend verlangender
　Sinn,
Hinab? Hinab?

Grüßender Sonne spielendes Gold,
Hoffende Wonne bringest du hold,
Wie labt mich dein selig begrüßendes
　Bild!
Es lächelt am tiefblauen Himmel so mild
Und hat mir das Auge mit Tränen gefüllt,
Warum? Warum?

3 Spring Longing

Whispering breezes, blowing so gently,
Exuding the fragrance of flowers;
How blissful to me is your welcoming
　breath!
What have you done to my beating
　heart?
It yearns to follow you on your airy path.
Where to?

Silver brooklets, babbling so merrily,
Seek the valley below.
Their ripples glide swiftly by!
The fields and the sky are deeply mirrored
　there.
Why yearning, craving senses, do you draw
　me
Downwards?

Sparkling gold of the welcoming sun,
You bring the fair joy of hope.
How your happy, welcoming countenance
　refreshes me!
It smiles so benignly in the deep-blue sky,
And yet has filled my eyes with tears.
Why?

Grünend umkränzet Wälder und Höh.
Schimmernd erglänzet Blütenschnee.
So dränget sich alles zum bräutlichen
    Licht;
Es schwellen die Keime, die Knospe
    bricht;
Sie haben gefunden, was ihnen gebricht:
Und du? Und du?

Rastloses Sehnen! Wünschendes Herz,
Immer nur Tränen, Klage und
    Schmerz?
Auch ich bin mir schwellender Triebe
    bewußt!
Wer stillet mir endlich die drängende Lust?
Nur du befreist den Lenz in der Brust,
Nur du! Nur du!

4 *Ständchen*
Leise flehen meine Lieder
Durch die Nacht zu Dir;
In den stillen Hain hernieder,
Liebchen, komm' zu mir!

Flüsternd schlanke Wipfel rauschen
In des Mondes Licht;
Des Verräters feindlich Lauschen
Fürchte, Holde, nicht.

Hörst die Nachtigallen schlagen?
Ach! sie flehen Dich,
Mit der Töne süßen Klagen
Flehen sie für mich.

Sie verstehn des Busens Sehnen,
Kennen Liebesschmerz,
Rühren mit den Silbertönen
Jedes weiche Herz.

Laß auch Dir das Herz bewegen,
Liebchen, höre mich!
Bebend harr' ich Dir entgegen!
Komm', beglücke mich!

5 *Aufenthalt*
Rauschender Strom, brausender Wald,
Starrender Fels, mein Aufenthalt.
Wie sich die Welle an Welle reiht,
Fließen die Tränen mir ewig erneut.

Hoch in den Kronen wogend sich's regt,
So unaufhörlich mein Herze schlägt.
Und wie des Felsen uraltes Erz,
Ewig derselbe bleibet mein Schmerz.

6 *In der Ferne*
Wehe dem Fliehenden
Welt hinaus ziehenden! —
Fremde durchmessenden,
Heimat vergessenden,

The woods and hills are wreathed in green.
Snowy blossom shimmers and gleams.
All things strain towards the bridal
    light;
Seeds swell, buds
    burst;
They have found what they lacked:
And you?

Restless longing, yearning heart,
Are there always only tears, complaints and
    pain?
I too am aware of swelling
    impulses!
Who at last will still my urgent desire?
Only you can free the spring in my heart,
Only you!

4 *Serenade*
Softly my songs plead
Through the night to you;
Down into the silent grove,
Beloved, come to me!

Slender tree-tops whisper and rustle
In the moonlight;
My darling, do not fear
That the hostile betrayer will overhear us.

Do you not hear the nightingales call?
Ah, they are imploring you;
With their sweet, plaintive songs
They are imploring for me.

They understand the heart's yearning,
They know the pain of love;
With their silvery notes
They touch every tender heart.

Let your heart, too, be moved,
Beloved, hear me!
Trembling, I await you!
Come, make me happy!

5 *Resting Place*
Surging river, roaring forest,
Immovable rock, my resting place.
As wave follows wave,
So my tears flow, ever renewed.

As the high tree-tops stir and heave,
So my heart beats incessantly.
Like the rock's age-old ore,
My sorrow remains forever the same.

6 *Far Away*
Woe to those who flee,
Who journey forth into the world,
Who travel through strange lands,
Forgetting their native land,

Mutterhaus hassenden,
Freunde verlassenden
Folget kein Segen, ach!
Auf ihren Wegen nach!

Herze, das sehnende,
Auge, das tränende,
Sehnsucht, nie endende,
Heimwärts sich wendende!
Busen, der wallende,
Klage, verhallende,
Abendstern, blinkender,
Hoffnungslos sinkender!

Lüfte, ihr säuselnden,
Wellen sanft kräuselnden,
Sonnenstrahl, eilender,
Nirgend verweilender:
Die mir mit Schmerze, ach!
Dies treue Herze brach —
Grüßt von dem Fliehenden
Welt hinaus ziehenden!

7 *Abschied*
Ade, Du muntre, Du fröhliche Stadt, Ade!
Schon scharret mein Rösslein mit lustigem
    Fuß;
Jetzt nimm noch denn letzten, den
    scheidenden Gruß.
Du hast mich wohl niemals traurig gesehn,
So kann es auch jetzt nicht beim Abschied
    geschehn.
Ade . . .

Ade, Ihr Bäume, Ihr Gärten so grün,
    Ade!
Nun reit' ich am silbernen Strome entlang,
Weit schallend ertönet mein Abschieds-
    gesang;
Nie habt Ihr ein trauriges Lied gehört,
So wird Euch auch keines beim Scheiden
    beschert.
Ade . . .

Ade, Ihr freundlichen Mägdlein dort, Ade!
Was schaut Ihr aus blumenumduftetem
    Haus
Mit schelmischen, lockenden Blicken
    heraus?
Wie sonst, so grüß' ich und schaue mich
    um,
Doch nimmer wend' ich mein Rösslein um.
Ade . . .

Ade, liebe Sonne, so gehst Du zur Ruh',
    Ade!
Nun schimmert der blinkenden Sterne
    Gold.
Wie bin ich Euch Sternlein am Himmel so
    hold;

Spurning their mother's home,
Forsaking their friends:
Alas, no blessing follows them
On their way!

The yearning heart,
The tearful eye,
Endless longing
Turning homewards!
The surging breast,
The dying lament,
The evening star, twinkling
And sinking without hope!

Whispering breezes,
Gently ruffled waves,
Darting sunbeams,
Lingering nowhere:
Send her, who broke
My faithful heart with pain,
Greetings from one who is fleeing
And journeying forth into the world!

7 *Farewell*
Farewell, lively, cheerful town, farewell!
Already my horse is happily pawing the
    ground;
Take now my final, parting
    greeting.
I know you have never seen me sad,
Nor will you now as I
    depart.
Farewell!

Farewell, trees and gardens so green,
    farewell!
Now I ride along the silver stream;
My song of farewell echoes far and
    wide.
You have never heard a sad song,
Nor shall you do so at
    parting.
Farewell!

Farewell, charming maidens, farewell!
Why do you look out with roguish, enticing
    eyes
From houses fragrant with
    flowers?
I greet you as before, and look
    back;
But never will I turn my horse back.
Farewell!

Farewell, dear sun, as you go to rest,
    farewell!
Now the stars twinkle with shimmering
    gold.
How fond I am of you, little stars in the
    sky;

Durchziehn die Welt wir auch weit und breit,	Though we travel the whole world, far and wide,
Ihr gebt überall uns das treue Geleit.	Everywhere you faithfully escort us.
Ade . . .	Farewell!

Ade, Du schimmerndes Fensterlein hell,
Ade!
Du glänzest so traulich mit dämmerndem
Schein
Und ladest so freundlich ins Hüttchen uns
ein.
Vorüber, ach, ritt ich so manches mal
Und wär' es denn heute zum lezten mal?
Ade . . .

Farewell, little window gleaming
brightly,
You shine so cosily with your soft
light,
And invite us so kindly into the
cottage.
Ah, I have ridden past you so often,
And yet today might be the last time.
Farewell!

Ade, Ihr Sterne, verhüllet Euch grau!
Ade!
Des Fensterleins trübes, verschimmerndes
Licht
Ersetzt Ihr unzähligen Sterne mir nicht;
Darf ich hier nicht weilen, muß hier vorbei,
Was hilft es, folgt Ihr mir noch so
treu!
Ade, Ihr Sterne, verhüllet Euch grau!
Ade!

Farewell, stars, veil yourselves in grey!
Farewell!
You numberless stars cannot replace for
us
The little window's dim, fading light;
If I cannot linger here, if I must ride on,
How can you help me, though you follow
me so faithfully?
Farewell, stars, veil yourselves in grey!
Farewell!

8 *Der Atlas*
Ich unglücksel'ger Atlas! eine Welt,
Die ganze Welt der Schmerzen muß ich
tragen.
Ich trage Unerträgliches, und brechen
Will mir das Herz im Leibe.

8 *Atlas*
I, unhappy Atlas, must bear a world,
The whole world of
sorrows.
I bear the unbearable, and my heart
Would break within my body.

Du stolzes Herz, du hast es ja gewollt!
Du wolltest glücklich sein, unendlich
glücklich,
Oder unendlich elend, stolzes Herz,
Und jetzo bist du elend.

Proud heart, you wished it so!
You wished to be happy, endlessly
happy,
Or endlessly wretched, proud heart!
And now you are wretched!

9 *Ihr Bild*
Ich stand in dunklen Träumen,
Und starrte ihr Bildnis an,
Und das geliebte Antlitz
Heimlich zu leben begann.

9 *Her Picture*
I stood in dark dreams,
Gazing at her picture;
And that beloved face
Began mysteriously to come alive.

Um ihre Lippen zog sich
Ein Lächeln wunderbar,
Und wie von Wehmutstränen
Erglänzte ihr Augenpaar.

Around her lips there played
A wondrous smile;
And her eyes glistened,
As though with melancholy tears.

Auch meine Tränen flossen
Mir von den Wangen herab —
Und ach, ich kann es nicht glauben,
Daß ich dich verloren hab'!

My tears, too, flowed
Down my cheeks.
And ah, I cannot believe
That I have lost you!

10 *Das Fischermädchen*
Du schönes Fischermädchen,
Treibe den Kahn ans Land;
Komm zu mir und setze dich nieder,
Wir kosen Hand in Hand.

10 *The Fisher Maiden*
Lovely fisher maiden,
Guide your boat to the shore;
Come and sit beside me,
And hand in hand we shall talk of love.

315

Leg an mein Herz dein Köpfchen,
Und fürchte dich nicht zu sehr;
Vertraust du dich doch sorglos
Täglich dem wilden Meer.

Mein Herz gleicht ganz dem Meere,
Hat Sturm und Ebb' und Flut,
Und manche schöne Perle
In seiner Tiefe ruht.

Lay your little head on my heart
And do not be too afraid;
For each day you trust yourself
Without fear to the turbulent sea.

My heart is just like the sea,
It has its storms, its ebbs and its flows;
And many a lovely pearl
Rests in its depths.

11 *Die Stadt*
Am fernen Horizonte
Erscheint, wie ein Nebelbild,
Die Stadt mit ihren Türmen
In Abenddämmrung gehüllt.

11 *The Town*
On the distant horizon
Appears, like a misty vision,
The town with its turrets,
Shrouded in dusk.

Ein feuchter Windzug kräuselt
Die graue Wasserbahn;
Mit traurigem Takte rudert
Der Schiffer in meinem Kahn.

A damp wind ruffles
The grey stretch of water;
With mournful strokes
The boatman rows my boat.

Die Sonne hebt sich noch einmal
Leuchtend vom Boden empor,
Und zeigt mir jene Stelle,
Wo ich das Liebste verlor.

Radiant, the sun rises once more
From the earth,
And shows me that place
Where I lost my beloved.

12 *Am Meer*
Das Meer erglänzte weit hinaus
Im letzten Abendscheine;
Wir saßen am einsamen Fischerhaus,
Wir saßen stumm und alleine.

12 *By the Sea*
The sea glittered far and wide
In the sun's dying rays;
We sat by the fisherman's lonely house,
We sat silent and alone.

Der Nebel stieg, das Wasser schwoll,
Die Möwe flog hin und wieder;
Aus deinen Augen liebevoll
Fielen die Tränen nieder.

The mist rose, the waters swelled,
A seagull flew to and fro;
From your loving eyes
The tears fell.

Ich sah sie fallen auf deine Hand,
Und bin aufs Knie gesunken;
Ich hab' von deiner weißen Hand
Die Tränen fortgetrunken.

I saw them fall on your hand,
I sank upon my knee;
From your white hand
I drank away the tears.

Seit jener Stunde verzehrt sich mein Leib,
Die Seele stirbt vor Sehnen;
Mich hat das unglücksel'ge Weib
Vergiftet mit ihren Tränen.

Since that hour my body is consumed
And my soul dies of longing.
That unhappy woman
Has poisoned me with her tears.

13 *Der Doppelgänger*
Still ist die Nacht, es ruhen die Gassen,
In diesem Hause wohnte mein Schatz;
Sie hat schon längst die Stadt verlassen,
Doch steht noch das Haus auf demselben
    Platz.

13 *The Wraith*
The night is still, the streets are at rest;
In this house lived my sweetheart.
She has long since left the town,
But the house still stands on the self-same
    spot.

Da steht auch ein Mensch und starrt in die
    Höhe,
Und ringt die Hände vor Schmerzens-
    gewalt;
Mir graust es, wenn ich sein Antlitz sehe —
Der Mond zeigt mir meine eigne Gestalt.

A man stands there too, staring
    up,
And wringing his hands in
    anguish;
I shudder when I see his face —
The moon shows me my own form.

Du Doppelgänger, du bleicher Geselle!
Was äffst du nach mein Liebesleid,
Das mich gequält auf dieser Stelle
So manche Nacht, in alter Zeit?

You wraith, pallid companion,
Why do you ape the pain of my love
Which tormented me on this very spot,
So many a night, in days long past?

14 *Die Taubenpost*
Ich hab' eine Brieftaub in meinem Sold,
Die ist gar ergeben und treu,
Sie nimmt mir nie das Ziel zu kurz,
Und fliegt auch nie vorbei.

14 *Pigeon Post*
I have a carrier-pigeon in my pay,
Devoted and true;
She never stops short of her goal
And never flies too far.

Ich sende sie viel tausendmal
Auf Kundschaft täglich hinaus,
Vorbei an manchem lieben Ort,
Bis zu der Liebsten Haus.

Each day I send her out
A thousand times on reconnaissance,
Past many a beloved spot,
To my sweetheart's house.

Dort schaut sie zum Fenster heimlich
    hinein,
Belauscht ihren Blick und Schritt,
Gibt meine Grüße scherzend ab
Und nimmt die ihren mit.

There she peeps furtively in at the
    window,
Observing her every look and step,
Conveys my greeting breezily,
And brings hers back to me.

Kein Briefchen brauch ich zu schreiben
    mehr,
Die Träne selbst geb ich ihr:
O sie verträgt sie sicher
    nicht,
Gar eifrig dient sie mir.

I no longer need to write a
    note,
I can give her my very tears;
She will certainly not deliver them
    wrongly,
So eagerly does she serve me.

Bei Tag, bei Nacht, im Wachen, im
    Traum,
Ihr gilt das alles gleich,
Wenn sie nur wandern, wandern kann,
Dann ist sie überreich.

Day or night, awake or
    dreaming,
It is all the same to her;
As long as she can roam
She is richly contented.

Sie wird nicht müd, sie wird nicht matt,
Der Weg ist stets ihr neu;
Sie braucht nicht Lockung, braucht nicht
    Lohn,
Die Taub ist so mir treu.

She never grows tired or faint,
The route is always fresh to her;
She needs no enticement or
    reward,
So true is this pigeon to me.

Drum heg ich sie auch so treu an der Brust,
Versichert des schönsten Gewinns;
Sie heißt — die Sehnsucht!
Kennt ihr sie? Die Botin treuen
    Sinns.

I cherish her as truly in my heart,
Certain of the fairest prize;
Her name is — Longing!
Do you know her? The messenger of
    constancy.

Schwanengesang / *Swan Song*

JOHANN SENN

D744 (1822?)

»Wie klag' ich's aus, das
    Sterbegefühl,
Das auflösend durch die Glieder
    rinnt,
Wie sing' ich's aus, das Werdegefühl,
Das erlösend dich, o Geist, anweht.«

'How shall I lament the presentiment of
    death,
The dissolution that flows through my
    limbs?
How shall I sing of the feeling of new life
That redeems you with its breath, o spirit?'

Er klagt', er sang,	It lamented, it sang,
Vernichtungsbang,	Fearful of extinction,
Verklärungsfroh,	Joyously awaiting transfiguration,
Bis das Leben floh.	Until life fled.
Das bedeutet des Schwanen Gesang!	That is the meaning of the swan's song!

Schweizerlied / Swiss Song

JOHANN WOLFGANG VON GOETHE

D 559 (1817)

Uf'm Bergli	I sat
Bin i g'sesse,	On the mountain side
Ha de Vögle	Watching
Zugeschaut;	The birds;
Hänt gesunge,	They sang,
Hänt gesprunge,	They hopped,
Hänt's Nästli	They built
Gebaut.	Their nests.
In ä Garte	I stood
Bin i g'stande,	In a garden,
Ha de Imbli	Watching
Zugeschaut;	The bees;
Hänt gebrummet,	They hummed,
Hänt gesummet,	They buzzed,
Hänt Zelli	They built
Gebaut.	Their cells.
Uf d'Wiese	I walked
Bin i gange,	In the meadow,
Lugt' i Summer-	Looking at
Vögle a;	The butterflies;
Hänt gesoge,	They sucked,
Hänt gefloge,	They flew,
Gar zu schön hänt's	And they did it
Getan.	Very prettily.
Und da kummt nu	Then Hansel
Der Hansel,	Comes along
Und da zeig i	And I show him
Em froh,	Gaily
Wie sie's mache,	How they do it,
Und mer lache,	And we laugh,
Und mache's	And do
Au so.	As they do.

Schwestergruß / Sister's Greeting

FRANZ VON BRUCHMANN

D 762 (1822)

Im Mondenschein	In the moonlight
Wall' ich auf und ab,	I wander up and down,
Seh' Todtenbein'	Seeing dead bones
Und stilles Grab.	And a silent grave.

Im Geisterhauch Vorüber schwebt's, Wie Flamm' und Rauch Vorüber bebt's;	In the ghostly breeze Something floats past, Flickering Like flame and smoke.
Aus Nebeltrug Steigt eine Gestalt, Ohn' Sünd' und Lug Vorüber wallt,	From the deluding mists A figure rises, Without sin or falsehood, And drifts past.
Das Aug' so blau, Der Blick so groß Wie in Himmelsau, Wie in Gottes Schoß;	Such blue eyes, Such a noble gaze, As in the fields of heaven, As in the lap of God.
Ein weiß Gewand Bedeckt das Bild, In zarter Hand Eine Lilie quillt.	A white garment Covers the apparition; From its delicate hand Springs a lily.
Im Geisterhauch Sie zu mir spricht: »Ich wand're schon Im reinen Licht,	In a ghostly whisper She speaks to me: 'Already I walk In the pure light.
»Seh Mond und Sonn' Zu meinem Fuß Und leb' in Wonn', In Engelkuß;	'I see the moon and the sun At my feet, And live in bliss, Kissed by angels.
»Und all' die Lust, Die ich empfind', Nicht deine Brust Kennt, Menschenkind!	'Your heart, child of man, Cannot know How great is the joy I feel.
Wenn du nicht läßt Den Erdengott, Bevor dich faßt Der grause Tod.«	Unless you relinquish The god of this earth Before fearful death Seizes you.'
So tönt die Luft, So saust der Wind, Zu den Sternen ruft Das Himmelskind,	Thus the air echoes, Thus the wind whistles; The child of heaven Calls to the stars.
Und eh' sie flieht, Die weiß' Gestalt, In frischer Blüt' Sie sich entfalt':	And before she flees Her white form Is enfolded In fresh flowers.
In reiner Flamm' Schwebt sie empor, Ohne Schmerz und Harm, Zu der Engel Chor.	She floats up In pure flame, Without pain or grief, To the choir of angels.
Die Nacht verhüllt Den heil'gen Ort, Von Gott erfüllt Sing' ich das Wort.	Night veils The holy place; Filled with God, I sing the Word.

Sehnsucht / Longing

JOHANN WOLFGANG VON GOETHE

D 123 (1814)

Was zieht mir das Herz so?	What is it that tugs at my heart so?
Was zieht mich hinaus?	What lures me outside,
Und windet und schraubt mich	Twisting and wrenching me
Aus Zimmer und Haus?	Out of my room and my home?
Wie dort sich die Wolken	Over there the clouds
Am Felsen verziehn!	Disperse around the rocks.
Da möcht ich hinüber,	I would like to cross over there,
Da möcht ich wohl hin!	I would like to go there!
Nun wiegt sich der Raben	Now the ravens hover
Geselliger Flug;	In gregarious flight;
Ich mische mich drunter	I join them
Und folge dem Zug.	And follow their course.
Und Berg und Gemäuer	We fly above mountains
Umfittigen wir;	And ruins;
Sie weilet da drunten,	She dwells below,
Ich spähe nach ihr.	I look out for her.
Da kommt sie und wandelt;	There she comes, strolling along;
Ich eile sobald,	I immediately hasten,
Ein singender Vogel,	Like a singing bird,
Im buschigen Wald.	To the bushy wood.
Sie weilet und horchet	She lingers and listens,
Und lächelt mit sich:	Smiling to herself:
»Er singet so lieblich	'He sings so charmingly,
Und singt es an mich.«	And sings to me!'
Die scheidende Sonne	The departing sun
Vergüldet die Höhn;	Gilds the hills;
Die sinnende Schöne,	The musing beauty
Sie lässt es geschehn.	Does not heed it,
Sie wandelt am Bache	She strolls by the brook,
Die Wiesen entlang,	Through the meadows;
Und finster und finstrer	Darker and darker
Umschlingt sich der Gang;	Grows her winding path.
Auf einmal erschein ich,	Suddenly I appear,
Ein blinkender Stern.	A shining star.
»Was glänzet da droben,	'What is that sparkling up there,
So nah und so fern?«	So near and yet so far?'
Und hast du mit Staunen	And when, with astonishment,
Das Leuchten erblickt,	You catch sight of its light,
Ich lieg dir zu Füssen,	I shall lie at your feet.
Da bin ich beglückt!	There I shall be contented!

Sehnsucht / Longing

JOHANN MAYRHOFER

D 516 (1817?)

Der Lerche wolkennahe Lieder	The songs of the cloud-soaring lark
Erschmettern zu des Winters Flucht,	Ring out as winter flees;
Die Erde hüllt in Samt die Glieder,	The earth wraps her limbs in velvet,
Und Blüten bilden rote Frucht.	And red fruit forms from the blossoms.

Nur du, o sturmbewegte Seele,
Nur du bist blütenlos, in dich gekehrt,
Und wirst in goldner Frühlingshelle
Von tiefer Sehnsucht aufgezehrt.

Nie wird, was du verlangst, entkeimen
Dem Boden, Idealen fremd,
Der trotzig deinen schönsten Träumen
Die rohe Kraft entgegenstemmt.

Du ringst dich matt mit seiner
    Härte,
Vom Wunsche heftiger entbrannt,
Mit Kranichen ein strebender Gefährte,
Zu wandern in ein milder Land.

You alone, storm-tossed soul,
Do not flower; turned in on yourself,
You are consumed by deep longing
Amid spring's golden radiance.

What you crave will never burgeon
From this earth, alien to ideals,
Which defiantly opposes its raw strength
To your fairest dreams.

You grow weary struggling with its
    harshness,
Ever more inflamed by the desire
To journey to a kinder land,
As aspiring companion to the cranes.

Sehnsucht / Longing

FRIEDRICH VON SCHILLER

First version: D 52 (1813)
Second version: D 636 (1821?)

Ach, aus dieses Tales Gründen,
Die der kalte Nebel drückt,
Könnt ich doch den Ausgang finden,
Ach, wie fühlt ich mich beglückt!
Dort erblick ich schöne Hügel,
Ewig jung und ewig grün!
Hätt ich Schwingen, hätt ich Flügel,
Nach den Hügeln zög ich hin.

Harmonien hör ich klingen,
Töne süsser Himmelsruh,
Und die leichten Winde bringen
Mir der Düfte Balsam zu,
Goldne Früchte seh ich glühen,
Winkend zwischen dunkelm Laub,
Und die Blumen, die dort blühen,
Werden keines Winters Raub.

Ach wie schön muss sich's ergehen
Dort im ewgen Sonnenschein,
Und die Luft auf jenen Höhen,
O wie labend muss sie sein!
Doch mir wehrt des Stromes Toben,
Der ergrimmt dazwischen braust,
Seine Wellen sind gehoben,
Dass die Seele mir ergraust.

Einen Nachen seh ich schwanken,
Aber ach! der Fährmann fehlt.
Frisch hinein und ohne Wanken,
Seine Segel sind beseelt.
Du musst glauben, du musst wagen,
Denn die Götter leihn kein Pfand,
Nur ein Wunder kann dich tragen
In das schöne Wunderland.

Ah, if only I could find a way out
From the depths of this valley,
Oppressed by cold mists,
How happy I would feel!
Yonder I see lovely hills,
Ever young and ever green!
If I had pinions, if I had wings
I would fly to those hills.

I hear harmonious sounds,
Notes of sweet, celestial peace,
And the gentle breezes bring me
The scent of balsam.
I see golden fruits glowing,
Beckoning amid dark leaves,
And the flowers which bloom there
Will never be winter's prey.

Ah, how beautiful it must be to wander
There in the eternal sunshine;
And the air on those hills,
How refreshing it must be.
But I am barred by the raging torrent
Which foams angrily between us,
Its waves tower up,
Striking fear into my soul.

I see a boat pitching,
But, alas! there is no boatman.
Jump in without hesitation!
The sails are billowing.
You must trust, and you must dare,
For the gods grant no pledge;
Only a miracle can convey you
To the miraculous land of beauty.

Sehnsucht / Longing

JOHANN GABRIEL SEIDL

D 879 (1826)

Die Scheibe friert, der Wind ist rauh,
Der nächt'ge Himmel rein und blau.
Ich sitz' in meinem Kämmerlein
Und schau' ins reine Blau hinein!

Mir fehlt etwas, das fühl' ich gut,
Mir fehlt mein Lieb, das treue Blut;
Und will ich in die Sterne seh'n,
Muss stets das Aug' mir übergeh'n!

Mein Lieb, wo weilst du nur so fern,
Mein schöner Stern, mein Augenstern?
Du weisst, dich lieb' und brauch' ich ja,
Die Träne tritt mir wieder nah.

Da quält' ich mich so manchen Tag,
Weil mir kein Lied gelingen mag,
Weil's nimmer sich erzwingen lässt
Und frei hinsäuselt, wie der West!

Wie mild mich's wieder grad' durchglüht!
Sieh' nur, das ist ja schon ein Lied!
Wenn mich mein Los vom Liebchen warf,
Dann fühl' ich, dass ich singen darf.

The window pane freezes, the wind is harsh,
The night sky clear and blue.
I sit in my little room
Gazing out into the clear blueness.

Something is missing, I feel only too well;
My love is missing, my true love.
And when I look at the stars
My eyes constantly fill with tears.

My love, where are you, so far away,
My fair star, my darling?
You know that I love you and need you;
Again tears well up within me.

For many a day I have suffered
Because no song of mine has turned out well,
Because none can be forced
To murmur freely, like the west wind.

How gentle the glow that again warms me!
Behold — a song!
Though my fate has cast me far from my beloved,
Yet I feel that I can still sing.

Sehnsucht der Liebe / Love's Yearning

THEODOR KÖRNER

D 180 (1815)

Wie die Nacht mit heil'gem Beben
Auf der stillen Erde liegt!
Wie sie sanft der Seele Streben,
Üpp'ge Kraft und volles Leben
In den süssen Schlummer wiegt!

Aber mit ewig neuen Schmerzen
Regt sich die Sehnsucht in meiner Brust.
Schlummern auch alle Gefühle im Herzen,
Schweigt in der Seele Qual und Lust:
Sehnsucht der Liebe schlummert nie,
Sehnsucht der Liebe wacht spät und früh.

Tief, im süssen, heil'gen Schweigen,
Ruht die Welt und atmet kaum,
Und die schönsten Bilder steigen
Aus des Lebens buntem Reigen,
Und lebendig wird der Traum.

Lo, how with solemn trembling
Night lies over the silent world.
How gently it lulls the soul, its strivings,
Its abundant strength and rich life,
To sweet slumber!

But with ever-new pain
Yearning stirs within my breast.
Though all feeling slumbers in my heart,
Though anguish and pleasure are silent in my soul,
Love's yearning never slumbers,
Love's yearning lies awake early and late.

In sweet, holy silence
The world rests deeply, scarcely breathing,
The loveliest images rise
From the brightly-coloured dance of life,
And dreams come alive.

Aber auch in des Traumes Gestalten
Winkt mir die Sehnsucht, die
   schmerzliche, zu,
Und ohn' Erbarmen, mit tiefen Gewalten,
Stört sie das Herz aus der wonnigen Ruh'.
Sehnsucht der Liebe schlummert nie,
Sehnsucht der Liebe wacht spät und früh.

But even amid the images of dreams
Painful yearning beckons to
   me,
And without pity, with violent force,
It wrenches the heart from blissful rest.
Love's yearning never slumbers,
Love's yearning lies awake early and late.

Sei mir gegrüsst / *I Greet You*

FRIEDRICH RÜCKERT

D 741 (1822)

O du Entriss'ne mir und meinem Kusse,
Sei mir gegrüsst, sei mir geküsst!
Erreichbar nur meinem
   Sehnsuchtsgrusse,
Sei mir gegrüsst, sei mir geküsst!

You who were torn from me and my kisses,
I greet you, I kiss you!
You, whom only my yearning greeting can
   reach,
I greet you, I kiss you!

Du von der Hand der Liebe diesem Herzen
Gegeb'ne, du von dieser
Brust Genomm'ne mir! Mit diesem
   Tränengusse
Sei mir gegrüsst, sei mir geküsst!

You who were bestowed on this heart
By the hand of love, you who were taken
From my breast! With this flood of
   tears
I greet you, I kiss you!

Zum Trotz der Ferne, die sich feindlich
   trennend
Hat zwischen mich und dich gestellt;
Dem Neid der Schicksalsmächte zum
   Verdrusse
Sei mir gegrüsst, sei mir geküsst!

Defying the distance that, hostile and
   divisive,
Has come between you and me;
Frustrating the envious powers of
   fate,
I greet you, I kiss you!

Wie du mir je im schönsten Lenz der Liebe
Mit Gruss und Kuss
   entgegenkamst,
Mit meiner Seele glühendstem Ergusse,
Sei mir gegrüsst, sei mir geküsst!

As in love's fairest spring
You once came to me with greetings and
   kisses,
So with all the fervour of my soul
I greet you, I kiss you!

Ein Hauch der Liebe tilget Räum' und
   Zeiten,
Ich bin bei dir, du bist bei mir,
Ich halte dich in dieses Arms Umschlusse,
Sei mir gegrüsst, sei mir geküsst!

One breath of love dissolves time and
   space,
And I am with you, you are with me;
I hold you closely in my arms' embrace,
I greet you, I kiss you!

Selige Welt / *Blessed World*

JOHANN SENN

D 743 (1822?)

Ich treibe auf des Lebens Meer,
Ich sitze gemut in meinem Kahn,
Nicht Ziel, noch Steuer, hin und
   her,
Wie die Strömung reisst, wie die Winde
   gahn.

I drift upon life's sea,
I sit comfortably in my boat,
Without destination, without tiller, moving
   to and fro
As the current takes me, as the winds blow.

Eine selige Insel sucht der Wahn,
Doch eine ist es nicht.
Du lande gläubig überall an,
Wo sich Wasser an Erde bricht.

Folly seeks a blessed isle,
But no such isle exists.
Be trusting, land wherever
Water breaks against the shore.

Seligkeit / Bliss

LUDWIG HEINRICH CHRISTOPH HÖLTY

D 433 (1816)

Freuden sonder Zahl
Blühn im Himmelssaal
Engeln und Verklärten,
Wie die Väter lehrten.
Oh, da möcht' ich sein
Und mich ewig freun!

Joys beyond number
Bloom in the vaults of heaven
For angels and the transfigured,
As our fathers taught.
Ah, there I should like to be,
Forever rejoicing!

Jedem lächelt traut
Eine Himmelsbraut;
Harf' und Psalter klinget,
Und man tanzt und singet.
Oh, da möcht' ich sein
Und mich ewig freun!

Upon each a heavenly bride
Smiles tenderly;
Harp and psalter sound,
There is dancing and singing.
Oh, there I should like to be,
Forever rejoicing!

Lieber bleib' ich hier,
Lächelt Laura mir
Einen Blick, der saget,
Daß ich ausgeklaget.
Selig dann mit ihr
Bleib' ich ewig hier!

I would sooner stay here
If Laura smiles on me
With a look that says
I have ceased grieving.
Blissfully then with her
I will remain forever here!

Selma und Selmar / Selma and Selmar

FRIEDRICH GOTTLIEB KLOPSTOCK

D 286 (1815)

Weine du nicht, o die ich innig liebe,
Daß ein trauriger Tag von dir mich
   scheidet!
Wenn nun wieder Hesperus dir dort
   lächelt,
Komm', ich Glücklicher, wieder!

Do not weep, my most truly beloved,
Because a sad day separates you from
   me.
When Hesperus once more smiles on you
   here
I shall return in happiness.

Aber in dunkler Nacht ersteigst du
   Felsen,
Schwebst in täuschender dunkler Nacht
   auf Wassern!
Teilt' ich nun mit dir die Gefahr zu ster-
   ben;
Würd', ich Glückliche, weinen?

But in the dark night you climb the
   rocks,
In night's deluding darkness you drift on
   the waters!
If I could now share with you the danger of
   death,
Should I, in my happiness, weep?

Seufzer / Sighs

LUDWIG HEINRICH CHRISTOPH HÖLTY

D 198 (1815)

Die Nachtigall	The nightingale
Singt überall	Sings everywhere
Auf grünen Reisen	On green boughs
Die besten Weisen,	Her loveliest songs,
Daß ringsum Wald	That all around woods
Und Ufer schallt.	And river banks resound.
Manch junges Paar	Many young couples
Geht dort, wo klar	Stroll where
Das Bächlein rauschet,	The limpid brook murmurs.
Und steht, und lauschet	They stop and listen
Mit frohem Sinn	Joyfully
Der Sängerin.	To the songstress.
Ich höre bang'	But gloomily,
Im düstern Gang	On the dark path,
Der Nachtigallen	I hear the nightingales'
Gesänge schallen;	Echoing song.
Denn ach! allein	For, alas, I wander
Irr' ich im Hain.	Alone in the grove.

Shilrik und Vinvela / Shilrik and Vinvela

JAMES MACPHERSON (OSSIAN), probably translated by EDMUND VON HAROLD, and
further adapted by FRANZ VON HUMMELAUER

D 293 (1815)

Vinvela
Mein Geliebter ist ein Sohn des Hügels; er verfolgt die fliehenden Hirsche; die Doggen schnauben um ihn; die Senn seines Bogens schwirrt in dem Wind. Ruhst du bei der Quelle des Felsen oder beim Rauschen des Bergstroms? Der Schilf neigt sich im Wind, der Nebel fliegt über die Heide; ich will ihm ungesehn nahn; ich will ihn betrachten vom Felsen herab. Ich sah dich zuerst liebreich bei der veralteten Eiche von Branno; schlank kehrtest du vom Jagen zurück, unter allen deinen Freunden der schönste.

Vinvela
My love is a son of the hill. He pursues the fleeing deer. His dogs are panting around him; his bow-string sounds in the wind. Dost thou rest by the fountain of the rock, or by the noise of the mountain stream? the rushes are nodding to the wind, the mist flies over the heath. I will approach my love unseen; I will behold him from the rock. Lovely I saw thee first by the aged oak of Branno; thou wert returning tall from the chase; the fairest among thy friends.

Shilric
Was ist's für eine Stimme, die ich höre? Sie gleicht dem Hauche des Sommers! Ich sitz nicht beim neigenden Schilfe; ich hör nicht die Quelle des Felsen. Ferne, ferne Vinvela, geh ich zu den Kriegen von Fingal: meine Doggen begleiten mich nicht; ich trete nicht mehr auf den Hügel. Ich seh dich nicht mehr von der Höhe, zierlich schreitend am Strome der Fläche; schimmernd, wie der Bogen des Himmels; wie der Mond auf der westlichen Welle.

Shilric
What voice is that I hear? that voice like the summer wind! I sit not by the nodding rushes; I hear not the sound of the rock. Afar Vinvela, afar, I go to the war of Fingal. My dogs attend me no more. No more I tread the hill. No more from on high I see thee, fair moving by the stream of the plain; bright as the bow of heaven; as the moon on the western wave.

Vinvela
So bist du gegangen, o Shilric! Ich bin
allein auf dem Hügel! man sieht die Hirsche am Rande des Gipfels, sie grasen
furchtlos hinweg; sie fürchten die Winde
nicht mehr; nicht mehr den brausenden
Baum. Der Jäger ist weit in der Ferne; er ist
im Felde der Gräber. Ihr Fremden! ihr
Söhne der Wellen! o schont meines lieb-
reichen Shilric!

Shilric
Wenn ich im Felde muß fallen, heb hoch, o
Vinvela, mein Grab. Graue Steine und ein
Hügel von Erde; sollen mich, bei der
Nachwelt bezeichnen. Wenn der Jäger
beim Haufen wird sitzen, wenn er zu
Mittag seine Speise geneußt, wird er sagen:
»Ein Krieger ruht hier;« und mein Ruhm
soll leben in seinem Lob. Erinnere dich
meiner, Vinvela, wenn ich auf Erden
erlieg!

Vinvela
Ja! ich werd' mich deiner erinnern; ach!
mein Shilric wird fallen! Mein Geliebter!
Was soll ich tun, wenn du auf ewig
vergingest? Ich werd' diese Hügel am
Mittag durchstreichen: die schweigende
Heide durchgehen. Dort werd' ich den
Platz deiner Ruh, wenn du von der Jagd
zurückkehrtest beschaun. Ach! mein
Shilric wird fallen; aber ich werd' meines
Shilrics gedenken.

Vinvela
Then thou art gone, O Shilric! I am alone
on the hill! The deer are seen on the brow;
void of fear they graze along. No more they
dread the wind; no more the rustling tree.
The hunter is far removed; he is in the field
of graves. Strangers! Sons of the waves!
Spare my lovely Shilric!

Shilric
If fall I must in the field, raise high my
grave, Vinvela. Grey stones, and
heaped-up earth, shall mark me to future
times. When the hunter shall sit by the
mound, and produce his food at noon,
'Some warrior rests here,' he will say; and
my fame shall live in his praise. Remember
me, Vinvela, when low on earth I lie!

Vinvela
Yes! I will remember thee; alas! my Shilric
will fall! What shall I do, my love! when
thou art for ever gone? Through these hills
I will go at noon: I will go through the silent
heath. There I will see the place of thy rest,
returning from the chase. Alas! my Shilric
will fall; but I will remember Shilric.

Skolie / Skolion (Drinking Song)

JOHANN LUDWIG VON DEINHARDSTEIN

D 306 (1815)

Laßt im Morgenstrahl des Mai'n
Uns der Blume Leben freun,
Eh' ihr Duft entweichet!
Haucht er in den Busen Qual,
Glüht ein Dämon im Pokal,
Der sie leicht verscheuchet.

Schnell wie uns die Freude küßt,
Winkt der Tod, und sie zerfließt;
Dürfen wir ihn scheuen?
Von den Mädchenlippen winkt
Lebensatem, wer ihn trinkt,
Lächelt seinem Dräuen.

Let us in the light of the May morning
Enjoy life's flower
Before its fragrance fades!
If it should breathe sorrows into our hearts
A spirit glows within the cup
That will effortlessly banish them.

No sooner does joy kiss us
Than death beckons, and it flees.
Should we fear death?
From maidens' lips the breath of life
Entices us; he who drinks it
Can smile at death's threats.

Skolie / Skolion (Drinking Song)

FRIEDRICH VON MATTHISSON

D 507 (1816)

Mädchen entsiegelten,
Brüder, die Flaschen;
Auf! die geflügelten
Freuden zu haschen,
Locken und Becher von Rosen
  umglüht.

The girls have unsealed
The bottles, brothers;
Come, let us snatch
Winged joys,
Curls, and cups rimmed with glowing
  roses.

Auf! eh' die moosigen
Hügel uns winken,
Wonne von rosigen
Lippen zu trinken;
Huldigung allem, was jugendlich blüht!

Come, before the mossy
Hills beckon to us,
Let us drink bliss
From rosy lips,
And do homage to all in the bloom of youth.

So laßt mich scheinen (Mignon's Gesang) | Thus Let Me Seem (Mignon's Song)

JOHANN WOLFGANG VON GOETHE

First version: D 727 (1821)
Second version: D 877 no. 3 (1826)

From *Wilhelm Meister*

So laßt mich scheinen, bis ich werde,
Zieht mir das weiße Kleid nicht aus!
Ich eile von der schönen Erde
Hinab in jenes feste Haus.

Thus let me seem till thus I become.
Do not take off my white dress!
I shall swiftly leave the fair earth
For that safe dwelling place below.

Dort ruh' ich eine kleine Stille,
Dann öffnet sich der frische Blick;
Ich lasse dann die reine
  Hülle,
Den Gürtel und den Kranz zurück.

There, for a brief silence, I shall rest;
Then my eyes shall open afresh.
Then I shall leave behind this pure
  raiment,
This girdle and this rosary.

Und jene himmlische Gestalten
Sie fragen nicht nach Mann und Weib,
Und keine Kleider, keine Falten
Umgeben den verklärten Leib.

And those heavenly beings
Do not ask who is man or woman,
And no garments, no folds
Enclose the transfigured body.

Zwar lebt' ich ohne Sorg' und Mühe,
Doch fühlt' ich tiefen Schmerz genung.
Vor Kummer altert' ich zu frühe;
Macht mich auf ewig wieder jung!

True, I lived free from care and toil,
Yet I knew much deep suffering.
Too soon I grew old with grief —
Make me young again for ever!

Son fra l'onde / I am among the Waves

PIETRO METASTASIO

D 78 (1813)

Son fra l'onde in mezzo al
  mare,
E al furor di doppio vento;

I am among the waves in the midst of the
  sea,
A prey to the fury of fierce winds;

Or resisto, or mi sgomento Fra la speme, e fra l'orror.	Now I am resolute, now I tremble, Vacillating between hope and terror.
Per la fè, per la tua vita Or pavento, or sono ardita, E ritrovo egual martire Nell' ardire e nell' timor.	Now I fear for your faith, for your life, Now I am emboldened; And yet I find equal suffering In boldness and in fear.

Sonett I / Sonnet I

PETRARCH, translated by AUGUST WILHELM VON SCHLEGEL

D 628 (1818)

Apollo, lebet noch dein hold Verlangen, Das an thessal'scher Flut die blonden Haare In dir entflammt, und ist's im Lauf der Jahre, Nicht unter in Vergessenheit gegangen:	Apollo, if the sweet desire With which her blonde hair inflamed you By the waters of Thessaly still lives; and if, in the course of the years, It has not sunk into oblivion:
Vor Frost und Nebeln, welche feindlich hangen, Solang' sich uns dein Antlitz birgt, das klare, Jetzt dies geehrte heil'ge Laub bewahre, Wo du zuerst, und ich dann ward gefangen.	Then preserve from the hostile frost and mist, Which appear when your bright face is concealed, This revered and hallowed tree, Where first you, then I, were taken captive.
Und durch die Kraft von dem verliebten Hoffen, Das in der Jugend dich nicht liess vergehen, Lass, von dem Druck befreit, die Luft erwarmen.	And, by the power of those impassioned hopes Which in your youth saved you from death, Let the air grow warm, freed from an icy grasp.
So werden wir, vom Staunen froh getroffen, Im Grünen uns're Herrin sitzen seh'n, Und sich beschatten mit den eignen Armen.	Thus, in joyful astonishment, We shall behold our mistress seated on the grass, Shading herself with her own arms.

Sonett II / Sonnet II

PETRARCH, translated by AUGUST WILHELM VON SCHLEGEL

D 629 (1818)

Allein, nachdenklich, wie gelähmt vom Krampfe, Durchmess' ich öde Felder, schleichend träge, Und wend' umher den Blick, zu fliehn die Stege, Wo eine Menschenspur den Sand nur stampfe.	Alone, pensive, as if paralysed by cramp, I trudge wearily across the desolate fields, And cast my gaze around, that I may avoid those paths Where human footprints are impressed in the sand.

Nicht andre Schutzwehr find' ich mir im Kampfe	I can find no other defence in my battle
Vor dem Erspäh'n des Volks in alle Wege,	Against people who observe me wherever I go;
Weil man im Tun, wo keine Freude rege,	For in my actions, devoid of joy,
Von aussen lieset, wie ich innen dampfe.	They see from without how I burn inwardly.
So dass ich glaube jetzt, Berg und Gefilde,	So that I now believe that mountains and pastures,
Und Fluss und Waldung weiss, aus welchen Stoffen	Rivers and forests, know what stuff
Mein Leben sei, das sich verhehlt jedweden.	My life is made of, though it is concealed from others.
Doch find' ich nicht so rauhe Weg' und wilde,	But I cannot find a path so rough and wild
Dass nicht der Liebesgott mich stets getroffen.	That the god of love does not constantly find me
Und führt mit mir, und ich mit ihm dann Reden.	And converse with me, and I with him.

Sonett III / Sonnet III

PETRARCH, translated by AUGUST WILHELM VON SCHLEGEL

D 630 (1818)

Nunmehr, da Himmel, Erde schweigt und Winde,	Now that heaven and earth are silent, and winds,
Gefieder, Wild des Schlummers Bande tragen,	Birds and beasts are fettered by sleep,
Die Nacht im Kreise führt den Sternenwagen,	Night drives the starry chariot in its orbit,
Und still das Meer sich senkt in seine Gründe:	And the sea sinks calmly into its depths.
Nun wach' ich, nun sinn' ich, glüh' und wein' und finde	Now I wake, think, burn and weep, and find
Nur sie, die mich verfolgt mit süssen Plagen.	Only her, who pursues me with sweet torment.
Krieg ist mein Zustand, Zorn und Missbehagen:	War is my state, anger and unease;
Nur, denk' ich sie, winkt Friede mir gelinde.	But when I think of her, peace beckons gently to me.
So strömt, was mich ernährt, das Süss' und Herb',	So all that nourishes me, both sweet and bitter,
Aus eines einz'gen Quell's lebend'gem Strahle,	Flows from the living radiance of a single source,
Dieselbe Hand gibt Heilung mir und Wunden.	And the same hand both heals and wounds me.
Und dass mein Leiden nie ein Ziel erreiche, sterb'	And since my suffering never reaches its end
Und ersteh' ich täglich tausendmale,	I die and rise again a thousand times each day,
So weit entfernt noch bin ich, zu gesunden.	So far am I still from being cured.

Sprache der Liebe / Language of Love

AUGUST WILHELM VON SCHLEGEL

D 410 (1816)

Laß dich mit gelinden Schlägen
Rühren, meine zarte Laute!
Da die Nacht herniedertaute,
Müssen wir Gelispel pflegen.
Wie sich deine Töne regen
Wie sie atmen, klagen, stöhnen,
Wallt das Herz zu meiner Schönen,
Bringt ihr, aus der Seele Tiefen,
Alle Schmerzen, welche schliefen;
Liebe denkt in süßen Tönen.

Let me touch you with gentle strokes,
My tender lute!
Now that the dewy night has fallen
We must talk in whispers.
As your notes vibrate,
As they breathe, lament, moan,
So my heart flows to my beloved,
And calls forth from her soul's depths
All the sorrows that were slumbering;
Love thinks in sweet music.

Ständchen / Serenade

LUDWIG RELLSTAB

see Schwanengesang no. 4

Ständchen / Serenade (from Cymbeline)

First verse by WILLIAM SHAKESPEARE, translated by AUGUST VON SCHLEGEL, EDUARD VON BAUERNFELD and FERDINAND MAYERHOFER; the second and third verses were added by FRIEDRICH REIL after Schubert's death.

D 889 (1826)
Shakespeare's original (first verse only) is printed below in italics.

Horch, horch, die Lerch' im Ätherblau!
Und Phöbus, neu erweckt,
Tränkt seine Rosse mit dem Tau,
Der Blumenkelche deckt.
Der Ringelblume Knospe schleußt
Die goldnen Äuglein auf;
Mit allem, was da reizend ist,
Du süße Maid, steh auf!
Steh auf; steh auf!

Hark, hark, the lark in the blue ether!
And Phoebus, newly awakened,
Waters his steeds with the dew
That covers the chaliced flowers.
The marigold's bud opens
Its little golden eyes;
With everything that is pretty,
Sweet maid, arise,
Arise, arise!

Wenn schon die liebe ganze Nacht
Der Sterne lichtes Heer
Hoch über dir im Wechsel wacht,
So hoffen sie noch mehr,
Daß auch dein Augenstern sie grüßt.
Erwach! Sie warten drauf,
Weil du doch gar so reizend bist;
Du süße Maid, steh auf!

Though throughout the sweet night
The radiant host of stars
Keep watch in turn high above you,
Yet they hope for still more:
That your starlike eyes should greet them.
Awake! They are waiting,
For you are surpassingly pretty;
Sweet maid, arise!

Und wenn dich alles das nicht weckt,
So werde durch den Ton
Der Minne zärtlich aufgeneckt!
O dann erwachst du schon!
Wie oft sie dich ans Fenster
trieb,
Das weiß sie, drum steh auf,
Und habe deinen Sänger lieb,
Du süße Maid, steh auf!

And if all this should not awaken you,
Then be teased awake tenderly
By sounds of love!
Then, for sure, you will awaken!
How often love has drawn you to the
window,
Love knows, so arise,
And love your minstrel;
Sweet maid, arise!

Hark! hark! the lark at heaven's gate sings,
And Phoebus 'gins arise,
His steeds to water at those springs
On chalic'd flowers that lies:
And winking Mary-buds begin
To ope their golden eyes:
With every thing that pretty is,
My lady sweet, arise:
Arise, arise!

Stimme der Liebe / Voice of Love

FRIEDRICH VON MATTHISSON

First version: D 187 (1815?)
Second version: D 418 (1816)

Abendgewölke schweben hell
Am bepurpurten Himmel;
Hesperus schaut, mit Liebesblick,
Durch den blühenden Lindenhain,
Und sein prophetisches Trauerlied
Zirpt im Kraute das Heimchen.

Evening clouds float brightly
Through the crimson sky.
Hesperus looks lovingly
Through the flowering lime grove,
And in the grass the cricket
Chirps his prophetic threnody.

Freuden der Liebe harren dein!
Flüstern leise die Winde;
Freuden der Liebe harren dein!
Tönt die Kehle der Nachtigall;
Hoch von dem Sternengewölb' herab
Hallt mir Stimme der Liebe!

The joys of love await you!
The winds whisper softly;
The joys of love await you!
Thus sings the nightingale.
From the high starry vaults
The voice of love echoes down to me.

Aus der Platanen Labyrinth
Wandelt Laura, die Holde!
Blumen entsprießen dem Zephyrtritt,
Und wie Sphärengesangeston
Bebt von den Rosen der Lippe mir
Süße Stimme der
    Liebe!

From the labyrinth of plane-trees
Comes fair Laura!
Flowers bloom at her airy footsteps,
And like the music of the spheres
The sweet voice of love
Floats tremulously towards me from the
    roses of her lips.

Stimme der Liebe / Voice of Love

FRIEDRICH LEOPOLD GRAF ZU STOLBERG-STOLBERG

D 412 (1816)

Meine Selinde!
Denn mit Engelsstimme singt die Liebe
    mir zu:
Sie wird die Deine!
Sie wird die Meine!
Himmel und Erde schwinden!
Meine Selinde!

My Selinde!
For love sings to me with an angel's
    voice:
She will be yours!
She will be mine!
Heaven and earth vanish!
My Selinde!

Tränen der Sehnsucht,
Die auf blassen Wangen bebten,
Fallen herab als Freudentränen!
Denn mir tönt die himmlische Stimme:
Deine wird sie, die Deine!

Tears of longing
Which quivered on pale cheeks
Fall as tears of joy!
For the heavenly voice sings to me:
She will be yours, yours!

Suleika I / Suleika I

MARIANNE VON WILLEMER, adapted by JOHANN WOLFGANG VON GOETHE

D720 (1821)

Was bedeutet die Bewegung?
Bringt der Ost mir frohe Kunde?
Seiner Schwingen frische Regung
Kühlt des Herzens tiefe Wunde.

What does this stirring portend?
Is the east wind bringing me joyful tidings?
The refreshing motion of its wings
Cools the heart's deep wound.

Kosend spielt er mit dem Staube,
Jagt ihn auf in leichten Wölkchen,
Treibt zur sichern Rebenlaube
Der Insekten frohes Völkchen.

It plays caressingly with the dust,
Throwing it up in light clouds,
And drives the happy swarm of insects
To the safety of the vine-leaves.

Lindert sanft der Sonne
    Glühen,
Kühlt auch mir die heißen Wangen,
Küßt die Reben noch im Fliehen,
Die auf Feld und Hügel prangen.

It gently tempers the burning heat of the
    sun,
And cools my hot cheeks;
Even as it flies it kisses the vines
That adorn the fields and hillsides.

Und mir bringt sein leises Flüstern
Von dem Freunde tausend Grüße;
Eh' noch diese Hügel düstern,
Grüßen mich wohl tausend Küsse.

And its soft whispering brings me
A thousand greetings from my beloved;
Before these hills grow dark
I shall be greeted by a thousand kisses.

Und so kannst du weiter ziehen!
Diene Freunden und Betrübten.
Dort wo hohe Mauern glühen,
Dort find' ich bald den Vielgeliebten.

Now you may pass on,
And serve the happy and the sad;
There, where high walls glow,
I shall soon find my dearly beloved.

Ach, die wahre Herzenskunde,
Liebeshauch, erfrischtes Leben
Wird mir nur aus seinem Munde,
Kann mir nur sein Atem geben.

Ah, the true message of the heart,
The breath of love, renewed life,
Will come to me only from his lips,
Can be given to me only by his breath.

Suleika II / Suleika II

MARIANNE VON WILLEMER, adapted by JOHANN WOLFGANG VON GOETHE

D717 (1824?)

Ach, um deine feuchten Schwingen,
West, wie sehr ich dich beneide:
Denn du kannst ihm Kunde bringen
Was ich in der Trennung leide!

Ah, west wind, how I envy you
Your moist wings;
For you can bring him word
Of what I suffer separated from him.

Die Bewegung deiner Flügel
Weckt im Busen stilles Sehnen;
Blumen, Auen, Wald und Hügel
Stehn bei deinem Hauch in Tränen.

The motion of your wings
Awakens a silent longing within my breast.
Flowers, meadows, woods and hills
Grow tearful at your breath.

Doch dein mildes sanftes Wehen
Kühlt die wunden Augenlieder;
Ach, für Leid müßt' ich vergehen,
Hofft' ich nicht zu sehn ihn wieder.

But your mild, gentle breeze
Cools my sore eyelids;
Ah, I should die of grief
If I had no hope of seeing him again.

Eile denn zu meinem Lieben,
Spreche sanft zu seinem Herzen;
Doch vermeid' ihn zu betrüben
Und verbirg ihm meine Schmerzen.

Hasten then to my beloved,
Speak softly to his heart;
But be careful not to distress him,
And conceal my suffering from him.

Sag ihm, aber sag's bescheiden:
Seine Liebe sei mein Leben,
Freudiges Gefühl von beiden
Wird mir seine Nähe geben.

Tell him, but tell him humbly,
That his love is my life,
And that his presence will bring me
A joyous sense of both.

Täglich zu singen / To be Sung daily

MATTHIAS CLAUDIUS

D 533 (1817)

Ich danke Gott und freue mich
Wie's Kind zur Weihnachtsgabe,
Dass ich hier bin, und dass ich dich,
Schön menschlich Antlitz habe.

I thank God, and rejoice
Like a child at Christmas.
That I am here, and that I possess
The fair countenance of mankind.

Dass ich die Sonne, Berg und Meer
Und Laub und Gras kann sehen,
Und abends unter Sternenheer
Und lieben Monde
   gehen.

That I can see sun, mountains and the sea,
Leaves and grass,
And can walk in the evening
Beneath the host of stars and the beloved
   moon.

Ich danke Gott mit Saitenspiel,
Daß ich kein König worden;
Ich wär' geschmeichelt worden viel
Und wär' vielleicht verdorben.

To the sound of strings I thank God
That I am not a king;
I would have been greatly flattered
And would perhaps have been corrupted.

Gott gebe mir nur jeden Tag,
So viel ich darf zum Leben.
Er gibt's dem Sperling auf dem Dach;
Wie sollt' er's mir nicht geben!

May God give me each day
Just so much as I need for my life.
He gives this to the sparrow on the roof;
Why should he not give it to me?

Thekla: eine Geisterstimme / Thekla: A Phantom Voice

FRIEDRICH VON SCHILLER

First version: D 73 (1813)
Second version: D 595 (1817)

Wo ich sei, und wo mich hingewendet,
Als mein flüchtiger Schatte dir ent-
   schwebt?
Hab' ich nicht beschlossen und geendet,
Hab' ich nicht geliebet und gelebt?

You ask me where I am, where I turned to
When my fleeting shadow
   vanished.
Have I not finished, reached my end?
Have I not loved and lived?

Willst du nach den Nachtigallen fragen,
Die mit seelenvoller Melodie
Dich entzücken in des Lenzes Tagen?
Nur so lang' sie liebten, waren sie.

Would you ask after the nightingales
Who, with soulful melodies,
Delighted you in the days of spring?
They lived only as long as they loved.

Ob ich den Verlorenen gefunden?
Glaube mir, ich bin mit ihm vereint,
Wo sich nicht mehr trennt, was sich
   verbunden,
Dort, wo keine Träne wird geweint.

Did I find my lost beloved?
Believe me, I am united with him
In the place where those who have formed a
   bond are never separated,
Where no tears are shed.

Dorten wirst auch du uns wieder finden,
Wenn dein Lieben unserm Lieben gleicht;
Dort ist auch der Vater, frei von Sünden,
Den der blut'ge Mord nicht mehr erreicht.

There you will also find us again,
When your love is as our love;
There too is our father, free from sin,
Whom bloody murder can no longer strike.

Und er fühlt, daß ihn kein Wahn betrogen,
Als er aufwärts zu den Sternen sah;
Denn wie jeder wägt, wird ihm gewogen,
Wer es glaubt, dem ist das Heil'ge nah.

And he senses that he was not deluded
When he gazed up at the stars.
For as a man judges, so he shall be judged;
Whoever believes this is close to holiness.

Wort gehalten wird in jenen
    Räumen
Jedem schönen gläubigen Gefühl;
Wage du, zu irren und zu träumen:
Hoher Sinn liegt oft im kind'schen
    Spiel.

There, in space, every fine, deeply-felt
    belief
Will be consummated;
Dare to err, and to dream:
Often a higher meaning lies behind child-
    like play.

Tiefes Leid / Deep Sorrow

ERNST SCHULZE

D876 (1826)

Ich bin von aller Ruh geschieden
Und treib' umher auf wilder Flut;
An einem Ort nur find' ich Frieden,
Das ist der Ort, wo Alles ruht.
Und wenn die Wind' auch schaurig sausen,
Und kalt der Regen niederfällt,
Doch mag ich dort viel lieber hausen,
Als in der unbeständ'gen Welt.

All peace has forsaken me;
I am tossed upon the stormy waters.
In one place alone I shall find peace:
The place where all things rest.
Though the wind may whistle eerily
And the rain fall cold,
I would far rather dwell there
Than in this fickle world.

Denn wie die Träume spurlos schweben,
Und einer schnell den andern treibt,
Spielt mit sich selbst das irre Leben,
Und jedes naht und keines bleibt.
Nie will die falsche Hoffnung weichen,
Nie mit der Hoffnung Furcht und Müh;
Die Ewigstummen, Ewigbleichen
Verheißen und versagen nie.

For as dreams float away without trace,
As one swiftly succeeds another,
So life is a dizzy whirl:
Everything draws near, nothing remains.
False hope never fades,
Nor with that hope fear and toil;
The ever-silent, the ever-pale
Never promise, and never deny.

Nicht weck' ich sie mit meinen Schritten
In ihrer dunklen Einsamkeit.
Sie wissen nicht, was ich gelitten,
Und Keinen stört mein tiefes Leid.
Dort kann die Seele freier klagen
Bei Jener, die ich treu geliebt,
Nicht wird der kalte Stein mir sagen,
Ach, daß auch sie mein Schmerz betrübt!

I shall not waken them in their dark solitude
With my footsteps.
They do not know what I have suffered,
My deep sorrow disturbs none of them.
There my soul can lament more freely
With her, whom I have truly loved;
There no cold stone will tell me,
Alas, that my suffering distresses her too.

Tischerlied / Joiner's Song

POET UNKNOWN

D274 (1815)

Mein Handwerk geht durch alle Welt
Und bringt mir manchen Taler Geld,
Des bin ich hoch vergnügt.

My craftsmanship travels the world over
And brings me many a thaler,
Which makes me very happy.

334

Den Tischler braucht ein jeder Stand,
Schon wird das Kind durch meine Hand
In sanften Schlaf gewiegt.

Das Bette zu der Hochzeitnacht
Wird auch durch meinem Fleiss gemacht
Und künstlich angemalt.
Ein Geizhals sei auch noch so karg,
Er braucht am Ende einen Sarg,
Und der wird gut bezahlt.

Drum hab' ich immer frohen Mut
Und mache meine Arbeit gut,
Es sei Tisch oder Schrank.
Und wer bei mir brav viel
    bestellt
Und zahlt mir immer bares Geld,
Dem sag' ich grossen Dank.

Men of all ranks need a joiner.
Even the baby is rocked to gentle sleep
In my own handiwork.

The bed for the wedding night
Is also built and finely painted
By my hard work.
However mean the miser may be
He still needs a coffin in the end,
And for it I am well paid.

So I am always cheerful,
And do my work well
Whether I am making a table or a cupboard.
And to all those who place good orders with
    me
And always pay in cash
I am deeply grateful.

Tischlied / Drinking Song

JOHANN WOLFGANG VON GOETHE

D 234 (1815)

Mich ergreift, ich weiß nicht wie,
Himmlisches Behagen.
Will mich's etwa gar hinauf
Zu den Sternen tragen?
Doch ich bleibe lieber hier,
Kann ich redlich sagen,
Beim Gesang und Glase Wein
Auf den Tisch zu schlagen.

Wundert euch, ihr Freunde, nicht,
Wie ich mich gebärde;
Wirklich es ist allerliebst
Auf der lieben Erde:
Darum schwör' ich feierlich
Und ohn' alle Fährde,
Daß ich mich nicht freventlich
Wegbegeben werde.

Da wir aber allzumal
So beisammen weilen,
Dächt' ich, klänge der
    Pokal
Zu des Dichters Zeilen.
Gute Freunde ziehen fort,
Wohl ein hundert Meilen,
Darum soll man hier am Ort
Anzustoßen eilen.

I am overcome, I know not how,
With a sense of heavenly well-being.
Shall I perhaps be borne aloft
To the stars?
But, to be honest,
I would rather stay here
Beating on the table,
With a song and a glass of wine.

Do not wonder, friends,
At my behaviour;
It is truly delightful
On this dear earth.
So I swear solemnly,
And without risking my soul,
That I shall not wantonly
Take my leave.

But since we are all
Gathered together,
I would have thought that the cup should
    resound.
To the poet's lines.
Good friends are going away,
A hundred miles or so,
So we must hasten to clink glasses
While we are here.

Todesmusik / Death Music

FRANZ VON SCHOBER

D 758 (1822)

In des Todes Feierstunde,
Wenn ich einst von hinnen scheide,
Und den Kampf, den letzten, leide,
Senke, heilige Kamöne,
Noch einmal die stillen Lieder,
Noch einmal die reinen Töne
Auf die tiefe Abschiedswunde
Meines Busens heilend nieder.
Hebe aus dem ird'schen Ringen
Die bedrängte, reine Seele,
Trage sie auf deinen Schwingen,
Dass sie sich dem Licht vermähle.

In the solemn hour of death,
When one day I depart hence
And suffer my last battle,
Then, sacred muse, let your tranquil songs
And pure tones
Descend one more time
To heal the deep wound of parting
Within my heart.
Raise my pure, anguished soul
From this earthly struggle;
Bear it on your wings
To be united with the light.

O da werden mich die Klänge
Süss und wonnevoll umwehen,
Und die Ketten, die ich sprenge,
Werden still und leicht vergehen.
Alles Grosse werd' ich sehen,
Das im Leben mich beglückte,
Alles Schöne, das mir blühte,
Wird verherrlicht vor mir stehen.

Then harmonies will enfold me
In sweet bliss,
And the chains which I shall break
Will vanish, silently, lightly.
I shall behold all the greatness
That gave me joy in life;
All the beauty that flowered for me
Will be glorified before me.

Jeden Stern, der mir erglühte,
Der mit freundlichem Gefunkel
Durch das grauenvolle Dunkel
Meines kurzen Weges blickte,
Jede Blume, die ihn schmückte,
Werden mir die Töne bringen.
Und die schrecklichen Minuten,
Wo ich schmerzlich könnte bluten,
Werden mich mit Lust umklingen,
Und Verklärung werd' ich sehen,
Ausgegossen über allen Dingen.
So in Wonne werd' ich untergehen,
Süss verschlungen von der Freude Fluten.

Those tones will bring back to me
Every star that shone for me,
That with its friendly light
Looked down upon my brief journey
Through the fearful darkness,
And every flower that adorned my path.
And those terrifying minutes
When I might have bled in agony
Will envelop me with joyous sounds.
I shall behold
All things transfigured.
Thus I shall go down in bliss,
Sweetly engulfed by waves of joy.

Totengräberlied / Gravedigger's Song

LUDWIG HEINRICH CHRISTOPH HÖLTY

D 44 (1813)

Grabe, Spaten, grabe!
Alles, was ich habe,
Dank' ich Spaten, dir!
Reich' und arme Leute
Werden meine Beute,
Kommen einst zu mir.

Dig, spade, dig!
All that I have
I owe to you, spade!
Both rich and poor
Become my prey,
Come to me in the end.

Weiland gross und edel,
Nickte dieser Schädel
Keinem Grusse Dank.
Dieses Beingeripppe
Ohne Wang' und Lippe
Hatte Gold und Rang.

Great and noble,
This skull once
Acknowledged no greeting.
This skeleton
Without cheeks or lips,
Possessed gold and high rank.

Jener Kopf mit Haaren	Only a few years ago
War vor wenig Jahren	That head with hair
Schön, wie Engel sind.	Was as lovely as the angels.
Tausend junge Fäntchen	A thousand young fops,
Leckten ihm das Händchen,	Would lick her hands,
Gafften sich halb blind.	And grow half-blind staring at her.
Grabe, Spaten, grabe!	Dig, spade, dig
Alles, was ich habe,	For all that I have
Dank' ich Spaten, dir!	I thank you, spade!
Reich' und arme Leute	Both rich and poor
Werden meine Beute,	Become my prey,
Kommen einst zu mir!	Come to me in the end.

Totengräbers Heimweh / Gravedigger's Homesickness

JACOB NICOLAUS CRAIGHER

D 842 (1825)

O Menschheit, o Leben! was soll's? o was soll's?	O mankind, o life! To what purpose, to what purpose?
Grabe aus, scharre zu! Tag und Nacht keine Ruh!	Dig out, fill in! No rest, day and night!
Das Treiben, das Drängen, wohin? o wohin?	This urgency, this haste, where does it lead? Where?
»Ins Grab, ins Grab, tief hinab!«	'Into the grave, into the grave, deep down!'
O Schicksal, o traurige Pflicht,	O fate, o sad duty,
Ich trag's länger nicht!	I can bear it no longer!
Wann wirst du mir schlagen, o Stunde der Ruh?	When will you strike for me, hour of peace?
O Tod! komm und drücke die Augen mir zu!	O death, come and close my eyes!
Im Leben, da ist's ach! so schwül, ach! so schwül!	Life, alas, is so sultry, so oppressive!
Im Grabe so friedlich, so kühl!	The grave is so peaceful, so cool!
Doch ach! wer legt mich hinein?	But ah, who will lay me there?
Ich stehe allein, so ganz allein!	I stand alone, quite alone.
Von allen verlassen, dem Tod nur verwandt,	By all forsaken, kin to death alone,
Verweil ich am Rande, das Kreuz in der Hand,	I tarry on the brink, cross in hand,
Und starre mit sehnendem Blick hinab	Staring longingly down
Ins tiefe, ins tiefe Grab!	Into the deep, deep grave!
O Heimat des Friedens, der Seligen Land,	O homeland of peace, land of the blessed!
An dich knüpft die Seele ein magisches Band.	A magic bond binds my soul to you.
Du winkst mir von ferne, du ewiges Licht,	You beckon to me from afar, eternal light;
Es schwinden die Sterne, das Auge schon bricht,	The stars vanish, my eyes already grow dim.
Ich sinke, ich sinke! Ihr Lieben, ich komm!	I am sinking, I am sinking! Loved ones, I come!

337

Totengräberweise / Gravedigger's Song

FRANZ XAVER VON SCHLECHTA

D869 (1826)

Nicht so düster und so bleich,
Schläfer in der Truhe,
Unter Schollen leicht und weich
Leg' ich dich zur Ruhe.

Wird der Leib des Wurmes Raub
Und ein Spiel den Winden,
Muss das Herz selbst noch als Staub
Leben und empfinden.

Denn der Herr sitzt zu Gericht;
Gleichend deinem Leben
Werden, dunkel oder licht,
Träume dich umschweben.

Jeder Laut, der dich verklagt
Als den Quell der Schmerzen,
Wird ein scharfer Dolch und nagt
Sich zu deinem Herzen.

Doch der Liebe Tränentau,
Der dein Grab besprühet,
Färbt sich an des Himmels Blau,
Knospet auf und blühet.

Im Gesange lebt der Held,
Und zu seinem Ruhme
Schimmert hoch im Sternenfeld
Eine Feuerblume.

Schlafe, bis der Engel ruft,
Bis Posaunen klingen,
Und die Leiber sich der Gruft
Jugendlich entschwingen.

Not so sad and pale,
Sleeper in your chest;
Beneath the soft, light earth
I shall lay you to rest.

Though the body is a prey to worms
And a plaything of the winds,
The heart, even as dust,
Will live on and feel.

For the Lord sits in judgement;
Resembling your life,
Dark or bright,
Dreams will hover about you.

Every sound that accuses you
Of being a source of pain
Will become a sharp dagger,
Piercing you to the heart.

But the dewy tears of love
That are sprinkled on your grave
Will be coloured by the blue of heaven,
And bud and flower.

The hero lives in song,
And to honour him
A flower of fire
Gleams high above in the field of stars.

Sleep until the angel calls,
Until the trumpets sound,
And the bodies rise from the grave
To new life.

Totenkranz für ein Kind / Wreath for a Dead Child

FRIEDRICH VON MATTHISSON

D275 (1815)

Sanft wehn, im Hauch der Abendluft,
Die Frühlingshalm' auf deiner Gruft,
Wo Sehnsuchtstränen fallen.
Nie soll, bis uns der Tod befreit,
Die Wolke der Vergessenheit
Dein holdes Bild umwallen.

Wohl dir, obgleich entknospet
   kaum,
Von Erdenlust und
   Sinnentraum,
Von Schmerz und Wahn geschieden!
Du schläfst in Ruh'; wir wanken irr
Und unstet bang im
   Weltgewirr,
Und haben selten Frieden.

In the evening breeze the spring grass
Waves gently upon your grave,
Where tears of longing fall.
Never, until death frees us,
Shall the mists of oblivion
Shroud your sweet image.

Happy you, though your blossom was
   barely unfolded,
For you left behind earthly pleasure and
   sensual dreams,
Sorrow and illusion.
You sleep in peace; we stumble,
Confused and troubled, through the
   turmoil of this world,
And seldom know peace.

Totenopfer / Sacrifice to the Dead

FRIEDRICH VON MATTHISSON

D 101 (1814)

Kein Rosenschimmer leuchet dem Tag zur Ruh!
Der Abendnebel schwillt am Gestad empor,
Wo durch verdorrte Felsengräber
Sterbender Lüfte Gesäusel wandelt.

Nicht schwermutsvoller bebte des Herbstes Weh'n
Durch's tote Gras am sinkenden Rasenmal,
Wo meines Jugendlieblings Asche
Unter den trauernden Weiden schlummert.

Ihm Tränen opfern werd' ich beim Blätterfall,
Ihm, wenn das Mailaub wieder den Hain umrauscht,
Bis mir, vom schönern Stern, die Erde
Freundlich im Reigen der Welten schimmert.

No rosy shimmer lights the day to rest!
The evening mist rises on the shore,
Where, through dried-up rocky graves,
Dying breezes whisper.

The breath of autumn was not more melancholy than this,
Quivering through the dead grass on the sinking sward,
A memorial of where the ashes of my youthful lover
Slumber beneath weeping willows.

I shall sacrifice tears to him when leaves fall,
And when May's leaves again rustle in the grove,
Until, from a fairer star,
The sweet earth shines in the dance of the spheres.

Trauer der Liebe / Love's Sorrow

JOHANN GEORG JACOBI

D 465 (1816)

Wo die Taub' in stillen Buchen
Ihren Tauber sich erwählt,
Wo sich Nachtigallen suchen,
Und die Rebe sich vermählt;
Wo die Bäche sich vereinen,
Ging ich oft mit leichtem Scherz,
Ging ich oft mit bangem Weinen,
Suchte mir ein liebend Herz.

O, da gab die finstre Laube
Leisen Trost im Abendschein;
O, da kam ein süsser Glaube
Mit dem Morgenglanz im Hain;
Da vernahm ich's in den Winden,
Ihr Geflüster lehrte mich:
Dass ich suchen sollt und finden,
Finden, holde Liebe, dich!

Aber ach! wo blieb auf Erden,
Holde Liebe, deine Spur?
Lieben, um geliebt zu werden,
Ist das Los der Engel nur.
Statt der Wonne fand ich Schmerzen,
Hing an dem, was mich verliess;
Frieden gibt den treuen Herzen
Nur ein künftig Paradies.

Where the dove, in silent beeches,
Chooses her mate,
Where nightingales seek one another
And vines intertwine;
Where streams meet
I often walked, in gentle melancholy,
Or with anxious tears,
In search of a loving heart.

There the dark foliage
Gave gentle comfort in the glow of evening;
With the light of morning
A sweet belief came to me in the grove;
I heard it in the winds,
Their whispering told me
That I should search
And find you, fairest love.

But alas, where on this earth
Did any trace of you remain?
To love, and be loved in turn,
Is the fate of angels alone.
Instead of happiness I found only sorrow,
And clung to that which deserted me;
Peace is given to faithful hearts
Only in a future paradise.

Trinklied / Drinking Song (from *Antony and Cleopatra*)

WILLIAM SHAKESPEARE, translated by AUGUST VON SCHLEGEL, FERDINAND
MAYERHOFER and EDUARD VON BAUERNFELD

D888 (1826)
A literal translation of the German is followed by Shakespeare's original, printed
in italics.

Bacchus, feister Fürst des Weins,
Komm mit Augen hellen Scheins,
Uns're Sorg' ersäuf' dein Fass,
Und dein Laub uns krönen lass.
Füll' uns, bis die Welt sich dreht!
Füll uns, bis die Welt sich dreht!

Bacchus, plump prince of wine,
Come with brightly shining eyes,
Let your vat drown our cares,
And your leaves crown us.
Fill us till the world spins round!
Fill us till the world spins round!

Come thou monarch of the vine,
Plumpy Bacchus, with pink eyne!
In thy fats our cares be drown'd,
With thy grapes our hairs be crown'd:
Cup us till the world go round!

Trinklied / Drinking Song

ALOIS ZETTLER

D183 (1815)

Ihr Freunde und du goldner Wein!
Versüsset mir das Leben:
Ohn' euch Beglücker, wäre fein
Ich stets in Angst und Beben.
»Ohne Freunde, ohne Wein
»Möcht' ich nicht im Leben sein.«

You, friends, and you, golden wine,
Make my life sweeter.
Without you, bestowers of joy,
I would live in fear and trembling.
Without friends, without wine,
I should not wish to live!

Wer Tausende in Kisten schließt,
Nach Mehrerem nur trachtet,
Der Freunde Not und sich
    vergißt —
Sei reich! von uns verachtet.
»Ohne Freunde, ohne Wein
»Mag ein andrer reicher sein!«

The man who locks thousands in his chest,
Who endeavours only to increase them,
Forgetting himself and the plight of his
    friends —
Let him be rich, despised by us!
Without friends, without wine,
Let another man be rich!

Ohn' allen Freund, was ist der Held?
Was sind des Reichs Magnaten?
Was ist ein Herr der ganzen Welt? —
Sind alle schlecht beraten!
»Ohne Freunde, ohne Wein,
»Mag ich selbst nicht Kaiser sein!«

What is the hero without a friend?
What are the great men of the realm?
What is the master of the whole world?
They are all poorly counselled!
Without friends, without wine
I should not even wish to be Emperor!

Und muss einst an der Zukunft Port
Dem Leib die Seel' entschweben:
So wink' mir aus der Sel'gen Hort
Ein Freund und Saft der Reben:
»Sonst mag ohne Freund und
    Wein,
»Ich auch nicht im Himmel sein.«

And if one day in the future
My soul must leave my body,
Then let a friend and the juice of the vine
Greet me in the refuge of the blessed.
Otherwise, without a friend and without
    wine
I should not even wish to be in heaven!

Trost / Consolation

JOHANN MAYRHOFER

D 671 (1819)

Hörnerklänge rufen klagend	Horn-calls sound plaintively
Aus des Forstes grüner Nacht,	From the green night of the forest;
In das Land der Liebe tragend,	Their magic power is at work,
Waltet ihre Zaubermacht,	Transporting us to the land of love.
Selig, wer ein Herz gefunden,	Happy he who has found a heart
Das sich liebend ihm ergab,	That yields itself in love;
Mir ist jedes Glück entschwunden,	For me all happiness has vanished,
Denn die Teure deckt das Grab.	For my beloved lies buried in the grave.
Tönen aus des Waldes	When horn-calls from the depths of the
Gründen	forest
Hörnerklänge an mein Ohr,	Ring in my ears,
Glaub' ich wieder sie zu finden,	I imagine I have found her once more,
Zieht es mich zu ihr empor.	And am drawn up towards her.
Jenseits wird sie mir	Beyond the grave she who gave herself to
erscheinen,	me in love
Die sich liebend mir ergab,	Will appear to me.
O welch seliges Vereinen!	Ah, what a blissful reunion!
Keine Schrecken hat das Grab.	The grave holds no terror for me.

Trost / Comfort

POET UNKNOWN

D 523 (1817)

Nimmer lange weil' ich hier,	I shall not tarry here much longer,
Komme bald hinauf zu dir;	Soon I shall come to you above;
Tief und still fühl' ich's in mir:	Deeply, silently I feel within me:
Nimmer lange weil' ich hier.	I shall not tarry here much longer.
Komme bald hinauf zu dir,	Soon I shall come to you above;
Schmerzen, Qualen, für und für	Sorrow and torment forever
Wüten in dem Busen mir;	Rage in my breast;
Komme bald hinauf zu dir.	Soon I shall come to you above.
Tief und still fühl' ich's in mir:	Deeply, silently I feel within me:
Eines heissen Dranges Gier	The flame of ardent desire
Zehrt die Flamm' im Innern hier,	Consumes my innermost being.
Tief und still fühl' ich's in mir.	Deeply, silently I feel it within me.

Trost, An Elisa / Consolation: To Elisa

FRIEDRICH VON MATTHISSON

D 97 (1814)

Lehnst du deine bleichgehärmte	Are you still resting your cheek, pale with
Wange	grief,
Immer noch an diesen Aschenkrug?	On this urn of ashes?
Weinend um den Toten, den schon lange	Weeping for the dead man, who long since,
Zu der Seraphim Triumphgesange	On the wings of perfection,
Der Vollendung Flügel	Soared up to the Seraphim's triumphant
trug?	song?

Siehst du Gottes Sternenschrift dort
flimmern,
Die der bangen Schwermut Trost
verheisst?
Heller wird der Glaube dir nun
schimmern,
Dass hoch über seiner Hülle Trümmern
Walle des Geliebten Geist!

Wohl, o wohl dem liebenden Gefährten
Deiner Sehnsucht, er ist ewig dein!
Wiederseh'n, im Lande der Verklärten,
Wirst du, Dulderin, den
Langentbehrten,
Und wie er unsterblich sein!

Can you see God's starry script
shimmering,
Promising comfort for anxious
sorrow?
Your faith will now shine more
brightly,
So that high above his mortal remains
Your beloved's spirit will live!

Happy the loving companion
Of your longing, he is for ever yours!
Patient sufferer, in the land of the blessed
You will see again the one you have long
yearned for,
And be immortal, as he is!

Trost im Liede / Comfort in Song

FRANZ VON SCHOBER

D 546 (1817)

Braust des Unglücks Sturm empor,
Halt' ich meine Harfe vor,
Schützen können Saiten nicht,
Die er leicht und schnell durchbricht:
Aber durch des Sanges Tor
Schlägt er milder an mein Ohr.

Sanfte Laute hör' ich klingen,
Die mir in die Seele dringen,
Die mir auf des Wohllauts Schwingen
Wunderbare Tröstung bringen.

Und ob Klagen mir entschweben,
Ob ich still und schmerzlich weine,
Fühl' ich mich doch so ergeben,
Dass ich fest und gläubig meine:
Es gehört zu meinem Leben,
Dass sich Schmerz und Freude eine.

When the tempest of misfortune roars
I hold up my harp.
Strings cannot protect,
The storm breaks them swiftly and easily,
But through the portals of song
It strikes my ear more gently.

I hear sweet sounds
That pierce my soul;
On the wings of harmony
They bring me mysterious comfort.

And even if threnodies escape my lips,
And I weep in silence and sorrow,
Yet I feel such humility
That I firmly and devoutly believe
It is part of my life
That pain and joy are mingled.

Trost in Tränen / Consolation in Tears

JOHANN WOLFGANG VON GOETHE

D 120 (1814)

Wie kommt's, dass du so traurig bist,
Da alles froh erscheint?
Man sieht dirs an den Augen an,
Gewiss, du hast geweint.

»Und hab ich einsam auch geweint,
So ists mein eigner Schmerz,
Und Tränen fliessen gar so süss,
Erleichtern mir das Herz.«

How come that you are so sad,
When everything appears so joyful?
One can see from your eyes,
For sure, you have been crying.

'And if, in solitude, I have been crying,
It is my own sorrow,
My tears flow so very sweetly,
Comforting my heart.'

Die frohen Freunde laden dich,
O komm an unsre Brust!
Und was du auch verloren hast,
Vertraue den Verlust.

»Ihr lärmt und rauscht und ahnet
    nicht,
Was mich, den Armen, quält.
Ach nein, verloren hab ichs nicht,
So sehr es mir auch fehlt.«

So raffe dich denn eilig auf,
Du bist ein junges Blut.
In deinen Jahren hat man Kraft
Und zum Erwerben Mut.

»Ach nein, erwerben kann ichs nicht,
Es steht mir gar zu fern.
Es weilt so hoch, es blinkt so schön,
Wie droben jener Sterne.«

Die Sterne, die begehrt man nicht,
Man freut sich ihrer Pracht,
Und mit Entzücken blickt man auf
In jeder heitern Nacht.

»Und mit Entzücken blick ich auf,
So manchen lieben Tag;
Verweinen lasst die Nachte mich,
Solang ich weinen mag.«

Your joyful friends bid you,
Come to our hearts!
And whatever you have lost,
Confide to us that loss.

'You revel and make merry, and cannot
    guess
What torments this poor man.
No, I have not lost what I grieve for,
Although I feel its absence sorely.'

Then quickly take heart.
You are a young man.
At your age men have strength
And the courage to achieve.

'Alas, I cannot achieve what I desire,
It lies too far away,
It dwells high and shines as fair
As yonder star.'

One does not covet the stars,
But rejoices in their splendour,
And gazes up in delight
On each clear night.

'I do gaze up in delight
On many a sweet day.
Let me weep away my nights
As long as I wish to weep.'

Über Wildemann / Above Wildemann*

ERNST SCHULZE

D884 (1826)

Die Winde sausen am Tannenhang,
Die Quellen brausen das Tal entlang;
Ich wandre in Eile durch Wald und
    Schnee,
Wohl manche Meile von Höh zu
    Höh.

Und will das Leben im freien Tal
Sich auch schon heben zum Sonnenstrahl,
Ich muss vorüber mit wildem Sinn
Und blicke lieber zum Winter hin.

Auf grünen Heiden, auf bunten Aun,
Müsst ich mein Leiden nur immer
    schaun,
Dass selbst am Steine das Leben
    spriesst,
Und ach, nur eine ihr Herz
    verschliesst.

The winds whistle over the pine-slopes,
The streams rush along the valley;
I hasten for many a
    mile
Through forest and snow, from peak to
    peak.

And though life in the open valley
Already rises to meet the sun's rays,
I must pass on, troubled in spirit,
Preferring to look towards winter.

In green fields, in many-coloured meadows
I would only contemplate my suffering
    ceaselessly,
Knowing that life burgeons from the very
    stones,
And, alas, that only one creature closes her
    heart.

*A town in the Harz mountains.

343

O Liebe, Liebe, o Maienhauch,
Du drängst die Triebe aus Baum und
    Strauch,
Die Vögel singen auf grünen Höhn,
Die Quellen springen bei deinem Wehn.

Mich lässt du schweifen im dunklen
    Wahn
Durch Windespfeifen auf rauher Bahn.
O Frühlingsschimmer, o Blütenschein,
Soll ich denn nimmer mich dein erfreun?

O love, o love, o breath of May!
You force the shoots from tree and
    bush.
The birds sing on green tree-tops,
The springs gush forth when you stir.

You leave me to roam with my dark
    imaginings,
Along the rough path, in whistling winds.
O gleam of spring, o sheen of blossom,
Shall I never again delight in you?

Um Mitternacht / *At Midnight*

ERNST SCHULZE

D 862 (1825)

Keine Stimme hör' ich schallen,
Keinen Schritt auf dunkler Bahn,
Selbst der Himmel hat die schönen
Hellen Äuglein zugetan.

I hear no voice,
No footstep on the dark path;
Even heaven has closed
Its beautiful bright eyes.

Ich nur wache, süßes Leben,
Schaue sehnend in die Nacht,
Bis dein Stern in öder Ferne
Lieblich leuchtend mir
    erwacht.

I alone am awake, sweet love,
Gazing longingly into the night
Until, in the bleak distance,
Your star awakens me with its lovely
    radiance.

Ach, nur einmal, nur verstohlen
Dein geliebtes Bild zu sehn,
Wollt' ich gern in Sturm und Wetter
Bis zum späten Morgen stehn!

Ah, if I could see your beloved image
But once, secretly,
I should gladly stand even until morning
In storm and tempest.

Seh' ich's nicht von ferne leuchten?
Naht es nicht schon nach und nach?
Ach, und freundlich hör' ich's flüstern:
Sieh, der Freund ist auch noch wach.

Do I not see it shining in the distance?
Is it not gradually approaching?
Ah, I hear it whispering gently:
'See, my beloved is still awake.'

Süßes Wort, geliebte Stimme,
Der mein Herz entgegen schlägt!
Tausend sel'ge Liebesbilder
Hat dein Hauch mir aufgeregt.

Sweet words, beloved voice,
At which my heart beats!
Your breath has stirred within me
A thousand blissful images of love.

Alle Sterne seh' ich glänzen
Auf der dunklen blauen Bahn,
Und im Herzen hat und droben
Sich der Himmel aufgetan.

I see all the stars gleaming
On their deep-blue course;
The sky has cleared, up above,
And within my heart.

Holder Nachhall, wiege freundlich
Jetzt mein Haupt in milde Ruh',
Und noch oft, ihr Träume, lispelt
Ihr geliebtes Wort mir zu!

Sweet echo, lull now
My head to gentle rest;
Dreams, whisper often to me
Her beloved words.

Uraniens Flucht / Urania's Flight

JOHANN MAYRHOFER

D 554 (1817)

»Laßt uns, ihr Himmlischen, ein Fest
 begehen!«
Gebietet Zeus —
Und von der Unterwelt, den Höh'n und
 Seen,
Steigt Alles zum Olympus unverweilt.

Der Rebengott verläßt, den er
 bezwungen,
Des Indus blumenreichen Fabelstrand;
Des Helikons erhabne Dämmerungen
Apoll, und Cypria ihr Inselland.

Die Strömerinnen moosbesäumter
 Quellen,
Dryadengruppen aus dem stillen Hain,
Und der beherrscht des Ozeanes Wellen,
Sie finden willig sich zum Feste ein.

Und wie sie nun in glänzenden Gewanden
Den ew'gen Kreis, an dem kein Wechsel
 zehrt,
Den blühenden, um unsren Donn'rer
 wanden,
Da strahlt sein Auge jugendlich verklärt.

Er winkt: und Hebe füllt die goldnen
 Schalen,
Er winkt: und Ceres reicht
 Ambrosia,
Er winkt: und süße Freudenhymnen
 schallen;
Und was er immer ordnet, das geschah.

Schon rötet Lust der Gäste Stirn' und
 Wange,
Der schlaue Eros lächelt still für sich:
Die Flügel öffnen sich — im sachten Gange
Ein edles Weib in die Versammlung
 schlich.

Unstreitig ist sie aus der Uraniden
Geschlecht', ihr Haupt umhellt ein
 Sternenkranz;
Es leuchtet herrlich auf dem lebensmüden
Und bleichgefärbten Antlitz Himmels-
 glanz.

Doch ihre gelben Haare sind verschnitten,
Ein dürftig Kleid deckt ihren reinen
 Leib.
Die wunden Hände deuten, daß
 gelitten
Der Knechtschaft schwere Schmach das
 Götterweib.

'Let us, Immortals, hold a
 feast!'
Commands Zeus.
And from the underworld, the hills and
 lakes,
All climb up to Olympus without delay.

The god of the vine leaves the fabled
 flowery banks
Of the Indus, which he has conquered,
Apollo the sublime shade of Helicon,
And Cypria her native island.

River-nymphs from mossy
 springs,
Dryads from the silent grove,
And he who rules the ocean waves
Gladly join the feast.

And as they now in radiant attire
Dance the eternal, unchanging, round-
 dance
About our
 Thunderer,
His eyes sparkle with the light of youth.

He gives the sign, and Hebe fills the golden
 cups;
He gives the sign, and Ceres offers
 ambrosia;
He gives the sign, and sweet hymns of joy
 resound;
Whatever he commands comes to pass.

Already the guests' brows and cheeks glow
 crimson with pleasure,
And sly Eros smiles silently to himself.
The doors open — and with soft steps
A noble woman creeps into the
 company.

Without doubt she is of the race
Of the Uranides; around her head is a
 bright crown of stars,
And a wonderful heavenly radiance shines
Upon her pale, life-weary
 face.

But her yellow hair is cropped,
And a wretched garment covers her pure
 body.
Her sore hands reveal that the divine
 woman
Has suffered the heavy shame of
 servitude.

Es spähet Jupiter in ihren Zügen:
»Du bist — du bist es nicht, Urania!«
»Ich bin's.« — Die Götter taumeln von den
   Krügen
Erstaunt, und rufen: wie? Urania!

Jupiter studies her features.
'You are — you are not Urania?'
'I am.' The gods lurch from their
   cups,
Astonished, and cry: 'What? Urania!'

»Ich kenne dich nicht mehr. In holder
   Schöne«
Spricht Zeus — »zogst du von mir der
   Erde zu.
Den Göttlichen befreunden ihre
   Söhne,
In meine Wohnung leiten solltest du.

'I no longer know you,' says Zeus. 'In your
   beauty and grace
You left me and went to the
   earth;
You were to acquaint her sons with the
   gods,
And lead them to my abode.

»Womit Pandora einstens sich
   gebrüstet,
Ist unbedeutend wahrlich und gering,
Erwäge ich, womit ich dich
   gerüstet,
Den Schmuck, den meine Liebe um dich
   hing.«

'The finery of which Pandora was once
   proud
Was truly meagre and insignificant
When I consider the jewels with which I
   adorned you,
And which my love hung about
   you.'

»Was du, o Herr, mir damals
   aufgetragen,
Wozu des Herzens eigner Drang mich
   trieb,
Vollzog ich willig, ja ich darf es sagen;
Doch daß mein Wirken ohne Früchte
   blieb.

'The task with which you entrusted me
   then,
To which my own heart, my lord, urged
   me,
I fulfilled willingly, if I may say so;
But my work remained
   fruitless.

»Magst du, o Herrscher, mit dem Schicksal
   rechten,
Dem alles, was entstand, ist untertan:
Der Mensch verwirrt das Gute mit dem
   Schlechten,
Ihn hält gefangen Sinnlichkeit und
   Wahn.

'You, my lord, may dispute with
   fate,
To which every living thing is subject:
Man confuses good with
   evil,
Lust and delusion hold him
   captive.

»Dem Einen mußt' ich seine Äcker
   pflügen,
Dem Andern Schaffnerin im Hause sein,
Dem seine Kindlein in die Ruhe wiegen,
Dem Andern sollt' ich Lobgedichte
   streu'n.

'For one I had to plough his
   fields,
For another I had to be housekeeper;
For one I had to rock his children to sleep,
For another I had to broadcast
   eulogies.

»Der Eine sperrte mich in tiefe Schachten,
Ihm auszubeuten klingendes Metall;
Der Andre jagte mich durch blut'ge
   Schlachten
Um Ruhm — so wechselte der Armen
   Qual.

'One locked me in deep shafts
To dig out jangling metal for him;
Another hunted me through bloody
   battles
For glory — thus were the varied torments
   of the poor wretches.

»Ja dieses Diadem — die goldnen Sterne —
Das du der Scheidenden hast zugewandt,
Sie hätten es zur Feurung ganz gerne
Bei winterlichem Froste weggebrannt.«

'Even this diadem — these golden stars
You gave to me when I departed,
They would gladly have burnt up as fuel
During the winter frosts.'

»Verwünschte Brut,« herrscht Zeus mit
   wilder Stimme,
»Dem schnellsten Untergang sei sie
   geweiht!«

'Accursed race,' cries Zeus with angry,
   imperious voice.
'It shall be condemned to swift
   ruin!'

Die Wolkenburg erbebt von seinem
    Grimme,
Und Luft und Meer und Land erzittern
    weit.

The palace amid the clouds quakes at his
    fury,
And air, sea and land tremble far
    around.

Er reißt den Blitz gewaltsam aus den
    Fängen
Des Adlers; über'm hohen Haupte
    schwenkt
Die Lohe er, die Erde zu versengen,
Die seinen Liebling unerhört gekränkt.

Violently he tears the lightning from the
    eagle's
Talons; high above his head he
    brandishes
The flames to burn the earth,
Which shamefully harmed his darling.

Er schreitet vorwärts, um sie zu verderben,
Es dräut der rote Blitz, noch mehr sein
    Blick.
Die bange Welt bereitet sich zu
    sterben —
Es sinkt der Rächerarm, er tritt
    zurück,

He steps forward to destroy it;
The red lightning threatens, his counten-
    ance is more menacing still.
The world, in trepidation, prepares to
    die —
But the avenger's arm sinks down, and he
    steps back.

Und heißt Uranien hinunter schauen.
Sie sieht in weiter Fern' ein liebend Paar,
Auf einer grünen stromumflossnen Aue,
Ihr Bildnis ziert den ländlichen Altar,

He bids Urania look down.
In the far distance she sees a loving couple
On a green meadow lapped by a stream;
Her own image adorns the rustic altar.

Vor dem die Beiden opfernd niederknieen,
Die Himmlische ersehnend, die
    entflohn:
Und wie ein mächtig Meer von Harmonien
Umwogt die Göttin ihres Flehens
    Ton.

Before this the pair kneel down in sacrifice,
Yearning for the goddess who fled from
    there.
And, like a mighty ocean of harmonies,
The sound of their entreaties envelops the
    goddess.

Ihr dunkles Auge füllet eine Träne,
Der Schmerz der Liebenden hat sie
    erreicht;
Ihr Unmut wird, wie eines Bogens Sehne
Vom feuchten Morgentaue, nun erweicht.

Tears fill her dark eyes;
The lovers' sorrow has touched
    her.
Like a bow string in the moist dew
Her displeasure is now softened.

»Verzeihe«, heischt die göttliche
    Versöhnte:
»Ich war zu rasch im Zorn, mein Dienst,
    er gilt
Noch auf der Erde: wie man mich auch
    höhnte,
Manch frommes Herz ist noch von mir
    erfüllt.

'Forgive me,' begs the goddess,
    appeased.
'I was too swift in my anger; my
    cult
Is still practised on earth; though I was
    scorned,
Many a pious heart still holds me
    dear.

»O laß mich zu den armen Menschen
    steigen,
Sie lehren, was dein hoher Wille ist,
Und ihnen mütterlich in Träumen zeigen
Das Land, wo der Vollendung Blume
    sprießt.«

'Oh let me descend to wretched
    mankind
To teach them your noble will,
And, like a mother, show them in dreams
The land where the flower of perfection
    blooms.'

»Es sei,« ruft Zeus, »reich will ich dich
    bestatten;
Zeuch, Tochter, hin, mit frischem
    starken Sinn!
Und komme, fühlst du deine Kraft
    ermatten,
Zu uns herauf, des Himmels Bürgerin.

'It shall be so,' cries Zeus. 'I shall deck you
    out richly.
Go forth, daughter, with new strength of
    purpose!
And should you feel your powers
    wane,
Return to us, citizen of heaven.

»Oft sehen wir dich kommen, wieder
    scheiden,
In immer längern Räumen bleibst du
    aus,
Und endlich gar — es enden deine
    Leiden,
Die weite Erde nennst du einst dein
    Haus.«

'Often we shall see you come and depart
    again;
For ever longer periods you shall remain
    away,
And finally your sufferings will
    cease,
And you will call the wide earth your
    home.

»Da, Dulderin! wirst du geachtet wohnen,
Noch mehr, als wir. Vergänglich ist die
    Macht,
Die uns erfreut; der Sturm fällt unsre
    Thronen,
Doch deine Sterne leuchten durch die
    Nacht.«

'You who have suffered, will dwell there
More highly revered than we are. The
    power we enjoy
Shall end; the storm shall destroy our
    thrones,
But your stars shall shine through the
    night.'

Vaterlandslied / Song of the Fatherland

FRIEDRICH GOTTLIEB KLOPSTOCK

D 287 (1815)

Ich bin ein deutsches Mädchen!
Mein Aug' ist blau und sanft mein Blick,
Ich hab ein Herz
Das edel ist, und stolz, und gut.

I am a German girl!
My eyes are blue, my gaze is soft,
I have a heart
That is noble, proud and good.

Ich bin ein deutsches Mädchen!
Zorn blickt mein blaues Aug' auf den,
Es haßt mein Herz
Den, der sein Vaterland verkennt!

I am a German girl!
My blue eyes look with anger on him,
My heart hates him
Who does not prize his fatherland.

Ich bin ein deutsches Mädchen!
Erköhre mir kein ander Land
Zum Vaterland,
Wär mir auch frei die große Wahl!

I am a German girl!
I would choose no other country
For my fatherland
Even if I had a free, wide choice.

Ich bin ein deutsches Mädchen!
Mein gutes, edles, stolzes Herz
Schlägt laut empor
Beim süßen Namen: Vaterland!

I am a German girl!
My good, noble, proud heart
Surges and beats loud
At the sweet name of the fatherland.

So schlägt mirs einst beim Namen
Des Jünglings nur, der stolz wie ich
Aufs Vaterland,
Gut, edel ist, ein Deutscher ist!

Thus it will beat one day only at the name
Of the youth who is as proud as I am
Of the fatherland,
And is good, noble, and a German!

Vergebliche Liebe / Futile Love

JOSEPH KARL BERNARD

D 177 (1815)

Ja, ich weiss es, diese treue Liebe
Hegt unsonst mein wundes Herz!
Wenn mir nur die kleinste Hoffnung
    bliebe,
Reich belohnet wär' mein Schmerz!

Yes, I know, my wounded heart
Harbours this true love in vain.
If only the slightest hope remained for
    me
My sorrow would be richly rewarded.

Aber auch die Hoffnung ist vergebens,
Kenn' ich doch ihr grausam Spiel!
Trotz der Treue meines Strebens
Fliehet ewig mich das Ziel!

Dennoch lieb' ich, dennoch hoff' ich,
     immer
Ohne Liebe, ohne Hoffnung treu;
Lassen kann ich diese Liebe nimmer!
Mit ihr bricht das Herz entzwei!

But even hope is in vain,
For I know her cruel game!
Despite my constant endeavour
My goal forever eludes me!

Yet I love, yet I hope
     unceasingly,
Faithful, even without love or hope;
I can never forsake this love,
Yet with it my heart breaks in two!

Vergißmeinnicht / Forget-me-not

FRANZ VON SCHOBER

D792 (1823)

Als der Frühling sich vom Herzen
Der erblühten Erde riß,
Zog er noch einmal mit Schmerzen
Durch die Welt, die er verließ.

When spring tore himself from the heart
Of the burgeoning earth
He walked sorrowfully one last time
Through the world that he was leaving.

Wiesenschmelz und Saatengrüne
Grüßen ihn mit hellem Blühn,
Und die Schattenbaldachine
Dunklen Walds umsäuseln ihn.

Radiant meadows and green cornfields,
Blooming brightly, greeted him,
And the shady canopy
Of the dark forest rustled about him.

Da im weichen Samt des Mooses
Sieht er, halb vom Grün verdeckt,
Schlummersüß, ein kummerloses
Holdes Wesen hingestreckt.

There, in the soft, velvet moss,
Half concealed by the greenery, he espied
A lovely, carefree creature
Stretched out in sweet slumber.

Ob's ein Kind noch, ob's ein Mädchen,
Wagt er nicht sich zu gestehn.
Kurze blonde Seidenfädchen
Um das runde Köpfchen wehn.

Whether it was a child still or a maiden
He was loath to say;
Short, blonde threads of silk
Waved about her little round face.

Zart noch sind die schlanken Glieder,
Unentfaltet die Gestalt,
Und doch scheint der Busen wieder
Schon von Regungen durchwallt.

Her slender limbs were still delicate,
Her figure undeveloped,
And yet her breast already seemed
To heave with emotion.

Rosig strahlt der Wangen Feuer,
Lächelnd ist der Mund und schlau,
Durch der Wimpern duft'gen Schleier
Äugelt schalkhaft helles
     Blau.

A rosy glow shone from her cheeks,
Her mouth smiled slyly,
Through the fragrant veil of her eyelashes
Her bright blue eyes looked out
     mischievously.

Und der Frühling, wonnetrunken
Steht er, und doch tief gerührt;
In das holde Bild versunken,
Fühlt er ganz, was er verliert!

And spring, drunk with ecstasy,
Yet deeply moved, stood up;
Enraptured by the sweet sight
He fully realized what he was leaving.

Aber dringend mahnt die Stunde,
Daß er schnell von hinnen muß.
Ach! da brennt auf ihrem Munde
Glühend heiß der Scheidekuß.

But the hour urgently reminded him
That he had to leave quickly.
Ah, his ardent parting kiss
Burned her lips!

Und in Duft ist er entschwunden,
Doch das Kind entführt dem Schlaf,
Tief hat sie der Kuß entzunden,
Wie ein Blitzstrahl, der sie traf.

Alle Keime sind entfaltet,
Die ihr kleiner Busen barg,
Schnell zur Jungfrau umgestaltet,
Steigt sie aus der Kindheit Sarg.

Ihre blauen Augen schlagen
Ernst und liebelicht empor,
Nach dem Glück scheint sie zu fragen,
Was sie ungekannt verlor.

Aber niemand gibt ihr Kunde,
Alle sehn sie staunend an,
Und die Schwestern in der Runde,
Wissen nicht wie ihr getan.

Ach sie weiß es selbst nicht! — Tränen
Sprechen ihren Schmerz nur aus,
Und ein unergründlich Sehnen
Treibt sie aus sich selbst heraus;

Treibt sie fort, das Bild zu finden,
Das in ihrem Innern lebt,
Das ihr Ahnungen verkünden,
Das in Träumen sie umschwebt.

Felsen hat sie überklommen,
Berge steigt sie ab und auf;
Bis sie an den Fluß gekommen,
Der ihr hemmt den Strebelauf.

Doch im Ufergras, dem feuchten,
Wird ihr heißer Fuß gekühlt,
Und im Wellenspiegel leuchten
Siehet sie ihr eignes Bild.

Sieht des Himmels blaue Ferne,
Sieht der Wolken Purpurschein,
Sieht den Mond und alle Sterne; —
Milder fühlt sie ihre Pein.

Denn es ist ihr aufgegangen:
Daß sie eine Seele fand,
Die ihr innigstes Verlangen,
Ihren tiefsten Schmerz verstand.

Gern mag sie an dieser Stelle
Sich die stille Wohnung bau'n,
Der verklärten sanften Welle
Kann sie rückhaltslos vertrau'n.

Und sie fühlt sich ganz genesen,
Wenn sie zu dem Wasser spricht,
Wie zu dem geahnten Wesen:
O vergiß, vergiß mein nicht!

And he vanished in a haze.
But the child awoke from her sleep;
The kiss had inflamed her deeply,
As if lightning had struck her.

Every bud concealed
Within her little bosom unfolded;
Swiftly transformed into a young woman
She rose from the coffin of childhood.

Her blue eyes opened,
Solemn and radiant with love;
She seemed to enquire after the happiness
That, unknowing, she had lost.

But no one brought her news of it;
All gazed at her in astonishment,
And her sisters in a circle
Did not know what had happened to her.

Alas, she herself did not know! Her tears
Expressed only their own sorrow,
And an unfathomable longing
Drew her out of herself;

Drew her away to find the image
That lived on within her,
That was conjured up by her imagination,
That hovered over her in her dreams.

She clambered over rocks,
She climbed up and down mountains
Until she reached the river
That checked her impetuous course.

But in the damp grass on the bank,
Her burning feet were cooled,
And she saw her own image shining
In the mirror of the waves.

She saw the distant blue of the sky,
Saw the crimson glow of the clouds,
Saw the moon and all the stars;
And she felt her pain less keenly.

For she realized
That she had found a soul
Which understood her innermost longing,
Her deepest sorrow.

She would gladly build herself
A tranquil dwelling on this spot;
She could trust implicitly
The gentle, radiant waves.

And she felt quite recovered
As she spoke to the waters,
As if to that figure of her dreams:
O forget, forget me not!

Verklärung / *Transfiguration*

ALEXANDER POPE, translated J. G. HERDER

D 59 *(1813)*
The text is a translation of Pope's poem 'The Dying Christian to his Soul'.
A literal rendering of Herder's translation is followed by Pope's original
poem, printed in italics.

Lebensfunke, vom Himmel entglüht,
Der sich loszuwinden müht!
Zitternd-kühn, vor Sehnen leidend,
Gern und doch mit Schmerzen
  scheidend —
End', o end' den Kampf, Natur!
Sanft ins Leben
Aufwärts schweben,
Sanft hinschwinden lass mich nur.

Spark of life, kindled by heaven,
That strives to twist itself free;
Bold yet trembling, aching with longing,
Parting gladly, yet with
  pain —
Cease, o cease this struggle, Nature!
Let me soar upwards
Gently into life,
Let me dwindle away gently.

Horch! mir lispeln Geister zu:
»Schwester-Seele, komm zur Ruh!«
Ziehet was mich sanft von hinnen?
Was ist's, was mir meine Sinnen,
Mir den Hauch zu rauben droht?
Seele, sprich, ist das der Tod?

Hark! Spirits whisper to me:
'Sister soul, come to rest!'
Am I drawn gently hence?
What is this, that threatens
To steal my senses and my breath?
Speak, soul, is this death?

Die Welt entweicht! Sie ist nicht mehr!
Engel-Einklang um mich her!
Ich schweb' im Morgenrot!
Leiht, o leiht mir eure Schwingen:
Ihr Bruder-Geister, helft mir singen:
»O Grab, wo ist dein Sieg?
Wo ist dein Pfeil, o Tod?«

The world recedes, it is no more!
Angelic harmonies surround me.
I float in the dawn.
Lend, o lend me your wings;
Brother spirits, help me sing:
'O grave, where is your victory?
O death, where is your sting?'

Vital spark of heav'nly flame!
Quit, oh quit this mortal frame:
Trembling, hoping, ling'ring, flying,
Oh the pain, the bliss of dying!
Cease, fond Nature,
Cease thy strife,
And let me languish
Into life.

Hark; they whisper; Angels say,
Sister spirit, come away.
What is this absorbs me quite?
Steals my senses, shuts my sight,
Drowns my spirits, draws my breath
Tell me, my soul, can this be Death?

The world recedes; it disappears!
Heav'n opens on my eyes! my ears
With sounds seraphic ring:
Lend, lend your wings! I mount! I fly!
O Grave! where is thy victory?
O Death! where is thy sting?

Versunken / Rapt Absorption

JOHANN WOLFGANG VON GOETHE

D715 (1821)

Voll Locken kraus ein Haupt so rund!
Und darf ich dann in solchen reichen
Haaren
Mit vollen Händen hin und wider
fahren,
Da fühl ich mich von Herzensgrund
gesund.
Und küss ich Stirne, Bogen, Augen,
Mund,
Dann bin ich frisch und immer wieder
wund.
Der fünfgezackte Kamm, wo sollt' er
stocken?
Er kehrt schon wieder zu den Locken.
Das Ohr versagt sich nicht dem
Spiel,
So zart zum Scherz, so
liebeviel!
Doch wie man auf dem Köpfchen kraut,
Man wird in solchen reichen Haaren
Für ewig auf und nieder fahren.
Voll Locken kraus ein Haupt so rund.

A head so round, so full of curly locks!
And when I am allowed to fill my
hands
With this abundant hair, and run them to
and fro,
Then I feel good from the depths of my
heart.
And when I kiss her forehead, eyebrows,
eyes and mouth
I am afflicted afresh and ever
again.
This five-toothed comb, where should it
stop?
Already it returns to your curls.
The ear, too, cannot refrain from joining in
the game;
So delicate it is in playful dalliance, so full
of love!
But he who fondles this little head
Will, in such abundant hair,
Move his hands up and down for ever.
A head so round, so full of curly locks!

Vier Canzonen / Four Canzonets

JACOPO VITTORELLI
D 688 nos. 1 and 2 (1820)

PIETRO METASTASIO
D 688 nos. 3 and 4 (1820)

1 *Non t'accostar all'urna*
Non t'accostar all'urna,
Che l'osse mie rinserra,
Questa pietosa terra
E' sacra al mio dolor.

Ricuso i tuoi giacinti
Non voglio i tuoi pianti;
Che giovan agli estinti
Due lagrime, due fior?

Empia! Dovevi allor
Porgermi un fil d'aita,
Quando traea la vita
In grembo dei sospir.

A che d'inutil pianto
Assordi la foresta?
Rispetta un'Ombra mesta,
E lasciala dormir.

1 *Do not Approach the Urn*
Do not approach the urn
Which contains my bones;
This compassionate earth
Is sacred to my sorrow.

I refuse your flowers,
I do not want your weeping;
What use to the dead
Are a few tears and a few flowers?

Cruel one! You should have come
To help me
When my life was ebbing away
In sighing and suffering.

With what futile weeping
Do you assail the woods?
Respect a sad shade,
And let it sleep.

2 *Guarda, che bianca luna*
Guarda che bianca luna!
Guarda che notte azzurra!
Un'aura non susurra,
Nò, non tremola uno stel.

L'usignuoletto solo
Va dalla siepe all'orno,
E sospirando intorno
Chiama la sua fedel.

Ella, ch'esente oppena,
Vien di fronda in fronda,
E par che gli dica,
Nò, non piangere: son qui.

Che gemiti son questi!
Che dolci pianti Irene,
Tu mai non me sapesti
Rispondere così!

2 *Look how Bright the Moon is*
Look how bright the moon is,
And how blue the night!
Not a breeze whispers,
Not a twig quivers.

A lone nightingale
Flies from the hedge to the elm-tree,
And sighing all the while,
Calls to his faithful love.

She, who scarcely hears him,
Flies from leaf to leaf,
And seems to say to him:
'No, do not weep. I am here!'

What tears,
What sweet laments, Irene!
You could never
Answer me thus.

3 *Da quel sembiante appresi*
Da quel sembiante appresi
A sospirand' amore
Sempre per quel sembiante
Sospirerò d'amore.

La face a cui m'accesi
Solo m'alletta e piace,
È fredda ogn' altra face
Per riscaldarmi il cuore.

3 *From that Face I Learnt to Sigh*
From that face I learnt
To sigh with love;
For that face
I shall always sigh with love.

The flame which kindled my love
Alone delights and pleases me.
Every other flame is too cold
To warm my heart.

4 *Mio ben ricordati*
Mio ben ricordati,
Se avvien, ch' io mora:
Quanto quest' anima
Fedel t'amò.

E se pur amano
Le fredde ceneri:
Nell' urna ancora
T'adorerò.

4 *Remember, Beloved*
Remember, beloved,
If it should happen that I die,
How this faithful soul
Loved you.

And if cold ashes
Can love
In the urn,
I shall still love you.

Viola / Violet

FRANZ VON SCHOBER

D786 (1823)

Schneeglöcklein, o Schneeglöcklein,
In den Auen läutest du,
Läutest in dem stillen Hain,
Läute immer, läute zu, läute immerzu!

Denn du kündest frohe Zeit,
Frühling naht, der Bräutigam,
Kommt mit Sieg vom Winterstreit,
Dem er seine Eiswehr nahm.

Snowdrop, snowdrop,
You ring through the meadows,
You ring in the silent grove.
Ring on, ring on for ever!

For you herald a time of joy;
Spring approaches, the bridegroom,
Victorious from his struggle with winter,
From whom he wrested his icy weapon.

German	English

Darum schwingt der goldne Stift,
Dass dein Silberhelm erschallt,
Und dein liebliches
  Gedüft
Leis' wie Schmeichelruf entwallt:
	So your golden rod swings
	That your silver bell shall resound,
	And your sweet fragrance wafts gently
	  away,
	Like an enticing call:

Dass die Blumen in der Erd' Steigen aus dem düstern Nest, Und des Bräutigams sich wert Schmücken zu dem Hochzeitsfest.	So that the flowers in the earth Rise from their gloomy nests, And to prove worthy of the bridegroom Adorn themselves for the wedding feast.
Schneeglöcklein, o Schneeglöcklein, In den Auen läutest du, Läutest in dem stillen Hain, Läut' die Blumen aus der Ruh'!	Snowdrop, snowdrop, You ring through the meadows, You ring in the silent grove, Ring the flowers from their sleep!
Du Viola, zartes Kind, Hörst zuerst den Wonnelaut, Und sie stehet auf geschwind, Schmücket sorglich sich als Braut,	Violet, tender child, Is the first to hear the joyful sound; She rises quickly, And adorns herself carefully as a bride.
Hüllet sich in's grüne Kleid, Nimmt den Mantel sammetblau, Nimmt das güldene Geschmeid, Und den Brillantentau.	She wraps herself in a green gown, Takes a velvety blue mantle, Her golden jewels And her dewy diamonds.

Eilt dann fort mit mächt'gem Schritt,
Nur den Freund im treuen
  Sinn,
Ganz von Liebesglut durchglüht,
Sieht nicht her und sieht nicht hin.
	Then she hastens forth with powerful gait,
	With thoughts only of her beloved in her
	  faithful heart,
	Inflamed with ardent love,
	Looking neither this way nor that.

Doch ein ängstliches Gefühl Ihre kleine Brust durchwallt, Denn es ist noch rings so still, Und die Lüfte weh'n so kalt.	But a feeling of apprehension Troubles her tiny breast, For all around it is still so quiet, And the winds blow so cold.
Und sie hemmt den schnellen Lauf, Schon bestrahlt von Sonnenschein, Doch mit Schrecken blickt sie auf, Denn sie stehet ganz allein.	She checks her rapid course. Already the sun shines on her, But she looks up in terror, For she is quite alone.

Schwestern nicht, nicht Bräutigam
Zugedrungen! und
  verschmäht!
Da durchschauert sie die Scham,
Fliehet wie vom Sturm geweht,
	No sisters! No bridegroom!
	She has been too pressing! She has been
	  rejected!
	Then she shudders with shame
	And flees, as if swept away by the storm.

Fliehet an den fernsten Ort, Wo sich Gras und Schatten deckt, Späht und lauschet immerfort, Ob was rauschet und sich regt.	She flees to the remotest spot, Where grass and shade conceal her; She constantly peers and listens To see if anything rustles or stirs.
Und gekränket und getäuscht Sitzet sie und schluchzt und weint, Von der tiefsten Angst zerfleischt, Ob kein Nahender erscheint.	Hurt and disappointed She sits sobbing and weeping, Tormented by the profound fear That no one will appear.

Schneeglöcklein, o Schneeglöcklein,
In den Auen läutest du,
Läutest in dem stillen Hain,
Läut die Schwestern ihr herzu!

Snowdrop, snowdrop,
You ring through the meadows,
You ring in the silent grove;
Call her sisters to her.

Rose nahet, Lilie schwankt,
Tulp' und Hyazinthe schwellt,
Windling kommt daher gerankt,
Und Narziss hat sich gesellt.

The rose approaches, the lily sways,
The tulip and hyacinth swell;
The bindweed trails along,
And the narcissus joins them.

Da der Frühling nun erscheint,
Und das frohe Fest beginnt,
Sieht er alle, die vereint,
Und vermisst sein liebstes Kind.

And now, as spring appears
And the happy festival begins,
He sees them all united,
But misses his dearest child.

Alle schickt er suchend fort,
Um die eine, die ihm wert,
Und sie kommen an den Ort,
Wo sie einsam sich verzehrt.

He sends them all off to search
For the one he cherishes,
And they come to the place
Where she languishes alone.

Doch es sitzt das liebe Herz
Stumm und bleich, das Haupt gebückt,
Ach, der Lieb' und Sehnsucht Schmerz
Hat die Zärtliche erdrückt.

But the sweet creature sits there
Dumb and pale, her head bowed;
Alas, the pain of love and longing
Has crushed the tender one.

Schneeglöcklein, o Schneeglöcklein,
In den Auen läutest du,
Läutest in dem stillen Hain,
Läut Viola sanfte Ruh'!

Snowdrop, snowdrop,
You ring through the meadows,
You ring in the silent grove;
Ring for Violet's sweet repose!

Vollendung / Fulfilment

FRIEDRICH VON MATTHISSON

D989 (1817)

Wenn ich einst das Ziel errungen habe,
In den Lichtgefilden jener Welt,
Heil, der Träne dann an meinem
    Grabe
Die auf hingestreute Rosen fällt!

When one day I reach my journey's end
In the radiant fields of the world beyond,
Then I shall hail the tears which fall on the
    roses
Scattered upon my grave.

Sehnsuchtsvoll, mit banger
    Ahnungswonne,
Ruhig, wie der mondbeglänzte Hain,
Lächelnd, wie beim Niedergang die Sonne,
Harr' ich, göttliche Vollendung, dein!

Full of yearning, with anxious joy of
    anticipation,
As calm as the moonlit grove,
Smiling, as at the setting sun,
I shall await you, divine fulfilment!

Eil', o eile mich empor zu flügeln
Wo sich unter mir die Welten drehn,
Wo im Lebensquell sich Palmen
    spiegeln,
Wo die Liebenden sich wieder sehn.

Hasten, o hasten to wing me on high,
To where the spheres turn beneath me,
Where palm-trees are mirrored in the
    spring of life,
Where lovers are reunited.

355

Vom Mitleiden Mariä / Mary's Suffering

FRIEDRICH VON SCHLEGEL

D 632 (1818)

Als bei dem Kreuz Maria stand,
Weh über Weh ihr Herz empfand
Und Schmerzen über Schmerzen;
Das ganze Leiden Christi stand
Gedruckt in ihrem Herzen.

Sie ihren Sohn muss bleich und tot
Und überall von Wunden rot
Am Kreuze leiden sehen.
Gedenk', wie dieser bitt're Tod
Zu Herzen ihr musst' gehen.

In Christi Haupt durch Bein und
   Hirn,
Durch Augen, Ohren, durch die Stirn',
Viel scharfe Dornen stachen,
Dem Sohn die Dornen Haupt und Hirn,
Das Herz der Mutter brachen.

As Mary stood by the cross
She felt woe upon woe in her heart,
And sorrow upon sorrow;
All Christ's suffering
Was impressed upon her heart.

She had to watch her son
Suffer on the cross, deathly pale,
His whole body red with wounds;
Ponder how this bitter death
Must have gone to her heart.

On Christ's head many sharp thorns
   pierced
Through bone and brain,
Through eyes, ears and brow;
The thorns broke the son's head and brain,
And the mother's heart.

Von Ida / Ida

LUDWIG KOSEGARTEN

D 228 (1815)

Der Morgen blüht,
Der Osten glüht;
Es lächelt aus dem dünnen Flor
Die Sonne matt und krank hervor.
Denn, ach, mein Liebling flieht!

Auf welcher Flur,
Auf wessen Spur,
So fern von Iden wallst du jetzt,
O du, der ganz mein Herz besitzt,
Du Liebling der Natur!

Vernimmst du auch
Im Morgenhauch
Das Ach, das Idens Brust entächzt,
Das Sehnen, drinn ihr Herz zerlechzt,
Im kühlen Morgenhauch?

Was ahndest du,
Der Idens Ruh
Und Idens Freuden mit sich nahm?
Ach, ahndest du wohl Idens Gram,
Und flehst für Idens Ruh?

O, kehre um!
Kehr' um, kehr' um!
Zu deiner Einsamtraurenden!
Zu deiner Ahnungschaurenden
Mein Einziger, kehr' um!

The morning blooms,
The east glows;
The sun smiles, weak and sickly,
Through a thin gauze of cloud.
For, alas, my beloved has fled!

On what meadows,
On what track
Do you tarry now, so far from Ida?
You, you possess my whole heart,
Darling of nature.

Do you also hear
In the morning breeze
The cry that escapes from Ida's breast,
The longing that pines within her heart
In the cool morning breeze?

What do you know,
You who took away Ida's peace
And her happiness?
Do you have an inkling of Ida's grief,
And do you pray for Ida's peace?

O return,
Return!
To her who grieves alone,
To her who shudders with foreboding!
Return, my one and only love!

Vor meiner Wiege / Before my Cradle

KARL GOTTFRIED VON LEITNER

D 927 (1827)

Das also, das ist der enge Schrein,
Da lag ich einstens als Kind darein,
Da lag ich gebrechlich, hilflos und stumm
Und zog nur zum Weinen die Lippen
    krumm.

Ich konnte nichts fassen mit Händchen
    zart,
Und war doch gebunden nach
    Schelmenart;
Ich hatte Füsschen und lag doch wie lahm,
Bis Mutter an ihre Brust mich nahm.

Dann lachte ich saugend zu ihr empor,
Sie sang mir von Rosen und Engeln vor,
Sie sang und sie wiegte mich singend in
    Ruh,
Und küsste mir liebend die Augen zu.

Sie spannte aus Seide, gar dämmerig grün,
Ein kühliges Zelt hoch über mich hin.
Wo find ich nur wieder solch friedlich
    Gemach?
Vielleicht, wenn das grüne Gras mein
    Dach!

O Mutter, lieb' Mutter, bleib' lange noch
    hier!
Wer sänge dann tröstlich von Engeln
    mir?
Wer küsste mir liebend die Augen
    zu
Zur langen, zur letzten und tiefesten Ruh'?

So this is the narrow chest
Where I once lay as a baby;
Where I lay, frail, helpless and dumb,
Twisting my lips only to
    cry.

I could grip nothing with my tiny, tender
    hands,
Yet I was bound like a
    rogue;
I possessed little feet, and yet lay as if lame,
Until mother took me to her breast.

Then I laughed up at her as I suckled,
And she sang to me of roses and angels;
She sang and with her singing lulled me to
    sleep,
And with a kiss lovingly closed my eyes.

She spread a cool tent of dusky green silk
Above me.
Where shall I find such a peaceful chamber
    again?
Perhaps when the green grass is my
    roof!

O mother, dear mother, stay here a long
    time yet!
Who else would sing to me comforting
    songs of angels.
Who else would close my eyes lovingly with
    a kiss
For the long, last and deepest rest?

Waldesnacht / In the Forest

FRIEDRICH VON SCHLEGEL

see Im Walde

Wandrers Nachtlied I / Wayfarer's Night Song I

JOHANN WOLFGANG VON GOETHE

D 224 (1815)

Der du von dem Himmel bist,
Alles Leid und Schmerzen stillst,
Den, der doppelt elend ist,
Doppelt mit Entzückung füllst,
Ach, ich bin des Treibens müde!
Was soll all der Schmerz und Lust?
Süsser Friede,
Komm, ach komm in meine Brust!

You who are from heaven,
Who assuage all grief and suffering,
And fill him who is doubly wretched
Doubly with delight,
Ah! I am weary of striving!
To what end is all this pain and joy?
Sweet peace,
Enter my heart!

Wandrers Nachtlied II / Wayfarer's Night Song II

JOHANN WOLFGANG VON GOETHE

D 768 (1822?)

Über allen Gipfeln	Over all the peaks
Ist Ruh,	There is peace,
In allen Wipfeln	In all the tree-tops
Spürest du	You feel
Kaum einen Hauch;	Scarcely a breath of air;
Die Vögelein schweigen im Walde.	The little birds in the forest are silent.
Warte nur, balde	Wait!
Ruhest du auch.	Soon you too will be at rest.

Wehmut / Melancholy

MATTHÄUS VON COLLIN

D 772 (1822?)

Wenn ich durch Wald und Fluren geh',	When I walk through the woods and fields
Es wird mir dann so wohl und weh	I feel so happy and yet so sad
In unruhvoller Brust.	In my unquiet heart;
So wohl, so weh, wenn ich die Au	So happy and so sad when I behold
In ihrer Schönheit Fülle	The meadows in the fullness of their
schau',	beauty,
Und all die Frühlingslust.	And all the joy of spring.
Denn was im Winde tönend weht,	For all that blows and echoes in the wind,
Was aufgetürmt gen Himmel steht,	All that towers up towards heaven,
Und auch der Mensch, so hold vertraut	And man himself, communing so fondly
Mit all der Schönheit, die er schaut,	With all the beauty he beholds —
Entschwindet, und vergeht.	All shall vanish and perish.

Wer kauft Liebesgötter? / Who will buy these Cupids?

JOHANN WOLFGANG VON GOETHE

D 261 (1815)

Von allen schönen Waren,	Of all the beautiful things
Zum Markte hergefahren,	Brought here to market,
Wird keine mehr behagen	None will please you more
Als die wir euch getragen	Than those we bring you
Aus fernen Ländern bringen.	From distant lands.
O höret was wir singen!	Hear our song!
Und seht die schönen Vögel,	See the fine birds!
Sie stehen zum Verkauf.	They are for sale.
Zuerst beseht den grossen,	First look at this big one,
Den lustigen, den losen!	This jolly, rakish fellow.
Er hüpfet leicht und munter	Chirpily, lightly,
Von Baum und Busch herunter;	He hops down from bush and tree,
Gleich ist er wieder droben.	Now he is up there again.
Wir wollen ihn nicht loben.	We are not going to sing his praises.
O seht den muntern Vogel!	Look at the chirpy fellow!
Er steht hier zum Verkauf.	He is for sale.

Betrachtet nun den kleinen,
Er will bedächtig scheinen,
Und doch ist er der lose,
So gut als wie der grosse;
Er zeiget meist im Stillen
Den allerbesten Willen.
Der lose kleine Vogel,
Er steht hier zum Verkauf.

Now take a look at this little one.
He pretends to be thoughtful,
But he's every bit as rakish
As the big fellow
In his quiet way he shows
The best will in the world.
This rakish little fellow
Is for sale.

O seht das kleine Täubchen,
Das liebe Turtelweibchen!
Die Mädchen sind so zierlich,
Verständig und manierlich;
Sie mag sich gerne putzen
Und eure Liebe nutzen.
Der kleine, zarte Vogel,
Er steht hier zum Verkauf.

See this little dove,
This sweet turtle dove.
Girls are so dainty,
So understanding and well-mannered.
She likes to spruce herself
And to serve your love.
This delicate little bird
Is for sale.

Wir wollen sie nicht loben,
Sie stehn zu allen Proben.
Sie lieben sich das Neue;
Doch über ihre Treue
Verlangt nicht Brief und Siegel;
Sie haben alle Flügel.
Wie artig sind die Vögel.
Wie reizend ist der Kauf!

We are not going to sing their praises,
You can try them out as you wish.
They love novelty,
But as for their constancy,
Do not ask for any promises!
They all have wings.
What charming birds!
What a delightful buy!

Wer nie sein Brot mit Tränen ass | *Who has never eaten his Bread with Tears*

JOHANN WOLFGANG VON GOETHE

see Harfenspieler: II

Wer sich der Einsamkeit ergibt | *He who gives himself up to Solitude*

JOHANN WOLFGANG VON GOETHE

see Harfenspieler: I

Widerschein / *Reflection*

FRANZ XAVER VON SCHLECHTA

D949 (1819–20)

Harrt ein Fischer auf der Brücke,
Die Geliebte säumt,
Schmollend taucht er seine Blicke
In den Bach und träumt.

A fisherman waits on the bridge;
His beloved is late.
Sullenly he dips his gaze
Into the brook, dreaming.

Doch die lauscht im nahen Flieder,
Und ihr Bildchen strahlt
Jetzt aus klaren Wellen wider,
Treuer nie gemalt.

But she is lurking in the nearby lilac bushes,
And now her image,
Never more truly portrayed,
Shines forth from the clear waters.

Und er sieht's! Und er kennt die Bänder,
Kennt den süssen Schein,
Und er hält sich am Geländer,
Sonst zieht's ihn hinein.

And he sees it! He recognizes the ribbons,
And her sweet radiance.
And he holds on to the railings,
For if he did not he would be drawn in.

Wie Ulfru Fischt / Ulfru Fishing

JOHANN MAYRHOFER

D 525 (1817)

Die Angel zuckt, die Rute bebt,
Doch leicht fährt sie heraus.
Ihr eigensinn'gen Nixen gebt
Dem Fischer keinen Schmaus.
Was frommet ihm sein kluger Sinn,
Die Fische baumeln spottend hin;
Er steht am Ufer fest gebannt,
Kann nicht ins Wasser, ihn hält das
    Land.

The rod quivers, the line trembles,
But it comes up easily.
You capricious water-sprites
Give the fisherman no feast.
What use is his cunning?
The fish glide away mockingly;
He stands spellbound on the shore,
He cannot enter the water, the land holds
    him fast.

Die glatte Fläche kräuselt sich,
Vom Schuppenvolk bewegt,
Das seine Glieder wonniglich
In sichern Fluten regt.
Forellen zappeln hin und her,
Doch bleibt des Fischers Angel leer,
Sie fühlen, was die Freiheit ist,
Fruchtlos ist Fischers alte List.

The smooth surface is ruffled,
Disturbed by the scaly shoals
That swim blithely
In the safe waters.
Trout dart to and fro,
But the fisherman's rod stays empty;
They feel what freedom is,
The fisherman's well-tried guile is in vain.

Die Erde ist gewaltig schön,
Doch sicher ist sie nicht.
Es senden Stürme Eiseshöh'n,
Der Hagel und der Frost zerbricht
Mit einem Schlage, einem Druck,
Das gold'ne Korn, der Rosen Schmuck;
Den Fischlein unter'm weichen Dach,
Kein Sturm folgt ihnen vom Lande nach.

The earth is surpassingly beautiful,
But safe it is not.
Storms blow from the icy peaks,
Hail and frost destroy
At one stroke, with one blow,
The golden corn, the roses' beauty;
The little fish beneath their soft roof
Are pursued by no storm from the land.

Wiedersehen / Reunion

AUGUST WILHELM VON SCHLEGEL

D 855 (1825)

Der Frühlingssonne holdes Lächeln
Ist meiner Hoffnung Morgenrot;
Mir flüstert in des Westes Fächeln
Der Freude leises Aufgebot.
Ich komm', und über Tal und Hügel,
O süße Wonnegeberin,
Schweb, auf des Liedes raschem Flügel,
Der Gruß der Liebe zu dir hin.

The sweet smile of the spring sun
Is the dawn of my hope;
In the stirring of the west wind
I hear joy's softly whispered call.
I am coming! And over hill and dale,
Sweet bestower of delight,
Love sails to greet you
On swift wings of song.

Der Gruß der Liebe von dem
    Treuen,
Der ohne Gegenliebe schwur,
Dir ewig Huldigung zu weihen

It is love's greeting from one who is
    devoted,
Who, without requital, swore
To pay eternal homage to you

Wie der allwaltenden Natur;
Der stets, wie nach dem Angelsterne
Der Schiffer, einsam blickt und lauscht,
Ob nicht zu ihm in Nacht und
  Ferne
Des Sternes Klang hernieder rauscht.

And to all-powerful nature;
Who forever watches and listens alone,
Like the sailor for the pole star,
For the sound of that star to come down to
  him
Through the remote expanses of the night.

Heil mir! ich atme kühnes Sehnen,
Und atm' es bald an deiner Brust,
Und saug' es ein mit deinen Tönen,
Im Pulsschlag namenloser Lust.
Du lächelst, wenn mein Herz, umfangen
Von deiner Näh', dann wilder strebt,
Indes das selige Verlangen
Der Güt' um deine Lippe schwebt.

What bliss! I sigh with bold yearning,
And shall soon sigh upon your breast,
And drink it in with the sound of your voice
As I pulsate with nameless pleasure.
You smile as my heart, enveloped
By your presence, beats more wildly,
Whilst a happy longing
To be kind hovers about your lips.

Du liebst mich, göttlich hohes Wesen!
Du liebst mich, sanftes zartes Weib!
Es gnügt. Ich fühle mich genesen,
Und Lebensfüll an Seel' und Leib.
Nein, noch mit dem Geschick zu
  hadern,
Das schnell mich wieder von dir reißt,
Verschmäht mein Blut, das durch die
  Adern
Mit stolzen leichten Wellen kreißt.

You love me, noble, celestial creature!
You love me, gentle, tender woman!
It is enough. I am made well again,
And abundant life fills my soul and body.
No, the blood, which ripples lightly,
  proudly
Through my veins, disdains
To struggle against the
  fate
That tears me so quickly from you again.

Wiegenlied / Lullaby

THEODOR KÖRNER

D 304 (1815)

Schlummre sanft! — Noch an dem
  Mutterherzen
Fühlst du nicht des Lebens Qual und Lust;
Deine Träume kennen keine Schmerzen,
Deine Welt ist deiner Mutter Brust.

Slumber softly! Close to your mother's
  heart
You do not yet feel life's torment and joy;
Your dreams know no sorrows,
Your world is your mother's breast.

Ach! wie süß träumt man die frühen
  Stunden,
Wo man von der Mutterliebe lebt;
Die Erinnerung ist mir verschwunden,
Ahndung bleibt es nur, die mich
  durchbebt.

Ah, how sweet are the dreams of those early
  hours,
When we live by our mother's love;
My memory of them has vanished,
They remain a mere impression to stir
  me.

Dreimal darf der Mensch so süß
  erwarmen,
Dreimal ist's dem Glücklichen erlaubt,
Daß er in der Liebe Götterarmen
An des Lebens höh're Deutung glaubt.

Three times a man may experience such
  sweet warmth;
Three times the happy man is permitted
To believe in the higher meaning of life,
Embraced by the divine arms of love.

Liebe gibt ihm ihren ersten Segen,
Und der Säugling blüht in Freud' und
  Lust,
Alles lacht dem frischen Blick entgegen;
Liebe hält ihn an der Mutterbrust.

Love gives him her first blessing,
And the infant blooms in joy and happi-
  ness.
All smile at his fresh gaze;
Love holds him to his mother's breast.

Wenn sich dann der schöne Himmel
  trübte,
Und es wölkt sich nun des Jünglings Lauf:
Da, zum zweiten Mal, nimmt als Geliebte
Ihn die Lieb' in ihre Arme auf.

Doch im Sturme bricht der Blütenstengel,
Und im Sturme bricht des Menschen
  Herz:
Da erscheint die Lieb' als Todesengel,
Und sie trägt ihn jubelnd himmelwärts.

Then, when the fair heavens
  darken,
And the youth's path becomes clouded,
Then, for the second time, love takes him
As her sweetheart in her arms.

But in the storm the flower's stem breaks,
And in the storm a man's heart
  breaks:
Then love appears as the angel of death,
And bears him jubilantly up to heaven.

Wiegenlied / Lullaby

JOHANN GABRIEL SEIDL

D867 (1826?)

Wie sich der Äuglein kindlicher Himmel,
Schlummerbelastet, lässig verschliesst!
Schliesse sie einst so, lockt dich die
  Erde:
Drinnen ist Himmel, aussen ist Lust!

How carelessly the eyes' childlike heaven
Closes, laden with slumber!
Close them thus, when one day the earth
  calls you:
Heaven is within you, outside is joy!

Wie dir so schlafrot glühet die Wange!
Rosen aus Eden hauchten sie
  an:
Rosen die Wangen, Himmel die
  Augen,
Heiterer Morgen, himmlischer Tag!

How your cheeks glow red with sleep!
Roses from Eden have breathed upon
  them;
Your cheeks are roses, your eyes are
  heaven,
Bright morning, heavenly day!

Wie des Gelockes goldige Wallung
Kühlet der Schläfe glühenden Saum.
Schön is das Goldhaar, schöner der Kranz
  drauf:
Träum' du vom Lorbeer, bis er dir blüht.

How the golden waves of your locks
Cool the edge of your burning temples!
Your golden hair is lovely, and even lovelier
  the garland upon it;
Dream of the laurel until it blooms for you.

Liebliches Mündchen, Engel umweh'n
  dich,
Drinnen die Unschuld, drinnen die Lieb!
Wahre sie, Kindchen, wahre sie
  treulich:
Lippen sind Rosen, Lippen sind Glut.

Sweet little mouth, the angels hover round
  you;
Inside is innocence, inside is love!
Guard them, my child, guard them
  faithfully:
Lips are roses, lips are warmth!

Wie dir ein Engel faltet die Händchen,
Falte sie einst so, gehst du zur
  Ruh'!
Schön sind die Träume, wenn man
  gebetet:
Und das Erwachen lohnt mit dem
  Traum.

As an angel folds your little hands,
Fold them thus one day when you go to
  rest!
Dreams are beautiful when you
  pray,
And your awakening rewards you no less
  than your dream.

Wiegenlied / Lullaby

POET UNKNOWN

D 498 (1816)

Schlafe, holder, süßer Knabe,
Leise wiegt dich deiner Mutter Hand;
Sanfte Ruhe, milde Labe
Bringt dir schwebend dieses
    Wiegenband.

Schlafe in dem süßen Grabe,
Noch beschützt dich deiner Mutter Arm,
Alle Wünsche, alle Habe
Faßt sie liebend, alle liebewarm.

Schlafe in der Flaumen Schoße,
Noch umtönt dich lauter Liebeston,
Eine Lilie, eine Rose,
Nach dem Schlafe werd' sie dir zum Lohn.

Sleep, dear, sweet boy,
Your mother's hand rocks you softly.
This swaying cradle strap
Brings you gentle peace and tender
    comfort.

Sleep in the sweet grave;
Your mother's arms still protect you.
All her wishes, all her possessions
She holds lovingly, with loving warmth.

Sleep in her lap, soft as down;
Pure notes of love still echo around you.
A lily, a rose
Shall be your reward after sleep.

Willkommen und Abschied / Hail and Farewell

JOHANN WOLFGANG VON GOETHE

D 767 (1822)

Es schlug mein Herz, geschwind zu Pferde!
Es war getan fast eh gedacht.
Der Abend wiegte schon die Erde,
Und an den Bergen hing die Nacht;
Schon stand im Nebelkleid die Eiche,
Ein aufgetürmter Riese, da,
Wo Finsternis aus dem Gesträuche
Mit hundert schwarzen Augen sah.

My heart was beating. Quick, to horse!
No sooner thought than done.
Evening was already cradling the earth,
And night hung about the mountains.
Already the oak stood in a cloak of mist,
A towering giant, there
Where darkness gazed from the bushes
With a hundred coal-black eyes.

Der Mond von einem Wolkenhügel
Sah kläglich aus dem Duft
    hervor,
Die Winde schwangen leise Flügel,
Umsausten schauerlich mein Ohr;
Die Nacht schuf tausend Ungeheuer,
Doch frisch und fröhlich war mein Mut:
In meinen Adern welches Feuer!
In meinem Herzen welche Glut!

From a bank of cloud
The moon gazed plaintively out through
    the haze;
The winds softly beat their wings,
Whistling eerily about my ears.
The night begot a thousand monsters,
Yet my mood was bright and cheerful;
What fire in my veins!
What ardour in my heart!

Dich sah ich, und die milde Freude
Floss von dem süssen Blick auf mich;
Ganz war mein Herz an deiner Seite
Und jeder Atemzug für dich.
Ein rosenfarbnes Frühlingswetter
Umgab das liebliche Gesicht,
Und Zärtlichkeit für mich — ihr Götter!
Ich hofft' es, ich verdient' es nicht!

I saw you, and a gentle joy
Flowed over me from your sweet gaze;
My whole heart was with you,
And my every breath was for you.
A rosy springtime
Enveloped your lovely face,
And tenderness for me — ye gods!
I had hoped for this, but never deserved it!

Doch ach, schon mit der Morgensonne
Verengt der Abschied mir das Herz:
In deinen Küssen welche Wonne!
In deinem Auge welcher Schmerz!

But alas, with the morning sun
Farewell already oppresses my heart.
In your kisses what ecstasy!
In your eyes what sorrow!

Ich ging, du standst und sahst zur Erden,
Und sahst mir nach mit nassem Blick:
Und doch, welch Glück, geliebt zu
  werden!
Und lieben, Götter, welch ein Glück!

I went, you stood looking down,
And gazed after me with moist eyes:
And yet, what happiness it is to be
  loved!
And to love, o gods, what happiness!

Winterlied / Winter Song

LUDWIG HEINRICH CHRISTOPH HÖLTY

D 401 (1816)

Keine Blumen blühn,
Nur das Wintergrün
Blickt durch Silberhüllen,
Nur das Fenster füllen
Blümchen, rot und weiß,
Aufgeblüht aus Eis.

No flowers bloom;
Only the winter green
Peeps through its silver mantle;
The window is filled
Only with red and white flowers,
Blossoming from the ice.

Ach, kein Vogelsang
Tönt mit frohem Klang,
Nur die Winterweise
Jener kleinen Meise,
Die am Fenster schwirrt,
Und um Futter girrt.

Ah, no birdsong
Rings out with joyous tones;
Only the wintry strains
Of the titmouse
That flutters at the window
Chirping for food.

Minne flieht den Hain,
Wo die Vögelein,
Sonst im grünen Schatten
Ihre Nester hatten;
Minne flieht den Hain,
Kehrt ins Zimmer ein.

Love flees the grove
Where the birds
Once made their nests
In the green shade;
Love flees the grove
And comes into this room.

Kalter Januar,
Hier werd' ich fürwahr
Unter Minnespielen
Deinen Frost nicht fühlen;
Walte immerdar
Kalter Januar!

Cold January,
Here, in truth,
Among love games,
I shall not feel your frost.
Reign for ever,
Cold January!

Winterreise / Winter Journey

WILHELM MÜLLER

D 911 (1827)

1 *Gute Nacht*
Fremd bin ich eingezogen,
Fremd zieh' ich wieder aus.
Der Mai war mir gewogen
Mit manchem Blumenstrauß.

1 *Good Night*
I arrived a stranger,
A stranger I depart.
May blessed me
With many a bouquet of flowers.

Das Mädchen sprach von Liebe,
Die Mutter gar von Eh' —
Nun ist die Welt so trübe,
Der Weg gehüllt in Schnee.

The girl spoke of love,
Her mother even of marriage;
Now the world is so desolate,
The path concealed beneath snow.

Ich kann zu meiner Reisen Nicht wählen mit der Zeit: Muß selbst den Weg mir weisen In dieser Dunkelheit.	I cannot choose the time For my journey; I must find my own way In this darkness.
Es zieht ein Mondenschatten Als mein Gefährte mit, Und auf den weißen Matten Such' ich des Wildes Tritt.	A shadow thrown by the moon Is my companion; And on the white meadows I seek the tracks of deer.
Was soll ich länger weilen, Daß man mich trieb' hinaus? Laß irre Hunde heulen Vor ihres Herren Haus!	Why should I tarry longer And be driven out? Let stray dogs howl Before their master's house.
Die Liebe liebt das Wandern, Gott hat sie so gemacht — Von einem zu dem andern — Fein Liebchen, gute Nacht.	Love delights in wandering — God made it so — From one to another. Beloved, good night!
Will dich im Traum nicht stören, Wär' Schad' um deine Ruh', Sollst meinen Tritt nicht hören — Sacht, sacht die Türe zu!	I will not disturb you as you dream, It would be a shame to spoil your rest. You shall not hear my footsteps; Softly, softly the door is closed.
Schreib' im Vorübergehen An's Tor dir gute Nacht, Damit du mögest sehen, An dich hab' ich gedacht.	As I pass I write 'Good night' on your gate, So that you might see That I thought of you.

2 *Die Wetterfahne*

Der Wind spielt mit der Wetterfahne Auf meines schönen Liebchens Haus. Da dacht' ich schon in meinem Wahne, Sie pfiff' den armen Flüchtling aus.	2 *The Weather-Vane* The wind is playing with the weather-vane On my fair sweetheart's house. In my delusion I thought It was whistling to mock the poor fugitive.
Er hätt' es eher bemerken sollen, Des Hauses aufgestecktes Schild, So hätt' er nimmer suchen wollen Im Haus ein treues Frauenbild.	He should have noticed it sooner, This sign fixed upon the house; Then he would never have sought A faithful woman within that house.
Der Wind spielt drinnen mit den Herzen, Wie auf dem Dach, nur nicht so laut. Was fragen sie nach meinen Schmerzen? Ihr Kind ist eine reiche Braut.	Inside the wind is playing with hearts, As on the roof, only less loudly. Why should they care about my grief? Their child is a rich bride.

3 *Gefrorne Tränen*

Gefrorne Tropfen fallen Von meinen Wangen ab: Ob es mir denn entgangen, Daß ich geweinet hab'?	3 *Frozen Tears* Frozen drops fall From my cheeks; Have I, then, not noticed That I have been weeping?
Ei Tränen, meine Tränen, Und seid ihr gar so lau, Daß ihr erstarrt zu Eise, Wie kühler Morgentau?	Ah tears, my tears, Are you so tepid That you turn to ice, Like the cold morning dew?
Und dringt doch aus der Quelle Der Brust so glühend heiß, Als wolltet ihr zerschmelzen Des ganzen Winters Eis.	And yet you well up, so scaldingly hot, From your source within my heart, As if you would melt All the ice of winter.

365

4 *Erstarrung*
Ich such' im Schnee vergebens
Nach ihrer Tritte Spur,
Wo sie an meinem Arme
Durchstrich die grüne Flur.

Ich will den Boden küssen,
Durchdringen Eis und Schnee
Mit meinen heißen Tränen,
Bis ich die Erde seh'.

Wo find' ich eine Blüte,
Wo find' ich grünes Gras?
Die Blumen sind erstorben,
Der Rasen sieht so blaß.

Soll denn kein Angedenken
Ich nehmen mit von hier?
Wenn meine Schmerzen schweigen,
Wer sagt mir dann von ihr?

Mein Herz ist wie erstorben,
Kalt starrt ihr Bild darin:
Schmilzt je das Herz mir wieder,
Fließt auch ihr Bild dahin.

5 *Der Lindenbaum*
Am Brunnen vor dem Tore,
Da steht ein Lindenbaum;
Ich träumt' in seinem Schatten
So manchen süßen Traum.

Ich schnitt in seine Rinde
So manches liebe Wort;
Es zog in Freud' und Leide
Zu ihm mich immer fort.

Ich mußt' auch heute wandern
Vorbei in tiefer Nacht,
Da hab' ich noch im Dunkel
Die Augen zugemacht.

Und seine Zweige rauschten,
Als riefen sie mir zu:
Komm her zu mir, Geselle,
Hier findst du deine Ruh'!

Die kalten Winde bliesen
Mir grad' in's Angesicht,
Der Hut flog mir vom Kopfe,
Ich wendete mich nicht.

Nun bin ich manche Stunde
Enfernt von jenem Ort,
Und immer hör' ich's rauschen:
Du fändest Ruhe dort!

6 *Wasserflut*
Manche Trän' aus meinen Augen
Ist gefallen in den Schnee;
Seine kalten Flocken saugen
Durstig ein das heiße Weh.

4 *Numbness*
In vain I seek
Her footprints in the snow,
Where she walked on my arm
Through the green meadows,

I will kiss the ground
And pierce ice and snow
With my burning tears,
Until I see the earth.

Where shall I find a flower?
Where shall I find green grass?
The flowers have died,
The grass looks so pale.

Shall I, then, take
No memento from here?
When my sorrows are stilled
Who will speak to me of her?

My heart is as dead,
Her image coldly rigid within it;
If my heart ever melts again
Her image, too, will flow away.

5 *The Linden Tree*
By the well, before the gate,
Stands a linden tree;
In its shade I dreamt
Many a sweet dream.

In its bark I carved
Many a word of love;
In joy and sorrow
I was ever drawn to it.

Today, too, I had to walk
Past it at dead of night;
Even in the darkness
I closed my eyes.

And its branches rustled.
As if they were calling to me:
'Come to me, friend,
Here you will find rest.'

The cold wind blew
Straight into my face,
My hat flew from my head;
I did not turn back.

Now I am many hours' journey
From that place;
Yet I still hear the rustling:
'There you would find rest.'

6 *Flood*
Many a tear has fallen
From my eyes into the snow;
Its cold flakes eagerly suck in
My burning grief.

Wenn die Gräser sprossen wollen,
Weht daher ein lauer Wind,
Und das Eis zerspringt in Schollen,
Und der weiche Schnee zerrinnt.

When the grass is about to shoot forth,
A mild breeze blows;
The ice breaks up into pieces
And the soft snow melts away.

Schnee, du weißt von meinem Sehnen;
Sag', wohin geht doch dein Lauf?
Folge nach nur meinen Tränen,
Nimmt dich bald das Bächlein auf.

Snow, you know of my longing;
Tell me, where does your path lead?
If you but follow my tears
The brook will soon absorb you.

Wirst mit ihm die Stadt durchziehen,
Muntre Straßen ein und aus;
Fühlst du meine Tränen glühen,
Da ist meiner Liebsten Haus.

With it you will flow through the town,
In and out of bustling streets;
When you feel my tears glow,
There will be my sweetheart's house.

7 Auf dem Flusse

Der du so lustig rauschtest,
Du heller, wilder Fluß,
Wie still bist du geworden,
Gibst keinen Scheidegruß.

7 On the River

You who rippled so merrily,
Clear, boisterous river,
How still you have become,
You give no parting greeting.

Mit harter, starrer Rinde
Hast du dich überdeckt,
Liegst kalt und unbeweglich
Im Sande ausgestreckt.

With a hard, rigid crust
You have covered yourself;
You lie cold and motionless,
Stretched out in the sand.

In deine Decke grab' ich
Mit einem spitzen Stein
Den Namen meiner Liebsten
Und Stund' und Tag hinein:

On your surface I carve
With a sharp stone
The name of my beloved,
The hour and the day.

Den Tag des ersten Grußes,
Den Tag, an dem ich ging,
Um Nam' und Zahlen windet
Sich ein zerbrochner Ring.

The day of our first greeting,
The date I departed.
Around name and figures
A broken ring is entwined.

Mein Herz, in diesem Bache
Erkennst du nun dein Bild?
Ob's unter seiner Rinde
Wohl auch so reißend schwillt?

My heart, do you now recognize
Your image in this brook?
Is there not beneath its crust
Likewise a seething torrent?

8 Rückblick

Es brennt mir unter beiden Sohlen,
Tret' ich auch schon auf Eis und Schnee,
Ich möcht' nicht wieder Atem holen,
Bis ich nicht mehr die Türme seh'.

8 Backward Glance

The souls of my feet are burning,
Though I walk on ice and snow;
I do not wish to draw breath again
Until I can no longer see the towers.

Hab' mich an jeden Stein gestoßen,
So eilt' ich zu der Stadt hinaus;
Die Krähen warfen Bäll' und Schloßen
Auf meinen Hut von jedem Haus.

I tripped on every stone,
Such was my hurry to leave the town;
The crows threw snowballs and hailstones
On to my hat from every house.

Wie anders hast du mich empfangen,
Du Stadt der Unbeständigkeit!
An deinen blanken Fenstern sangen
Die Lerch' und Nachtigall im Streit.

How differently you received me.
Town of inconstancy!
At your shining windows
Lark and nightingale sang in rivalry.

Die runden Lindenbäume blühten,
Die klaren Rinnen rauschten hell,
Und ach, zwei Mädchenaugen glühten! —
Da war's geschehn um dich, Gesell!

The round linden trees blossomed,
The clear fountains plashed brightly,
And, ah, a maiden's eyes glowed;
Then, friend, your fate was sealed.

Kommt mir der Tag in die Gedanken,
Möcht' ich noch einmal rückwärts sehn,
Möcht' ich zurücke wieder wanken,
Vor ihrem Hause stille stehn.

9 *Irrlicht*
In die tiefsten Felsengründe
Lockte mich ein Irrlicht hin:
Wie ich einen Ausgang finde
Liegt nicht schwer mir in dem Sinn.

Bin gewohnt das Irregehen,
'S führt ja jeder Weg zum Ziel:
Unsre Freuden, unsre Leiden,
Alles eines Irrlichts Spiel!

Durch des Bergstroms trockne
   Rinnen
Wind' ich ruhig mich hinab —
Jeder Strom wird's Meer gewinnen,
Jedes Leiden auch sein Grab.

10 *Rast*
Nun merk' ich erst, wie müd' ich bin,
Da ich zur Ruh' mich lege;
Das Wandern hielt mich munter hin
Auf unwirtbarem Wege.

Die Füße frugen nicht nach Rast,
Es war zu kalt zum Stehen,
Der Rücken fühlte keine Last,
Der Sturm half fort mich wehen.

In eines Köhlers engem Haus
Hab' Obdach ich gefunden;
Doch meine Glieder ruhn nicht aus:
So brennen ihre Wunden.

Auch du, mein Herz, in Kampf und Sturm
So wild und so verwegen,
Fühlst in der Still' erst deinen
   Wurm
Mit heißem Stich sich regen!

11 *Frühlingstraum*
Ich träumte von bunten Blumen,
So wie sie wohl blühen im Mai,
Ich träumte von grünen Wiesen,
Von lustigem Vogelgeschrei.

Und als die Hähne krähten,
Da ward mein Auge wach;
Da war es kalt und finster,
Es schrieen die Raben vom Dach.

Doch an den Fensterscheiben
Wer malte die Blätter da?
Ihr lacht wohl über den Träumer,
Der Blumen im Winter sah?

When that day comes to my mind
I should like to look back once more,
And stumble back
To stand before her house.

9 *Will-o'-the-Wisp*
A will-o'-the-wisp enticed me
Into the deepest rocky chasms;
How I shall find a way out
Does not trouble my mind.

I am used to straying
Every path leads to one goal;
Our joys, our sorrows —
All are a will-o'-the wisp's game.

Down the dry gullies of the mountain
   stream
I calmly wend my way;
Every river will reach the sea,
Every sorrow, too, will reach its grave.

10 *Rest*
Only now, as I lie down to rest,
Do I notice how tired I am.
Walking kept me cheerful
On the inhospitable road.

My feet did not seek rest,
It was too cold to stand still;
My back felt no burden,
The storm helped to blow me onwards.

In a charcoal-burner's cramped cottage
I found shelter.
But my limbs cannot rest,
Their wounds burn so.

You too, my heart, so wild and daring
In battle and tempest;
In this calm you now feel the stirring of
   your serpent,
With its fierce sting.

11 *Dream of Spring*
I dreamt of bright flowers
That blossom in May;
I dreamt of green meadows
And merry bird-calls.

And when the cocks crowed
My eyes awoke;
It was cold and dark,
Ravens cawed from the roof.

But there, on the window panes,
Who had painted the leaves?
Are you laughing at the dreamer
Who saw flowers in winter?

Ich träumte von Lieb' um Liebe,
Von einer schönen Maid,
Von Herzen und von Küssen,
Von Wonne und Seligkeit.

Und als die Hähne krähten,
Da ward mein Herze wach;
Nun sitz' ich hier alleine
Und denke dem Traume nach.

Die Augen schließ' ich wieder,
Noch schlägt das Herz so warm.
Wann grünt ihr Blätter am
  Fenster?
Wann halt' ich mein Liebchen, im Arm?

12 *Einsamkeit*
Wie eine trübe Wolke
Durch heitre Lüfte geht,
Wenn in der Tanne Wipfel
Ein mattes Lüftchen weht:

So zieh' ich meine Straße
Dahin mit trägem Fuß,
Durch helles, frohes Leben,
Einsam und ohne Gruß.

Ach, daß die Luft so ruhig!
Ach, daß die Welt so licht!
Als noch die Stürme tobten,
War ich so elend nicht.

13 *Die Post*
Von der Straße her ein Posthorn klingt.
Was hat es, daß es so hoch aufspringt,
Mein Herz?

Die Post bringt keinen Brief für dich.
Was drängst du denn so wunderlich,
Mein Herz?

Nun ja, die Post kommt aus der Stadt,
Wo ich ein liebes Liebchen hatt',
Mein Herz!

Willst wohl einmal hinübersehn,
Und fragen, wie es dort mag gehn,
Mein Herz?

14 *Der greise Kopf*
Der Reif hat einen weißen Schein
Mir über's Haar gestreuet.
Da glaubt' ich schon ein Greis zu sein,
Und hab' mich sehr gefreuet.

Doch bald ist er hinweggetaut,
Hab' wieder schwarze Haare,
Daß mir's vor meiner Jugend graut —
Wie weit noch bis zur Bahre!

I dreamt of mutual love,
Of a lovely maiden,
Of embracing and kissing,
Of joy and rapture.

And when the cocks crowed
My heart awoke;
Now I sit here alone
And reflect upon my dream.

I close my eyes again,
My heart still beats so warmly
Leaves on my window, when will you turn
  green?
When shall I hold my love in my arms?

12 *Loneliness*
As a dark cloud
Drifts through clear skies,
When a faint breeze blows
In the fir-tops;

Thus I go on my way,
With weary steps, through
Bright, joyful life,
Alone, greeted by no one.

Alas, that the air is so calm!
Alas, that the world is so bright!
When storms were still raging
I was not so wretched.

13 *The Post*
A posthorn sounds from the road.
Why is it that you leap so high,
My heart?

The post brings no letter for you.
Why, then, do you surge so strangely,
My heart?

But yes, the post comes from the town
Where I once had a beloved sweetheart,
My heart!

Do you want to peep out
And ask how things are there,
My heart?

14 *The Grey Head*
The frost has sprinkled a white sheen
Upon my hair;
I thought I was already an old man,
And I rejoiced.

But soon it melted away;
Once against I have black hair,
So that I shudder at my youth.
How far it is still to the grave!

Vom Abendrot zum Morgenlicht
Ward mancher Kopf zum Greise.
Wer glaubt's? Und meiner ward es nicht
Auf dieser ganzen Reise!

Between sunset and the light of morning
Many a head has turned grey.
Who will believe it? Mine has not done so
Throughout this whole journey.

15 Die Krähe

Eine Krähe war mit mir
Aus der Stadt gezogen,
Ist bis heute für und für
Um mein Haupt geflogen.

15 The Crow

A crow has come with me
From the town,
And to this day
Has been flying ceaselessly about my head.

Krähe, wunderliches Tier,
Willst mich nicht verlassen?
Meinst wohl bald als Beute hier
Meinen Leib zu fassen?

Crow, you strange creature,
Will you not leave me?
Do you intend soon
To seize my body as prey?

Nun, es wird nicht weit mehr gehn
An dem Wanderstabe.
Krähe, laß mich endlich sehn
Treue bis zum Grabe!

Well, I do not have much further to walk
With my staff.
Crow, let me at last see
Faithfulness unto the grave.

16 Letzte Hoffnung

Hie und da ist an den Bäumen
Manches bunte Blatte zu sehn,
Und ich bleibe vor den Bäumen
Oftmals in Gedanken stehn.

16 Last Hope

Here and there on the trees
Many a coloured leaf can still be seen.
I often stand, lost in thought,
Before those trees.

Schaue nach dem einen Blatte,
Hänge meine Hoffnung dran;
Spielt der Wind mit meinem Blatte,
Zittr' ich, was ich zittern kann.

I look at one such leaf
And hang my hopes upon it;
If the wind plays with my leaf
I tremble to the depths of my being.

Ach, und fällt das Blatt zu Boden,
Fällt mit ihm die Hoffnung ab,
Fall' ich selber mit zu Boden,
Wein' auf meiner Hoffnung Grab.

Ah, and if the leaf falls to the ground
My hopes fall with it;
I, too, fall to the ground
And weep on the grave of my hopes.

17 Im Dorfe

Es bellen die Hunde, es rasseln die Ketten.
Es schlafen die Menschen in ihren Betten,
Träumen sich manches, was sie nicht
haben,
Tun sich im Guten und Argen
erlaben;

17 In the Village

Dogs bark, chains rattle;
People sleep in their beds,
Dreaming of many a thing they do not
possess,
Consoling themselves with the good and
the bad.

Und morgen früh ist Alles
zerflossen—
Je nun, sie haben ihr Teil genossen,
Und hoffen, was sie noch übrig ließen,
Doch wieder zu finden auf ihren Kissen.

And tomorrow morning all will have
vanished.
Well, they have enjoyed their share,
And hope to find on their pillows
What they still have left to savour.

Bellt mich nur fort, ihr wachen
Hunde,
Laßt mich nicht ruhn in der Schlummer-
stunde!
Ich bin zu Ende mit allen Träumen—
Was will ich unter den Schläfern säumen?

Drive me away with your barking, watchful
dogs,
Allow me no rest in this hour of
sleep!
I am finished with all dreams;
Why should I linger among slumberers?

18 *Der stürmische Morgen*
Wie hat der Sturm zerrissen
Des Himmels graues Kleid!
Die Wolkenfetzen flattern
Umher in mattem Streit.

Und rote Feuerflammen
Ziehn zwischen ihnen hin.
Das nenn' ich einen Morgen
So recht nach meinem Sinn!

Mein Herz sieht an dem Himmel
Gemalt sein eignes Bild —
Es ist nichts als der Winter,
Der Winter kalt und wild.

19 *Täuschung*
Ein Licht tanzt freundlich vor mir her;
Ich folg' ihm nach die Kreuz und Quer;
Ich folg' ihm gern und seh's ihm an,
Daß es verlockt den Wandersmann.
Ach, wer wie ich so elend ist,
Gibt gern sich hin der bunten List,
Die hinter Eis und Nacht und
 Graus
Ihm weist ein helles, warmes Haus,
Und eine liebe Seele drin —
Nur Täuschung ist für mich Gewinn!

20 *Der Wegweiser*
Was vermeid' ich denn die Wege,
Wo die anderen Wandrer gehn,
Suche mir versteckte Stege
Durch verschneite Felsenhöhn?

Habe ja doch nichts begangen,
Daß ich Menschen sollte scheun —
Welch ein törichtes Verlangen
Treibt mich in die Wüstenein?

Weiser stehen auf den Wegen,
Weisen auf die Städte zu,
Und ich wandre sonder Maßen,
Ohne Ruh', und suche Ruh'.

Einen Weiser seh' ich stehen
Unverrückt vor meinem Blick;
Eine Straße muß ich gehen,
Die noch Keiner ging zurück.

21 *Das Wirtshaus*
Auf einen Totenacker
Hat mich mein Weg gebracht.
Allhier will ich einkehren:
Hab' ich bei mir gedacht.

Ihr grünen Totenkränze
Könnt wohl die Zeichen sein,
Die müde Wandrer laden
In's kühle Wirtshaus ein.

18 *The Stormy Morning*
How the storm has torn apart
The grey mantle of the sky!
Tattered clouds fly about
In weary conflict.

And red flames
Dart between them.
This is what I call
A morning after my own heart.

My heart sees its own image
Painted in the sky —
It is nothing but winter,
Winter, cold and savage.

19 *Illusion*
A light dances cheerfully before me,
I follow it this way and that;
I follow it gladly, knowing
That it lures the wanderer.
Ah, a man as wretched as I
Gladly yields to the beguiling gleam
That reveals to him, beyond ice, night and
 terror,
A bright, warm house,
And a beloved soul within.
Even mere delusion is a boon to me!

20 *The Signpost*
Why do I avoid the roads
That other travellers take,
And seek hidden paths
Over the rocky, snow-clad heights?

Yet I have done no wrong,
That I should shun mankind.
What foolish yearning
Drives me into the wilderness?

Signposts stand on the roads,
Pointing towards the towns;
And I wander on, relentlessly,
Restless, and yet seeking rest.

I see a signpost standing
Immovable before my eyes;
I must travel a road
From which no man has ever returned.

21 *The Inn*
My journey has brought me
To a graveyard.
Here, I thought to myself,
I will rest for the night.

Green funeral wreaths,
You must be the signs
Inviting tired travellers
Into the cool inn.

Sind denn in diesem Hause
Die Kammern all' besetzt?
Bin matt zum Niedersinken
Bin tödlich schwer verletzt.

O umbarmherz'ge Schenke,
Doch weisest du mich ab?
Nun weiter denn, nur weiter,
Mein treuer Wanderstab!

22 Mut
Fliegt der Schnee mir in's Gesicht,
Schüttl' ich ihn herunter.
Wenn mein Herz im Busen spricht,
Sing' ich hell und munter.

Höre nicht, was es mir sagt,
Habe keine Ohren,
Fühle nicht, was es mir klagt,
Klagen ist für Toren.

Lustig in die Welt hinein
Gegen Wind und Wetter!
Will kein Gott auf Erden sein,
Sind wir selber Götter.

23 Die Nebensonnen
Drei Sonnen sah ich am Himmel stehn,
Hab' lang' und fest sie angesehn;
Und sie auch standen da so stier,
Als wollten sie nicht weg von mir.
Ach, meine Sonnen seid ihr nicht!
Schaut Andren doch in's Angesicht!
Ja, neulich hatt' ich auch wohl drei:
Nun sind hinab die besten zwei.
Ging' nur die dritt' erst hinterdrein!
Im Dunkeln wird mir wohler sein.

24 Der Leiermann
Drüben hinter'm Dorfe
Steht ein Leiermann,
Und mit starren Fingern
Dreht er was er kann.

Barfuß auf dem Eise
Schwankt er hin und her;
Und sein kleiner Teller
Bleibt ihm immer leer.

Keiner mag ihn hören,
Keiner sieht ihn an;
Und die Hunde knurren
Um den alten Mann.

Und er läßt es gehen
Alles, wie es will,
Dreht, und seine Leier
Steht ihm nimmer still.

Are all the rooms
In this house taken, then?
I am weary to the point of collapse,
I am fatally wounded.

Pitiless tavern,
Do you nonetheless turn me away?
On, then, press onwards,
My trusty staff!

22 Courage
When the snow flies in my face
I shake it off.
When my heart speaks in my breast
I sing loudly and merrily.

I do not hear what it tells me,
I have no ears;
I do not feel what it laments,
Lamenting is for fools.

Cheerfully out into the world,
Against wind and storm!
If there is no God on earth,
Then we ourselves are gods!

23 The Mock Suns
I saw three suns in the sky;
I gazed at them long and intently.
And they, too, stood there so fixedly,
As if unwilling to leave me.
Alas, you are not *my* suns!
Gaze into other people's faces!
Yes, not long ago I, too, had three suns;
Now the two best have set.
If only the third would follow,
I should feel happier in the dark.

24 The Organ-grinder
There, beyond the village,
Stands an organ-grinder;
With numb fingers
He plays as best he can.

Barefoot on the ice
He totters to and fro,
And his little plate
Remains forever empty.

No one wants to listen,
No one looks at him,
And the dogs growl
Around the old man.

And he lets everything go on
As it will;
He plays, and his hurdy-gurdy
Never stops.

Wunderlicher Alter,
Soll ich mit dir gehn?
Willst zu meinen Liedern
Deine Leier drehn?

Strange old man,
Shall I go with you?
Will you grind your hurdy-gurdy
To my songs?

Wonne der Wehmut / *Delight in Melancholy*

JOHANN WOLFGANG VON GOETHE

D 260 (1815)

Trocknet nicht, trocknet nicht,
Tränen der ewigen Liebe!
Ach, nur dem halbgetrockneten Auge
Wie öde, wie tot die Welt ihm erscheint!
Trocknet nicht, trocknet nicht,
Tränen unglücklicher Liebe!

Do not grow dry, do not grow dry,
Tears of eternal love!
Ah, even when the eye is but half-dry
How desolate, how dead the world appears!
Do not grow dry, do not grow dry,
Tears of unhappy love!

Zufriedenheit / *Contentment*

MATTHIAS CLAUDIUS

D 501 (1816)

Ich bin vergnügt, im Siegeston
Verkünd' es mein Gedicht,
Und mancher Mann mit seiner Kron
Und Szepter ist es nicht.
Und wär' er's auch; nun, immerhin!
Mag er's! so ist er, was ich bin.

I am happy, my verses
Proclaim it triumphantly,
And many a man with his crown
And sceptre is not.
And even if he is, well, all the better!
Let him be: he is as I am.

Des Sultans Pracht, des Mogols
    Geld
Des Glück, wie hieß er doch,
Der, als er Herr war von der Welt,
Zum Mond hinauf sah noch?
Ich wünsche nichts von alle dem,
Zu lächeln drob fällt mir bequem.

The sultan's splendour, the mogul's
    wealth,
The good fortune of — what was his name?
He who, when ruler of the world,
Still gazed up at the moon.
I desire none of that;
I prefer to smile at it.

Zufrieden sein, das ist mein Spruch!
Was hülf' mir Geld und
    Ehr?
Das, was ich hab', ist mir genug,
Wer klug ist, wünscht nichts sehr;
Denn, was man wünschet, wenn man's
    hat,
So ist man darum doch nicht satt.

To be content, that is my motto!
What use would I have for wealth and
    honour?
What I have is enough for me.
He who is wise does not desire much;
For when people have what they
    desire
They are still not satisfied with it.

Und Geld und Ehr ist oben drauf
Ein sehr zerbrechlich Glas.
Der Dinge wunderbarer Lauf,
(Erfahrung lehret das)
Verändert wenig oft in viel
Und setzt dem reichen Mann sein Ziel.

Moreover, wealth and honour
Are like fragile glass.
The strange course of events
(As experience teaches)
Often turns little into much
And thwarts the rich man.

Recht tun und edel sein und gut
Ist mehr als Geld und Ehr;
Da hat man immer guten Mut
Und Freude um sich her,
Und man ist stolz und mit sich eins,
Scheut kein Geschöpf und fürchtet keins.

To do right, to be generous and good,
Is more than wealth and honour;
Such a man is always in good spirits,
With joy around him;
He is proud and at one with himself,
Shuns no creature and fears nothing.

Zum Punsche / *In Praise of Punch*

JOHANN MAYRHOFER

D 492 (1816)

Woget brausend, Harmonien,
Kehre wieder, alte Zeit;
Punschgefüllte Becher, wandert
In des Kreises Heiterkeit!

Swell, ring out, harmony!
Old times, return!
Let cups brimming with punch pass
Around the cheerful circle!

Mich ergreifen schon die Wellen,
Bin der Erde weit entrückt;
Sterne winken, Lüfte säuseln,
Und die Seele ist beglückt!

The waves already engulf me,
I am far removed from this world;
Stars beckon, breezes whisper,
And my soul is enraptured!

Was das Leben aufgebürdet,
Liegt am Ufer nebelschwer;
Steure fort, ein rascher Schwimmer,
In das hohe Friedensmeer.

The burden of life
Lies on the mist-laden shore;
Head off, fast swimmer,
Towards the high sea of peace.

Was des Schwimmers Lust vermehret,
Ist das Plätschern hinterdrein;
Denn es folgen die Genossen,
Keiner will der Letzte sein.

What enhances the swimmer's pleasure
Is the splash that ensues;
For his companions follow him,
No one wants to be the last.

INDEX OF FIRST LINES

375